Lynn W9-AEW-456

Subjects: 1) Religion and Society

2) Religion – U.S. – 1960

RELIGION IN CONTEMPORARY SOCIETY

H. PAUL CHALFANT

Texas Tech University

ROBERT E. BECKLEY

West Texas University

C. EDDIE PALMER

Texas Tech University

ALFRED PUBLISHING CO., INC.

To my parents
  Irene and the late Paul E. Chalfant, D.D.
and to my wife and children
  Lois, Marsha, and Craig

H. P. C.

To my parents
  Adele and the late C. E. Beckley
and to my wife and son
  Cheryl and Brian

R. E. B.

To my parents and stepparents
  Faye Crane and Eddie
  Shelby Palmer and Mina
and to my wife
  Ann

C. E. P.

        Alfred Publishing Co., Inc.
        15335 Morrison Street
        Sherman Oaks, California 91403

Current printing last digit: 10   9   8   7   6   5   4   3   2   1

Library of Congress Cataloging in Publication Data

Chalfant, Paul H. 1929–
    Religion in contemporary society.

    Includes bibliographical references, index.
        1.   United States—Religion—1960-   2.   Religion
and society.   I.   Beckley, Robert E., joint author.
II.   Palmer, C. Eddie., joint author.   III.   Title
BL2530.U6C47   261.8'0973   80–27999
ISBN 0-88284-126-2

ACKNOWLEDGMENTS

P. 6: Report #145 from "Religion in America" 1978 The Gallup Opinion Index. Used by permission.

Pp. 14, 47, 54: Extraordinary People by William Kephart, St. Martin's Press, Inc. Used by permission.

Pp. 41, 42, 67: Excerpts from The Sacred Canopy by Peter L. Berger. Copyright © 1967 by Peter L. Berger. Reprinted by permission of Doubleday & Company, Inc.

P. 51: Reproduced by permission of the American Anthropological Association from American Ethnologist 2(3):517-519, 1975.

Pp. 55, 56-58: From "Individualism, societalism, worldliness, universalism: Thematizing theoretical sociology of religion" by Roland Robertson. 1977 Sociological Analysis 38:281-308. Used by permission.

P. 57: From "Weberian theory and the ideological function of religion" by Francois Houtart and Genevieve Lemencineir. Copyright © 1976 Social Compass 23:345-354.

Pp. 75-77: These excerpts from "Becoming a World Saver Revisited" by John Lofland are reprinted from Conversion Careers, J. T. Richardson, Editor (Sage Contemporary Social Science Issues, Vo. 47) copyright 1977, by permission of the publisher, Sage Publications, Inc.

P. 109: "Me and Jesus" by Tom T. Hall © 1971 Hallnote Music Company. Used by permission.

P. 124: From SOCIOLOGY OF RELIGION by Glenn Vernon. Copyright © 1962 McGraw-Hill. Used by permission.

P. 125: From Social Class in American Protestantism by Nicholas J. Demerath, III. Used by permission of author.

P. 128: Reprinted with permission of Macmillan Publishing Company, Inc. from The Scientific Study of Religion by J. Milton Yinger. Copyright © 1970 by J. Milton Yinger.

Pp. 244, 460: From Why Conservative Churches Are Growing by Dean M. Kelley. Copyright © 1972 by Dean M. Kelley. Reprinted by permission of Harper & Row, Publishers, Inc.

Pp. 267, 270, 271: From The Jesus People: Old Time Religion in the Age of Aquarius by Ronald M. Enroth, Edward E. Ericson, Jr., and C. Breckinridge Peters. Copyright © 1972 William B. Eerdmans Publishing Company. Used by permission.

Pp. 273, 274, 275, 279, 280: From "Postscript: Jonestown; the Face of the Eighties" from Snapping: America's Epidemic of Sudden Personality Change by Flo Conway and Jim Siegelman (Delta paperback edition). Copyright © 1978, 1979 by Flo Conway and Jim Siegelman. Reprinted by permission of Harper & Row, Publishers, Inc.

Pp. 261, 262, 263, 278: From "Cult information: Three compatible models" by William Sims Bainbridge and Rodney Stark. 1979 Sociological Analysis 40 (Winter) 283-95.

P. 291: From "Cults of America: A reconnaisance in space and time" by Rodney Stark,

Contents

Chapter 5
Leadership and Participation in Religious Groups   141

PART THREE
RELIGION IN CONTEMPORARY SOCIETY   173

Chapter 6
The Development of American Pluralism   175

Chapter 7
Current Trends in Religious Life   201

Chapter 8
Fundamentalism as a Social Movement   227

Chapter 9
New Expressions of Christianity   259

Chapter 10
New Expressions from Nontraditional Sources   289

TABLE OF CONTENTS

Preface

Writing a sociology of religion text is a most challenging task. We undertook the project with the feeling that no existing text met our needs in teaching our particular courses. At this point, we are certainly more in sympathy with those who have preceeded us in attempting to confine this broad, varied and rich field to the space of three or four hundred pages. It is a sensitive undertaking in which one is continually attempting to balance the perspective of the student with the whole scope of the field of the sociology of religion. In one sense, while students are familiar with religion as they have always known it, they find it difficult to look at it in the objective manner in which one views other social phenomena. In another way, many of the terms and concepts necessary to unfold the sociological perspective, being appropriated from theology and philosophy, are unfamiliar and difficult for a large number of students. Presenting this material, then, in a way which really reaches the student and yet adequately presents the sociological interpretation of religion is not easy. While it will be obvious that we have not solved every problem, we do think we have taken steps which go some way toward relieving the difficulties inherent in communicating the importance and contributions which a sociological study of religion makes to our understanding of the world in which we live.

First, we are concerned that the subject matter be presented clearly as a *sociology* of religion, resisting temptations to get side-tracked into psychology, anthropology, or theology. We are particularly careful to avoid the pitfall of either siding with or lining up against institutional religion. Some have used the subject as a pulpit to promote religion and others as a platform to denounce "superstition." But the sociology of religion is clearly neither an attempt to convince or discourage those taking the course with regard to their personal faith, or lack of it.

Second, we have concentrated on religion as it is expressed in *American* society, using comparative material only as it is important in understanding religion in this society. It is quite true that material on religion in other cultures is important—and extremely interesting. However, to us it seems best to analyze the familiar in sociological terms as a way of appreciating what that perspective contributes to our understanding.

Third, we feel that there are several rather "unique" features of this text which contribute to the usefulness of the book. We have included some topics which are not usually considered or are given only slight attention in other texts. We include a separate chapter on fundamentalism, or evangelical Christianity, which we feel highlights one of the most significant religious movements of this time. The discussion of the role of the clergy is more extended than is the case in most texts, and, in addition, we have added special material on the process by which ministerial students are socialized into the professional role. The dilemmas and problems of the clerical role seem especially crucial at this period in the history of institutional religion. Another critical issue has to do with the role of women in the leadership of religious groups, and we have given this matter special attention.

In addressing these and other issues we have attempted to provide some historical flavor to our discussion. While we do not want to be led away from a sociological analysis, we feel it unfortunate that sociological interpretations so often forget the importance of the historical development of the phenomena they study. Both fundamentalism and religious pluralism, for example, cannot be considered apart from the socio-historical context in which they developed.

In writing this book we must acknowledge the assistance of a number of persons. We are appreciative of the efforts of a number of individuals at Alfred Publishing Company who have contributed to the production of this book. In the end, Steven Manus and Joseph Cellini helped us through the final stages and we have been encouraged by both Sue Ann Stark and Cindy Lieberman. We are grateful to our secretaries, Ellen Venable and Janet Wright, who, while not so directly involved with the book, have kept a variety of other matters under control, thus allowing us time to work on this project. We also appreciate the work of our typists—M. H. Montgomery, Ann Palmer, Linda Shelley, Christine McGlasson, and Lee Stribling. Finally, we thank our wives—Lois, Cheryl, and Ann—who suffered, with great restraint, our frustration and the hours of work which it took to produce this volume.

H.P.C.
R.E.B.
C.E.P.

PART ONE

THE SOCIOLOGICAL
STUDY OF
RELIGION

Chapter 1

The Study of
Religion and
American Society

The title of this chapter depicts the focus of this book—religion and society in America. This simple statement establishes our boundaries, defining both the opportunities and limitations of our work. Several things may be implied about this volume from this statement.

Use of the term "society" here implies a particular viewpoint to be taken concerning religion; we take a sociological perspective on the subject. Four characteristics distinguish this angle of vision from others which we might use (Demerath and Hammond, 1969:4,5). First, sociology requires empirical observation (direct observation through the physical senses) to support its theories and propositions; this means that much of what is considered religious will be beyond our gaze. Second, events, persons, and groups are viewed in terms of their relationship to more general social phenomena rather than as having worth in and of themselves; the Moonies and the Hare Krishnas, for example, are viewed in terms of their general place in the understanding of cult behavior rather than for their unique and special meaning. Third, the behavior of groups, in terms of their social structure and processes, are the center of concern rather than the individual. And, finally, we are concerned with the relationship of religion, as a social phenomenon, with all other social phenomena; religion cannot be viewed apart from such social institutions as the family, education, politics, and the economy.

It seems important to stress that our major focus is on religion as one aspect of *group* behavior. It is not that the individual response to and expression of what is known as the religious is unimportant or that we have no interest in it. As Williams (1962) has noted, there is a secret and private aspect to "being religious," and this is an important part of the whole. From our perspective, however, religion is viewed as it expresses itself in group behavior; the patterns, roles, structures, and behaviors which result from the activity of the group. The *individual's* religious experience is studied here only as it can be related to the *group* experience. In other words, we are concerned with religion as it reflects both the social structures and social processes of the group which give rise to, sustain, and instill in the individual, the beliefs, attitudes, and practices of the religious group.

In these limiting characteristics of the sociological approach lie some of the difficulties of and objections to such an investigation; given the necessary restrictions, the subject of religion seems too varied and rich to many to be comprehended within such narrow boundaries. Surely, only a combination of theology, philosophy, anthropology, history, psychology—and sociology—can even begin to comprehend such complex subject matter. The student approaching religion from only one discipline cannot hope to deal with the entire range of things which humans have designated "religious" over the years.

Some would say that such an abstraction, particularly when it comes from someone "outside" religious faith, never really embodies religion's essence. Certainly, in Yinger's imagery (1970), we cannot have the same view of the "stained-glass window" of religion from the outside as do those who are inside the building; for these it is the "light of faith" shining through the window that makes it visible. However, those viewing the window from the outside can also see many things which might be missed by those who never step outside. Just as the view from the inside provides a part of the picture, so does the outside view furnish knowledge important to understanding the whole.

In sum, we intend to look at religion as one aspect of socially constructed reality. In so doing, we can look at only that part of religion which is available to our physical senses. We cannot view the inner, intimate world of personal religious faith. Our view is that of religion as it expresses itself in the interaction between individuals and both the real and symbolic results of that interaction.

Given the complexity of religion, as such, and the complications of applying the sociological perspective, we have limited our attention in this book to religion as it finds social expression in the United States. Obviously such a limitation keeps us from a full inquiry into the subject of the sociology of religion; religion is more than the sum of the ways in which it is expressed in American society. A complete understanding of religion as a social phenomenon would require looking at the broad horizons of human behavior and beliefs concerning what can be defined as the religious.

Why then limit our scope? It is our feeling that Americans—from high church Episcopalians to Pentecostal sectarians—are interested in religions throughout the world because they consider them, especially the Eastern varieties, exotic. The theodicies, concepts, and languages of most non-Western religions are so alien to most Americans that to include them in this volume could possibly detract from our major purpose, which is to aid the student in understanding religion as a social phenomenon. We feel that by concentrating on those religious expressions most familiar to the American student, albeit, from an unfamiliar perspective, that we can help the student understand that generic patterns of religious expression can be revealed by the sociological approach.

In this chapter, we hope to provide an introduction which will set out our frame of reference for the sociological investigation of religion. In doing so, we

4

will want to look at several things: some comments on the relationship between religion and American society in general; sociology's interest in religion as a societal institution, both in the past and now; something about the specific techniques of looking at the world which the sociologist uses; and the problems associated with developing a sociological definition of religion.

RELIGION AND AMERICAN SOCIETY

Almost from the beginning, religion has played a significant part in the development and life of American society. To some degree, those who first journeyed to America from their European homes did so for religious reasons; indeed, each separate colony, with some exceptions, was formed around a particular interpretation of Christian faith. Yet, when the nation was finally united into one state, religious freedom was a necessary part of the compromises which resulted in the union, and freedom of religious belief as a principle led to the enunciation of the separation of church and state. Somewhat ironically, that doctrine was hammered out by individuals who themselves had only the most philosophical conception of the place of a deity in the conduct of human affairs.

Despite official comments on the neutrality of the government concerning religious organizations, there has never been, as Winter (1977) points out, a disparagement of religion by American government; indeed, there has always been a preference for religion over irreligion in the American system. What has been meant by religion, however, has not always been clear. At times former President Eisenhower's statement that our nation needed some religious faith, but that it did not matter what kind, seems to be the bottom line of our national faith.

Much of the society's respect for religion is traced by Winter to the three-community system of religion in the nation (Herberg, 1955). According to this thesis, we encourage participation in one of the three major religious communities—Protestant, Catholic, or Jewish—as a means of providing both self-identification and self-placement in a heterogeneous society. The matter simmers down to the idea that religion, in America, is a way of belonging. For Herberg, it is seen as *the* way Americans answer the questions, "What are you?"

The existence of three general religious communities in America connotes a situation of some complexity. When we attempt to look at the variations within each of the communities—from staid Presbyterians to the more emotional members of such as the Assembly of God; from Italian Catholics to those of Irish descent; from Hassidic Jews to the members of a suburban reformed synagogue—the situation is even more bewildering. As a nation we comprehend more religious interpretations of the Judaeo-Christian tradition than any other human society. It might be thought that religious belief in such a situation would

5

be of minor significance, but religion is, and always has been, a matter of considerable importance to Americans; from those who support and cherish it as well as for those who would see its influence in national life diminish. Whether it is the election of a new pope, the latest crusade of Billy Graham, the machinations in the legal arena of Madelyn Murray O'Hair seeking a block religious exercises in the public school, or sensational events surrounding an "exotic" cult like that at Jonestown, Guyana, religion makes the news.

Regardless of any overall evaluation of its worth as a conservative or dynamic force within society, it is certain that religion occupies a respected place in the United States. This can be documented in part by the results of a 1978 Gallup Poll which reports on the attitudes of Americans toward "the church."

> Americans have more confidence in the churches than in eight other key institutions of society, an extensive study has found. But churchgoers trust organized religion much more than those not involved in it.

> The study . . . found that 80 percent of church participants have a "great deal" or "quite a lot" of confidence in organized religion—more than feel that way about any other major institutions, from big business to the U.S. Congress.

> [Even] among the unchurched, 73 percent had at least "some" confidence in organized religion . . . (Associated Press, Lubbock, Texas, *Avalanche Journal*, June 25, 1978).

A quick survey of the "religion" section of daily newspapers or national newsmagazines, such as *Time* and *Newsweek*, easily confirms the fact that religion can be big news in the United States. When a major denomination debated the ordination of homosexuals and when a Mormon (Latter Day Saints) woman was excommunicated because of her support of the Equal Rights Amendment, the coverage by the national news media was extensive. The issue of the ordination of women to the Episcopal priesthood received more coverage in the secular press than it did in religious periodicals (Chambers and Chalfant, 1978), and the firing of an evangelical religious broadcaster by his church, and incidentally by his father, rated several pages in *Time* (June 19, 1978).

It seems clear that religious values, behaviors, and beliefs are intertwined with numerous attitudinal and behavioral configurations of institutional life in the larger society. Regardless of whether affiliation, attendance, or strength of religious preference is used to measure religiosity, we find that the way in which one is religious is strongly correlated with a number of views toward various segments and problems in society. For example, attitudes toward members of radical groups, voting behavior, tolerance of communism, views of homosexuality, and even happiness in marriage are significantly associated with religious variables, as are attitudes concerning euthanasia, abortion, and the Equal Rights Amendment (National Opinion Research Center, 1978).[1]

Interaction between religion and other aspects of society is multidirectional. Religion is affected by the dominant patterns of the culture; its organization and theology in a particular place are in some measure shaped by the characteristics of the society in which it is found. On the other hand, religion has an effect on most other aspects of that same society.

This dialectic of interdependence and responsiveness for religion in society can be articulated by reference to Max Weber's analysis of the interconnectedness of religion and the economic system of a society. He states that it was improbable that capitalism would develop except under the particular religious ethos associated with a Calvinistic version of Protestantism, the so-called Protestant ethic. According to this thesis, the influence of a particular attitude toward the world and worldly success was essential to such development. Indeed, one might trace many current conservative attitudes toward the poor and the governmental programs which aid them to a somewhat secularized version of this same attitude.

On the other hand, nonreligious variables can influence religious beliefs and organizations. It can be demonstrated, for example, that the American emphasis on democracy and participation in voluntary associations has drastically affected the character of the Roman Catholic Church in this country. Similarly, the perceived threat of communism in the United States influenced a number of religious movements to make opposition to this threat a major part of their ministry.

Simple statements about causation, however, are always precarious when dealing with complex historical forces and broad, sweeping macro-sociological variables. Even with the most seemingly simple variables the relationships are not clear cut. To make the point more salient, let us look at some of the supposedly obvious data concerning religious preference.

Note, for example, in Table 1-1 that religious preference varies considerably with region of the country in which the respondent lives. It is appropriate to say that religious preference causes individuals to see certain areas of the country as desirable places in which to live, or that living in a certain region influences the tendency to prefer particular religious groups, or both? Or are there other, in-

---

1. The National Opinion Research Center annually conducts what it refers to as the General Social Survey. Using proven sampling techniques a sample of between 1,500 and 2,000 persons is drawn, each year, which is representative of the total population of the United States. We are grateful for the information provided by that survey and use it often in this book. The data is furnished us through the Institute for Secondary Analysis of Texas Tech University. From now on we will generally refer to the Center as NORC.

tervening variables at work in this relationship? In this case, historical data could be important for a fuller understanding of this phenomenon of "regional" religion. For instance, Episcopalians and Presbyterians ("old line" religious groups) are more likely to be found in the Middle Atlantic states than in other regions of the country. This probably represents the maintenance of historic religious ties of the Middle Atlantic settlers to their European areas of origin. We can note also that persons with Jewish preference are overly represented in those regions of the country, such as the Middle Atlantic and Pacific states, where the major cities have traditionally been found; we know that Jews tended to settle first in large cities and have tended to remain in urban areas. Similarly, Baptists are over-represented in the population of the southern regions of the country. This geographic pattern is possibly reflective of early decisions concerning the location of frontier settlements. In fact, we shall later refer to such settlements in our description and treatment of frontier religion.

When we look at other "simple" data, as presented in Table 1-2, we observe that there is a significant relationship between religious preference and attitudes toward homosexuality. While most respondents are overwhelmingly opposed to such a sexual orientation, considering it to be "always wrong," we can also note that Jews and Episcopalians are grouped near those who have no religious preference in being less likely to find such behavior wrong in all cases. Why do these three apparently quite disparate groups tend to be similar in their attitudes toward the homosexual? Are there elements of religious doctrine which dictate such attitudes? If so, why do those having no religious preference agree with the Jews and Episcopalians? Are there other variables at work here?

Such problems as these always haunt the social scientist, and great analytical skill is necessary to avoid the pitfalls which confront those looking for objective information concerning religion. However, given enough data, enough theoretical grounding, and enough conceptual ability, sociologists are able to provide very relevant insights concerning this complicated subject. Concerning the questions posed above, it is not our purpose to offer answers at this time, but to demonstrate that any attempt to determine the more complex relationship between society and religion is frought with problems which have intrigued, motivated, and baffled scholars for some time. The message we would give is simply that we need to use great caution in evaluating the evidence and accepting conclusions.

THE SOCIOLOGICAL INTEREST IN RELIGION

Religion and its relationship with the rest of society was a major area of interest in the early years of the emerging discipline of sociology. Standing out among early sociologists are Emile Durkheim (1858-1917) and Max Weber

Table 1-1. RELIGIOUS AFFILIATION AND REGION OF INTERVIEW

Region of Interview	Catholic		Jewish		Baptist		Methodist		Lutheran		Presbyterian		Episcopalian		Other		No Preference		Total
New England	36	9.7	1	2.9	2	0.6	0	0.0	1	0.7	3	4.5	2	5.4	8	3.2	8	8.6	4.1
Middle Atlantic	84	22.5	16	45.7	18	5.6	24	12.4	30	22.1	18	27.3	9	24.3	22	8.9	9	9.7	15.3
East North Central	113	30.3	1	2.9	33	10.2	48	24.9	55	40.4	6	9.1	2	5.4	61	24.6	18	19.4	22.4
West North Central	21	5.6	1	2.9	22	6.8	15	7.8	19	14.0	3	4.5	2	5.4	22	8.9	8	8.6	7.5
South Atlantic	32	8.6	4	11.4	134	41.4	64	33.2	10	7.4	14	21.2	3	8.1	35	14.1	15	16.1	20.7
East South Central	3	0.8	0	0.0	34	10.5	10	5.2	1	0.7	6	9.1	1	2.7	16	6.5	5	5.4	5.0
West South Central	21	5.6	0	0.0	49	15.1	9	4.7	4	2.9	2	3.0	6	16.2	23	9.3	5	5.4	7.9
Mountain	14	3.8	0	0.0	13	4.0	6	3.1	4	2.9	1	1.5	2	5.4	15	6.0	5	5.4	4.0
Pacific	49	13.1	12	34.3	19	5.9	17	8.8	12	8.8	13	19.7	10	27.0	46	18.5	20	21.5	13.2
Total N	373		35		324		193		139		66		37		248		93		1505

Source: NORC General Social Survey, 1977. Courtesy of Institute for Secondary Analysis, Texas Tech University.

Table 1–2. RELIGIOUS AFFILIATION AND ATTITUDE TOWARD
HOMOSEXUALITY BY PERCENTAGE

| | Attitude Toward Homosexuality | | | | |
	Always Wrong	Almost Always Wrong	Sometimes Wrong	Not Wrong At All	Total N
Catholic	68.2	7.0	9.6	15.2	355
Jewish	37.5	0.0	6.3	56.3	32
Baptist	80.8	4.9	4.2	10.1	308
Methodist	76.8	7.0	8.1	8.1	185
Lutheran	75.6	6.1	4.6	13.7	131
Presbyterian	69.4	9.7	8.1	12.9	62
Episcopalian	53.3	6.7	20.0	20.0	30
Other	76.4	4.5	6.2	12.8	242
No Preference	47.6	4.8	13.1	34.5	84
Total	71.9	5.9	7.5	14.7	1429

Source: NORC General Social Survey, 1977. Courtesy of Institute for Secondary Analysis, Texas
Tech University.

(1864-1920). Both focused much attention on the relationship of religion and
society. Each was concerned with trends in the drastically changing society of
their day and interested in the role which religious beliefs, attitudes, and structures would play in these changes and in the emerging industrial society.

Durkheim was almost obsessed with the question of how society was held
together; how humans came to accept and obey the dictates of their group. He
believed that religion was one of the central cohesive factors binding individuals
to their society and wondered what effect the loss of religion might have. In
Suicide (1951), for example, he argued that societies embracing individualistic
Protestantism (low cohesiveness) had a higher ratio of suicide than those societies
in which Catholicism (high cohesiveness) was the predominant religion.

Throughout Durkheim's work he sees religion as an essential ingredient for
society. In his study of Australian totemic religion, he concluded that the seeming sacredness of a religion is really the power attributed to the society itself. The
elementary form of religion is nothing other than the society personified.
Religion is seen as a force because the idea of it is inspired by the group and pro-

jected outside the individual. This identification of religion and society led to the conclusion that religion served to emphasize the power of society over the individual members of the group.

Weber, too, made religion a major subject of study. He was concerned with showing, in contrast to Marx, that a noneconomic fact could have a decisive effect on the shape of society in general, and on the economic system in particular. Whereas Marx saw the religious institution developing from the particular economic system, Weber reversed the argument and traced the development of a particular economic system to the influence of a religious ethos. In *The Protestant Ethic and the Spirit of Capitalism* (1958), he attempted to show that Protestantism promoted, to some extent, a set of values and beliefs which stressed rationality and ascetic devotion to work, and which in turn promoted the development of capitalism.

Actually, Weber explicitly repudiated any idea that society could be interpreted through a single factor, insisting always that many mutually dependent conditions were necessary. While he was intent on showing that religion could have an independent effect, he did not believe that it was independent of other aspects of society. He contended, for example, that the social class of those who developed a religion profoundly influenced its nature. This was because, as he saw it, a central problem dealt with by the religious institution or religious belief is that of giving meaning to the position of the individual in society. Thus, religious movements which grew out of the soil of the urban, lower classes would emphasize escape from an unfriendly world and place importance on the rewards to be obtained in some future—better—existence. Lower-class sects tend to stress the evils of the riches of this world as compared to the glories of the next. On the other hand, middle-class founders—as in many forms of Calvinism—will stress those theological strains which place a premium on gaining status in terms of worldly rewards, a theme prominent in the Protestant ethic.

Weber saw these emphases as present in the type of religious organization which took shape in groups with particular theologies. He introduced the idea of two *ideal types* of such organization—the *church* and the *sect*—as a way of trying to understand the relationship between a particular religion, Christianity, and the larger social system. He was interested in how this might result in the kind of pluralizing, secularization processes common in the industrial world. For Weber, the single most important distinguishing element between the two types of organizations was the manner in which membership was established; by conversion in the sects, by birth in the church. Whether an individual belonged to a church or sect was seen as a reflection of the social status of the individual and, thus, futher indicated that religious expressions were tied into social forces other than those that were strictly religious.

While the founders of sociology made major contributions to our understanding of religion as a social phenomenon, and to our comprehension of society itself, this initial interest in the study of religion from the sociological perspective waned considerably. At least partially this may have been due to an evolutionary perspective common to most early social scientists which gave rise to the assumption that religion was "dying out" as human knowledge increased.

While some undoubtedly still hold such a view and downplay the importance of the scientific study of religion, others have come to see the easy disparagement of the field as in itself unscientific, and, since the Second World War, there has been a vital and renewed interest in the study of religion as one of the continuing, important presences in social life. Charles Glock (1973:1) observed, in introducing a book of readings on the sociology of religion, that religion is now generating more attention from sociologists than has been true since the last century, and that this renewed interest has brought forth a considerable amount of quality empirical research. In addition to significant continuations of the theoretical and historical work of the early sociologists of religion, new scholars have produced a large amount of work based on actual investigations of religious attitudes, behaviors, and organizations as they occur in society.

The Focus of Sociological Study

If, as noted above, interest in the sociological study of religion is increasing, and if researchers are taking a more empirical stance, how can we best understand the recent focus and conceptualizations of the researchers concerning religious life?

The interest of the sociologist in religion is obviously quite different from that of the theologian. It is not the value or validity of religious belief systems in general or of any individual system of theological belief which the sociologist seeks to study. Rather, sociologists see religious systems as networks of norms, values, and patterns of action similar to other social systems which center around the solution to essential problems of survival in society. It is the behavior which results from these norms, values, and patterns of action which provide the sociologists' data. Included in such data are expressed beliefs, affiliations with particular religious groups, types of religious organizations, as well as material concerning the relation of such standard demographic and sociological variables as social class, age, and sex, to religious behavior.

Put in two simple phrases, the sociologist is interested in *social structures* and *social processes*. That is, our concern is with the means by which human beings structure social life—norms, values, institutions—and the processes whereby individuals are channeled into positions in those structures and come to internalize for themselves the patterns as reality. To paraphrase Berger and Luckmann (1967), we are concerned as sociologists with how social interaction constructs the reality both individuals and the group accept.

Looking at religion as one of the patterns of role and role relationships, we see one of what sociologists refer to as social institutions. These institutional patterns of norms, roles, and patterns of interaction become more or less integrated systems which merge to provide the fabric of any society. Some would argue that in many industrial societies disintegration is more prevalent than many realize and that traditional patterns are breaking down. Clearly, any society which does not find ways of organizing and integrating its various elements to some degree must face the possibility of extinction or radical social change. And even though changes are characteristic of human relationships, some semblance of order, stability, and predictability is necessary (at both concrete and abstract levels) for their continuation. The maintenance of these patterns in social life is due to the fact that persons devise and utilize particular methods and techniques to meet their basic needs.

From a point of view which sees the various elements of culture as functioning to deal with the basic problem of adaptation to one's environment, it is assumed that societies develop the basic institutions of family, government, education, economy—and religion—to solve some of the most basic problems they face. However, such institutions are not necessarily mutually exclusive; that is, their functions may overlap, or certain institutions may assume tasks traditionally carried out by others.

Institutional arrangements, thus, are not totally static, but fluctuate according to perceived needs and sociohistorical time period. In general, institutional arrangements are supportive of one another and, thus, supportive of the general culture. For example, Western industrial society has an institution for dealing with problems of health and illness that leans upon scientific information and techniques; Azande society, in Africa, deals with and defines the same problems in terms of supernatural forces. Each approach fits its particular social system and thus is basically concordant with other elements in the society. American medicine is based on the scientific skill and knowledge that is highly valued in the United States; Azande healing takes its shape and form from the dominant religious beliefs of a religious society. Neither way is "correct" in the sociological sense. It is correct only in terms of the larger social context.

In some cases, the various institutional arrangements may appear to compete with one another. Even then the structures remain as *generic* forms in the overall scheme of things. They are so "institutionalized" that a topical change or two in function does not alter their total significance. Changes in the family functions in the United States, for example, have been documented by social scientists and historians for years, and, even though radical changes have occurred in some cases, the "family" has not disappeared from American society. We can see not only the *flexibility* but the *interconnectedness* of institutions in the following statement of Kephart (1976:37-38) concerning changes in the family:

> A number of years ago, William F. Ogburn, a sociologist interested in the study of cultural change, made an interesting observation apropos of the American family. From the colonial period to the present, he said, the family has been characterized by a progressive *loss of functions*. He went on to list the declining functions as education, religion, protection, recreation, and the economic function. . . . Thus, the function of religion, once centered in the home, had been taken over by the church. Education had become the province of the schools. . . . The economic function had been lost because the family was no longer a producing unit—due largely to the fact that child labor laws and compulsory school laws prohibited children from working. [Emphasis in original.]

Similar arguments can be made about the changing functions of organized religion in American society. Indeed, several sociologists have suggested that religion is becoming more privatized (Luckmann, 1967; Berger, 1967) or simply relegated to the task of embellishing large, public ceremonies (Berger, 1967). In other words, it may be losing some functions in integrating the community and providing a means of social control. At the same time, it has adopted some of the functions of the family such as moral education of the young in closely graded age groups. And, as we will see later, religious participation also serves educational, economic, and political needs.

In our study of religion as a social institution our subject matter ranges from the broad theoretical concerns about the meaning of religion in society to an understanding of how individuals come to internalize a particular religious system as their own. Such concerns, of course, are not always easy to discuss and study. A number of problems arise when we attempt a scientific study of religion.

Some Problems with the Sociological Study of Religion

In covering this broad area, some difficulties and special problems appear. In one sense the very nature of religion makes scientific approaches difficult. As sociologists, we are limited to those things which we can observe empirically. This means that while we can study attitudes which people express, beliefs which they say that they hold, ritual behavior such as attendance at worship services, the organization of the religious group, and so forth, we cannot go beyond that which can be seen. If we were to claim that studying such matters comprised *all* that was important in religion, we would be sadly mistaken, and, as Yinger (1970:2) has pointed out nonscientific ourselves. We do not, and cannot, study everything which might be considered religion.

The fact that the subject matter is religion has brought misunderstandings with regard to its offering as a course in the university curriculum. Some see such a course as a thinly veiled way in which to introduce religion into the content of the university curricula. When the senior author taught such a course at one church-related university, the registrar refused to schedule it in any building which had been built with federal funds, reasoning that it was really a course in theology and, as such, would violate federal regulations concerning the separation of church and state if it were taught in a building constructed with money from the government—a position from which no amount of argument or logic would dissuade him.

On the other hand, the sociology of religion course has also been seen as one which sought to attack religion at a number of levels. It is true that some instructors of the course have seen it as a "platform" from which to attack and denigrate the religious beliefs and practices of their students, as well as the established church itself. On more than a few occasions students have been subjected to an *exposé* of the simple-mindedness of religious beliefs and those who ascribe to them, rather than getting an objective introduction to a particular field of knowledge.

A study of the sociological perspective on religion should be neither an attempt to convince nor an effort to discourage those students taking the course in regard to their religious faith or to their beliefs and feelings about the religious structures of the society. Neither is it a course which merely compares the "great" religions of the world, except as such a comparison relates to the basic problems of social structure and social process. In short, a course in the sociology of religion should be seen primarily as just that—a course in sociology of which the subject matter at hand is the religious institution, looked at in the same way sociologists look at the institution of the family or medicine.

All of this has been well summarized by Vernon (1962:16–17). He indicates that it must be made clear that the sociology of religion is not: (1) a study of the truth or falsity of religion or religious ideas; (2) a promotion of the correctness of one set of ideas over against another such set; (3) an attack upon religion, since the realm of the "beyond" cannot be attacked by a scientific discipline; (4) an attempt to answer the question of whether or not religion is a good thing; or (5) a program of reform—either of society or of religion. It will be well for students with deep religious convictions, those who have rejected them, and those falling somewhere between, to keep these five points in mind during the progress of the study of this book, and the taking of such a course, so that statements made and evidence presented may always be understood in proper context.

TOWARD A SOCIOLOGICAL DEFINITION OF RELIGION

In any scientific or scholarly enterprise, it is important that a well-developed and appropriate definition of the subject matter be given: a definition which meets the needs of the inquiry. Certainly in actual empirical research an "operational" definition, which can be used to specify just what is measured and how, is essential. But even to consider in a theoretical framework the matter of a sociology of religion, it is necessary to come to some understanding of what we mean when we speak of "religion."

One thing is obviously necessary. In developing a sociological definition of religion we need to be able to differentiate between what *is* and what *is not* religion. In a common sense way of thinking this does not seem too difficult. Everyone knows that religion is . . . what? When one begins to think about all of the possibilities involved in separating religion from all other phenomena, the number of criteria possible for making such a distinction can be staggering.

It is almost a truism to state that all, or most, societies throughout history have had some kind of religion. Such a commonplace statement, however, covers an amazing variety of behaviors, practices, and beliefs, all categorized together under the single umbrella term, religion. It is useful to think for a few moments about this extreme diversity. Religion is applied to such differing practices as the high pageantry of a Roman Catholic mass and also to a snake-handling ceremony in a crude wooden church in the mountains of West Virginia; it may be seen as the basis for ritual cannibalism as well as the absolute silence of a Quaker meeting; it results in the intellectual discourse found in the services of a Unitarian-Universalist fellowship, as well as the emotional fervor of an "old fashioned" camp meeting which has led some of the "revived" to roll on the floor and bark at the moon like dogs; it is the staid services and organization of the middle-class Presbyterian congregation, as well as the superbly choreographed performances of the "electronic" church which possesses our television screens on Sunday mornings. Today we even hear some refer to the various political creeds such as communism, as "religion" and to a basic belief in the rectitude of the American way of life in a similar manner. With such an assortment of behaviors to be considered, it is small wonder that the student of the sociological study of religion is hard put to propose precise definitions of that subject matter.

As we approach the task of definition, then, a number of questions come to mind. Is there any special characteristic which ought to be considered concerning the nature of that which is at the center of this thing we call religion? Can a religion be separated from group activity? Are there practices which are peculiar to "religion?" What sorts of goals seem peculiarly appropriate to that which we call religious behavior?

These questions relate to some of the basic elements that have been found important in distinguishing religion from nonreligion. While some, such as Weber, have suggested that no real definition of religion can be developed until the phenomenon has actually been studied, most would follow Durkheim in suggesting that at least a provisional definition is needed. A definition given by

16

Durkheim has come to be seen as one benchmark for those attempting to develop such a sociological definition. He describes religion as (1947:62):

> ... a unified system of beliefs and practices relative to sacred things, that is to say, things set apart and forbidden—beliefs and practices which unite into one single moral community called a Church all those who adhere to them.

This definition tells us three things about that which is to be called religion. First, it marks as religious the concern for those things which are referred to as sacred, the chief marks of this being that it is something that is set off from daily activity and considered, somehow, foreboding. For the Australian Arunta, about whom Durkheim wrote, the totem object, which symbolized the object of worship, was the "sacred"; the Roman Catholic sees it portrayed in the crucifix; and the Jew evinces a certain amount of awe for the scroll of the Torah.

Second, a religion involves sets or complexes of beliefs and practices directed in some fashion at this "sacred." Such beliefs may range from the extremely unsophisticated to the highly complex. Primitive religions may center on only a few beliefs while the religions of highly industrialized societies, such as those of the Western world, may result in the complex and highly intellectual reasoning of John Calvin's theory of "double predestination," the idea that some are chosen before birth for either glory or damnation. Regardless of the complexity, each religion will have developed a set of beliefs and practices defining the sacred and practices related to appeasing or relating to it.

Finally, Durkheim's definition insists that religion is a property of the group, not the individual; that is, there cannot be religion unless there is a unifying community of some sort built around the phenomenon. While some (e.g., Williams, 1962) make a place for religion as an individual enterprise, the focus of the sociological study of religion is the group and the individual's relationship to the group. In this view, religion is never a completely solitary matter—even when the individual is engaging in behavior of a religious nature and is alone. It is the product of the group; the group is central in its formation, formulation and future.

While it might be said that Durkheim's definition "begs" the question, leaving much still vague and uncertain, the elements of his definition have been used by many investigators as a starting point in developing other definitional statements. The points Durkheim makes have been elaborated and considered by most of those engaged in the sociological study of religion. Glock and Stark (1965:4) suggest that all of this manipulaltion of Durkheim's definition can be summarized in one brief generalization:

> Religion, or what societies hold to be sacred, comprises an institutionalized

system of symbols, beliefs, values and practices focused on questions of ultimate meaning.

It can be seen that the three basic elements found in Durkheim's definition are also included in this summary statement, although the area of belief, values, and practices is somewhat differently defined. What is new here is the qualification that the kinds of questions which religion is set to address are those concerning "ultimate meaning," that is, questions related to matters of the significance of life and the explanation of those things which threaten this significance. What does life mean? How can we deal with the tragedies that occur in all our lives? How can we face the death of loved ones, or look forward to our own death? These, and many similar questions, are here viewed as the kind which religion addresses.

Accepting Glock and Stark's summary, then, we have four elements which can be considered bedrock for a definition of religion—or can they? As seemingly simple as this brief list of criteria seem, the questions which can be raised concerning their appropriateness for a sociological definition of religion are many. For instance, should we confine our definition of religion to those sets of beliefs which deal with supernatural realms in some way, or should it be broadened to include anything seen as providing some form of answer to problems of ultimate meaning? Are we to see religion as specifically referring to the functions associated with a particular set of symbols and beliefs, or is there a unifying, universalistic meaning attached to the concept of religion?

Purposes of a Sociological Definition

As we ponder questions such as these, it is important to understand the purpose of a sociological definition; the reason or reasons that such a definition is being formulated. It is possible, as Yinger (1970:3) reminds us, to create such rigid pigeonholes by the definitions we construct that they cease to represent reality, or hide much of reality in the service of the definition. Thus, in looking for the absolute idea of religion we might well consider religion not as a series of sharp, two-fold divisions, but as a flowing continuum in which some things are merely more or less religious than other things. However, our concern, in a sociological study of religion, is with increasing the ability to explain accurately the social fact of religion and to make predictions on the basis of these findings. Thus, we are really interested in what might be called a working, pragmatic sort of definition, one which will aid us in our research and study. To the extent that a definition does aid this process it is a useful one. If it does not help in this task, or if it makes the concept of religion become so cluttered with contradictions that no one can identify what it means, or if it seems to be something different to everyone who uses it, then it no longer serves our purpose (Osborne, 1977:2).

What we are looking for in a definition will depend upon the particular question we are asking. For example, if we are interested in finding out how people find meaning in their lives it will be important to decide if we classify certain political philosophies as "religions"; because these sometimes give meaning to people's lives. If, however, we want to determine the effects on individuals of having *no* ideology concerning the significance of life, we may not be interested in how carefully we exclude some phenomena from under the religious umbrella. Again, if we wish to investigate the way in which religious norms function to undergird the traditional ways of a society, we will be concerned with the broadness of the definition to the extent that we want to differentiate between kinds of norms that serve such a function.

Some further insight into the kind of definition constructed is provided if we make a distinction between two types of definition. The question to be raised, in this context, is that of whether there is any value in attempting to advance a definition of religion for "all purposes." As noted, we need at least some implicit, working definition in order to know the object of our investigation. But, we may make a distinction between two types of definition. One could be called a *nominal* definition, the other a *real* one. Both are potentially useful to the sociological researcher; however, they are useful for different purposes. Nominal definitions make quite clear what phenomena are under scrutiny. For example, if we agree to call only those behaviors which focus on the supernatural realm religion, we are clear that communism and other political ideologies are not to be included as they do not meet the requirements of the nominal definition. The object of investigation is thus clearly specified.

On the other hand, real definitions derive from empirical statements about a phenomenon and are useful in that they contain information about its essential properties. Thus, in the real world, we know that to certain respondents the term religion means only what goes on inside the institutional church, whereas for another group, such as some of those interviewed by Machalek and Martin (1976) in Louisiana, there is a much broader conception of the term. For certain purposes it might be well to consider communism under the definition of religion, if that made sense within a particular context.

Such considerations lead to the suggestion that different definitions and definitional strategies provide different kinds of information about the social world. We need to evaluate definitions in terms of their usefulness for specific types of information. It is inappropriate to criticize nominal definitions for not fitting the real world perfectly; likewise, it is not proper to downgrade functional definitions (real) for obscuring differences in the subjective meanings of religion for individuals. Different definitions are constructed to different ends. In practice, definitions are adopted most frequently for operational purposes, and we may gain little in attempting to construct a definition which would suit all situations and all needs. As Machalek notes (1977:400):

> ... definitions must be evaluated in terms of their utility with regard to the intellectual tasks at hand or in terms of the adequacy with which they purportedly represent an empirical phenomenon.

Given the tentative nature of many definitions, it is well to look more fully at what is involved in the choices made in constructing the definitional strategies used.

Two Definitional Questions

As could be inferred from what we have already noted, there are two major questions which confront us in deciding what does fit under the "sacred canopy" of religion (Berger, 1967). First, should religion be so defined as to emphasize the substance of religion, or should it be described in terms of the functions which it serves? Then, a second and related question: should the definition be inclusive of all that might possibly be seen as religion, or limited to some narrow range of things which more or less fit traditional or common sense approaches to what we mean by religion? In answering these questions, it is well to heed the comment of Hargrove (1971:5):

> ... some of the most miserable failures in the attempt to understand sociologically that phenomenon we call "religion" have occurred through the literal and narrow application of those principles. To limit the study of the sociology of religion to the observation of behavior in organized groups labeled as religious and generalized into categories of faith, denomination, geographical area, or social class, is to deal with so small a segment of the meaning of religion as to be almost useless.

In other words, we should not be too quick to accept one or the other answers to these questions, which are complex and important for the way in which we will come to understand religion. The answers, by directing where we shall look when we analyze religion, will determine what we see.

Substantive vs. functional definitions. Are we, then, to define religion in terms of substantive qualities which it has (such as relation to some transcendent realm) or is it better to see it in terms of what it does for society and individuals (such as providing ultimate meaning). The issue may be better understood if examples of the two kinds of approaches are given.

In *The Sacred Canopy,* Berger (1967) defines religion in a way that focuses on the substantive qualities which are essential to the classification of some phenomenon as related to religion. Berger speaks of religion as "the human enterprise by which a sacred cosmos is established." (1967:26) The emphasis here is on the activity of human beings related to a specific kind of realm—the *sacred*—which is different in every way from that of the mundane world. The substance of religion, and its important defining point, then, is that it must partake of or be related to something which can be termed sacred. It focuses on the importance of transcendental or supernatural objects—or the existence of such an order which can be addressed to human problems.

As can be seen, when we speak of substantive definitions, the focus is on some aspect of what the group has set apart in a very special way, in such a special way, in fact, that it is defined as the sacred. This usually implies that it is an area (generally represented by various symbols) which invokes form the individual both fear and love. It is a realm which is totally different from the normal, everyday life which we lead. As Durkheim has described the matter (1951:52):

> All known religious beliefs, whether simple or complex, present one common characteristic: they presuppose a classification of all the things, real and ideal, of which men think, into two classes or opposed groups, generally designated by two distinct terms which are translated well enough by the words *profane* and *sacred*. This division of the world into two domains, the one containing all that is sacred, the other all that is profane, is the distinctive trait of religious thought; the beliefs, myths, dogmas and legends are either representations or systems of representations which express the nature of sacred things, the virtues and powers which are attributed to them, or their relations with each other and with profane things.

Certainly such substantive types of definition provide us with a key characteristic by which we can distinguish between that which is religion and that which is not. Yet, it is possible that the emphasis on the particular substance, sacredness, may be so subject to definitional bias what we miss things which would meaningfully be referred to as religion if we thought in terms of something other than sacredness. For example, Berger (1967), Herberg (1955), and Bellah (1967) have all described devotion to, and faith in, the American way of life as a set of religious beliefs. Where can this fit into something which supposedly is defined in terms of its sacredness? Or, how does the so-called "death of God" theology (which called us to continue worship and believe in some eternal, transcendent power, even though the God of our traditions was dead) meet this standard?

Such consideration leads to the suggestion that religion might best be defined in terms of the *functions* which it performs for both the society and the individual. Yinger (1970) defines religion in such terms, centering his attention on what religion does for society and for the individual. For him, religion is to be seen as the set of beliefs, practices, and symbols human groups evolve in order to deal with the ultimate problems of existence.

Religion functions for human beings as a way of dealing with what O'Dea (1966:5) refers to as "the three brute facts of contingency, powerlessness, and scarcity" in human activity. In a perspective such as this, what ever serves to explain these breaking points of life may be called religion. This way of looking at religion, and other social phenomena, began within anthropology as a counter to the ethnocentric attitudes of many of the early students as primitive cultures who equated what was primitive with what was superstitious or false. The functional approach sees any social structure as aimed at performing certain functions. It looks at the issue of why religion exists and what difference it makes, rather than at the issues of truth and falsity, right and wrong. It is an attempt to see what functions in various societies to solve certain kinds of problems, a perspective which obviously calls for a different kind of definition than the substantive one given above.

Sociologists probably do, in fact, define religion very frequently in terms of its functions; Bellah (1964), for example, sees religion as those symbols, beliefs, and behaviors by which people attempt to relate their lives to some ultimate condition of existence. In many ways, the functional definition is a useful one for the purposes of sociological analysis. It clearly allows for shifts in religious style and even content does not limit the conception of religion to the perspective of any particular group. Using such a definition, it is possible to postulate that all societies will have some value system common to the group as a whole which serves the general functions of religion, and which can be designated by that term.

The conceptualization of religion in terms of functions, however, does raise the question of what happens in societies where religion has been suppressed or for individuals who have rejected traditional religious interpretations. It is possible to suggest that in a society such as ours, where many members bypass the traditional religions, "functional alternatives" are found. That is, some set of values, beliefs, and symbols replace for such individuals (and for whole groups) the more customary types of religious beliefs; faith in America, a political ideology, or even belief in the efficacy of science may serve as such an alternative. It seems that in some cases such "secular" ideologies have swallowed up and used the religious institution. For example, in one southwestern city, a whole congregation became so consumed with John Birch ideology that this became the *raison d'être* for the group and they withdrew from the objecting parent denomination.

But it must be asked whether these alternatives are to be seen as different from religion, or as just another form of it? That is, how inclusive should our definition of religion be? Should it include all things that function for a certain purpose, or should there be boundaries which mark off for us what will be classified as religion?

Inclusive vs. exclusive definitions. Inclusive views of religion tend to see it as a "force" in the life of the individual and the group which may be present in may ways across the broad spectrum of cultures. In a view such as this, communist ideology, for example, would certainly be seen as a religious faith. If one wishes to play with the terminology involved, it is possible for us to find a number of such "alternative" concepts which match those of Christian faith. The Proletariat stands as the "Savior" who lead the faithful into the "Battle of Armageddon" (the class war) in the struggle to free society and mankind from the evil clutches of the "devil," the bourgeoisie. The "classless society" then is "heaven" or "eternity." Likewise, one could take the belief systems found in a political ideology such as Nazism, or the mental illness model found in Freud, and find values which appear to serve, for some, the same functions that religion has traditionally served. There seem to be any number of such "secular" religions which might be considered if we define religion inclusively.

The exclusive view, on the other hand, would restrict the term "religion" to only those beliefs and behaviors intentionally directed to the supernatural or transcendent as a way of fulfilling these functions. In other words, religion may be seen as that which serves certain functions, but only with reference to a realm which transcends our empirical existence.

The problem, as Demerath (1974:6) reminds us, is that too inclusive a view of religion may lead to defining the term out of all meaningful existence. Once we start the process of including any value system related to ultimate meaning or societal integration under the rubrick of religion, we may lose touch with conventional meanings of the term to such an extent that we are no longer really doing anything which has significance. Under such a description, the atheist who subscribes to the objectivity of science as a "value system" would have to be called religious—even though such an appelation runs against common sense and our preconceived notions.

It has been suggested by some scholars in the sociology of religion that we are faced today with what could be referred to as *nontheological* religions. Yinger (1969), for example, postulates the existence of what he refers to as *nondoctrinal* religion. He suggests that many people in this time may be religious, but in ways which are quite different from the traditional patterns. According to this view, there is religion wherever individuals are concerned with ultimate problems, the basic human condition, or have hope for "better" relations with other human beings. He also finds that there is some pattern or order to existence.

Luckmann (1967) rather similarly formulates the existence of what he calls "invisible religion." He concludes that the traditional forms of religious belief and expression are less relevant to modern society. Seeing religion as that which provides ultimate meaning to existence, he notes that this has traditionally been confined to explanations with a transcendent referent. However, he contends that there are other systems of meaning which have the same function as traditional religion; these systems he refers to as "invisible religion,"—religion which is not visible to us in terms of the usual practices and structures associated with religion. It is not that people are no longer religious, or are not as frequently religious as they once were, but that they are religious in different ways; ways which are not observed because they do not fit the traditional models.

There have been some attempts to do research which would either confirm or reject the notion that such religions exist for large segments of our population. Some, like Nelson et al. (1971), can find no support for the ideas expressed by Yinger and Luckmann's contentions. However, others do find evidence that such nontheological systems of belief exist and serve traditionally religious functions for individuals in our society. Machalek and Martin (1976), going even beyond Yinger's suggestions, have carried such an inclusive definition to what seems its logical extreme. They suggest that Yinger's definition is limited because he insists that religion contain "elements of ritual and shared beliefs as well as organized groups." They contend that we should include under the term anything or anyone except the individuals who *specifically* do not ever acknowledge the existence of any "ultimate" problems in life and thus make no attempt to cope with them. Only these would be seen as having no religious belief system. In research in Baton Rouge, Louisiana, these scholars found evidence that a sense of the ultimate problems of existence is found in individuals other than those with traditional religious beliefs. Further, they found that individuals have many mechanisms for coping with such problems which are unrelated to the religious institution. Thus, they conclude that there is credibility in Luckmann's observations about the existence of a privatized religion in modern society which justifies the tendency to spread the term religion so as to cover a broader range of behavior.

Our discussion of these two basic questions cannot really lead us to some final solution. However, it does sensitize us to the various nuances that exist when we use the term, religion, and the various ways in which the word is used by sociologists. We need to understand that the answer to our questions may vary in terms of the problem being addressed, and that no one answer can be right at all times.

In summary of our discussion of the definition of religion, from the sociological perspective, we can say that most will accept the four basic points which we discussed earlier in this chapter: religion is that which is held to be sacred (with broad variations in definition of *that* term); that which contains beliefs and practices directed at this sacred aspect (sometimes limited to that which has a supernatural referent); that which is a group endeavor; and that which is directed toward solving problems of ultimate meaning. As we shall see, while most definitions fall within these four points, there is considerable variation in the emphases which are put upon each of them.

SUMMARY

Religion is important for most people in American society. For some it is the most pervasive aspect of their daily lives; these people are confident in the meaning, intent, and communal operation of religious affairs. As one of the basic societal institutions having far-reaching social psychological consequences for individuals, religion is important as a topic for research by sociologists and other social scientists. Any analysis of macro-level human behavior would be incomplete without attention paid to religious beliefs, expressions, and structures. In that religious beliefs are interwoven throughout the social fabric, influencing and being influenced by other institutional arrangements (family, government, education, economy), the study of religion and religious impact remains a necessity for students of society.

The sociological perspective, however, forces us to investigate interrelationships between institutions themselves as well as historical forces and, as such, place no more importance or meaning on religion than other societal arrangements. Similarly, sociology looks for explanations in terms of social forces and processes and does not look to individual psychology or biology alone to explain the human condition. We also assume that social forces, structures, and processes are not random events but are, rather, patterned responses to human existence brought about by socialization within a particular socio-historical milieu. Additionally, we assume that truth is a relative concept which presently represents the "state of the art" of human understanding and problem solving within particular groups. For all science, truth is not absolute but subject to reexamination and further testing. Religious truth, though, is a matter of faith and belief and cannot be easily subjected to empirical testing or refutation; such possibility of refutation being a bulwark of scientific truth. For those who consider sociology a science, it is scientific only through its method and only then to the degree it proceeds through systematic research procedures. Science cannot test the ultimate truth of religious beliefs, but it can systematically test propositions *about* people's beliefs and the characteristics of those who profess them. It can test hypotheses about the strength of beliefs and religious behavior of, for example, Christians and Moslems; it cannot test which religion is correct or true.

Along these lines, Vernon (1962) indicates what the sociology of religion is *not*. As sociologists, our study is not involved with the truth or falsity of religious beliefs nor do we posit the correctness of one set of beliefs over another. Likewise, we are not reformers stating religion is a "good" thing for society or individuals. In fact, we consider both the functions and dysfunctions of religion and try to maintain an objective stance toward the operation of belief systems within society. Our chore is to explore, not expound; to proposition, not prosely-

25

tize; to theorize, not theologize, and to consider rather than convert.

To approach the sociology of religion it is necessary to have a definition of religion which is adequate to the sociological purpose. "Religion" may be seen as an umbrella term covering a wide variety of beliefs, attitudes, behaviors, and practices. In that it covers such a variety of phenomena, it oftentimes involves many ambiguous, nonobjective special problems for our investigation related to the definition of the term itself and of the measurement of numerous concepts related to it.

While clear definitions are important in all scientific inquiry, the precise boundaries of the term "religion" will depend, to a certain extent, upon the purpose for which the definition is used. However, those who have wrestled with the definitional problem concerning religion have sensitized us to at least three *interrelated* questions which appear again and again. First, shall religion be defined in terms of some special *substance*, such as a supernatural order? Or, secondly, shall it be defined in regard to the *functions* which it performs for individuals and the society, such as helping one cope with the ununown or with death?

As can readily be seen, numerous questions arise concerning what is to be called religion. In fact, one may not be able to choose "a" correct definition which will fit all times and purposes. However, there are four aspects that we think should be considered in any "sociological" definition (1) religion is that which is concerned with what is seen as sacred; (2) has a complex of beliefs and practices directed in some fashion toward this sacred; (3) is concerned with group, rather than solely individual activity and belief; and (4) deals with what can be termed problems of ultimate meaning.

REFERENCES

Bellah, Robert N.
1964   "Religious evolution." *American Sociological Review* 29:358-74.

1967   "Civic religion in America." *Daedalus* 96:1-21.

Berger, Peter
1967   *Sacred Canopy—Elements of Sociological Theory of Religion.* New York: Doubleday.

Berger, Peter and
Thomas Luckmann
1967   *The Social Construction of Reality.* New York: Doubleday.

Chambers, Patricia Price
and H. Paul Chalfant
1978   "A changing role or the same old handmaidens: Women's role in today's church." *Review of Religious Research* 19 (Winter): 192-97.

Demerath, Nicholas J.
1974   *The Tottering Transcendence.* Indianapolis: Bobbs-Merrill.

Demerath, Nicholas J.
and Phillip S. Hammond
1969   *Religion in Social Context: Tradition and Transition.* New York: Random House.

Durkheim, Emile
1947   *The Elementary Forms of Religious Life.* New York: The Free Press.
1951   *Suicide.* New York: The Free Press.

Glock, Charles
1973   *Religion and Sociological Perspective.* Belmont, Cal.: Wadsworth.

Glock, Charles and
Rodney Stark
1965   *Religion and Society in Tensions.* Chicago: Rand McNally and Company.

Hargrove, Barbara
1971   *Reformation of the Holy.* Philadelphia: F. A. Davis Company.
1979   *Sociology of Religion.* Arlington Heights, Ill.: AHM Publishing Co.

Herberg, Will
1955   *Protestant— Catholic— Jew: An Essay in American Religious Sociology.* New York: Doubleday.

Hodges, Harold M.
1971   *Conflict and Consensus. An Introduction to Sociology.* New York: Harper and Row.

Kephart, William
1976   *Extraordinary People.* New York: St. Martin's Press.

Luckmann, Thomas
1967   *The Invisible Religion: The Problem of Religion in Modern Society.* New York: Macmillan.

Machalek, Richard
1977   "Definitional strategies in the study of religion."
                    Journal for the Scientific Study of Religion 16
                    (December):395-402.

Machalek, Richard and
Michael Martin
1976   " 'Invisible' religions." *Journal for the Scientific
                    Study of Religion* 15 (December):395-402.

National Opinion
Research Center
1977   *General Social Survey.* Chicago: National Opin-
                    ion Research Center.
1978   *General Social Survey.* Chicago: National Opin-
                    ion Research Center.

Nelson, Hart, Raytha
Yokeley, and Thomas
Madron
1971   "Rural-urban differences in religiosity." *Rural
                    Sociology* 36:389-96.

O'Dea, Thomas F.
1966   *The Sociology of Religion.* Englewood Cliffs, N.J.:
                    Prentice-Hall.

Osborne, Thomas M.
1977   "A sociological approach to religion: Another
                    consideration." Paper presented at the meetings
                    of the Society for the Scientific Study of
                    Religion.

Time
1978   "Strong-Arming Garner Ted: The Ins and Outs
                    of the Worldwide Church." (June 19): 54–55.

Vernon, Glenn
1962   *Sociology and Religion.* New York: McGraw-Hill.
Weber, Max
1958   *The Protestant Ethic and the Spirit of Capitalism.*
                    New York: Scribners.

Williams, J. Paul
1962   "The nature of religion." *Journal for the Scien-
                    tific Study of Religion.*

Winter, J. Alan
1977   *Continuities in the Sociology of Religion: Creed,*
        Congregation and Community. New York: Harper
        and Row. 2:3-14.

Yinger, J. Milton
1969   "A structural examination of religion." *Journal*
        for the Scientific Study of Religion 8:88-99.
1970   *The Scientific Study of Religion.* New York: Mac-
        millan.

Chapter 2

Theoretical Approaches to the Sociology of Religion

It should be clear from what we have said in our introductory chapter that we see sociology as one of a number of perspectives which can be used in viewing the phenomenon of religion. As a particular angle of vision on religion it reveals only certain parts of the totality of that phenomenon, missing aspects visible to other disciplines such as theology. None of these perspectives, by itself, provides us with a total picture of religion. Our knowledge of that phenomenon, as with all others, is simply a montage of what is seen from the different points of view.

There is an analogy from this to the situation within sociology itself. While some individual sociologists would contend that their own theoretical assumptions provide a more nearly total picture than do others, only the most fanatic would argue that one perspective alone provides the true or full view. In other words, each of these special theoretical positions reveals some knowledge concerning religion as a social phenomenon, but all are needed in order to get as full a picture as possible.

In this chapter we shall look at several of these theoretical points of view to understand the contributions which they can make to our sociological understanding of religion. We begin with consideration of the earlier views, many of which have been virtually discarded, and then proceed to the more influential contemporary views.

EARLY APPROACHES TO THE SCIENTIFIC STUDY OF RELIGION

As sociology began to take shape as a separate academic discipline it carried the "intellectual baggage" of its time. It was greatly influenced by the popular Darwinian theory of evolution, and social life was interpreted in terms of a sort of *Social Darwinism.* This explanation affected the early scientific study of religion. For example, Comte's theory of the three stages was an evolutionary theory which viewed theology or religion as something appropriate to the childhood of humanity which would be displaced first by philosophy, and then by science, as our rational understanding of the universe gradually increased. Such a "negative," early interpretation has obvious significance for later sociological interpretations.

The Search for Origins

This evolutionary strain in the thought of the time made it nearly inevitable that the sociological approach to religion would begin with a search for the primitive origins of religion from which the contemporary forms had evolved. These early students were caught in the trap of confusing origins with ultimate causes; that is, they attempted to explain religion in terms of the way in which it was thought to originate (Demerath, 1974:4).

Early scholars, then, turned to the evidence of primitive societies in order to find the "bare essentials" of religious life in the simplest of societies. From such studies two specific theories arose to explain religion as simply a stop-gap for inadequate explanations of things in nature which the primitives did not understand.

Animism is an explanation of religion which traces the origin of belief in "spirits" to common experiences that so-called primitive people could not explain. Examples of this are not difficult to find. We all have dreams in which we seem to move about in a different world or observe a reflection of ourselves in a pond of calm water. The animists proposed that such events or experiences for the primitive society required an explanation, and that in the attempt to explain these experiences the primitive individuals posited the existence of a totally separate order of existence. Such an order was peopled with other kinds of beings—spirits. From this the conclusion was drawn, according to the animists, that there was a spirit which lived in the individual which was released during times of sleep and which permanently left the body at the time of death. This latter kind of spirit became especially important, because it represented the dead individual. Rituals for the dead and beliefs about life in another existence developed. From these beliefs developed the idea of groups of spirits—and eventually the development of the concept of gods. Religion, thus, was seen by the animists as an irrational response to the rational quest for explanation.

Naturism is similar to, and a variation of, animism. It too explains religion as a result of the primitive's inability to understand what we would see as natural occurrences. That is, once again, the explanation or the "cause" of religion is seen as existing in the need for explanation. In naturism, the origin of religion is not generally in the kind of events which lead to belief in spirits. Rather, the need for explanation is to be found in certain mystifying events of nature—thunderstorms, sunrises, tides, and a variety of awe-inspiring events or physical acts of nature. Primitive groups, being at the mercy of such events, created beliefs in the existence of agents which controlled the forces—and which could be appeased into controlling them for the benefit, or at least the safety, of the group. It is claimed that primitives, or perhaps all humans, have difficulty in seeing action as "uncaused." Thus if it "pours" rain, someone must be doing the pouring; if a boat is rocked in a storm, the rocking is caused by some agent. Thus there developed a belief in the existence of gods or divine agents that were responsible for these actions and could be worshipped or manipulated to ward off evil or gain advantage.

Neither animism nor naturism is considered a viable explanation for the origin of religion today. The evolutionary hypothesis clearly distorted much of the thinking of these early sociologists of religion, even though they did contribute some relevant material to the sociology of religion. The chief problem of the evolutionary hypothesis, at least as used here, is to be found in the assumptions of inevitable evolutionary progress. One of the fallacies of this perspective, as Demerath and Hammond (1969) suggest, is that primitive societies are simple, small in population, limited in geography, uncomplicated by politics and economics, and generally preliterate. It is simply not possible to draw conclusions about contemporary religion in complex, modern societies based upon the evolutionary interpretations of primitive societies.

The evolutionary hypothesis, also, assumes generally that religion is the result of ignorance and that progression up the evolutionary trail will result in a lesser need for it in society. Religion was explained and then seen as withering away. Clearly this has not happened, and explanations based upon such assumptions are obviously less than adequate.

Religion as society worship. The fullest and most productive attempt to explore religion in its most elementary forms was provided by Emile Durkheim who went beyond a simple, evolutionary hypothesis to discover what was common to primitive religion that was also important in all religious expression. Durkheim discarded prior theories concerning religion, including both animism and naturism. He believed that these did not touch the most elementary forms of religious behavior and beliefs. For him, religion has two essential characteristics: (1) the division between the sacred and profane, and (2) the idea of a church or group. From these elements Durkheim defines religion as a unified system of belief and practices concerning sacred things, i.e., things set apart and forbidden. These beliefs and practices are then united into one single moral community to which all adherents belong. But this twofold division or characterization of religion leads to a central question for Durkheim. How did it happen that human beings first came to make such a division and then form groups around it?

To answer this question, Durkheim studied the form of religion he considered to be the most primitive—totemism. He based his study on reports concerning the Arunta of Australia, a tribe which practiced this ritual or belief. Totemism derives its name from a root word relating to the relationship between half-brothers and sisters. Basically it refers to a society composed of clans united by real or fictitious kinship (Hartland, 1951). Any object which serves as a totem generally belongs to either the animal or vegetable world and gives its name to the clan. Actually, the object provides more than a name; it is an emblem, a veritable coat of arms. Images of the totemic object are placed on the walls of houses, the sides of canoes, on weapons, utensils, and even tombs. These totemic decorations are employed in the course of religious ceremonies as part of the liturgy, indicating the fundamentally religious character of the totem. The totem also serves as the basis for the division between the sacred and profane.

The totemic images, however, are not the only sacred things for the Arunta. Because of the relation which they have to the totem, the species which correspond to the totem and the members of the clan adopting such a totem are also considered sacred. Thus, three classes of things can be recognized in totemism which are considered sacred: (1) the totemic emblem; (2) the animal or plant that this emblem represents; and (3) the members of the totemic clan. It is in the fact that all of these are sacred that Durkheim finds the clue to the real meaning of sacred and the origin of beliefs in the sacred.

Such beliefs are, according to Durkheim, obviously of a religious nature, as they imply the division between the sacred and the profane. However, they are also inseparable from a social organization on a clan basis, the simplest form known. The religious character of any of the things sacred in totemism cannot be due to any special attributes to these things, as these play no part in the division. It must come from some principle common to the totemic emblem, the people of the clan, and the corresponding plant or animal. From this, Durkheim concludes that totemism is the religion not of animals, people, or images, but of anonymous and impersonal forces found in each of these things.

This force or power is not definite or definable; it is *power* in the absolute sense. This makes clear how thoroughly the idea of an impersonal religious force enters into the meaning and spirit of Australian totemism. The totemic clan is addressed to a power spread through all things. This power is the original matter out of which every sort of being that religion consecrates was built. Thus what we find at the origins of religious thought are not determined and distinctive objects and beings, but indefinite powers and anonymous forces.

But where do these indefinite powers and anonymous forces originate? It would seem that the totem is the symbol of *both* the sacred and the society. If so, is it not so because the sacred and the society are *one*? The totemic principle *can be nothing other than the clan itself personified.*

Unquestionably, society has all that is necessary to arouse the sensation of the divine in our minds, because it is the source of authority and dependence for all of us. However, because it also has a nature peculiar to itself, it seems like something outside of us which demands our allegiance. When we yield to its orders, it is not merely because it is strong enough to triumph, but primarily because we give it our venerable respect.

We are thus brought to an understanding of how the totemic principle, and in general every religious force, comes to be thought of as outside the object in which it resides. It is because the idea of it is inspired by the group, projected outside of the consciousness of the individual, and objectified. For Durkheim, the primitives' religion is the expression in symbolic terms of their awareness of the social system upon which they are dependent for both material and psychic necessities of life. In short, Durkheim indicates that we feel the presence of another world, the world of social forces.

Durkheim explains the necessity for the objectification of social forces by pointing to the needs of the clan; the clan needs a constant reminder of its value which the totemic religion provides. Social life is made possible and continuous by this symbolism, which takes practical expression through ritual practices.

Durkheim assumed that the unanimous sentiment of so many believers in all times could not be purely illusory. This reality, represented in many forms by many mythologies, is the universal and eternal expression, *sui generis,* of society. Indeed, it can be said that nearly all great social institutions have been born of religion. Religious forces are, therefore, human and moral forces.

The Search for Causes

Yinger (1970:88-89) has suggested that the search for the origins of religion was, in fact, a search for causes. We cannot find adequate evidence of the total historical development of religion, but we can attempt to find clues to the sources of religious belief and behavior and how these continue to influence the lives of individuals and society as a whole. We will look only briefly at two attempts to explain religion in terms of causes.

Freudianism. While obviously not basically sociological in nature, the theories of Freud concerning the motivation for religious beliefs and behavior present an interesting example of the search for a cause of religion. Freud sought, by looking into the "beginnings" of human existence, some clue as to what continued to bring out the religious response in individuals and societies. Freud treated the subject of religion in a variety of ways, but basically he saw it as a sort of universal neurosis, mainly resulting from the Oedipus complex. For in religion Freud saw a mixture of love and dependence, respect and fear, hostility and love which he found characteristic of the Oedipus complex. Freud then traced religious drive to a biological heritage of crime and guilt, positing some great primal crime that took place in the childhood of the human race.

Essentially, Freud explained religion in terms of a "myth" or "parable" concerning primitive humanity. He posited that some primal father was slain by his sons in order that they might gain control of the women that the father kept to himself. However, once they had committed the patricide they were filled with deep remorse, and with great anguish for the feelings of love which they felt for the father. The brothers "undid" their deed by declaring that the killing of the father substitute, the totem, was forbidden. They also renounced their rights to the women (thus creating the incest taboo). They did, however, according to the myth, accomplish an identification with the father by eating him and acquiring part of his strength. This feast would then represent and become the memory of the criminal act and would be, according to Freud, the beginning of many of the restrictions of society. In *Civilization and its Discontents* (1930), Freud claimed that civilization is built on human renunciations of the satisfaction of instinctual drives. Religion, then, is seen as primarily a narcotic which gives spurious meaning to a heartless world. Religious beliefs are illusions, but the fact that they are learned from society, and held in common with other persons, protect the believer from individual neurosis at the cost of mass neurosis.

Marxism. In one sense it may not be totally germane to consider Marx at this point, because his interest in religion was far more minimal than is generally assumed. He thought that religion was a burden placed upon humanity that would eventually be lifted as the human's true position was established. Thus, he did not give it extensive consideration. Indeed, it is to be remembered that Marx sought *only* to relate Protestantism in nineteenth century Western Europe to the development of industrial capitalism. Thus, any explanation given by Marx of the cause of religion can only be seen in terms of that one particular system of beliefs (Winter, 1977:33).

Insofar as Marx attempted to explain religion, he tied his explanations to the particular means of production in society; that is, it was the result of the economic structure of the society. As such, religion was a tool used by the owners of the means of production to control those whom they exploited—in our society, the proletariat. In a sense, religion helped individuals cope with the frustrations of the capitalist society, and this dulled their impetus to fight that system. To him religion was made by people and corresponded to nothing eternal or superempirical; it was only a sign of the alienation of people in a society which oppressed and dehumanized them.

Winter has neatly summarized Marx's position with regard to religion (1977:35):

> ... the Marxian position is (1) that God, as conceived by the bourgeoisie, is a metaphoric representation of the basic characteristics of the economic order; that is, of the alien inexplicable denomination of the capitalistic system over the members of the bourgeoise society; and (2) that belief in such a God helps one cope with the distresses or frustrations of life in such a society.

In reality, Marx regarded religion as all but dead and considered intellectual attacks upon it valueless. It remained for his follower, Engels, to elaborate on the role which new religious sects might play in bringing about revolutionary social change.

We will return to the Marxian approach in the latter part of this chapter; suffice it to say now that there is a connection between Marxian thought, conflict theory and the dysfunctions of religion.

Symbolic Interactionism. Another perspective, or set of conceptual "lenses," with which one might approach religious beliefs is symbolic interactionism. This approach is more concerned than the Marxian with micro-level occurrences and does not deal as readily with large scale social structures or "classes" of people. Rather, attention is focused upon more minute, immediate, forms of social interaction which occur within smaller groups. In other words, person may be citizens of large geopolitical structures but their interaction remains, basically, at a much more primary level. By studying such minute levels of interactional discourse we are really studying what is meant by phrases such as "how a person fits into society," or "how a person becomes a group member," or in some sense, how a biological being becomes human and develops the ability to internalize norms and fulfill role obligations. A recent volume confronts these issues and concludes by calling upon symbolic interactionists to "work out better the logic of the relationship between social structure and individual behavior, between macro and microsocial processes" (Stryker, 1980:155). Even though we deal with the microsocial process of socialization more in Chapter 3, certain foundational premises are necessary here for our treatment of the search for causes of religious belief and behavior.

Symbolic interaction refers to the cognitive, informational, decisional and, of course, symbolic nature of human behavior. Several key terms are associated with the perspective: self and personality, definition of the situation, role and role internalization, and taking the role of the generalized other. Symbolic interactionism studies the social-psychological processes involved in shaping the individual into a member of society and, therefore, into a somewhat predictable person.

The often quoted concept of the "looking-glass self" (Cooley, 1902) refers to the reflective nature of the processes involved in the development of a self-concept. Rather than positing an imprinted identity and self-concept which unfold according to a biological pattern, the symbolic/reflective perspective states that we learn self-concepts through interaction with others. We are pliable actors capable of modification and, through such modification, continually in the process of changing selected aspects of our self-concept. Cooley (1976:20) put it this way:

> A self-idea of this sort seems to have three principal elements: the imagination of our appearance to the other person; the imagination of his judgement of that appearance, and some sort of self-feeling, such as price or mortification . . . the thing that moves us to pride or shame is not the mere mechanical reflection of ourselves, but an imputed sentiment, the imagined effect of this reflection upon another's mind.

Implicit in Cooley's ideas is that "significant others" may have an impact on our self-concept. If we conceptualize the self as being made up of different facets according to the informational feedback we get from members of our important reference groups, then the idea of a "religious self" (along with a work-self, family-self, school-self, etc.) easily emerges. That the social self is multifaceted and dependent upon groups of others we consider important is a mainstay of the symbolic interaction perspective.

George Herbert Mead (1934) contributed to our understanding of human behavior by developing the concept of the "generalized other." Mead believed that many of our actions are guided by the awareness we have of others' values and their expectations of us as we engage in the "game stage" of human development. As Horton and Hunt (1976:91-92) summarize:

> It is through this awareness of others' roles, feelings and values that the *generalized other* takes form in our minds. This generalized other is roughly equated with the standards or values of the community. By repeatedly "taking the role of the generalized other," one develops a concept of self—of the kind of person he or she is—while repeatedly applying the judgments of this generalized other to one's own actions. [Emphasis in original]

The game articulated by Mead forms the bases of our empathy and sympathy with other persons. It also allows one to develop a conscience in the sense that the internalized "values of the community" offer one a gyroscope with which to compare one's behavior to normative standards. Introspection provides a measure of self-worth or self-esteem based upon compliance with what is considered moral, right or appropriate cognitive and behavioral prescriptions.

Another concept important to symbolic interaction is the "definition of the situation" articulated by W. I. Thomas (1937). Stressing the interpretive character of thought and action, Thomas sensitized us to the mental processes which mediate between various stimuli and our responses to such stimuli. As Stryker (1980:31-32) has noted:

> Thomas makes abundantly clear the fundamental significance of definitions of the situation in that they precede all "self-determined" acts . . . Children, for example, are always born into an ongoing group that has developed definitions of the general kinds of situations faced and has formulated rules of conduct premised on these definitions: moral codes are the outcome of "successive definitions of the situation."

Moral codes and religious beliefs, then, are produced by historical fact and the manner in which these facts are interpreted or defined; they are implemented through teaching and learning from one generation to the next. The W. I. Thomas theorum (Thomas and Thomas, 1928), which states that if people "define situations as real, they are real in their consequences," elaborated upon the subjective nature of our interpretation of events and ideas. Therefore, if a group considers a Christian theodicy, for example, to be factual, they will interpret situations and events on the basis of that theodicy; it is, therefore, *real* in its consequences. Along this same line, consider the following treatment of the subjective nature of symbols (Karp and Yoels, 1979:31-32):

> We should stress that our range of responses to an object are dependent on the social and cultural circles in which we live our daily lives . . . consider the case of religious symbols. Here the physical characteristics of the symbols are irrelevant to their meaning. To Christians, a crucifix has meaning because it represents (or better, re-presents) an historical event—the crucifixion of Christ—that has been designated by Christians as a divine event. Whether a crucifix is made out of gold, iron, or wood is irrelevant to the Christian who defines it as a holy object and responds to it reverently . . . if strangers from another culture, never having heard of Christianity, were to come to America and happen upon a crucifix there is no way that the physical characteristics of the object would indicate to them what the crucifix represents. They would have to learn that through communications with others. In addition, the crucifix will evoke a different response (that is, have a different meaning) for members of groups with alternative religious views, such as Jews, Moslems, or atheists. Humans, we are arguing, live in a world where they alone have assigned meanings to things. Symbols mobilize our responses to the world. They help us bring together, or conceptualize, aspects of the world.

So, what can we draw from the symbolic interactionist tradition that helps in our search for the sources of religious belief? Very simply, that persons, through a process of mental development involving conditioning and internalization of values, learn to "define the religious situation," develop as part of a multifaceted personality a "religious self," and communicate more readily with others of a like mind, thereby reinforcing their structure of belief. The importance of interacting with others who share the same beliefs is pointed out by Bibby (1978) in his explanation of the recent growth of conservative churches. In his contention that conservative church growth is due to factors *other than* providing an "ultimate answer" and being characterized by a seriousness necessitating "personal commitment" (Kelley, 1972), Bibby (1978:133-134) declares:

> . . . .the ability to socialize and retain offspring looms as the vital determinant of the size of these religious groups. The data indicate that there the Conservatives are outdistancing the Mainliners. Not only do the Conservatives have a higher birth rate . . . but they further are increasingly more likely than Mainliners to expose their offspring to formal and presumably informal . . . religious education.

The symbolic interactionist could interpret Bibby's findings by pointing out that systems of *meaning* are bestowed upon the young through religious socialization which provides not only ideas that are reinforced, but interpretive examples of the truth of those ideas. Adverse circumstances come to be seen as "God's will," as a test of the strength of one's commitment to the religious principles of the church. Prayer can be interpreted as a cognitive dialogue between a person and the internalized conception of God (similar to Freud's concept of the superego). The need to "belong" to the church can be seen as a need to be accepted as a member of a positive reference group whereby one could maintain a positive self-image and avoid ostracism by cherished significant others. One's religious *Weltanschauung* would be primarily provided by the tenets of religious instruction instilled in the person by family, peers, and clergy.

In fact, symbolic interactionists could point to the utility of their perspective by referring to the *diversity* of religious belief sytstems. Such diversity could be seen as evidence of the myriad ways in which persons interpret, and pass on to others, religious doctrine and religious norms of propriety. Diversity in religious belief occurs because of different definitions of the religious situation.

Again, if one defines situations, religious or otherwise, as real, they are real in their consequences. The consequences of the definitions allow for strong in-group formations and, sometimes, hostility toward out-groups that fail to accept definitions, or interpretations, isomorphic to those of the in-group. The symbolic interactionist could remind us of the fact that socialization is a continuing process and that the personality is constantly in the process of "becoming" and that the roles we are expected to play are variable from stage to stage in our lives. The tentative character of the cognitive, evaluative and group processes in which we become engaged throughout our lives allows one to also change and adjust according to new information, or new intepretations of old information, and according to new situations and new definitions of those situations.

These contentions—in essence, that interacting persons creating their own reality, religious or otherwise—bring us to another perspective that may contribute to our search for the causes of religious beliefs. In some ways, as we will see, this perspective, called phenomenology, is similar to symbolic interactionism.

Phenomenology. We would be remiss if we did not acknowledge the confusion surrounding the phenomenological perspective in sociology today. Phenomenology means different things to different people. Thevenaz (1962:37) mentions that phenomenology has been seen, among other things, as an inquiry into the logic of meanings, a theory of abstraction, an analysis of consciousness, as a method for approaching concretely lived existence, and as similar to existentialism. More recently Heap and Roth (1978:286-289) have identified four different types of phenomenology. These "phenomenological sociologies" include (1) perspective involving the symbolic interactionist concern with subjective meaning, (2) the Schutzian (1967) approach to social action and "formal" structures of the "life-world," (3) the first person approach to researching the social world (reflexive sociology), and (4) ethnomethodology, which tries to find out how people make sense of their daily lives. We cannot go into an extended treatise here on the meaning(s) of phenomenology. We hope that our articulation of the principles found in Berger's (1967) *The Sacred Canopy* will, however, provide the "essence" of what we consider to be the phenomenological approach to religion.

Berger (1967:3-4), in explicating the notion of the dialectic process of society, identifies the three steps of externalization, objectivation and internalization as essential to an understanding of society:

> Externalization is the ongoing outpouring of human being into the world, both in the physical and the mental activity of men. Objectivation is the attainment of the products of this activity (again both physical and mental) of a reality that confronts its original producers as a facticity external to and other than themselves. Internalization is the reappropriation by men of this same reality, transforming it once again from structures of the objective world into structures of the subjective consciousness. It is through externalization that society is a human product. It is through objectivation that society becomes a reality *sui generis*.

Through the learning of language and success in socialization the individual actively "appropriates" parts of the social world in order to make sense of one's own biography. In the course of this internalization, an individual takes on knowledge that has been generated by society; thus learning to live an ordered and meaningful life by structuring consciousness according to the nomos (laws) of the parent society. To lose the norms, or to become anomic, implies the separation of the person and his world. In extreme cases, according to Berger (1967:23), this may cause the person to lose "his sense of reality and identity." In "marginal" situations (such as being anomic, separable from society and aware of and fearful of death) the society offers the individual protection by offering meaningfulness. In Berger's (1967:25-26, 28) words:

> Whenever the socially established nomos attains the quality of being taken for granted, there occurs a merging of its meanings with what are considered to be the fundamental meanings inherent in the universe. Nomos and cosmos appear to be co-extensive. . . . It is at this point that religion enters significantly into our argument. . . . Religion is the human enterprise by which a sacred cosmos is established. . . . Put differently, religion is the audacious attempt to conceive of the entire universe as being humanly significant.

This "audacious attempt" to make sense of one's existence and the existence of

41

the world as an objective reality and as a perceived object is, to us, the underpinning of phenomenological inquiry. When persons are asking questions such as "Who am I?," "What is the nature of the universe?," and "How am I to conceive of and relate to God?," they are asking questions that can be studied phenomenologically. *That we try to make sense of phenomena*, is phenomenologically relevant and can be taken as a point of departure. How we "make meaning" out of the world and the cosmos is a phenomenological study. For Berger (1967), the approach would be to recognize that persons fear chaos, or separation from the meaning provided by the nomos, and believe and act to shield themselves from the meaninglessness inherent in such a separation. Persons appropriate meaning (for their lives and the cosmos) by being guided by well-defined "plausibility structures" (legitimations of existence contained within institutionalized social process). Berger (1967:47) reflects upon meaning systems (as does the symbolic interactionist) in his treatment of the nature of plausibility structures:

> The reality of the Christian world for example depends upon the presence of social structureswithin this reality as taken for granted and within which successive generations of individuals are socialized in such a way that this world will be real *to them*. When this plausibility structure loses its intactness or continuity, the Christian world begins to totter and its reality ceases to impose itself as self-evident truth. . . . The firmer the plausibility structure is, the firmer will be the world that is "based" upon it [emphasis in original.]

Phenomenologically we may contend that a prime consideration in the search for causes of religious belief, or, for that matter, any belief system, is predicated upon the search for meaning *vis à vis* our recognition of the inevitability of death. In speaking about the works of another phenomenologist, Ernest Becker, Scimecca (1979) points out that Berger (1967) and Becker (1973; 1975) take a social constructionist position—one that involves the active, phenomenological *creation* of meaning through dialectical relationships between culture and the individual. Thus, as we stated earlier, phenomenology is akin to symbolic interactionism in that it involves introspection, reflectivity, and interpretation of events—in essence the *bestowal* of meanings upon phenomena by humans (which includes the human characteristic of apperception). In the final analysis, phenomenology contends with the multi-faceted techniques through which persons (individually and collectively, or in Berger's term, dialectically) strive for understanding and legitimacy in a precarious mental and physical world. Thus, the phenomenologist, as we see it, could take as subject matter the tribal practices involving anunism, totemism, and multitheism, as well as the more modern practices of worshipping an abstract deity and following philosophically oriented church doctrines. In short, and oversimplified, the phenomenologist approaches religious belief just as any other belief or "attitude": through a study of the perceptual, cognitive, intellectual, and behavioral trial-and-error processes we utilize in "making" the universe, our social worlds, or our own consciousness humanly significant and understandable.

In our brief treatment of Freudianism, Marxism, symbolic interaction, and phenomenology, we have attempted to reveal ideas relevant to the search for the causes of religious belief. Our treatment is not to be considered exhaustive but, rather, heuristic, in that one should realize that different perspectives, or "glasses," concentrate upon different aspects of religious life.

Our task is now to turn to analysis of the impact of religious beliefs (regardless of their causes) and to show how such beliefs operate on the group or societal level. We will concentrate on the functions and dysfunctions of religion for groups (as well as for individuals within those groups) and will address some of the current concerns of religious practice within the United States.

Before presenting some of the functions and dysfunctions of religion, however, it is necessary to briefly review the tenets of functionalism and the conflict perspective of human relationships. Such a discussion will be particularly important when we speak of the conceptual notion of dysfunction of religion.

FUNCTIONALISM AND CONFLICT: THE SOCIETAL VIEWS

As a theory of society, functionalism arose in anthropological thought to deal with the "ethnocentrism" of early students. They found the ways of "savages" incomprehensible and quickly dismissed them as primitive, or naive, or just plain wrong. Functionalism opened up the notion that in all societies the various features, mores, ways of doing things, are tied together in a "functional whole" which works toward the solution of the society's various problems of adaptation, integration, tension managment, and pattern maintenance.

Most simply put, there are three basic principles underlying the functionalist view. First, it is assumed that for any society there are problems which need to be solved if the society is to maintain itself. Also, it must pass on its patterns and ways of doing things to the next generation of "societal members." Each society, then, must develop ways in which these traditions can be passed on *and* ways to enforce among the new members the traditional manner of doing things.

Second, society is conceived of in terms of an "ongoing equilibrium." That is, the society is seen as being a somewhat precarious balanced of a number of elements, all of which must maintain a certain degree of consistency lest the society itself be thrown out of balance. In this regard, the functionalists spend a great deal of time exploring the problems of "re-equilibrating" societies and

THE SOCIOLOGICAL STUDY OF RELIGION

handling deviances that might threaten this balance. Third, each part of the society, seen as a system, is viewed as making a contribution to the solution of the problems. Thus, each part is also seen as "necessary" to the maintenance of the equilibrium. Obviously, this shows a conservative tendency to enshrine existing parts.

In summary, functional theory views society as an interdependent system of parts all aimed at the basic problem of societal survival. A society, or the pattern of beliefs, values, and actions of a society, is the result of a careful balancing of different parts of the whole which form an equilibrium that must be maintained. The balance of equilibrium is considered necessary for the solution of societal problems. Each part of the society is viewed as having necessary participation in the solution.

The conflict perspective is at odds with the functionalist view of society for a variety of reasons. As a view of historical change, conflict theory maintains that rather than cooperative equilibrium as the normal state of affairs, that conflictual power struggles have dominated societal change. Conflict theorists warn that viewing elements of society (such as stratification systems) as necessary and inevitable places one in a narrow-minded mold from which one then selectively perceives human relationships. As Perrucci et al. (1977:345) have summarized:

> As an alternative to functionalism, the conflict view focuses upon class conflict and coercion as the basic element in social life. Derived from the statement of Marx about class dynamics, this view suggests that change, not integration, is the significant fact in society. This continuous and pervasive change results from basic inequalities that exist in society.

While functionalism and conflict theory are not the only major perspectives of social life, as we have seen, they have probably resulted in more scholarly discourse within the discipline of sociology than any others, at least during the twentieth century. This voluminous discourse has possibly resulted in the recognition by most scholars that neither view is adequate as a grand theory of social arrangements nor as an explanation of individual or group behavior. However, both remain conceptually rich and provide basic points of departure for the study of social change and social and institutional stability.

THE FUNCTIONAL PERSPECTIVE AND RELIGION

O'Dea (1966) cites three specific conditions of life which find some answer in the "religious" institution—the contingency of life, that is, the very conditional sense in which we may live one moment and be dead another; powerlessness, our inability to answer many problems; and scarcity, the problem of allocating scarce resources in some fashion that is seen as "just" to the members of society. The so-called functionalist view of religion would emphasize the way in which religion is used by the society to solve both group and individual problems.

As noted, the function of religion in society has frequently been summarized in terms of its integrative aspects. That is, its chief function has been seen as its ability to achieve a successful melding of the individual members and groups of the society into a whole which can function effectively to solve the basic problems of the maintenance of society. O'Dea (1966), in expanding the ideas presented above, notes that religion can be seen as having six *basic* functions. These, and others, are discussed below.

Support, consolation, and reconciliation. Because religion provides human society with a point of reference that transcends the everyday world, that is, the divine or supernatural, it also provides individuals and groups with the sense that this "beyond" is concerned with the meaningfulness of life. Thus, they can find support, consolation and reconciliation for the events of their lives. For example, however lowly the status of an individual might be, one can justify this status and the meaninglessness of this one's existence by reference to some eternal "pie-in-the-sky-bye-and-bye" reward which one will receive. And, looking at the other side, those who have spent their lives accumulating goods may find deeper meaning in this as the sign of supernatural support or approval. Religion may also be used to explain the many tragedies and sorrowful happenings that befall individuals by "explaining" them.

New security and firmer identity. Again, the relationship to the transscendental realm can lead to a feeling of security and a sense or worth as a result of an identity provided by beliefs concerning this transcendental realm. O'Dea refers to this as the "priestly" function of religion and notes that it contributes to stability, order, and generally, the maintenance of the status quo. In short, having this reference point beyond the present life can give individuals and groups a sense that there is an order to life beyond what appears to them in the present. Again, a seemingly senseless occurrence, such as the death of a very young child, may be given some meaning if that child's family believes thay may see that child again in another realm.

Sacralizing norms and values. Religion tends to give an added emphasis or importance to the norms and values of the society and thus helps to maintain their dominance over the individual or individual groups. That is, those social values and the norms are given not only a legal sanction but also a "divine" one. In past times, going to war when asked by the society has been a social norm for young men. However, it has also taken on, particularly during the Second World War, religious overtones. That war, for example, was seen as a sacred one in which we were fighting for "God's will," and thus to fail to fight was to "let God down." Therefore, religion reinforced the societal norm and very few openly refused to take up arms against God's enemies.

THE SOCIOLOGICAL STUDY OF RELIGION

The prophetic function. Religion can, however, perform a function contrary to the above. It can also provide standards of values against which the existing norms of the society can be critically examined and called into question. Thus, during the 1950s many used religion as the reason for calling into question the norms of the society concerning segregation and discrimination; in the 1960s large numbers of people felt it a religious duty to oppose the draft and the war in Vietnam. In both cases, religion was used to call into account the assumed way in which things worked.

Identity functions. Religion can also be seen as assisting the individual to perform certain identity functions. That is, it provides the individual with an answer to the question, "Who am I?" Frequently, the answer that is most meaningful to the individual is in terms of a religious group point of reference. "I am a Catholic," "I am a Presbyterian," or, even, "I am an agnostic." In any of these cases the individual defines himself with reference to the religious group and finds his identity in this relationship.

Growth and maturation. Finally, religion can be seen as related to the processes of growth and maturation of the individual. As individuals pass through the various age categories constructed by the society, religion provides symbols and ceremonies which effectively mark off these new positions in society.

O'Dea's listing does not exhaust all possibilities for the functions performed by religion, as our continuing discussion illustrates. In one sense, as Jacobs (1971) points out, we can simply look at religion as providing a general sense of morality and responsibility. He decries the fact that in the more or less secularized society of today there is a negative character to much of our lives: a defiance of authority, a contagious irresponsibility, a kind of moral delinquency, no longer restrained by religion or ethical faith. He sees these attitudes as threatening personal serenity and public order in many parts of the world. He points to the paradox of an increasingly secular order, particularly within individualized protestantism, that is led by a Christian morality based upon spiritualism. In short, religion may be fulfilling as many critical functions as it possibly could.

One specific function of religion, that of providing comfort, has been investigated by Glock et al. (1967). They attempted to determine the extent to which social deprivation underlies involvement in contemporary churches. Basing their results on a study of church members, they reported that the "comfort thesis" was supported in that the poor among church members tended to be more involved.

A similar "comfort" which may be provided by religious belief and participation is physical comfort. Missions many times provide food, shelter, and clothing, as do collectivities such as the Salvation Army and other active religious agencies. One movement in our recent history remarkably demonstrates that "comfort" may come in various physical forms. The Father Divine movement peaked in this country in the 1930s and early 1940s and still maintains a few followers. The movement was led by a charismatic black man that claimed to be God and admonished his followers to abstain from sexual behavior, drinking, smoking, and obscenity. Father Divine established an employment network, chains of hotels in which his followers could work, and prepared elaborate feasts for true believers. During the depression years, for example, a typical "communion banquet" was described as follows:

> And what a banquet it is! A dozen different vegetables, roast beef, fried chicken, baked ham, roast turkey and duck, meat loaf, steak, cold cuts, spare ribs, liver and bacon, four different kinds of bread, mixed salad with a choice of dressing, celery and olives, coffee, tea, and milk, and a variety of desserts, including layer cake, pie, pudding, fresh fruit, and great mounds of ice cream. (Kephart, 1976:108).

The practical comforts, or functions, of religious participation are many times intertwined with other functions. As Kephart (1976:126) points out below, these are real-life considerations and influence numerous people regarding religious participation.

> Things were so bad for black Americans in the 1930s that a feeling of alienation often prevailed. . . . More than any other leader of his time, it was Father Divine who fought against the spread of alienation, and he was a superb practitioner. He understood the masses. He could talk to them. He could engender feelings of self-respect, and he could play the role of God. Most important, he never lost sight of two basics: food and jobs. These were the bedrock. As long has he was helmsman, his followers would have ample food at little or no cost. And—through his employment service or within his own economic establishment—they would have jobs.

Numerous other studies also provide evidence of the interplay of the social structure, religion, religious institutions, and the individual. Some have seen religion as functioning to provide a substitute for the primary ties broken down by increased urbanization and industrialization. As early as 1940, Holt suggested that Holiness sects developed in response to the cultural disorganization produced by the urban migration of rural southerners to the industrial centers. Such religious movements, he claimed, provided a new form of community for the displaced and disoriented. Likewise, Frazier (1974) saw such groups as functioning to give rural, southern blacks a replacement for their ritual communities, thus providing escape from the anonymity of the city.

Willems (1967) has also noted that the Pentecostal sect in Latin American nations, and among Latin Americans in the Southwestern United States, are making great inroads into formerly Roman Catholic Latin populations which have moved from the rural to the urban areas. The economic and social needs of these groups find their response in such sectarian groups. In response to the need for new, close, personal relationships, the sectarian groups provide what might be seen as a new family—even the terminology most favored in such groups stresses the "brotherhood" of the members.

Flora (1973) has commented on the relationship of socal dislocation and Pentecostalism. Noting that social disloation gives rise to mass movements, she attempts to relate individual histories of social dislocation to adherence to religious movements. Using respondents from Palmira in the Cauca Valley of Columbia, she sees Pentacostalism as a mass movement involving lower class individuals caught up in a total change of lifestyle. Analysis of the responses demonstrates that individuals of low socio-economic status who have experienced personal social dislocation in terms of migration and employment are more likely to be Pentecostals than their fellows without similar experiences. Primary ties are seen as mechanisms for introducing lower class individuals to Pentecostalism. However, they are no more important for Pentecostals who had not suffered personal dislocation than for those who had.

Another example of the impact of social structure on religion is to be found in the shape which American Catholicism has increasingly taken in the United States. In short, the societal values of democracy and participation have brought about a response in the structure of the Catholic church in our society. Roche (1968) comments that the laity of the Catholic church are bringing about the greatest transformation in the Church since the Reformation. There is clearly a crisis of confidence in the leadership of the Church; freedom is the key word for the "reforms" of the Vatican Council.

Photiadis and Schnabel (1977) have examined some of the reasons that religious fundamentalism persists in Appalachia even more strongly than it endures in the rest of the United States. Their major hypothesis is that it persists because it forms a buffer for the rural and low income residents of the Appalachians who feel alienated because of dislocations that have taken place in that region in the last few decades. Their findings show that dimensions of religiosity which involve potential for reducing anxiety (for instance, need to use religion as a buffer to the outside world) tend to be associated not simply with lower socioeconomic status but also with alienation in terms of bewilderment and confusion. The authors contend (1977:40) that religion provides meaning for those of low socioeconomic status and enables them to avoid "the anomie of dislocation and alienation from self." For those who have risen in status it provides recognition and identity functions, "offering social recognition for what has already been achieved."

These functions mentioned above are basically adaptive and integrative, serving both the needs of the individual psyche and the needs of the larger social structure. We must remember that religious beliefs and participation may have negative consequences for individuals and groups. Put differently, religion is a two-sided coin having both functional and dysfunctional components.

THE OTHER SIDE: DYSFUNCTIONS AND CONFLICT

If the functionalist perspective can be described in any sense as that which sees the function of religion in society as integrating the society, the conflict perspective is best seen in terms of the segmenting effects of religion. As mentioned earlier, accepting either the functionalist *or* conflict approach as one's *total* viewpoint tends to make one narrow-minded. Elements of functionalism *and* conflict, synthesized into a broader perspective, usually provide a more epistemologically appropriate theoretical and ideational springboard. Reminding us of the problems with a purely functional interpretation of religion, Eister (1957:387) contends that any attempt to apply most of the available functional theories of religion to complex societies rather than to primitive ones will be more likely to lead to frustration than to useful understanding. He contends that despite the impressive array of opinion supporting the idea that religion is primarily an integrating social force, it is difficult to accept this pattern of interpretation as valid or appropriate for the contemporary scene. Indeed, the interpretation is hard to accept for any society where there is a high degree of specialization and functional autonomy among institutions, or where religion itself is organized on a basis which tolerates a variety of faiths. For each of the integrative or support functions of religion cited in the popular theories it is possible to find similar dysfunctions of religious ideology and practice.

In our brief discussion of the dysfunctions of religion, one might keep in mind two basic levels at which dysfunction might occur, individual and group. Keep in mind, also, that function and dysfunction must be seen in context; what is functional or dysfunctional depends upon taking the conceptual role of the other. In other words, what is perceived as functional (or dysfunctional) depends upon where the interpreter is "coming from" intellectually, conceptually, and ideologically. Robert Merton (1967:91-100) has sensitized numerous students of religion and functionalism to the very import of separation of functional analysis from functional (or conflict) ideology. Our purpose here, however, is to entice the reader into engaging in these intellectual exercises with us; to think about various instances in one's own life where religion might be conceptualized as dysfunctional, hindering rather than aiding one's overall well-being. Again, we may utilize individual and group levels.

The Individual Level

Most people, if they are human beings in the usual sense of the word, have undergone the process of socialization—learning the norms (folkways, mores, laws) of their culture. The socialization process involves conditioning, which may or may not be intentionally carried out by socialization agents (parents, teachers, peers). Conditioning involves not only sensorimotor behavior (do not stick your hand in the fire) but ideas of appropriate and inappropriate conduct toward others (it is not nice to kick Mom's shins). Numerous social and developmental psychologists have immersed themselves in the study of the socialization process and have produced sensitizing concepts with which to better understand this phenomenon. Freud spoke of the id, ego, and superego; Cooley of the looking-glass self; Mead of the generalized other; Piaget of the various developmental stages. Implicit in these studies are notions of the internalization of psychological mechanisms which guide peoples' behavior in the "appropriate" direction. Pleasure, shame, fear, guilt, and approval are vehicles for keeping the person on the "right track" psychologically and socially. Adherence to the norms promotes "healthy" personal development and makes for comformity, which is, of course, necessary for a "healthy" society. Such are the bases of the conservative nature of society.

What happens, though, when the proscriptions and prescriptions of a society are not followed? Are there dysfunctional elements to conformity in general, and religious conformity in particular? The answer is, "maybe." Psychopathologists have long chronicled the damaging impact of unrelieved guilt and feelings of unworthiness present in the psyches of those who have violated certain religious proscriptions. Religious beliefs may "drive a person crazy" if that person cannot resolve concomitant dilemmas and contradictions. Striking out against what one has been taught may also entail damaging individual behavior, especially if it encompasses an emotional trauma in the process. Durkheim's classic study on suicide informs us that, in addition to the above, individuals who are involuntarily or accidentally separated from group-supported religious beliefs may be unable to cope with the void and turn to drastic means of adjustment which are unhealthy and dysfunctional to the living organism. Similarly, religion often plays the role of institutionalizing immaturity and develops in its adherents dependence upon religious beliefs, religious institutions, and religious leaders rather than an ability to assume individual responsibility and self-direction.

Religiously induced psychic stress, then, is a common dysfunction of religion. Chesen (1972) in his book *Religion May Be Hazardous To Your Health* has addressed the relationship between emotional instability and authoritarian religious practices, and Rokeach (1979:173) has commented that "people with formal religious affiliation are more anxious. Believers, compared with nonbelievers, complain more often of working under great tension, sleeping fitfully, and similar symptoms." Additionally, novels, plays, and movies abound with the theme of religiously induced psychic stress. If "religious toilet training" is not conducted properly (which is rather variable in itself), then individuals may develop numerous types of neuroses and psychoses associated in some way with religious socialization. Dealing with guilt, indecision, and frustration produced by religious doctrine has actually become big business in American society today, as a quick glance through bookstores will attest. Competing alternatives abound.

While numerous biographies, autobiographies, and literary classics could be cited as exemplary of the frustration and "crises of identity" provoked by religious beliefs, the following comments by an anthropologist seem to adequately get our point across. Miles Richardson (1975:517-519), in speaking (somewhat allegorically) of his association with Southern Baptists states:

> You would think that a person with an intense religious upbringing would become someone compatible with that background . . . one of my brothers was a preacher, and my sister married one. But it didn't work out that way with me. Actually, that's not too uncommon either. I suspect that for every minister the Southern Baptists have produced, they have turned out five atheists. Pound for pound, the Baptists have probably put more souls in hell than any other religion. And I'm one of them. It was in my early adolescence that I discovered I was evil. Because I was evil, I was going to die. . . . I tried hard not to be evil. I did not swear, I did not smoke, and certainly I did not drink. . . . I went to church twice on Sunday plus attending the morning Sunday School and the evening Training Union. I tried to think pure thoughts . . . and here I was, looking at girls with lust on my mind and even stealing glances at the big-bosomed preacher's wife. How could I be saved? . . . "Look to Jesus," the preacher said. But Jesus was a Levi-Strauss paradox. Jesus-Christ-God was perfect feminity. He was kind, sweet, and full of love. . . . Jesus-Christ-God was perfect masculinity. . . . He was victor over death and his blood was full of power. He taught gentleness and peace; he sent people to burn forever in hell. How could I touch such a figure? . . . I have never tried anything harder nor wanted anything more. But I did not succeed, and then I knew I hated God. . . . [Anthropology] was going to free me from the view of man groveling before a God that, on the one hand was sweetly sissy and on the other remotely brutal, from a religion that makes the gentle touching between a man and a woman evil. . . . My freedom from the things that nearly destroyed me (and that continue to haunt me) would come from studying them, from wrestling with them in order to expose their secret. At that point, just short of stomping on them and destroying them, for some reason my private battle stops. Today, I have no love for the Southern Baptists, but I can almost say "Billy Graham" without sneering.

This narrative only scratches the surface of the ways in which frustration and indecision may "haunt" a person. However, Richardson himself may not consider his turmoil as totally dysfunctional. Such may simply be the price one pays for intellectual growth. These problems *can*, however, result in debilitating consequences for individuals.

Indirectly, the strict internalization of religious mores may limit the individual's receptivity to new and possibly correct ideas. Religious doctrine may promote hostility to critical, open-minded thought but, to again indicate the contextual nature of the argument, such hostility and intellectual conservatism may also be functional for the individual in that it provides *some* interpretation of reality. Individuals may, nevertheless, find themselves in particular situations in which their conservatism becomes individually dysfunctional. Feelings of superiority (or of inferiority) of one's religious self, and the prejudices which result, may place individuals in hostile circumstances which may be psychologically, even physically, dangerous. Martyrs may benefit from their deaths in other worldly salvation and in the foreknowledge of martyrdom, but torture and death can hardly be seen as functional for the individual organism.

Even following some religious prescriptions may be harmful to the biological well-being of the individual. Overzealous fasting may have deleterious effects on the body as well as on the mental health of the individual. Religious pilgrimages, if over rough terrain at unfamiliar altitudes, may prove hazardous to life and limb. Certain beliefs in the inefficacy of modern medicine may allow diseases to spread and wounds to fester. And among certain congregations (Gerrard, 1968:11, 23) scriptural interpretations propel certain adherents to handle poisonous snakes.

> The serpent-handling ritual was inaugurated between 1900 and 1910, probably by George Went Hensley .... He died in Florida at age 70—of snakebite. To date, the press has reported about 20 such deaths among the serpent-handlers ....For their part, the serpent-handlers say the Lord causes a snake to strike in order to refute scoffers' claims that the snakes' fangs have been pulled. They see each recovery from snakebite as a miracle wrought by the Lord ....

While these examples may border on the extreme, they do serve to make our point—in certain circumstances and from certain perspectives religious beliefs and practices can be dysfunctional to the individual as a biological and psychological organism. These dysfunctions may be more or less group-induced and may be suffered singularly or in conjunction with other group members. Or, in some senses, the group itself, as a sociological entity, may engage in beliefs and practices which are dysfunctional. This brings us to the next level of analysis—the group level.

The Group Level

The group level, as used herein, ranges across the continuum from small scale (dyads, cliques, church groups, congregations) to large (religious bodies, religious organizations, societies). The groups at the large end of the scale might even be considered to be national or international in scope.

To set the stage for brief discussion of how dysfunctions and conflict may emerge at the group level, we can consider the term *religiocentrism*. A common word used in sociological literature is "ethnocentrism," which refers to the tendency to take for granted the rightness and superiority of one's own sub-culture or culture. In the same vein, we might refer to feelings of rightness and superiority resulting from religious affiliation as religiocentrism. Religious beliefs and religiously induced behaviors are not all "positive" in regard to adaptation, integration, and goal-attainment. As Horton and Hunt (1976:58) state:

> In an age of atom bombs and push button warfare, when the nations must probably either get together or die together, ethnocentrism helps to keep them tied to concepts of national sovereignty. Under some circumstances, then, ethnocentrism promotes cultural stability and group survival; under other circumstances, ethnocentrism dooms the culture to collapse and the group to extinction.

On the community level, numerous instances of religious squabbles, splits, and schisms have had real consequences for participants caught up in the conflict. Bitterness, gossip, and hostility have more than once divided a community. Families, social clubs, and even neighborhood schools have been victimized as a result of religiocentric values. These conflicts may arise within a basically homogeneous religious group or may involve different, heterogeneous, groups such as Protestant, Catholic, Jewish, or Muslim. Or, such conflict may arise from generalized religious views. The current controversy over prayer in public schools is one example. While the net effect of such conflict may be a merger or synthesis, it is nevertheless, at one point on the continuum, social "conflict" which may promote or impede social adjustment.

Religiocentric views may also keep people in the dark intellectually. They may hamper individual adjustment, as mentioned previously, or harm the group as a whole. Millenarian groups, such as the Jehovah's Witnesses, have had to modify their original spiritual insights in order to continue when the world did not end when expected (Zygmunt, 1970). Some groups have been so steadfastly religiocentric as to damage their very survival. The United Society of Believers in Christ's Second Appearing—or "Shakers"—have held to their beliefs, including the prohibition of marriage and sexual relations, until there existed, as of 1976, only twelve members. As Kephart (1976:191) states:

It is true that there are still two families of Shakers—one at Canterbury, New Hampshire, the older at Sabbathday Lake, Maine. But while their buildings and grounds are in excellent condition, the membership is dying off. There are eight sisters at Sabbathday Lake, and only four at Canterbury. Most of them are quite elderly—in their seventies and eighties—and some are in poor health. While it is conceivable that new members might be admitted, no applicants are presently being considered; in fact, it has been fifteen years since the last admission.

Even though there could possibly occur a revival of Shakerdom, the present membership of just twelve people is a far cry from the seventeen thousand plus all-time membership (Kephart, 1976:168) claimed for the group. In this vein, the religiocentric views of the Shakers, involving celibacy, economic communism, and separation from the world, drastically influenced their demise as a viable religious group.

Religious groups may sometimes be confronted with problems of adaptation which do not immediately threaten their very survival. Even though the system of courtship and marriage practiced by the Amish may continue for some time as "successful," Kephart (1976:30) mentions an interesting facet of the religious prescriptions surrounding an Amish marriage.

Amish parents forbid their young people to date the "English" (non-Amish). As a matter of fact, the only permissible dating is (a) within the district or (b) between districts that have full fellowship with one another. Endogamy among the Amish, therefore, does serve to limit the number of eligible mates. In outlying districts, this limitation may present some real problems.

These few examples demonstrate that religious groups may confront problems which arise from *within* and which necessitate adjustment of beliefs and operations if the groups are to continue. The sociological perspective called conflict theory, however, deals primarily with conflict *between* groups, whether religious or secular. A rather recent conflict in this country concerns the rights of a religious group to prescribe certain behaviors which are contrary to the law of the land. The Amish, who do not heartily accept frills and modern inventions, have been forced by state law to install night lights and turn signals, powered by under-the-seat batteries, on their horse-drawn buggies (Kephart, 1976). Amish parents have also been convicted, in Wisconsin, for refusing to send their children to local schools. Even though on appeal the Amish were found to be in the "right" (Kephart, 1976:40), they were, nevertheless, originally victimized by state laws which assumed the "rightness" of a formal, bureaucratic, and standardized educational system. The conflicts between institutional arrangements and beliefs (in this case between religion, education, and government) have not escaped sociological attention; in fact, much of the early writing of Karl Marx, dedicated to just such analysis, deserves additional attention at this juncture.

Institutionalized procedures often collide with one another. In such a collision power becomes of paramount importance in the handling of such conflict. Some theorists maintain that power, within the United States at least, is of a pluralistic nature—power is spread out among individuals who have a voice regarding the use of power and authority. Others contend that there exists some sort of elite which controls most societal operations. Such an elite may be of a conspiratorial nature or it may be nonconspiratorial. However, due to historical circumstance the elite maintains control, in one form or another, over large portions of people's lives. So, then, where does religion fit into such a theoretical schema? The functionalists would tell us that religion serves basically integrative functions. The power theorists would probably agree that such is the way religion has been *used*, but at the expense of those not in powerful societal positions. Through some societal con game, the powerful have utilized religious values to keep people pacified and nonrevolutionary. Dominant religions are conservative and even reactionary in emphasizing and maintaining the status quo, particularly the economic and political status quo. As Robertson (1977:3723) writes:

> The conflict approach to religion derives mainly from the writings of Karl Marx, who saw religion as a form of false consciousness and as a tool of the powerful in the struggles between competing social classes.

> To Marx, belief in religion was the profoundest form of human alienation. By *alienation* Marx meant the process through which people lose their sense of control over the social world that they have created, so that they find themselves "alien" in a hostile social environment . . . people create gods, lose their sense of social authorship of religion, and then worship or fear the very gods that they themselves have created. . . . Moreover, Marx claimed, the *dominant* religion in any society is always the religion of its economically and politically dominant class, and it always provides a justification for existing inequalities and injustices. . . . As Friedrich Engels caustically remarked, religion tends to make the masses "submissive to the behests of the masters it had pleased God to place over them." [Emphases in original].

Boughey (1978:22-3) articulates how religion would be viewed through an "Activist sociological lens" (similar to a conflict lens).

> Institutionalized religion from this perspective, is and always has been a counterrevolutionary force in human society. The demands and the struggles of the masses for concrete benefits, such as economic and social justice and freedom from domination by others, have traditionally been met with

offers of "spiritual" rewards instead. You save your soul, and I'll invest my profits, say the elites through their religious spokesmen. Be patient, slave, you'll get justice in heaven. Blessed are the poor. Your sufferings under my heel are the expression of God's will, so take your complaints to the head office. You'll never get justice, so try bliss instead, you'll feel better.

From the preceding examples it should be clear that institutionalized patterns (macrolevel elements) are not always harmonious. People may not be allowed and/or do not demand full participation in the economic, political, and social arena. They have been cooled out, have *allowed* themselves to become cooled out by an "opium of the people" (religion) and have developed a mistaken sense of their value as human beings—their sociopolitical consciousness is of a "false" nature, pliably accepting and passively experiencing their "station" in life ("The meek shall inherit the earth"). In the sense that religion hinders individuals and groups from achieving their "full potential," religion is seen as socially dysfunctional.

One must remember that the above discussion is heavily laden with ideological biases and represents a particular theoretical stance. That the proletariat is such a passive group, or that an elite is so conspiratorial and self-seeking, has provided impetus to numerous arguments. The pluralists *and* the power theorists both have elements of logical consistency in their arguments as well as supporting data. Houtart and Lemencinier (1976), for example, have suggested that rather than looking at the total society in regard to the impact religion has on the masses, that we might consider, as did Weber, that the function of religion appears to be essentially tied to, in segmental fashion, several identifiable groupings within the society. These ideas are presented in Table 2-1.

One other dysfunction of religion on the group level should be pointed out—that of the conflict, bloodshed, and warfare prompted by religiocentrism. Such conflict may occur at both the intranational and international levels. History is full of evidence concerning the direct and indirect effects of religiocentric views. Religious persecution and attempts at religious genocide still linger in the memories of many Americans and citizens of other countries. However, one should, for scientific accuracy, be careful of such seemingly obvious direct casual links. As Robertson (1977:374) has stated:

Wars fought on ostensibly religious grounds are often marked by extreme bloodiness and fanaticism, but religious differences are not necessarily the *causes* of the wars, even though the participants themselves may take this view. The medieval crusades, for example, appear at first sight to have been a purely religious conflict between Christians and Muslims. A closer analysis suggests, however, that the crusades were initiated in Europe partly to divert the considerable unrest that existed among the peasantry at the

Table 2-1. SOCIAL STRATA AND RELIGIOUS FUNCTION

Social Strata	Cultural Traits Related to the Place Held in the Religious Field	Religious Form	Function of the Religious Demand	Justification
Peasants	absence of rationalism (dependence on nature)	(animism)	protection	insecurity
Warrior nobility	absence of rationalism (challenges irrationality of fate) — love of danger	no ethical religion (of salvation) but ceremonial rites	protection against evil spells — recognition of the dignity of order	need to conquer, status
Merchant bourgeoisie	rationalism	more or less strict ethics	legitimization of its own excellence	psychological
Bureacracy	rationalism	ritualistic religiosity	recognition of order	psychological
Craftsmen	rationalism	no homogeneity, atypical feature of demand, tends toward an ethical religion (of salvation) and emotional community	compensation or reward for one's situation, need to replace primary family relationships	psychological
Modern proletariat	rationalism and knowledge of the relationships of social forces	Nil	Nil	replaced by ideologies
Capitalist bourgeoisie	rationalism and control of production and knowledge and of social relationships	Nil	Nil	replaced by ideologies

Source: Houtart and Lemencinier, 1976:348.

time. Similarly, the continuing conflict in Northern Ireland seems on the surface to be simply one between Protestants and Catholics, but its roots lie deeper in a conflict between classes and nationalisms. For historical reasons, the Protestants are primarily members of the middle and upper classes and are pro-British, while the Catholics are primarily members of the working class and favor secession from Britain. Religious differences may thus serve as a justification for rather than a cause of the conflict: the real origin of the conflict often lies elsewhere. [Emphasis in original].

With such a caveat noted, we can conceptualize religiocentricity as being dysfunctional to the degree that it promotes needless violence, intolerance, and hostility toward others. In that religious differences may serve as justifications for conflict, they serve as dysfunctional facets of social life. This, again, must be interpreted in context. The judgment of holy wars, or of other attempts at religious genocide, as functional or dysfunctional depends upon one's perspective and level of analysis. We hope we have shown, however, that there *are* different perspectives and that religious values and behaviors *can* be interpreted as functional *as well as* dysfunctional.

SUMMARY

In this chapter we have taken a look at a few of the ways in which religion, other institutions, and the individual are intertwined. A sociological stance is, by necessity, a relativistic position regarding the nature of the "correct," "true," or the "chosen" religion. To sociologists, religions are best studied as human beliefs and social patterns which become institutionalized within a society and which exist for some socially constructed reason; this general statement is compatible with all of the different perspectives utilized herein (Freudianism, Marxism, symbolic interactionism, phenomenology, functionalism, and conflict theory).

Even by utilizing all of these theoretical perspectives, however, sociology cannot deal with the "ultimate" nature of religion. We can, however, study religious beliefs and religious behaviors and ask questions about how religion operates as one of the basic institutions in a society. We can answer questions about the functioning of religious beliefs and practices and can catalog various elements of such beliefs and practices. We can demonstrate that, under certain conditions, religion functions to aid an individual's adjustment to a socially constructed world and helps the society maintain itself as a more or less integrated system. We can also demonstrate that religion is dysfunctional, under certain circumstances, to both the individual and to the society as a whole. As perspectives within sociology, "functionalism" deals with the integrative aspects of religion and the "conflict perspective" deals with the dysfunctional and oppressive features of religion. Both perspectives have objective merit as conceptual viewpoints of the ways religion, and other institutions, operate in society.

We have also shown that studies of macrolevel systems, such as religious systems, must be constantly on guard concerning the imputation of "causation" to singular variables. Even "simple" relationships (i.e., the impact of religious values on "holy" wars) may prove to be spurious and complicated beyond our original thinking. Probably the most important point to remember is that religion, society, and the individual are interrelated. The individual, on one hand, sometimes influences religious beliefs (through charismatic leaders, for example), is also the recipient of religious indoctrination in varying degrees, and is a member of the general society and a member of a particular religious organization. From our point of view the intriguing and perplexing point of departure is the interactional nature of these three variables—religion, society, and the individual. This chapter has hopefully aided in sensitizing the reader to such a point of view. The next chapter continues the sensitization process by addressing problems which confront specific groups and by looking at techniques utilized in the solutions to particular problems.

REFERENCES

Becker, Ernest
    1973   *The Denial of Death.* New York: The Free Press.
    1975   *Escape from Evil.* New York: The Free Press.
Berger, Peter L.
    1967   *The Sacred Canopy: Elements of a Sociological Theory of Religion.* New York: Doubleday.
Bibby, Reginald W.
    1978   "Why conservative churches *really* are growing: Kelley revisited." *Journal for the Scientific Study of Religion* 17 (June):129-137.
Boughey, Howard
    1978   *The Insights of Sociology: An Introduction.* Boston: Allyn and Bacon, Inc.
Chesen, Eli
    1972   *Religion May Be Hazardous To Your Health.* New York: Peter Wyden.
Cooley, Charles Horton
    1902   *Human Nature and Social Order.* New York:

Scribner's.

1976   "The looking-glass self." Pp. 16-22 in Henslin, James M. (ed.), *Down to Earth Sociology: Introductory Readings*. New York: The Free Press.

Demerath, Nicholas J.
1974   *The Tottering Transcendence*. Indianapolis: Bobbs–Merrill.

Demerath, Nicholas J.
and Phillip S. Hammond
1969   *Religion in Social Context: Tradition and Transsition*. New York: Random House.

Eister, Allan W.
1957   "Religious institutions in complex societies: difficulties in the theoretic specification of functions." *American Sociological Review* 22 (August):387-391.

Flora, Cornelia Bretler
1973   "Social dislocation and pentecostalism: a multivariate analysis." *Sociological Analysis* 34:296-304.

Frazier, E. Franklin
1974   *The Negro Church in America*. New York: Schocken Books.

Gerrard, Nathan L.
1968   "The serpent-handlers of West Virginia." *Transaction* 5 (May):22-28.

Glock, Charles Y., Benjamin B. Ringer, and E. R. Babbie
1967   *To Comfort and To Challenge: A Dilemma of the Contemporary Church*. Berkeley and Los Angeles: University of California Press.

Hartland, E. Sidney
1951   "Totemism." Pp. 393–407 in Hastings, James (ed.), *Encyclopedia of Religion and Ethics, Vol. II. New York: Charles Scribners Sons.*

Heap, James L. and Phillip A. Roth
1978   "On phenomenological society." Pp. 279-293 in Alan Wells (ed.), *Contemporary Sociological Theories*. Santa Monica, Cal.: Goodyear.

Holt, J. B.
1940   "Holiness religion—cultural shock and social reorganization. *American Sociological Review* 5(5):740-747.

Horton, Paul B. and
Chester L. Hunt
1976   *Sociology.* New York: McGraw-Hill, Inc.

Houtart, Francois and
Genevieve Lemencinier
1976   "Weberian theory and the ideological function of religion." *Social Compass* 23:345-354.

Jacobs, Jerry
1971   "From sacred to secular: the rationalization of Christian ideology." *Journal for the Scientific Study of Religion* 10:1-9.

Karp, David A. and
William C. Yoels
1979   *Symbols, Selves and Society: Understanding Interaction.* New York: Lippincott/Harper and Row.

Kelley, Dean M.
1972   *Why Conservative Churches Are Growing.* New York: Harper and Row.

Kephart, William M.
1976   *Extraordinary Groups: The Sociology of Unconventional Life-styles.* New York: St. Martin's Press, Inc.

Mead, George Herbert
1934   *Mind, Self, and Society.* Chicago: University of Chicago Press (Published posthumously; collected and edited by Charles W. Morris).

Merton, Robert K.
1967   *On Theoretical Sociology.* New York: The Free Press.

O'Dea, Thomas F.
1966   *The Sociology of Religion.* Englewood Cliffs, N.J.: Prentice-Hall.

Perrucci, Robert, Dean
D. Knudsen and Russell
R. Hamby
1977   *Sociology: Basic Structures and Processes.* Dubuque, Iowa: Wm. C. Brown Company

Publishers.

Photiadis, John D. and
John F. Schnubel
1977   "Religion: a persistent institution in a changing Appalachia." *Review of Religious Research* 19:32-42.

Richardson, Miles
1975   "Anthropologist—the myth teller." *American Ethnologist* 2 (August):517-533.

Robertson, Roland
1977   "Individualism, societalism, worldliness, universalism: thematizing theoretical sociology of religion." *Sociological Analysis* 38:281-308.

Roche, Douglas
1968   *The Catholic Revolution.* New York: David McKay.

Rokeach, Milton
1979   "Paradoxes of religious belief." Pp. 172-177 in Cargan, Leonard and Janne H. Ballantine (eds.), *Sociological Footprints.* Boston: Houghton Mifflin Company.

Scimecca, Joseph A.
1979   "Cultural hero systems and religious beliefs: the ideal-real social science of Ernest Becker." *Review of Religious Research* 21 (Fall):62-70.

Schutz, Alfred
1967   *The Phenomenology of the Social World* (George Walsh and Frederick Lehnert, Trans.). Evanston, Ill.: Northwestern University Press.

Stryker, Sheldon
1980   *Symbolic Interactionism: A Social Structural Version.* Menlo Park, Cal.: Benjamin/Cummings.

Thevenaz, Pierre
1962   *What is Phenomenology?* (James M. Edie, Trans.). Chicago: Quadrangle Books.

Thomas, William Isaac
1937   *Primitive Behavior.* New York: McGraw-Hill.

Thomas, William Isaac
and Dorothy S. Thomas
1928   *The Child in America.* New York: Knopf.

Willems, Emilio
1967   *Followers of the New Faith. Culture Change and*

the Rise of Protestantism in Brazil and Chile.
Nashville, Tennessee: Vanderbilt University
Press.

Winter, J. Alan
    1977

Continuities in the Sociology of Religion:
Creed, Congregation and Community. New
York: Harper and Row.

Yinger, Milton
    1970

The Scientific Study of Religion. New York: Macmillan.

Zygmunt, Joseph F.
    1970

"Prophetic failure and Chiliastic identity: the
case of Jehovah's witnesses." *American Journal
of Sociology* 75 (May): 926-948.

PART TWO

THE SOCIAL
ORGANIZATION OF
BECOMING RELIGIOUS

Chapter 3

The Individual and Becoming Religious

Emphasis has been given in the previous chapters to the sociology of the group and group behavior. We have indicated that those aspects of religion which are personal and private are not within the scope of our interest unless they are expressed as attitudes or behavior in the social arena.

This concentration on the social does sometimes lead the sociologist to view the group as a reality which is over and above any involvement with the individual. Dennis Wrong (1961) has accused us of taking an "oversocialized" view of persons in society which sees the individual as almost "at the mercy" of social forces over which they have no control and in the formation of which they have no part.

Certainly, as Parsons (1951) contends, the individual members of a society tend to develop needs and motivations which are shaped by the patterns of their society and by their particular status. However, any view of the interaction between society and the individual which reduces that transaction to the all-encompassing coercion of society over the individual fails to account for many meaningful aspects of social life. In our eagerness to make our central assertion that individual life is strongly affected by the group, we should not make the mistake of seeing the interaction as a one-way street.

Berger and Luckmann (1967:89) remind us of the dangers of reifying a concept such as society, that is, of treating the products of human being *as if* they were something more than that. In fact, this reification tends to treat *human beings* as the product, thus reversing the true situation. As Berger notes elsewhere (1967:3):

> Society is a dialectic phenomenon in that it is a human product, and nothing but a human product, that yet continuously acts upon its producer. Society is a product of man. It has no other being except that which is bestowed upon it by human activity and consciousness. . . .

In this process, we tend to externalize that which we have created. We then experience it as a force of its own making, a fact apart from human creation. Through the process of socialization, then, we again appropriate these forces as reality, but not the awareness that they really have their origin in the activity and interaction of humans.

In this chapter, we want to place the individual in the group or social setting, showing the two faces of social experience. In particular, we will look at two questions: (1) How does the individual come to be religious (or nonreligious)?; and, (2) How can we apprehend the various ways in which the individual experiences and expresses the religious.

BECOMING RELIGIOUS

How does one become religious? In keeping with our general theme of how the group affects the individual, we can note, with Finney (1978:19), that the religiosity of individuals is best seen as the consequence of the norms of religious groups with which the individual has contact. All of the "norms, surveillance, and sanctions" which form part of any group life operate also in religious groups and affect the members of the group in a particular way. Thus religious behavior is most fully explained when we give attention to the patterns of interaction prevalent in the religious groups with which one has contact.

A question such as "how does one come to be religious?" will receive a variety of answers depending upon who is asked and in what region of the country it is asked. There are sections of American society in which it is almost assumed that one will be religious, at least to the extent of identifying with some religious group. For example, in at least one southwestern city, religious affiliation is routinely printed in the city directory along with other routine items of personal information. Being a religious person is simply a part of belonging to society in this area of the country. In fact, it is so important that some belong to and attend a Unitarian fellowship in order to be able to say that they have such an identification.

The answer to this question also depends upon the orientation of the particular religious group. Members of small, conservative, fundamentalist groups, for example, would probably insist that "becoming religious" is a matter of conversion, and that only through such a very intimate and personal experience can one really become a believer. Those affiliated with groups that are large and middle-class, on the other hand, would be more inclined to see one's religious affiliation as one of a series of natural steps in the process of growing up.

In some ways, neither of these particular perspectives gives us the whole picture. Becoming religious is seldom the thundering experience of instant conversion it is sometimes taken to be, nor is it really the inevitable, automatic progress of the young into the religion of their elders. However we see the process coming about, the prospective "religionist" undergoes some period of instruction, learning by word and observation, and experimentation with ritual, ideas, and practices.

Socialization and Religion

What is involved in "becoming religious," of course, is that process which sociologists refer to as "socialization." To be "religious," in one sense of the term, is to take on the "role" of member of a religious group or perhaps the role of "believer." Suggesting that one "becomes religious" by learning to take on the roles of member or believer is to say that one comes to know and internalize the expected behaviors, patterns of interaction, attitudes, and values of those who are already believers and members of the group. Without such expectations, smooth and efficient social interaction could not go on; a social fact which is as true for roles within the religious group as it is for roles that one plays in other parts of society. Just because these expectations are so very important to the success of the group, it is vital that "new recruits" to a religious movement have transmitted to them the "ways of life" of the group. Thus, socialization is an all important aspect of learning to be religious.

Socialization is simply the means by which an individual learns the expectations society has for particular statuses and internalizes them. It is the way in which the individual comes to take on the values, beliefs, and attitudes characteristic of a particular position or status; that is, the process by which persons learn to "play" the particular role the group attaches to that status. As a result of the socialization process, individuals acquire the knowledge, skills, and dispositions that enable them to participate as more or less effective members of the group (Brim and Wheeler, 1966). The process is life-long (Duberman, 1975), certainly so in the case of religious socialization.

Berger and Luckmann (1967) make a distinction between primary and secondary socialization. Primary socialization occurs during childhood when the individual becomes a member of society. Significant others during this period, principally parents, impose definitions of reality upon the child which the child internalizes; the roles and attitudes of these others become the child's world. Secondary socialization is the process by which the institutional, generalized world, with its roles and attitudes, is internalized.

The individual experiences both steps in religious socialization. There are discernable stages in the process. At first, in the primary sense, such socialization occurs in the family as parents initiate the child into their particular view of what being religious means, even if their view is a totally negative one. At an early stage of life, however, the formal organization—through church school groups and other forms of association—takes a hand in shaping the institutional version of norms and values. Peer groups, at every stage of development, also influence the perspective of the individual. Of course, some do not experience this smooth development. At some time in their lives there comes a moment called "conversion," which can be seen as a process of re-socialization, a time when previous socializations are discarded for those newly earned. As we shall see, even a conversion experience is the result of the internalization of the perspective of some other.

69

Johnstone (1975:79) suggests that there are four steps involved in this secondary socialization whereby one "becomes religious" (or not religious, for that matter) in the institutionalized sense. First, some formal religious group or community attempts to convince the "initiate" that the organization and its values are worth a commitment which will lead to the investment of time, money, and effort. Second, after an initial commitment, the group norms are further instilled in the individual so that they are more deeply internalized as part of the individual's basic values and beliefs. Third, the religious group attempts to see that the norms of the group so influence the new recruit that even when not in direct contact with the group, the behavior of the newcomer will follow its norm. Finally, there is continual reinforcement and encouragement aimed at undergirding and strengthening these norms.

Different religious groups will vary in how and with what intensity they proceed in this process. Still the essential process is followed. As Westerhoff (1972:121) notes, the process consists of both formal and informal mechanisms operating through the life of the individual. New members come to identify themselves with the faith and value systems of the religious group through participation in the rites, beliefs, and symbols of the "community of faith"; the faith reality for them.

Through the religious socialization of the individual, a religious identity forms. For most, as Wilson (1978:113) notes, this process is as "natural and as taken for granted as learning sex roles" is for most people. It proceeds in a number of different ways, however, including what Westerhoff (1973) calls a "hidden curriculum." We now turn our attention to some of the formal and informal mechanisms through which religion is transmitted; the agents which knowingly or unknowingly pass the "faith" on.

Agents of Religious Socialization

The term "agents of socialization" refers to all of those means—persons, groups, media, institutions—through which the process of "becoming religious" takes place. We shall look principally at the three most obvious agents of socialization: the family, various organized religious groups, and peer groups.

The family. There is clearly no aspect of an individual's life in which the influence of the family is not felt. Generally, it can be seen as the most important factor in the development of a religious *persona*. The immediate family, the significant others as Cooley (1902) called them, is of such importance that it is the principal example of the primary group. Cooley referred to it as a *primary* group in the sense that it was first, in time and importance, in the formation of the individual as a social being. As the family is the key factor in the development of a general identity, it is also the cornerstone in the development of the religious identity.

The importance of the family in the process of becoming religious is well illustrated by the many traditional rituals which focus on the home; the formal religious ceremonies which revolve around family life, the practices of parents in the home, and, in some cases, special familial ceremonies. The Jewish faith provides an example, although one which is rather exceptional, of the role of the family in traditional rituals which have their focus in the home rather than in the synagogue or the church. For instance, one of the holiest of all times in the Jewish faith is the Passover season. Central to this is the *seder* meal; a meal which reenacts the events of the first Passover in Egypt when, the Jews believe, Yahweh, God, delivered the Hebrew people from Egyptian captivity. Although for some the meal takes place in the synagogue or temple, this is a poor substitute for the home meal. It is in the heart of the family that *seder* takes place. There, in a dialogue between the youngest child and the father of the house, the events and symbols of that first Passover are recited. Clearly, the family is engaged in teaching or in "socializing" the children into the basic tenets of the faith. There are really no corresponding Christian practices that are so focused in the home, although the practice of home devotions, or of Christmas services in many homes, serve the same purpose. Certainly the religious group—Catholic or Protestant, liberal or conservative—continually mounts campaigns aimed at increasing such family-based expressions of religious faith, a testimony to their perception of the importance of such acts.

Many of the formal religious ceremonials related to the various "faiths" attempt to tie the youngster to the religious community through the family. Infant baptism, with its attendant responsibilities for the father and mother in some communions, certainly operates to tie the family into a process of religious training for the child. This is seen as such an important ritual that many of those congregations which do not believe in the practice of infant baptism have instituted "dedication" ceremonies. These perform the same function of encouraging parents to undertake responsibility for inculcating religious beliefs and attitudes in their children. Confirmation, first communion, and other practices which vary from group to group, also involve the family formally in such training.

Other rituals of the religious community take place with some kind of family reference. Weddings, and even funerals, guide the family into a situation where its action can reinforce religious socialization. Scarcely any stage in human maturation is neglected in the procession of religious rituals. In such events, the family reaffirms its religious beliefs and values.

The effects of the family are probably felt most strongly in the informal practices (or "hidden curriculum") which underlie the life of the family rather than in formal occasions. These underscore for the child the importance, or lack of it, which religion has for the family. If the family regularly goes to church, if there is the practice of saying grace before meals, or if other religious practices are stressed, the child is more likely to be religious then and in later life. If, on the other hand, religion is merely a label, or a vestigial rite infrequently practiced, the child will most likely not be religious, unless some other factors intervene.

This assertion of the signal importance of the family in religious socialization is borne out in the variety of studies of the effects of parochial school experience on the religious beliefs and practices of those who attend. Greeley and Gockel (1971), for example, note that their strongest findings on the effects of such religious education indicate that its effects are generally reinforced by the teachings of the family. It does seem that parochial education is most effective when it functions to confirm what has already been taught by the family experience. Greeley and Rossi (1966) report, for example, that education under church auspices strengthens religious practices, but that religious training in the family does more to increase religiosity in offspring than does parochial education.

The religious organization. While suggesting that the family is *the* most important group in the socialization of individuals in religion, it should not be assumed that it is the only influence. Clearly the various religious organizations, denominations, sects, and so forth, are set up to foster, emphasize, and initiate the socialization process, providing the more general, institutionalized roles and attitudes concerning religious faith.

What is frequently referred to as the "program" of a local congregation is actually a plan whereby the religious beliefs and values of the group can be learned, sustained, and deepened. The worship services, church or Sunday school classes, women's associations, men's groups, and so forth, are all designed to further the task of internalizing the religious faith in the individual. Even the "fellowship supper" is a means of binding members together around the values of the group. Of course, the less formal the group, the less formal will be its methods for promoting this socialization. The very small sectarian group probably relies mostly on "fellowship," which is a primary feeling of the group. However, such fellowship is promoted, also, in the most formal of religious organizations through such devices as pot luck suppers and family nights. From the youngest child entering kindergarten class to the members of the senior citizens' group, socialization is both accomplished and reinforced.

An examination of a number of Sunday church bulletins or programs gives some indication of the fervor with which most present day churches devise organizations and meetings to pursue this socialization process. A summary of just one month's sampling of such programs in the bulletins of various churches in a southwestern city reveals an almost bewildering array of "events." Included are: women's visitation groups, Bible studies, roller skating parties, men's prayer breakfasts, bowling leagues, evangelistic task groups, fund raising programs, youth fellowships, Mothers' day outs, social problems discussions, visitation of nursing homes, prayer meetings, choir practice, Church school Boy and Girl Scout troops, pizza parties, and many, many others. A number of these have overt purposes that seem quite unrelated to some process for the internalization of religious values; however, the latent or underlying purpose of each is still that of undergirding the individual's acceptance of group norms and values.

In some religious organizations this attempt at socialization is broadened to include the whole educational experience for the young, through the parochial school. The effects of parochial education for Catholics as reviewed by Greeley and Gockel (1971) indicate that such education does have an effect in strengthening the religious faith of those who attend such schools and increasing their participation in the rites of the church (although, as noted, the family practice of religion has an important effect on this). Johnstone (1966) studied Lutheran parochial education in St. Louis and Detroit and found that a significant association exists between such education and the tendency to attend church services, the livelihood of praying, attending church school, and involvement in a variety of church-related organizations. Also, individuals who attended parochial schools showed greater knowledge of the Bible and of Lutheran doctrine. However, returning to the impact of the family, it was also found that the influence of parochial schooling was only significant for those students who came from marginal Lutheran families. That is, if the family provided religious training, the school's religious training had less of an impact.

In another study, Greely and Rossi (1966) looked at both an adult and an adolescent sample of American Catholics. They found that such indications of religiosity as knowledge about the religious beliefs and doctrinal orthodoxy were affected in a positive way by an "all Catholic" education. Like Johnstone, however, they also found that those adolescents who came from very religious Catholic families were less likely to be influenced by the Catholic education than those who came from less religious families. In other words, those who had little faith to begin with gained more than those already firmly established through family influence; however, those beginning with a family-inherited belief system had the strongest faith and were most consistent in observing the rituals of their particular faith.

Looking at the adult sample, the authors conclude that there is only a modest association between parochial education and religiosity in the adult years. As in other studies, it is here apparent that parental religiosity is seen as the most important factor in the long term effects of parochial education. They conceive of the effect of such education, over time, as that of a "multiplier" (1966:86-69). That is, a family environment that is religiously strong is probably necessary if parochial education is to have a positive effect over the long run. The school, therefore, appears to act as a reinforcer. They note (1966:101):

> Something of a pattern begins to emerge: religious education does indeed have an impact on the adult lives of its students, but only when the social context of childhood or adulthood supports and emphasizes

the values learned in the school. Religious education apparently works when there is constant reinforcement from outside the school.

Thus, although in the short run parochial schooling may increase religious knowledge and practice, it takes the influence of the family to make it last.

The peer group. While the family and the religious organization are the prime agents of religious socialization, the effect of the peer group, especially for teenagers, is not to be forgotten. The "youth fellowship group" is often a recruiting device for the congregation, and the more permanent values of the individual may be altered or reshaped through such a group. Many parents have been shocked to find that their children have gotten some "strange" ideas through the youth fellowship. Further, family socialization may be forgotten, or at least ignored, if the young person joins a group of peers whose norm is not to be religious.

The influence of the peer group on young adults can be seen in those studies which examine the effects of college attendance on religious behavior. Becker's (1977) longitudinal studies indicate that students in college and universities of all sizes were less involved in religious associations as they continued their education; in the large schools, students also tended to be less concerned about particular religious groups. His data strongly indicate that peer attitudes have a strong impact on religiosity. Those with friends who are inactive in religion were generally less involved in religion and also less particularistic about a given religious belief system. On the whole, he found that the college experience affected the religiosity of students. "What seems to happen is that students change their behavior first, then change the ways they think about themselves and their religious beliefs. The clear implication is that maintaining the behavior is essential to maintaining the belief systems." (1977:72-73).

Conversion

As indicated, "becoming religious" is, in the main, such a subtle part of the person's total socialization process that except for formalized ceremonies, one is seldom really conscious that anything is happening. However, there are instances, some of them quite dramatic in nature, where there does appear to be a sudden change in religious orientation, or a sudden decision to "become religious" through the process referred to as conversion. As the converted one might say, "It happened in a flash!"

Although that moment at which the individual senses that a decision has been made, or announces such a decision, appears to have happened at a single moment, it is highly unlikely that conversions happen so suddenly. Although, as Conway and Siegelman (1979) indicate in their book, *Snapping,* when conversion happens it seems to "snap," "flash," "boom," the event really does not come "out of the blue." Like any process of becoming religious, conversion is also a matter of socialization, and a number of factors are involved in turning to a new life perspective.

Actually, we can look at the process of conversion—turning it another way—as a matter of *resocialization*. That is, it is an instance of socialization in which the individual unlearns old ways while learning a new perspective. The whole act of conversion can be viewed in terms of the dual process of learning the beliefs, values, and attitudes of the group to which the individual turns, while unlearning those of previous religious reference groups or of those obtained in a nonreligious milieu.

It would appear, from the sociological perspective, that there are generally aspects of previous socialization which lead the prospective convert to an interest in turning to new values and beliefs of particular kinds, as well as circumstances in the immediate social situation of the individual, which "trigger" the new declaration of faith. This is what Lofland (1966) and Lofland and Stark (1965) reported concerning their study of what they called the Divine Precepts movement, a group which resurfaced in the 1970s as the Unification Church or, more popularly, the Moonies.

They noted, first, that for converts to this radically different view of religious faith, there were factors in previous socialization which had already turned them to some kind of a change in a religious direction. Three things seemed to characterize their situation prior to the conversion. First, they tended to be persons who for some time had felt frustrated, deprived, and under tension and strain. Second, they were individuals who possessed an orientation which looked for religious solutions to felt problems. Third, they tended to define themselves as people who were "religious seekers."

Such a predisposition, however, was not seen as sufficient to bring about the conversion; something in the immediate situation had to work to "trigger" the acceptance of the new religious perspective. Again, Lofland and Stark (1965) suggest some of the situational factors which were operating in the lives of the converts to the Divine Precepts (Moonies) movement. First, they suggest, that these converts had reached what they felt to be a "turning point." Their old ways of dealing with their problems were no longer workable. At this time they made contact with members of the DP's (as Lofland and Stark refer to the movement). Second, feelings of liking, or friendship bonds, were developed among members of the DPs and the "pre-convert." Third, as these new friendships developed, older ties with those not among the DPs were weakened, or at least neutralized. Fourth, the interaction with the members of the DPs became more and more intensive until the new recruit was able to make the final, full commitment and "convert," becoming an active member and recruiter for the DPs in his own right.

More recently, Lofland (1978) has attempted to modify some of the steps in this resocialization process. Feeling that the terminology in the older study was not particularly incisive, he has suggested five new terms for the stages in the process: picking up, hooking, encapsulating, loving, and committing. Following his work, we can describe each of these stages in the route to conversion as they apply to this one movement.

The term "picking-up" refers to that time in the life of the pre-convert when contact is made with the movement. DPs spend much time in trying to make just such pick-ups through a variety of means, as Lofland (1978:11) indicates.

> Indeed, DPs spend time almost daily giving hitchhikers rides and approaching young men and women in public places. Display card tables for front organizations were regularly staffed in the public areas of many campuses as a way to pick up people.

According to Lofland, when contact was made; it was usually followed by an invitation to some social gathering or to a DP lecture.

"Hooking" is the stage wherein the prospective convert is brought more under the influence of the DP movement with elaborate "promotion tactics." Lofland reports one instance of such hooking where the prospect was invited to a dinner and on arrival found a large crowd of very personable, outgoing young people. The prospect was assigned a "buddy" and then (Lofland, 1978:13):

> . . . various people stopped by my table, introduced themselves and chatted. They seemed to be circulating like sorority members during rush.

The DP members are taught to find out all that they can about the prospective members and pass it on. They are told to "write down their hooks so that the whole center knows in follow up." (Lofland, 1978:13). The prospects are made to feel that they are being served and are the full center of attention.

The next step is referred to as "encapsulating," that is, the envelopment of the prospect with both ideology and "affective bonds." Lofland suggests that there are basically five lines along which the total immersion is accomplished: absorption of attention; focus of the individual's attention on the group; limitation of conversation and other "inputs" to the pre-convert to matters of DP movement; creation of fatigue on the part of the prospect; and presentation of "logical comprehensive cognitions."

"Loving" is the movement of the prospect into a feeling of being loved and, as Lofland puts it, a desire to "melt together" into the embrace of the total group. One woman who went to a DP center for a weekend is reported to have seen her experience in this way (Lofland, 1978:16-17):

> When I did hold back in some small way, and received a look of sorrowful, benevolent concern, I felt guilt and a desire to please as though it were God

himself whom I had offended. What may really have been wisdom on my part (trying to preserve my own boundaries in a dangerous and potentially overwhelming situation) was treated as symptomatic of alienation and fear; and withholding of God's light. Those things are sometimes true of me, and I am unsure enough of my own openness in groups that I tended to believe they were right. Once, when (the workshop leader) spoke to us after a lecture, I began to cry. She'd said something about giving, and it had touched on a deep longing in me to do that, and the pain of that wall around my heart when I feel closed off in a group of people. I wanted to break through that badly enough that right then it almost didn't matter what they believed—if only I could really share myself with them. I think that moment may be exactly the point at which many people decide to join (the DPs).

The final stage in the process (that point which popularly would be seen as the conversion) is referred to as "committing." Gradually, the convert is drawn more and more into the enveloping atmosphere of the movement, filled by the "love bombs" of the movement, as they are called. The prospect at this stage expressed commitment by doing such work as street-peddling and becomes a full time, believing participant in the DPs.

Of course, it would be misleading to suggest that the description of conversion to the Moonies is one which fits every conversion. The steps cited from Lofland's work are basically illustrative of a fact which seems central to most conversion experiences—they do not represent a full turning around so much as they do an alteration of a perspective with which the individual generally tends to view the world.

Traviasano (1969) has suggested, in fact, that we need to make a distinction between "conversion," as a *total* change in perspective, and what he refers to as "alternation." The latter term would refer to instances wherein individuals do not change the general orientation through which they approach problem solving, but simply change the particular "solution" within that "general orientation." Thus Lofland and Stark's conclusion that the majority of the DP converts were already looking at the world in a religious perspective, considering themselves "religious seekers," probably means, in Traviasano's terms, that this was not so much a conversion to a new perspective as it was an alternation to a different set of beliefs, but still within a religious perspective.

This same sort of phenomenon would appear to be operating in the number of conversions of young people to the Jesus Movement (Richardson and Stewart, 1978). They found that the majority of the members of the Jesus Movement were, in fact, "returning fundamentalists." That is, they tended to be individuals with conservative religious backgrounds who had drifted into drug use and a hippie lifestyle. Similarly, Bibby and Brinkerhoff (1974), in their study of evangelism and conversion in fundamentalist churches in a metropolitan area, concluded that most of these "conversions" were the result of a good deal of predisposition and may have represented alternation more than they did actual resocialization to a totally new world view. They found that the majority of the converts made were actually already "insiders," that is, they were the children or other family members of people who were already inside the fundamentalist, evangelical religion.

The Effects of Religious Socialization

There are several ways in which the effects of religious socialization might be measured, and, in a sense, much of the material that follows in this book is a discussion of such effects. At this point we want to look specifically at several aspects of these effects: the ability of specific faiths or communions to maintain members over time; the influence of such socialization on continuing religiosity; the effects on social attitudes and behaviors of various kinds and the formation of values concerning the society in general; and, the relationship between particular religious faiths and marriage and family life.

Maintenance of members. It is obvious that each particular religious group, in its socialization, attempts to instill a particularism relative to that communion; a loyalty not only to religious faith in a generalized sense but also to the specific beliefs of that group. Therefore, one measure of the effectiveness of such socialization would be the success of the group in maintaining the affiliation of their youth in later life. Table 3-1 provides some information about the success of various religious communions in maintaining this loyalty from the time of age 16 to adult life.

The greatest consistency in affiliation is found among those who are Jewish. However, since this might also be seen as an ethnic designation, from which one "escapes" only at the cost of group pride, there may be little "religious" socialization reflected in this case. The fact that 11.1 percent of those who described themselves as Jewish at the age of 16 now see themselves as having no preference may be indicative of the lack of religious meaning in these figures.

Of the Christian religious groups, Roman Catholics have the highest retention rates (85.5 percent), while Episcopalians have the lowest (61.1 percent). Lutherans and Presbyterians do not do too much better; 63.8 and 63.6 percent, respectively, remain in the faith of their childhood. However, the largest "loss" of Episcopalians does not represent a movement to another denomination or group at all, but a lack of religious preference altogether. That is, 16.7 percent of those who considered themselves Episcopalians at the age of 16 now cite no preference or affiliation with a religious group. The approaches, beliefs, and attitudes of some groups, then, appear to be more successful than those of others in maintaining the "faith" of their young.

Table 3-1. COMPARISON OF RELIGIOUS AFFILIATION AT AGE OF 16 AND AS ADULTS, BY PERCENTAGE

Affiliation at 16	Affiliation at Time of Interview								
	Catholic	Jewish	Baptist	Methodist	Lutheran	Presbyterian	Episcopalian	Other	No Preference
Catholic	85.5	0.3	1.3	1.8	1.3	0.8	0.0	4.4	4.7
Jewish	0.0	88.9	0.0	0.0	0.0	0.0	0.0	0.0	11.1
Baptist	3.0	0.0	72.8	4.9	1.1	1.1	0.5	10.5	6.0
Methodist	1.4	0.0	11.8	63.8	3.6	2.3	0.5	10.0	5.9
Lutheran	6.2	0.0	2.8	1.4	75.2	0.7	1.4	9.0	3.4
Presbyterian	9.1	0.0	3.8	6.5	2.6	63.6	1.3	10.4	2.6
Episcopalian	8.3	0.0	0.0	5.6	5.6	0.0	61.1	2.8	16.7
Other	2.1	0.0	7.2	8.8	0.5	2.1	3.6	70.1	5.7

Source: Data from 1977 General Social Survey, NORC. Supplied by Texas Tech University Institute for Secondary Analysis.

Continuing religious practice. As to the maintenance of ritual behavior and other religious practices, there are several kinds of evidence. Some indications come from the studies on the effects of parochial education. As noted, Greeley and Rossi (1966) found relatively little relationship between the formal socialization of the parochial schools and later religious practices. The example set by parents, however, did seem to have the strongest significant effect on the chances that individuals would continue the practices of their religious faith in their adult years.

Others have viewed such continuation in terms of the natural processes of development in adult life (see Maves, 1971). It is reported that age has a marked effect on church attendance, although there seems to be no clear-cut conclusion as to what that effect is. Some report that those over 65 attend much less frequently, while others have noted that church attendance drops in the middle years of life but picks up again in the later years (see Fichter, 1961).

The confusion in this matter may well come from trying to draw conclusions by looking only at particular groups, or looking at attendance for all groups as if it were a homogeneous whole. When data from National Opinion Research Center polls (NORC, 1978) are examined, it becomes clear that the relationship between age and attendance varies considerably by the religious preference of the individual. For Lutherans, Presbyterians, Episcopalians, sectarians, and Jews, age does not have a great effect on patterns of attendance. These patterns are quite different, however, for each of these groups considered separately. Jews at any age seldom attend services except for High Holy Days, while sectarians maintain steady attendance throughout life, again regardless of age. As we can see from Table 3-2, however, for Catholics, Baptists, and Methodists age does affect the rate of attendance. For Roman Catholics, in the two older age categories (including persons from 45 to 65 and over), nearly one-half attend regularly, while only a quarter of the young (18-24) and just over one-third of those in the early middle years (25-44) attend on a regular basis. Attendance patterns classified as "often" (two or three times a month) and "some" (several times a year to two or three times a month) follow patterns congruent with the findings for "regular" attenders as do the figures for those who rarely attend. A similar pattern is found for Baptists and Methodists although the rate of attendance even for the aged in these groups is considerably lower than for the Catholics. We may conclude, however, that for these three preference categories, attendance at religious services increases as age increases, except that for those indicating Methodist preference there remains a fairly large proportion even of "aged" who attend only rarely. In these three groups, socialization into religious beliefs seems to have been effective in the sense that the "aging" find some value in attendance during their later years. It is apparent, too, that attendance takes on a special significance for those related to such groups.

Table 3-2. AGE AND ATTENDANCE FOR CATHOLICS, BAPTISTS, AND METHODISTS, BY PERCENTAGE*

		Catholics		
	Young 18–24	Early Middle 25–44	Late Middle 45–64	Aged 65 +
Rare	35.6	28.7	20.2	24.2
Some	25.9	21.7	17.8	12.6
Often	13.1	12.1	11.2	9.2
Regular	25.4	37.4	50.7	53.9
Number	343	964	67	293
		Baptists		
	Young 18–24	Early Middle 25–44	Late Middle 45–64	Aged 65 +
Rare	37.1	28.4	24.8	19.3
Some	25.0	24.3	24.6	16.6
Often	19.9	19.7	19.1	22.1
Regular	18.0	27.6	31.5	42.1
Number	272	765	549	290
		Methodists		
	Young 18–24	Early Middle 25–44	Late Middle 45–64	Aged 65 +
Rare	43.9	39.6	34.4	34.7
Some	26.5	24.4	22.6	16.5
Often	16.3	18.8	21.9	17.3
Regular	13.3	17.2	21.1	31.5
Number	98	361	393	248

*Note: All relationships significant at the .001 level.
Source: Data from NORC General Social Surveys. Courtesy of Institute for Secondary Analysis, Texas Tech University.

A somewhat similar picture develops when we look at whether the region of the country in which individuals live influences their tendency to practice ritual acts; that is, "Is there stronger socialization in some areas for individuals to practice religious acts such as attending church services?" As we can see from Table 3-3, we are faced with a situation not totally unlike that we have seen with regard to age. Region makes a difference for some preference groups but not for others. In this case, however, there are only three groups for which it does not make a difference: Jewish, Episcopalians, and sectarians. Again, these three groups differ in terms of their attendance pattern in general. Sectarians have high rates of attendance, while attendance for the other two groups is low in general. It should be noted, also, that these two preference categories have fewer members in one region of the country, the South, than do the other groups.

Table 3-3. REGION OF THE COUNTRY AND ATTENDANCE FOR CATHOLICS, BAPTISTS, METHODISTS, LUTHERANS, AND PRESBYTERIANS, BY PERCENTAGE*

	Catholics			
	Northeast	Midwest	South	West
Rare	29.3	20.4	23.5	35.7
Some	19.0	16.3	24.4	25.2
Often	11.3	11.7	13.2	11.3
Regular	40.4	51.6	38.9	27.8
Number	852	711	357	353
	Baptists			
	Northeast	Midwest	South	West
Rare	33.3	35.3	22.2	39.7
Some	22.9	22.0	23.8	22.9
Often	20.1	17.3	21.8	11.7
Regular	23.6	25.1	32.2	25.7
Number	144	346	1214	179

Table 3-3. REGION OF THE COUNTRY AND ATTENDANCE FOR CATHOLICS, BAPTISTS, METHODISTS, LUTHERANS, AND PRESBYTERIANS, BY PERCENTAGE* (cont.)

Methodists

	Northeast	Midwest	South	West
Rare	33.1	39.0	30.9	56.8
Some	28.1	23.1	20.6	20.5
Often	15.7	19.5	22.0	13.6
Regular	23.1	18.4	26.5	9.1
Number	121	364	486	132

Lutherans

	Northeast	Midwest	South	West
Rare	41.3	23.3	20.9	44.2
Some	27.5	24.9	27.5	24.4
Often	15.6	27.7	22.0	15.1
Regular	15.6	24.1	29.7	16.3
Number	167	386	91	86

Presbyterians

	Northeast	Midwest	South	West
Rare	40.0	30.6	34.4	58.8
Some	25.0	27.0	14.8	17.5
Often	17.0	20.7	22.1	12.5
Regular	18.0	21.6	28.7	11.3
Number	100	111	122	80

*Note: All relationships significant at the .001 level, except for Presbyterians which is significant at the .01 level.

Source: Data from NORC General Social Surveys. Courtesy of Institute for Secondary Analysis, Texas Tech University.

For the groups in which there is some regional variation in attendance patterns, all, except the Catholics, show highest attendance rates in the southern region, with the Midwest providing the next highest rates, except for Baptists. Catholic attendance rates are highest in the Northeast and Midwest, probably reflecting the larger percentage of Catholics in those populations which possibly has led to more established norms about attendance. Baptist attendance is poorest in the Northeast, a finding which probably reflects the differences in stress on attendance between the more literal American Baptist convention, strong in the Northeast, and the Southern Baptist Convention, which has more influence elsewhere. Except for those giving Baptist as a preference, the West shows the poorest attendance rates. Even for the Baptists that is the area in which the greatest percentage indicate that they attend rarely. In short, with some variations, it does appear that some regions of the country provide an atmosphere which is more conducive, as in the South, or nonconducive, as in the West, to the continuance of a regular pattern of church attendance.

It has frequently been noted, also, that women are more likely to attend church than males; that is, in our terms, that some socialization efforts seem to be more effective in persuading females, rather than males, to continue church attendance. Our data from the National Opinion Research Center confirm this general impression, but, again, only for some of the eight preference categories. For Catholics, Baptists, Methodists, and Lutherans, women are found to attend church "regularly" more often than males. Although there are some slight differences for the other groups, sex of the respondent does not seem to make a significant different in rate of attendance. For a variety of reasons, we can assume that the socialization efforts which promote regular attendance at religious services are better internalized by women than men in these four groups, but that no such differences appear for the others. Once more, for those groups in which there is difference, we are dealing with communions with widely different norms about attendance. For example, Jews are equally likely *not* to attend regardless of sex, while sectarians of both sexes are equally likely to be regular attenders.

Social attitudes and behaviors. Most religious groups in the Judaeo-Christian tradition believe that religion should have *some* effect on how one behaves and the attitudes one takes regarding certain social issues. But they are by no means in agreement as to what these attitudes and behaviors should be. For instance, for some denominations, particularly Southern Baptists and Methodists, there has been a strong official emphasis on adopting a position of total abstinence with regard to alcoholic beverage use. If the socialization of the religious group is effective, then, one would expect to find relatively little use of alcoholic beverages among the members of these two denominations. While NORC data reveal that Baptists and Methodists use alcoholic beverages less often than members of other major denominations, over one-half of the Baptists (53.1 percent) and more than two-thirds of the Methodists have used alcohol as a beverage. Of course, this is no measure of the extent of drinking, or when the drinking occurred, but it does to some extent indicate less than full acceptance of the value of abstinence. A further indication is found in the fact that, except for Episcopalians, Baptists, and Methodists who drink are no less likely than others to indicate that they have on occasion had too much to drink. The findings are similar with regard to another supposed Methodist and Baptist "taboo"—smoking.

It has been shown that a variety of key social attitudes are significantly affected by religious preference (Chalfant, 1978). Members of the Episcopal church, and those with Jewish preference, are the most likely to have "liberal" attitudes with regard to such issues as abortion, suicide, race relations, and freedom of speech. Chalfant has also shown that, with such factors as social class controlled, racial attitudes (1979) and stance with regard to both the Equal Rights Amendment (ERA) and other feminist issues (1980) vary with religious affiliation. The general comments regarding the more liberal stance of the Episcopalians and Jews are born out in these studies, as is a somewhat lesser tendency for Catholics to be nonracist. On the other hand, Baptists and sectarians show the most racist and sexist attitudes. The NORC data also reveal that, not surprisingly, Catholics are less accepting of both abortion and suicide. It seems clear that religious socialization has some effect on attitudes toward social issues, with some groups inculcating liberal views and others more conservative attitudes.

Formation of values. As we have seen, Weber's studies indicated an interaction between religious ideology and an economic system. In his thesis, certain dominant societal values and attitudes had their origins and found support in a particular set of religious beliefs. Others have gone further to suggest that whether or not societal views have their origins in the particular religious system, religious socialization does tend to provide, for many, the opportunity for the internalization of such dominant values.

Benton Johnson (1961) provides an intriguing argument that such socialization is provided even in certain religious groups generally defined as being in opposition to the dominant culture of the society. He contends that an important aspect of the religious groups known as parts of "Holiness" religion is that they do provide socialization into dominant societal values for a largely lower-class membership. Although the "Holiness churches" vary in many important aspects from the staid, middle-class denominations, they share a similar value orientation; the values into which the members of these Holiness sects are socialized are like that of middle-class America in that they encourage thrift, hard work, and an asceticism which develops work-attitudes which make them "good employees." Indeed, it is suggested that middle-class mill owners in Gastonia (Pope, 1942) help establish such "churches" in order to have a pool of "well-behaved" workers.

Following up work done by Willems (1967) in Chile and Brazil, Weigert et al.

(1971) reported a similar effect on the socialization of Pentecostal sects on Chicanos in south Texas. They found, in particular, that some Mexican Americans who migrated to cities abandoned their traditional Catholicism in favor of Pentecostalism. The result of conversion and adoption of the Pentecostal ascetic values was upward mobility for the converts since these new value orientations were in line with dominant values of Anglo society. Also, as in Gastonia for example, it made them better workers.

Marriage and the family. Several aspects of marriage and family life are related to religious socialization. Religious preference or affiliation appears to be particularly important in this area. For example, religious membership has been seen as important in the choice of marital partner. There are some indications that membership in or preference for a particular religious group is related to whether or not a person will get married at all. As can be seen from looking at Table 3-4, those who profess no religious preference are far less likely to have ever been married; three times as many of those without a religious preference have never been married as those with Protestant preference, and twice as many as compared to Catholics and Jews. Of course, it is possible that this may be because those without a preference are more likely to be young or that the non-married may not be as religious as the married.

If we look only at individuals who attend church at least several times a year (see Table 3-5), we note that the few who attend, but have no preference, are still by far the most likely not to have ever been married. There are also differences with regard to specific groups in terms of the rate of marriage. Lutherans, Presbyterians, and Jews are most likely to be married, while Episcopalians have the highest percentage of those currently divorced. More nonmarried appear among the Catholics, where one would expect religious identification to be high regardless of marital status.

Generally speaking, religious preference tends to define the pool from which one will choose a partner for marriage. Although this is not as true as it once was, there is still a strong tendency to marry within one's broad religious group—Protestant, Catholic, or Jew. Norms which prescribe marriage within one's own religious group do vary with the different organizations. Both the Jewish and Catholic faiths have strong norms of endogamy, as do several conservative Protestant groups. As Wilson (1978) points out, such norms have a dual purpose. While they make a contribution to family solidarity, they also increase commitment to the particular religious group. Certainly, marriage between persons of different groups weakens the ties of both partners to their faith, and also makes it less likely that children will be adequately socialized into the beliefs of either parent (Vincent, 1964; Trent and Golds, 1967; Sklare, 1971).

Despite the norms which discourage interfaith marriage, the number of such alliances has increased steadily over the last half-century. According to Bumpass (1970), it is twice as likely now that persons will marry outside their own

Table 3-4. MARITAL STATUS AND RELIGIOUS PREFERENCE, BY PERCENTAGE

	Catholic	Jewish	Baptist	Methodist	Lutheran	Presbyterian	Episcopal	Sects	None
Married	66.9	70.5	66.8	68.6	74.4	70.2	62.1	69.3	51.2
Widowed	9.1	12.5	10.0	12.5	8.9	9.9	13.7	9.7	3.3
Divorced	5.2	3.5	6.6	6.8	4.4	6.1	10.9	7.1	7.1
Separated	2.7	0.5	5.5	2.1	2.1	1.7	2.4	4.3	4.7
Never married	16.2	13.0	11.1	10.1	10.3	12.1	10.9	9.5	33.7
Number	2274	200	1888	1107	731	413	248	462	635

Table 3-5. MARITAL STATUS AND RELIGIOUS PREFERENCE, BY PERCENTAGE OF THOSE ATTENDING CHURCH AT LEAST "SOME"

	Catholic	Jewish	Baptist	Methodist	Lutheran	Presbyterian	Episcopal	Sects	None
Married	68.3	76.6	67.3	69.3	76.7	76.0	65.8	72.1	43.3
Widowed	9.6	11.7	11.4	13.2	8.8	8.4	11.8	10.5	6.7
Divorced	4.3	—	5.2	5.5	4.1	4.8	11.2	5.1	5.0
Separated	1.9	—	5.8	2.3	1.9	0.8	2.0	3.7	6.7
Never married	16.0	11.7	10.2	9.8	8.6	10.0	9.2	8.5	38.3
Number	1668	94	1372	696	514	250	152	354	60

religious group as it was in the early part of the twentieth century. Wilson (1978:243) cites a number of factors which seems to play an important part in this increase:

> ... the waning influence of religion: the decline in the number of first generation immigrants; the increase in the number of people in college, the increase in the number of women who work; changing family values, including greater equality of the sexes, weaker extended kinship ties, and greater popularity of the romantic love idea; and increased urbanization, which raise the rate of religious intermixing.

Among the different Protestant denominations, there is some variation in the rates with which individuals marry outside their "faith." According to Greeley (1971:88), Presbyterians are the most likely to marry outside of their own group. In part, this might be explained by the higher educational level of members of that group, although the more liberal outlook of the denomination probably also plays a part.

Whether or not a marriage will end in divorce is also related to religious preference. According to National Opinion Research data (see Table 3-6), those without any religious preference are most likely to have divorced at some time, which might lead to the suggestion that being religious binds families together. However, two of the more conservative religious affiliations—the Baptists and that loosely defined grouping known as the sects—have nearly as high a percentage of adherents who have been once divorced as is found among those with no religious preference. Jewish respondents have the lowest rate of divorce, with Catholics very near the same rate. Both socioeconomic status and particular religious norms concerning the family are certainly involved to some extent in these varying rates.

When we look at the figures for those who attend church at least several times a year (see Table 3-7), we find a still higher rate of dissolution for those without a religious preference who attend church at least "some" than for those who rarely if ever attend church. Baptists and sectarian members still have slightly higher rates than do respondents preferring other Protestant groups, but the difference has been reduced for those who attend church at least several times a year. Again, Jews have the lower rate of divorce, with Catholics remaining in the second position. In both cases, the rates of divorce are lower than when all persons with such a preference are considered regardless of attendance, as is true for all groups. More regular church attendance is related to a greater likelihood of marital stability to some degree.

McCarthy (1979) notes that traditionally Catholics have been seen as far less likely to divorce than non-Catholics. He reports that several studies have shown convergence of these differences, reporting that Catholics are increasingly more

Table 3-6. DIVORCE AND RELIGIOUS PREFERENCE, BY PERCENTAGE

	Catholic	Jewish	Baptist	Methodist	Lutheran	Presbyterian	Episcopal	Sects	None
Ever divorced	9.5	7.3	18.1	15.3	13.2	14.5	15.4	18.1	19.9
Never	90.5	92.7	81.9	84.7	86.8	85.5	84.6	81.9	80.1
Number	1718	164	1443	887	607	330	188	364	342

Table 3-7. DIVORCE AND RELIGIOUS PREFERENCE, BY PERCENTAGE, FOR RESPONDENTS ATTENDING CHURCH "SOME"

	Catholic	Jewish	Baptist	Methodist	Lutheran	Presbyterian	Episcopal	Sects	None
Ever divorced	7.2	3.7	15.8	10.4	12.3	12.4	13.6	16.1	24.1
Never	92.8	96.3	84.2	89.6	87.7	87.6	86.4	83.9	75.9
Number	1294	82	1076	568	438	210	118	292	29

like Protestants with regard to divorce rates (McRae, 1977). Obviously, Catholics have shown the greater change in this regard. McCarthy concludes that dissolution of marriage rates for Catholics—both through divorce and separation—have increased more than have rates for Protestants, but that they have by no means reached the level of that for Protestants. He does point out, however, that separation is more likely for Catholics than it is for Protestants.

The low rates of marital dissolution for Catholics and Jews are related to norms in these groups. Both stress family solidarity, with Catholics maintaining rigid proscriptive norms concerning the remarriage of those who are divorced. It is probable that the high rates for the fundamentalist Christians (sects) and Baptists are related to the lower socioeconomic status of these groups, as marital dissolution is generally associated with lower status. The fact that separation is also higher for these groups is somewhat supportive of the supposition concerning the effect of lower status.

Finally, we can look at the relationship between religious preference and happiness in marriage and the satisfaction of the individual with family life. Does being religious have an effect on such happiness and satisfaction? Table 3-8 presents NORC data with regard to this question. Those with no preference are least like to describe their marriage as very happy and, conversely, most likely to view their unions as not happy. There is little difference between the other groups, although Baptists and sectarians are somewhat less likely to see their marriages as "very happy." This, again, may be related to the lower socioeconomic status of many Baptists and sectarians in that those of lower status tend to be less happy. When we control for attendance (Table 3-9), we find surprisingly little difference in reported mental happiness except for Jews and those with no preference. This is an interesting finding since these groups are unlikely to be frequent attenders. It would seem that the few persons with no preference who attend at least "some," and the half of the Jewish respondents who report attendance several times a year, find a special meaning in attending services since there are few pressures on them to do so. Thus, attendance may also have special effect on the quality of marital relations.

Looking at satisfaction with family life in general, a rather similar pattern is found. Those with no preference are least satisfied with their family life, while those who report preferences for Judaism, Presbyterianism, and Episcopalianism are the most like to report that they are happy with their family life (see Table 3-10), although the differences are rather small. Those who attend religious services somewhat regularly (see Table 3-11) are a bit more likely to be satisfied than those who do not, with about the same relationship existing between the variant religious preferences. Again, the factor of socioeconomic status probably plays a fairly important part in these findings, and may be more influential than religious belief. Certainly the groups which report that they are most happy with their family are those which generally have the higher socioeconomic status, and

Table 3–8. MARITAL HAPPINESS AND RELIGIOUS PREFERENCE, BY PERCENTAGE

	Catholic	Jewish	Baptist	Methodist	Lutheran	Presbyterian	Episcopal	Sects	None
Very happy	68.2	73.4	64.6	69.1	67.1	70.9	70.8	64.7	54.8
Pretty happy	29.5	25.9	30.6	28.9	31.3	27.3	27.9	31.9	39.3
Not happy	2.2	0.7	4.8	2.0	1.7	1.7	1.3	3.5	5.9
Number	1513	139	1253	758	544	289	154	317	323

Table 3–9. MARITAL HAPPINESS AND RELIGIOUS PREFERENCE, BY PERCENTAGE, OF THOSE ATTENDING CHURCH "SOME"

	Catholic	Jewish	Baptist	Methodist	Lutheran	Presbyterian	Episcopal	Sects	None
Very happy	69.8	80.3	66.8	71.4	70.3	70.4	73.0	66.1	64.0
Pretty happy	28.3	18.3	29.0	27.0	28.7	28.0	26.0	30.7	24.0
Not happy	1.9	1.4	4.2	1.7	1.0	1.6	1.0	3.1	12.0
Number	1134	71	918	482	394	189	100	254	25

Table 3-10. SATISFACTION WITH FAMILY LIFE AND RELIGIOUS PREFERENCE, BY PERCENTAGE

	Catholic	Jewish	Baptist	Methodist	Lutheran	Presbyterian	Episcopal	Sects	None
Very great	45.0	54.1	41.9	46.9	45.1	48.4	53.6	44.8	34.6
Great	36.5	30.8	38.1	35.4	37.1	35.4	29.5	36.2	35.0
A bit	10.6	10.8	11.4	10.2	11.3	10.4	11.2	9.9	20.1
Fair	7.8	4.3	8.5	7.5	6.5	5.7	5.8	9.2	10.3
Number	2151	185	1757	1037	708	384	224	426	543

Table 3-11. SATISFACTION WITH FAMILY LIFE AND RELIGIOUS PREFERENCE, BY PERCENTAGE, OF THOSE ATTENDING CHURCH "SOME"

	Catholic	Jewish	Baptist	Methodist	Lutheran	Presbyterian	Episcopal	Sects	None
Very great	46.5	59.8	42.8	46.5	48.1	52.3	64.7	45.2	33.3
Great	36.4	29.3	38.5	37.0	36.0	35.4	21.6	37.8	25.5
A bit	10.1	8.7	11.1	9.9	9.9	9.3	7.9	8.9	25.5
Fair	7.0	2.2	7.6	6.6	5.9	3.0	5.8	8.0	15.7
Number	1594	92	1287	665	505	237	139	336	51

it seems reasonable that such high status would incline one to more satisfaction with the family. Of course, considering the Jewish faith, there may be a tendency to "grin and bear it" regardless of the actual situation, given the strong norms for family life found among the Jewish. The Catholics, on the other hand, do not seem to have this same stoicism with regard to their family life.

We have discussed the effects of religious socialization, repeatedly noting differences among those of different affiliations. We have also seen that even within these specific groups there is tremendous variation. Implicit in these statements is the fact that all people are not equally religious or religious in the same way. To understand the social aspects of religion, we need to be able to understand the patterns which characterize these variations.

VARIATIONS IN INDIVIDUAL RELIGIOSITY

Anyone who takes notice of religious behavior at all certainly notices how differently people express their religion. There simply is not a single way of being religious, let alone a single intensity; religion is not an "either-or" proposition. We have to look at religious behavior, belief, and attitudes as varying along a continuum, or perhaps on several continuums. Our task is to attempt to understand what general patterns of religiosity may exist, so that we can conceptualize different categories of such behaviors, beliefs, and attitudes. In one sense, we need to determine the major elements in religiosity. Early scholars provided some distinctions. In *The Elementary Forms of Religious Life*, Durkheim (1947) distinguished simply between *beliefs* and *rites* as aspects of religious behavior, while Wach (1944) added a social or fellowship aspect to being religious. In these distinctions we have one way of looking at the matter of being religious—what kind of activity is involved: believing, ritual, or social life? There are, however, other ways in which being religious can be viewed.

Another aspect which might be considered is the way people "obey" the dictates for practising their faith in terms of attending church and other observances expected of members. An early attempt to deal with this problem was made by Joseph Fichter (1951, 1954). He took the concept, church member, and proposed four ways in which such members might be characterized. Based on his study of Roman Catholic parishioners in the south, he suggested that members could be categorized as "nuclear Catholics," "modal Catholics," "marginal Catholics," or "dormant Catholics." Obviously, these terms move, in order, from highly involved members to members with no real participation. Nuclear Catholics are those who go beyond the minimal requirements and are active in parish life—including attendance at Holy Communion every week. Modal Catholics are seen as falling between nuclear and marginal ones, and, according to Fichter (1954:41) live their religion in a "middling" sort of way. Generally such a church member meets the minimal requirements. The marginal Catholics see themselves as members of the Catholic Church; however, they do not meet such standards as attending mass or participating in confession. They also do not send their children to a Catholic parochial school. The dormant Catholics are those born Catholic; they were baptized in the church and might ask for a priest when death approaches. However, they are not members of any parish in a formal sense. This distinction between types of membership helps us to understand this further dimension of ways in which one can be, or not be, religious.

Yet another aspect of being religious might involve the "quality" or orientation of one's religious faith and practice. A frequently used distinction is that between "intrinsic" and "extrinsic" religiosity. This basic dichotomy is the work of Allport and others (Allport, 1950, 1954, 1959, 1960; Allport and Ross, 1967). It suggests that there are two qualitatively different orientations to one's religion. For the person with an extrinsic orientation, religion serves and rationalizes several forms of self-interest. However, the full teachings and ethical implications of the religion are not accepted. The main motive of the extrinsically religious individual is self-interest. On the other hand, for the person described as having an "intrinsic" orientation to religion, the full implications of the religious faith are internalized, and religion serves as a "master motive." This simple dichotomy does provide us with a great deal of insight. However, it does not seem likely that this, or a similar distinction Allport and Ross (1967) make between committed and consensual religion, can adequately describe the whole range of qualities with which one apprehends religion. While these terms are useful, the attempts to use them as a "religious orientation scale" (Allport and Ross, 1967) have been heavily criticized even by some who have used them in other forms (e.g., Dittes, 1971; Hunt and King, 1971; Spilka et al., 1977). In short, what is useful in these terms is another look at one aspect of religious quality, but in a way that is quite limited. The terms are not necessarily mutually exclusive in all regards. The quality of being religious is more complicated than this supposed opposition.

Our purpose is not to discuss at length the validity of this or other particular distinctions. Rather we use this debate as one of many indications that any attempt to discuss patterns of religiosity must consider a number of different facets. The consideration of this complexity in religiosity has led to the contention, by many, that religion is multidimensional. Considerable attention has been given to attempts to define such dimensions and, while the results are not conclusive, the work provides further valuable insight into the nature of religiosity.

DIMENSIONS OF RELIGIOSITY

As we have noted, the difficulties involved in finding any single measure or continuum along which religious behavior can be arrayed leads to the general proposition that there are a number of factors, which have come to be known as "dimensions," involved in the ways in which individuals express their religiosity. Further, it has been found that these dimensions do not, in fact, "hang together." That is, people who are religious in some respects may not be at all religious in others. For example, individuals who attend Sunday morning worship services each and every Sunday may, in reality, be attempting to boost a political career or an insurance business, while neither knowing much about the principles of that particular religious faith, or having any commitment to it.

One of the earlier attempts to outline the dimensions involved in individual religiosity was made by Glock (1959) who suggested that as a concept, religiosity could be divided into four separate aspects: the experiential, the ritualistic, the ideological, and the consequential. For Glock, these referred, respectively, to religious feelings, practices, beliefs, and works and were seen as inclusive of the major ways in which church members could be said to be religious. Three years later (1962) he added a fifth dimension—the intellectual—dealing with information about one's religion.

In 1961, Fukuyama reformulated and elaborated Glock's (1959) proposal. He put the matter this way:

> Religion is a phenomenon which can be described in terms of at least four major dimensions; the cognitive, the cultic, the creedal, and the devotional; these dimensions represent distinctive styles of religious orientation and provide meaningful categories for the sociological study of religion. (Fukuyama, 1961:2).

The cultic dimension has to do with the practice of the faith; the creedal with what a person believes; the cognitive with what people know about religion; and the devotional, which parallels Glock's category of the experimental, with feelings and experiences.

Yet another attempt to define aspects of religiosity is that of Lenski (1961). The four which he proposed were: "Associational involvement," as reflected by frequency of church attendance and participation in subgroups of the religious organization; "communal involvement," the degree to which people's primary relations are restricted to persons of one's own religious group; and "devotionalism," the importance people place on personal contact or communion with God, a concept which Lenski operationalized as frequency of prayer and the act of seeking to determine God's will when important decisions have to be made.

To this day the most often used statement of "dimensions of religiosity," built upon Glock's 1962 statement, is found in Glock and Stark's book, *Religion and Society in Tension* (1965). Five dimensions are listed: experiential, ideological, ritualistic, intellectual, and consequential. The *experiential* dimension is that which examines expectations concerning the direct knowledge individuals may feel they have had of the object of worship, the sacred, and the emotional feelings they have experienced. This dimension would include all those feelings, perceptions, and sensations which are experienced by an individual or defined by a religious group as involving some communication, however slight, with the sacred.

We might ask if a person had ever felt that God was somehow especially present with them. If such was the case, we would say that the individual had had some religious experience. Those members of charismatic groups who "feel" that they have been "filled" with the Holy Spirit and begin to speak strange sounds (speaking in tongues) can be said to have had a rather strong religious experience. The experiential dimension is clearly, then, a category which goes from quite mild feelings to powerful "overtaking" of the individual.

Glock and Stark have attempted to describe various attributes of this dimension of "experience" in terms of its increasing levels. The least involved kind of religious experience is that which they term "the confirming experience." This is the most general kind of religious feeling, the one most frequently reported by individuals. "Confirming" indicates experiences which provide a sudden feeling, knowing, or intuition that one's beliefs are real. There are two subtypes of such experience noted by Glock and Stark: a generalized sense of sacredness and a specific awareness of the presence of divinity. The next "level" in the order of varying religious experience is termed "the responsive experience." Three basic means by which the divine may be seen as noticing the individual are involved: salvational, miraculous, and sanctioning experiences. The feeling that the divine has chosen the individual is indication of the salvational means. The miraculous experience involves such instances as that of a healing miracle; the experience affects the sensate world. If the divine is seen as intervening in negative ways, this is referred to as sanctioning experience. The third level of experience is designated "ecstatic"; it involves all the experiences of the less intimate types plus a deepening of this mutual awareness into an emotional personal relationship. The best example of this kind of religious encounter is the "glossolalia," or speaking in tongues, common to many Pentecostal groups and typical of the newer charismatic movements. The "highest" type or most intense experience is the "revelational" one. Here the sacred responds to the individual and, in addition, provides "confidential" messages or "special" knowledge.

The *ideological* dimension refers to the set or kinds of beliefs which the individual holds. While the particular content and range of beliefs will vary between religions, and often even within the same religion, every religion sets forth some range of beliefs to which its followers are expected to adhere. Generally this dimension has been measured in terms of standard church doctrine. In fact, it is usually measured along the lines of a "liberal-orthodox" continuum, with those professing the greatest number of "traditional beliefs" being seen as the most orthodox.

Questions concerning beliefs in the virgin birth, the literal truth of scripture, the necessity of belief in Christ for salvation are frequently used in measuring this dimension for Protestants. For Catholics, questions might be expanded to include questions concerning specific Church doctrine. An obvious shortcoming here, as mentioned previously, is that the nonorthodox individuals are frequently simply classified as low in belief even though they may have a great range of beliefs, but not orthodox ones. Another problem is that belief is seldom measured in terms of its depth of significance for the respondent. Thus, one may profess to believe a number of things, but place no great importance on these beliefs. Many Americans profess a belief in God, but the real significance of that belief is very uncertain.

The *ritualistic* dimension deals with those activities and practices which are performed in the name of the religious faith. We sometimes think of ritual as only the "high church" acts of worship involving elaborate ceremonies, costumes, and practices. Here by ritual we mean the "routines" through which individuals attempt to come into contact with the object of worship, strengthen their faith, call down the favor of the object or deity worshipped, and so forth. In practice, it is probably the dimension of religiosity most frequently measured, as it includes such easily quantified matters as religious affiliation, church attendance, and participation in church activities.

A great variety of activities can be included under this dimension. Prayer, fasting, carrying a religious charm, and the like would all be included. We can think of the higher church Episcopalian attending a Christmas Eve mass, the Roman Catholic going into the confessional, the member of a charismatic group "speaking in tongue," the Southern Baptist coming forward to the altar, or the Presbyterian sitting quietly in the church pew as the bread and wine of communion are passed by the elders. We can think also of the man and woman having devotions with their children at the breakfast table; the baseball player crossing himself as he comes to the plate; the business person attending a prayer breakfast. In short, anything we *do* in the name of our religion is part of our ritual society.

The *intellectual* dimension concerns the level of knowledge and information which the individual has about the scriptures and other basic matters of the particular religious faith. Such a dimension is clearly related to the ideological dimensions, but here we measure actual knowledge of the creeds, doctrines, and scriptures of the faith reader than actual belief in them.

For the Christian faith, classification of this dimension would probably be measured by such things as knowledge of *facts* about the Bible and its contents; for example, how many books are contained in the Old Testament, or the ability to identify such Biblical characters as Abraham, Moses, Abimelech, and so forth. In some cases, a measure of knowledge concerning the history of a particular church might be part of this dimension of religiosity.

The final dimension, the *consequential* one, is of a somewhat different type than the first four. It is concerned with the effects of religious belief, practice, experience, and knowledge in the secular world. Included in this dimension are all those things one ought to do or the attitudes which one should hold as a result of "being religious." The "good works" idea comes through very strongly on this dimension, as well as the denial of certain activities because of religious faith.

Because we tend to believe that religious belief should have consequences for one's life, we look for relationships between levels of the other dimensions of religiosity and results in the real world. Thus, we may want to look at the question of whether students who are active in religious activities are more or less likely to cheat on exams. Many have looked at the issue of whether or not being religious makes one less bigoted or more prejudiced toward people of other faiths and toward people of other races. Again, there have been studies of the relationship between delinquency and religious activity. All of these are trying to measure the extent to which religious belief has consequences for the individual who holds them.

Again, Peek et al. (1979) ask a key question concerning the consequences of religiosity. Does involvement in religious subcultures deter such deviance as juvenile delinquency? The widely recognized role of religion in reinforcing group values, as well as its emphasis on moral conduct, make a positive response seem obvious. However, in spite of extensive research on this question, a clear answer has yet to emerge. While its failure to do so is partly due to methodological shortcomings in this research, Peek et al. contend that a major reason is the neglect of a major theoretical approach to deviance—deterrence theory. Although a few researchers have examined the deterrent effects of religious beliefs and the possibility of being sanctioned (Hirschi and Stark, 1969; Burkett and White, 1974; Albrecht et al., 1977), the vast majority of explanations focused on whether religious norms prevent deviance. Specific religious beliefs about the severity, and especially the inevitability, of particular sanctions have simply not been examined, even though it is just such kinds of beliefs that are critical in recent efforts of deterrence theory to explain differences in deviant behavior. In fact, "sanction fear"—beliefs which specify that particular sanctions are likely to result from deviance—now seems to be a greater factor in producing conformity than is commitment to norms (Shoham et al., 1976; Tittle, 1977). To the extent, then, that differences in sanction fear exist among religious subcultures, a potentialy strong theoretical approach for explaining the effects of these subcultures on deviance is unexplored.

Research has demonstrated the usefulness of the Glock and Stark "religion in five dimensions" idea. Nelson et al. (1971), for example, made use of the concept in assessing rural-urban differences in religiosity. Their basic problem was that of answering the question of whether urban residence brings a different view of religion and its importance. In measuring the responses of urban and rural residents they utilized four Gallup Poll surveys conducted between 1954 and 1968; operationalizing the "religiosity" of residents in terms of four of Glock and Stark's dimensions in a rather literal way. They defined the ideological dimension by a four-item index in which they saw orthodox individuals believing in life after death, hell, heaven, and the devil. Individuals seen as low on the intellectual dimensions were those who could only answer less than four items of rather basic religious knowledge concerning Christianity. For the experiential dimension they measured response to a direct question concerning religious or mystical experience, and for the ritualistic dimension they were concerned with differences in prayer activity and church attendance. They dropped the consequential dimension, as had Glock and Stark by that time. They were able to show that residential differences occurred only on the ideological dimension, that is, in terms of orthodoxy. Thus, by use of the dimensional approach they were able to "pinpoint" what aspect of religiosity tended to differ. Urban residents were not necessarily nonbelievers; they were, however, not tending to hold to all of the traditional beliefs in their most literal form.

While this statement on the five dimensions has become a standard point of reference in the sociology of religion, it certainly is not seen as the final and complete statement on the various aspects of religiosity. In fact, as noted, Glock and Stark themselves have dropped the consequential dimension as a separate aspect of religiosity. Nevertheless, the presentation of the five dimension hypothesis has sparked much discussion, research, and reformulation on the part of those studying religion from the sociological perspective, leading most to affirm that religion is, in fact, multidimensional, although there is less agreement as to the number and the types of dimensions that exist.

One study (Faulkner & DeJong, 1969) attempted to measure the salience of the dimensions proposed. Testing interrelationships among the given dimensions, it was found that the ideological or belief dimension is the most pervasive of the five. On the other hand, the consequential dimension was of relatively little importance, suggesting that it may reflect a qualitatively different measure of religiosity. The authors concluded that the diversity found supported the view that religious involvement is multidimensional, although some dimensions are more closely related to one another than others. Perhaps the most important of the findings of this study is the significant grouping of scores on the ideological dimension, which indicates support for other findings that college students are not making a marked departure from traditional beliefs. The most important question, however, concerned the interrelationships among the five dimensions; the strongest relationship exists between ideological and intellectual dimensions and the weakest between the experiential and consequential.

Davidson (1975) found that, while dimensions do not always hang together, there are some intriguing relationships between them. For instance, based on his sample of Baptist and Methodist church members, he concluded that the ideological and intellectual dimensions were not only separate dimensions, but were also negatively related to one another. That is, members who had very strong orthodox beliefs tended to be the ones who *know* the least about their faith in terms of content. Thus, the person who believes in the Bible "from cover to cover" may actually know little of what is actually between those covers.

Somewhat differently, he found that the ritualistic and experiential dimensions, while analytically separate, were positively related to each other. Thus, members who regularly performed acts of religious practice were those most likely to have reported having religious experiences. Obviously, in many cases the scene of religious ritual—the praise service in a charismatic group—is fertile ground for the occurrence of a religious experience. It is also interesting that the consequential dimension seemed unrelated to the other dimensions. In short, members tended to be religious in four ways without that having any consequences for their lives.

The most thorough attempt to approach the dimensionality of religiosity is probably that of King (1967) and King and Hunt (1969, 1975). King's original findings support the contention that religiosity is not unidimensional. He found nine dimensions which could be identified. Some are similar to the ones already proposed in the literature, such as creedal assent (belief) and personal commitment, participation in congregational activities, personal religious experience, and personal ties in the congregation. Other dimensions proposed or found were commitment to intellectual search despite doubt, openness to religious growth, dogmatism, and talking and reading about religion. In a later article, King and Hunt (1969) postulated the existence of two additional religious variables making eleven rather than the original nine dimensions: (1) creedal assent; (2) church attendance; (3) organizational activity; (4) personal religious experience; (5) church work with friends; (6) orientation to religious growth and striving; (7) orientation to religious security or dogmatism; (8) extrinsic orientation; (9) financial support; (10) talking and reading about religion, and; (11) religious knowledge.

In summation of this extended debate, it seems sufficient to note that while religion is multidimensional, the exact nature and number of its dimensions is clearly "up for grabs." Nevertheless, the perception of religiosity as having several, or many, different dimensions is an important guide as we consider the social nature of religion.

SUMMARY

In this chapter we have focused on the process of becoming religious as one in which the individual comes to take on the attitudes, beliefs, and behaviors appropriate to a particular religious group. Most people "become religious" as a result of the powerful influences of their family, although other agents such as religious organizations and peer groups are usually involved, too. Most studies indicate that it is the religious practices of the parents which have the most lasting effect on the religious behavior of the adult. Some people, however, do go through a process of re-socialization; they are converted to a new religious group or belief. It is argued, however, that most "conversions" really do not represent a change from a nonreligious perspective but simply an alternation from one religious perspective to another. We have also noted some of the varying effects of such socialization, particularly in terms of the success of the different religious groups. In one way or another we looked at the ability of the group to maintain the loyalty of members over time, the extent to which individuals continued to practice aspects of their faith, the success of groups in inculcating attitudes toward social issues and certain social behaviors, the general ability to provide for the formation of values, and the effects of religious socialization on marriage and the family.

The variations found in the effects of religious socialization lead to a consideration of variation in individual religious behavior. Making the assumption that, in some way, religious behavior is based upon several continuums, or dimensions, we looked at various manners in which these dimensions have been conceptualized. In particular, we examined the five dimension hypothesis of Glock and Stark; religion is seen as involving experiential, ideological, intellectual, ritualistic, and consequential dimensions. Various other schemes which both add to and detract from this basic "religion in 5-D" hypothesis are also discussed. In the end, it would seem that religion is, indeed, multidimensional, and to such an extent that it is difficult to determine just what these dimensions may be.

A great deal has been said in this chapter about socialization into religious groups. Some references have been made to differences that could be found between these groups. In the next chapter we shall take a look at the rather complex nature of such variation and different patterns of organization that we find for such groups.

REFERENCES

Albrecht, S. L., B. A
Chadwick, and D. S.
Alcorn
    1977   "Religiosity and Deviance: Application of an Attitude-Behavior Contingent Consistency Model." *Journal for the Scientific Study of Religion* 16:263-274.

Allport, G. W.
    1950   *The Individual and His Religion.* New York: Macmillan.

1954	*The Nature of Prejudice.* Cambridge, Mass.: Addison-Wesley.
1959	"Religion and Prejudice." *Crane Review* 2:1-10.
1960	*Personality and Social Encounter.* Boston: Beacon Press.
1966	"The religious context of prejudice." *Journal for the Scientific Study of Religion* 5:447-457.

Allport, G. W. and J. M. Ross

1967	"Personal religious orientation and prejudice." *Journal of Personality and Social Psychology* 5:432-443.

Becker, Lee B.

1977	"Predictors of change in religious belief and behaviors during college." *Sociological Analysis* 38:65-74.

Berger, Peter

1967	*The Sacred Canopy—Elements of Sociological Theory of Religion.* New York: Doubleday.

Berger, Peter and Thomas Luckmann

1967	*The Social Construction of Reality.* New York: Doubleday.

Bumpass, Larry

1970	"The trend of interfaith marriage in the United States." *Social Biology* 17:253-59.

Brim, Orville G., Jr. and Stanton Wheeler

1966	*Socialization after Childhood: Two Essays.* New York: John Wiley.

Bibby, Reginald and Merlin B. Brinkerhoff

1974	"When proselytizing fails: An organizational analysis." *Sociological Analysis* 35 (Fall):189-200.

Burkett, S. R. and M. White

1974	"Hellfire and Delinquency: Another Look." *Journal for the Scientific Study of Religion* 13 (December):455-462.

Chalfant, H. Paul

1978	"Religious preference and attitudes toward social issues." Paper presented at the meetings of the Mid-South Sociological Association, Jackson, Miss., November.

1979	"Socioeconomic status, religious affiliation and social issues." Paper presented at the meetings of the Association for the Sociology of Religion, Boston, August.
1980	"Attitudes toward feminist issues, socioeconomic status and religious affiliation." Paper presented at the meetings of the Association for the Scientific Study of Religion/Southwest, Houston, February.

Conway, Flo and Jim
Siegelman
1979 *Snapping: America's Epidemic of Sudden Personality Changes.* New York: Dell Publishing.

Cooley, Charles Horton
1902 *Human Nature and the Social Order.* New York: Scribners.

Davidson, James D.
1975 "Glock's model of religious commitment: Assessing some different approaches and results." *Review of Religious Research* 16:83-93.

Dittes, James E.
1971 "Typing the typologies: Some parallels in the career of church-sect and extrinsic-intrinsic." *Journal for the Scientific Study of Religion* 4:3-13.

Duberman, Lucille
1975 *Gender and Sex in Society.* New York: Praeger.
Durkheim, Emile
1947 *The Elementary Forms of Religious Life.* New York: Free Press.

Faulkner, Joseph E. and
Gordon F. DeJong
1969 "On measuring the religious variable: rejoinder to Weigert and Thomas." *Social Forces* 48 (December):263-67.

Fichter, Joseph
1954 *Social Relations in the Urban Parish.* Chicago: University of Chicago Press.
1961 *Religion as an Occupation: A Study in the Sociology of Professions.* Notre Dame: University of Notre Dame Press.

Finney, John M.
1978 "A theory of religious commitment." *Sociological Analysis* 39 (Spring):19-35.

Fukuyama, Yoshio
1961   "The major dimensions of church membership." *Review of Religious Research* 2:154-61.

Glock, Charles Y.
1959   "The religious revival in America." Pp. 25-42 in Zohn, J. (ed), *Religion and the Face of America.* Berkeley: University Extensions, University of California.
1962   "On the study of religious commitment." *Religious Education* 42 (July-August):98-110.

Glock, Charles Y. and
Rodney Stark
1965   *Religion and Society in Tension.* Chicago: Rand McNally and Company.

Greeley, Andrew
1971   *Why Can't They Be Like Us? America's White Ethnic Groups.* New York: Dutton.

Greeley, Andrew and
Galen Gockel
1971   "The religious effects of parochial education." Pp. 265-301 in Merton Strommen (ed.), *Research on Religious Development.* New York: Hawthorne Books.

Greeley, Andrew and
Peter Rossi
1966   *The Education of Catholic Americans.* Chicago: Aldine.

Hirschi, T. and R. Stark
1969   "Hellfire and Delinquency." *Social Problems* 17 (Fall):202-213.

Hunt, Richard A. and
Morton King
1971   "The intrinsic-extrinsic concept: A review and evaluation." *Journal for the Scientific Study of Religion* 10:338-56.

Johnson, G. Benton, Jr.
1961   "Do holiness sects socialize in dominant values." *Social Forces* 39:309–16.

Johnstone, Ronald L.
1966   *The Effectiveness of Lutheran Elementary and Secondary Schools as Agencies of Christian Education,* St. Louis: Concordia Seminary.

1975	*Religion and Society in Interaction.* Englewood Cliffs, N.J.: Prentice-Hall.

King, Morton B.
1967	"Measuring the religious variable: Nine proposed dimensions." *Journal for the Scientific Study of Religion* 6:173-90.

King, Morton B. and
Richard A. Hunt
1969	"Measuring the religious variable: Amended findings." *Journal for the Scientific Study of Religion* 8:321-23.
1975a	"Religious dimensions: Entities or constructs?" *Sociological Focus* 8 (June):57-63.
1975b	"Measuring the religious variable: National replication." *Journal for the Scientific Study of Religion* 14 (March):14-22.

Lenski, Gerhard E.
1961	*The Religious Factor.* Garden City, New York: Doubleday.

Lofland, John
1966	*Doomsday Cult.* Englewood Cliffs, N. J.: Prentice-Hall.
1978	"Becoming a world saver revisited." Pp. 10-23 in J. T. Richardson (ed.), *Conversion Careers,* Beverly Hills: Sage.

Lofland, John and
Rodney Stark
1965	"Becoming a world saver: A theory of conversion to a deviant prospective." *American Sociological Review* 30:862-74.

Maves, Paul B.
1971	"Religious development in adulthood." Pp. 777-97 in Merton Strommen (ed.), *Research on Religious Development.* New York: Hawthorne Books.

McCarthy, James
1979	"Religious commitment, affiliation, and marriage dissolution." Pp. 179-97 in Robert Wuthnow (ed.), *The Religious Dimensions: New Directions in Quantitative Research.* New York: Academic Press.

McRae, J. A.
1977   *Patterns of Marriage Dissolution in the United States.* Unpublished doctoral dissertation, Princeton University.

National Opinion
Research Center
1978   *General Social Survey.* Chicago: University of Chicago.

Nelson, Hart, Raytha
Yokeley, and Thomas
Madron
1971   "Rural-urban differences in religiosity." *Rural Sociology* 36:389-96.

Parsons, Talcott
1951   *The Social System.* New York: The Free Press.

Peek, Charles, H. Paul
Chalfant and Edgar V.
Milton
1979   "Sinners in the hands of an angry God: Fundamentalist fears about drunk driving." *Journal for the Scientific Study of Religion* 18 (March):29-39.

Pope, Liston
1942   *Millhands and Preachers.* New Haven: Yale University Press

Richardson, J. T. and
Mary Stewart
1978   "Conversion process models and the Jesus movement." Pp. 24-42 in J. T. Richardson (ed.), *Conversion Careers.* Beverly Hills: Sage.

Shoham, G. S., E. Segal,
and G. E. Rahav
1976   "Secularization, deviance and delinquency among Israeli Arab villagers." *Megamot* 22:202-209.

Sklare, Marshall
1971   *America's Jews.* New York: Random House.
Spilka, B., L. Stout, B.
Minton and D. Sizemore
1977   "Death and personal faith: A psychometric investigation." *Journal for the Scientific Study of Religion* 16:167-78.

Tittle, C. R.
1977   "Sanction fear and the maintenance of social
                        order." *Social Forces* 55(March):579–96.

Traviasano, Richard
1969   "Alternation and conversion as qualitatively dif-
                        ferent transformations." Pp. 594-606 in Gregory
                        Stone and Harvey Faberman (eds.), *Social
                        Psychology through Symbolic Interaction.*
                        Waltham: Mass.: Ginn-Blaisdell.

Trent, James and Jenette
Golds
1967   *Catholics in College: Religious Commitment and
                        Intellectual Life.* Chicago: University of Chicago
                        Press.

Vincent, Clark
1964   "Interfaith marriages." Pp. 50-59 in Earl Raab
                        (ed.), *Religious Conflict in America.* New York:
                        Doubleday.

Wach, Jacob
1944   *Sociology of Religion.* Chicago: University of
                        Chicago Press

Weigert, Andrew J.,
William V. D'Antonio,
and Arthur Rubel
1971   "Protestantism and assimilation among Mexican
                        Americans: An exploratory study of ministers'
                        reports." *Journal for the Scientific Study of
                        Religion* 10:219-32.

Westerhoff, John H., III
1973   "A changing focus: Toward an understanding of
                        religious socialization." *Andover Newton Quarter-
                        ly* 14 (November):118-29.

Willems, Emilio
1967   *Followers of the New Faith: Culture Change and
                        the Rise of Protestantism in Brazil and Chile.*
                        Nashville: Vanderbilt University Press.

Wilson, John
1978   *Religion in American Society: The Effective
                        Presence.* Englewood Cliffs, N. J.: Prentice-Hall.

Wrong, Dennis
1961   "The oversocialized conception of man in
                        modern sociology." American Sociological
                        Review 25 (April): 183–43.

Chapter 4

The Organization
of Religious Groups

Some years ago, when buttons with clever sayings were something of a fad, one proclaimed: "God is not dead—Church is!" In a sense, that mirrors a great deal of the American way of thinking about our religion. We believe in God, but we are not at all sure about the structures built to service that belief. We are comfortable dealing with individual religiosity, but suspicious of groups that channel that religiosity.

This attitude blends well with the theme of rugged individualism which runs strongly through the American value system. We seem to have the feeling that religion is something so essentially personal and individualistic that organizational structures are more likely to "get in our way" than they are to help. Recall such favorite gospel songs as "My God and I" and "In the Garden" and you see that they clearly express a religiosity unfettered by group constraints. An extreme example of this feeling is expressed in the words of a comparatively recent "cowboy" gospel song:

> Well, Me and Jesus got our own thing going,
> Me and Jesus got it all worked out;
> Me and Jesus got our own thing going,
> We don't need anybody to tell us what it's all about.
> (Hall, 1971)

This sort of individualistic expression may be appealing, but it is far from realistic. Religion, like all human behavior, is essentially a group enterprise; as human beings we are never truly alone. All that we do, even when physically separated from others, is deeply influenced by the present or past action of some group or groups within our society. Even to think of God is to use a gift of the group—the very language by which we think. Thus, our conceptions of God, sin, virtue, redemption, proper behavior, all depend upon definitions supplied by the group.

The simple fact is that the religious group is a basic necessity for the existence and maintenance of belief, practice, values, and ritual. As it is only through the agency of the group that we can become "truly human," so it is only in the interaction with the religious group that we can be said to become "truly religious."

In this chapter we shall look at two aspects of the life of religious organizations: (1) the way in which such groups develop and problems attendant to that development; and (2) the various types of religious organizations.

Any human group is presented with numerous problems associated with growth and development which must be solved if the group is to continue. It is possible that the religious group has some particular problems which arise out of the nature of its goals and values. Three questions need to be addressed in regard to the development of such groups: (1) Is there any pattern of development that seems standard?; (2) What dilemmas are confronted by the group as it grows?; and (3) How does the growing group relate to the larger society?

THE PATTERNS OF GROWTH FOR RELIGIOUS GROUPS

Religious groups tend to develop according to some broad general patterns. Although they face different problems and solve them in their own way, these groups seem to share clear stages of organization which characterize their development. The first stage, marking the emergence of a new movement, is usually characterized by *informality of leadership and operation.* New groups tend to begin through the leadership of a strong individual who by the power of personal gifts attracts supporters to his particular program—a "recall" to a "purer" form of the faith, a new interpretation of the faith, or a different organizational form. This style of leadership is referred to as "charismatic,"[1] a term borrowed from the Greek Biblical word meaning gifts, especially of the spirit. This person-centered organization of the group is indicative of the lack of formal structure characteristic of this phase of the group's life.

Reaching back into the history of our country, we can look at some of the beginnings of frontier religion as illustrative. Following a period of relative religious apathy in our nation, the Second Awakening began in various parts of the nation and represented a revival of religious interest for many. On the western frontier—Kentucky and Tennessee, for example—the religious styles of the more settled areas did not seem appropriate, and many sought a reinterpretation or renewal of them. Actually there was a tendency for adherents to see it as a return to New Testament Christianity.

Among such movements, one in particular took hold. Known to some as the Campbellite movement, it was initiated by two Presbyterian ministers, Alexander and Thomas Campbell, who felt the need to "call back" Christians on the frontier to a religion unfettered by the rules, laws, and structures characterizing established, "eastern" religion. The point for us is that at this stage the movement centered on their personal gifts, as well as those of a few other such disgruntled clergy, and the movement proceeded as a result of their personal

1. "Charismatic" is used here to refer to personality characteristics of leaders. Elsewhere it will relate to groups which believe in such "spirit-filled" practices as speaking in tongues.

ability to attract followers. There were no rules, no legislation, no elections, in short, no formality.

But religious movements do not stand still; they either grow or wither. If the group continues it generally faces a crisis of leadership as the original leader or leaders die or otherwise leave active direction of the movement. The tendency is to resort to what is called "traditional" leadership. That is, there are still no rules or creeds, but the teachings of the charismatic leader become "policy," and interpretations of these teachings become the benchmark for the group. Interpretations are needed, of course, because as the group has grown and matured new problems have arisen. For example, the original followers now have families and a desire that their children be brought up in the faith, so "education" may be needed to instruct the new generation in the tradition.

In the case of the so-called Campbellite movement, this was a time of schism, or separation of differing segments from each other. Two large factions in the movement (then calling itself simply Christian) could not agree on what the tradition might say about the relatively minor issue of the use of instrumental music in church. Over this issue the two groups split: the Church of Christ declaring instruments to be unbiblical; the Christian Church (Disciples of Christ) allowing such use. The point for the growth of the group is that there were still no "official" rules but that the tradition and its interpretation were used to decide this issue.

Usually, if a religious group continues into the second and third generation, it will take on a much more formal style of leadership; a style which we refer to as "legal-bureaucratic." Now the rules, laws, and strictures against which the movement may have first protested become a part of the group's life. Although a variety of terms may be used to disguise the fact, the movement is now established, its policies "routinized," and there are official rules and channels for making decisions.

This appears to happen even to those groups which protest that they are not so formally controlled. The Church of Christ, for example, claims to be free of the twin "error" of distinctions between laity and clergy and connections beyond the local congregation. Yet a body as strong as this group in such areas of the country as the Southwest, cannot exist without routinizing, formalizing its patterns of operation. Thus, for example, "Christian" colleges have been established to train the leadership of the group, and pastors have assumed official positions which in large congregations may take on an hierarchial nature. Also, congregations do, indeed, cooperate with one another according to unwritten, but acknowledged, rules.

The Dilemmas of Growth

This pattern of growth creates a dilemma or a set of dilemmas, particularly for the older, more faithful members. With each stage of growth there seems to be a diminution of the original spirit of the movement and a solidifying of organization. Further, the message of the movement may seem less unique and inspiring when used to attract more converts. O'Dea (1966:90-97) has listed a number of choices which maturing religious groups must make. Following his lead, we look at three such choices which create dilemmas for the maturing group.

First, there is the matter of *structure*. If a group is to function as it becomes larger, it must have structure; however, the effort to maintain that structure may actually displace the principles it seeks to uphold. The formal organization may become an end in itself as those with "vested interests" seek to maintain the *status quo*. This may, however, alienate rank and file members insofar as it is seen as irrelevant to their needs. For example, strict adherence to the traditional system of authority in the Roman Catholic Church has led to the alienation of large numbers of laypersons in this country and has reduced their loyalty to the organization.

A second dilemma comes with the investiture of *formal positions with powers and privileges*. Such investiture is necessary for the functioning of the group, but again may alienate the group from its ideal goals. What happens is that leaders, now occupying positions with some "pay-off," seek such positions out of motivations which are less than pure. Certainly there are a number of instances where the motives of professionals in religion have been questioned. The leaders of the so-called Protestant Reformation certainly saw the motivations of the Roman Catholic clergy of that time as far from pure. To some, the motives of any "full-time" church workers are suspect: especially doubtful are the motives of the seemingly compromising pastor of the Church of the Blessed Rich or the television evangelist "hawking" healing and deliverance on a quasi-commercial basis.

Finally, there is a dilemma related to the way in which *new recruits* to the group might be attracted. Clearly, such recruits are necessary for growth, but the very lack of the group's original inspiration in these recruits may mean the necessity of "watering down" the strict message of the original followers. As Nottingham (1971:218) suggests, in order to have any impact on the outsiders the group seeks to attract, it must make modifications in both its program and structure. Generally, this means that aspects of the "ideal" patterns of discipline and belief will have to be relaxed. Also, the more extreme aspects of its general program or "message" must be changed so that it will seem less strange to the nonmembers. A strict adherence to "standards" will be much less appealing to prospective recruits, but if standards are lowered the goals and ideals of the organization may be so changed that it will no longer meet the needs of the original or existing membership.

This dilemma appears to have been faced by those groups whose main focus was on a healing ministry. In becoming successful in terms of numbers, they have relinquished some of their major emphasis on healing and turned to a message promising success in a number of other areas. It seems certain that while this increases their attractiveness to outsiders it also alienates some of the original followers of the movement.

RELATING TO THE LARGER SOCIETY

A serious problem faced by religious groups today is that of relating to what may be a disinterested, even potentially hostile, secular world. In simple societies the religious institution and the society are so nearly identical that there is little question about how one shall relate to the other. As societies become complex, and institutions are differentiated, the religious group must face the problem of how it shall deal with these other, now differentiated, parts of society; a society which may welcome religion with less open arms.

Because of this, Demerath and Hammond (1969) suggest that religious groups in contemporary society face some serious functional problems. They assume that the religious organization in today's world is really *deviant*. That is, while religion may be seen as the repository of basic societal values, the values tend to be the ideal ones which are no longer completely consistent with the real values.

To the extent that this is true, religious groups need to deal with this "deviant" status. Demerath and Hammond (1969:168-73) suggest that one problem to be dealt with concerns maintaining the traditional patterns of the group; seeing that those norms and values which have sustained the group in the past are continued. How, for example, can the religious emphasis on revealed truth be maintained in a society which increasingly stresses the importance of empirical verification as the means to knowledge? It is not a question of whether the two are actually or even necessarily opposed; the point is that to an increasing number of persons science and religion seem to be at odds, and this means that for many in society the old patterns, goals, and beliefs seem increasingly irrelevant to everyday life.

The serious problem of dealing with this challenge to the established pattern has been handled by religious groups in a number of ways, as Demerath and Hammond suggest. The most radical of such strategies is exemplified by those who, in the early 1960s, proclaimed "the death of God." Their strategy was to radically alter the symbols and belief system of Christianity in order to make it as compatible as possible with contemporary thought. Thus Anglican Bishop Robinson, one of the several prominent Church leaders to question traditional doctrine, proclaimed that we should be "honest to God." By this he meant that we should admit that we no longer believe in the traditional, transcendent meaning behind our religious symbols, thereby making ancient formulas consistent with contemporary value systems. The probability that most readers of this book have never heard of "death of God" theology is adequate commentary on the effectiveness of this strategy.

A related, but by no means as extreme, strategy attempts to modernize doctrine in order to make it more appealing and less obviously at odds with contemporary ways of thinking. This has led to the highly philosophical theology of Paul Tillich which borrows heavily from the existentialist movement in philosophy and redefines God as "Ground of All Being." Similarly, scholars like Rudolf Bultmann have conceptualized the Biblical narratives as "myths." That is, these Bible stories are symbols which contain divine truth, but by no means should be taken as literal accounts of reality.

A more popularized (some would say vulgarized) version of this approach can be seen on the shelves of many bookstores under the general rubric of "popular religion." Here God and traditional doctrine take on an extremely familiar sort of tone, and we are asked not to believe in abstract doctrine but in our "old Daddy god" who just wants to help us if we will only plug into him in the right way. Such a strategy seems to run from Norman Vincent Peale's "power of positive thinking" to the chumminess of such "gospel songs" as "Drop Kick Me Jesus through the Goal Posts of Life."

By far the most common organizational strategy is to underplay traditional doctrine, leaving it understated or unmentioned whenever possible. Thus the group or its leaders may "appear" to be maintaining the pattern while actually not accepting the traditional meaning of the words. Young clergy, in particular, have frequently adopted such an approach so that they will not be thought hopelessly agnostic by their older, more conservative flocks.

It is interesting to note that the single most effective strategy seems to be to act as if there is no problem, or to make a virtue out of "holding" on to "old time religion." Many point to the continuing success of fundamentalist and Pentecostal groups in the late 1970s as an example of the success of this strategy. While the death of fundamentalist doctrine has been confidently predicted by "liberal" theologians for some time, it has simply refused to die. Indeed, as Roof (1978) points out, while the "liberal" groups (those trying hardest to be consistent with contemporary thought patterns and values) are steadily decreasing in membership, fundamentalism is flourishing, and "born again" Christians appear to dominate media reports on the religious world, even if they do not really constitute a majority of Christians.

This apparent contradiction may not be as real as it seems. There is some indication that the increasing numbers embracing a fundamentalist view of the faith consist of a hard core of true believers, while the masses may simply be dropping out. In fact, it has been noted that membership in liberal churches may represent a move toward a religious perspective. The seemingly successful strategy, of attracting converts with old time religion then, may only work on a limited audience; the others are buying none of the strategies.

A second problem for the religious group in contemporary society is that of convincing prospective clientele that religious goals are attainable and worth attaining, and dealing with problems resulting from nonattained goals. Demerath and Hammond (1969:173-80) view the issue as one in which organizations need to have goals related to the values of the societal system which can be thought of as valuable. Traditional religious values, such as that of "ultimate, otherworldly" salvation, are in trouble at this point. Such values seem unsuitable or at least unimportant in light of many contemporary values. For more and more persons such a goal seems incongruous, or, at best, far from a matter of immediate importance: "Salvation is not so much spurned as it seems to be losing any sense of urgency" (Demerath and Hammond, 1969:174).

Goals are also better pursued when they are concrete so that progress toward reaching them can be assessed. But it is just this sort of objectivity which religious goals lack. They are otherworldly, unattainable in this order of existence.

It is suggested that for this reason segments of religious organization have latched on to new, determinate goals. For example, those clergy, and others, who supported the civil rights movement in the 1950s could be seen as substituting this concrete, obtainable goal for the vague, less proximate one of otherworldly salvation. In a similar way, many more socially conservative religionists have linked their faith to the problem of fighting "godless" communism.

Another way of dealing with these problems is through *goal displacement*. That is, the original programs or procedures intended as a way to reach a goal become goals in themselves. A clear example is the way in which "numbers" have often become the real goal of religious groups. Thus, having the biggest Sunday School attendance becomes the goal of the church rather than teaching people religious doctrine. Large churches have been known to wage intercity contests to see who would reach this sort of goal most effectively. Similarly, specific subgroups within the congregation can often take on the character of ends in themselves. The woman's organization in many congregations has taken such a complexion; its success becomes a sign of the vitality of the whole group.

A third problem is that of adapting to the surrounding environment while maintaining the strength or boundaries of the group. Demerath and Hammond (1969:180-187) conceptualize this problem in terms of the need religious organizations have to recruit new members while maintaining the interest of those already a part of the group. Since individuals can be members of just so many groups (generally only one religious group) and can only give so much of their time, there is a real competition among religious and nonreligious organizations. Insofar as competition with other religious groups is concerned, the available pool of potential members may be so small that denominational types are led to make comity agreements. That is, areas of a city may be assigned to one of the more standard denominations, and others agree not to establish congregations in that area. Denominational mergers are another way in which denominations seek to deal with competition, and recent history has seen a number of such mergers. Indeed, the whole ecumenical movement might be seen in terms of attempts to lessen the competition and spread potential recruits around (Berger, 1967).

Competition still exists, however, and groups may be driven to rather extreme attempts in seeking to attract new members. Competition with secular groups can be even more fierce. The service club, the family, the political party, occupational and professional involvement, and many other interests, all demand the time and effort of members. In some smaller communities this contest is handled by having a specific time set aside for religion; for example, Sundays and one night of the week may be "cleared" of nonchurch activities. The desire to involve more and more of the member's time, however, may be so intense that the church attempts to gain increased involvement.

A final functional problem for religious organization is referred to as that of "integration" (Demerath and Hammond, 1969:189-95). It is the job of taking the various roles and positions in the organization and seeing that they fit together to accomplish necessary tasks. This can mean the need to integrate the church's parishioners and their various viewpoints with the denomination's program to ensure loyalty to the church organization. It is also the problem of integrating the various roles of the official full-time clergyperson. While we discuss some of the dysfunctional aspects of the role of the clergy in today's church in the next chapter, it is useful here to point to this as a major problem. The demands of heterogeneous parishioners on the church and its officials, as well as demands from denominational authorities, may be so severe that members of the clergy suffer a great deal of role strain.

Religious organizations also face the problem of allocating roles, that is, integrating people rather than roles. No religious group, not even the small sectarian one, is completely homogeneous. There are important differences in the religious needs and inclinations of the various members. An extreme example was seen in one congregation in the inner city of Chicago. It drew its diverse membership from residents of the area around the church who were black, Italian, and Puerto Rican. But, the church was near a large medical and professional center associated with a state medical school and several large hospitals. Parishioners also came from the student body of the school, the faculty, and practicing medical people who lived in nearby luxury apartments. Then, too, old time residents now living in the suburbs as well as "liberals" from other parts of the city came to the older location to make their church home. Imagine the problems of devising a program that would suit such a variety of social statuses, ethnicity, education, and interest. Just to decide how to pitch a sermon was a major problem for the pastor of the church.

In summary, like most groups, the religious association faces a number of problems and is confronted with a number of dilemmas. The solutions offered frequently draw the group away from its original "purity" and drastically change its nature. The results of these changes are so significant that the group sometimes takes on a totally different character.

The different styles which characterize religious groups have generally been seen as the basis for developing a typology or classification of different types of religious groups, and it is to a fuller elaboration of this aspect of religious phenomena that we now turn.

TYPES OF RELIGIOUS ORGANIZATIONS

While in everyday language we call any sort of religious body in Christendom a "church," such an unreflective designation is far from helpful to a sociological study of religious groups. That is because such groups vary in a number of important ways which help us understand the different effects of religiosity, the relationship between the group and the secular world, the involvement of the membership, and the attitudes and beliefs of the membership. All of these factors are significant in understanding the social aspects of religiosity and the religious institution.

The Traditional Dichotomy: Church and Sect

The oldest attempt to differentiate types of religious organizations divides them into two polar types called the *church* and the *sect*. This distinction is generally attributed to a theologian, Ernst Troeltsch, and also appears in the work of his teacher, Max Weber, whose concepts of the role of the prophet and the priest were influential in the development of the classification. Although this simple dichotomy is not fully applicable to the contemporary religious world, its basic formulation of polar types of associations helps us to think about the differential nature of particular religious groups.

As Troeltsch (1931) defined it, the church is a type of religious group at peace with the ways of the secular world. It neither rejects the values of the world nor denies its power. Rather, it attempts to have an influence in secular matters through its very acceptance of the secular realm. In brief, the church is built on compromise and accommodation with the secular power. Membership in the church is by virtue of birth and all those living in a particular region are considered to be "members." What Troeltsch had in mind was the Roman Catholic Church of the thirteenth century. At that time one simply was a Catholic by virtue of being born and living in a particular region where power was shared by both secular and religious authorities. Although it exercises universal domination in religious matters, the church is closely aligned with its secular world; it is more concerned with correct ritual, rightly administered sacraments, and an orthodox creed than it is with ethics and behavior.

The sect reflects one part of what Troeltsch conceptualized as a perpetual dialogue in the history of the Christian church; a dialogue between the tendency of religion toward accommodation with the secular world and that of protest against such accommodation. The sect is essentially a protest movement. It's chief tenet is objection to the church's surrender to the secular authorities (as the sectarian views it). It may also be seen as an expression of the failure of the church to meet the needs of its total membership, usually of its less prestigious segment. Troeltsch refers to it (1931:336) as:

> . . . lay Christianity, personal achievement in ethics and in religion, the radical fellowship of love, religious equality and brotherly love, indifference toward the authority of the State and the ruling classes, dislike of technical law and of the oath, the separation of the religious life from the economic struggle by means of the ideal of poverty and frugality . . . the directness of the personal religious relationship, criticism of official spiritual guide and theologians, the appeal to the New Testament and the Primitive Church. . . .

As we ponder this simple church-sect dichotomy, we need to understand, as Beckford (1975:73) reminds us, that Troeltsch and Weber used these terms to refer to specific, albeit variant, aspects of the differences in organizational life. It was not meant as some final form of classification, but was tied to given historical situations and the particular interests of these men.

Swatos (1976) has suggested that Weber introduced the concept as part of the attempt to understand how religion in general, and Christianity in particular, developed its relationship with the secular social system. He was concerned with how this relationship "resulted in the pluralistic, secularizing process to be found in the modernizing Western world" (1976:17). For Weber, the one all important factor separating the polar types has to do with whether membership is based on birth or conversion. That is, were individuals members simply because they could not avoid it as a member of the society, or were they members because of a conscious decision which they made and a definite step which they took? Troeltsch saw the basis of the distinction as having to do with accommodation to or compromise with the world. The church is the spirit of compromise as opposed to the protest against the ways of "the world" which marks the sect. If sociologists of religion use only one measure, they generally refer to the compromise vs. protest distinction; all descriptions of the sect stress that "protest" is at the center of its nature.

The difficulties with the simple dichotomy have been indicated by the results of a number of research efforts, and many sociologists of religion have dealt with the questions of the adequacy and relevance of the concept in contemporary society (see Berger, 1954; Demerath, 1967; Eister, 1967, 1973; Goode, 1967;

Gustafson, 1967; Johnson, 1963; Martin, 1962; O'Dea, 1966, 1970; Wilson, 1967; and Yinger, 1970). Some of these critics have frankly arrived at the conclusion that the dichotomy is no longer meaningful. Eister (1957; 1967) charges that the whole business of trying to use this particular typology is a "fruitless argument," and Goode calls the typology a "dead concept, obsolete, sterile and archaic" (1967:77).

In sum, there is almost no agreement about how the concept should be understood and how we can properly use it. Because Weber and Troeltsch formulated the theory for specific purposes at a particular time, it seems inappropriate to apply it directly to the American scene in any way; this is clearly the principal difficulty with using it. However, even though we cannot use the concept *per se*, a long heritage in the sociological study of religion has found that some modifications of the basic principle of differentiation between groups can provide the student with a useful tool.

Contemporary American Typologies of Religious Groups

A number of attempts have been made to adapt the concept in order to understand the origin and development of variant religious groups in contemporary society. The "church-sect" dichotomy was first applied to the religious scene in America in the work of a theologian with an interest in society, H. Richard Niebuhr. He wrote *The Social Sources of Denominationalism* (1932) as an exploration of the problem of differences in religious groups. Using the term church in a sense much modifed from that of Troeltsch and Weber, his work implicitly polarized the two terms. That is, church and sect were seen at opposite ends of a continuum of religious organizations with most of the existing religious bodies falling between. Some groups may be "more" like the ideal type of church while others are "more" sectlike in character. One concern of Niebuhr was to try to understand the processes which occur as groups appear to move along the continuum. Niebuhr hints that the direction of such transitions was generally, if not always, in the direction of becoming more church-like. This suggestion was made explicit by Pope (1942) in his analysis of the development of religious groups in *Preachers and Millhands*, the story of the development of religious groups in a North Carolina milltown.

The suggestions concerning what categories of religious organizations are most appropriate and useful for the American religious scene have come from the work of Howard Becker (1932) and Milton Yinger (1946, 1969, and 1970). Both elaborate on the basic church-sect dichotomy and articulate a number of different types of religious associations which generally tend to be ranged along the continuum suggested by Niebuhr's work.

Becker's suggestion is that there are four basic types of religious organizations to be found in American religious life; the *ecclesia*, the *denomination*, the *sect*, and the *cult* (Becker, 1932). Yinger accepted much of this but made a few useful additions (1946, 1969, and 1970). While he speaks of two types of the "Universal Church" (Institutionalized and Diffused) he also notes that these two types do not really exist in any practical sense in American life. To the rest of Becker's typology he adds a new category of sect—the *established sect*—and also differentiates between the "types" of sects: *acceptance sects, aggressive sects,* and *avoidance sects.* We will use Becker's four types along with Yinger's added category of the established sect to consider the problems of differentiating between various kinds of religious groups which exist in America today.

The Ecclesia

The ecclesia is a religious association which attempts to expand its realm so as to claim as members everybody within the boundaries of a particular society. However, it is not really able to make such a widespread appeal. For example, it is not totally effective in dealing with the sectarian tendencies of those groups in society who feel that they have been deprived in some sense. Becker's classic description of the ecclesia is in these terms (1932:624):

> The social structure known as the ecclesia is a predominantly conservative body, not in open conflict with the secular aspects of social life, and professedly universal in its aims. . . . The fully developed ecclesia attempts to amalgamate with the state and the dominant classes, and strives to exercise control over every person in the population. Members are born into the ecclesia; they do not have to join it. It is therefore a social structure somewhat akin to the nation or the state, and is in no sense elective. . . . The ecclesia naturally attaches a high importance to the means of grace which it administers, to the system of docrine which it has formulated, and to the official administration of sacraments and teaching by official clergy.

In summary, the ecclesia is a religious body characterized by: (1) the inclusion of all members of society in its membership; (2) a sense of monopolistic right to the religious realm within that society; (3) a close alliance with the power of the secular world; (4) a social organization which is quite formal and in which there is great specification of roles and relationships; (5) leadership from officially designated, full-time clergy who alone have rights over the sacramental means of grace; and (6) membership based more upon birth and socialization than upon the conversion of individuals, whether children or adult, to its particular perspective.

As a type of religious organization, the ecclesia appears only occasionally today. There are concrete organizations to which we can point, however, which are more or less close to the ideal type of the ecclesia. The Anglican church (Church of England) in England comes somewhat close to the model as does the Roman Catholic Church as found in a country like Spain. The situation of some Lutheran churches in Scandinavian countries also gives some indication of what an ecclesia is. The policies of separation of church and state and of religious tolerance in this country, of course, preclude the possibility that any religious group could claim status as an ecclesia in our society.

The Denomination

The Denomination, sometimes referred to as "the class church," is certainly the most common organizational form to be found on the American religious scene. Yinger (1970:264-66) defines the denomination as a type of religious group that does not have general appeal to the total society. That is, its attraction is for only a limited segment of the population. The denomination is limited by the boundaries of class, race, ethnicity, and, sometimes, regional area. For example, the African Methodist Church is limited mainly to blacks; the Episcopal church draws its participation from the upper classes; and Baptists have their greatest concentration in the South. While it is clear that membership in "denominational" type bodies is not strictly limited particular social classes, there is a tendency for the attitudes and styles of the middle class to influence the life and order of the "denominational" type of religious body.

The major characteristics of the denominational type are:

(1) Compromise and accommodation with the secular "world" and the authority of the state.

(2) Heavy reliance on birth (infant baptism) and socialization as a means of increasing membership.

(3) More liberal (less literal) interpretation of doctrines.

(4) More or less formal worship services with varying degrees of ritual and standardization.

(5) Leadership through a formal, trained clergy usually "approved" by denominational bodies and persons operating from a "headquarters."

(6) Tolerant and even friendly relationships with similar religious bodies, frequently involving a great deal of cooperation and joint efforts.

(7) A membership dominantly drawn from the ranks of the middle and upper socioeconomic strata of society.

In defining and discussing both the denomination and the sect, it should be remembered that no single "real" group matches either polar type perfectly. Some, such as Presbyterians and Episcopalians, fit the type more than others, such as Baptists and members of the Church of the Nazarene. The concept of a continuum stretched between the two extremes, with actual organizations ranged between them, has a great deal of validity. There are sectarian qualities in the most austere denomination, and the sect group will display characteristics associated with the more formal group.

It is important that we note the wide range of variation to be found within the denominational type of religious group. Tolerance is a key characteristic of such groups, but this tolerance does not necessarily follow a straight line progression from denomination to sect; the degree of formality may also be seen as differing widely from one group categorized as a denomination to another.

Thus (while both are classified as denominations), the formality of the worship service in an American Baptist congregation and that found in an Episcopal service will be considerably different both in quantity and quality. Again, the degree of "liberalness" in the interpretation of the doctrine will vary between congregations of the church of Nazarene and those of the United Church of Christ. Clergy in the Presbyterian Churches are more formally defined than in the Church of Christ. While all of these are definitely "denominations" (at some point along the continuum) they are really quite different from one another.

It is important to note also that *within* denominations there will be considerable variation. Sometimes such variation is related to the region of the country in which the congregation is found, to the socio-economic level of the group, or even to whether it is in a rural or an urban setting. Most frequently the variation may be traced to the particular history of the specific congregation. A Presbyterian church begun as a mission congregation in a poorer section of town, and drawing members from many other religious bodies, will tend to be more like a Baptist church than to be like the wealthier suburban congregations of the same denomination located not far from it. Similarly, a wealthy Southern Baptist congregation in a downtown site may seem much like its Methodist neighbor across the street. There does appear to be a tendency for religious bodies of the denominational type to increase their cooperation with one another, almost to the point of blunting some of their original distinctiveness, as they continue and prosper.

The key distinguishing characteristic of the denomination has always been accommodation—to the state, the secular power, and other religious groups. That is, the denomination is comfortable in its world. However, it has been argued (Johnson, 1971:131-35) that we tend to overplay the accommodation of the denomination to society, as if it were a one-way street. Johnson contends that it may be possible for denominations to gain some of their own goals through the process of working out the compromise. After all, compromise does imply that there will be give and take from both sides. It does not mean that the denomination is totally swallowed by the society.

Still the weight of the literature suggests that the denominations are, indeed, very widely accommodated to the world around them. At the very least they have given up traditional claims to their own comprehensivity and supremacy. However, it would be wrong to suggest that the denomination is totally dominated by the world.

The Sect

Sect type groups probably interested sociologists more and have been studied by them more frequently than any other type of religious organization. It was the existence of this other polar type of religious organization which initially called Troeltsch's attention to potential variations in types of religious groups, and this extreme protest type of group raises sharply the issue of the existence of a differentiation unique to the contemporary world. At the same time, it provides us with the most insight into the processes whereby religious organizations develop and the direction in which this development tends to move. Sects are the deviant type of group and, as is true in so much sociological investigation, the deviant type tells us more than does the expected pattern.

The sect is, above all, characterized by protest. Generally it is a group or body which has seceded or withdrawn from a more traditional, accommodated, compromised group. For example, the early Methodist movement was a protest against the formality of the established Church of England. When, however, the Methodist Church itself became accommodated to the dominant values of the society, sectarian groups such as the Wesleyan Methodists and the Free Methodists seceded. While what Wilson (1978) refers to as a "sectarian spirit" may appear in individuals and small groups in what are otherwise denominational type groups, it usually expresses itself in the formation of new groups who purport to embody the "true" version of the faith and who see themselves as a kind of pure elite of God's people.

A rather standard list of the characteristics of the sect would include the following points:

(1) Opposition to the world and refusal to compromise.

(2) A sense of elitism in which the sect is seen as stressing the pure doctrine, calling people back to some original sect of principles.

(3) Informal, often emotionally directed services, worship, or gatherings.

(4) Leadership by means of lay people, with no formal clergy, and a deemphasis on organization as such.

(5) Small size.

(6) Emphasis on coming into the group by conversion rather than by birth.

(7) Members drawn largely from the lower socioeconomic strata.

As in the case of the denomination, no real group matches exactly all the characteristics of the sect. Some, such as the small holiness groups, some of which engage in rather exotic practices like snake-handling, come very close to the ideal type of the sect. They protest the status values of the secular world, have small, poor congregations, and no specified clergy. Jehovah's Witnesses, on the other hand, have moved in many ways from the strict sectarian stance. Still the sect type is generally seen as in direct contrast to the denomination.

Contrast with denominations. If the denominations can be seen as the typical kind of religious organization in contemporary society, the sect is the most common alternative. As we have indicated, denomination and sect are frequently defined in contrast to one another. The outline provided by Vernon (1962:186) gives us a rather clear perspective on the two groups and the way in which they differ from one another (see Table 4-1).

Some, however, have called our attention to the possibilities that the differences are overrated. The tendency to polarize the two groups has blurred some of the ways in which they are not so completely opposite. Demerath (1965)

Table 4-1.

Characteristic	Sect	Denomination
Size	Small	Large
Relationship with other religious groups	Rejects—feels that the sect alone has the "truth"	Accepts other denominations and is able to work with them in harmony
Wealth (church property), buildings, salary of clergy, income of members	Limited	Extensive
Religious services	Emotional emphasis—try to recapture conversion thrill; informal, extensive congregational participation	Intellectual emphasis; concern with teachings, formal; limited congregational participation
Clergy	Unspecialized; little if any professional training; frequently part-time	Specialized, professionally trained, full time
Doctrines	Literal interpretations of scriptures; emphasis upon other-worldly rewards	Liberal interpretations of scriptures; emphasis upon this worldly rewards
Membership recruitments	Conversion experience; emotional	Born into group or ritualistic requirements; intellectual commitment
Relationship with secular world	"At war" with the secular world which is defined as being "evil"	Endorses prevailing culture and social organization
Social class of members	Mainly lower class	Mainly middle class

Source: Vernon, 1962:186.

has demonstrated that even the most church-like groups contain members with a sect-like orientation (see Table 4-2). Snook (1975:203) also raises this question, suggesting that what really differentiates the sect from the denomination is mainly a matter of the ability of the sect to gain a higher degree of commitment to its authority and positions than do the denominations. In short, we need to guard against the tendency to reify the concepts. While there are clear differences between the denomination and the sect, there are probably as many similarities. Both are, after all, organized for the same general purpose. Further, if we are correct in suggesting that religion is deviant in our society, it may be that protest is only a matter of degree.

Deprivation and the rise of sectarian groups. How do sects actually come into being? One obvious answer would be that they develop out of protests against theological "impurity." Individuals begin to feel that the "true" faith is not being preached, lived, and upheld in the established or traditional groups. Certainly the public pronouncement of sectarian leaders tend to play up the lack of spirituality, the perversion of beliefs, and the low level of commitment found among members of the dominant religious groups. In fact, no topic seems closer to the heart of the sect member than the evils and waywardness of the more "respectable" churches. Traveling evangelists for such groups have been known to make whole messages out of the supposed foibles of the local denominational clergy, all aimed at indicating a lack of "real" faith in the established groups.

Table 4-2. SECT-LIKE RELIGIOSITY AND INDIVIDUAL STATUS AMONG CONGREGATIONALISTS, PRESBYTERIANS, DISCIPLES OF CHRIST, AND BAPTISTS

Religiosity	Individual Status				
	Upper	Middle	Working	Low	Denominations
% High Sect-Like Involved	22	27	32	37	Congregationalists
N	(1386)	(1145)	(572)	(102)	
% High Sect-Like Involved	33	41	51	52	Presbyterians
N	(711)	(674)	(471)	(129)	
% High Sect-Like Involved	36	45	43	56	Disciples of Christ
N	(387)	(396)	(284)	(52)	
% High Sect-Like Involved	42	48	50	56	Baptists
N	(171)	(233)	(218)	(75)	

Source: Demerath, 1965:119.

But are the reasons for the rise of sectarian groups totally religious? Obviously, sociologists cannot answer such a question, but it would seem that the reasons are to some extent other than religious. For one thing, religious disagreement, and even protest, need not mean a break or schism in the organization. The rise of the "charismatic movement" in the 1960s and 1970s (not to be confused with the charismatic activity long present in Pentecostal sects) could certainly be viewed as a protest against the supposed lack of fervor and the shallowness of traditional religious groups and their leadership.Yet, no new charismatic or Pentecostal sects have been formed as a result of the increased charismatic activity. Staid Presbyterians, wealthy Episcopalians, conservative Baptists, ritualistic Catholics, and formal Lutherans have all felt the force of the "new charismatics" but have been able to contain the movement *within* the organization. For example, while the "charismatics" in the United Presbyterian Church have formed as association of like-minded people across the denomination, as a group they have shown no inclination to form the Charismatic Presbyterian Church. Theological and spiritual shortcomings alone do not appear to be sufficient causes for the establishment of new sectarian groups.

The common knowledge in sociology has generally been that such groups arise among poor people who are seen as cut off from the main stream of society and for whom the establishment docrine is not appropriate. In other words, economic deprivation and its attendant problems are seen as the root cause for the development of the new sectarian groups. The poor are protesting their economic plight by seeking status in a moral realm which they cannot find either in the secular world or in the spiritual world of the established churches.

Certainly the majority of the members of sectarian groups are from the lower classes, and sectarian groups are generally located in the lower income sections of the community. They particularly abound in the slum areas of larger cities. Also, the ethos of many such groups is one which decries worldly wealth and possessions and looks for ultimate rewards in a future realm—a heaven with ivory palaces and streets of gold. In such groups the secular status system is reversed and the first do become last, while the last have become first. It is by no means wide of the mark to indicate that economic deprivation has played a major part in sectarian protests from the medieval ages unto the present.

But can it be said that economic matters alone bring out the rise of sects? Clearly not, for not all sectarians are made up of the bitterly poor and, as we shall see, not all sectarian groups hold to the doctrine of "pie in the sky by and by." Again, not all poor are members of sect groups. Both the Roman Catholic and Episcopal Churches have numerous lower-class members.

Dynes (1956) has suggested that two factors are involved in the rise of the sect and sectarian values. Following Holt's (1940) thesis concerning culture shock and the rise of sects, Dynes correlates the sense of being in an alien, unfamiliar culture with lower socioeconomic level. Thus, sectarian groups are apt to arise when rural emigrants of a low socioeconomic status move to an urban place they perceive as alien.

Johnstone (1975:118-19) goes beyond what Dynes has suggested and notes that while deprivation may be the cause for the development of new sect groups, such deprivation need not necessarily be economic. He would add, for our consideration, social, organismic, ethical, and psychic deprivation, each contributing to the felt need for protest. Actually, the type of deprivation which is felt will also influence the type of sect which is formed in order to deal with that deprivation. Those who feel ethical deprivation are more likely to belong to a sect with a program for reforming the world here and now; those experiencing economic deprivation may join a sect which displaces "rewards" from the secular realm to a more heavenly place.

Types of sects. In other words, different kinds of needs and different sorts of deprivation lead individuals into different types of sects. Thus, sects have a variety of form and content. Clearly, we cannot conceptualize the whole vast array of different kinds of bodies which we classify as sects as fitting under one umbrella. They are far from a homogeneous set. Looking at such varied groups as the Amish, Jehovah's Witnesses, the Quakers, Pentecostal Holiness, and Foursquare Gospel, we find much more diversity than similarity. It might well be said, then, that sect is a genus with many species, and it is necessary to distinguish between the various species.

To say that we need such distinctions is a good bit easier than making them. The array of such groups is so great, especially when the definition of sect is broad, that most typologies or classifications fall under their own weight. However, it is useful to look at two attempts which have contributed to our understanding of the sect. First, Milton Yinger (1970) has analyzed sects in terms of their approach to dealing with the secular world. Second, a modification of a typology presented by Bryan Wilson (1963) seeks to classify sectarian groups in terms of their central means for adapting to deprivation.

Yinger's classification (1970:257-78) of responses to the world is threefold. Basically it deals with the manner in which the sectarian groups relate to the secular world: some accept the secular world and its values; others aggressively seek change in that world; and still others avoid or withdraw from it. Table 4-3 gives an overview of the characteristics of the three categories.

Acceptance sects are ones in which the members believe they face significant problems which are not solved by the doctrines and practices of estimated religious organizations. However, they do not interpret these problems as resulting from bad social structures. Members of this type of group have not suffered from economic deprivation to any significant extent and are primarily from the middle or upwardly mobile lower class. Their "protest" is not so much against the conditions of the world, as it is against an inability to handle problems of alienation, meaninglessness, and suffering.

Table 4–3. COMPARATIVE QUALITIES OF TYPES OF SECTS

Type name	Characteristic form of deprivation	Characteristic type of leadership and experience	Strategy toward society	Principal objective	Extreme or "pure" expression	Illustrative groups
1. Acceptance	Individual Morale	Mystical	Disregard or or accept	Individual poise and participation	Downgrading of normal sense experience	Early Christian Science; League for Discovery
2. Aggressive	Structural	Prophetic	Attack	Power	Religious military movement	Munsterites; Ghost Dance
3. Avoidance	Cultural values	Ascetic	Withdraw	Achievement of values	Communist community	Hutterites; Amana Community

Source: Yinger, 1970:279.

THE ORGANIZATION OF RELIGIOUS GROUPS

For this type of sect the problems of the world are seen more in terms of a "lack of faith, selfishness, ignorance, and isolation, not an evil society" (Yinger, 1970:275). Thus, their attack is not so much on the principles of the world, as on shortcomings in it. They try to deal with these shortcomings by focusing on ways of overcoming individual suffering, alienation, and a sense of insignificance.

Christian Science provides a good example of this kind of sect. "Sin" is a lack of faith, and such lack is the reason for the individual suffering that the world calls "sickness." By studying and employing the methods of Mary Baker Eddy, its founder, this group believes that its members will be better able to overcome illness.

Aggressive sects are oriented toward the use of power to change the world —either through changes in individuals or by some drastic alteration in the world. Yinger places both the Salvation Army, which seeks to convert people to a new way of life, and the Adventist Jehovah's Witnesses, which look for a coming of a new world, into this particular category.

Such groups appear to be responses to economic deprivation. Religious answers are given to the powerlessness and apathy which result from poverty. However, Yinger notes, such an aggressive approach will more probably be taken by individuals who feel that they have some hope for improving the conditions of their lives. Therefore, aggressive sects are more likely to be found in societies in which there are major revolutionary pressures for social change. We would expect to find them in developing nations more than in countries where there is a settled economy.

Avoidance sects are most likely to be found in a developed nation. Although they do not seek to reform the world (or they have little hope of that), neither do they accept values of the secular world. Their approach is to transform the values of this world, devaluing the meaning of "success" symbols and focusing their hopes on a kind of success which will come in a future existence to those who have "kept the faith." Logically, they can be expected to appear among groups where there is little hope that life will get better. Disprivileged minority groups—blacks, Chicanos, Puerto Ricans, Appalachian whites—provide fertile ground for the development of this kind of sect. A drive through the main thoroughfares of any urban slum or the backways of the poorer sections of smaller cities will give ample evidence of their existence as you see the crudely lettered signs and storefronts turned into "temples."

As we have implied, there are ample illustrations of this type of sect in American religious life. Some white and black Pentecostal groups in rural areas and cities can also be classified in this way. Avoidance for these groups is largely in terms of symbols whereby they deny the reality of the secular world. The use of the "gift of speaking in tongues" has long been a mark of such groups who, in

Liston Pope's (1942) terms, are substituting religious status for social and economic prestige. The majority, perhaps the vast majority, of sectarian groups in this country could be classified as avoidance sects.

This last remark suggests that Yinger's typology does not provide all of the meaningful distinctions that we might want in looking at sect life in this country. Wilson (1963), looking mainly at the sectarian scene in England, has provided classification for seven types of sectarian groups. While each of these clearly represents a type, sect groups in the "real" world tend to cross the boundaries of this typology and partake of more than one type of approach. For our purpose, it is important to look at three types which can be derived from Wilson's categories. Classification of these types is based on how the sect group deals with the problem of adjusting to its environment, that is, of living with the secular world around it. The specific classification would focus on those groups which seek to change the present order; those which withdraw from that order; those which find ways of dealing with the order of existence.

Reforming the present order. The focal point of sects classified in this manner would be to somehow change the world so that it would be a better place, more in accord with God's will. There are two ways in which this might be done—through converting individuals or through changing the world itself. Many sectarian groups in this country follow the former option. These groups tend to embrace an evangelical, fundamentalistic approach to Christian faith and feel that the world is an evil place because individuals are corrupt. Changing things requires that the individuals in it be changed, one by one if necessary. Attention is focused on seeking conversions which will lead individuals to live the way "God intended" that they should. Clearly, early periods in the life of the Salvation Army and the church of the Nazarene provide examples of sectarian groups which had such an approach.

Other sects try the second approach—converting the world itself. That is, the focus in these sects is on changing the world so that it will be possible for individuals in the world to lead a better life. Contemporary Quakers, for example, do try to change the present world both by convincing individuals to change and by attempting to influence the power structures of the world.

Withdrawing from the present order. These groups, retreatist in some ways, are much like Yinger's category of avoidance sects. They deny the validity of the present world and look for an existence better than that which they feel they have found in the secular world. Again there are two major types, depending upon the extent and kind of withdrawal which they make.

One type retreats into pietistic and ascetic practices to declare its superiority to the ways of the world. That is, though a lifestyle of self-denial and avoidance of many of the pleasures of the world, they attempt to develop a personal holiness that will be the means to a new kind of security, a spiritual security with which to face the world. Those groups bearing the name Holiness in their title fit into such a classification as do many of those whose Pentecostal patterns are aimed at developing a "holier" life.

For other such groups, there is a total withdrawal and the formation of a new community. These sects attempt to set up "perfect" communities, sometimes as a model for others. At some points in their existence types of Amish and Mennonite groups have fit into this category, as might Trappist Monks if they could be called sectarian.

Managing the present order. Wilson's concept of manipulation sects fits into this category. These sects believe that they have a hold on some special ability, some unique knowledge, that enables them to manage problems confronting the secular world. They do not deny the ideals of the world, but lift them to a higher category and offer special techniques for assurance of success in certain areas of life. The Christian Science movement, again, fits into this category because it emphasizes special ways of practicing the "science" as a means of dealing with illness.

Creating a new order. Such sects propose to be rid of the present social order when the appropriate time comes, whether by violence or the intervention of divine power. Adventist groups, such as the Jehovah's Witnesses, which look for the immediate, usually dramatic "second coming" or the establishment of a divine order on earth, fit into this category.

Any attempt to categorize sectarian groups, of course, eventually will be less than adequate. There are two reasons for this failure. First, sectarian groups, if they persist, do tend to undergo a process of change. As they are never totally cut off from the world, they cannot totally ignore its impact upon them. Further, internal factors, such as the change of leadership when the charismatic leaders die, bring about some kind of changes. In short, almost by definition, sects are not the most stable of religious groups and cannot be put into a category once and for all. Also, the whole nature of sectarian protest may change so as to make some types obsolete.

Second, the sectarian protest is far from formally organized and cannot be neatly shoved into any particular pigeon hole. That is, sectarian groups tend to borrow from more than one strategy and utilize more than one approach. Thus, although logically strange, the adventist Jehovah's Witnesses spend a great deal of their time in attempting to convert people—thus taking on the character of the conversionist types like the Salvation Army.

In summary, while the typologies help call attention to the wide variation in sectarian groups which we can observe, they do not really account for all the variables involved. They do, however, provide useful ways in which to think about this kind of reaction to the compromises of established religion. In the end, such typologies are probably most useful in discovering the ways in which variation in sect type affects a number of factors and behaviors in the social world. What typology will be most useful will depend upon the purpose of the research.

The Development of Sectarian Groups

For some time, the common assumption has been sects which persist for more than a generation will begin a movement along a supposed sect-denomination continuum toward the denominational end of that continuum. An early study of sect groups, Liston Pope's *Millhands and Preachers* (1942), bluntly states that such is the inevitable fate of the sect. It either "dies" or becomes more accommodated to the secular world, becoming more like a denomination. In Pope's formulations, the direction is always one way. Sects arise through schism from a church, but never as a result of the decline or reconstitution of a denomination or church. He suggests that, in their desire to achieve some measure of success, the new groups lose their *extreme* sectarian qualities and perspectives. There is a move to build more expensive and permanent buildings, an insistence on a full-time, educated clergy so that it becomes necessary to build training schools, and the development of tolerance of older denominations and community leaders. All of these represent attempts to achieve more prestige and power in the "world," and, thus, a move away from the sectarian spirit of protest. Clearly, a large number of such sectarian groups have undergone this kind of transformation. The Church of the Nazarene, the Church of Christ, some Pentecostal holiness groups, and the array of Assemblies of God seem to have followed such a path to some degree.

Even that branch of evangelical Christianity which emphasized faith healing and seemed so sectarian in nature can be seen to have undergone a process of compromise and accommodation to the world. Indeed, many suggest that its most popular message today deals with gaining worldly success from faith. It is forgivable, then, to assume that such transformation is a common feature of sectarian groups.

A number of scholars have begun to question the orthodox conclusion that such movement is inevitable and in one direction only. Wilson (1963), contends, indeed, that such a movement is only characteristic of those kinds of sects which he calls conversionist, and that it tends to be true only where there is an expanding economy in which sectarian members can hope to improve their economic status and thus find themselves contending with the dominant society for the "goodies" of money, prestige, and power. In other situations, the groups may evolve into other kinds of sects rather than into a denomination.

Established Sects

For the sect, one clear alternative to becoming a denomination is to develop into what Yinger (1970) has called an "established sect." In fact, Redekop (1974) contends that this is especially likely to occur when the sectarian group's protest is aimed at the basic norms of the society.

Yinger's definition of the established sect is that it is a group which has grown out of the less stable sectarian movements and becomes "somewhat more inclusive, less alienated, and more structured than the sect" (Yinger, 1970:266). However, it does not make the full change into a denominational type of group. As he notes, while Methodists and Quakers both began as sectarian protests, and while both have since moved away from the extremes of such protest, they clearly cannot be considered similar today. The Methodists have gone the full route of transformation to take their place with the denominational groups of today. But the Quakers have not made this change. They cannot be comfortably classified as a denomination but they do not fully fit the sect category either. The Quakers, then, are an example of what would be called the established sect, as are several Amish and Mennonite groups and the Hutterites. In each case the groups considered "established sects" have accommodated to the world to a degree, but *only* to that degree essential to survival.

Yinger (1970) suggests that where a group is characterized by a "middle-class" tone, and where the problems seen by the group have an individualized nature (as in Methodism), the movement into a denomination may be rather quick. However, those sects concerned with the corrupt nature of the secular world (like the Amish and Quakers) cannot so easily make this accommodating movement, and are more likely to become established sects.

The Cult

One final type of religious body remains—the cult. Yinger (1970:279) contends that such a group develops where there is alienation from the traditional religious system as well as alienation from the society itself. In such a situation new religious systems or movements borrowing principles from other religious systems often appear.

Wallis (1975:91) argues that these new religious movements we call cults represent way stations toward becoming sects. According to him, cults take form out of a broad background which can be seen as a "cultic milieu"—a range of possible ideas and practices. The new cult draws from this reservoir in merging a more or less defined group of seekers around one or several common interests. He notes several features which are typical of the cult type group: (1) focus on individual problems; (2) loose structure; (3) tolerance of other religious groups; (4) nonexclusion; (5) no clear distinction between members and nonmembers; and, (6) no clear focus of authority. If we were to put a cult column next to those of the sect and denomination in Table 4-1, we would find it similar in some respects to the denomination and in others to the sect. There are, however, significant differences from both. In terms of relationship with other groups it is tolerant almost to the point of indifference; its services really fit the pattern of neither sect nor denomination; doctrine is specific on only a few points and quite loose on most others; and membership is not a matter taken very seriously.

Wallis suggests that cults are subject to a number of problems not necessarily faced by other groups. First, it is difficult for the cult to have much control over members. The groups tend to be transient; and when new, temporary leaders attempt to change the activities of the cult they cause dissension. A central problem is that members share a relatively limited set of beliefs.

Cults, then, are very delicate organizations and face a number of problems of survival. Wallis (1975:92) lists these as, first, "doctrinal precariousness"; there is generally little difference between the beliefs of a specific cult and the general "cultic milieu." Thus, there can be little loyalty to specific beliefs. Second, cults have a problem controlling members. The members tend to be general seekers who can visualize a number of paths to truth or salvation. Thus, they cannot be held to a particular path through the threat of any kind of "excommunication." Third, the cults tend to face a situation in which the level of commitment of its members is relatively low. In short, for the members of sects, any number of beliefs may be seen as legitimate, making allegiance to a particular cult exceedingly ephemeral.

It is probably more difficult to find a "pure" cult type as an example than either a pure sect or denomination. Because transitoriness is part of the definition of the cult, groups seldom last long enough to be "pinned down." As far as organized groups are concerned, Scientology and Spiritism come as close as any. Loosely organized groups, such as all those who believe in astrology or practice transcendental meditation, have been seen as cults (Robertson, 1977). Like the many sects, those cults which exist over time tend to change their nature. In its origin, Christian Science was very close to the "ideal type" of the cult; it centered on a single idea, it had no formal membership, was tolerant of others, and attracted a middle-class group of "seekers." Today, of course, it has, in many ways moved in the denominational direction and would at least have to be seen as an "established cult" (Yinger, 1970).

Because of the many difficulties involved in "typing" specific empirical groups, some have suggested that we abandon the use of these distinctions. Certainly one is tempted to suggest the use of a number of continua along which to array the various groups rather than a rigid classification of specific types. However, the classification does provide us with a useful way of thinking about the differences between groups and thus helps us to understand the meaning and nature of these variations. To this extent it continues to be important and helpful.

SUMMARY

We have been concerned in this chapter with the religious group as an organization that takes form and structure in society. Two aspects of this structural existence have been discussed: (1) the development of religious groups and the problems attendant to such development; and, (2) the various types of religious groups which emerge.

Religious groups, if they persist over time, seem to follow a broad general pattern. Basically, the pattern is a movement from the informal, charismatic style of leadership and loose structure to the formal, bureaucratic style of organization. This pattern presents problems to the continuing religious group in a number of ways. First, continued group life necessitates the development of structure, but that structure may become an end in itself and the vitality of the original movement become lost. Second, the power and privilege that attach to the positions in the now structured religious movement may be the objects of "mixed motivation," that is, offices and positions may be sought for their perceived power rather than for spiritual motives. Finally, the new recruits, the very source of the growth and development, do not share the experiences of the original group and bring with them their own needs, threatening to change the original inspiration and ideology of the group.

Even when these problems are sufficiently met, the religious group is faced with the problem of relating to the larger society. It is suggested that in many ways religious values are deviant in contemporary, industrial society. This deviant status may make it difficult for the religious group to solve the functional problems of maintaining traditional patterns, tension management and goal attainment, adaptation, and integration. A variety of techniques used to handle these basic problems has been discussed.

The classification of religious groups into "types" has fascinated students of religion since the time of Ernst Troeltsch, who first divided Western Christianity into two types, the church and the sect; a dichotomy based largely on whether the particular group's values were harmonious with the secular world or if it protested against the entrapment of the church by the secular world. Contemporary students of religious groups, however, have found it necessary to divide the world of religious groups into more than these two polar types. Generally, four types of such groups are discussed; ecclesia, denomination, sect, and cult. Most of the attention in the United States focuses on the differences between the denomination and the sect; they are seen as something like polar types, with the denomination accommodating to the secular world and the sect making a religious protest.

The world of sectarian religion has been the subject of much sociological investigation. It is readily apparent that not all sectarian groups are alike; sects actually display a dazzling diversity. Both Yinger and Wilson have attempted to categorize the array of sects into a few types. Yinger refers to the acceptance, avoidance, and aggressive sects, while Wilson lists a number of types according to the way in which the sect deals with the world. We have suggested that perhaps four such types can be formulated: sects seeking to reform the world, those withdrawing from it, those attempting to manipulate it, and those seeking to create new worlds or new orders within the world.

Attention has also been drawn to the question of the development of sectarian groups. The common rule has been that sects, if they last, will give up their "protestant" stance and become like the accommodating denominations. A number of researchers, however, have raised doubt that such is necessarily the case, although it does seem to occur with great frequency. It is suggested that if sects change at all they may simply change into other kinds of sects. Also, some sects seem to change in only relatively minor ways. Thus Yinger suggests that we need to talk about "established sects." The Amish, for instance, have existed for many years with only minor modifications to their beliefs, norms, and values; in short, they have retained basically sectarian qualities despite their long existence.

In the next chapter we continue our examination of the organizational structure of religious groups by concentrating on the impact of the type of leadership present in certain religious collectivities. We will examine the tendency of organizations to bureaucratize offices and roles and investigate the effect of certain kinds of leadership upon lay participation in religious activities. Also we will look at some of the problems faced by ministers as they attempt to perform numerous functions for their congregations.

REFERENCES

Becker, Howard
1932   *Systematic Sociology.* New York: Wiley.
Beckford, James
1975   "Two contrasting types of sectarian organization." Pp. 70-85 in Roy Wallis (ed.), *Sectarianism: Analyses of Religious and Nonreligious sects.* New York: John Wiley.
Berger, Peter
1954   "The sociological study of sectarianism." *Social Research* 21:467-476.
1967   *The Sacred Canopy—Elements of a Sociological Theory of Religion.* New York: Doubleday.
Demerath, Nicholas J., III
1965   *Social Class in American Protestantism.* Chicago: Rand McNally.
1967   "Son of sow's ear." *Journal for the Scientific Study of Religion* 6 (Fall):275-277.

Demerath, N. J., III and
Phillip E. Hammond
    1969   *Religion in Social Context.* New York: Random House.

Dynes, Russel R.
    1956   "Rurality, migration and sectarianism." *Rural Sociology* 21:25-28.

Eister, Allan W.
    1957   "Religious institutions in complex societies." *American Sociological Review* 22:387-91.
    1967   "Toward a radical critique of church-sect typology." *Journal for the Scientific Study of Religion* 6 (Spring):85-90.
    1973   "H. Richard Niebuhr and the paradox of religious organization: A radical critique." Pp. 355-408 in Charles Glock and Phillip Hammond (eds.), *Beyond the Classics? Essays in the Scientific Study of Religion.* New York: Harper & Row.

Goode, Erich
    1967   "Some critical observations on the church-sect dimension." *Journal for the Scientific Study of Religion* 6 (Spring)69:77.

Gustafson, Paul M.
    1967   "UO-US-PS-PO: A restatement of Troeltsch's church-sect typology." *Journal for the Scientific Study of Religion* 6 (Spring):64-68.

Hall, Tom T.
    1971   "Me and Jesus." Hallnote Music.

Holt, J. B.
    1940   "Holiness religion—Cultural shock and social reorganization." *American Sociological Review* 5 (5):740-747.

Johnson, Benton
    1963   "On church & sect." *American Sociological Review* 28:539-549.
    1971   "Church-sect revisited." *Journal for the Scientific Study of Religion* 10:124-37.

Johnstone, Ronald L.
    1975   Religion and Society in Interaction. Englewood Cliffs, N. J.: Prentice-Hall.

Martin, D. A.
    1962   "The denomination." *British Journal of Sociology* 13 (1):1-14.

Niebuhr, H. Richard
1932   *The Social Sources of Denominationalism.* New York: Holt.

Nottingham, Elizabeth
1971   *Religion: A Sociological View.* New York: Random House.

O'Dea, Thomas T.
1966   *The Sociology of Religion.* Englewood Cliffs, N.J.: Prentice-Hall.
1970   *Sociology & the Study of Religion: Theory, Research, Interpretation.* New York: Basic Books.

Pope, Liston
1942   *Millhands & Preachers.* New Haven, Conn.: Yale University Press.

Redekop, Calvin
1974   "A new look at sect development." *Journal for the Scientific Study of Religion* 13:345–53.

Robertson, Ian
1977   *Sociology.* New York: Worth.

Roof, Wade Clark
1978   *Community and Commitment.* New York: Elsevier.

Snook, John B.
1975   "An alternative to church-sect." *Journal for the Scientific Study of Religion* 13 (June):191-204.

Swatos, William H. J.
1976   "Church-sect theory. Weber or Troeltsch?" *Journal for the Scientific Study of Religion* 15 (June):129-144.

Troeltsch, Ernst
1931   *The Social Teaching of the Christian Churches.* New York: Macmillan.

Vernon, Glenn
1962   *Sociology & Religion.* New York: McGraw-Hill.

Wallis, Roy
1975   "Scientology: Therapeutic cult to religous sect." *Sociology* 9 (June):89–100.

Wilson, Bryan R.
1963   "A typology of sects in a dynamic and comparative perspective." *Archives de Sociologie de*

Religion 16:49-63. Translated by Jenny M. Robertson.

1967   *Patterns of Sectarianism.* London: Heinemann.

Wilson, John

1978   *Religion in American Society: The Effective Presence.* Englewood Cliffs: Prentice-Hall.

Yinger, J. Milton

1946   *Religion and the Struggle for Power.* Durham, N.C.: Duke.

1969   "A structural examination of religion." *Journal for the Scientific Study of Religion* 8(1):88-99.

1970   *The Scientific Study of Religion.* New York: Macmillan.

CHAPTER 5

Leadership and Participation in Religious Groups

In the last two chapters we have discussed, respectively, the process by which individuals become religious and the nature and types of religious organizations. Now we need to look at the way in which the individual fits into the organization.

Religious organizations, like all formal groups, necessarily have a structure by which they are governed. Such structures, or *polities* as they are sometimes called, vary according to broad types, and the individual is related to the organization differently according to the variation in the type of organization.

In Chapter 3 we indicated that being religious involved having a particular status, with accompanying role expectations. Actually, within the specific organization, individuals have varying status-roles. Some are simple members, others lay officers, and still others hold the status of formal leader—usually known as pastor, priest, minister, or some other "sub-clerical" title. There is also some indication that women, regardless of other status-roles they may play in the religious group, occupy a special sex-role status.

Our attention in this chapter will be focused on these issues. First, we will look at one method of categorizing the ways in which religious groups are governed, including the tendency of such organizations to be bureaucratically structured. Then, we will examine the place of laypersons in the structure, moving on to the specialized formal leadership roles. Finally, consideration will be given to the important issue of the place of women in the religious organization.

THE FORMS OF RELIGIOUS ORGANIZATION

Whether a group is a sect, a cult, a denomination, or an ecclesia, it must take some particular form of government. Three such forms, or polities, have commonly been delineated in American Christianity—*congregational, presbyterian,* and *episcopal*. It might be noted, however, that despite the original shape of the polity or government of the group, in the contemporary world there is a bureaucratizing tendency to be found in any such group as it continues to exist. Further, it is equally clear that local parishes do not necessarily operate as the

141

"book" or constitution of the particular parent bodies would prescribe they operate.

Types of Polity

Polity is a term which refers to the rules by which groups are governed. While there are variations within each of the general types, it is, as noted, possible to characterize three major approaches to "running" the religious organization. The three types most commonly used center on where the major focus of control is to be found for the groups. That is, congregational type organizations place ultimate authority in the congregation itself; presbyterian types place control in the hands of *elders* or a representative form of government consisting of elected lay leaders; and episcopal types put ultimate authority in an hierarchy of bishops.

In the congregational type of church, the stress is on the specific, separate congregation as the ultimate, and essentially the only, source of authority. While churches of the congregational type may belong to conferences or conventions, each separate congregation is theoretically a law unto itself. Further, in such groups, all important decisions are made in theory by the total congregation. Although there is generally an official board of some kind, all *major* decisions are theoretically up to the entire congregation. In the true congregational type such a board would be subject to ratification by the group as a whole. In this organizational type, the role of the pastor is that of democratic leader, subject totally to the will of the congregation for his or her position. While conferences or convention boards may make recommendations about standards for clergy, and circulate the names of pastors who might be looking to make a move, they have no control over such matters. Each year, for example, the whole congregation votes on the question of the continuation of the pastor and on the terms of the contract with the pastor.

The traditional Congregational Church of New England was an example of such a polity, but since its merger with the Evangelical and Reformed Church—to form what is now known as the United Church of Christ—it has evolved a form of polity somewhat modified from the pure congregational type, with more control over local affairs given to outside bodies. The Southern Baptist Convention, largest of all Protestant bodies, is a good example of congregational polity in its purer form, as is the Christian Church (Disciples of Christ). In both cases, despite the presence of regional and even national associations, the congregations make their own decisions and pastors are really only the leaders of these "officially" independent fellowships. Most sectarian groups are also organized according to this congregational type of polity. In general, groups so governed deemphasize the importance of formal creeds and confessions.

Presbyterian churches are those so organized that authority resides in a *session* composed of *elders*; they derive their name from the Greek word for elder, *presbuteros*, and the pastor is sometimes known as a *teaching elder*. Both pastor and lay members of the session are considered, preeminently, elders, and both are ordained to that particular office although a distinction is made between the *ruling*, or *lay*, and *teaching* elder. With some exceptions, as in the call of the pastor in some presbyterian groups and approval of the annual budget, authority at the local level rests in this group of representatives of the congregation. Like the form of democracy embodied in the United States Constitution, presbyterian churches are governed by elected representatives who are then free to act in accordance with their own consciences and wisdom. However, the local session is also subject to a higher body, generally called a *presbytery*, and composed of all ordained clergy and ruling or lay elders representing each congregation. Much of the authority in such churches rests in this group which has some of the powers given the bishop in the episcopal type of polity.

The session of the local church in the presbyterian system has control of that congregation, but this authority is subject to the review of the higher courts or judicatories of the church, particularly the presbytery. When trouble or complaints occur in such congregations, the presbytery may exercise its authority and actually take over the duties of the session. In churches governed by such a polity the minister is typically called (hired) by the church, but the local congregation must have the approval of the presbytery which ultimately has the authority to maintain or dissolve the relationship between the pastor and the local congregation. Thus, while responsible to the session for many things, the pastor in a presbyterian system must also be responsible and attentive to the higher authority of the presbytery.

The United Presbyterian Church in the United States of America and the Presbyterian Church in the United States, as well as most smaller bodies with "presbyterian" in their name, have some variation of this form of organization. Generally, too, churches carrying the term "reformed" in their names also have such a form of government.

The episcopal form of polity also takes its name from a Greek word, *episcopus*, meaning shepherd or bishop. Thus, episcopal types of churches are those which have in their structures the provision for some form of a bishopric. Episcopal polities are theoretically dominated by the hierarchy which controls the appointment of local clergy and exercises much authority over the local congregation. While authority clearly flows from the top, there is some room for decisions at the local congregational level. Ultimately, however, the bishop and other higher church officials can overrule the congregation. Local clergy in the pure type of episcopal polity are almost totally dependent upon the hierarchy; technically, clergy are appointed to parish positions by the bishop's office and at the will of the bishop. The Episcopal church, as might be obvious, has such a polity, as does the Roman Catholic Church. The official polity of The United Methodist (formerly Methodist Episcopal) Church also follows such governmental policies, although with some modifications.

It is apparent that there are a number of denominations which have blunted some of the extreme features of each type of polity and some which represent a mixture of the pure types. In the former case, the United Methodist Church seems to be moving away from episcopal authority in the case of the appointment of pastors and adopting a style not totally different from that of the presbyterian type of polity. Some of the Lutheran churches in this country have also tended to have a mixture of polities, combining elements of the presbyterian and congregational types. The models of government which we have described really represent extreme cases, and a given denomination or group does not necessarily follow one to the exclusion of elements of others. It is probably true, however, that the Southern Baptist Conference represents very well the congregational type; the United Presbyterian Church follows the presbyterian model nearly perfectly; and the Roman Catholic Church is a good example of the episcopal system.

It might also be noted that both congregations and denominational superstructures often subvert official policy. Wood and Zald (1966) demonstrated this tendency on the part of Methodist congregations with regard to policies concerning racial integration, and Harrison (1959), as we shall see, showed how a set of denominational executives develop power in a congregational polity. In short, religious organizations are subject to the same "push" and "pull" of all bureaucratic organizations with regard to the "official rules."

The Bureaucratic Tendency

The fact that "pure" embodiments of the various ideal types do not in fact exist may be attributed partly to the realistic facts of operating a church in contemporary society. It is not unfair to say that churches, beyond the early sectarian stage, are corporations (most are, in fact, legally so) and that they have organizational problems not unlike those of any complex organization. So, regardless of polity model officially embedded in their constitution, the realities of organizational life force upon congregations and denominational groups faces of organization that are not really true to that model.

In this vein, the most striking feature of church life in contemporary America has to be the increasing bureaucratization to be found there. That is, increasingly, American denominations and their congregations are being operated, regardless of polity, on models approximating the bureaucratic ones used in operating governmental agencies, businesses, and most any large scale organization. In this regard, Demerath (1974:23) notes:

> In short, American religion has been *bureaucratized* even as it has been differentiated, delocalized, and secularized. The romantic Norman Rockwell

144

portrait of Americans at worship in the neighborhood church of their choice must now be placed side by side with an image of denominational headquarters as a business enterprise and a portrait of the clergyman as a harassed professional torn between different roles and conflicting demands.

This tendency seems to affect all churches, regardless of their basic form of government. This can be seen as we look at examples of bureaucratization in each of the three general types.

The best known study of the bureaucratic tendency, especially as it is to be seen in a denomination having a congregational polity, is Paul Harrison's *Authority and Power in the Free Church* (1959). In this study of the American Baptist Convention (sometimes referred to as the "northern" Baptist church), Harrison claims that the "fences" built to control central authority have been largely futile and that the attempt to maintain the "pure" congregational ideal has led to a situation in which some leaders of the convention have "grabbed" extralegal, personal power.

Harrison suggests that a means for bridging the gap between national boards and local independent congregations in the American Baptist Church is the action of the executive who heads a board or agency. If the executive secretary or administrator of some national board or commission has powerful personal, charismatic leadership qualities, he or she can find strength from clergy and laypeople which allows greater autonomy and substantial authority for the executive even in the affairs of the local congregation. In any event, the denominational executive will have some autonomous power because most of the work of the agency is unseen and unknown by rank-and-file members.

Chalfant (1967) provides a study of the operation of a presbyterian polity within local congregations. Studying five different United Presbyterian congregations in a southwest community, he found that levels of bureaucratic organization in the various congregations were dependent upon both the size and affluence of the congregations. Small, relatively poor (in terms of budget) congregations tended to a much more informal type of operation in which the rules of the church constitution were frequently subverted, and personal power and relationships were involved in decisions that should, according to the rules, have been made by the session. The larger and wealthier congregations, however, violated the rules differently by forming more organizational structures which frequently went beyond the letter of the law as expressed in the Book of Order, and, in a sense, usurped authority belonging to the session. Likewise, such groups had some tendency to become highly organized laws unto themselves.

In a study of perhaps the most extreme form of an episcopal form of government, that of the Roman Catholic Church, Robert Szafran (1976) investigated the distribution of influence in determining policies and actions in eighty-five Catholic dioceses. He concludes that the basic structure of influence and authority in the diocese studied is extremely centralized, with clear domination by the bishopric. In a system which is officially very highly structured on an hierarchical basis, the bureaucratic mold seems to be well internalized by the participants in the system. Not a single diocese, according to Szafaran, had proposed changes in the basic system which might have led to a more democratic style of authority and influence. In short, the bureaucratic tendency is well-established and accepted.

FORMAL LEADERSHIP IN RELIGIOUS ORGANIZATIONS

Religious groups, as we have said, are composed of people who, in the sociological perspective, occupy status-roles. The most obvious is that of church member, and that particular position varies considerably from group to group. Then, some members take on special roles of formal leadership, statuses which go by various names such as steward, deacon, elder, or vestryman. Of course, the most highly specialized position is that of the clergyperson, a position which also takes on quite different overtones from communion to communion.

As we have just indicated, most religious organizations in our society fall into that type of organization Weber referred to as legal-bureaucratic. That is, they are organized according to rules, and positions in the organizations are formally ordered. Most Protestant groups provide for a considerable amount of voluntary leadership by laypersons, and are generally governed by some official board such as a session, board of stewards, or board of deacons. Of late, the Catholic church has also relied more on lay advice, if not rule, in the operation of their parishes. In addition, there are many other part-time lay roles to be played in the religious organization, and persons filling such roles, such as Sunday School Superintendent, occupy a special status within the group.

Lay Participation

In our chapter on the individual becoming religious (Chapter 3), we noted that taking a particular religious stance is the result of a socialization process. Yet, such socialization which leads to the holding of certain beliefs and attitudes usually needs some reinforcement or support if the individual is to become a regular participant in the particular religious group.

Another way of looking at this matter is to remind ourselves that not all of those who simply prefer a particular church or sect actually worship with that group on a regular basis. Why, beyond the variations in socialization, do some people take an active part in the church or sect to which they belong, while others do not, or show only moderate interest? Hoge and Carroll (1978) have pointed to five different answers to that question which can be discovered by examining the results of social research. First, there is *deprivation theory* which holds that individuals who suffer from some form of dispossession are more likely to participate in religious activities than others as they seek to compensate for their felt deprivation. Second, the desire to give one's children some form of ethical and religious training has been seen by some as an adequate explanation; it is held that the presence of young children in the family causes parents to become more active in the affairs of the church in order that their children will receive the desired training. Third, the particular kind of beliefs an individual holds and the strength of these beliefs, particularly those which relate to the church, are the important determinants of religious participation. Fourth, the enhancement of status given by the religious group, as well as the opportunity for identification bestowed by such participation, are seen as reasons for taking an active part in a church. Fifth, it has been suggested by Roof (1978) that participation in the religious group is related to having the local community, rather than a more cosmopolitan view, as the point of reference for one's life. This localism is seen as giving greater support to participation in the life of the church.

In reviewing the first four of these theories, Hoge and Carroll conclude that none of the theories actually receive very strong support. Indeed, deprivation theory, which has frequently been advanced as "the" explanation for participation, seems to contribute nothing to explaining variation in participation in the religious organization. Why does this favorite explanation not "work out," and why do none of the other theories really provide any significant support in explaining religious participation? The answer, suggested in part by Hoge and Carroll, may be in the fact that the meaning of membership, and the obligations which attend it, vary from group to group, and any attempt to explain participation behavior which does not take particular norms into account will have relatively little explanatory power.

To a certain extent we might say that the degree of membership expectation varies along the same continuum which stretches from church at one polar point to sect at the other. Sect members certainly have heavier obligations than do those who belong to the more well-established denominations; obligations ranging from ascetic regulations for their daily lives to the amount of time they are expected to spend in doing church work and attending the various services and activities of the group. Yet, it isn't quite that simple. The kind, number, and intensity of requirements put upon the lay member vary within each category. What is expected of the Roman Catholic laypersons is quite different than what the devout Presbyterian layperson might be expected to do; a member of the Church of Christ is obliged to give far more time to church activities than is even the conservative counterpart in a Southern Baptist congregation; and so it goes from group to group. In short, we cannot really explain *all* participation by any single theory, not only because individuals differ in their reasons for participation, but also because each particular religious group requires different things of its members. The motivations which lead individuals to undertake these different duties may well vary from one set of obligations to another.

Turning from observations concerning general church membership to the more specialized roles involved in running the organization, it is apparent that here, too, groups differ on the extent to which the layperson is allowed (or has been able to grasp) some power in the process of governing. Actually, American society has seen all possible variations in the amount of power permitted. Those who came first to this country were strongly influenced by the Protestant doctrine of the priesthood of all believers; thus they felt that the laity was endowed with the same priestly authority as the clergy and should have a strong, if not totally dominant, voice in the operation of the religious group. Some, indeed, felt that there should be no control beyond that of the local democratic assembly in which all laypersons have an equal voice. Most of the original religious groups in the country had some such view. At the opposite end of the spectrum is the Catholic tradition which has always stressed the authority of the hierarchy. Indeed, the authority of the Catholic hierarchy was originally a source of great distrust of the Catholic church on the part of Protestant church people who saw it as exercising foreign control over the affairs of the church.

In actual practice, of course, most groups are arrayed at different points along the continuum of lay participation. No church, however, seems to be totally congregational in form of leadership, at least if it has gone beyond the early sectarian stage. Even the Catholic church is not so completely hierarchical in government as to leave the laity no place in its decision-making.

The real situation seems to be that, as has been noted for almost all instances of the bureaucratic form of organization, the formal rule structure is frequently abrogated, and persons with no place in the formal table of organization have real power in the operation of the group. This is what Chalfant (1967) found for those small churches which he described as failing to live up to all the rules of the Book of Order. In these congregations, individuals without formal leadership roles had much influence: the husband of an elder could really determine the church school curriculum; the couple who gave the most money, although neither held any position in the particular church, had to be consulted on most decisions; and the old-time member who literally opened up the church in another instance still determined much church policy, despite not having served on the official board for years. At times the unofficial leadership seemed to have virtual veto power over some areas of congregational life.

This kind of informal power has been noted by others, also. Hougland and Wood (1979) have referred to it as the "inner circles in social churches"—groups of individuals which actually exercise considerable control over the affairs of these local churches, despite the fact that this control is not in line with what is spelled out in the church's constitution. They studied a sample of fifty-eight

Protestant churches in the Indianapolis, Indiana, area which included congregations of seven denominations from what could be considered mainline denominations in that area. It was found that such inner circles did exist in a large number of these congregations and were "real" powers in the management of the congregations. Far from seeing some conspiratorial plot aimed at subverting the rules, Hougland and Wood seem to feel that the inner circles operated in the absence of other strong leadership as well as in cases where the size and complexity of the congregation, in terms of members and budget, made control by official boards difficult. In such instances, control by this inner circle was made possible, if not necessary. Only in cases where the minister's activism offended some in the inner circle could there be an accusation of an attempt to exercise ideological control. The authors note (1979:235):

> Inner circles seem most likely to develop when relatively little control is being exercised elsewhere in the church and when ministers lack attributes that would expedite their exercising strong leadership. Thus, inner circles may be particularly likely to emerge in organizations when other potential mechanisms of control (ministerial, leadership, united congregational action, etc.) are not performing effectively.

Thus, these authors tend to see the inner circles developing as a means for filling a leadership vacuum.

In another study, Balswick and Layne (1973) demonstrated that formal church leaders may not have central places in the power structure of a congregation. In analyzing the power situation for one local church, whose formal leadership consisted of an eighteen member council and two professional staff persons (along with other minor functionaries), they found that only three persons reputed to have authority and power in the congregation actually held any sort of formal leadership position—two members of the council and the assistant minister. The other twenty-one individuals said to have power were not in any formal position, although, in an intriguing finding, eight of these leaders were the *wives* of members of the church council.

In the Roman Catholic Church the assumption has generally been that there is a rather definite hierarchical structure which officially leaves lay participation with activity but little power. However, as we have previously noted, the nature of American voluntary associations in general has brought about some movement toward more lay participation in decision making as have the prinicples set forth in Vatican II. As Rosenberg (1979) points out, there has been a movement toward shared responsibility in the Catholic church which involves a lessening of the barriers which traditionally existed between the clergy and the laity, as well as between the nonclergy in religious orders and the laity. Another reason, of course, is the growing shortage of full-time clergy and religious[1], and the need for lay people to "fill in the gaps." There has been, too, as Rosenberg points out, a tendency on ideological grounds to make more opportunities open to the laity. Such functions as reading parts of the mass, distributing the elements in communion, doing pastoral counseling, and working with other types of groups are now being performed by Catholic laypeople.

Regardless of the role which is given to laity, most religious organizations in our society have as their major role that of the full-time, formally appointed, ordained pastor or priest (as well as that of other "professionals" in the field of religion). This is for a majority of groups the most significant role or roles within the organization. The nature of such leadership roles obviously varies from one type of religious group to another. In the near "ideal type" sectarian group, there would be no formally appointed functionary such as pastor, minister, or rabbi, although such a group probably has one or several members who, in reality, assume what amounts to pastoral leadership. Frequently, such groups are led by what is referred to as a charismatic leader who functions on the basis of personal characteristics.

Nevertheless, it is clearly the ministerial status where the burden of leadership, and problems thereof, are focused. As Demerath and Hammond (1969:188) have observed:

> If a researcher were confined to analysing only one of Parson's four problems and sought the one that would best predict and reveal underlying tensions and difficulties in the church as a whole, his choice might well be the integrative "box." Here is where many of the previous issues come home to roost. No one is more aware of this than the minister in charge. In fact, his daily routine involves him in crucial and agonizing integrative problems of two sorts. First, there is the integration of the church's various activities and hence the minister's various roles. Second, there is the need to intergrate the church's various parishioners, the minister's variegated clients, and the denomination's various types and levels of structure.

Thus, it is appropriate to focus attention on this one particular status—with all of its variations and all of the attendant problems.

The Role of the Minister

The problem which arises in attempting to describe the role that goes with the status of minister is that there is *not* just one role, but a multiplicity of them. Blizzard (1956:508), who has written what remains the major work on this issue

---

1. Religious is used in the Roman Catholic church as a term to apply to all those who have taken some form of Holy Orders, for example, nuns, brothers, priests.

As manager of the parish, he is an administrator, when he is involved in leadership of, and participation in, the work of the local church associations and community organizations, he is an organizer. As a pastor, he is involved in the interpersonal relations with individuals, often in an intimate way. As preacher, he is expected to prepare and deliver sermons that are once brilliant, witty, and spiritually edifying—but they must not be too brilliant, lest they be over people's heads, and not too witty, since this might be though of as out of character, and not too painfully, edifying lest the gospel be though of an offense. Even in the churches where the word "liturgy" is seldom, if ever heard, the minister functions as liturgist. He leads the worship and sets its mood, whether this be high or low, formal or informal. Church social instruction, confirmation or membership classes, and leadership of study groups involve minister in being a teacher.

He indicates that the ministerial role in our time is not as clear as it might once have been. He suggests that while there is a "master role" which the minister plays which separates it from other occupations there are a number of choices which can be made as to how that master role should be played (Blizzard, 1958:374-80).

He contends that there are basically five expectations of the work of the minister. First, he is expected to be a preacher, composing and delivering fifty or more sermons a year. Second, the minister operates as a priest; he must conduct worship services properly and perform the various rites of his particular communion with some skill and familiarty. Third, community relations—in many formal as well as informal ways—must be maintained. The minister is really spokesperson for the congregation. Fourth, many members (increasingly it seems) call upon the minister for pastoral counseling, and the expectation is that there will be some skill, with insights from psychology, in this rather difficult task. Finally, administration of the church's program, finances, and other aspects of the group are usually left almost entirely in the hands of the ministers.

What is interesting about this rather prosaic list of duties, Blizzard comments, it that there is purpose in the ordering of them; it corresponds to the amount of time spent on each of the sub-roles during the period of ministerial training. Indeed, in accredited seminaries, the bulk of the education centers on courses in Biblical studies and theology, with much less attention paid to other areas. In fact, administrative skills are seldom taught, even though the need to perform such tasks is rather frequently bemoaned. There is some indication that seminaries are making adjustments to this need, although those who regularly visit seminaries to interview students report that what changes there are seem more cosmetic than real.

The rub, as it were, comes in the fact that this listing of ministerial tasks is in the opposite order of the amount of time ministers end up spending on them in the actual parish experience. Blizzard's research showed that over one-third (40 percent) of the parish clergyperson's time is spent in the somewhat distasteful task of administration, a fourth is devoted to pastoral counseling, 15 percent to operating in the community as agent of the congregation—and only 20 percent, together, on the most favored roles of preacher and priest. In other words, what the seminary has trained the minister to do are precisely those tasks which take up the least of the parish minister's time; and that which will take up most of the hours of the clergyperson's day has received little, if any, preparation during the seminary years. What seems particularly frustrating is that laypeople are no more satisfied with the amount of time spent on such things as administration than is the clergyperson (see Glock and Roos, 1961). They, too, would prefer that their minister be primarily a preacher and a priest, but bow to the need for certain tasks to be done.

A corresponding piece of research on ministerial role for Catholic priests has been done by Mary Ellen Reilly (1975). She determined that there are six prime aspects of the priestly role; priest and teacher, prophet, pastor, administrator, organizer, and priest-ritual. As she notes, there are great similarities between these factors and those which Blizzard described. The only new factor not described by Blizzard is that of the prophetic component, an aspect suggested by Fichter (1968), Hall and Schneider (1973), and Koval (1970). She found that perceptions of the priestly role varied strongly by age. Younger priests were heavily committed to the prophetic role, despite a general feeling that there was great dissatisfaction with priestly duties and threats of clerical resignation. Still, these young priests had been trained at a time when the changes of Vatican II affected their thinking. Further, they were influenced by the currents of social action which, as we have seen, deeply affected Protestant churches. She notes:

> For the youngest men a period of rapid religious and social change has occurred concurrently with their training; therefore, in addition to their age, which may be sufficient to incline them to innovation, they have received church and societal sanctions for their excursions into other areas of interest.

Priests in their early middle years who could be considered still looking for advancement were more completely organization-type men and more concerned about their future. Most of those priests over 45 years of age are pastors and are probably instilled into routines established over the years.

Whitley (1964), in a good review of work concerning the minister's role, notes that Blizzard's research underlines the fact that there is a great deal of "role-ambiguity" for the contemporary clergyperson. He suggests three contexts in which this is true. First, with the multiplicity of expectations, containing some contradictions, there is no clear concept of what the minister's role is in the minds of either clergy or laity. Second, such ambiguity makes it difficult for the minister, as an individual, to develop an appropriate image of the role. Finally, the minister must try to understand the role as seen by American culture in general, and by the particular parish being served.

Adding to this strain is the fact, as Brannon (1971:30) has observed, that the American clergyperson is really in a precarious status. The minister does not have much power to oppose the people who hire him (the laypeople) on important issues, especially social ones. The clergyperson is really very dependent, psychologically and economically, on the whims of the congregation. He needs approval from them more than from fellow clerical peers.

Strains and Conflict in the Ministry

Clearly the ministry, as a profession, is not without its problems. One can easily get a picture of extreme strain and considerable conflict for those in the ministerial role. While it would be an exaggeration to suggest that the occupation is mostly filled with such strain and conflict, it is clear that there are many pushes and pulls operating on the person occupying that status in contemporary society.

It might well be that at the center of these strains and conflicts is the difficulty which the minister has in developing an appropriate professional identity and self-image. Gustafson (1954:187) called attention to this in remarking:

> . . . the problem the minister faces in any social context is that of determining *who he is* and *what he is doing* within the complexity of his functions.

He goes on to suggest that the image of a valid and "authentic" ministry is difficult because of the large number of possible definitions available in a heterogeneous society. There is, of course, the particular denomination's image of the ministry, but his is seldom totally congruent with it. Further, the parish clergyperson is faced with the myriad ministerial images reflected in the mass media; the images of such newsworthy figures as Billy Graham, Robert Schuler, Oral Roberts, and even the Reverend Moon.

With regard to the conflicting values within the role of the ministry, Whitley (1964) points to three studies which emphasize different kinds of conflict which clergypersons face. The first of these studies deals with the special strains faced by ministers in a sectarian group which, by official ideology, finds the presence of a formally appointed pastor an embarrassment, even if it is a necessity. Wilson (1958-59) studied an English Pentecostal group, the Elim movement, and the contradictions in role expectations experienced by clergy in that movement.

The problem, of course, is that in a Pentecostal group, the idea of a trained and appointed person as a minister is out of keeping with the pure Pentecostal spirit which would say that only a spirit-filled person can occupy such a role. However, the minister in the Elim group is now trained, specialized, and paid. As Wilson sums it up (1958-59:504):

> The status of the Pentecostal minister is contradictory because of a lack of consensus among those for whom his role has significance. . . . The contradictions in his status arise from the marginality of his role both within the profession and within the movement.

In another study Whitley (1964) notes that the minister is a living contradiction of the values of the movement. In addition, and again contrary to Pentecostal tradition, the minister must represent the group's "headquarters," while at the same time trying to build up a primary group feeling among the members of the congregation. In a sense, the Elim minister described by Wilson (1958) is cut off from professional identification because of the structure of the movement, but he is also in touch with the status of the ministry in the surrounding community.

A second sort of conflict is explored by Waldo Burchard (1954), a conflict coming from the contradictions between two roles played at once. His study deals with the potential problem which a military chaplain has in balancing the two statuses, minister and military officer. He did, indeed, find such conflict and determined that the chaplains tended to handle it through a process of compartmentalization. Thus, with regard to a possible conflict between military regulations and religious ideology, it was found that the chaplains saw themselves in the moral context of the religious ideology only when they were actually performing clerical tasks; at other times they considered themselves to be in a "nonreligious" situation, and dealt with the situation in terms of the military ideology. There was, however, considerable ambiguity in their minds concerning their status as military officers. While they felt that this cut them off, to some extent, from enlisted personnel, they also had a considerable interest in maintaining the officer status.

A third kind of conflict can occur when the beliefs and values held by the clergyperson are opposite to those of the general community. An example of this is reported in Pettigrew and Campbell's (1958-59) study of ministers in Little Rock, Arkansas, at the time of the school integration crisis. Utilizing the concept of behavioral systems, they explored the conflict between the self-reference system and the membership system, in the sense that the latter represented members of their congregations as well as the general position of Little Rock. The obvious point of interest were those clergypersons whose self-reference system held integration up as a desirable, Christian end. While these clergy might get some support from their professional (denominational) reference system, it was not adequate or even very strong. It was the membership system with which they most had to deal. Certainly the "prosperity" of the local congregation was a prime matter for the minister, and anything that would upset this represented a danger. How, then, did these ministers deal with the conflict. Basically, those clergy interested in integration tended to placate their values by simply calling attention to the need for brotherly love, but not getting involved in action.

Some have called attention to a conflict existing between segments of the clergy and the laity in general. Jeffrey Hadden (1969) has referred to it as "the gathering storm in the churches." His central thesis, reflecting on events in the late sixties, was that the Protestant churches were involved in a deep and entangling crisis which threatens to disrupt or change conceptions of the nature of the church. The civil rights crisis, and activity centering around it, is seen as the issue which has unleashed the sources of latent conflict. Hadden summarizes the matter (1969:6):

> The deception . . . cuts deeply along two dimensions. The first dimension is a struggle over the very *purpose* and *meaning* of the church. Clergy have developed a new meaning of the nature of the church; but for a variety of reasons, laity have not shared in the development of this new meaning. . .
> The second dimension of unrest is a crisis of *belief* . . . Christian theology has been shaken at the foundation. But again, the laity have largely been left out of this painful struggle. . . .
>
> Yet a third dimension of crisis in the church grows out of the first two, and that is a struggle over *authority*. Clergy have long been vested with authority to run the church as they have seen fit. Today, laity are discovering that they have grave reservations about the way clergy have handled their authority, and the evidences of power struggles are beginning to be apparent.

A later discussion of this same issue of the division between the laity and a new breed of socially activist clergy is presented by Hoge in *Division in the Protestant House* (1976), the report of a study made of United Presbyterian laity and clergy. Hoge suggests that the main division in the United Presbyterian Church is one that centers around the *mission* priorities of the denomination. Two almost opposite factions exist in the church—one which stresses the need for personal evangelism and the maintenance of moral standards, and another which sees social activism as the real purpose of Christianity as expressed through the church. Actually, Hoge notes, the real issue is not whether there should be social action, but whether it should be done in the name of the organized church. However, the white middle class feels threatened and generally will not support social action.

The main battleground, then, is really over the protection of the commitments of the middle class. Hoge notes that they are mainly to the "family, career, and standard of living, plus health whenever it appears in danger." These interests are so strong for the typical middle-class church member that church commitment will be forsaken unless it is an instrument for the attainment of these ends. Thus, Hoge concludes that the problem of the United Presbyterian Church, and by implication other mainline Protestant denominations, is a conflict over the priorities of the institution. Clearly, a theological division between two polar positions underlies it. Also problematical is a social division over whether or not white middle-class commitments will be affirmed.

A third study of the division caused by activist clergy is that presented by Quinley (1974). He made a study of 1,580 parish ministers in California at a time when social activism, for clergy and others, was fairly near its height. His data indicated a strong sense of prophetic leadership among California clergy, even from such typically conservative denominations as Southern Baptist and Missouri-Synod Lutheran. But, liberal ministers have been turned away from the activist role and are now less certain about what their role should be in public affairs. The mood of the church members is decidedly more conservative, and large financial cutbacks from liberal programs, among other things, has led to the adoption of more conservative policies in general.

Actually, the rank-and-file membership of these churches never did accept the active public role for the clergy or the organized church. They have not accepted the social action mission as having high priority, nor have they felt it the church's mission to provide leadership on such issues as race, poverty, and peace.

The problem for ethically committed clergy in the 1960s was the need to overcome the complacency and conservatism that commonly grips Protestant churches and to utilize the church's potential to provide critical leadership on public issues. Certainly, we must acknowledge that the church of the middle and late 1960s was not the conservative status quo oriented organization that existed historically. However we choose to assess the significance of these rates of new breed activism, it is evident that they are strongly influenced by the minister's theological position. We have seen that the lay members of Protestant churches in California are no less antagonistic to church activism than they have been said to be. More importantly, they possess substantial authority within all Protestant denominations, and they do not hesitate to use the sanctions at their disposal to punish parish ministers who speak out on controversial public issues.

In sum, then, the "gathering storm" seems to have passed through the mainline church without changing its basic conservative nature. However, those ministers whose self-reference system incline them to see social action as having high priority for the church are caught in an increasing conflict. The "lay backlash" demands conformity to a priority these clergy do not feel.

Socialization into the Ministry

Some denominations, from their very beginnings in this country, have emphasized an educated clergy. Thus, much higher education in our country was created mainly for the purpose of providing such an educated clergy. In times past, however, this was not true for every communion, with many stressing only the "call of God" as sufficient to prepare an individual for ministry. As the trend toward increasingly greater bureaucratization of the religious organization has progressed, however, those groups which can be seen as nearing the status of denomination, as opposed to sect, increasingly require more training for their clergy—ranging from the "preaching schools" of the Church of Christ to the essentially graduate education required by such groups as the Presbyterian church, with an increasing number of clergy pursuing doctoral degrees.

In essence, then, to the degree that specialized training is the mark of a profession, it can be said that the ministry should be classified along with law and medicine in this category. There are reasons to qualify this classification; the periods of training are not necessarily long and there is less autonomy and control over the "tools of the trade" for the clergyperson (see Jarvis, 1975). However, whether it is seen as a full profession, as it rather consistently has been, or one of the subprofessions (like social work), today most preachers are "made," not "born" or "born again." To become a minister today is more than to receive a call; it is to undergo a period of socialization, of varying lengths, in which the recruit comes to take on the professional self of the clergyperson, learning to play the role as well as gaining more knowledge about the faith and its practice.

What happens during this process though? Common sense tells us that we might expect several things to be happening. At a minimum, we assume that ministerial students learn the basics of their religious belief and value system, and how to perform those tasks which make up the core of their responsibility; tasks discussed under the role of the minister. However, it is likely that much more is happening in this learning process than just ministerial education. Although the literature on the sociology of seminary education is relatively limited, analogies can be made to the training of physicians. It seems safe to paraphrase Coe (1970:203) in saying that seminary education is a time of intensive contact with others seeking to join the "brotherhood" of the ministry and, thus, a period which serves as a crucial one in guiding the prospective clergyperson in taking on the professional role.

It has been suggested (Armstrong, 1977:245) that there is a "hidden curriculum" in the medical school; a curriculum which provides more than the learning of the technical skills of medical knowledge. It is an agenda aimed at the *internalization* of the beliefs and values thought important to the medical profession. It seems likely that, to some extent, the same statement can be made concerning the socialization into the ministry which occurs in seminary.

One study of the process of socialization into the ministry has been done by Berg (1969). He suggests that seminary works to develop a professional outlook. In essence he sees four factors in such an outlook: (1) a less charismatic orientation to the ministry; (2) a more extrinsic religiosity; (3) a lesser degree of intrinsic

157

religiosity; and (4) greater skill in communication abilities. He suggests further that both the social prestige of a denomination and the university orientation of a seminary will increase this professional orientation. While his findings are not perfectly consistent, they do indicate that seminary has the effect of developing just such a professional orientation.

In one of the few studies regarding theological education, Carroll (1971:61) has commented on the effect of the theological orientation of the particular seminary in shaping the student's socialization process. He sees this orientation as a part of the social climate of the school which shapes the students development. He suggests that there are great variations in seminaries depending on this orientation. Those schools which emphasize spiritual formation and a mastery of the religious tradition he sees as more like a religious community; those interested in spiritual formation and practical competence are likened to a vocational school; and those concerned with practical competence over mastery of the tradition, and secular awareness over spiritual formation, are seen as like graduate schools. Obviously the way in which these variables operate in a particular school will have an effect on the product of that school.

One thing given much stress in the studies of education for a medical career is the importance of *student culture*. Several major studies have been done concerning the effects of this culture, with somewhat contradictory results. For instance, one study sees students as "boys in white" (Becker et al., 1961) while another refers to them as "student physicians" (Merton et al., 1957). What is common to these studies is the emphasis upon the way in which the student culture organized to respond to the academic and social pressures of learning this role and how that culture then appears to develop a "life of its own." While no corresponding work has been done on the "boys in black" or "student minister" it seems likely that something of the same sort of student organization does exist in the seminaries and that through this organization much of the process of identification with the role occurs.

The Clergy Dropout

One final note seems in order with regard to the clerical role. That is the assumption in the media, and in many denominational headquarters, that there is an increasing tendency for those already in the ministry to leave it. Although individuals have obviously given up their vocation in every period of time, there seems little doubt that either the drop out rate has increased or defections from the ministry (and other religious life) are more publicized in our day. It is also suggested by some that many more would "drop out" if only they had another way of making a living; a suggestion perhaps supported by the speed with which many seek the nonparish positions, such as campus ministries or chaplaincies, available in almost every denomination.

What is the source of such defection? Older studies, such as those of Fichter (1961) suggested that defections, at least from the priesthood, were the result of some spiritual deficiency, an inability to "hold the faith" strongly enough. However, more recently it has been indicated that "loss of faith" is simply not the answer, but that the problem lies in facets of the ministerial role, its requirements, and its status in contemporary society (see Schoenherr and Greeley, 1974).

Much of the problem probably relates to the general flux in the status of the ministry in general. As Goldner et al. (1973:119) have noted, the Catholic priesthood and the ministry in general, are in what amounts to a near state of crisis. They suggest that this crisis results from a confusion over exactly what services the clergy are to perform and what services are to be "referred" to other types of professionals. Potvin (1976) also refers to such role ambiguity as a problem for increasing the number of clergy. Others suggest that the crisis is one of identity emerging from the changes in the value system of the society which often leaves the clergy with little idea of how to define, sustain, and transmit the values when they are in a state of flux (Hadden, 1969). Richardson (1969) identifies one specific problem as that of the role of celibacy in the increasing defection of priests.

In the end it may be as simple as the answer suggested by Schoenherr and Greeley (1974). They have built a model based on the net balance of rewards and costs of remaining in the ministry. They conclude that the net rewards of remaining in the ministry (suggesting, for example, lesser prestige in our time) are not worth the costs arising from role confusion and the variety of pressures obtaining in the present day ministerial role.

THE ROLE OF WOMEN IN RELIGIOUS ORGANIZATIONS

One of the major issues facing America in the 1970s has been that of the status of women. With the increasing concern over the role which women play in society has also come a concern for the place of women in the religious organization. Questions of women's liberation, feminism, and equal rights for women are having an effect on the religious organization just as they are on all other aspects of the institutional life of society.

In one sense, the matter is really one of role and the expectations which go with the status of female and male. Gove and Tudor (1973) have noted that the sex role is a "master status" or identity for both men and women, and, as such, influences all other facts of their activities. The traditional role definitions associated with sexual status, then, can be seen as providing an effective block to social and occupational mobility for women (Laws, 1975). Attempts by women to engage in occupational activities which violate traditional role stereotypes are generally met by tokenism, which permits some entry into male dominated activity without any change in the basic role definition. Laws notes that this approach is used as a means by which a female may actually enter a male-dominated role while leaving the status quo or traditional stereotype virtually unchanged.

Generally, the religious institution has been seen as one of the major barriers to changes in the definition of the female role (Reuther, 1974). In looking at this issue we can look at two aspects of the role of women in the life of the religious organization: (1) the status of women in the church in general, as well as the views of the place of women held in religious ideology, and (2) the role of women in the leadership of the church, particularly the formal leadership role of clergyperson.

Religion and the Role of Women

The bulk of both sociological the theological literature on the status of women indicates that the traditional, subservient or inferior role for women is reflected in the ideology of most Christian and Jewish groups and that this ideology is reflected in the practices of the various bodies. There exist practices which tend to exclude women from the fullest participation in the group and assign them to basically servant and nurturant roles.

In one sense, it can be seen that both the Old and New Testaments do assign women to such statuses, a fact typical of the practices in most lands of Biblical times. Certainly Pauline theology reflects such a low opinion of the status of women that feminists are inclined to see misogynism in Paul's attitudes. There does appear to be a strong Biblical bias for the traditional status of women, a bias now woven deeply into the subcultural fabric of nearly all Protestant groups. In short, there is a sexist attitude in the warp of Christian thought, deriving from the first century, Eastern view of the role of women.

This low status is expressed in both the language and the symbolism of the Bible. It has been pointed out that this common Biblical heritage tends to portray men in all sorts of leadership roles—kings, prophets, and priests. Women, on the other hand, are almost always portrayed in terms of a family or home status, or in the role of servants (Crabtree, 1970; Wilson, 1973; Neville, 1974). There is, as Morton (1974) and Pagels (1970) have both suggested, a concept of a God ordained "pecking order" which goes—God-Christ-man-woman-child. Undergirding these beliefs about female inferiority is a heavily masculine symbol system in the Bible. Not only is God referred to exclusively in masculine terms, but such terms—king, master, lord, judge, father—barely grace Biblical reality with the current presence of females, as would be true if descriptive words like husband or lover which are almost totally absent (Morton, 1974; Pagels, 1970) were used.

While this is the traditional or conservative view of the Bible's conception of the role of the woman, such an interpretation does not go unchallenged (see Sapp, 1979). Feminists are bringing the concept of a Biblical foundation for male social superiority under question, challenging a number of beliefs about man, society, and the world. The argument is that the traditional view is really an interpretation of what the Bible is saying, and that it is largely based on the patriarchal system of the time and misunderstandings which flow from this. Leaders in this reinterpretation insist that Jesus actually changed this patriarchal view, giving women direct involvement in his ministry, and that the Pauline statements concerning the man as head of the woman are actually misinterpretations of commands that all should fall under the headship of Jesus.

In noting the traditional Christian view—and attempts to introduce a new paradigm, as Sapp writes—it should also be indicated that not all traditional churches have taken this literalist view of the place of the woman. Actually, a great number of churches, particularly those seen as liberal in their interpretation of scripture, have been in the vanguard of the battle for the Equal Rights Amendment, at least at the official denominational level. It is basically the denominations that are literalist in their interpretation of scriptures and conservative in theology that have been seen as opposing women's rights. Peek and Brown (1978) studied denominational differences in attitudes toward a number of feminist issues. They found that when all persons giving a religious preference were considered the differences between the denominations were slight, and no great chasm formed between the fundamentalists and the nonfundamentalists. However, when the analysis was restricted to a consideration of those who were high in religiosity (measured in terms of church attendance and strength of religious preference), there was support for the proposition that those individuals coming from fundamentalist groups who were high in religiosity were also more likely to oppose issues involving the granting of rights to females. Although the association was not very strong, it was strong enough to conclude that such affiliation, coupled with high participation, led to anti-feminist attitudes. That in the mid-1970s hundreds of women from evangelical or fundamentalist congregations marched on the Texas capital of Austin to support the rescinding of the approval of the Equal Rights Amendment is probably a fair example of the kinds of attitudes toward women generated in such theological traditions.

In sum, then, the religious ideology of the Judaeo-Christian tradition tends to reinforce, and give religious sanction, to the general societal position or understanding of the rule which women have and should have in society. There is little impetus, except in some of the most liberal denominations, to seek change for the status of women. Indeed, a content analysis of leading Protestant and Catholic religious journals during the early seventies indicates that there was than one percent of the space in these magazines was given to the issue of women's status (Chambers and Chalfant, 1978).

Leadership Roles and Women in the Church

Clearly the religious organizations in our society tend to undergird the general societal appraisal of the position of women. That this is true becomes more apparent as we look at the participation of women in the leadership of the religious organization, even though it should be noted that churches were among the first to allow women any significant leadership roles in some of its subgroups.

While most Protestant denominations allow women a place on their official boards, this is not true of all groups. Moreover, when women are elected to such boards it is frequently in an inferior status, and can be taken as a kind of tokenism. Many official boards would seem to be saying, "We need to let the women feel they have a part in governing the church, but we know they will understand that they aren't to get carried away with their positions and actually try to do anything." In truth, women laity working in the church do tend to be relegated to duties that relate to aesthetic matters (such as flower and music committees), working with children, and church school rather than being given key organizational responsibility and decision-making roles (Crabtree, 1970).

We have previously noted that the key to leadership in the religious organization is the formal role of minister or priest. Here, clearly, the role of the female is inferior, if women are allowed to be a part of the clergy at all. For, even when allowed to assume "full ministry," as Jacquet (1978) puts it, they are generally assigned to an inferior kind of ministry or one of the less desirable posts. Actually, even where the ordination of women to the full ministry is allowed, few women avail themselves of the opportunity. The United Presbyterian Church, for example, has granted ordination to women since 1954, but less than one percent of its clergy are female, and about one-half of these are not serving in any official church post (General Assembly Minutes, 1977).

The status of women and the ministry has been explored in some detail in a report to the National Council of Churches by Constant H. Jacquet, Jr. (1978). Jacquet[2] comments that we have very little information, in a statistical sense, concerning the extent to which women are ordained to the full ministry, or concerning what kinds of positions they hold or what benefits they receive compared with male counterparts. It is even hard to determine what denominations actually ordain women to the *full* ministry.

There have been studies in the past which attempted to answer questions concerning the ordination of women. For example, in 1927 the Federal Council of Churches produced a report which showed that only 44 of the 114 religious

2. The material concerning women and the church, particularly as it relates to Protestantism, is paraphrased from Jacquet's work, with permission.

bodies surveyed in 1925 granted full ordination to women. Sixty of these denominations did not grant such ordination and ten were "uncertain" of their stand. Twenty years later (1949), Cavert published material on women in American church life and stated that "of all denominations for which information could be secured, 41 ordain women and 7 license them" (1949:69). She also indicated that there had been little, if any, increase in the number of women who were in the ministry in spite of what was described as a "critical" lack of ministers, with thousands of churches vacant. Further, what women ministers there were served only the smaller, outlying churches which could not be "choosy" about their ministers.

Another estimate of the actual number of female clergy is found in the *Yearbook of American Churches* for 1951 where it is reported that 78 religious bodies granted ordination to women; however, much of this was presumption. The latest edition of the Yearbook indicates that out of 211 religious groups, there are 87 which do *not* ordain women, 76 which do, and 10 which fall into a special category because there is no officially ordained clergy. There is no information available on the remaining denominations.

Looking at the 76 groups reported as ordaining women to the full ministry it is found that women clergypersons represent only about 4 percent of their total clergy. Of the 10,470 women reported to be ordained in 1977, nearly one-third (31.8 percent) were in 14 bodies of the Pentecostal sect type and another third (29.9 percent) were in three groups with an emphasis on holiness doctrines and social service (i.e., the Salvation Army, Volunteers of America, American Rescue Workers). Ten major Protestant denominations account for another 17.4 percent while the remaining 20 percent are ordained in a wide variety of Protestant groups. Of the major Protestant denominations ordaining women, only three ordained women before 1956, and these three account for the majority of women clergy in the ten denominations. The three are the American Baptist Churches, Disciples of Christ, and United Church of Christ. The remaining major denominations which ordain women are the American Lutheran Church, The Episcopal Church, The Lutheran Church in America, The Presbyterian Church in the United States, local congregations of the Southern Baptist Convention, The United Methodist Church, and the United Presbyterian Church in the United States of America.

A survey done by Bonn and Kelley (1973) on clergy support in salary, income, and attitudes, included data on female ministers. In all, 124 female ministers completed the research instrument, and it was found that while the average congregation served by a male minister had 313 communicant members, that of the female had only 128. Further, such congregations had an average expense budget of $17,000 compared to $35,800 for congregations with male ministers. Obviously, this meant, too, that salaries for female clergy were lower than for males, approximately $4,000 less.

The job market for the female minister. There has been an increase in enrollment in seminaries, and this increase has been 5 times that for women as for men. Carrol and Wilson (1978) report, in a survey of the clergy labor market, that seminary students plan to be ordained by a ratio of 9 to 1, and half of them plan to enter the pastorate. Women students, however, are seen as different in that just under one-fourth of them plan to become pastors. About a third plan to become assistants as compared with only 23 percent of the men. This means that about 56 percent of the women plan to enter the pastorate (in either full or assistant roles) as compared to 78 percent on the male seminarians.

However, due to a slowing down of birth rates and the relative lack of new church "starts," along with decline in membership and increased longevity for existing pastors, the absorption of new pastors is not easy in the major denominations. The Episcopal church and the two major Presbyterian bodies have the most serious surplus of ministers. With such a tightening job market for both men and women some efforts are being made to work on placement of women in parish ministeries. For example, The Rockefeller Family Fund has given a grant in the Boston area to facilitate such employment in the American Baptist, African Methodist, United Methodist, and United Churches.

Changing attitudes. Will the attitudes toward female clergy change? It is possible that there will be a slow growth in the number of women employed in local churches. This will depend, in large measure, on the local pulpit committee and its attitudes toward women ministers. Women's causes have developed in a number of denominations; they monitor the progress of employment for female clergy and work toward changing attitudes.

In sum, the question raised with regard to the ordination of women to the full ministry has to do with right of women to this position based on interpretation of the Scriptures according to current theological norms and also on social norms in the contemporary church and society. The right of women to be ordained to the full ministry has not been recognized by many denominations on grounds of Biblical injunctions, traditional church practices, sexist biases, or a combination of these factors. The question of whether to ordain women has tended to follow liberal-conservative theological and social orientations that cut across many confessional groupings (e.g., Baptists, Lutherans, and Presbyterians) as well as across the whole spectrum of denominational life in the United States.

Florence Rosenberg (1979) has reported on the status of "women in ministry" in the Catholic church in describing a proposed study by the Leadership Council of Women Religious. The status of women, particularly in regard to their ordination to the priesthood, has been an issue which has occupied much of the attention of those investigating women's rights within the Catholic church. However, it should not be concluded that lack of such ordination, and the apparant rigid resistance of the papacy against such a move, means that there is no change in the status of women in that church. The changes that accompanied Vatican II, as well as some parish needs, have brought new opportunities for service within the church, or ministry as Rosenberg defines it. While in some parishes women are still limited to traditional tasks, in others they take part, with men, in the increasing role of the laity in the church. There would seem to be, according to Rosenberg, a trend toward the expansion of the participation which women have in the Catholic church. This seems particularly true because laity are being asked to do more in the face of a shortage of priests, and women religious are most frequently those with the time to devote to ministry which has no financial rewards connected with it.

Having noted these changes and new places for women in the church, she goes on to note that this has relatively little to do with any radical changes in sex-role beliefs and attitudes. It is probably true, also, that it has very little to do with any changes in official power in the structure of the church.

SUMMARY

Religious groups are sometimes classified as having one of three forms of government or polity, although a number might be seen as combining elements from two or even all three forms. The three forms are "episcopal," "presbyterian," and "congregational." The epsicopal form is one in which power is vested in a hierarchy of bishops and little formal power is left at the local level. Presbyterian polity is something like a representative democracy in that representatives of the congregations (elders) are elected. Authority is vested in the elders at the local level as well as in higher judicatories to which elders may be elected as representatives. The congregational form places rule and authority in the local congregation, with no decisions, technically, being made above that level, and with all members having an equal voice.

However, as stated, it is clear that no one church or group follows these forms to the letter. In particular, it is noted that where a group has attained some size and continuity, the tendency is to develop legal-bureaucratic forms of authority.

Religious organizations are obviously structured into a number of different roles: clergy, member, officer, teacher, and so forth. It is clear that the formal leadership role of the clergyperson is the one of dominant interest, although attention can be given to the way in which the laity participate in the governmental activities of congregations. We have called attention to the fact that frequently such participation is based on informal power elites within the congregations rather than on official rules. Considering the clergyperson, although some groups may have no clearly specified clergy, few groups can maintain themselves over time without such leadership.

There have been several attempts to delineate general expectations for the incumbents of the clerical role. Perhaps the best accepted notes five tasks ordered by increasing amount of time clergy devote to them: preacher, priest, community relations person, pastoral counselor, and administrator. Problems arise for the clergyperson, however, in that this ordering of roles is pleasing to neither clergy nor laity. It is also a role in which many conflicting demands are placed upon the occupant, resulting in much strain and frustration. Considerable attention has been focused on the division in many Protestant groups between a liberal, activist clergy and a more conservative laity seeking spiritual comfort rather than political reform from their church. It is certainly a task of the theological seminary, the agent for "socialization into the ministry," to help students learn not only the "tools of their trade," but also to develop a sense of the role dimensions and how to cope with them. Some evidence of the difficulty of this task is to be seen in the rather high "drop out" rate for clergy.

Along with the generalized societal concern for the status of women goes an attentiveness to the role of women in the religious organization. As a sex role is a master role controlling most aspects of life it is also a dominating concern with regard to religious matters. There is strong indication that religious organizations tend to be sexist; women have generally been seen in a subservient position in the Judaeo-Christian tradition. Clearly the symbol system of that tradition is replete with evidence of this male domination.

The subservient status of women in the religious organization can be seen in the kinds of roles which they play in the leadership of such groups. While most groups elect women to their governing boards, their positions on these boards are frequently inferior ones. Some organizations allow women in the formal role of the clergy; however, even in those bodies which permit female ministers only, four percent of clergypersons are women. It is also clear that female clergy tend to occupy subordinate roles (assistant pastor, director of Christian education, and so forth) or have pastorates that are too small or too poor to support a male clergyperson.

In this chapter we have generalized as much as possible about style of polity and leadership roles in American religious groups. However, the great variation which exists in the demands and organization of the numerous such groups makes it impossible to describe each different form. This very diversity in American religious life is unique in religious life among the world's societies. In the next two chapters we will discuss the development and nature of this diversity.

REFERENCES

Armstrong, J.
1977   "The structure of medical education." *Medical
                         Education* 11 (July):244-48.

Balswick, Jack and Nor-
man Layne
1973   "Studying social organization in the local

church: A socio-metric approach." *Review of Religious Research* 14:101-09.

Becker, Howard S.,
Blanches Geer, Everett C.
Hughes and Anselm L.
Strauss
1961   *Boys in White: Student Culture in Medical School.* Chicago: University of Chicago Press.

Berg, Philip L.
1969   "Socialization into the ministry: A comparative analysis." *Sociological Analysis* 30:59-71.

Blizzard, Samuel W.
1956   "The minister's dilemma." *Christian Century* 73 (April 25):508-9.

1958   "The Protestant parish minister's integrating roles." *Religious Education* 53 (July-August):374-80.

Bonn, Robert L. and
Sheila M. Kelley
1973   *Clergy Support 1973: Salary, Income and Attitudes.* New York: National Council of Churches.

Brannon, Robert C. L.
1971   "Organizational vulnerability in modern religious organization." *Journal for the Scientific Study of Religion* 10 (Spring):27-32.

Burchard, Waldo W.
1954   "Role conflicts in military chaplains." *American Sociological Review* 19:528-35.

Carroll, Jackson W.
1971   "Structural effects of professional schools on professional socialization. The case of protestant clergyman." *Social Forces* 50:61-72.

Carroll, Jackson W. and
Robert L. Wilson
1978   *The Clergy Job Market: Over-Supply and/or Opportunity.* Hartford, Hartford Seminary Foundation.

Cavert, Inez M.
1949   *Women in American Church Life.* New York: Friendship Press.

Chalfant, H. Paul
1967   *Classification of the Variables of Socioeconomic Class, Ecological Place and Leadership Style in Urban Church Congregations.* Stillwater, Okla.: Oklahoma State University. Unpublished master's thesis.

Chambers, Patricia Price
and H. Paul Chalfant
1978   "A changing role or the same old handmaidens: Women's role in today's church." *Review of Religious Research* 19 (Winter): 192-97.

Coe, Rodney
1970   *Sociology of Medicine.* New York: McGraw-Hill.

Crabtree, Deirde F.
1970   "Women's liberation and the church." Pp. in Sarah B. Doely (ed.), *Women's Liberation and the Church.* New York: Association Press.

Demerath, N. J., III
1974   *A Tottering Transcendence.* Indianapolis: Bobbs-Merrill.

Demerath, N. J., III and
Phillip E. Hammond
1969   *Religion in Social Context.* New York: Random House.

Fichter, Joseph H.
1961   *Religion as an Occupation: A Study in the Sociology of Professions.* Notre Dame: University of Notre Dame Press.

1968   *America's Forgotten Priests.* New York: Harper.

General Assembly
1977   *Minutes of the General Assembly. Statistics.* Philadelphia: General Assembly of the United Presbyterian Church.

Glock, Charley Y. and P.
Roos
1961   "Parishioners' views of how ministers spend their time." *Review of Religious Research* 2:170-75.

Goldner, F. H., T. P.
Ference and R. R. Ritti
1973   "Priests and laity: A profession in transition." *Monographs of Sociology Review* 20 (Fall).

Gove, Walter R. and
Jeanette F. Tudor
 1973   "Sex roles and mental illness." *American Journal of Sociology* 78 (January):812-35.

Gustafson, James
 1954   "An analysis of the problem of the role of the minister." *Journal of Religion* 34:187.

Hadden, Jeffrey K.
 1969   *The Gathering Storm in the Churches.* Garden City, N.Y.: Doubleday.

Hall, Douglas and Ben-
jamin Schneider
 1973   *Organization Climates and Careers: The Work Lives of Priests.* New York: Seminar Press.

Harrison, Paul M.
 1959   *Authority and Power in the Free Church Tradition.* Princeton: Princeton University Press.

Hoge, Dean
 1976   *Division in the Protestant House: The Basic Reasons Behind Intra-Church Conflict.* Philadelphia: Westminster Press.

Hoge, Dean and Jackson
W. Carroll
 1978   "Determinants of church commitment and participation." *Journal for the Scientific Study of Religion* 17 (June):107–27

Hogland, James G., Jr.
and James R. Wood
 1979   "Inner circles in local churches: An application of Thompson's theory." *Sociological Analysis* 40 (Fall):226-39.

Jacquet, Constant H.
 1978   *Women Ministers in 1977.* New York: Office of Research, Evaluation and Planning, National Council of Churches.

Jarvis, Peter
 1975   "The parish ministry as a semi-profession." *Sociological Review* 23:911-22.

Johnstone, Ronald L.
 1975   *Religion and Society in Interaction.* Englewood Cliffs: Prentice-Hall.

169

Koval, John P.
1970   "Priesthood as career: Yesterday and today." Pp. 85-100 in William Bartlett (ed.), *Evolving Religious Careers*. Washington, D.C.: Center for Applied Research in the Apostolate.

Laws, Judith
1975   "Psychology of tokenism." *Sex Roles* 1:51-67.

Merton, Robert K.,
George Reader and
Patricia L. Kendall
1957   *The Student Physician*. Cambridge, Mass.: Harvard University Press.

Morton, Nelle
1974   "Preaching the word." Pp. 12-20 in Alice L. Hageman (ed.), *Sexist Religion and Women in the Church*. New York: Association Press.

Neville, Gwen K.
1974   "Religious socialization of women within U.S. subcultures." Pp. 20–31 in Alice L. Hageman (ed., *Sex Religion and Woman in the Church*. New York: Association Press.

Pagels, Elaine H.
1970   "What became of God the Mother? Conflicting images of God in early Christianity." *Signs* 2 (Winter):293–303.

Peek, Charles W. and
Sharon Brown
1978   "Affiliation, religiosity and political prejudice toward women among white protestants." Paper presented at the meetings of the Southern Sociological Society. New Orleans, La.

Pettigrew, J. and Ernest
Q. Campbell
1958–   "Racial and moral crisis: The role of the Little
59   Rock ministers." *American Journal of Sociology* 64:509–16.

Potvin, Raymond H.
1976   "Role uncertainty and commitment among seminary faculty." *Sociological Analysis* 37 (September):45–52.

Quinley, Harold
1974   *The Prophetic Clergy: Socialization Activism*

Among Protestant Ministers. New York: John Wiley.

Reilly, Mary Ellen
1975   "Perceptions of the priest role." *Sociological Analysis* 36:347–56.

Reuther, Rosemary
1974   *Religion and Sexism: Images of Women in the Jewish and Christian Tradition.* New York: Simon and Schuster.

Richardson, H.
1969   "The symbol of virginity." Pp. 775-811 in D. Cutler (ed.), *The Religious Situation.* Boston: Beacon.

Roof, Wade C.
1978   *Community and Commitment: Religious Plausibility in a Liberal Protestant Church.* New York: Elsevier.

Rosenberg, Florence
1979   "Catholic women in ministry: Ideological and functional origins." Paper presented at the annual meetings of the Association for the Sociology of Religion, Boston.

Sapp, Stephen G.
1979   "Biblical interpretations on women's roles: A sociological perspective." Paper presented at the annual meetings of the Association for the Sociology of Religion, Boston.

Schoenherr, R. A. and A. M. Greeley
1974   "Role commitment processes and the American Catholic priesthood." *American Sociological Review* 39 (June):407-26.

Szafran, Robert F.
1976   "The distribution of influence in religious organizations." *Journal for the Scientific Study of Religion* 15 (Dec.):339-50.

Whitley, Oliver R.
1964   *Religious Behavior: When Sociology and Religion Meet.* Englewood Cliffs, N. J.: Prentice-Hall, Inc.

Wilson, Bryan R.
1958-59   "The Pentecostalist minister: Role conflicts and

status contradictions." *American Journal of Sociology* 64:497.

Wilson, Martha M.
1973

"Women, religion, and the Bible." Pp. 15-27 in Judith Goldenberg (ed.), *Women and Religion: 1972.* Missoula, Montana: University of Montana Press.

Wood, James R. and
Mayer N. Zald
1966

"Aspects of racial integration in the Methodist Church: Sources of Resistance to Organizational Policy." *Social Forces* 45:255–65.

PART THREE

RELIGION IN CONTEMPORARY SOCIETY

CHAPTER 6

The Development
of American Pluralism

It is not difficult to perceive the great diversity in American religious life. Almost any almanac will list hundreds of separate religious groups, and the telephone Yellow Pages present a variety of different groups sufficient for almost anyone's religious tastes. Or, you might simply wander through any community of any size and observe the churches of all sizes and faiths holding public services and sessions of religious instruction. A person can see ornate Gothic cathedrals, simple colonial-style buildings, and store-front buildings given over to the activities of a Pentecostal sect. One can choose to follow the faith of the Catholics, Jews (Orthodox, Conservative, or Reformed), or more than 200 varieties of Protestants—or to give allegiance to no religious faith.

Probably nowhere else in the world is diversity of religious belief so widespread or do the various groups live with each other in such harmony. Such has not always been the case in our society, however. Pluralism in American religion, the concept of coexisting different groups, evolved historically from a state-church situation in colonial America.

THE DEVELOPMENT OF RELIGIOUS PLURALISM

The first English colonists, the Pilgrims, came to New England ostensibly to escape religious persecution in Europe for their Calvinistic beliefs. They were followed shortly by other Puritans, and these early settlers of Massachusetts made a serious attempt to enforce religious uniformity (Hudson, 1961:10). This theocracy mixed religious law and church law; dissenters from the Puritan religious point of view were dealt with swiftly. Roger Williams was banished to neighboring Rhode Island, where he established the first Baptist congregation in the New World (Littell, 1962:22). Religious dissenters from the Church of England also settled in other areas: the Quakers in Pennsylvania and the Roman Catholics in Maryland. On the other hand, in the proprietary colonies of Virginia, the Carolinas, and Georgia, the Church of England became the state church (Littell, 1962:12). New York began as a Dutch colony with the Dutch Reformed Church as the state church, but later became English and Anglican. In 1689, Anglicanism was established in Maryland and, as a result, Catholics were persecuted there. Littell (1962:17) sums up the colonial religious order as an oppressive establishment of mixed Congregational and Presbyterian order in New England and the dominance of the Church of England in the Southern colonies. Only in Pennsylvania, New Jersey, and Delaware was the shift to religious liberty and voluntary support accomplished without severe readjustment. In fact, Pennsylvania was considered a "swamp of sectarianism" by New Englanders and Southerners alike.

To this "swamp" migrated the German lowland Lutherans, the Moravians, the Dutch Calvinists, and the Amish. In 1707, the Baptists chose Philadelphia as their headquarters (Hudson, 1961:21). Religious ferment in these middle colonies provided the base for the First Great Awakening, begun in 1734, which further developed the concept of religious pluralism.

The First Great Awakening

The first evangelical preaching in the colonies was done by Domine Greylinghausen, a Dutch Calvinist. Jonathan Edwards was influential in New England, and George Whitefield preached the message of evangelicalism among all the colonies from New Hampshire to Georgia. Calvinistic theology dominated the evangelistic efforts of these men, but in spite of this, the Congregationalists of New England and the Presbyterians of several colonies divided as to the propriety of such "mass evangelistic efforts." The revivalists among Congregationalists were named "New Light" and among Presbyterians, "New Side." The antirevivalists were called "Old Light" Congregationalists and "Old Side" Presbyterians (Hudson, 1961:31-32). Littell sees the Great Awakening as "the first major manifestation of a motive, which, more than any other, has shaped modern American church life: mass evangelism" (1962:19). Beginning with the Great Awakening in 1734, the revivalist wing of the Presbyterians (the "New Side") and the Methodists began to play an important role in American religious life. The Methodists were most effective in the mission to the de-churched in the Southern colonies which were dominated by the Anglican Church. During the same period, Baptists also became more prominent. Under the Puritan-Congregationalist Establishment of New England, they suffered whippings, jailings, and other persecutions. During the Great Awakening, however, many Congregationalists and Anglicans were forced out of state-church parishes and joined the Baptists (Littell, 1962:20-21). This further contributed to the concept of *denominationalism*, an important necessity to religious pluralism. As explained by church historian Winthrop S. Hudson (1961:33-34), the word *denomination* is an inclusive term—an ecumenical term. The word implies that the group referred to is but one member, called or *denominated* by a particular name, of a larger group. In this case that larger group is the chruch. Denominationalism is the opposite of the exclusive term, *sectarianism*. The basic contention of denominational theory of the church is that the true church is not to be identified exclusively with any single ecclesiastical body. Furthermore, Hudson states that no denomination claims to represent the whole Church of Christ. No denomination claims that all other churches are also churches. Each is regarded as constituting a different "mode" of expressing in the outward forms of worship and organization the larger life of the universal church in which they all share (1961:34).

The use of the word came into vogue during the early years of the Great Awakening. John Wesley's famous quote sums up an early expression of denominations:

> I . . . refuse to be distinguished from any other men by any but the common principles of Christianity . . . I renounce and test all other marks of distinction. But from real Christians, of whatever denomination, I earnestly desire not to be distinguished at all . . . Dost thou love and fear God? It is enough! I give the right hand of fellowship

The revivalists of the Great Awakening were ready to preach their messages in meetinghouses of various denominations. The religiously indifferent colonial population was this mission. Hudson (61:45) quotes a portion of evangelist George Whitefield's sermon preached from a balcony in Philadelphia:

> Father Abraham, whom have you in heaven? Any Episcopalians? No! Any Presbyterians? No! Any independents or Methodists? No, no, no! Whom have you there? We don't know those names here. All who are here are Christians . . . Oh, is this the case? Then God help us to forget party names and to become Christians in deed and truth.

This early pluralistic concept was applied in rather limited ways. Only evangelical-type Christians granted each other tolerance. The few Roman Catholics in the colonies were disenfranchised; Jew were so few in number that they were almost invisible. Black slaves (and free blacks) were overseen religiously through white paternalism. The communal settlements of the Moravians and the Amish were self contained; and therefore, they posed no threat to the evangelical Protestants. Nevertheless, this early concept of denominationalism allowed for the development of religious tolerance, religious liberty, and later formal separation of church and state. These revolutionary religious principles provided the base from which religious pluralism evolved.

Religious Tolerance, Religious Liberty, and the Separations of Church and State

Even though many of the colonial settlers had come to the English speaking colonies to seek religious freedom, they had, in many ways, become a religious establishment. At the time of the Declaration of Independence in 1776, there were thirteen "small nations" trying to become one out of many. Nine of these former colonies recognized official establishments of religion. All of the colonies had a significant number of religious dropouts and dissenters. Between the time of winning freedom from England and of framing the United States Constitution, no single church body had enough strength to prevail in the new United States (Marty, 1970:36). Formally, the new nation was a "Christian nation," and for most this meant a "Protestant Christian nation." Out of a population of approximately 3,500,000, only about 20,000 were Roman Catholic and only about 6,000 were Jews. Furthermore in 1776, only about 5 percent of the colonial population were participating members of churches (Littell, 1962:29-32). The members of the huge nonchurched majority in the new nation had to find a way to assert their freedom *from* religion; the people who were church-going wished to preserve this right; and the few passionate defenders of religion needed a formulation which they could endorse (Marty, 1970:37). The proponents of *denominationalism* were in actuality contending among themselves.

Some of the political leaders of the new nation, notably James Madison, took comfort from the division of churches. He and fellow framers of the Constitution were nominal church members, but they embraced the enlightened philosophy of the eighteenth century including the religious philosophy of *Deism*. Deism viewed God as benign, content to let the world go by controlled only through natural law which the deity had fashioned. In a very real sense, organized religion in American was weaker at the time of our national beginnings than in any other time in history. While religion was deeply stamped on colonial institutions and minds, few people really bothered to observe religious customs and practices. Still, few citizens wished to harm religion. Apathy, not antipathy, was the rule (Marty, 1970:38-39). While Benjamin Franklin, John Adams, James Madison, and particularly Thomas Jefferson wished to prevent the churches from "meddling in civil affairs," evangelical church leaders and dissenters from the established religion were pressing for a method to guarantee freedom *from* governmental intrusion into religion. Shortly after the ratification of the Constitution in 1789, the first ten amendments, or Bill of Rights, were added. Included was the important First Amendment guaranteeing *freedom of religion*. The new nation was officially *nonreligious*, but religious tolerance and freedom were unique features of the religiously neutral nation. The compromises of the intellectuals of politics and the proponents of religious tolerance gave rise to what we now refer to as the *historic separation of church and state*.

Wilson (1978:194) lists ten reasons for the development and implementation of the separation of church and state, ranging from the fact that the United States was originally settled by those seeking freedom from religious persecution to the fact that Freemasonry strongly advocated religious toleration and was popular among many moving spirits of the American revolution. Three of Wilson's ten reasons seem particularly relevant to the establishing of the church-state separa-tion. First, the dominant values in the infant nation were liberalism and pluralism. Both emphasized freedom of choice and individual responsibility, an emphasis that extended into the area of religion. Second, the First Great Awakening, which began in 1734, strengthened the nonconformist spirit in the United States and helped break down the constraints of the old parish system upon which the Anglican Church largely depended. Third, the sheer number and variety of religious groups present by the time of the nation's founding made some sort of accommodation to pluralism necessary if the nation were not only to become united, but also to remain united. In addition, the voluntarism of most of these groups paved the way for religious pluralism and militated against a church in which citizenship and religious affiliation would be synonymous.

As we stated earlier, religious toleration, *chiefly* among Protestants, had begun before the ratification of the first amendment to the Constitution. Even in the Anglican and Congregationalist-dominated colonies, other religious groups coex-isted. The religious groups which gained most from the Great Awakening—the Presbyterians, the Methodists, and the Baptists—were anxious to receive this new "charter" which elevated their status and enhanced their sense of mission to the unchurched masses (Marty, 1970). Soon after the nation's founding, they began to move west to the frontier in an effort to fight the already existing religious apathy of the nation. The *voluntarism* of these groups, so necessary for the support of pluralistic religious groups, became the underpinning of the many religious bodies which gained an almost coequal status with the now disestab-lished colonial state churches.

Voluntarism

Established religion in America as well as in Europe had depended upon finan-cial support from the state. In exchange for the right to remain free from state control or interference, the churches of the United States had to be completely self-supporting and self-perpetuating. An emasculated establishment of religion, with each taxpayer assigning his tax rates to the church of his choice, continued in existence in three New England states. However, the other ten states of the new nation incorporated the principle of separation of church and state into their constitutions. Voluntary support allowed the revival churches (the Baptists, the Methodists, some Presbyterians, and later the Disciples of Christ) to attempt mass evangelism in the expanding frontier. Voluntary support from the wealthy planter class of Virginia saved the newly-named Protestant Episcopal Church (the American successor to the Anglican Church) from oblivion. When state sup-port of the Congregationalists finally came to an end in New England in 1832, those churches also survived through voluntarism.

Winthrop Hudson (1961:81-84) reports that voluntary societies sprang up first in New England and later in other seaboard states. Sunday schools, religious tracts (or pamphlets), religious periodicals, schools, colleges, and missionaries to the frontier territory were to be the beneficiaries of voluntary societies. The American Home Missionary Society was founded in 1826, its stated purpose was to promote "home missions" essential to the moral advancement and the political stability of the United States. There followed a series of frontier campaigns that stressed Bibles for every family, schools for all, and an abundance of pastors for the western settlers. These new churches, as well as the more established ones in the original thirteen states, depended heavily on voluntary support (Hudson, 1961:84-86).

The concept of voluntarism was a necessary complement to separation of church and state. In the premises of functional theory, this separation contributed to the stability of the nation by neutralizing any potential conflict to the state because of religion. Voluntarism, despite early nineteenth century efforts for united voluntary societies and financial support, did maintain a fragmented religious presence, albeit one with public tolerance. The churches which flourished supported the nation, its leaders, and its new political system; all in all, these groups supported the status quo. Voluntarism also allowed for some accommodation of more peculiar religious groups such as the Moravians, the Amish, and the Mennonites—whose exclusivity and communitarian characteristics stood in direct contrast to the more established and culturally approved Protestant denominations. Voluntarism also allowed for the beginnings of separate black Protestant churches, such as the African Methodist Epsicopal Church which began in 1816, in spite of the fact that white slave owners and non-slave owners alike agreed that the black American was no equal to the Anglo-Saxon. However, their feelings of paternalism led to the financial support for a separate denomination for free black Americans (Marty, 1970:27-28). Finally, voluntarism became the "salvation" of those most opposed to it: the New England Congregational Establishment. When Congregational churches began to embrace Unitarianism, or the disbelief in the Trinitarian view of God, they still enjoyed state support in Massachusetts, which resulted in tax monies going to "Unitarian Congregationalists." By disestablishing the churches, orthodox Congregationalists muted the growth as well as the influence of Unitarians, reducing them, in the end, to what Littell calls a "permanent minority" in America (1962:88). As the republic moved into its second fifty years, religious pluralism was tenuously established. Voluntarism had proven successful, allowing influential Protestant expansion into the western territories of the nation. The separation of church and state seemed to pose no threat to either party, since the state did not actively discourage religious beliefs and practices. "Freedom of religion was seen as belonging to the *individual* rather than to any religious group to which he might or might not belong . . ." (Pfeffer, 1974:13). There was genuine diversity in American religious life, but this was within a framework of Protestant unity. *Real* religious diversity, which would test the boundaries of pluralism, of church-state separation, and of voluntarism was about to unfold. The tensions—produced by conflicting religious groups, by a civil war, and by internal Protestant bickerings—were about to begin.

REASONS FOR RELIGIOUS DIVERSITY

Four historical processes can be seen as constituting the main reasons for the presence of religious diversity in America. The first was the influx of a large immigrant population into the United States, which was largely Roman Catholic. The second was the divisive effect of the Civil War, which divided many of the dominant Protestant denominations into northern and southern branches and which led to the further creation of separate churches for blacks. The third process was the division within evangelical Protestantism brought about by doctrinal differences among the frontier revival churches, the Unitarian schism in New England, the millenarian movement within Protestantism, and liberal theological developments which led to the Social Gospel and to the fundamentalist-modernist controversy. Finally, there was the immigration of large numbers of Jews into the country whose refusal to believe that Christ was the Messiah provided another foil to Christianity. Within the Protestant-dominated religion these historical processes created conflict during the nineteenth century which did not begin to subside until the 1930s. In addition to these major historical processes, the persistence of fringe sects, the recurring awakenings and revivals in religion, the ebb and flow of dominance by one particular religious group or another have also contributed to religious diversity within the United States.

From a functionalist theoretical perspective, religious pluralism that allows for religious diversity promotes social integration. No single religious group does, or can, dominate; and religious diversity diffuses moral and ethical values throughout the various levels of social class. Functionalism tends, then, to play down social conflict, particularly that of an earlier era, which seemingly has worked itself out so that equilibrium once again exists (Wilson, 1978:273-275). The competing (or complementary) conflict theoretical perspective plays up the potentiality for conflict that is caused by religious differences. Historical events provide the data by which an analysis based upon conflict theory, with its Marxist legacy, can provide an alternative explanation for religious diversity. The presence of a dominant Protestant establishment which equated itself with national expansionism, *laissez faire* capitalism, industrialization, and Christian manifest destiny provides some evidence that "religious differences" were used as tools to keep the growing numbers of urban workers economically depressed.

It can also be demonstrated that religious arrogance and paternalism maintained the economic and political oppression of black Americans, even after the same paternalism precipitated the abolition of slavery. The assumption of conflict theory, that conflict is a major source of social change, can help explain the fratricidal battles within Protestantism concerning the gloomy predictions of millenarian Protestants that the world's end was imminent; concerning the idealism of the Social Gospel that society, rather than individual souls, could be saved; and concerning the reconciliation of scientific knowledge and the inerrancy of the Bible. From these battles came at least two distinctive camps of Protestants which Martin Marty (1970) labels the "public Protestants" concerned with social action and political involvement, and the "private Protestants" concerned with pietistic living, personal salvation, and heavenly reward. Also altered was the overwhelming dominance of the American social structure by a rather monolithic Protestantism. Finally, there is an assumption of conflict theory that religion can operate to mask real divisions (such as economic and political divisions) by substituting racial and ethnic "differences" that are specious. The anti-Semitism that has surfaced from time to time in the United States can be seen as a means of preventing domination by Jews of parts of the economic order. Yet conflict theory does not explain that the historical processes which furthered religious diversity resulted finally in a rather peaceful, religiously diversified public, with representative members of most of the major religious groups within the higher levels of the stratification system. An analysis of these processes reveals both conflict and consensus, both social destructiveness and social change, and both intolerance and real accommodation.

The Growth of Roman Catholicism

At the time the nation began, Roman Catholics numbered only 20,000 and had but 56 parishes (Hudson, 1961). Their numbers did not begin to increase until the first immigration of Irish and continental Europeans, beginning in the 1880s. It did not take long for American Protestants to strike out against this other branch of Christianity. Politically, the Know Nothing Party sought to prevent economic and political pluralism insofar as it applied to Catholics. Several prominent Americans, including Samuel F. B. Morse, the inventor of the telegraph, published anti-Catholic tracts and made anti-Catholic speeches. The main theme was that Roman Catholics constituted a *foreign conspiracy*. Although the waves of immigrants included continental European Protestants (Lutheran and Reformed Church members), Jews, and infidels, these groups were assimilated by the national consciousness before the Civil War. The Catholic "hordes" posed the main threat to the Protestant establishment. Many spokesmen for Protestantism were to spend years in agitation for immigration laws and in attempts at legal limitation on Catholicism. The sheer number of

Irish and German Catholics who came was awesome. By 1850, there were 1,606,000 Roman Catholics. In 1816 there were only 6,000 Irish in the United States; by 1850, there were 961,719. German immigration was smaller, but did include a sizeable portion of German Catholics (Marty, 1970:124-128).

Proper evangelical Protestants were offended by the Germans' observance of the continental Sabbath. This nonpietistic custom included beer drinking and other robust entertainment, all held on Sunday. The Irish were viewed as poor, undependable, and untrustworthy drunkards. In general, the alien culture of a vast majority of Catholics provided a convenient target of blame for the increasing problems of poverty, unrest, and crime in the expanding population of the nation. The Know Nothing Party (properly named the American Party) disclosed lurid information concerning illicit sexual activities behind the doors of the Catholic convents. Best known of these phony exposes were *Six Months in a Convent* (1834) and *The Awful Disclosures of Maria Monk* (1836) (Myers, 1960:92). Shortly thereafter, in 1844, the Methodist bishops said that "Romanism is now laboring, not only to recover what it had of its former supremacy in the Reformation, but also to assert and establish its monstrous pretentions in countries never subject either to its civil or ecclesiastical authority"(Marty, 1970:129). It appears that the establishment Protestants, such as the Methodist bishops and other Protestant clergy, joined in the anti-Catholic crusade with almost as much vigor as the extremist "Know Nothings." When an occasional moderate Protestant spokesman dared to plead for tolerance of the Roman Catholics, his logic was usually met with further examples that "proved" conspiracy. Typical is the quote from the *Protestant Vindicator* in 1834:

> Jesuits are prowling about all parts of the United States in every possible disguise ... to disseminate Popery ... including puppet show men, dancing masters, music teachers, peddlers of images and ornaments, barrel organ players, and similar practitioners. (Marty, 1970:129-130)

During the 1850s, the political power marshalled against Roman Catholic immigration reached a frenzy. In 1854, the Know Nothing Party seated 8 of 62 United States Senators and 104 of 234 United States Representatives. It also controlled the governorships of 9 states (Myers, 1960:144). However, their extremist viewpoints failed to halt Catholic increase; and the extremist rhetoric proved too much for the majority of Americans. Moreover, the events leading up to the Civil War preoccupied most citizens. Protestant fanatics had failed to prove that a vast majority of the foreign-born Catholics were un-American (Marty, 1970:130).

After the Civil War, immigration continued at an even more rapid pace. As in the preceding decades, the cities became the repositories of the alien populations. Between 1820 and 1900, nineteen million immigrants arrived; one-fourth of these were Irish who landed in the urban cities of the East (and later the Midwest). Although it was their muscle that built much of the cities and fired the industrial machines, Protestants, in general, despised them. Because of religious (and ethnic) prejudice, most of the foreign-born stayed close together, particularly the Irish Catholics. Although they had been indifferent about the Church in Ireland, many contributed pennies and nickels from sacrifice wages in order to build the imposing edifices of urban Catholicism. The church became the center for a neighborhood under local Irish control. The Irish Catholics also built parochial schools to avoid too much Protestant influence upon their children (Marty, 1970:159).

These exclusive patterns were followed by other Catholic immigrant groups, due in large part to the dominance of the Catholic hierarchy and priesthood by Irishmen. Josiah Strong, a public relations agent for the Congregationalist Church and a Protestant moderate, wrote a book, *Our Country*, published in 1891. He revealed the extent to which Protestants feared, mistrusted, and resented Roman Catholics. Catholicism opposed the bases of national life; it was critical of popular sovereignty, free speech, free press, free conscience, free schools, and separation of church and state. Strong had heard the Catholic archbishop of St. Paul, Minnesota, announce the desire to make America Catholic. Such inflammatory statements suggested to Protestants that Catholics were out to destroy church-state separation. The decree of Papal Infallibility, issued in 1870-1871, demonstrated to Protestants that Catholics would be more responsive to a foreign infallible religious leader than to the civil leaders of the United States. Catholic numbers were estimated by spokesmen of the Catholic hierarchy at anywhere from 9 million to 13 million in 1889-1890. Strong also reported that there was one Protestant church organization to every 438 people of the population in 1890. In Boston, however, the ratio was 1 to 1,778; and in St. Louis, the ratio was 1 to 2,662. Worse. In Chicago, the ratio was 1 to 3,061 people of the 1890 population (Marty, 1970:155-160).

Protestants, however alarmed and distrusting they might be, were realizing that the Catholic presence was for real. The factory and the city were not going to disappear. Also, the problems of the city were not just the problems of a non-Protestant, alien population, because the agrarian economy of the United States was evolving into an industrial system which also attracted native-born rural Americans. The growing agitation for unionization by urban workers was interpreted by most middle-class Protestants as agitation for socialism. Intemperance, particularly on the part of the urban Catholic immigrant population, was viewed as a dangerous threat to rural, Christian values. The Democratic Party was again becoming influential by capturing the growing urban vote, and evangelical Protestants dubbed it the Party of "Rum, Romanism, and Rebellion." Catholic bishops and priests were at first cautious. By urging political participation they countered the charges that they were subservient to a "foreign power."

However, the highest-ranking Catholic cleric, Cardinal Gibbons, refused to condemn the Knights of Labor in 1887, and thereby gave tacit approval for Catholics to join in labor organizing. Affluent Protestantism, which in large part was antilabor, mistrusted and feared the Catholic masses *even more* after this. The efforts of Protestants, first to prevent and later to temper Catholic influence, can be seen as efforts to preserve Protestant hegemony. Their antiunionism can also be seen as an effort to preserve owner-dominated capitalism at the expense of the masses of the largely Catholic urban working class. Their attacks upon the city as a place of evil and irreligion can be seen as an effort to preserve the rural, conservative, and Protestant dominance in the political realm.

The War Between the States and the Growth of Black Churches

The second major historical process that contributed to religious division and diversity was the society-wide conflict that divided North and South in the United States. Slavery and the economic system that spawned it were attacked by abolitionist religious leaders in the North and defended by proslavery clergy in the South. Marty (1970:57:58) states that southern church leaders defended the two-nation theory of the secessionists as "God's plan for America." God was seen as a proslavery deity by southerners and as an antislavery deity by northerners. Historically, the influence of the Episcopal church and the eighteenth century deistic philosophy had contributed to the preeminence of the Southern colonies (and later states) in politics and in intellectual leadership. As a result of the First and Second Great Awakenings, Methodists, Baptists, and other more evangelical religious groups became the dominant churches of the southern states. Marty (1970:60-61) states also that in 1860, within the South and the Southwest, one-third of southern church members were Methodist, one-fourth were Baptist, one-fourth were Roman Catholic, and the rest were mostly Presbyterian and Disciples of Christ. Revivalism was as strong in the southern region as it was in the new territories of the northern section of the country.

Littell (1962) generally agrees with Marty's interpretation concerning the tension that developed between "Southern" and "Northern" religion even in the same denomination. Breakdown of communication between the sections of the country started with a breakdown of communication within the Methodist, Baptist, and Presbyterian churches. This created a situation in which the most strenuous efforts were made to suppress discussions concerning slavery, pro and con. This culminated in the Gag Law passed by the United States House of Representatives in 1832. This law tabled without discussion all petitions against slavery (Littell, 1962:62). Other religious issues entered the argument between the branches of the different Protestant denominations, but the issue of slavery and the economic survival of the agrarian South was always present. For example, Presbyterians in the southern states split initially concerning the propriety

185

of revivalism. The Presbyterians of the South allied themselves with the antirevivalism of the "Old Side" or "Old School" Presbyterians. In contrast, the prorevival "New Side" or "New School" Presbyterians were also abolitionists (Littell, 1962:64-65).

Methodists and Baptists, however, did not mask the issue of slavery as well as Presbyterians did. Even though most southerners did not own slaves, the perpetuation of this "peculiar institution" was seen as necessary by a majority of ordinary southerners. At the root of the southern defense was the fact that the Bible did not proscribe slavery. As the growing and exporting of cotton continued to increase in the South, the association of religion with race came to be a distinctive feature of southern thinking and economic rationalization. It contributed to the defense of the southern way of life (largely agrarian) and to the isolation of the rural South from the urbanizing and industrializing North (Marty, 1970:63-64). In 1845, Southern Baptists withdrew from their northern counterparts over the question of slavery. In that same year, the Methodists in the South became the Methodist Episcopal Church, South. In 1857, the Old School alliance between Presbyterians of both sections gave way to a formal Presbyterian Church within the southern states.

As the Civil War was fought, these divisions were exacerbated. During the war, the Emancipation Proclamation added further fuel to the division. Lincoln's "religious language" (although he was a member of no formal church) perpetuated the idea within the Union that the war was a "holy war" to preserve the common society. This belief was countered with the South's version of a "holy war" to create two distinctive nations (Marty, 1970). Although President Abraham Lincoln wanted the victorious Northern states to heal the deep wounds inflicted by the war, his death resulted in the ascension of radical Republican leaders who implemented vindictive reconstruction policies. As a result, the economically devastated South suffered even greater personal and political humiliation than would have occurred under Lincoln. In addition, the emancipation of slaves left the Southern region with about 4 million largely untrained, free people (Marty, 1970:134).

Northern church people saw their abolitionist cause vindicated; southern church people could only be confused and make vague references to "God's will." Largely left out of the religious thought of the South were the newly enfranchised black citizenry. The northern churches began concentrating on educational missions among blacks. Previously Protestant churches of the South had provided for the spiritual needs of the slaves through the establishment of some slave edifices, but largely through segregated seating in their own church buildings. During the Civil War, however, a mass exodus of blacks from the dominant southern churches began. In 1860 there had been 207,000 Southern Methodist blacks; in 1866, there were only 78,000 still on the church membership rolls. Southern Presbyterians experienced a 70 percent decline in black membership during the war years. This Presbyterian trend continued into the twentieth century and left almost no blacks within the Presbyterian church in the United States (the "Southern" Presbyterian church). Southern Baptists saw a similar black exodus, but because of the local autonomy of Baptist churches, their statistics are more tenuous (Marty, 1970:137).

For the remainder of the nineteenth century, and well into this one, the split between northern and southern Protestants continued to further divide the Protestant religious fraternity of the United States. The two dominant southern denominations, Methodist and Baptist, became the recipients of the evangelical and revivalistic traditions of nineteenth century Protestantism after the social gospel debates and the fundamentalist-modernist doctrinal controversy of the 1920s (these issues are discussed in greater detail in Chapter 8.) "Rural Protestantism" was the legacy left to southern Protestants after the Civil War and Reconstruction.

During the same period, the new status of blacks as office-holders in southern states aided in the further establishment and growth of all-black churches. As was stated earlier in this chapter, the African Methodist Episcopal Church was founded in 1816, and a rival group was formed out of the denomination a few years later. However, these churches were predominantly northern with members who were free blacks. After the Civil War, the black exodus from southern Protestant churches was welcomed by whites; the black person in the South was seen by the Protestant establishment as an ally of Republican reconstruction. Any mission to blacks was largely abandoned by southern church people, who established the policy of segregation in religion as well as in all other areas of social life (Marty, 1970:140). The blacks who remained within the Presbyterian and Methodist churches were members of segregated congregations. The emergence of a fourth religious community, a black religious community, followed this rigid segregation in the South and subsequent discrimination against blacks in the North (Winter, 1977:268-269). The subculture of black Americans included subcultural religion as well. (The black church is examined in greater detail in Chapter 13.)

It can be stated, then, that the economic and political conflict of sectionalism that resulted in the American Civil War had a divisive effect upon the dominant Protestant religious establishment. A division, almost as deep as that between Roman Catholics and Protestants, developed as a result of the slavery issue before the Civil War and of the racism that developed in the South after the conflict. This division resulted in a separate kind of culture religion in the southern states which emphasized segregation in religion, in education, and in daily social contacts. The evangelistic tradition of nineteenth century Protestantism remained firmly but separately embedded in the religious consciousness of southerners, both black and white. In a real sense, this further diversity in American religious life has perhaps perpetuated the caste system affecting black

Americans by providing "caste churches" for this largest of American minorities (Wilson, 1978:322). White supremacy reigned in the South, unthreatened by the presence of the children of God who happened to be nonwhite. Political reconstruction did end, and the South was fully restored to the Union. In the realm of "religious reconstruction," however, black Protestants did not win full participation in the religious affairs of either the South or the rest of the country. Other historical events which had begun before the Civil War continued to divide the dominant Protestant establishment of the United States.

The Divisions Within Evangelical Protestantism

The evangelical fervor of the Great Awakenings had become the dominating feature of American Protestantism by the early part of the nineteenth century, but the revival techniques characteristic of evangelicalism were not universally accepted. Even during the First Great Awakening of the late colonial period of history, the Puritan Congregational establishment divided itself into prorevival and antirevival segments. Likewise, Presbyterians suffered a similar schism following the Second Great Awakening of the early nineteenth century. As we stated earlier in this chapter, the primary recipients of these evangelical efforts were Baptists, Methodists, and the newly formed Disciples of Christ churches. The American frontier became the arena for Protestant revival efforts, and this common purpose of evangelizing the people in the new territories united these divergent Protestant groups for several decades. The concept of voluntarism, discussed earlier, provided financial support for these undertakings. The growth of an alien and Catholic population further unified Protestant efforts and provided a common foil which minimized Protestant differences in doctrine and church polity. Even the introduction of millenarianism, the belief in the imminent return of Christ to earth, into most American Protestant denominations did not fragment them at first. However, there did develop differences both in theology and in the nature and purpose of the Christian tradition that ultimately divided the Protestant denominations and weakened their dominance of the religious realm of the United States. The first of these was the doctrinal dispute concerning the concept of the Trinity—God the Father, God the Son, and God the Holy Spirit.

The nineteenth century opened with anti-Trinitarianism enjoying rather widespread support in the new nation. The enlightened thinkers of the eighteenth century had partially embraced "Unitarianism" through their infatuation with Deism. Thomas Jefferson stated in 1822, "I trust that there is not a young man now living in the United States who will not die a Unitarian" (quoted in Littell, 1962:42). John Calhoun, the distinguished senator from Kentucky, predicted that within fifty years Unitarianism would be the religion of the country. The rejection of a Trinitarian formula as a test of religious orthodoxy brought together not only intellectuals and New England elitists, but also many who opposed the rigid theological scholasticism of Calvanistic doctrine. As early as 1785, the historic Kings Chapel (Episcopal) in Boston altered its prayer book and embraced Unitarian ideas (Chworowsky and Raible, 1975:274). Because Massachusetts still provided state monies for churches (predominantly Congregational churches), those congregations which rejected Trinitarianism were able to obtain control of their buildings. In 1819, William Ellery Channing voiced this literal view in a sermon entitled "Unitarian Christianity." More churches joined the exodus from Congregationalism. The final result was the end to state support of churches in New England and the division of the old established church in New England into two smaller denominations, Congregationalism and Unitarianism (Marty, 1970:70).

The elitism of the Unitarians was to become their hallmark. They remained centered intellectually in eastern cultural circles and in literary and philosophical interests. They refused to participate in missionary activity both in the eastern states and on the frontier because such activity seemed incompatible with their views of the dignity of man (Littell, 1962:44–45). The doctrinal controversy between the New England Trinitarians and Unitarians was a hint of what was to develop within the ranks of Protestantism. A kind of religious toleration was permanently within Unitarianism but it did not quickly spread to the more exclusive denominations. On the frontier a similar controversy further divided Protestantism.

In the restitution movement which began under Thomas and Alexander Campbell, the goal was a restoration of primitive Christian unity. The Campbells believed that sectarian divisions among Christians were un-Christian and the cure for such divisions was the restoration of the New Testament church. For several years the new movement sought fellowship with both Presbyterians and Baptists, but these efforts failed. As a result, the movement became known as the "Christian Church" or the "Disciples of Christ." Like the Unitarians of New England, they refused to enforce the Trinitarian formula as a test of orthodoxy. There was some speculation that Unitarianism and the restitutionism of the Disciples of Christ would join forces, but there were too many differences between these groups. The Disciples were evangelical and used revival techniques. They were common folk who were largely uneducated, and they also were removed geographically and philosophically from New England. Finally, during the second generation of Unitarianism, German idealistic philosophy became dominant. As a result, transcendentalism, as exemplified through the writings of Ralph Waldo Emerson, moved the Unitarians further from the Disciples' goal of simple Christian unity (Littell, 1962:43–45).

As these attempts toward Protestant unity disintegrated, the support of a united Protestant ministry in the expanding nation fragmented into more sectarian voluntary efforts. Baptists, Methodists, Presbyterians, and the weakened

Congregationalists pursued similar, but nonetheless, different paths in extending Christianity. At the end of the Civil War, no attempts toward reunification of the split evangelical denominations were successful. As we said earlier, the defeated South continued a culture religion which excluded black Christians and included the isolated traditions of rural Protestantism. A different kind of culture religion developed in the northern tier of states. As immigrants (largerly Catholic) poured into the cities, so also did rural, native-born Americans. The virtures of the work ethic and *laissez-faire* capitalism were the features of transplanted urban Protestantism. The unique and obvious destiny of a Protestant America in the world provided a common goal for these denominations in the last three decades of the nineteenth century. To limit Catholic influence and to convert as many Catholic immigrants as possible were publicly stated aims. However, even these common efforts did not prevent further division within Protestantism.

As Protestant immigrants came to the Midwest, they were also viewed as somehow different and threatening to the evangelical denominations. Lutherans from the German states and members of European reformed churches practiced the customs of continental Sabbath just as did Roman Catholics. Furthermore, the Lutherans sought to preserve their liturgical traditions. Although Germans had been well-regarded in school textbooks, their arrivals in large numbers made them hard to absorb or to comprehend. Marty (1970:126) quotes a Methodist mission superintendent on the need to proselytize these Lutherans: "The Germans almost all belong to some church, and are strongly attached to what they call their faith. Hence, we have to preach their religion out of their heads in order to preach Bible religion into their hearts." These efforts largely failed, for few Lutherans of the German tradition converted to evangelical denominations, particularly those who settled into cities. Lutherans from Scandinavian countries settled in the upper Midwest and on the Great Plains. Among those immigrants an alliance with the larger evangelical bodies did develop. Their fear of Catholics and the sinfulness of the urban areas led to their adoption of the Protestant culture religion of the day. Still, the Lutherans remained apart from Methodists, Baptists, Presbyterians, and other evangelicals largely divided along ethnic lines. It was within the more established evangelical churches that the major issue would fragment American Protestantism for many decades. That issue consisted of two parts: a doctrinal dispute concerning Biblical inerrancy and an internal dispute over the mission of the church.

The rise of science and scientific discovery led to disputes over the creation of man and the universe. Biblical literalists insisted upon the accuracy of the account given in the book of Genesis. Proponents of Biblical criticism argued that this need not be a test of orthodoxy. Internal disputes within the Protestant evangelical bodies continued into the twentieth century. The applications of science that developed the mighty industrial machine in the cities provided the second part of the major divisive issue.

Washington Gladden of Ohio and Walter Rauschenbush of New York became known as proponents of the "social gospel." Basically, the social gospel involved ministering to the economic, political, and social needs of the rising number of urban poor. This was seen by complacent and conservative Protestants as a subversion of the Gospel. The old evangelical mission was concern for the salvation of the individual first, not an improvement of his or her living conditions. This was the position taken by the great evangelist of the late nineteenth century, Dwight L. Moody. Moody also preached a millenarian message that Christ would soon return to earth. Although his evangelism was supposedly aimed toward all the urban immigrants, Catholic and Protestant, he mainly preached to an already churched Protestant crowd (Marty, 1970).

Ultimately, the Protestant world would split into two distinct groups, "public" and "private" Protestants. The "public" Protestants sought to improve the conditions within the social order. Gradually, they rejected more and more the techniques of revivalism and personal conversions. On the other hand, the "private" Protestants cherished the "evangelical" traditions that had characterized all Protestants early in the nineteenth century. These church people accented individual salvation, or personal moral life characterized by piety, and heavenly rewards (Marty, 1970:179). The causes of this ultimate division and the consequences for Protestantism in the twentieth century are discussed in detail in Chapter 8. The inability of the two factions to reconcile their internal differences contributed to further diversity in American religious life. Minor splits involving "holiness" in living occurred within Methodism. Baptists in both the North and the South suffered schisms involving doctrinal disputes. The Disciples of Christ split into two camps, one conservative and one moderate. The present day Churches of Christ are the extremely conservative group, and the Disciples of Christ are moderate-to-liberal in their theological and social stances. In the end there developed a "third force in Christendom" (McLoughlin, 1967:43-68) composed of "private" Protestants in mainline denominations, fundamentalists, and members of small sects. Together these formed, at the beginning of the twentieth century, a pietistic culture religion which has competed, however unequally, with the social culture religion of mainstream Protestantism in this century.

This internal conflict created deep and permanent divisions within Protestant America. Some of the wounds did heal, but Protestants battling each other, particularly conservative and fundamentalist bodies fighting against the more moderate churches, has been second only to Protestants battling Roman Catholics. The absolute dominance of American religious life by Protestantism was permanently weakened by internal divisiveness. No longer able to stand united against Catholic growth, American Protestantism was faced with a fourth historical process which further promoted religious pluralism.

The Growth of Judaism in America

At the time of the disestablishment of the colonial state churches, Jews were present in the new nation, but they numbered only one-twentieth of one percent of the citizenry. Before the Civil War, they made little impact on the national consciousness; by 1848 only fifty congregations of Jew existed. Although anti-Semitism was a feature of the early post-Civil War Ku Klux Klan, this anti-Jewish prejudice did not fully bloom until much later. In the 1880s, the first large migration began to occur following pogroms against Jews in Russia; and almost all of the Jewish immigrants gravitated to the urban areas. Most of these Jews were secularized as a result of their Russian and Eastern European experiences. Some, but by no means all, were politically radical. They did not embrace the rural American virtues sustained by Protestants (Marty, 1970:38, 124-125, 160-161). Judaism offered the benefits of a homogeneous community against ethnic and religious bigotry; and as a result, Judaism in America has always seemed to be an ethnic subculture as well as a religion. This was aided in large part by the fact that the many immigrant families were by no means orthodox Jews. Most of the almost two million Jews who came between the end of the Civil War and the outbreak of World War I (1914) were influenced by the ideals of the European Enlightenment of the late eighteenth century. These rather secular Jews had undergone considerable emancipation from traditional Jewish observances. The earlier arriving German Jews, through their rabbis, developed what is now known as Reform Judaism. The appeal of this "branch" of the Jewish faith to the secularists among the migrants lay in its emphasis upon a liberal humanism and its adaptation of certain features of American Protestantism, notably voluntarism and religious education of the young (McNamara, 1974:211). However, this dose of humanism did not satisfy all of the newly arrived Jews. By the end of the nineteenth century, a reaction developed among Jews dissatisfied with such an amalgamation of liberalism and Protestantism. This produced the branch of that faith now known as Conservative Judaism. Emphasis was upon Jewish traditions, but not upon strict orthodoxy. Fidelity to Jewish law, literature, and language was preeminent; but flexibility concerning American traditions was also included (Sklare, 1971:269). The conservative position, however, was not the compromise that would provide unification of America's growing Jewish populations. The Eastern European Jews who formed the second wave of Jewish immigration at the end of the nineteenth century were a mix of people who adhered to religious orthodoxy and to political radicalism such as socialism and anarchism (McNamara, 1974:212).

Both the orthodoxy of some of these Eastern European Jews and the widely publicized unorthodox political views of other Jews served as impediments to the quiet assimilation of earlier Jewish immigrants. The strict customs of Orthodox Judaism seemed repugnant to both American Protestants and Catholics. Because the Roman Catholic Church still blamed the death of Christ upon all Jews, tensions quickly developed between Catholic and Jewish enclaves within the growing cities. In addition, American evangelical Protestants were also mildy anti-Semitic, based upon historical interpretations of Biblical teachings. The growing presence of Judaism, particularly in the cities, added fuel to the smoldering fires of anti-Jewish prejudice.

Throughout history, the form and substance of anti-Semitism has varied. The long association between Jews and banking and finance in certain European nations was certainly a factor in much of the anti-Semitism directed against them as more and more arrived in the United States. This was particularly true of the anti-Semitism demonstrated by other European immigrants. As early as the 1880s, Jews were suspected in some quarters of economic manipulation and exploitation. Curiously, the later immigrants were relatively poor, and most were crowded into tenement houses in New York City's lower east side and in other urban areas. Several decades passed before the upward mobility of Jews took place on a large scale. (This phenomenon is discussed in greater detail in Chapter 13.) Nevertheless, anti-Jewish prejudice, so long a part of Western civilization, became a part of the religious as well as the economic and political fabric of the United States.

Although there were no European-style pogroms against Jews, their acceptance by Protestants and by Roman Catholics was long in coming. Partly as a reaction to these hostilities, American Jews, unlike the majority of Catholics who came from Europe, have rejected the idea that assimilation is the end toward which they should strive (Sklare, 1971:4). Thus, while there were fewer public conflicts between Jews and others than there were between Protestants and Catholics, their addition of a third dimension to American religious diversity did not come easily.

The Growth of Exclusive Religious Groups and Sects

A final process that contributed to religious diversity in the United States was the ebbing and flowing of communitarian experiments, religious sects adhering to particularistic beliefs, and subsequently the development of three uniquely American sects. These three are Mormonism, Christian Science, and Jehovah's Witnesses. In addition, there are many more, smaller, bodies which have split from the larger Protestant groups. Within Judaism there are smaller exclusive groups which adhere to the historical traditions of that religion more than most American Jews do. Even within Roman Catholicism there are old order churches such as Polish Old Catholics and the Byzantine Rite Church (Clark, 1947). But the three groups of "American origin" are generally seen by religious historians as the best examples of American religious originality in the infinite variety of the world's religions (Littell, 1962:83).

Exclusive religious communities date back to colonial times. In the late 1600s, Mennonites and Amish arrived in Pennsylvania. In the early 1700s, Moravians (or German pietists) migrated to Pennsylvania and later to North Carolina. During the early decades of America, several communitarian experiments with religious overtones were established. Marty (1970:123) states that the Shakers, Rappities, Zoar, Oneida, Amana, Owenites, and others tested the limits of religious consensus and encountered various degrees of ostracism, persecution, and martyrdom.

None of these communities, however, was as disturbing as was Mormonism, which began in the western part of New York. Littell (1962:83-84) states that it is best understood as one of the many variant movements which came from theocratic Puritanism. Its founder, Joseph Smith, advocated polygamy because it was present in the Old Testament. Latter day revelations, or an extension to Biblical teachings, became a part of the tradition of Mormonism. The early Mormons viewed America as the continent upon which the Ten Tribes of Israel would be restored and would be reigned over personally by Christ. When the followers of Smith were driven from New York to Illinois, many establishment Protestants viewed them as a greater threat to religious life than Roman Catholics (Marty, 1970:124-125). Smith was killed by an armed mob in Carthage, Illinois, in 1844; and his successor, Brigham Young, led the group into the Salt Lake Valley in the Utah territory in 1847. During the 1850s and 1860s, some 80,000 Mormon pioneers migrated west. Of these, more than 6,000 died in route (Evans, 1975:187-188).

The Church of Jesus Christ of Latter-Day Saints' settlement in the western part of the United States—chiefly in Utah, southern Idaho, and most of Nevada—now claims almost a monopoly in the political, economic, and religious spheres (Hargrove, 1979:202). This was accomplished by the church's "giving up" polygamy in exchange for statehood. In 1870, in *Reynolds v. the United States*, the Supreme Court unanimously ruled that while Mormons were free to believe what they wished regarding plural marriages, their actions must stay within the laws of the state (Hargrove, 1979:210-211). Through extensive proselytizing, the Church of Jesus Christ of Latter-Day Saints has increased its membership not only in those states, but throughout the United States. The church's emphasis upon large families, the subservience of wives to husbands, and the virtues of the work ethic have attracted many converts to this conservative approach to life.

Christian Science, by contrast, did not proselytize but claimed that its possession of an esoteric body of knowledge would lead people to a new vision of the world. Intellectually, it was based on a simplified reading of the tenets of German Idealism: evil has no real existence; and positive, manifest prosperity is a mark of triumphant living and divine favor. When Mary Baker Eddy founded this movement in 1875, she had only a small number of followers in a poor suburb of Boston (Littell, 1962:89). Mrs. Eddy published *Science and Health with Key to the Scriptures*. She and her followers stressed the reinstatement of primitive Christianity and its lost element of healing. Unity of mind between God and people became the chief tenet of faith—a kind of simplified transcendentalism (Stokes, 1975:69-70). Her quiet zeal led to the formation of churches in all of the major cities of the United States and Europe. Her stress on the evidence of spiritual well-being, as well as on spiritual healing, fit in with an upper middle-class belief in prosperity. While Christian Science grew rather slowly in the first half of the twentieth century, it now has influence far beyond its estimated 300,000 members. For example, *The Christian Science Monitor* remains an influential newspaper. The legality of Christian Science Practitioners in healing is now unquestioned, since fees paid to them are tax deductible. In spite of their influential role in America's religious development, the exclusivity of Christian Science is seen by its lack of interdenominational cooperation and its attempts at supression of books and articles deemed unfriendly to its cause (Littell, 1962:90).

The third "American" contribution to religious bodies is the Jehovah's Witnesses, a millenarian movement founded by Charles Taze Russell in 1872. In 1831, this former Congregationalist incorporated it as the Watch Tower Bible and Tract Society. It, like Mormonism and Christian Science, claimed to represent a restitution of primitive Christianity. Teachings included an imminent second coming of Christ followed by a millennium, or thousand year reign upon the earth (Littell, 1962:90-91). In the beginning, the Jehovah's Witnesses were proletarian, and they have remained that way throughout their history. Their original appeal was to the dispersed working people and to the poor. According to Zygmunt (1970:926-948), Witnesses have maintained and intensified their opposition to worldly life. In spite of continuing failures in predicting accurately the Second Coming of Christ, they have become more vigorous and militant over time. Jehovah's Witnesses have always cited the Biblical authority for their name and particularly for their belief that only 144,000 will ultimately be saved and permitted to live in Heaven (Henschel, 1975:132). The central preoccupation of this sect was, and is, proselytism. Their evangelism has become a warning and rescue operation, with deliverances from the world as a major theme (Zygmunt, 1970:946). In a way similar to the Mormons, the Witnesses have experienced organized opposition by government and by private groups. During 1940 alone, more than 335 cases of mob violence against Jehovah's Witnesses in 54 states was documented. Arrests of group members were widespread; and because of this, court action was sought by the sect. They finally won the right *not* to salute the American flag in 1943 (Wilson, 1978:197). Thus, their right to exist as an alternative to traditional forms of Christianity has been hard fought. More than most millenarian organizations, the Jehovah's Witnesses have survived organizationally, have maintained their "last days" appeal, and have continued to convert thousands of people to their peculiar beliefs (Zygmunt, 1970:947).

THE ASCENDANCE OF RELIGIOUS PLURALISM

The historical processes which account for religious diversity in the United States were each marked with religious and political conflict. By the twentieth century, however, Protestant dominance of American religious life was almost finished. Roman Catholic populations in the cities began to exercise political power through urban Democratic Party machines, which culminated in the largely anti-Catholic Temperance Movement as a reaction against growing Catholic power. The coercive side of this crusade drew a heavy line between the Anglo-Saxon Protestantism of rural and small town American and the non-Anglo-Saxon Catholicism of the cities. Rum, Romanism, and rebellion were pitted against Prohibition, Protestantism, and patriotism. The passage of the Eighteenth Amendment to the Constitution was the last time that Protestants were to attempt to preserve their brand of American morality (Wilson, 1978:313-314). Prohibition, of course, was a failure almost from the start. Not only did Roman Catholics violate the laws against drinking, but so also did Protestants. In addition, the Prohibition decade saw an upswing in overt anti-Catholicism: ethnic differences as perceived among Catholics continued to be important to middle-class Protestants, and the Roman Catholic Church in America continued to be viewed as the church of immigrants (McNamara, 1974:167).

The Protestant middle class during the 1920s also gave its support to a revived Ku Klux Klan. This resulted partially as an outgrowth of extreme xenophobia manifest during World War I and partially as a continuing fear of Catholics' foreign allegiances and their perceived desire to unite church and state. By 1922, the Klan was operating in all states; and by 1925, it had grown to a membership of eight million (Wilson, 1978:314). Roman Catholic leaders reacted to that atmosphere in one of two ways. A minority of them tried to further "Americanize" the church. They emphasized freedom and democracy as a climate in which Roman Catholicism would flourish. The majority of Catholic leaders, however, reacted much more defensively. They sought to protest Catholics from a continuing Protestant hostility and warned communicants against cooperating with non-Catholics in political and social ventures (McNamara, 1974:167-168). Parochial schools were continued, the ethnic diversity among Catholics was encouraged through the maintenance of neighborhood parishes, and ties to Rome and to international Catholicism were stressed. Social, charitable, and religious activities were the features of the typical urban neighborhood parish. All in all, a common Catholic front against Protestant prejudice was the dominant response of American Catholicism until World War II (Greeley, 1977:189-190).

The same Protestant middle class also continued some hostility toward Judaism. The Ku Klux Klan was also anti-Semitic, both for religious and economic reasons. Beginning in the 1920s, American Jews began to practice an upward mobility. By using the mechanism of higher education, they began to enter many professions and occupations that were formerly hard for them to enter. Still, there remained difficulties for Jews in gaining entrance into top corporate-management positions, governmental posts, and political offices (Wilson, 1978:317). Covenant agreements in exclusive neighborhoods and suburbs prevented Jewish home ownership. Private clubs and resorts often were "closed" to Jews. The reaction of Americans who were Jewish was usually one of withdrawal. The synagogue became more and more a social as well as a religious meeting place. In ways similar to Roman Catholics, Jews began their own charitable organizations, social service agencies, and social clubs (McNamara, 1974:212-213). It was not until World War II and the subsequent knowledge of Nazi atrocities perpetrated against European Jews that anti-Semitism in the United States became more muted.

In the midst of anti-Catholic and anti-Jewish sentiment, Protestantism continued to fight among itself. The outcome of the fundamentalist-modernist controversy of the 1920s resulted in the dominance of a complacent moderate-to-liberal Protestant culture religion everywhere but in the South. Southern Protestantism, along with the fundamentalism of the North, continued to emphasize narrow doctrinal views, personal evangelism, and piety. Black Protestant churches were largely ignored in all parts of the society. During the 1930s the economic depression preoccupied most Americans. With the outbreak of World War II, however, religion once again supported the national war effort, but with less overt fervor than in World War I or in the Civil War (Wilson, 1978:200). Persecution of fringe sects such as the Jehovah's Witnesses did take place; but by the end of World War II, religious diversity was a permanent reality in the United States. Loyalty to the nation had been demonstrated by Catholics, by Jews, by blacks, and even by Japanese-Americans whose religion was outside the Judeo-Christian tradition.

SUMMARY

Religious pluralism implies a coequal existence of diverse religious groups within one society. Such coequality was not always characteristic of American society. Religious discrimination against dissenters was widespread in the New England colonies and in the Southern colonies. A suspicion of the political liability of theocratic states as well as agitation from nonestablishment religious groups led the early political leaders of the new American nation to guarantee religious freedom within the United States through an amendment to the Constitution.

Even this legal guarantee did not automatically assure the coexistence of different and unique religious groups. The citizens of the early United States were overwhelmingly Protestant; and, to them, religious diversity meant Protestant diversity. Not until Catholics began migrating to the United States after 1830 in increasing numbers did the religious persons within the United States accept this other branch of Christianity. This acceptance was slow and was also aided by the preoccupation of native-born Americans with the Civil War and Reconstruction.

As a result of this national trauma several Protestant denominations split into "Northern and Southern" bodies. The southern groups for the most part excluded the free slaves who were overwhelmingly Protestant. This resulted in the formation of more separate black Protestant denominations continuing a trend which began with "free" blacks forming separate Methodist Churches before the Civil War.

Intra-Protestant divisiveness over orthodox doctrine, scientific explanations of creation versus Biblical explanations, and revivalism versus social action further contributed to religious diversity. So also did the formation of groups which either rejected or modified traditional Christian doctrine, such as the Unitarians, the Mormons, the Christian Scientists, and the Jehovah's Witnesses. Each of these unorthodox bodies overcome hostility from traditional American Protestants and took over their place in the religious realm of America.

Finally, the influx of large numbers of Jews, first from Germany, and subsequently from Eastern Europe, added an additional dimension to religious groups, the Reform, the Conservative, and the Orthodox. Unlike Protestants, the divided groups within Judaism were able to maintain a sense of community which was both ethnic and religious.

By the end of World War II, religious pluralism was a reality in America. By demonstrating loyalty to the United States, Catholics, Jews, and members of Protestant fringe sects won begrudging acceptance from the formerly dominant Protestant establishment.

REFERENCES

Clark, Elmer T.
 1947   *The Small Sects in America.* Nashville, Tennessee: Abington Press.

Chworosky, Karl M. and
Christopher Gist Raible
 1975   "What is a Unitarian Universalist?" Pp. 263-276 in Leo Rosten (ed.), *Religions of America: Ferment and Faith in an Age of Crisis.* New York: Simon and Schuster.

Evans, Richard L.
 1975   "What is a Mormon?" Pp.186–199 in Leo Rosten (ed.), *Religions of America: Ferment and*

Faith in an Age of Crisis. New York: Simon and Schuster.

Greeley, Andrew M.
1977   *The American Catholic: A Social Portrait.* New York: Basic Books.

Hargrove, Barbara
1979   *The Sociology of Religion: Classical and Contemporary Approaches:* Arlington Heights, Illinois: AHM Publishing Corp.

Henschel, Milton G.
1975   "Who are Jehovah's Witnesses?" Pp. 132-141 in Leo Rosten (ed.), *Religions of America: Ferment and Faith in an Age of Crisis.* New York: Simon and Schuster.

Hudson, Winthrop S.
1961   *American Protestantism.* Chicago: University of Chicago Press.

Littell, Franklin
1962   *From State Church to Pluralism: A Protestant Interpretation of Religion in American History.* Chicago: Aldine.

Marty, Martin
1970   *Righteous Empire: The Protestant Experience in America.* New York: Dial Press.

McLoughlin, William C.
1967   "Is there a third force in Christendom?" *Daedalus* 96 (Winter):43:68.

McNamara, Patrick H.
1974   *Religion American Style.* New York: Harper and Row

Myers, Gustavus
1960   *The History of Bigotry in the United States.* New York: Capricorn Books.

Pfeffer, Leo
1974   "The Legitimation of marginal religions in the United States." Pp. 9-26 in Irving Zaretsky and Mark Leone (eds.), *Religious Movements in Contemporary America.* Princeton, New Jersey: Princeton University Press.

Sklare, Marshall
1971   *America's Jews.* New York: Random House
Stokes, J. Buroughs
1975   "What is a Christian Scientist?" Pp. 69-82 in

Leo Rosten (ed.), *Religions of America: Ferment and Faith in an Age of Crisis.* New York: Simon and Schuster.

Wilson, John
1978

Religion in American Society: The Effective Presence. Englewood Cliffs, New Jersey: Prentice-Hall.

Winger J. Alan
1977

Continuities in the Study of Religion: Creed, Congregation, and Community. New York: Harper and Row.

Zygmunt, Joseph F.
1970

"Prophetic Failure and Chiliastic Identity: The Case of Jehovah's Witnesses." *American Journal of Sociology* 75 (May):926-948.

Chapter 7

Current Trends
in Religious Life

At the end of World War II, Americans of virtually all religious groups defined worldwide communism as the common enemy of American religion. "Godless, atheistic, communism" provided a common foil for the religious. The most militant expression of this sentiment came from the Protestant fundamentalists, but other Protestants, conservative Catholics, and even liberal, humanistic Jews joined in a defense of the "American Way of Life" which was procapitalistic and proreligious. As the decade of the 1950s began, a new culture religion extremely popular with almost all segments of the American population emerged. There were really three representative people involved in this popularization of religion. For moderate Protestants, Norman Vincent Peale, a Reformed church minister, was the chief proponent of "religious positive thinking"; for Catholics, Bishop Fulton J. Sheen of New York used the new medium of television as a vehicle for popular inspiration and advice; and for conservative and fundamentalist Protestants, Billy Graham used the techniques of revivalism to further promote America's religious heritage and its need for continuing religious commitment. Brotherhood Weeks and interfaith observances included Jews as well as Christians. At no time in the history of the United States had American society demonstrated so much overt religiosity.

By 1950, 57 percent of Americans were church members; and by the end of that decade, 63 percent were members. Public opinion polls revealed that almost 50 percent of the American people claimed to attend church weekly. Table 7-1 illustrates this increase. Although Catholic attendance increased, Protestant churches were the chief beneficiaries of this apparent religious revival. This generalized religion and morality adapted the Protestant doctrine of God and portrayed him as a convenient and benign figure (Marty, 1970:259). Cooperation, an acceptance of religious pluralism, and the complacency of religious organizations produced what has come to be known as *ecumenicism*. The concept has a number of meanings. It can mean no more than interdenominational cooperation, or it can mean common work through federation or corporate bodies. Finally, it can mean an organic union of separate denominations (Wilson, 1978:424). The ecumenical movement emerged as one response to religious pluralism in the United States.

1978:424). The ecumenical movement emerged as one response to religious pluralism in the United States.

ECUMENICISM

The reversal of the nineteenth century pattern of division began with the establishment of the Federal Council of Churches in 1908. However, because of continuing Protestant in-fighting, this interdenominational organization made little historical impact. In the 1930s the theological position known as "neo-orthodoxy" gained a wide following among American Protestants. Under the leadership of Reinhold Niebuhr, this doctrinal interpretation became a synthesis of the socioeconomic liberalism of the social gospel, with stress on the fall of man and the judgment of God (Rosten, 1975:619). Its acceptance led to the reduction of theological differences characteristic of Protestant denominationalism. In 1939, the Methodist Episcopal Church, the Methodist Episcopal Church-South, and the Methodist Protestant Church reunited. This was the first of several denominational mergers and paved the way for further plans of union and interdenominational cooperation. At the end of World War II, this cooperation began on a much larger scale.

Figure 7-1: Church Membership and Church Attendance 1940–1960*

*Data for this figure are taken from Benson Y. Landis, editor. *Yearbook of American Churches, 1964* (New York: National Council of Churches in the U.S.A.)

The National Council of Churches in Christ

In 1950 and 1951, the moribund Federal Council of Churches was supplanted by the newly formed National Council of Churches in Christ. In addition to the original twenty or more Protestant denominations that were members of the old Federal Council, some of the Lutheran bodies also joined. Between 1951 and 1968, ten more denominations, including the Eastern Orthodox Church, became members of the Council. Previously independent ventures in missions, in education, in stewardship, and in mass communications were absorbed by the new council (Wilson, 1978:427). The popular culture religion of the 1950s which blurred denominational differences promoted the practice of *comity* among the participating Council denominations. This process encouraged various churches to develop joint planning and strategy in order to avoid overlap. This "staking out of the territory" also fostered denominational "switching" by an increasingly mobile and suburbanite people. The mainline Protestant churches deemphasized membership requirements; accepted certificates of transfer from other denominations; and promoted common points of unity in the form of ecumenical Thanksgiving services, world-wide Communion Sundays, and, occasionally, the creation of union community churches with pan-denominational support. The ecumenical spirit of the National Council of Churches also furthered the development of the World Council of Churches, which was a larger, but more loose-knit, world federation of cooperating denominations. Even more than the national federation, this example of international ecumenicism concentrates on the practical side of church work: missionary work in the non-Christian world, disaster relief and charity, and attempts at doctrinal agreement (Wilson, 1978:428).

Denominational Mergers

The reunion of the three major Methodist denominations in 1939 served as an example to other Protestant Christians. Beginning in 1957, a unique merger took place between the Congregationalist-Christian Church (the successors to New England Puritanism) and the Evangelical and Reformed Church (the transplanted European Reformed Church). Although each merging denomination possessed a tradition of polity that was different, the local autonomy of the Congregationalist, and the synodical relationship of the Evangelical and Reformed congregations, became a loosely-knit, connected system. In 1958, two of the four Presbyterian bodies united. The Presbyterian Church in the United States of America and the United Presbyterian Church became the United Presbyterian Church in the United States of America. (The "southern" Presbyterian Church in the United States and the rural Cumberland Presbyterian Church remained separate denominations.) This uniting trend continued throughout the 1960s.

Lutheran churches of Norwegian, Danish, and German background united in 1960 to form the American Lutheran Church. Two years later the United

Lutheran Church, whose history traced back to colonial times, joined the Augustana (Swedish) Lutheran Church, and smaller synods of Finnish and Danish backgrounds. They became the Lutheran Church in America. Both of these Lutheran denominations practice aspects of ecumenicism, but the Lutheran Church in America is the more ecumenical of the two bodies. The Lutheran Church-Missouri Synod did join with the other two large Lutheran bodies to form the Lutheran Council in the United States of America in 1965, but it did not participate in larger ecumenical activities (Raff and Standerman, 1975:157). At about the same time, the two most liberal of Christian groups joined together. The American Unitarian Association merged with the Universalist Church of America to become the Unitarian Universalist Association in 1961 (Rosten, 1975:620). This represented a common religious community that stressed liberal humanism and, generally, liberal political activities.

The decade of the 1960s finally saw the merger of the Methodist church with the smaller but similar Evangelical United Brethren. In 1967 the two denominations became the United Methodist Church. An important feature of this unification was the elimination of the all-black Central Jurisdiction of the Methodist Church. That internally segregated component of Methodism was a necessary compromise with southerners in the original Methodist merger of 1939. As important as these church unions were, they usually involved the reuniting of similar groups, with the United Church of Christ as the exception. Another more dramatic plan of union was also proposed at the close of the 1950s. In 1960, the Consultation of Church Union (COCU) was initiated by Presbyterians, Episcopalians, Methodists, and the United Church of Christ. In 1962, the Disciples of Church joined, and formal negotiations began. The southern branch of Presbyterianism, the Presbyterian Church in the United States, affiliated with COCU in 1966. In that same year and the next, two large black Protestant denominations participated in the discussions: the African Methodist Episcopal Church and the African Methodist Episcopal Zion Church. They were followed by the third largest black Methodist body, the Christian Methodist Episcopal Church, in 1967. So far, negotiations have proceeded cautiously and no sweeping Christian merger is in sight. Its goal remains an organic union of mainline Protestantism (Wilson, 1978:429).

Ecumenicism Between Christian Groups and Judaism

Because of the historical processes of immigration, which fostered interfaith prejudices, ecumenicism among the three major faiths of America has proceeded cautiously. The defensive response of ethnic Catholics to Protestant suspicion and overt discrimination precluded any rush toward embrace. Likewise, the subcultural aspects of American Judaism minimized religious fraternization for many decades. Charitable endeavors and symbolic days of interfaith cooperation were about the only examples of ecumenicism until the 1960s. However, the gradual lowering of religious barriers in the 1950s, the eventual tolerance of Billy Graham by the Roman Catholic hierarchy, and the end to the political intolerance of Protestants toward Catholics through the election of Catholic John F. Kennedy to the Presidency in 1960 set the scene for Christian interfaith cooperation.

The Catholic church sent its first official observers to the assembly of the World Council of Churches in 1961. Protestants were official observers at the Second Vatican Council, 1962-1965, convened by Pope John XXIII, which fostered new Catholic and Protestant working relationships at an institutional level. The hierarchy of the Roman Catholic Church moved closer to the position that church divisions are harmful not only to Protestants but also to Catholics. Vatican II also affirmed support for the World Council of Churches and acknowledged the ecclesiastical reality of non-Catholic denominations (Wilson, 1978:429-430). The translation of Catholic liturgy from Latin into vernacular languages made Catholic observances and services more comprehensible to non-Catholics. Also, the end of the practice by which a non-Catholic marriage partner agreed that the children of such a union would be reared in the Catholic faith diminished Protestant prejudice toward Catholics. Finally, the participation of Catholics in Protestant and Jewish services promoted interfaith ecumenicism. Still, Jews have remained the weakest of the three interfaith partners. Protestant-Catholic cooperation has seemed to progress at a more rapid pace than has Christian-Jewish cooperation. Whereas serious discussion concerning doctrinal reconciliation between Protestants and Catholics is occurring, only cultural and charitable ventures are conducted by Jews and Christians. There are limits, obviously, to interfaith ecumenicism. Interfaith limitations involve the lack of cooperation among Christian bodies and differences over whether or not religious pluralism in America is a true "melting pot" of religions.

Limits to Interfaith Ecumenicism

While the mainline Protestant denominations do exhibit a cooperative spirit, significantly large minorities of Protestant Christians *do not* share in this venture. The largest of Protestant denominations, the Southern Baptist Convention (with 13 million members), remains outside of the National Council of Churches. Likewise, another strong evangelical body, the Churches of Christ (with 2.4 million members), believe that they are the only "real" New Testament Church and therefore refuse cooperation with other Protestants. The Lutheran Church-Missouri Synod (with 3 million members) also exhibits almost no interfaith cooperation because of beliefs concerning Biblical literalism and orthodox Lutheran doctrinalism. All of the sectarian bodies (such as Seventh Day Adventists, Pentecostal groups, and the Assemblies of God) that can be classified as growing conservative churches (Kelley, 1972) are also outside the ecumenical movement. Thus, even within Protestant Christianity, serious divisions remain. Among those who express some support for Christian unity, there remains some pessimism concerning ultimate union. James Kelly (1971) provides one empirical study of attitudes toward ecumenicism.

The majority of each congregation questioned by Kelly, with the exception of Jews in two synagogues, accept the convergence theory of Protestant and Catholic doctrinal development. This concept is simply the idea that Protestant-Catholic dialogue will produce a blend of agreement on religious essentials and freedom of differences on religious nonessentials. The first statement to which people responded simply said, "It seems to me that Protestants and Catholics are becoming more and more alike in their religious beliefs and practices." All Protestants and all Catholic respondents overwhelmingly agreed with the statement. However, the issue of future Protestant-Catholic union produced a different response among the survey population. The statement involved was, "Unity among Protestant, Roman Catholic, and Eastern orthodox churches will always prove to be impossible." Such a union was seen as impossible by the great majority of sect members (72 percent), and by a slight majority of Unitarians (54 percent), and of Jews (54 percent). Mainline Protestants were uncertain on this question. A sizeable plurality (48 percent) felt that such union would always be impossible. The majority of Protestants either expressed uncertainty (22 percent) or expressed its possibility (30 percent). By contrast, Roman Catholics either felt that church union is possible (48 percent) or expressed uncertainty concerning it (22 percent). When questioned concerning a Protestant union, only sectarian groups (57 percent) disapproved of this (Kelly, 1971:341-351).

Quinley (1974:91) indicates that only 29 percent of his sample of California clergy supported the eventual union of all Protestant denominations. Sixty percent, however, indicated that they would favor the merger of their local congregation with one of another denomination if financial exigencies dictated this. Although an overwhelming majority of church people who know of the activities of the National Council of Churches looked favorably on its goals and its work (Johnson and Cornell, 1972:108), opposition to ecumenicism is nevertheless present, even within those denominations that support it.

Hadden (1969) uses the Glock and Stark data (1968) concerning religious beliefs of Christian laypeople to illustrate the existence of important doctrinal differences within denominations. He shows that *denominationalism* (the antithesis of ecumenicism) is a powerful force in influencing what people believe about Christian doctrine. Furthermore, an important fact is that within denominations and even within individual congregations that is a significant degree of dissension. For Hadden, this represents a dilemma for Protestantism: "There is no consensus as to what is believed, as to what is central and what is peripheral, nor is there any clear authority to resolve the uncertainty" (Hadden, 1969).

These differences, mainly between pietists and humanists, probably account for the fact that in terms of social issues, clergy were more "liberal" than were lay respondents in attitudes toward the Vietnam War and toward increased racial integration (Hadden, 1969:198-205). Since the ecumenical movement generally has been identified with cooperative social activism, those laypersons more conservative in both doctrinal beliefs and political beliefs tend to show less enthusiasm for ecumenical activities. Such individuals are not necessarily opposed to intrafaith cooperation, but they simply are more cautious concerning an expanding (and less controllable) religious bureaucracy that is responsible to a variety of religious denominations. Such an organization is viewed as more likely to promote "liberal" causes such as increased welfare spending, support of women's rights, abortions, and international religious cooperation (McNamara, 1974).

Consequently, conservative lay organizations have developed within the United Methodist, the United Presbyterian, and the Protestant Episcopal denominations in order to slow down ecumenical cooperation and to promote more traditional moral and spiritual values (Pratt, 1972:84). Financial retribution by conservative laity resulting in cutbacks in church contributions began in earnest in 1969. The most socially activistic (and ecumenical) denominations experienced the largest financial declines (Johnson and Cornell, 1972). Because of these pressures by laypeople, the ecumenicity of the 1970s has begun to emphasize personal evangelism and its compatibility with social concerns. The rise of contemporary evangelicalism, discussed in Chapter 8, is no doubt influential in this new convergence. Neo-Pentecostalism among both Protestants and Catholics further contributes to a convergence. Nevertheless, there remain important differences both in religious beliefs and practices that account for the limitations on interfaith ecumenicism during the 1970s.

The Three Culture Hypothesis

Because of the strides made by various ethnic groups toward assimilation by the 1950s, a popular thesis was advanced by Will Herberg (1960). According to Herberg, the bond between religious affiliation and ethnic identity was supposed to have loosened; and, consequently, those second and third generation immigrant Americans were expressing more generalized feelings of religious identification with one of the three major American faiths (1960:34). The three major faiths were seen as different cultural manifestations of a basic American unity, and central to this unity was a common set of values related to the American way of life. The "religiousness" characteristic of that era was a way of sociability and of "belonging" (Herberg, 1960:260). Herberg's thesis attracted much attention. Interfaith cooperation was proceeding, church attendance was high, and knowledge of specific and individual religious beliefs were low. Greeley (1974:108) paraphrased the Herberg thesis by stating that America's religious communities

207

help their members "define who they are and where they stand in a large and complex society."

Although Herberg's analysis appears to apply to all Americans, it is most directly applicable to the largely eastern and southern European ethnics. Among those ethnics of second generations, differences did *appear* to be disappearing. However, since religious identification *is* a part of ethnicity, Herberg seemed to ignore that ethnic barriers to intermarriage and friendships, for example, remained intact (Winter, 1977). Many divisions within Roman Catholicism remained fixed along ethnic lines particularly in large eastern and midwestern cities. Certainly there is evidence that Catholics think of themselves as simply Catholics, but a sizeable number still identify as a German-Catholic, an Italian-Catholic, or a Polish-Catholic.

Protestant denominational differences have remained important to many in spite of the developing ecumenicity. There is, to be sure, "a kind of 'melting pot' " Protestantism, as exemplified by community churches such as Robert Schuler's Garden Grove Community Church (California); and the nationwide telecasts of his "Hour of Power" attest to the appeal of this kind of culture religion. His popularity does not lie with the more evangelical Protestants of the 1970s, but instead lies with the heirs to Norman Vincent Peale's culture religion of the 1950s (Mariani, 1979). Nevertheless, to be a Baptist or a Presbyterian or a Lutheran still means something to many people in the United States. This "something" may be a class identification, a regional identification, or an ethnic identification. It may even be a "theological identification," as in the case of a Pentecostal.

Furthermore, Herberg's thesis tends to ignore racial differences. During the civil rights revolution of the 1960s, a black Methodist or a black Baptist was something greatly different from his white counterpart. There are also a large number of blacks in the ghettos of large cities who have abandoned religious identification altogether, or who have traded their black Christian affiliation for a commitment to black Muslimism.

It is for Jews that Herberg's thesis seems to apply best. To be a Jew in America is something vastly different from being a Protestant or a Catholic, for it immediately suggests ethnicity as well as religion (Wilson, 1978:311). In terms of the ecumenical movement, none of the three branches of Judaism has joined (Glazer, 1972:158). Sklare (1971) suggests that in varying degrees the synagogue remains a source of spiritual and social identification. The less the Jewish population is, the greater is synagogue participation. In small communities, affiliation commonly reaches 80 percent. Significantly, the rate of affiliation among the foreign born is no higher than it is among the native born (Sklare, 1971). In those larger communities where affiliation and attendance are lower, there are many organizations and causes of a specifically Jewish nature available outside the orbit of the synagogue. Thus, to be a Jew is to suggest a rich and unique spiritual and ethnic heritage, regardless of the person's affiliation with one of the three branches of Judaism or of the person's status as "secular" or "cultural" Jew.

Samuel Mueller has suggested that the American Jews, the American nonreligious, and perhaps the American Unitarians may be forming a white non-Christian culture apart from a single white Christian group composed of Protestants and Catholics. A third culture would consist of the blacks (1971). However, the resurgence of Jewish identification in the early and middle 1970s offers some contrast to Mueller's research which analyzed patterns of intermarriage, friendship patterns, residential segregation, occupation, and political participation (1971:18-33).

Regardless of whether or not the three-culture hypothesis is the "correct" analysis of religious pluralism, it does help to explain the relatively peaceful coexistence of diverse religious bodies in the United States. Tensions between Roman Catholics, Protestants, and Jews still exist. Old hostilities and suspicions can at any time be resurrected, particularly by the fundamentalist Protestants. McLoughlin (1967:43-68) states that anti-Catholicism and anti-Semitism are still characteristic of what he calls a third force in Christianity, consisting of those denominations outside of the ecumenical movement. But the fact remains that religious diversity does exist, that no one religious body or faith dominates the others, and that even the most opposite of established religious groups limit their "holy wars" to verbal and written attacks.

EXAMPLES OF RELIGIOUS DIVERSITY

Religious diversity in America is reflected in the number of religious groups present. There are 280 different bodies which have at least 50 thousand members. The total number of church members (including Jewish congregations) for 1974 is 171 million (*1975 Yearbook of American Churches*). Table 7-1 illustrates present day religious diversity.

Included within the mainline Protestant bodies is the Eastern Orthodox Church which also is a member of the National Council. In addition, those predominantly black churches which are NCC members are a part of the total. Conservative Protestants include all those religious groups such as Mormons, Jehovah's Witnesses, and Churches of Christ that consider themselves to be either the only true church or more perfect than other churches. The Jewish total includes all three groups—Reform, Conservative, and Orthodox.

It is difficult to verify the accuracy of these figures, because different groups have different ways of counting members. Some include infants and young children; others enumerate only older teenage and adult members. Furthermore, many people suspect that the Catholic total is too high. Greeley (1974:42), by us-

Table 7-1. DISTRIBUTION OF MEMBERSHIP IN RELIGIOUS
ORGANIZATIONS IN THE UNITED STATES

Mainline Protestants (Members of the National Council of Churches)	Roman Catholics
42,000,000	49,000,000

Conservative Protestants (Non-members of the National Council of Churches	Jews (Orthodox, Conservative and Reform Groups)
33,000,000	6,000,000

ing National Opinion Research Center surveys, estimates a Catholic total that would be 24.7 percent instead of the 37 percent indicated by these figures. Also, racial segregation is demonstrated by an examination of membership statistics. Wilson (1978:283) also estimates that 10 million of the church membership are blacks who belong to black denominations. Less than 2 percent of blacks belong to predominantly white Protestant churches or the Roman Catholic Church (Greeley, 1974:42). Obviously, there are many examples of religious diversity among these 280 religious bodies, ranging from differences in beliefs to differences in practices. Even within the three major faiths, diversity exists in differing degrees. Protestants are divided between *mainline Protestantism* and *conservative/fundamentalist Protestantism*. Although no such division exists within Roman Catholicism, there remain ethnic differences within that church. American Judaism is divided into three branches—Orthodox, Conservative, and Reform. The social characteristics of each of these groups, the central tenets of religious belief, and the extent to which members practice the beliefs provide a glimpse of religious diversity within the United States.

Mainline Protestantism

Approximately twenty-nine Protestant denominations are members of the National Council of Churches in Christ; and of these, the United Methodist Church is the largest. Among these mainline religious bodies, there are varying degrees of ecumenical cooperation. For the most part they consist of a membership that is middle-class and above, although there are members whose social class levels are below the middle. This is particularly true for the largest of the all-black Protestant denominations which belong to the Council. However, mainline Protestantism is predominantly white.

While distinctive doctrinal differences are still found between member bodies, there is convergence in terms of nondistinctive generalized religious beliefs. Glock and Stark's study of American piety (1968:28-29) indicates that a sizeable majority of those mainline Protestants surveyed believed in the absolute existence of God. The exception was the Congregationalists whose belief in the absolute existence of God totaled only 41 percent. Most of these Protestants, by a sizeable majority, also believed in the divinity of Christ, with the exception of Congregationalists. Fewer accepted the belief of "life beyond death," and only a minority of those surveyed believed in the existence of "the devil."

In terms of ritual practices of the Christian church, only the liturgical Protestant denominations, the Episcopalians, and the Lutherans placed great emphasis upon baptism and the Sacrament of the Lord's Supper (or the Eucharist). The United Methodists, the United Church of Christ, the Disciples of Christ, the Presbyterians, and the American Baptists tend to de-emphasize such ritualistic practices (Stark and Glock, 1968). More recent surveys by Gallup and others tend to confirm these earlier findings (Rosten, 1975).

Mainline Protestants show less commitment to religious practices than do either "conservative/fundamentalist Protestants" or Roman Catholics. For example, Stark and Glock report that between 41 to 49 percent of the membership of those denominations which are within the National Council of Churches attend services weekly or almost weekly (1968). This percentage has remained about the same throughout the 1970s. Even the contemporary evangelical "movements" within the mainline Protestant churches have failed to increase this proportion except in localized instances. Neither an emphasis on sociability nor an emphasis upon revivalistic evangelism have changed church attendance patterns.

Wilson (1978:434-435) reports that, since its inception, the National Council of Churches has consistently sought to enforce a liberal, middle-class social policy on the membership of participating denominations. He further states that this kind of ecumenical movement is a class movement which reflects a division between mainline Protestantism and the evangelical lower class. However, not all of the middle-, upper middle-, and upper-class members of these religious bodies adhere to such policies. The liberal social activism of the National Council of Churches during the 1960s and early 1970s alienated many of the denominations' more conservative members. Beginning in 1969, denominational income began to decline, and the bureaucracies of the denominations began to respond to grass roots complaints (Wilson,1978:435). Such organizations as the Presbyterian Lay Committee within the United Presbyterian Church and the Methodist Lay Witness Movement within the United Methodist Church have diverted some denominational attention to more conservative political causes and to individualistic revivalism. In addition to these efforts to redirect mainline Protestantism toward individualistic evangelicalism, most of these denominations have experienced varying degrees of the charismatic renewal movement involving *gifts of the spirit* and *glossolalia* (speaking in unknown tongues). Most of the churches in which this movement has occurred have adopted a tolerant addition on the denominational level, but in local congregations and parishes animosities between procharismatics and anticharismatics have developed. For many reasons, including the reaction against liberal social action, mainline Protestant denominations have experienced either declines in membership or stagnation. Kelly (1972) states that the similarity of generalized beliefs, the ease of religious commitment, and the secularization of these religious bodies have contributed to this decline and to the growth of the conservative Protestant groups.

The ease of changing membership from one denomination to another is another characteristic of most denominations within the National Council of Churches. Although an inquirers or communicants class is required for membership in Episcopal and Lutheran churches, such extended sessions are not generally required for membership in the other Protestant bodies. Transferring church membership betwen denominations is often as easy as transferring church membership within churches of the same denomination. The ease of affiliation has further blurred the distinctive doctrinal beliefs and religious practices of mainline Protestantism. The phenomenon of the "cultural community church," chosen more for its convenience, the verbal skills of the minister, the music, or the educational and social programs for the young, continues today within mainline Protestantism.

Conservative/Fundamentalist Protestantism

In contrast to the churches of mainline Protestantism, those Protestant denominations which are outside of the National Council of Churches in Christ have more distinctive doctrinal beliefs, a higher level of church attendance, and more exclusive requirements for church membership. The approximately 33 million people who belong to these denominations generally are of a lower social class level than are the members of the predominantly white mainline Protestant churches. There are, however, some important exceptions to this general social class ranking.

In the South, Southern Baptists have more middle- and upper middle-class members than do Baptists in other areas of the country; and with approximately 13.5 million members the Southern Baptist Convention accounts for over one-third of all conservative and fundamentalist Protestants. Likewise, members of the Lutheran Church-Missouri Synod also have more middle- and upper middle-class members than do most conservative and fundamentalist groups (Rosten,

1975:449-450). The third largest group of conservative and fundamentalist Protestants is the Church of Christ. Most of the congregations which form the Church of Christ are located in the South and Southwest. These churches are the result of a split between the Churches of Christ and the mainline Disciples of Christ churches. Although there are many middle and upper middle-class members of the Church of Christ, more of their membership is lower middle-class and lower-class than are the memberships of both Southern Baptists and Missouri Synod Lutherans. Another larger religious group that generally is included with conservative and fundamentalist Protestants is the Church of Jesus Christ of Latter Day Saints (the Mormons). In states in which Mormons are the dominant group, they are likely to come from all social class levels.

On the other hand, Pentecostal and Holiness groups, groups who identify themselves as "Bible Churches," and groups which emphasize a new revelation such as the Jehovah's Witnesses include a preponderance of members from lower social class levels. These groups also tend to require more commitment to their particular religious institution as a requirement for membership; consequently, a higher proportion of their membership is regular in attending religious services, often more than just once a week. Kelley (1972:57-58) uses a model which consists of goals, controls, and communication traits seen as descriptive of religious groups. Commitment to goals, effective discipline, and a missionary goal in terms of communicating the "good news" of the organization are all necessary traits of a strong religion. He (1972:84) further specifies that strong religious groups also include traits of strictness in terms of goals, controls, and communication. One trait is absolutism, or a belief that one group has the truth. Conformity is another trait which reflects the individual member's submission to the religious organization's controls. Fanaticism is the trait that describes the communication of the organization's beliefs. Although sect-like Protestants are most characterized by these six traits, all of the conservative and fundamentalist Protestant denominations share in some of these.

Kelley also proposes an ecumenical gradient (1972:88-90) which indicates the exclusivist feelings of a religious group as opposed to its ecumenical feelings. According to this gradient, those conservative and fundamentalist Protestants which are most exclusive are Jehovah's Witnesses, Evangelicals, Pentecostals, Churches of Christ, Mormons, and Seventh Day Adventists. By contrast the mainline Protestants (and liberal religious bodies) who are most ecumenical are Unitarian-Universalists, the Ethical Culture Society, the United Church of Christ, and the United Methodist Church. At the pivotal point of the gradient is the Roman Catholic Church. Significantly, according to Kelley, two of the largest conservative Protestant denominations—the Southern Baptist Convention and the Lutheran Church-Missouri Synod—are near the middle of the gradient and are growing at a lower rate than the more exclusivistic groups. Finally, Kelley contends that the reason that most of these groups remain outside of the ecumenical movement is that cooperation with the less exclusivistic groups is seen as leading to a compromise in their central beliefs. Such a compromise would dilute the commodities which they offer: absolute salvation and the security which such a belief gives to an individual.

The other facet of conservative and fundamentalist Protestant bodies which makes them different from other religious groups in the United States is their tendency to reject the liberal, middle-class social policy which led to the social action policies of the denominations within mainline Protestantism. In fact, there has been little internal cooperation within the conservative and fundamentalist sphere. When cooperation has occurred, it has generally involved antidrinking, antigambling, and pro-Sunday closing law issues. In the few conservative denominations which have clergy and laypeople who are interested in closer ties with other denominations and in more social action programs (notably the Southern Baptist Convention and the Lutheran Church-Missouri Synod), conservative forces within the denominations have generally prevented such policies. In the case of the Missouri Synod Lutherans, a schism developed between moderates and conservatives which resulted in a separate Lutheran religious group.

All in all, the intensity of religious beliefs, the exclusivity of membership requirements, the emphasis upon salvation, and the suspicion of any religious compromise remain the hallmarks of the conservative and fundamentalist Protestant denominations and sects. It is within these groups that the contemporary evangelical movement has its strongest support. As a result, conservative and fundamentalist Protestants simply say to mainline Protestants that the evangelical movement is a vindication of their exclusivity and their emphasis upon personal salvation. In Chapter 9, this contemporary movement is examined in greater detail.

Roman Catholicism

Since the end of World War II, the "church of immigrants" has become more and more the church of native born Americans (McNamara, 1974:167). Whereas Roman Catholicism was once characterized by a majority of working-class and lower class members, it is little different today from the class differentiation found within mainline Protestantism. With few exceptions, the proportionate distributions of Catholics by education, occupation, and income parallels those distributions of the United States population at large (Rosten, 1975:449-450). Like both mainline Protestants and conservative/fundamentalist Protestants, Roman Catholics have a very small number of black members: in 1971, only 3 percent of Roman Catholics were black (Rosten, 1975:448).

Although Catholicism remains distinctively different in terms of doctrine and religious practices from Protestant Christianity, the Second Vatican Council in

1961 caused profound changes within the Church (McNamara, 1974:168). These changes resulted in a church that began to officially recognize the existence of other Christian bodies and that gave up exclusive claim to "all religious truth" (Kelley, 1972:32). The mass celebrated in vernacular languages, the introduction of broader congregational participation through the use of hymns and musical liturgies, the option of communicants taking the wine as well as the host (or bread) are also major innovations in the public religious rites of the Roman Catholic Church.

In terms of basic beliefs, Roman Catholics still overwhelmingly subscribe to the orthodox and traditional doctrines of their faith. Stark and Glock (1968:28, 33, 37) found that 81 percent of Roman Catholics in their sample believed in the existence of God, 86 percent believed in the divinity of Christ, and 75 percent believed in life beyond death. Furthermore, almost twice as many Catholics believed in the existence of the Devil (66 percent). Those beliefs that are distinctively "Catholic" as opposed to "Protestant" are not as readily accepted today as they were in the past, however. An absolute belief in original sin was seen in only 68 percent of Stark and Glock's sample (1968:40). Furthermore, only 65 percent of the Catholic sample believed that holy baptism was a requirement for salvation. Membership in the Catholic church as a requirement for salvation was believed by only 28 percent of the same sample of Roman Catholics (1968:45).

A Gallup Poll commissioned by *Newsweek* in 1971 revealed further change among American Catholics in their willingness to accept the more exclusivistic teachings of the church, particularly those that related to social issues. Fifty-eight percent believed that a good Catholic could ignore the Pope's condemnation of artificial birth control, and 60 percent did *not* believe that a divorced Catholic who remarries is living in sin.

Significantly, 53 percent of Roman Catholics also thought that priests should be permitted to marry (Rosten, 1975:393-394). Joseph Fichter, who is both a sociologist and a Jesuit priest, polled 3,000 priests in the United States in 1967. Two-thirds said that they preferred to be free to choose whether to remain celibate or to marry (Rosten, 1975:403). A Gallup Poll taken in 1971 revealed that priests under the age of forty overwhelmingly believed that priests should be permitted to marry (77 percent). Furthermore, the National Opinion Research Center found in 1975 that some 79 percent of American Catholics favored permitting priests to marry (Rosten, 1975:403-404).

Also, survey research compiled by McCready and Greeley (McNamara, 1974:195-204) indicates that a majority of Catholics would approve of a legal abortion for a woman who had become pregnant by rape, who expected a defective child, or whose life was threatened by the birth of the child. McCready and Greeley found that these changes in attitudes concerning abortion, as well as attitudes which reject the traditional moral teachings of the church regarding sexual behavior, occurred chiefly among Roman Catholics under the age of thirty.

The two researchers concluded that the organizational loyalty given to the Roman Catholic Church in America by the various Catholic ethnic groups who migrated to the United States has greatly diminished.

In a more recent work, Greeley (1977) views the declining loyalty and church participation of Roman Catholics as a result of an eroding confidence in church leadership and growing differences between church hierarchy and the people over sexual issues such as birth control.

These changes within the membership of America's largest single religious body have come about as Catholics have achieved virtual parity with Protestants in educational attainment, occupational prestige, and income. The ethnicity so characteristic of Catholics prior to World War II has not been a barrier to these achievements (Greeley, 1977). However, the ethnicity of many Roman Catholics *does* make for a difference between various Catholic family units such as Italian and Irish. All Catholic families, however, show more social support for family members than do Protestant families, but less than do Jewish families.

In spite of such findings as these, Greeley states that there are more similarities of moral style among Protestants, Catholics, and Jews than there are dissimilarities. Additionally, many of the religious activities that Catholics participated in and used as ways of defining themselves as distinctively religious as compared to Protestants—devotions and observances of certain Holy Days—have been eliminated. Nevertheless, in the practice of religion, Roman Catholic attendance at religious services is still greater than is either Protestant or Jewish attendance, in spite of an overall decline in Catholic attendance. In 1973, 55 percent of Catholics attended church in a given week, in contrast to an average Protestant attendance of 37 percent for the same year (Rosten, 1975;431).

On the other hand, the renewal of interest in ethnicity has rekindled some of the past ethnic divisions within the Roman Catholic Church. Hargrove (1979) suggests that some of the distinctive characteristics of ethnic Catholicism may reappear to sharpen once again the distinctiveness of Roman Catholicism as compared to American Protestantism. Furthermore, Pope John Paul II is a more vibrant papal leader than his predecessor Pope Paul, and his conservatism and traditionalism could become more appealing to the American Catholic church than was Paul's. In summary, the Roman Catholic Church in contemporary America remains a church in transition—less traditional than in the past, less influential in terms of moral authority—but, nevertheless, a tremendously important religious body containing a neo-Pentecostal (charismatic renewal) movement, conservative and radical priests and nuns, parishes representative of all social class levels, and a stable membership.

Judaism

As we illustrated earlier in this chapter, a sizeable migration of Jews into the United States between the end of the Civil War and the end of World War I resulted in the expansion of religious pluralism to include a "third faith," Judaism. The first wave of this immigration was almost entirely from Germany. They joined a numerically insignificant population of Jews already present who were primarily of Spanish, Dutch, German, and Portuguese descent (McNamara, 1974:211). These later German Jews practiced assimilation much more effectively than the early Catholic immigrants. Later waves of Jewish immigration, however, consisted more of people from the "peasant" Jewish communities of Eastern Europe. For many of them, the synagogue had been a central place of worship and activity in their homeland; for others, the Jewish faith had given way to ideas of radical social reform—socialism and anarchy. The religious among both groups of immigrants who became dissatisfied with the American form of Judaism found *Reform Judaism*. Late in the nineteenth century, *Conservative Judaism* was born. It stressed loyalty to the Jewish law, literature, and language, but it was not as strict or as legalistic as traditional Judaism.

When the second wave of immigration occurred, however, the peasant Jews were not completely satisfied with Conservative Judaism. These people had a desire to continue the strict observance of Jewish law and dietary customs ("keeping Kosher"); and this desire, as well as their emphasis on national origin, impeded the absorption of most Eastern European Jews into the existing religious structure of Judaism in the United States. Instead, *Orthodox Judaism*, with its own organizational forms and synagogues began. There were bitter arguments between the branches, but there never developed the kind of permanent alienation that characterizes the relationship between fundamentalists and nonfundamentalist Protestantism. By 1924, American Jews, despite their internal division, constituted a well defined ethnic group (Herberg, 1960;182), and this ethnicity often overshadowed the religious aspect of Judaism. The Yiddish language, a peculiar possession of Jews, remained a cultural mark of Jewishness, particularly for the Eastern European immigrants.

During the early decades of the twentieth century, *Conservative Judaism* became the larger of the three bodies, mainly because it appealed to sons and daughters of the immigrants. It stressed not only Judaism but also liberalism in politics, human rights, and religious rights. Today, however, the largest membership is found within the congregations of the Union of Orthodox Jewish Congregations of America. These 3,000 congregations have 3 million members. Conservative Judaism is known as the United Synagogue of America and has 835 congregations with 1.5 million members. The most "American" of the branches, the Reform branch, counts 1 million members within the 686 congregations of the Union of American Hebrew Congregations (Rosten, 1975:439).

The relative smallness of both Conservative and Reform Judaism as compared to Orthodox Judaism probably reflects the secularization of many Jews who have simply left Jewish religious organizations while maintaining Jewish cultural ties. For example, some Jewish people, because of their humanism and political liberalism, have become Unitarians; others may observe the High Holy Days of

217

Judaism, but may not participate regularly in weekly synagogue or temple activities; but they do express their Jewishness, do identify with Jewish people, and do carry on Jewish tradition (Lasker, 1971:241-248). By contrast, Orthodox Jews observe religious customs and practices on a much more regular basis. In the same study concerned with motivations for attending High Holy Day services, Lasker (1971:241-248) found that his subjects who were Orthodox ranked "relationship with God" and "influence on God" as their highest motivations for attending. All of the Orthodox respondents consider as a very important reason for observing the Holy Days their desire "to comply with God's requirement that we observe Rosh Hashanah and Yom Kippur." These expressions reflect both the orthodox emphasis upon a personal God and His requirements for the Jewish people to practice legalistically the religion. These tenets of faith are less emphasized in both Conservative and Reform Judaism.

The inconsistency of the regular practice of religion among American Jews is reflected in weekly attendance rates at synagogues and temples. In 1973, the Gallup Poll indicated that only 19 percent of Jews in the sample attended services in a typical week, as compared with 17 percent in 1964 (Rosten, 1975:565). In spite of this, Jewish identity remains strong. The attendance for High Holy Day services is much higher, sometimes as high as 57 percent. This identity is also refected in the Bar Mitzvah of Jewish boys. Although it has become a social occasion as much as a religious observance, nominal as well as active Jewish families tend to observe this traditional rite of passage (Herberg, 1960:191).

In parallel fashion to Protestantism, affiliation as well as attendance with a synagogue or temple seems to vary according to location. Although the overwhelming majority of American Jews live in urban areas, it is in the smaller communities that affiliation commonly reaches over 80 percent of all Jews in a given area (Sklare, 1971). Sklare points out that as the number of Jews forming a "Jewish Community" increases, synagogue affiliation decreases. He further states that lack of affiliation or lack of regular attendance does *not* reflect opposition to synagogue life or activities. Instead it probably reflects great secularization on the part of the unaffiliated (Sklare, 1971). While Sklare is writing primarily of Conservative synagogues, his observations also apply to Reform congregations as well. These affiliation and attendance patterns are also related to differences in beliefs and ritual between the three branches of American Judaism.

The Orthodox Jew regards his faith as the mainstream of a tradition that has been unaltered for three thousand years. The Bible (Old Testament) is seen as the revealed word of God. For the Orthodox, the Sabbath is strictly observed. There is no work, no travel, no writing, no business dealings, and no carrying of money; all details of the dietary laws are also observed; women are segregated in seating from men in the synagogue; and only Hebrew is used in prayer and ceremonial services. Furthermore, a hat or a skull cap is worn at all times.

The Conservative Jew follows the pattern of traditional Judaism, but regards the religion as evolving and ever-growing. The practicing conservative follows the dietary laws, but with minor relaxations. The Sabbath is observed, as are the High Holy Days; but the Sabbath observance is likely to be on late Friday evening. Also, many Conservative congregations use English in prayers.

The Reform Jew is quite different in the practice of religion from the Orthodox and somewhat different from the Conservative. In matters of the revelation of the will of God to mankind, the Reform branch accepts as binding only the moral laws of the Bible and those ceremonies which elevate and sanctify the lives of people. A religious faith that is rational and that is capable of withstanding the scrutiny of reason and science is the important tenet in Reform Judaism. In the temple, there is a complete equality of the sexes; prayer is largely in English; and flexibility in the choice of prayers is great. Organs, and sometimes choirs, are used in worship services. Rarely does a worshipper cover his head during prayer (Kertzer, 1975:142-151).

In addition to these differences in both beliefs and in worship practices, there are common beliefs among Orthodox, Conservative, and Reform Judaism. The *Torah*, consisting of the five books of Moses in the Bible (Genesis to Deuteronomy) and the *Talmud*, consisting of sixty-three books of legal, philosophical, ethical, and historical writings of the ancient rabbis are accepted· by all three branches. The Jewish prayer book also speaks of three basic principles of Jewish faith: the first is the love of learning; the second is the worship of God; and the third is the performance of good deeds. Jews are also generally in agreement in *not* accepting the principle of incarnation: God becoming man. In contrast, a cardinal tenet of Jewish faith is that God is spiritual and has no human attribute. Obviously, Jews reject the divinity of Jesus Christ; and Judaism generally does not accept the principle of atonement by Christ for the sins of the whole world (Kertzer, 1976:143-145). In spite of this rejection of Christianity, modern American Judaism is not a proselytizing religion. However, converts to the Jewish faith are welcome (many of these converts are the non-Jewish spouses of an interfaith marriage). These commonly held beliefs, along with the strong sense of Jewish community and culture unite American Jews in a way that few religious faiths in the United States experience.

Of all the religious groups in this society, Jews are least likely to intermarry. Catholic-Protestant marriages are increasing rapidly, but Jewish-Gentile marriages are not (Mueller, 1971). Greeley (1970:949-952) reported that Jews are least likely to marry members of other religious faiths, but *The New York Times* reported in 1973 that almost one-third of American Jews who married between 1966-1971 took non-Jewish spouses (Rosten, 1975:568-569). Clearly, there is more intermarriage than in the past.

Like immigrant Catholics, American Jews of the second and third generations have achieved much upward social mobility. By comparison with Catholics and

Protestants, 30 percent of American Jews are in the top income bracket and 56 percent are in the two highest income levels. (Gallup Opinion Index for 1971; cited in Rosten, 1975:450). This was in comparison to 34 percent of all Protestants and 42 percent of Roman Catholics in the two highest income levels. Glazer (1972) views this overrepresentation in the higher socioeconomic levels as one reason for a decline in Jewish radicalism (as evidenced by some of the eastern European immigrant Jews' affinity for socialism), and some dissolution with traditional Jewish political and economic liberalism. Since their stake in the American economic (and political) system is so great, America's Jews have looked with dismay as younger secular Jews (as well as black militants and white radicals) have advocated radical economic and social reform of American society. Jews in the late 1960s and early 1970s were not so much subjected to classical anti-Semitism as they were to anti-Jewish economic and political sentiment. Glazer states that, all in all, anti-Semitism is at a very low level. Still, past historical experiences with this particularistic form of prejudice causes America's Jewish community to remain vigilant against its resurfacing.

The sense of community that solidified among Jews as a result of the Nazi Holocaust was further strengthened with the formation of the nation of Israel following World War II. An overwhelming majority of America's Jews support Israel emotionally, and many support its defense efforts financially. More recent accounts of human rights violations against Jews in the Soviet Union have also promoted Jewish unity. This contemporary pogrom by the Soviet Union has also led to militant (and sometimes illegal) activities on the part of committed Jewish Americans. This renewed sense of self-identity is in line with Herberg's hypothesis that the "third generation" American Jew would closely identify with the religious heritage that his or her father or mother (the "second generation" Jew) consciously avoided (1960). However, this phenomenon has been less than widespread. Wilson (1978:321) summarizes contemporary Judaism as consisting of a Jewish middle class that is becoming more like the Protestant middle class than the Jewish working class.

Still, important differences remain between American Judaism and Christianity. Although the Roman Catholic Church has officially reannounced its anti-Semitic accusation of deocide against Jews, little substantive rapprochement between Catholics and Jews has occurred, except for ecumenical Thanksgiving services and the like. Protestant-Jewish relationships are more relaxed except among fundamentalist Protestantism and Judaism. According to Himmelfarb (1967:220-236), American Jews who are traditional or orthodox in the observance of their religious faith feel that the overt and covert Christian symbols and practices of the United States erode Jewish religious faith and promote further secularization. Nevertheless, to be Jewish and American means something unique in the history of Judaism. It means a sense of loyalty to a religious and to an ethnic heritage; it means an historical identification with the oppressed; and it means perseverance in overcoming vast social, economic, political, and religious discrimination. Today's American Jews are no longer subjected to covenant restrictions that exclude them from neighborhoods or from social clubs. Jewish people experience only sporadic outburst of anti-Semitism; and usually then only from fringe political groups like the Ku Klux Klan, the John Birch Society, and Neo-Nazi groups. Still, Jewish representation in the highest echelons of predominantly Gentile corporate organizations remains low. Certain country clubs still admit no Jews or only a few Jews. Because of these exceptions to complete acceptance of Jews in American society, the three branches of American Judaism remain a solidified third religious community in the United States.

Diversity in American religious life is paradoxical. Cooperation and conflict are both products of the process of religious pluralism. Protestant denominations hold the allegiance of a majority of America's religious population. Roman Catholics command the second largest membership and constitute the largest single religious body in this society. Jews form a small but significant minority of citizens who claim religious affiliation. All of the three major faiths have minority group members, but racial minorities constitute only small proportions of members within predominantly white denominations. Because of this, Allen Winter (1977:265) sees the religious organizations and the religiosity of blacks as constituting a "fourth religious community." (The religion of black Americans is presented in Chapter 13). Tensions between the three (or four) religious faiths, as well as between the Christian-Judaic faiths and other faiths, have subsided over the years, but still surface from time to time. The rights of religious nonbelievers in society continue to be subjected to court tests involving the concept of church-state separation. Religious pluralism has been achieved, resulting in a kind of parity between the major religious groups, but *only* as the result of the achievement of parity in nonreligious spheres such as social class level, political participation, and social participation. Another pluralistic development is the emergence of what several scholars view as American civil religion. It knows no denominational or religious boundary, but instead is embraced by millions of Americans.

CIVIL RELIGION

Civil religion, a term that can be traced to Rousseau, has been used by Robert Bellah to describe "a set of religious beliefs, symbols, and rituals growing out of the American historical experience interpreted in the dimension of transcedence" (Bellah, 1967:389). Beginning with the Founding Fathers and the early presidents of the United States, Bellah cites historical examples that refer to "Providence," the "Deity," the "Almighty Being," and "God" as guiding the destiny of the United States. Bellah (1967:7) states that the "God of the civil religion is not only rather 'unitarian'; he is also on the austere side, more related to order, law, and right than to salvation and love. . . . He is actively interested and involved in history, with special concern for America. . . ." Bellah continues his argument by pointing out that there has been, from the early years of the United States, a collection of beliefs, symbols, and rituals with respect to sacred things that have become institutionalized (1967:8). American civil religion, Bellah states, makes reference to God's special concern for the "chosen people" of the United States (1975:36-40). Furthermore, this civil religion celebrates the "American Way of Life"—economically, politically, and ethically.

Bellah views the American Civil War as an important milestone in enhancing the moral and intellectual meaning of an American civil religion. The Civil War raised very deep questions concerning national purpose and meaning; and subsequently, Abraham Lincoln became a high priest of this religion. For him, the issue was not slavery but "whether that nation, or any nation so conceived, and so dedicated, can long endure." (Lincoln quoted in Bellah, 1967:9) Bellah states also that the two national cemeteries that were the product of the Civil War, Gettysburg and Arlington, have become shrines of civil religion. Memorial Day and Thanksgiving Day have also become sacred days in the celebration of this civil religion. Other sacred days include Independence Day, Veterans' Day, Washington's Birthday, and Lincoln's Birthday. Less frequent, although just as important, are the inaugurations of American presidents.

In his initial article concerning civil religion, Bellah (1967:1-2, 13-14) illustrates the religious solemnity of John F. Kennedy's inaugural address, and the references to God and to his approval of American causes in Lyndon B. Johnson's address. Additionally, Bellah illustrated that Kennedy's inaugural address pointed to the religious aspect of the Declaration of Independence. Other ceremonies are also crucial but unpredictable. For example, funeral ceremonies for national figures are a time for national mourning and for reaffirmation of America's commonly-held values. Bellah (1967) and Cherry (1970) both acknowledge this quasi-sacred phenomenon. In recent years the funerals of John F. Kennedy, of Martin Luther King, Jr., of Robert F. Kennedy, of Dwight D. Eisenhower, and of Lyndon B. Johnson were important ceremonies that showed civil religion in operation. Wilson (1978:178), in discussing civil religion, points out that true civil religion is present in the minds of all who have faith in democracy as it is defined by the American System. In this faith the goals of freedom, of equality, and of justice are made sacred. The "sacred ceremonies" simply undergird this faith.

In their exposition of civil religion, Bellah and others have referred to civil religion in the context of Durkheim's premise concerning religion and societal integration. Hammond (1974:116) explains that the phenomenon of social cohesion has a religious quality about it and is therefore not produced by religion. Civil religion embodies the symbols of cohesion and unity of American society.

Wilson (1978:178-179) also argues that Bellah is not equating this religion with either the churches or Christianity. Instead, he views civil religion as an interpretation of America's major religious faiths in the light of political experience. Winter (1977:88) states that the existence of such a civil religion supports Durkheim's notion that religion contains an eternal quality. In an advanced industrial society like that of the United States the Durkheimian religious function is being performed with the help of religious content, although such a content now seems to have more political symbols and content than traditional Judaeo-Christian symbols and ceremonies.

Not all empirical studies of religion within the context of the political realm agree upon the importance of American civil religion. Social differentiation and pluralism may reduce civil religion to a far less important role in societal integration. Civil religion could still exist, but exist only on the periphery of a society whose integration is very functional in nature (Winter, 1977:88-89). For example, Bellah (1974, 1975) states that perhaps the content of contemporary American civil religion is no longer as adequate in its integrative task as it once was.

SUMMARY

By the middle of the twentieth century, religious diversity within the United States seemed a stabilizing force in society. Herberg advanced the three-culture hypothesis which implied religious parity between Protestants, Catholics, and Jews. American Catholics were less ethnic and exclusive than in the past. The mainline Protestant denominations, both white and black, promoted unity by reorganizing the old Federal Council of Churches into the National Council of Churches in Christ. Conservative and fundamentalist Protestant bodies, however, remained outside of this new expression of cooperation and ecumenicism. Church attendance reached an all-time high. During the 1960s the liberal social activism of mainline Protestantism and Judaism was tested in the arena of civil rights and opposition to the Vietnam War. Many Catholics also joined in these efforts. The result for the 1970s was a conservative reaction in mainline Protestantism.

Still, the ecumenicism of the Roman Catholic Church as a result of the Second Vatican Council brought Protestants and Catholics into new dialogue and closer cooperation. Even a convergence between new Pentecostal and Charismatic Renewal movements in Protestant and Catholic churches occurred. Furthermore, a renewed interest in evangelicalism (or revivalism) appeared. The result of these events is a renewed interest in religion, however diverse that religion happens to be in America. That diversity includes two distinctive Protestant alliances, the mainline denominations and the conservative/fundamentalist denominations; a different kind of Roman Catholic church; Judaism; and perhaps, a distinctive black religious grouping. Finally, civil religion permeates many institutional arrangements without regard to particularistic religious creeds or beliefs.

REFERENCES

Bellah, Robert N.
1967   "Civil religion in America." *Daedalus* 96 (Winter):1-21.
1974   "American civil religion in the 1970's." in Russell E. Richey and Donald G. Jones (eds.), *American Civil Religion.* New York: Harper and Row.
1975   *The Broken Covenant: American Civil Religion in Time of Trial.* New York: Seabury Press.

Cherry, Conrad
1970   "American sacred ceremonies." Pp. 303-316 in Phillip E. Hammond and Benton Johnson (eds.), *American Mosaic: Social Patterns of Religion in the United States.* New York: Random House.

Glazer, Nathan
1972   *American Judaism.* Chicago: University of Chicago Press.

Greeley, Andrew M.
1970   "Religious intermarriage in a denominational society." *American Journal of Sociology* 75 (Fall):949-952.
1974   *Ethnicity in the United States: A Preliminary Reconnaissance.* New York: John Wiley.
1977   *The American Catholic: A Social Portrait.* New York: Basic Books.

Hadden, Jeffrey K.
1969   *The Gathering Storm in the Churches.* Garden City, New York: Doubleday.

Hammond, Phillip E.
1974   "Religious pluralism and Durkheim's integration thesis." Pp. 115-142 in Alan W. Eister (ed.), *Changing Perspectives in the Scientific Study of Religion.* New York: Wiley.

Hargrove, Barbara
1979   *The Sociology of Religion: Classical and Contem-*

porary Approaches. Arlington Heights, Ill.: AHM Publishing Corp.

Herberg, Will
1960   *Protestant, Catholic, Jew.* Garden City, New York: Doubleday Anchor Books.

Himmelfarb, Milton
1967   "Secular society? A Jewish perspective." *Daedalus* 96 (Winter):220-236.

Johnson, Douglas W. and
George W. Cornell
1972   *Punctured Preconceptions.* New York: Friendship Press.

Kelley, Dean M.
1972   *Why Conservative Churches are Growing: A Study in the Sociology of Religion.* New York: Harper and Row.

Kelly, James R.
1972   "Attitudes toward ecumenicism: an empirical investigation." *Journal of Ecumenical Studies* 9 (Spring):341-351.

Kertzer, Morris N.
1975   "What is a Jew?" Pp. 142-155 in Leo Rosten (ed.), *Religions of America: Ferment and Faith in an Age of Crisis.* New York: Simon and Schuster.

Lasker, Arnold A.
1971   "Motivations for attending High Holy Day services." *Journal for the Scientific Study of Religion* 10 (Fall 1971):241-243.

Mariani, John
1979   "Television evangelism: milking the flock." *Saturday Review* (February 3):22-25.

Marty, Martin
1970   *Righteous Empire: The Protestant Experience in America.* New York: Dial Press.

McCready, William C.
and Andrew M. Greeley
1974   "The end of American Catholicism," in Patrick H. McNamara (ed.), *Religion American Style.* New York: Harper and Row.

McLoughlin, William C.
1967   "Is there a third force in Christendom?" *Daedalus* 96 (Winter):43-68.

McNamara, Patrick H.
1974   *Religion American Style.* New York: Harper and Row.

Mueller, Samuel A.
1971   "The new triple melting pot: Herberg revisited." *Review of Religious Research* 13 (Fall):18-33.

Pratt, Henry J.
1972   *The Liberalization of American Protestantism.* Detroit: Wayne State University Press.

Quinley, Harold
1974   *The Prophetic Clergy: Social Activism among Protestant Ministers.* New York: John Wiley.

Raff, G. Elson and Albert P. Standerman
1975   "What is a Lutheran?" Pp. 156-169 in Leo Rosten (ed.), *Religions of America: Ferment and Faith in an Age of Crisis.* New York: Simon and Schuster.

Rosten, Leo
1975   *Religions of America: Ferment and Faith in an Age of Crisis.* New York: Simon and Schuster.

Sklare, Marshall
1971   *America's Jews.* New York: Random House.

Stark, Rodney and Charles Glock
1968   *American Piety: The Nature of Religious Commitment.* Berkeley, Cal.: University of California Press.

Wilson, John
1978   *Religion in American Society: The Effective Presence.* Englewood Cliffs, N.J.: Prentice-Hall.

Winter, J. Alan
1977   *Continuities in the Study of Religion: Creed, Congregation, and Community.* New York: Harper and Row.

Chapter 8

Fundamentalism as a Social Movement

Fundamentalism as a religious tradition is a peculiar Protestant phenomenon. As a social movement, it began with agitation to return to the fundamentals of the Christian faith—Christianity must be defined in terms of Biblical doctrine; it presents a great saving fact; the Bible is the sole authority for mankind for it is the Word of God; God created man as a moral personality; sin is universal and powerful; God provided historical redemption for all persons through Jesus Christ; the Holy Spirit is everywhere, available for cleansing and quickening; and in the end, there will be a final consummation of the world. With the exceptions of Anglicanism and Lutheranism, all evangelical Protestant traditions were influenced by these so-called fundamental doctrines of the Old and New Testaments as stated in those writings. As an outgrowth of this agitation, some Protestant leaders emerged who debated the issues with others who held modified views of the nature and purpose of Christianity. Various historians, sociologists, and journalists view the decade of the 1920s as the battleground between the churchmen called "fundamentalists" and those labeled "modernists;" but an analysis of this portion of American religious history from a sociological perspective indicates that the social processes which led to this public religious battle—expansionism, urbanization, and the Social Gospel—began early on in the collective life of the United States. A rather telescoped summary of these historical processes provides a more accurate understanding of fundamentalism as a movement which ultimately fragmented the Protestant establishment of America

RELIGIOUS APATHY AND EARLY AMERICAN LIFE

Although many people still view religion and the founding of America as constituting a "cause-and-effect relationship," historical evidence indicates that a general apathy existed toward organized religion as the new nation began. By 1775, it is estimated that only 5 to 7 percent of the colonial population were members of organized churches (Knudten, 1967:58). Despite this lack of religiosity among the colonial population, the intellectuals behind both the little interest in feminism in these "news" outlets of organized religion. Less American Revolution and the formation of the federal system were keenly aware of the political advantages that came from an accommodation of various religious groups, and religious pluralism was carefully guaranteed by the First Amendment to the Constitution of the United States.

At the time of the First Great Awakening, which was discussed in Chapter 6, the Puritan Congregationalists and the Anglicans constituted state churches in most of the various colonies. This Great Awakening has been described as "the first major manifestation of a motif which, more than any other, has shaped modern American church life: mass evangelism . . . " (Littell, 1962:19). Although the New England establishment resisted the Great Awakening rather successfully, its effect in the southern colonies lasted right up to the Revolutionary War. By the time the new states were writing their constitutions (and proclaiming religious liberty), the revival emphasis was fairly advanced in Methodist, Baptist, and "New Side" Presbyterian circles. This technique, so closely identified today with fundamentalism, evangelicalism, and Pentecostalism, was eminently suited to work under frontier conditions as the new nation expanded westward. The peculiar institutions of Methodism— itinerant preachers, lay preachers, and the class meeting — widened the gap between the staid cultural-religion of the coastal areas whose main concerns were order, tradition, propriety, and education (Littell, 1962:18-22).

It can be stated, then, with historical accuracy that the agitation for mass conversion of the religiously apathetic citizenry by the less established religious groups (Methodists, Baptists, and "New Side" Presbyterians) and the suspicious view of the established churches generally held by the constitutional framers worked hand in hand to mold into shape a new concept of religious toleration—and even competition. While Franklin, Adams, Madison, and Jefferson were interested in a means to prevent the churches from "meddling in civil affairs," the evangelical leaders and dissenters were pressing for a method to guarantee freedom from governmental interference in religion (Marty, 1970:35-39). Marty further observes that the dissenters, in their evangelical fervor, used these new "charters" to prepare for religious expansion as the new nation expanded. In a sociological context, the apathy of a majority of American society toward organized religion provided a social vacuum into which the evangelical groups rushed. The "closeness" of the Methodist or Baptist group, its "consciousness of kind" mentality, and its emphasis upon personal redemption, equipped the newer and lower-status religious denominations with the precise tools necessary to build Protestant Christian communities on the frontier.

THE EFFECT OF THE FRONTIER

These Baptist and Methodist groups, as well as some Presbyterians, were prototypes of the "religious citizens" who moved west. An assumption was made that the religious apathy of the new nation would also move westward. It was the "holy task" of "chosen people" to counteract such religious apathy. Support for frontier religious establishments was necessary. As we mentioned in Chapter 6, the concept of voluntarism in religion became the chief means of religious support. Lyman Beecher, a distinguished Presbyterian minister of New England, wrote an eloquent appeal to the churches to recognize that "the religious and political destiny of the nation would be decided in the continually multiplying frontier communities" (Hudson, 1961). Revivals were seen as the chief vehicles for Christianizing the western states and territories. The Second Great Awakening in New England (and later on the frontier), beginning in the early 1800s, again stimulated interest in the revivalism tools of the Methodists and Baptists. Home missionary societies were founded to provide financial support as well as personnel for mass evangelism. These tactics were primarily responsible for personally-oriented, simplistic Protestant Christianity flourishing in the southern and western frontier areas. What truly began as an early social movement later became an institutionalized religious structure.

As was discussed in Chapter 5, the first stage of growth for new religious groups is characterized by informality of leadership and operation. The new religious group tends to begin through the leadership of a strong individual who, by the power of personal gifts, attracts supporters to the particular cause. In the emerging frontier, one particular movement caught on, initiated by two Presbyterian ministers—father and son. Alexander and Thomas Campbell were interested in the restoration of primitive Christian unity. For a few years, the new movement sought alliance with the Presbyterians and Baptists, but it ultimately failed in this mission. Thomas Campbell authored an historic *Declaration and Address* in 1809 which states that the "Church of Christ" had essential unity; sectarian divisions among Christians were un-Christian; and the cure for such divisions was the restoration of the New Testament Church (Littell, 1962:43–44). The movement became more settled in the form of a "brotherhood" of locally organized churches, with the Bible viewed as the chief cornerstone of faith and truth. Theologically, the Campbellite churches were strongly Wesleyan, but not Methodist in terms of organization. Although these churches were confined almost entirely to the Ohio Valley area, their zeal in opposing an educated clergy and their opposition to the missionary societies of the more established religious groups were an early sign of later Protestant fragmentation over the fundamentals of the faith (Hudson, 1961:94).

On the other hand, Baptists, Methodists, and fragmented groups of Presbyterians worked in consort to fight against infidelity on the frontier. The Mississippi Valley was the target of a religious campaign during the years 1829-1831. When the American Home Missionary Society was founded in 1826, the circular which announced its formation declared that "a more extended effort for the promotion of Home Missions is equally indispensable to the moral mainline denominations and 33.5 million are distributed within conservative advancement and the political stability of the United States" (Hudson, 1961:84-86). Although there was friendly rivalry between churches for converts won in jointly sponsored revivals, cooperation was the hallmark of their evangelistic efforts. The great valley campaign stressed Bibles for every family, schools for all, and an abundance of pastors for the western settlers.

Baptists, on the other hand, were never truly comfortable in this joint effort, and they eventually formed a separate society. Nevertheless, the Methodists contributed to the establishment of orthodox (and later fundamentalist) Protestantism through their farmer-preachers, circuit riders, and camp meetings. These groups served primarily those who went to the new territories from the southern states. The frontiersmen and their families were characterized by less education and lower cultural standards and by more active frontier "godlessness" than was true of the New Englanders who settled the upper Midwest and Mississippi Valley (Hudson, 1961:90-91). By the middle of the nineteenth century, these revival churches predominated and put their imprimatur on public life—in spite of the warnings of Unitarians, Congregationalists, Episcopalians, Orthodox Presbyterians, and Confessional Lutherans that such fervor made a mockery of sober religion (Littell, 1962:50-51). Still, it is true historically that the churches which were before the public eye and which followed people westward to the new frontiers were the Methodists, Baptists, Disciples of Christ, and the "missionary" Congregationalists and Presbyterians.

The effect of religion on the frontier was primarily to advance the pluralistic concept of American religion. As we illustrated in Chapter 6, frontier cooperation among Protestants gave way to narrowing sectarianism. The pluralistic arrangement of American religion actually encouraged dissident viewpoints among Protestant Christians. The seeds of fundamentalism as a social movement were nurtured historically through the existence of dissident viewpoints that evolved through the concept of religious pluralism. As Protestant Christianity butted heads against the emerging Roman Catholic urban presence during the second half of the nineteenth century, Biblical orthodoxy became a tool for opposing the social and political accommodation of the urban industrial workers (largely Catholic), for preserving the political power of the rural segments of the nation, and for standing against improving the economic position of working-class Americans regardless of their religious identification. Mass evangelism of the American public remained the chief vehicle for preserving the "Godly" nature of the United States.

THE CHANGE FROM RURAL TO URBAN EMPHASIS IN AMERICAN SOCIETY AND RELIGION

The fuel for America's industrial machine was a steady stream of European immigrants who settled in the industrial cities of the East and Midwest. As was indicated in Chapter 6, they were largely Catholics who, following the Civil War, came in ever increasing numbers. Their Catholicism served not only as a religious base, but as a culturally cohesive base as well. Protestant alarmists greatly exaggerated the numerical strength of the Catholics in order to gain support for organized efforts to evangelize them. The foremost Protestant evangelist of the late nineteenth century, Dwight L. Moody, aimed his orthodox Biblical message at the urban Catholics. Earlier, other more establishment-type Protestants (notably Samuel F. B. Morse and the Methodist bishops), were equally concerned about converting immigrant Catholics. Most of these mainline Protestant "anti-Catholics" believed in the manifest destiny of a Protestant, Christian United States, in the words of Martin Marty (1970), they sought to extend the "righteous empire" of Protestant Christianity.

On the other hand, there existed in this same era a *millenarian* movement within the United States. Millenarianism is the belief that Christ's return to Earth is imminent, and that when he does return there will exist a thousand years during which holiness will prevail and Christ will reign on Earth. This concept is based, in part, upon the writings in the twentieth chapter of the Book of Revelation in the Bible. This movement attempted to function as a correction to "perverse beliefs" in different Protestant denominations. It possessed a distinct identity and all of the characteristics of a new sect. The millenarian movement developed as a "church within a church." Because of this, it was more similar to eighteenth century Methodism than to the nineteenth century Campbellite movement (Sandeen, 1970:xv). The leadership for this apocalyptic vision of society's destiny came largely from Episcopal, Presbyterian, and Baptist clergy of good standing and considerable pulpit abilities. This group, who believed in the imminent Second Coming of Christ, spread their doctrinal interpretations through annual summer conferences, periodicals, and winter conventions. Sandeen states that their aim was to "awaken the sleeping church to the imminence of judgement and to call sinners to repentance before the day of salvation had passed away" (1970:xvii). They campaigned *against* Biblical liberalism and *for* the belief in the "infallibility of the Holy Scriptures." These were seen as the tools for salvation of the masses. Dwight L. Moody treated the urban masses in his revival meetings to large dosages of Christ's Second Coming; only this would bring in a new order; and until this second advent occurred, Christians should occupy themselves by saving others' souls and tending to their own (Marty, 1970:162:63). Moody's preaching fame, however, overshadowed his programs for the urban masses.

In spite of his concern with immigrant Catholics, evidence indicates that his audiences were largely already-settled Americans who had traded the farm for the factory or urban business, and were not the hardened secularists or papists that he implied they were. Moody really did not convert many of the new Irish, or eastern and southern European immigrants of the Roman Catholic tradition; but like so many orthodox Protestants of the era, he adopted a stance of protecting the faith from reformers and their theological questioning of the Holy Scriptures. The fittest would survive the harshness of city living largely by coming under the care of the Great Shepherd (Marty, 1970:162:62). Moody's revival song leader, Ira Sankey, presented the same theme in the most famous gospel song of the Moody revivals, "The Ninety and Nine."

Still, the Catholic urban population continued to bother conservative Protestants. As we pointed out in Chapter 6, Josiah Strong in a best selling book named *Our Country*, observed the following: "Because our cities are so largely foreign, Romanism finds in them its chief strength." Furthermore, Catholics were a visible presence in Protestant areas because they did not keep the Sabbath, were often given to intemperance, and were perceived as raucous rioters. The decree of Papal Infallibility in 1870-71 further fueled anti-Catholic sentiment (Marty, 1970:155-59).

Finally, free-thinkers began publically to question religious truths and fundamentals. Robert Ingersoll, the son of a Presbyterian minister, became the most celebrated platform speaker against God and Christianity. Church people went to his lectures to boo and hiss the villain; liberated thinkers went to have their reasons for opposing superstitions and man-shaped dieties confirmed. Although Ingersoll was little more than a tempest in a teapot (for he filed no court suits against established religion as has Madelyn Murray O'Hair), he did help to congeal among conservative Protestants the ideas that eventually led to the emergence of fundamentalism as a religious movement.

Historically it seems that the society-wide changes which reflected the shift from a rural to an urban emphasis made their mark upon American Protestantism. Immigrant Catholics threatened the established religious order because "true" biblical beliefs were not the foundation of their faith. Individual salvation and concern for a person's soul were the keys to the kingdom—both on earth and in heaven. The urban masses, one by one, had to be reached in the name of salvation; the more narrow view of the impending Apocalypse held by the millennialists caused a collective nervousness since the cities loomed as godless Babylons; and the impact of science and free-thinking upon the infallibility of the Bible further caused a need for fundamentalist entrenchment.

It is important, then, to place the fundamentalist movement into proper historical perspective. As an organized campaign against urbanization and the impact of science upon Biblical truths. Both mass evangelism and millenarianism characteristic of late nineteenth and early twentieth century fundamentalism were rural reactions against the cities and their immigrant populations. Later, when fundamentalist beliefs were defended in the "Scopes Trial," William Jennings Bryan, former candidate for President and a populist leader, was special prosecutor for the anti-evolution forces.

Finally, those branches of moderate and progressive Protestantism which sought to reconcile the message of Christianity with the social, economic, and political needs of the urban population began to make an impact within the main religious denominations. The Social Gospel became first, a complement, and later, an alternative to mass evangelism and revivalism. As the social gospel movement began to be perceived as a genuine threat to orthodox Protestant Christianity, southern Protestants became allies of the "Yankee" fundamentalists. It was, after all, social reformers from the northern tier of states who came into the South after the Civil War and set up educational facilities for blacks. These religious reformers also saw the defeat of the Confederacy as a moral and spiritual victory. Consequently, feelings against the reform movement ran high among southern Protestants, and the alliance with northern religious conservatives was a comfortable arrangement. The Social Gospel movement, while aimed at cities, threatened further the rural population of the United States.

THE SOCIAL GOSPEL AND ITS FOES

The ideals of the *Social Gospel* stressed the progressive side of human behavior. It took root in the "postmillennial side" of earlier revivalism. The leaders, such as Walter Rauschenbusch and Washington Gladden,[1] both argued and agitated for social reform, labor reform, and political reform. What the movement set out to do was to show that the "private Protestants" (those who stressed individual salvation, pietistic personal behavior, and the future benefits of heavenly life) also "meddled in politics" by constantly taking stands against gambling and drinking and for Sunday closing laws and other similar issues. Furthermore these conservative Protestants supported the *laissez-faire* economic system and, in general, the status quo. Those who supported the social gospel argument believed that Christianity should work to change laws so that all persons, rich and poor, would be treated in a humanitarian way. Although they advocated reshaping the collective social condition of urban dwellers, their methods were an extension of earlier evangelical traditions: they did *not* want a social involvement at the expense of historic evangelical concerns with individuals, souls, and morality. In a sense they were the "public Protestants" of the decades on either side of 1900. The world, as well as individuals, needed transforming (Marty: 1970:177-79, 204-06).

This overall goal of the Social Gospel, however, was not uniformly received in spite of the sincerity of its leaders. Since some of these leaders supported the effort of the labor movement as a means of helping the urban workers, big business strongly opposed the extension of religion into the social arena. Most of the membership of Protestant churches was composed chiefly of persons in the mid-

[1]Rauschenbusch reacted to the poverty-stricken immigrant population in the Hell's Kitchen area of New York City; Gladden was a well-known minister in Columbus, Ohio.

dle class; and many of these members feared that the churches would support socialism, which they then identified with the labor movement and unionization (Olmstead, 1961).

The alternative to the Social Gospel remained a kind of Christian social service that was individual-oriented. Notable was an import from England, the Salvation Army. Founded in 1878 by William Booth, its program stressed witnessing to Christ by informal preaching and outdoor evangelistic missions which featured brass bands. Its theology was conservative, emphasizing sin, redemption, and holiness in living. When the Salvation Army reached the United States in 1889, it began its ministry in the tenement sections of cities through highly publicized Slum Brigades. These "troops," organized along quasi-military lines, went into the deteriorating city neighborhoods, held services in saloons, brought relief to the destitute, and preached against sinful vice (Olmstead, 1961). Since this kind of approach was in line with the older, evangelical style of church ministry, it gradually won the support of conservative Protestants and served as a foil to the Social Gospel. Personal redemption was an alternative to the Social Gospel's collective redemption, and individual perfection was more important than society-wide perfection.

Although the proponents of the Social Gospel hoped to build a broad base of support through all of Protestantism, they saw it gain only limited acceptance within Presbyterian, Northern Baptist, Congregationalist, Methodist, and Disciples of Christ denominations. Its capstone was the issuance of a Social Creed in 1908 by the newly founded Federal Council of Churches. The creed called for equal rights for all men, child labor laws, laws against the liquor traffic, protection for workers in their place of employment, old age benefits, labor arbitration, reduction of working hours, guaranteed living wages, and "the application of Christian principles to the acquisition and use of property." Although these positions seem rather mild by contemporary standards, they were perceived by a majority of affluent Protestant laity as inflammatory. Furthermore they served to drive fundamentalist Protestant clergy and laity into further intransigence regarding orthodoxy, piety, and personal evangelism.

The Social Gospel continued to be viewed by its foes as an unscriptural perversion of the gospel and as an extremely liberal political philosophy masquerading as religion. The only issue on which there was general agreement was the temperance movement and National Prohibition. With the exception of Lutherans of German background, virtually all Protestant groups fought the "evils of liquor" (and politically, the power of urban Catholics). This issue alone was not strong enough to keep the fundamentalists and the progressives within the mainline Protestant denominations together. The first two-and-one-half decades of the twentieth century constituted the era during which "fundamentalist Christians" emerged as different kinds of "believers" than their less conservative counterparts. They were antisocial gospel, anti-intellectual, and anti-Biblical criticism. Some were ardent *pre-millenialists* (an American term for millenarianism) who believed that God would end the evil world momentarily; others were orthodox conservatives who simply believed that man should not tamper with the revelations of God to mankind as recorded in the Scriptures. Still a broad-based plurality of Protestants simply believed that religion should consist of living a holy and pietistic life, of saving the souls of unbelievers through the techniques of revivalism, and of working hard during a person's earthly life in order to obtain heavenly rewards. These latter beliefs were the older, familiar tenets of American Protestantism; and, in the eyes of many, fundamentalism preserved their familiar frontier and rural qualities.

THE FUNDAMENTALS AND THE FUNDAMENTALISTS

The specific events that eventually led to a series of written expositions entitled *The Fundamentals* can be traced to the various Bible conferences that were held between 1865 and 1910 to foster pre-millenarian interpretations of Scripture and historical events. As noted earlier, these early meetings enjoyed broad-based mainline Protestant support. However, in the early 1900s, much of this leadership disappeared through death or change in belief (Sandeen, 1970:208-210). Nevertheless, a strong millenarian tradition remained to be incorporated into fundamentalism. Another event during this period that contributed directly to fundamentalism was the establishment of numerous Bible Schools. According to Goen (1959), there were twenty-three such schools by 1910. Furthermore, numerous heresy trials in those churches whose governmental systems allowed such procedures proceeded. By 1910, the clash concerning nonliteral Biblical interpretations, the social gospel ideology, and liberal theology had erupted into open controversy.

Between 1910 and 1912, twelve paperback pamphlets, *The Fundamentals*, were published and distributed by two wealthy brothers from California. Virtually all of the contributing writers were scholarly students of the Bible, and they gave sober and serious defenses for the main beliefs of orthodox Protestant Christianity. Over 300,000 copies were distributed which served the purpose of bringing the issues involved in the controversy out in the open (Goen, 1959:88). On the other hand, Sandeen explains that the primary purpose of *The Fundamentals*, that of checking the spread of modern and liberal theology, was a failure. He views the writing as the "last flowering of a millenarian-conservative alliance dedicated at all costs to the defense of the cardinal doctrines of nineteenth century American evangelicalism" (1970:206-207).

Nevertheless, those conservative Protestants who subscribed to the doctrinal points outlined in *The Fundamentals* began a movement within organized churches which later would lead to parting of the ways for many of them. The years leading up to World War I saw continued success for revivalism. Billy Sunday, an ex-baseball player-turned-evangelist, followed in the footsteps of Dwight L. Moody. Prohibition became the law of the land through constitutional amendment. Morality, albeit of a Protestant variety, seemed ascendant. In a sense, conservative Protestants believed that traditional Christianity had been preserved. In 1919 the World's Christian Fundamentals Association was formed. A prominent Baptist minister from Minneapolis, William Bell Riley, led its formation and urged all who wanted cooperative action against liberalism and the Social Gospel to join (Goen, 1959:88). Represented were orthodox theological conservatives, pre-millenialists," and a few people from holiness or Pentecostal sects. Their common bond was a holy war on "modernism" within the organized churches and their theological schools.

As the decade of World War I gave way to the decade of the 1920s, two significant controversies began to unfold. The first was a northeastern urban tempest, while the second was a southern rural phenomenon. The former was the famous sermon preached in 1922 from the pulpit of New York's First Presbyterian Church by Harry Emerson Fosdick. Its title was "Shall the Fundamentalist Win?" Fosdick, a liberal Baptist, was then the supply pastor for that Presbyterian church. His controversial message flung down the gauntlet to fundamentalists, daring them to fight to the finish. In the ensuing uproar, Baptists demanded Fosdick's resignation from the ministry, and Presbyterians urged his removal from the pulpit of the New York church. The fundamentalists did not win either of these battles (Goen, 1959:88).[2] However, the controversy concerning fundamentalist doctrine continued in several denominations, including Presbyterians, for several more years.

The second controversy concerned science and religion. Fundamentalists viewed the theory of evolution as a direct threat to the omnipotence of God and to the Genesis account of the creation of the universe. Therefore, the fundamentalists sought to root the theory out of the public schools. The antievolution campaign concentrated upon southern states for the most part and drew rather strong support from Methodists and Disciples of Christ as well as southern Presbyterians and Baptists. All in all, thirty-seven antievolution bills were introduced into twenty state legislatures between 1921 and 1929 (Sandeen, 1970:266-67). The climax of the controversy occurred in 1925 in the small town of Dayton, Tennessee. Known as the "Monkey Trial," it involved the prosecution of John T. Scopes for teaching evolution in the high school in direct violation of Tennessee state law against promoting evolutionary theory. William Jennings Bryan, three time presidential candidate, was the special prosecutor. Clarence Darrow of Chicago was Scopes' defense attorney. Bryan really defended Christianity as he understood it and was in turn attacked by the agnostic Darrow. Scopes was

---

[2]Fosdick became the minister of New York City's Riverside Church, built by John D. Rockefeller. He also gained national acclaim as a radio preacher.

convicted, but the "war against modernism" was not won with this one victory.[3]

Both of these controversies simply added to the intransigence of the fundamentalists in their defense of conservative Protestantism. In 1929, the Presbyterian Seminary at Princeton University became the object of a last ditch effort for control by fundamentalist J. Gresham Machen. In 1923, he had published a volume entitled *Christianity and Liberalism.* Its central issue was the supernatural nature of Christianity. According to Goen, Machen's formulation amounted to the following:

> Christianity must be defined in terms of doctrine derived from the Bible rather than in terms of life growing out of religious experience. It is a message rather than a movement. It presents a great saving fact, not merely the description of a feeling. Life is important, to be sure, but doctrine is not derived from religious experience but rather from conditions that determines such experience. This is why so much must be made of Biblical authority: the Bible represents the essentially trustworthy transmission of the message—it is the Word of God. Its central truths are the transcendence of the living God, the special creation of man as a moral personality, the universality and power of sin, the historical redemption provided by Jesus Christ the Son of God, the need of every person for cleansing and quickening by the Holy Spirit, the incompleteness of time forms and the necessity for a final consummation (Goen, 1959:91).

Machen and those who agreed with him viewed all of the doctrinal statements as necessary. The dilution of any one would allow the concept of Biblical fallibility to prevail which, in turn, would humanize God and deify man.

By 1930 the mainline Protestant faiths had rather well repudiated the narrow stance of fundamentalism. Fundamentalist Presbyterians withdrew and formed Westminster Seminary in Philadelphia, and extremely conservative Northern Baptists likewise established the Eastern Baptist Seminary (Goen, 1959:89). Although many fundamentalists remained within the established denominations, their influence was diluted. Outside of the South, Protestant denominations began to implement the new version of "cultural religion" discussed in Chapter 6. In place of the older nineteenth century model of evangelical revivalism, the mainline churches substituted a broad "community" religion. Doctrinal differences tended to be minimized. Glorification of America's destiny and its prosperity prevailed, although the Great Depression somewhat altered this belief. The heritage of evangelical Protestantism remained with the Protestants of the South: Methodists, Baptists, Presbyterians, and Disciples of Christ.

[3]The famous journalist, H. L. Mencken, of the *Baltimore Sun* used the trial to portray the South as a backward, "redneck," unsophisticated region ruled mainly by religious intolerance and ignorance.

Fundamentalism in the South

Even as the nation prospered in the 1920s and stumbled economically in the 1930s, the states of the old Confederacy remained essentially rural. Few urban Catholics could be found in southern cities with the exception of New Orleans and San Antonio. Although the oil industry in Texas was booming, agriculture and agricultural products formed the base of the southern economy. What few industries that did move South recruited cheap labor from rural white southerners who would move to the cities and towns. These workers brought with them a rural Protestantism in much the same way that northern and midwestern rural-to-urban immigrants had done in the nineteenth century.

This rural religious tradition, whether Baptist or Methodist, emphasized personal redemption, pietistic living, and evangelistic fervor. Even southern Presbyterians shared in these beliefs to some extent. The "brush arbor revivals" of rural Baptists and the small-town "protracted meetings" of Methodists were transplanted to the southern cities. Although most of the major Protestant denominations of the South, particularly Baptist and Presbyterians, were somewhat exclusive concerning membership requirements, a community-wide cooperation prevailed during seasonal evangelistic efforts. To "save the lost" was a common goal for southern Protestants. According to Martin Marty (1970) the most popular southern Protestant sermon topic during the twenties and thirties was "Eternal Life." Although Presbyterians and Methodists used ritualistic services of worship, an air of informality prevailed. Baptists and Disciples of Christ congregations generally had no formal order of service, except in their largest urban churches.

In this atmosphere, the fundamentalist-modernist controversy was not much of an issue. Only in isolated instances did the battle gain much attention. Alumni of Wake Forest College, a Southern Baptist school in North Carolina, successfully defended William Louis Poteat for his efforts to reconcile scientific theory and Biblical scriptures. Professor Lulu Pace held onto her post as a distinguished biologist at the Baptist's Baylor University in Waco, Texas, despite anti-evolutionists' efforts to remove her. After southern Methodists lost their battle to prevent Vanderbilt University's Divinity School from slipping into the hands of liberal theologians, they simply retreated to Duke University, Emory University, and Southern Methodist University, then newly formed. Famed Bishop Warren A. Candler of the Methodist Church stated southern Protestantism's evangelical mission as follows: "The hope of mankind is in the keeping of the Anglo-Saxon nations, led by the United States; and evangelical Christianity, with Methodism in the forefront, is the hope of these nations" (Marty, 1970:222-23). The reform of society should follow individualistic lines and should not tamper with the established social order. If there were poor, then convert the rich man who would then, through Christian charity, take care of the needy. Although Candler did not represent all of southern religion, he did give eloquent support to the widely shared religious symbols of the South: the Bible, the hymnal (or songbook), the revival, and the prayer meeting. Although the Methodist tradition never advocated a literalist interpretation of the Bible, many of the undereducated Methodist ministers of the South accepted the infallibility of the Scriptures.

It was, however, within the ranks of Southern Baptists that some of the earlier northern fundamentalist controversies occurred in the South. Although about 95 percent of Southern Baptist ministers rejected Biblical criticism as un-Godly, they were not as united in interpretations of certain portions of the New Testament. Those portions of the scriptures which underscored the millenarian position were interpreted in a variety of ways. The pre-millenialists within the denomination were vocal critics of the non-millenialists. The leading Southern Baptist fundamentalist and pre-millenialist, J. Frank Norris, eventually led his First Baptist Church of Fort Worth, Texas, from the Southern Baptist fold. This followed many years of disrupting annual conventions of Texas Baptists and weekly telegrams each Sunday morning condemning the work of his rival, George W. Truett, for forty years the pastor of the First Baptist Church in Dallas. Other Baptist congregations holding extreme millenarian viewpoints also withdrew to become "Bible Baptist Churches" and "independent Baptist churches." Another internal controversy involved the local autonomy of churches: the Baptist Missionary Association was a schismatic movement that erupted over who would support missionaries—the local church or the denominational missionary board. Other issues related to local autonomy included the exclusivity of baptism and the "Lord's Supper."

Many fundamentalist congregations restricted these "ordinances" to *local* members only and even excluded other Baptists. Even the less fundamentalist Baptists were nonetheless conservative in doctrinal practices. In an overwhelming majority of Southern Baptist churches, only "Baptist" Christians were invited to communion, and baptism by total immersion under the auspices of a Baptist church was the requirement of membership. Also, certain churches continued to "de-fellowship" (or to expell) members who strayed from pietism by drinking, by dancing, or by otherwise leading a "worldly" life. Even a child reared in a Baptist home was required to "profess faith in Jesus Christ," to be "born again," and to be baptized into the faith. The twice-yearly revivals so characteristic of Southern Baptists during the first four decades of the twentieth century, usually "saved the souls" of younger Baptist off-spring and offered older members a chance to publically "re-dedicate their lives to Christ."

Though there was no evangelist of national prominence to succeed Billy Sunday during these decades, there were many Southern Baptist ministers whose preaching reputations were regional or statewide. A major part of southern Protestantism had always involved the pulpit appeal of the clergy, and Southern Baptists continued this legacy. One well-known Baptist pastor, Joseph M. Dawson, who served the historic First Baptist Church of Waco, Texas, for over thirty years, said that the ability to bring in converts during a revival was a primary measure of a minister's worth. The Baptists of the South did then, preserve the tradition of revivalism.

The southern branch of the Methodist church also stressed revivalism, at least until their merger with northern Methodists in 1939. Evangelistic preaching in revivals and in summer camps remained a part of their tradition for twenty or more years, but gradually became less important. In the 1930s Methodist seminary students began to be exposed to less conservative theological education and the "preaching mission" of that tradition gave way to a community cultural religion characteristic of the northern branch of the church. In many respects, however, the clergy were ahead of the laity who wanted old-fashioned preaching and hymn-singing to continue. A distinguished Methodist minister who held important pastorates in Arkansas and Texas, Dr. Homer Fort, once invited the famous Harry Emerson Fosdick to preach in the Central Methodist Church of Hot Springs, Arkansas, in the late 1930s. Dr. Fosdick had traveled from New York to that spa to "take hot mineral baths" for his health and had attended a Sunday morning service at Fort's downtown Methodist church. After some coaxing from Dr. Fort, Fosdick agreed to deliver the sermon the following Sunday. With appropriate fanfare Fosdick's guest pulpit appearance was announced. His fame through radio had become nationwide, overcoming much of the earlier controversy concerning his famous antifundamentalist sermon of 1922. Nevertheless, several of the parishioners of Central Methodist Church were offended that such a "liberal" preached from this pulpit. It is probably true, however, that neither southern Baptists nor southern Presbyterians would have invited Fosdick to preach at that time. The regional conservatism of southern Protestantism still permeated those denominations, although the Presbyterians were becoming more of a cultural and accommodating body than the Baptists.

Thus, while fundamentalism remained very much a restricted social movement in northern Protestant denominations, its southern counterpart continued to flourish under the end of World War II. While the Orthodox Presbyterian Church (one of the sect-like groups to be formed out of the fundamentalist-modernist controversy) attracted only a few thousand members, the conservative Southern Baptist Convention experienced rapid growth between 1940 and 1960. Other conservative religious groups such as the Church of Christ, which split from the more moderate Disciples of Christ, also expanded in the southern and southwestern regions of the United States. Pentecostal and Holiness sects, some of which were the heirs to the pietism and holiness once present in Methodism, likewise flourished in the South. The exclusivity of all these groups and their narrow doctrinal beliefs became the symbols of southern fundamentalism. Still, there was and is, little affinity between northern fundamentalist sects and small denominations and the larger conservative and fundamentalist religious bodies in the South.

The most vocal fundamentalists, such as Carl McIntyre and Billy James Hargis, used the National Council of Churches, the World Council of Churches, and the spread of worldwide communism as centers for attack. Ministers and laity who were pre-millenial in their views continued to argue with other fundamentalists who were not like themselves. For the most part, fundamentalist sects outside of the South attracted a working-class and lower middle-class following. Still, there is evidence that church members with conservative, if not fundamentalist, beliefs remained within the denominations of mainstream Protestantism (Sandeen: 1970). Their collective voices, however, were muted until recently.

They and the departed fundamentalists probably formed a large part of the audience for a more moderate spokesman for the conservative Protestant cause, Charles H. Fuller of California. From the late 1930s until the middle 1960s, Fuller broadcast the "Old Fashioned Revival Hour" on nationwide radio. Although he was strongly pre-millenialist in his beliefs, Fuller never became a spokesman for causes of the far right. He founded Fuller Theological Seminary which has become a respectable, conservative theological school. Like the mass evangelists that preceded him, he used gospel music and a theme song. Fuller also read letters and testimonies from listeners that further personalized his evangelism. Finally, for most of the time the programs were broadcast, they were done "live" from the Long Beach, California, Municipal Auditorium. That such an undertaking could be sustained financially without a denominational base is a tribute to the viability of fundamentalism after the fundamentalist-modernist controversy withered away.

The Rise of Billy Graham

Fuller's success with radio evangelism led to numerous imitations, but none were as successful as Billy Graham. In the late 1940s, the man who was to become the most widely-known evangelist in the world appeared as just another tent revivalist preaching the millenarian message of Christ's imminent return to earth. Born in North Carolina, he first attended Bob Jones University, a fundamentalist college in the South. Graham then transferred to Wheaton College in Illinois, also a conservative religious school. He married the daughter of A. Nelson Bell, a well-known conservative southern Presbyterian missionary. However, in a California evangelistic tent meeting, Graham received nation-wide publicity through the conversion of two Hollywood personalities: actress Coleen Townsend and song-writer Stuart Hamblin. As the result of his experience, Hamblin wrote a song, "It Is No Secret What God Can Do," which became a nationwide hit. By the early 1950s, Billy Graham's crusades began attracting overflow crowds in arenas, coliseums, and stadiums in cities throughout the country. Motion pictures, beginning with "Oil Town, U.S.A." were produced to further promote the fundamentalist-evangelical cause. A nationwide program, "The Hour of Decision," began its broadcasts (Frady, 1979:194-196;231).

As Graham became more successful, he became more respectable. He would hold no "crusade" in any city without support from the mainline churches of the area. Converts in these revivals were urged to join a local church. Graham refrained from competing with already organized religious groups. His message remained basically pre-millenialist and Biblically-literal, but his "success" won him respect even from liturgical Protestants and Roman Catholics. He became an invited guest of American presidents beginning with Dwight D. Eisenhower. The National Prayer Breakfast held annually in Washington usually featured a Graham talk. According to Marty (1970), he gradually modified his time-table for the Second Coming of Christ, but he never abandoned the basic millenarian belief (McLoughlin, 1960).

That Graham's evangelical approach would flourish in the 1950s is seen as somewhat of a paradox. While the United States was more visibly religious than at any other time in its history, it was a religiosity that thrived mainly upon a culture religion which stressed progress, positive thinking, the spiritual and material blessing of God, and cooperation among religious groups. In contrast, the evangelical Graham preached repentance from sins, pietistic living through Christ, and heavenly life. Still, Americans of the 1950s seemed to thrive on both of the religious themes. Although his crusades were filled with mostly a white audience, he did insist that audiences be integrated after the Supreme Court decision in 1955 which pronounced an end to school segregation. The phenomenal success of Billy Graham's mass evangelism served to reassert fundamentalist and evangelical theology. His fame and his acceptance by national leaders gave evangelicalism a respectability that it had lacked for twenty or more years.

The leader of fundamentalist extremism, Carl McIntyre, denounced Graham as a compromiser of the true faith because Graham was not as vocal as McIntyre in his denouncing of Communism and was cooperating with Protestants of the National Council of Churches. This type of action by right-wing fundamentalists separated them even further from mainstream Protestant Christianity and allowed more accommodation between the more moderate fundamentalists and the major denominations.

Southern Baptist Expansion

This accommodation between the moderate fundamentalists and the major denominations did not lead to real cooperation. Southern Baptists, the Missouri Synod Lutherans, and the lesser fundamentalist groups outside the South remained suspicious of the growing ecumenical spirit of Christianity which developed in the 1950s. The Baptists of the South began to open churches in the

West, the Midwest, and even the Northeast. This ended an informal demarcation between them and their Northern Baptist counterparts that had prevented competition between the denominations. This "Mason-Dixon Line" of Baptists crumbled as Southern Baptists migrated North, East, and West. Since many of those who left the South were skilled and semi-skilled laborers, most of the Southern Baptist churches that were built in the northern and western states were working-class congregations, with a strong emphasis upon distinctive doctrines, exclusiveness, and political conservatism. Those more educated Southern Baptists who left the South also gravitated to these outpost churches. They felt a lack of warmth, informality, and Baptist "distinctiveness" among the American (or northern) Baptist congregations; and the newer Southern Baptist churches filled this need.

The Baptist revival technique continued to flourish in the 1950s and the southern migrants exported it to other parts of the nation. "Bigness" and "growth" were Southern Baptist goals. Slogans and attendance techniques were promoted through the denomination. One catch-phrase which appeared for 1954 and which summed up the Southern Baptist goal was "A Million More in '54." The goal was achieved. In the larger congregations, techniques to increase Sunday School attendance were adopted. Church staffs of these churches began to include, in addition to the pastor, an associate pastor, a "Minister of Education," a "Minister of Music," a "Minister of Youth," elementary and junior high coordinators, and often other staff members. Even the congregations of medium size often employed a second full-time staff member who directed religious education or music or both. Graded choir programs from kindergarten through adulthood were promoted and often implemented. In short, the once regional, once provincial, and once fundamentalist Southern Baptist Convention successfully copied the organization techniques of mainline Protestantism, modified them for their own use, and combined them with mass evangelism. The result was an unprecedented growth, an elevation in the prestige of the denomination, and a new competing culture religion that demanded more commitment from active members than other Protestant churches could expect.

This occurred in the era of religiosity, the 1950s; but as we indicated in our discussion of pluralism (Chapter 7), the appeal of Norman Vincent Peale, Bishop Fulton Sheen, and the comfortable community culture religion of the era began to fade during the turmoil of the Civil Rights movement and the Vietnam War expansion in the 1960s. However, no such fading occurred among the evangelicals, particularly the Southern Baptists. In 1967, the Southern Baptist Convention with 11 million plus members, surpassed in total membership its long-time rival, the Methodists. This was in spite of the fact that the Methodist Church had experienced growth throughout the 1950s and half of the 1960s (Kelley, 1972:20-25). Figure 8-1 illustrates this growth. Other churches in the category of "evangelical sects and denominations" also experienced growth.

Figure 8-1: Membership Comparison: 1958-1975

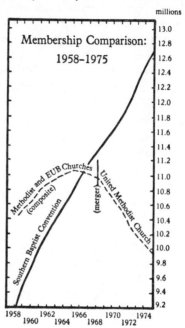

Kelley, 1972:22.

All of these fundamentalist and conservative groups achieved this without adandoning fundamentalist doctrine, conservative political stances, or their exclusivity. As the more "liberal" Protestant denominations asserted themselves in the realm of civil rights and political protest, the conservatives, for the most part, maintained the stance of "private Protestantism," referred to earlier. They continued to oppose political issues involving private morality—legalized gambling, liquor-by-the-drink, and the repeal of Sunday closing laws—but they remain virtually silent regarding the rights of minorities and the issue of the war in Vietnam. As clergy from Methodist, Presbyterian, United Church of Christ, and Episcopalian denominations spoke out and demonstrated on behalf of these national issues, only mild resolutions endorsing desegregation were adopted by the Southern Baptists. The anger of the conservatives within the mainstream churches was often seen as "proof" by the fundamentalist and conservative churches that political activism, instead of personal evangelism, was non-Christian. The mainline Churches' preoccupation with social and political issues led to the prediction of fragmentation and decline at the end of the 1960s, but the continued success of the fundamentalists would prove otherwise.

In a real sense, "contemporary evangelicalism" was born out of the frustrations inherent in the 1960s. Although the nation made real gains in the area of

Civil Rights and finally disengaged from the Vietnam conflict in 1973, the "liberal" influence of mainline Protestantism failed again to produce the Kingdom of God on earth. A sizeable minority within the mainline denominations called for a return to theological conservatism, personal evangelism, and Biblical enlightenment. In other words, the conservatives' anger translated into direct programs, small movements, and agitation for a return to evangelicalism. No denomination with Protestantism escaped these pressures. By the mid-1970s most had reached accommodation with their own "evangelicals," who saw themselves as in the vanguard of a genuine Christian renewal of nationwide size. Popular journals, religious journals, and scholars call this movement *contemporary evangelicalism*.

CONTEMPORARY EVANGELICALISM

The main point of agreement between the many evangelicals of various denominational affiliations in the 1970s is a subjective experience of personal salvation which they describe as being "born again." This generally means conversion or regeneration. More particularistic interpretations vary from one group to another. For example, members of the churches which make up the Southern Baptist Convention have always emphasized the idea of being "born again"; the baptism of infants has never been a part of their tradition, but the conversion of children, teenagers, and adults has. By contrast many Missouri Synod Lutherans embrace the authority of the Bible—a major tenet of the evangelicals, but keep the tradition of infant baptism. Holiness congregations, such as the Wesleyans, Pentecostals, and Assemblies of God, stress a continuing emotional experience that includes the charismatic phenomenon of glossolalia (speaking in Apostolic tongues), rededicating of a person's life to Christ, and rhythmic music. United Methodist, Presbyterian, and Disciples of Christ congregations which are evangelical are more likely to embrace conservative doctrine, personal morality, and Biblical authority as an alternative to the social activism and involvement of their parent denominations. They stress what was once an integral part of their tradition, particularly in the South: "making a conscious, personal commitment to Christ," a spiritual encounter that can be either sudden or gradual. In addition, many individuals within these denominations participate in the charismatic renewal movement, once the exclusive province of the Holiness sects and churches. This aspect of contemporary evangelism is more controversial and, therefore, is not a point of unity among the evangelicals. Even certain "non-evangelicals" such as some Episcopalians and Roman Catholics are enthusiastically following this movement too.[4]

This basically loose-knit minority within American Christianity numbers an estimated 45.5 million people. Twelve million are within the Protestant

[4]This aspect of the evangelical movement is discussed later in this chapter.

Protestant denominations outside of the National Council of Churches (*Newsweek*, 1976:68). Unlike the successors to fundamentalist controversy of the 1920s, many of these newer evangelicals are prosperous business and professional people. They are confined neither to the southern nor midwestern "Bible Belts"; instead they seem to be a part of a nationwide Bible Belt that has neither geographical nor social class boundaries.

The common appeal of this newer religious social movement seems to be a sense of close-knit community. The formalism of established rituals in mainline Protestant churches and the growing reserve of many large Southern Baptist congregations has contributed to the perceived need of many for a more intimate small group atmosphere in the religious arena. This, along with the reaction against the public activism of American Protestantism, accounts for the continuing success of "born again" Christianity. The new respectability of the evangelicals has been aided also by large numbers of businessmen and professionals who engage in organized Bible study, small prayer meetings, and personal evangelism.

The growing base of people committed to these activities began during the successful Billy Graham Crusades of the 1950s. Over the years, the number of such individuals has increased. According to William Martin, a sociologist from Rice University, as many as 1,500 people, many of whom are laypeople, receive fairly intensive instruction in preaching, soul-winning, and church leadership prior to any contemporary crusade by Graham. Their training eventually leads to a continuation of their involvement. Furthermore, Martin has reported that Graham's decision to hold a crusade in New York City was reached in the board room of Mutual Life Insurance of New York. That revival's executive committee included the board chairman of MONY, a Chase Manhattan National Bank, and the presidents of RCA and Genesco (Martin, 1978:152). Other prominent business men who support Graham included J. Howard Pew of Sun Oil Company and W. Maxey Jarman. Well-known politicians are also listed as evangelicals: President Ronald Reagan, former President Jimmy Carter, former President Gerald Ford, United Nations Ambassador Andrew Young, former Senator Harold Hughes, United States House of Representatives Minority Leader John Rhodes, and United States Senator Mark Hatfield. These individuals, who form a miniature composite of the evangelical movement, are dispersed throughout various Protestant denominations, both mainline and conservative. Although not all are counted as ardent supporters of Billy Graham, they are committed to the principles of evangelicism of which Graham is the unquestioned symbol and the single most dominating influence and power within the movement. He stands also as a symbol of consensus among many who think of themselves as the "decent people" of America (Martin, 1978:97-99). In addition, the symbolism of Biblical authority and the decency of living a good Christian life are of primary importance to evangelicals.

This reflects the results of previous studies that demonstrate the sense of community that serves as a motivation for people to attend fundamentalist churches. Robert R. Monaghan (1967) used both interviews and questionnaires to identify reasons for such religious participation in a fundamentalist church in the Midwest. He identified three "ideal types" of members. Each type found the intimacy of their religious experience enhanced by participation in conservative congregation. The first type, "the authority seeker," believed in the absolute pronouncements of the minister and saw them as the only guide to living a Christian life, particularly in family affairs. Monaghan identified the second type as the "comfort seeker." This individual expressed satisfaction that the church provides the way to eternal life and peace of mind. He or she was also stronger than the other two types in expressing a desire for intimate personal relationships. Finally the "social participator" as an ideal type enjoyed the church intrinsically. This individual saw himself or herself as a leader and felt that the church provided him or her with an opportunity to use talents through Sunday School teaching, visitation, and other activities. Although all three types of participants differed on certain basic feelings about their reasons for attending the church, they all, to a large extent, expressed the notions of "intimacy" and "community" as motivating factors for their religious behavior. Monaghans' study probably reflected the feeling of many people during the 1960s who saw conservative religion as a secure base during that turbulent decade. The intimate communal spirit of evangelicism contributed to its reemergence as a highly visible alternative to the "culture religion" of social activism which had replaced the comfortable community religion of the 1950s.

A further example of the symbolic community aspect of the evangelicals is the use of certain phrases which indicate (1) intimacy with each other, (2) piety as a demonstration of religiosity, and (3) the necessity of evangelism. For example, "God loves you," "Jesus loves you," and "Praise the Lord" repeated to each other serve as means to show familiarity. Phrases such as "surrendering to the Lord," "lifting him or her up to the Lord," and "my life has been changed by Jesus Christ" tell others of a new found personal faith and relationship. The use of slogans and phrases that stress the importance of mass evangelism and personal evangelism are also employed. These include "witnessing for Christ," helping someone who is "under conviction of the Holy Spirit," and urging someone to "let Jesus come into your heart." None of these words are new since most have come out of the revivalism of the past, but they are new to the vocabularies of many of the "born again" evangelicals. Such phrases are similar to those used in the past by the Moravian pietists of the seventeenth century and by John Wesley who at Aldersgate Chapel "felt his heart strangely warmed."

Because of the success of evangelicalism, there seems to be a new ecumenical spirit that allows more cooperative efforts and fewer doctrinal differences. Their exploration of common interests stresses the similarities of the present movement with historical movements of the past. Not only the German pietism of the seventeenth century, but also the great Awakenings in England and America are viewed as recurring events in history. In a sense, the evangelicals are united in this view of dispensationalism—or the belief that God orders history according to a divine plan and intervenes in the affairs of mankind. The arena of politics is one example of the evangelicals' common efforts.

Dr. James Sullivan, former president of the Southern Baptist Convention, said in 1976:

> "There never was a time when our nation sensed the need for what Baptists can deliver more than now. . . . A world that had thought we were an ignorant, barefooted, one gallused lot was jarred out of its seat when it found out that. . . . our voluntary gifts in a year are approximately $1.5 billion, and that on an average Sunday our churches baptize about three times as many people as were baptized at Pentecost. . . . If we do not seize this opportunity, I think God's condemnation will be upon us. . . ." (*Newsweek*, 1976:70)

Other evangelicals are also interested in influencing the nation through politics, through publicizing social issues, and through influencing consumer patterns. In the 1976 presidential campaign, both Gerald Ford and Jimmy Carter emphasized their evangelical beliefs. In that same election year an estimated thirty congressional candidates, including several clergy, sought office on political platforms which stressed evangelical Christianity—particularly its commitment to traditional morality. Of course, this is ironic for many evangelicals since they have, during most of the existence of the United States, benefited from religious pluralism that resulted from the separation between church and state. However, as we demonstrated both in Chapter 6 and in the earlier discussion of the historical roots of fundamentalism, evangelicals and fundamentalists have always participated in politics when issues involved personal morality. Contemporary examples of other social issues in which the evangelicals are involved include the anti-abortion campaign, opposition to the ratification of the equal rights amendment, and opposition to homosexual rights. In addition, they are opposed to certain kinds of "sexual programming" on television, and they are currently putting pressure on the three commercial networks and their program sponsors. Finally there is a small but concerted effort to once again debunk the evolutionary theory of man's creation. However, in all of these issues there is division as well as unity among the evangelicals.

Anti-Abortion Campaign

Although this movement is seen as a largely Catholic effort, many evangelical Protestants are very opposed to "abortion-on-demand." The Lutheran Church-

Missouri Synod strongly opposes the Supreme Court decision which allows such abortions. Smaller churches of the Calvinist tradition, such as The Reformed Church in America and the Christian Reformed Church, are on record as favoring a constitutional amendment to outlaw all but therapeutic abortions. The Southern Baptist Convention on three occasions has debated resolutions concerning abortion without consensus. Individual congregations of the two main Presbyterian denominations have pressed the issue at regional presbytery and synod meetings and at the national general assemblies. Annual conferences of the United Methodist Church have also heard from their more conservative, evangelical congregations about opposition to abortion. In a very real sense, the "self-righteousness" and "absolutism" of fundamentalism precludes toleration of varying viewpoints and deeply felt beliefs about abortion. Many of the contemporary evangelicals demonstrate these "fundamentalist" personality characteristics in regard to abortion.

Opposition to the Equal Rights Amendment

This organized effort is closely akin to the antiabortion campaign, but is also uniquely different. Since most fundamentalists and evangelicals believe in a literal interpretation of the Bible, they read the writings of St. Paul as authoritative on the position of women as related to men. Subservience of women to men in both religious and nonreligious activities is viewed as the only "Christian" lifestyle. Any activity that takes women away from serving their husbands is seen as unscriptural. The most well-known contemporary expression of this belief is the "total woman" concept. What is interesting about this small social movement is that it largely involves middle-class and upper middle-class women. They are well-educated and are involved in the affairs of their community; but the one thing that sets them apart from other well-educated and community-oriented women is that the traditional (and Biblical) woman's role serves as their model. Great emphasis is placed on strict discipline of children. To be permissive in the realm of child-rearing is to be un-Christian, as is inattention to the moral and social needs of husbands. Among women committed to these ideas is a strong, well-articulated opposition to the ratification of the Equal Rights Amendment to the United States Constitution. In the view of those who subscribe to the "total women" concept, the fate of the United States is riding on the outcome of the Equal Rights Amendment. For the fundamentalist-evangelicals who are a part of this effort, the fate involves whether or not the United States will survive as a "Christian" nation.

Opposition to the Civil Rights of Homosexuals

The issue of rights for homosexuals is seen by many people as a new cause for old-line fundamentalists and some contemporary evangelicals. It is new only because the issue has never before surfaced so publically. Those conservative Christians who oppose public acceptance or tolerance of homosexuality cite Old Testament scriptural passages condemning homosexuality as a grievous sin. In addition, they use the scriptural passages of St. Paul as further justification of their opposition to "gays" and "gay rights." While Anita Bryant's 1977 crusade against homosexual rights is the best publicized of evangelical efforts, the moderate success of the antihomosexual crusade seems to be built upon the existence of strong opposition within and without evangelical Christianity to open, homosexual behavior.

Opposition to the Evolutionary Theory of Creation

Concern with the Book of Genesis versus the widely accepted scientific perspective of the beginnings of life has again surfaced as an issue within the evangelical movement. Although it never really died among die-hard fundamentalists, a new "creationist" position has achieved a new sophistication. Contemporary proponents of the literal interpretations of Genesis, such as a professor of physics at the University of Texas-El Paso, attempt to buttress their position with quasi-scientific data. One large public school system, the Dallas (Texas) Independent School District, now provides for the use of a textbook that presents the "creationist" point of view along with more standardized textbooks which subscribe to the "evolutionary" point of view.

These issues, each of which can be seen as a separate social movement to resist new points of view or prevailing points of view are, from time to time, skillfully promoted by evangelicals through mass media. The widespread use of television and radio is another characteristic of contemporary evangelicalism.

Evangelicalism and Mass Media

Television evangelism has become a booming business. As we stated earlier, the success of Billy Graham's "Hour of Decision" and Charles H. Fuller's "Old Fashioned Revival Hour," demonstrated the success of radio as an evangelistic medium. While most Protestant mainline denominations are content to present television and radio broadcasts of worship services, the evangelicals are presenting full-scaled productions that use the format of variety shows and talk shows. According to John Mariani (1979:22-25) there are at least 25 television stations almost wholly devoted to religious programming today. In addition, the Christian Broadcasting Network reaches 130 commerical stations, 4,000 cable stations in North America, and 60 satellite stations. In addition, individual evangelists' packaged shows such as those of Oral Roberts, are watched by millions throughout the world. Billy Graham's organization usually purchases prime time, preempting commercial network programs for periodic video-taped programs from his crusades.

Mariani considers the PTL (originally, Praise the Lord) Club to be the most polished evangelical show, which buys $7.4 million of air time each year. The PTL Club uses a talk-show format and is hosted by Jim Baker. He mixes Christian testimony with musical acts. A typical PTL Club show will involve celebrities, preachers, and simple folk (1979:24). A similar undertaking is the "700 Club," whose host is Pat Robertson, founder of the Christian Broadcasting Network. His talk-show format is more likely to include discussions concerning abortions, homosexuality, and the Equal Rights Amendment. Also popular (and successful) are the modified worship services presented by the Thomas Road Baptist Church of Lynchburg, Virginia.

Another successful example of the variety show format is the weekly half-hour series produced by Oral Roberts University in Tulsa, Oklahoma. Roberts also produces occasional "specials" which have the sophistication of Hollywood productions (Mariani, 1979:24). Music, preaching, and testimonies are a part of these shows. Little remains of the "old" Oral Roberts who was more of a brash faith healer than an evangelist with mass appeal.

Many observers of this phenomenal growth in media-based religion refer to all of these efforts as the *Electric Church*. The term implies a separate religious organization with little connection to established Protestant and Catholic churches. Critics, even within evangelical congregations, see collective programs siphoning off members and money from traditional churches and denominations. Others, however, within evangelical congregations are producing and airing their own programs which are in the same vein as the shows of the Electric Church.

Still there remain the more traditional evangelistic television and radio programs that have been associated with the evangelical appeal. Included are those whose legacy is the healing and charismatic revivals. It is this aspect of the evangelical movement that remains controversial among evangelicals.

The Charismatic Renewal Movement

American *Pentecostalism*, the original name associated with glossolalia and faith healing, began to emerge at the end of the nineteeneth century. Around the turn of the century, some of the reformers within Methodism and other Protestant bodies began to teach that the "baptism of the Holy Ghost, accompanied by speaking in tongues, was the final, and Pentecostal, work of grace to be sought by every Christian" (Harrell, 1975:11). Harrell reports that this "amorphous movement" slowly took shape in the 1920s as a "confusing patchwork" of small sects frequently divided by seemingly trivial points of doctrine. Pentecostal religion was especially successful in the South, but small churches began to spring up throughout the United States drawing members from the poor and from those discontented in more traditional Protestant churches (1975:11).

Because of their emphasis upon faith healing, glossolalia, and Jesus (as opposed to an emphasis upon the Trinity), Pentecostal bodies were refused admission to the World's Christian Fundamental Association in 1928. Still this tradition associated with Pentecostalism and the Holiness movement continued, although various sects split and resplit because of internal divisions over Biblical interpretations on marriage, divorce, and other moral issues. The relatively poor and obscure churches—Pentecostal, Assembly of God, and the Church of the Nazarene—offered distinctive alternatives to other Protestant churches, liberal and conservative, through the emotionalism of their music, glossolalia, and healing activities.

After World War II, two prominent Pentecostal evangelists gradually dominated the entire movement: A. A. Allen and Oral Roberts. Both continued the Pentecostal tradition of the test revival meeting featuring both personal salvation and personal healing. Loose affiliations with local congregations were present but these evangelists ran their own operations. Even though they were prosperous enough to purchase radio time, Allen, Roberts, and lesser Pentecostal evangelists continued to suffer the same skepticism and derision from the major Protestant denominations that had been leveled at earlier evangelists of their type (Harrell, 1975).

During the 1960s, however, Pentecostal religion began to appeal to certain members of traditional Protestant churches and of the Roman Catholic Church. These people, most of whom were affluent and educated, chose to remain in their respective churches. In Protestant denominations, certain congregations and parishes came to be known for their "charismatic" or "neo-Pentecostal" emphasis. Liturgical denominations, such as the Lutheran churches and the Episcopal church, gradually adopted a tolerant attitude toward their charismatics. Presbyterians, United Methodists, and Disciples of Christ studied the issue and were, at least, benign toward manifestation of the movement within their congregations. On the other hand, Southern Baptists and the Churches of Christ were generally intolerant. Wilson (1978:59) reports that during 1975 various state conventions affiliated with the Southern Baptist Convention voted to either disavow or to remove from cooperative fellowship local congregations and their pastors engaged in the charismatic movement. Harrell (1975:230) states that the Churches of Christ produced thousands of tracts denying the Biblical validity of the charismatic experience. Also attacked were the "quality" of the healing miracles. Generally, Southern Baptists also condemned charismatic activities as unscriptural.

The Roman Catholic Church saw groups urging a "charismatic renewal" within the church beginning to form in the 1960s. These scattered groups came together for the first time in 1967. From a total of 100 people attending the first conference, attendance increased to 22 thousand at the 1973 meetings. These were reportedly drawn from 1,250 separate Catholic Pentecostal groups around the United States (Harrison, 1974:49-63). Joseph Fichter (1975:53) states that the Catholic Pentecostals generally appear to be uninterested in affecting structural reform within the church. Instead, they are rather conservative both theologically and socially. Bord and Faulkner (1975:257-270) report that Catholic charismatics are actively involved with their religion, often attending weekly meetings, engaging in public religious behavior, and attending mass frequently. Participants can be described as highly orthodox, and their charismatic involvement tends to reinforce involvement with the formal church and their respect for the church authority. There is, however, a tenuous relationship between church authority and neo-Pentecostalism. In spite of the fact that Catholic bishops are tolerant of the charismatic renewal movement (O'Connor, 1971:21), the hierarchical arrangement of the Roman Catholic Church could quickly ban the movement if it should become too excessive. Thus, even though Catholic neo-Pentecostalism appears to benefit from church approval, it does have internal divisions between participants who are liberal Catholics and conservative Catholics. The liberals tend not be embrace the fundamentalist aspects of traditional and Protestant neo-Pentecostalism, while the conservatives are more likely to find affinity with non-Catholic charismatics (Fichter, 1975: 303-310).

This division, as well as other divisions, exists within the general charismatic renewal movement. Although some 47,000 charismatics from traditional Pentecostal sects and denominations, from mainline Protestant denominations, and from the Roman Catholic Church gathered in Kansas City, Missouri, in 1977, their common interest and belief in the "gifts of the spirit" was their major point of unity. The sacramental nature of the Catholic and Episcopalian charismatic experience is basically incompatible with the spontaniety of the same phenomenon for a Pentecostal or for a charismatic Presbyterian. The music of the Catholic Folk Mass, which includes "speaking in tongues" after receiving the eucharist is not an emotional experience for the charismatic of the Assembly of God tradition. Finally there is a division between charismatics which has become a point of controversy between them and noncharismatic Christians. Many who share in the beliefs of neo-Pentecostalism are adamant about its rightness, and they question not only the beliefs but also the sincerity of noncharismatics. They believe that no religious experience is valid unless it is a charismatic religious experience. This exclusivity has threatened the unity in not a few congregations and parishes which have neo-Pentecostal groups. Coupled with the theological opposition of most Southern Baptists, the charismatic movement remains a controversial aspect of contemporary evangelicalism.

Divisions within Contemporary Evangelicalism

The charismatic renewal movement within Protestantism (and its counterpart within Roman Catholicism) is not the only issue that divides evangelicals. Those predisposed toward extremely conservative political, economic, and social views remain skeptical of the more socially activistic "born-again" believers, as are represented by the radical evangelical journal *Sojourners*. The "Chicago Declaration" of 1973, held by an ecumenical group of evangelical scholars and activists called for a greater commitment to social reform in the tradition of the great reforms in England that followed the Wesleyan awakening. Many younger evangelicals agree with United States Senator Mark Hatfield that political liberalism is scripturally sound. This zeal for social reform stands in direct contrast to the right-wing political ideology of fundamentalists Carl McIntyre, and W. A. Criswell, pastor of the largest Southern Baptist church—the First Baptist Church in Dallas. It is also far more activistic than the political and economic conservatism of the Presbyterian Lay Committee—the conservative movement within the United Presbyterian Church. The evangelical and fundamentalist Southern Presbyterians who left their denomination to form the newer Presbyterian Church in America also are characterized by theological, political, social, and economic conservatism. Even with the rather culturally isolated Southern Baptist Convention there are diverse opinions concerning social activism (*Newsweek*, 1976:76-78).

Furthermore, many Southern Baptists dislike the label "evangelical." The Reverend Foy Valentine, a social activist who has headed for many years the Southern Baptist Christian Life Commission says:

> ... we are not evangelicals. ... That's a Yankee word. They want to claim us because we are big and successful and growing every year. But we have our own traditions, our own hymns, and more students in our own seminaries than they have in all of theirs put together. We don't share their politics or their fussy fundamentalism, and we don't want to get involved in their theological witchhunts." (*Newsweek*, 1976:76)

That there is disunity within the evangelical ranks is obvious. The inerrancy of the Bible remains a smoldering issue. This issue caused a schism within the Lutheran Church-Missouri Synod during the early 1970s. More traditional and fundamentalist evangelicals, particularly those with a Calvinistic theological framework, are still fighting among themselves on the literalness of the Bible. All of these issues—social activism vs. conservatism, charismatic renewal vs. conservatism, charismatic renewal vs. noncharismatic renewal, Biblical inerrancy vs. errancy—are similar to the doctrinal, political, and social issues that divided the fundamentalists toward the end of the 1920s. These in-house battles demonstrate the ferment of a social movement more than the solidification of likeminded groups who are bringing about a genuine revival and renewal within American Protestantism. Most mainline Protestant denominations are accommodating the conservatives, the evangelicals, and the charismatics within their churches. Some evangelicals and fundamentalists who feel alienated within the historical Protestant churches are joining more fundamentalist churches, and Kelley (1972) and others seem to be correct in their analyses that conservative church growth comes from disenchanted members of the mainline Protestant denominations rather than from "unchurched" Americans.

The ecumenical spirit of contemporary evangelicalism remains tenuous; and the aloofness of the Southern Baptist Convention, the Churches of Christ, and the Lutheran-Missouri Synod from other conservative and evangelical Christian groups seems to preclude any genuine pan-church movement of Great Awakening proportions. The two camps of American Protestantism, private and public, are still present. Each group sees its purpose as pre-eminent. While the historical toleration by public Protestants of the private Protestants' piety and conservatism is still practiced, no real rapprochement by the private Protestant groups to the more liberal mainline denominations has yet to emerge.

SUMMARY

The roots of fundamentalism extend back to the beginnings of America. At one time, most of the Protestant denominations of the religious establishment were fundamentalist to the extent that they were orthodox in doctrine. The First and Second Great Awakenings in the eighteenth and nineteenth century provided a tool, revivalism, through which the expanding nation could be made more religious. This religiosity was an evangelical Protestant kind stamped by the frontier revivals of the Methodists, the Baptists, the Disciples of Christ, and certain of the Presbyterians and Congregationalists.

The relative success of evangelicalism on the frontier produced a comfortable Protestant culture religion complete with the idea of Protestant manifest destiny. However, the immigration of vast numbers of Europeans, mainly Roman Catholic, to the expanding industrial cities threatened the dominance of the evangelicals. Along with the immigrant migration there also occurred a general rural to urban migration of native-born Americans. These people brought their revivalistic religion with them. The latter decades of the nineteenth century saw a continuation of revivalism with an element of millenarianism included. This belief in the imminent return of Christ to earth served as a reason for many evangelicals to ignore the emerging social problems of urban America.

In the South, the defeat suffered in the Civil War created a hostility between southern and northern Protestants. Those Protestants who challenged the comfortableness of complacent Protestantism by advocating a social Gospel as well as an individualistic gospel, met with resistance not only from the pietistic revivalists of the North but also from almost all of southern Protestantism.

The Social Gospel along with "higher Biblical criticism" created strife and division within the Protestant ranks in the early twentieth century. The *Fundamentals* were published in the first decade, and a World Christian Fundamentalist Association was formed in 1919. Both of these occurrences had as their goal the preservation of orthodox Christianity, personal piety, and revivalistic emphasis. In the 1920s, Harry Emerson Fosdick preached a famous sermon entitled *Shall the Fundamentalists Win?* In a real sense these liberal views set the stage for a fundamentalist withdrawal from mainline Protestantism outside of the South.

In the South, fundamentalism and evangelicalism continued to flourish as the chief characteristics of Protestantism. This cultural religion of the twentieth century South regularly held revivals and kept fundamentalism alive in the churches. This, in part, accounted for the steady growth of the most evangelical of the southern Protestant denominations, Southern Baptists. This denomination eventually surpassed the rival Methodists as the largest Protestant body. While many other Protestants within the southern region deemphasized revivalism, the Southern Baptist Convention used it, exported it to other regions, and increased this membership through it.

When a renewed interest in evangelical Christianity appeared in the late 1960s, Southern Baptists provided a model for many to follow. The "born again Christian," new to mainstream Protestants of the twentieth century, has always been a conventional idea to Southern Baptists. The charismatic renewal movement, which is a parallel to contemporary evangelicalism, has introduced another dimension of personal piety into Christianity. These ideas which were once rejected by more moderate and liberal Protestants have created a renewed interest in the tenets of evangelicalism: piety, revival, witnessing, and conventional morality. Whether or not this movement will become a more permanent facet of Christianity remains to be seen.

REFERENCES

Bord, Richard J. and
Joseph E. Faulkner
  1975   "Religiosity and secular attitudes: case of
                  Catholic Pentecostals." *Journal for the Scientific
                  Study of Religion* 14(3):257-270.

Fichter, Joseph H.
  1975   *The Catholic Cult of the Paraclete.* New York:
                  Sheed and Ward.

Frady, Marshall
    1979   *Billy Graham: A Parable of American
                            Righteousness.* Boston: Little, Brown and Com-
                            pany.

Goen, C. C.
    1959   "Fundamentalism in America." In Phillip E.
                            Hammond and Benton Johnson (eds.), *American
                            Mosaic: Social Patterns of Religion in the United
                            States.* New York: Random House.

Harrell, David Edwin, Jr.
    1975   *All Things Are Possible: The Healing and
                            Charismatic Revivals in Modern America.* Bloom-
                            ington: Indiana University Press.

Harrison, Michael I.
    1974   "Sources of recruitment to Catholic
                            Pentecostalism." *Journal for the Scientific Study
                            of Religion* 13(1):49-63.

Hudson, Winthrop S.
    1961   *American Protestantism.* Chicago: University of
                            Chicago Press.

Kelley, Dean M.
    1972   *Why Conservative Churches Are Growing: A
                            Study in Sociology of Religion.* New York: Harper
                            and Row.

Knudten, Richard D.
    1967   *The Sociology of Religion.* New York: Appleton-
                            Century Crofts.

Littell, Franklin Hamlin
    1962   *From State Church to Pluralism: A Protestant In-
                            terpretation of Religion in American History.*
                            Chicago: Aldine.

Mariani, John
    1979   "Television evangelism: milking the flock."
                            Saturday Review (February 3):22-25.

Martin, William
    1978   "The power and the glory of Billy Graham."
                            Texas Monthly (March):97-100, 151-154,
                            156-162.

Marty, Martin E.
    1970   *Righteous Empire: The Protestant Experience in
                            America.* New York: Dial.

McLoughlin, William C.
    1960   "Is there a third force in Christendom?"

Daedalus 96 (Winter):43-68.

Monaghan, Robert R.
1967

"Three faces of the true believer: motivations for attending a fundamentalist church." In Phillip E. Hammond and Benton Johnson (ed.), *American Mosaic: Social Patterns of Religion in the United States.* New York: Random House.

O'Connor, Edward
1971

The Pentecostal Movement in the Catholic Church. Notre Dame, Indiana: Ave Maria Press.

Olmstead, Clifton E.
1961

"Social religion in urban America." In Phillip E. Hammond and Benton Johnson (ed.), *American Mosaic: Social Patterns of Religion in the United States.* New York: Random House.

Sandeen, Ernest R.
1970

The Roots of Fundamentalism. Chicago: University of Chicago Press.

Wilson, John
1978

Religion in American Society: The Effective Presence. Englewood Cliffs, New Jersey: Prentice-Hall.

Woodward, Kenneth, John Barnes and Laurie Lisle
1976

"Born again!" *Newsweek* 88 (October):68-78.

Chapter 9

New Expressions
of Christianity

The term "new expressions" in the title of this chapter (and in Chapter 10) requires certain qualifications. What is a new religious expression for one generation may be "old hat" for others, or it may be an example of "old wine in new
bottles." Our concern in this chapter is to deal with selected happenings, behaviors, or movements involving Christianity which have surfaced very recently.
We will concentrate on new expressions from less traditional (non-Christian)
sources in the next chapter.

Another qualification is that we will be drawing heavily upon topical rather
than generic matters, or, if you will, content rather than form. For example, the
November 18, 1978, Guyana Massacre involving the suicide and murder of over·
900 persons in Jonestown, Guyana, is a "new expression" in terms of the actual
circumstances and personalities involved; as a generic form of expression, however, it is not completely new. As reporters noted when covering the story, other
masses have taken their lives when faced with certain circumstances involving
religious beliefs. According to Morrow (1978:30):

> Jonestown, for all its gruesome power to shock, has its religious (or quasi-
> religious) precedents ... The Jewish Zealots defending the fortress of
> Masada against the Roman legions in A.D. 73 chose self-slaughter rather
> than submission; 960 men, women and children died ... In the 17th cen-
> tury, Russian Orthodox dissenters called the Old Believers refused to ac-
> cept liturgical reforms. Over a period of years some 20,000 peasants in pro-
> test abandoned their fields and burned themselves.

In other stories (*Time*, December 4, 1978:16) we are reminded that hundreds
of Japanese civilians jumped to their deaths off the cliffs of Saipan as American
forces approached in World War II. Still others (*Newsweek*, December 4,
1978:72) contend that there is a similarity between "mind-bending" in Jonestown and that in which induced Japan's *kamikaze* pilots to give their lives for
their beliefs. The point of all this, again, is to qualify the material in this chapter
as "apparently" new, or "seemingly" new with regard to religious expression,
ritual, or belief systems.

Scholars have recently documented, written about, and reviewed research on
new expressions in religious life in America. For example, one exhaustive article

(Robbins et al., 1978) contains more than 260 references pertaining to recent accents and developments in religious and quasi-religious behavior in the United States. Books with titles such as *The New Religions* (Needleman, 1970), *New Gods in America* (Rowley, 1971), *Religious Movements in Contemporary America* (Zaretsky and Leone, 1974), *Conversion Careers: In and Out of the New Religions* (Richardson, 1978), and *The New Religious Consciousness* (Glock and Bellah, 1976) all reflect the idea that something has happened recently to give American religious life a flavor unlike that of the past. Popular magazines and periodicals also reflect this viewpoint. Much of this material focuses upon youth and religious behavior as well as behavior prompted by the youth movement of the 1960s and early 1970s. This is not to say that the youth movement is responsible for all the newness in religious expression, nor that all novel expressions began with young participants; it does demonstrate, however, that many young persons are searching for, finding, and developing religions not commonplace in the past in the United States. Neither is this to say that the *main line* churches and organizations have lost their appeal for younger participants; just some of them for some youngsters and older members as well.

EMERGENCE OF NEW EXPRESSIONS

One may encounter numerous vocabularies and conceptual frameworks when searching for material on the emergence of religious expression. An examination of one rather exhaustive work by LaBarre (1971) points to the complexity of the question of why religious movements get started. Centering his attention on "crisis cults" and addressing theories of causality, LaBarre 1971:36) concludes that no "particularist explanation" can explain cult formation and/or transformation and that "reductionism" is to be guarded against. Before this conclusion, however, LaBarre lists several theories or approaches that have been used by various writers in an attempt to further our understanding of certain religious and quasi-religious movements. These theoretical attempts fall into the following categories: (1) political, (2) military, (3) economic, (4) messianism, (5) the "great man" theory, (6) acculturation, (7) psychological stress and (8) other theories. Each of these emphases, separately or conjointly, may offer important clues to the causes of new movements, religious or otherwise. Also, they provide the student of religion with a wealth of variables to consider in the analysis of new religious expressions.

In writing of "cult formation" Bainbridge and Stark (1979) also avoid reductionism by proposing three different, but compatible, models of how religious ideas are generated and made social. Drawing upon numerous ethnographies, these authors, in summary fashion, identify and elaborate upon the (1) psychopathology model, (2) the entrepreneur model, and (3) the subculture-evolution model. Viewing religions as exchange systems, Bainbridge and Stark (1979:284) rely heavily upon their concept of "compensators," stating: "Faced with rewards that are very scarce, or not available at all, humans create and exchange compensators—sets of beliefs and prescriptions for action that substitute for the immediate achievement of the desired reward." Thus, the main ideas of the psychopathology model (Bainbridge and Stark, 1979:285) are:

1. Cults are novel cultural responses to personal and societal crisis.

2. New cults are invented by individuals suffering from certain forms of mental illness.

3. These individuals typically achieve their novel visions during psychotic episodes.

4. During such an episode, the individual invents a new package of compensators to meet his own needs.

5. The individual's illness commits him to his new vision, either because his hallucinations appear to demonstrate its truth, or because his compelling needs demand immediate satisfaction.

6. After the episode, the individual will be most likely to succeed in forming a cult around his vision if the society contains many other persons suffering from problems similar to those originally faced by the cult founder, to whose solution, therefore, they are likely to respond.

7. Therefore, such cults most often succeed during times of societal crisis, when large numbers of persons suffer from similar unresolved problems.

8. If the cult does succeed in attracting many followers, the individual founder may achieve at least a partial cure of his illness, because his self-generated compensators are legitimated by other persons, and because he now receives true rewards from his followers.

The psychopathology model deals with cult founders who invent compensator-systems for their own use and differs from the entrepreneur model in the emphasis placed on cult formation and organization as a "business." Bainbridge and Stark (1979:288) identify the following ten points of the entrepreneur model:

1. Cults are businesses which provide a product for their customers and

receive payment in return.

2. Cults are mainly in the business of selling novel compensators, or at least freshly packaged compensators that appear new.

3. Therefore, a supply of novel compensators must be manufactured.

4. Both manufacture and sales are accomplished by entrepreneurs.

5. These entrepreneurs, like those in other businesses, are motivated by the desire for profit, which they can gain by exchanging compensators for rewards.

6. Motivation to enter the cult business is stimulated by the perception that such business can be profitable, an impression likely to be acquired through prior involvement with a successful cult.

7. Successful entrepreneurs require skills and experience, which are most easily gained through a prior career as the employee of an earlier successful cult.

8. The manufacture of salable new compensators (or compensator-packages) is most easily accomplished by assembling components of pre-existing compensator-systems into new configurations, or by the further development of successful compensator-systems.

9. Therefore, cults tend to cluster in lineages. They are linked by individual entrepreneurs who begin their careers in one cult and then leave to found their own. They bear strong "family resemblances" because they share many cultural features.

10. Ideas for completely new compensators can come from any cultural source or personal experience whatsoever, but the skillful entrepreneur experiments carefully in the development of new products and incorporates them permanently in his cult only if the market response is favorable.

Both the psychopathology and entrepreneur models concentrate on the innovative behavior of an individual while the subculture-evolution model stresses group behavior. The nine points of the subculture model mentioned by Bainbridge and Stark (1979:291) are:

1. Cults are the expression of novel social systems, usually small in size but composed of at least a few intimately interacting individuals.

2. These cultic social systems are most likely to emerge in populations already deeply involved in the occult milieu, but cult evolution may also begin in entirely secular settings.

3. Cults are the result of sidetracked or failed collective attempts to obtain scarce or nonexistent rewards.

4. The evolution begins when the group of persons commits itself to the attainment of certain rewards.

5. In working together to obtain these rewards, members begin exchanging other rewards as well, such as affect.

6. As they progressively come to experience failure in achieving their original goals, they will gradually generate and exchange compensators as well.

7. If the intragroup exchange of rewards and compensators becomes sufficiently intense, the group will become relatively encapsulated, in the extreme case undergoing complete social implosion.

8. Once separated to some degree from external control, the evolving cult develops and consolidates a novel culture, energized by the need to facilitate the exchange of rewards and compensators, and inspired by essentially accidental factors.

9. The end point of successful cult evolution is a novel religious culture embodied in a distinct social group which must now cope with the problem of extracting resources (including new members) from the surrounding environment.

These models, while articulating processes involved in cult formation, do not address completely the ways in which followers become active members of new religious groups. To continue our exploration of how new groups attract followers we will now turn to material on conversion—such material being important to our understanding of new expressions of Christianity and to new expressions from nontraditional sources that will be covered in the next chapter.

CONVERSION THEORY

Sociological and psychological literature demonstrates that conversion (either to an idea, ideology, or religion) has interested scholars for many years. The most recent theories, or at least those which have gained the most attention in new religious expressions, concern the "world-saver model" addressed by Lofland and Stark (1965) and additions and reflections concerning that model.

The model consists of certain "predisposing characteristics" (felt needs, a problem-solving perspective, rejection of traditional religion) and "situational factors" (reaching a turning point in one's life, meeting and liking a cult member, and intensive interaction with cult members). This model views the convert as essentially static or passive and as one to whom the conversion process essentially takes over the person's life and influences his or her thinking. However, some theorists (i.e., Richardson and Stewart, 1978) believe this model to be too simplistic and places the actor in too much of a passive stance. Even Lofland (1978:22) modified the notions involved in the theory by stating:

> Stepping back yet further, I have since come to appreciate that the world-saver model embodies a thoroughly "passive" actor—a conception of humans as "neutral medium through which social forces operate," as Blumer (1969) has so often put it. . . . It is with such a realization that I have lately encouraged students of conversion to turn the process on its head and to scrutinize how people go about converting themselves.

Thus, the actor may be more than putty in the hands of a moulding society or group and may actually become an active participant in social life by seeking out religious conversion. Even questioning traditional religious values and vaguely looking around for new ideas may constitute "seekership" or "creative bumbling" (Straus, 1976) which eventually allows one to push oneself into a newly found ideology or religious belief system. But the conversion process is more than just "being pulled" (by social forces) or "pushing oneself" (by individual seekership) into a new religious participation. There are numerous possible factors involved in the process, a few of which will be delineated below.

Possible Factors in Conversion

Given that we are in part products of our culture, we may identify certain cultural factors instrumental to conversion experiences. As Cloward and Ohlin (1961) demonstrate, persons must have an "opportunity" to engage in certain forms of behavior. Unless the person has access to a system of beliefs, that person cannot convert to that belief system. The views of Leslie White (1959) similarly indicate that until the cultural base is sufficiently developed to allow something to come into being, it will not gain fruition in society. Thus, many of the factors possibly involved in the creation and fulfillment of new expressions in religious life have a decidedly cultural or social basis. However, the *interplay* between the individual and his/her cultural milieu is the conceptual plane that many studies of religion have utilized. Such a blending of social and psychological processes leads one to the study not just of individual characteristics per se but to an analysis of how the group affects the individual and of the impact of the individuals upon the group.

Given this perspective, it is not surprising that as one inspects elements thought to be instrumental in conversion experiences, one may find it difficult to completely separate the individual from society. In an excellent review of theory and research on new religions, Robbins et al. (1978:95-99) identify four basic variables explaining the "why" of recent religious movements. These are secularization, crisis of community, value crisis, and the increasing need for holistic self-definition in a differentiated society.

Secularization, as a societal construct, refers to the breaking up of society into various parts which do not have a religious ideology as a guiding principle. The often used sacred-secular dichotomy points to how these elements are often juxtaposed for purposes of clarification. Secularization, however, means more than just antireligion, it refers, to some extent, to a societal condition characterized, usually, as complex, bureaucratized, fragmented, and impersonal. As persons are not encapsulated by a sacred set of traditional rules and principles, they are diverted to and seek out "new" ways of psychological and social expression. As Wilson (1975:80) contends, secularization produces "a supermarket of faith . . . . But all of them coexist because the wider society is so secular, because they are relatively unimportant consumer items." Therefore, if a society experiences a change to a secular society, it can be expected that traditional religious values will lose some of their strength and a certain kind of social and religious experimentation will take place. One should remember, however, that the sacred-secular dichotomy represents ideal types which may not exist in pure form in reality. Therefore, no modern society may exist as a secular society; societies do, however, vary along a continuum representing sacred-secular dimensions. For this reason, among others, secularization is not a necessary and sufficient condition for the emergence of new religious expressions.

Similarly, the second factor mentioned by Robbins et al. (1978), that of "quest for community," does not alone explain religious change. The quest for community on the part of individuals supports the idea that as societies become more impersonal, persons seek to establish (or perhaps re-establish) a feeling of "belongingness" to certain groups and ideas. The theory posits that as the family becomes less traditional, encompassing less of the individual's field of experiences, and as the primary groups lose out in importance to secondary concerns, the persons may experience feelings of anomia. There follows an attempt to replace the vague feelings of frustration and aloneness with an involvement with a primary surrogate which may be a new religion. This thesis, again, is not comprehensive, but it buttresses the notion of the interplay between societal conditions and individual action concerning finding a "place" in society.

The third and fourth themes identified by Robbins et al. continue the basic social psychological perspective of the first two. "Normative breakdown and value dissensus" as well as the search for groups offering a more "holistic conception of self" indicate that the person is "reacting" to a set of social circumstances. With social change comes a sense of the breakdown of old belief systems and a questioning of the appropriateness of traditional ways of thinking. As one becomes more aware of alternative values, and of the plethora of such values, one may try to reorient oneself to particular beliefs which offer "meaning" to one's life. The interest in a holistic conception of self refers to the need to "get it all together," so to speak, spiritually, mentally, and sometimes, physically.

Other factors which might be mentioned vary in the degree of psychological involvement experienced by the convert. One may find oneself in a particular situation in which certain things "just happen" without one planning for the happening. One may encounter a street proselytizer and, having nothing better to do, strike up a conversation which leads to more and more involvement. One may be enticed into initial contacts by curiosity concerning chanting, dancing, or activities at a public gathering. One may make acquaintances in a variety of situations (parties, work settings, college classes) which offer the first contact with a new religion. One may be "down" and experience the warmth and friendship of a person or persons who "cheer you up"; a situation which may provide later contact with an organized religious group. Then one may consciously find faults or flaws with the religion in which one was raised and consciously explore new ideas offered by whatever groups are handy. Another factor may simply be curiosity or a need for something new or exciting in one's life. One may engage in "religion-hopping," as it were, either out of active rebellion towards parents or society or some less causal, more situational reasons.

Certain combinations and permutations of the above ideas provide numerous factors which could possibly influence one to embrace new ideas concerning religion. Students are urged to expand this listing by asking themselves how they or their friends arrived at their present religious beliefs and if the processes involved could not be present in regard to numerous faiths, regardless of whether the beliefs are old or new, "weird" or "straight." Later we will consider processes currently referred to as "programming," as well as the counterpart, "deprogramming." Presently, however, we turn to a brief discussion of selected new Christian-based religious expressions on the American scene.

THE JESUS PEOPLE

To some it may be that the Jesus movement started with Jesus, and that the history of Christianity is synonymous with the history of the Jesus movement. In current vernacular, however, the Jesus People movement means a recent social phenomenon involving numerous young people whose activities center around a strict literal interpretation of the Bible and other accoutrements of a conservative theology. This phenomenon had its start in the United States in the mid-1960s and continues to this day.

The sociological exactitude of applying the term "social movement" to this phenomenon, however, has been questioned by various writers. Balswick (1977:167), for example, writes:

> The Jesus movement contains very diverse, loosely organized groups and is not a social movement in any organized sense. Their peculiar unifying characteristic is the belief that man can overcome his alienation and find real meaning in life only through a personal relationship with Jesus Christ.

The myriad names of the groups generally subsumed under the umbrella term Jesus People movement points to the diversity of the phenomenon. A few of the generic names taken from various sources are Street Christians, Jesus Freaks, and Jesus People. Names of organizations with identifiable leaders and locations are: Children of God, Texas Soul Clinic, Christian World Liberation Front, Jesus People's Army, The Way, Tony and Susan Alamo's Christian Foundation, His Place, the East Coast Jesus People, the Jesus People Church, Inc., Calvary Chapel, and Jews for Jesus. This variety of organizations indicates the difficulty of speaking of one social movement as the Jesus People movement although some are apparently comfortable with a qualified use of the term. Enroth et al. (1972:11-12), for example, writes:

> Most treatments currently in print assume, mistakenly, that the Jesus People present a unified front, so that one may generalize from a part of the movement to the whole. Actually, there is so much diversity within the movement that some elements of it consider others non-Christian, even demonic. Also, there is a surprising isolation of groups, so that one group usually knows little about others, especially those separated geographically . . . . Nevertheless, there are some unifying threads that run through all segments and make it proper to consider the Jesus People as one movement.

While different organizations may require a particular regimen for its members and a different emphasis upon scriptures, some of the "unifying threads" concerning the Jesus People revolve around the following: (1) experiential relationships with Jesus, (2) emotional religious services, (3) the power of prayer, (4) a belief in the healing powers of Jesus, (5) denouncing the secular world as evil, (6) anti-intellectualism, (7) the Bible as inerrant, (8) witnessing for Jesus, (9) proselytizing, and (10) speaking in tongues or "glossolalia."

There appears to be a rough dichotomy discernable in the Jesus movement. The "electronic" movement dealing with T.V. and radio ministries is composed of business persons and energetic evangelists somewhat different than the Jesus Freaks emerging from the counterculture. Rather than sustaining a separation from the world, the electronic establishment element is reformational and continues to work for Jesus through business channels. Dwayne Walls (1979) describes the zeal with which the establishment side of the movement is operating in this country in his article "The Jesus Mania: Bigotry in the Name of the Lord." We will return to the "street people" aspect of the movement after a brief summary of Walls' paper.

Walls (1979) provides, in the first of his article, a scenario concerning a businessman about to close a deal when the client said "There is one other thing ... Are you a born-again Christian?" Walls (1979:177-178) comments:

> This scene ocurred in Charlotte, North Carolina, last spring. The business deal went through, but Roy Brown (a pseudonym) wishes now he had never seen that particular client. By refusing to kneel in the office for a word of prayer, by declining to discuss his religion because he believes it is a personal matter (he is a practicing Christian), Brown opened himself to a systematic missionary effort by representatives of various evangelical organizations. At first it was merely annoying, but as Brown's resistance stiffened, the calls and visits become threatening. After three months, the campaign against him had turned to downright harassment.

Walls continues by stating that what is happening to Brown is happening, with variations, to businessmen, professionals, laborers, students, and others across the country. According to Walls (1979:178), "Brown is but one victim of the militance and overzealousness—'the mean streak,' a noted theologian has called it—that has at times accompanied the astonishing 'Jesus movement.' "

The march of the movement has gone into the "marketplace and the counting-house," according to Walls (1979:180-181) and has produced a nationwide 'buy Christian' campaign reminiscent of those the Jews have been subjected to periodically throughout their history, notably in Nazi Germany." This campaign involves a "Christian Business Directory" and a "Christian Yellow Pages." According to Walls (1979:181-182):

> To be included in either of the directories, an advertiser must sign a statement saying that he is a "Born-again Christian believer" and that he "accepts Jesus Christ as ... personal Lord and Saviour and acknowledges Jesus as the Son of God." For that and a fee ranging up to $900, the advertiser gets space in the listings and the publisher's stamp of approval as a fellow to be trusted by all good Christians.

As to the electronic media, Walls (1979:180) states:

> Among the new stars in the Holy Hit Parade are Robert Schuller, who broadcasts from his drive-in church in Disneyland; Virginia's M.G. (Pat) Robertson, whose offerings include the "Top 40" in religious tunes; Jim Bakker, whose "PTL Club" broadcasts out of Charlotte are heard in every state ... Meanwhile, Oral Roberts, Rex Humbard, and other familiar voices have gained new audiences since the Jesus movement hit full stride.

As we will see below, some Jesus People organizations would not claim any association with the kind of secular activity described above. Some would even say that the electronic/business aspect of Christianity is antithetical to their purpose. However, the fundamentalistic proselytizing, based upon a rather literal interpretation of the Bible, makes both sides of the continuum similar in purpose if varying in degree and emphasis.

Jesus Movement Organizations

Enroth et al. (1972) provide an insightful history into the beginnings of the Jesus movement in this country. Their data concern the street or counterculture aspect of the movement mentioned above. We will examine only a couple of the Jesus movement organizations mentioned in Enroth et al. (1972) and encourage the reader to consult the original source for a more detailed picture of the early activities of numerous organizations.

The Children of God (COG) represent an antiestablishment form of Christianity and see themselves as true followers of God through a belief in the King James version of the Bible. The sect was formed by David Berg in Huntington Beach, Los Angeles, California, in the fall of 1968 and was originally called Teens for Christ. According to Davis and Richardson (1976:321) "By mid-1976 the COG claimed approximately 4,500 full-time members (not counting some 800 young children of members), and they had organized into more than 600 colonies in over 70 countries."

Some of the early activities of COG (before Berg had a vision of California dropping into the ocean which eventually led him to abandon Huntington Beach) consisted of descending *en masse* on a church service in progress, marching in, and generally creating a disturbance. After leaving the California property the COG wandered around the country and finally camped at Fred Jordan's ranch in Texas. Fred Jordan was Berg's ex-boss who ran the Texas Soul Clinic on a ranch near Thurber, Texas. While Jordan's motivation for having the COG set up headquarters at his clinic may have been to draw support for his own ministerial work, it provided instead a geographic base from which the COG could expand. (Several sources, when mentioning the COG, refer to the "Texas-based Children of God.") After a conflict with Jordan, the COG moved to several new locations (San Diego, Boulder, Austin, Dallas) and, after being joined by the "Jesus People Army" and the "House of Judah," soon branched out worldwide.

Among the beliefs of COG are (1) seeing themselves as the only Christians "sold out one hundred percent" for Christ, (2) separation from the world through communal living, (3) giving up their worldly possessions to the elders, (4) memorizing scripture, (5) witnessing, (6) destroying one's former identity, (7) aggressive recruiting of new members, (8) protesting events they do not agree with, (9) receiving the correct interpretation of the Bible, and (10) a fast approaching doomsday.

According to Enroth et al. (1972:44) there are at least four types of young people particularly susceptible to the COG: (1) those at the end of their rope and who have tried all the other "trips," (2) those with a fundamentalist background who do not have sufficient Biblical knowledge to feel confident of their positions, (3) those who strongly need a sense of belonging, and (4) those who came from permissive backgrounds and feel a need for discipline.

The recent structure of the COG is outlined in detail in Davis and Richardson (1976). Ideally the structure has eight major levels. From the smallest to the largest unit, the structure consists of (1) colonies, (2) district, (3) region, (4) bishoprics, (5) archbishopric, (6) ministry, (7) prime ministry, and (8) the King's Counsellorship, of which David "Moses" Berg is a member. Berg is said, however, not to dictate policy for the organization and has allowed the organization to undergo numerous recent changes (Davis and Richardson, 1976: 336-338).

Another organization, the Christian Foundation of Tony and Susan Alamo, was founded in 1966. Tony Alamo, who was born Bernie Lazar Hoffman in Montana, was a "successful" Hollywood impressario until "one day during a business meeting he received an audible message from God threatening to kill him unless he gave up his lucrative business and began to preach the Gospel" (Enroth et al., 1972:61). The Alamo Foundation requires its members to forego any physical contact with one another and to talk to each other only at meal time. Marriage is permitted if approved by the Alamos only after a separation of ninety days reserved for praying and fasting. Drugs, drinking, and social dancing are prohibited, and daily life is strictly regimented. The King James version of the Bible is considered the only inspired Bible, and the return of Christ is considered imminent. Meetings are similar to old-time fundamentalist gatherings involving music, foot-stomping, dancing in the Spirit, speaking in tongues, frenzied prayer, verbal testimonials, and rousing sermons by Tony and Susan Alamo.

This type of enthusiasm is characteristic of many people within the Jesus movement, whether in their worship services, daily rituals within the commune, witnessing on the street corner, or trying to obtain converts to their religion. The intensity of their involvement and the sensory stimulation attendant upon constant reinforcement from fellow members brings about a cultic milieu rather different in character from the mainline Christian community. Members are said to see visions, receive visits from the Spirit, observe miracles, perform healings of the sick, and to have "warm feelings" come over them. This ethos supposedly developed, at least for some, due to a desire or need for direct *experience* in religious living; a desire to *see* miracles, to *feel* spiritual stimulation, to *hear* the word of God and to *touch* the supernatural, to *hunger* and *thirst* for religious experiences. Speaking about such sensory involvement, Enroth et al. (1972:241) state that in talking with some Jesus People "we felt that Christ had better come soon, because they could not long sustain the emotional high and the intensity of life that they were presently enjoying."

As mentioned previously, not all organizations in the Jesus movement agree with each other; each may be openly hostile to religious emphases and interpretations other than their own. In fact, some groups "define the situation" of other groups as con artistry and hucksterism.

Some also criticize the "faddish" nature of parts of the Jesus movement. The "one way" gesture of raising one finger pointed at the sky; cheerleaders shouting "Gimme a *J*; gimme an *E*; gimme an *S*; gimme a *U*; gimme an *S*"; and the wearing of Jesus tee shirts, marks for some an insincere attitude toward Jesus. The epitome of such an attitude is mentioned by Enroth et al. (1972:154):

> Among the most grotesque examples of faddish commercialization of the recent wave of interest in Jesus are Jesus Christ jockey shorts and Jesus Christ bikinis. A new Jesus watch is advertised as follows: "Hi kids, it's me, Jesus. Look what I'm wearing on my wrist. It's a wristwatch with a five-color picture of me on the dial and hands attached to a crimson heart."

The impact of the Jesus movement has not yet been assessed. Some contend that the whole thing is faddish and will fade away without lasting consequences. Some say the movement has produced new recruits for mainline Christianity after they "burn out" on the intense emotionalism of a Jesus People experience. Others say the movement has scarred young people for life and has done irrevocable psychological damage to the participants. Still others predict that the movement will continue to splinter and form more established types of religious expression akin to a real "spiritual awakening."

PEOPLE'S TEMPLE

Probably the most awesome religiously related occurrence of the century took place in Jonestown, Guyana, in November, 1978, when over 900 persons were murdered or committed suicide as a result of their involvement with Jim Jones and the People's Temple. Scores of magazines and newspaper articles have been written about Jonestown. In addition, several books and scholarly articles, hours of radio and television coverage, and at least two movies have been produced about the incident at this writing.

According to published accounts,[1] James Warren Jones was born in Lynn, Indiana, on May 13, 1931 and early in his life became involved in religious activities by "playing church" and "holding services." In 1950 Jones became a pastor at Sommerset Southside Church in Indianapolis and worked for racial equality by operating a nearby integrated community center (Kilduff and Javers, 1978:15). After leaving Sommerset, Jones founded his Community Unity Church in Indianapolis and was also associate pastor at the Laurel Street Tabernacle. Fighting financial difficulties, Jones engaged in door-to-door selling and raised enough money to open the first People's Temple in 1956 on North New Jersey Street in Indianapolis (Anonymous, 1979).

Jim Jones adopted seven children (black, white, and Asian) and persuaded several of his congregation to do likewise. Jones was interested in combining church and family life and started "assembling families and arranging relationships within the church" (Kilduff and Javers, 1978:17) at his first People's Temple. He continued his civil rights activities and searched for a ministerial style to appeal to the blacks and lower-class whites in the neighborhood. Jones visited other preachers to learn of their styles and was impressed with Father Divine's manner and control over his following. Shortly thereafter he instituted an "interrogation committee" to aid in solidifying his leadership and "to surround himself with a loyal cadre of followers who could police the congregation" (Kilduff and Javers, 1978:18).

One of the first political roles played by Jones was in 1969 when he was appointed director of the Indianapolis Human Rights Commission by Mayor Charles Boswell. His politics and religious activities soon drew hostile and harassing reactions from segregationists in Indianapolis. Despite his politics and faith-healing demonstrations, The People's Temple Full Gospel Church became a Disciples of Christ congregation in 1963; Jones was ordained as a Disciples of Christ minister in 1965. Soon thereafter, he moved to Ukiah, California, with several members of his congregation. Some say he left to escape mounting financial and political problems. Others contend he journeyed to Ukiah because it was supposedly one of the ten safest places in the world in the event of a nuclear war. He had previously visited, in 1963, Belo Horizante, Brazil, one of the other "safest" places to live in case of a nuclear attack. During that trip he also briefly visited the colony of British Guiana (now Guyana).

From 1965 to 1972 Jones and his followers lived and worked in and around

---

[1]Most of the material herein on People's Temple comes from published journalistic accounts and information supplied by the electronic media. While we wish for more systematic data for our analysis, it is not available to us at the time of this writing.

Redwood Valley, a small community 125 miles north of San Francisco. Jones began working with American Indians in Mendocino county and operated a 40-acre home for boys and three convalescent centers (Kilduff and Javers, 1978: 29). In 1967 he was appointed to the county grand jury and became a director of Mendocino and Lake Counties Legal Services Foundation. Continuing to attract followers, Jones soon started his "road shows." He began visiting San Francisco and Los Angeles with his emotional, faithhealing religious sermons.

In 1972 Jones moved his headquarters to San Francisco and started attracting local blacks to his church. Jones also began publishing a newspaper, *Peoples Forum*, and broadcasting a thirty-minute religious program on a religious radio station in San Francisco. Jones was appointed to the San Francisco Housing Authority in 1976 and moved up to Chairman of the Housing Authority in February, 1977. Some claim this was due to his part, through the bloc voting of People's Temple members, in helping George Moscone get elected San Francisco's mayor.

For awhile, Jones continued to attract followers in San Francisco to his soup-kitchen, faith-healing, emotionally pitched sermonizing and religious revivals. During this time, however, Jones began to perform more "miracles," required his followers to call him "Dad" or "Father," denounced the Bible and the outside world, required members to turn over their possessions to the Temple, demanded more involvement in Temple activities, and asked members of his planning commission (inner circle) to sign loyalty oaths. Conway and Siegelman (1979:237) describe some of the activities of this period:

> While the temple grew rapidly . . . Jone's declarations and behavior became more extreme. He stepped up his preaching about imminent earthquakes and nuclear holocausts and of a coming race war between blacks and whites. He established a "relationship committee" to preside over his methodical splitting up of marriages and families, and, while he declared sex evil, he solicited temple members to engage in relations with him as a sign of their loyalty . . . in the early seventies, Jone's punishments became . . . progressively more severe to the point of brutality. . . . Older members deemed slack in their duties might be compelled to fight in "boxing matches," sometimes for several hours, with up to three or four bigger, stronger opponents. . . . the children, would be subjected to the "blue-eyed monster"—a secret disciplinary weapon that was said to be a kind of electric cattle prod that sent a severe shock through the child's body.

During this period Jones claimed to be God and/or the reincarnation of Christ and Lenin with the power to bring dead persons back to life. In 1976 Jones "tested his first suicide drill on Planning Commission members. He explained afterward that the drill was designed to test their loyalty" (Conway and Siegelman, 1979:240). Jones did this by telling members that the wine he had just given them was poison and that they had but one hour to live.

Possibly as a result of this extremism several members withdrew from the People's Temple. One person who argued with the doctrine of Jim Jones was Robert Houston, Jr., who was to play a very significant role in the latter happenings at Jonestown. Houston, while a follower of Jones and a steady contributor to the People's Temple, was once severely beaten by another church member for questioning the activities of Jones and the doctrine of the cult. According to Krause (1978:9), Robert Houston, Sr., on October 5, 1976, learned that his son's body had been found alongside the railroad tracks where he had worked—"How this bizarre accident happened was never explained to the family's satisfaction." Robert Jr. had previously been a student of Congressman Leo Ryan and Robert Sr., a photographer for Associated Press, was an acquaintance of Congressman Ryan. At the urging of Robert Houston, Sr., Ryan started an investigation into the activities of the People's Temple; an investigation that eventually led him to Jonestown, Guyana, and to his death.

Jones and a few followers had actually visited Guyana in 1973 (Krause, 1978:92). In 1974 they established a modest commune and cleared several fields for agricultural production (Anonymous, 1979:46). When Jones' "extremism" began to attract media attention to San Francisco, Jones and approximately 800 followers migrated to the Guyanese jungle and expanded the commune. The events surrounding the actual move to Guyana involved the bad press Jones was beginning to receive due to the stories being told by ex-members. In August, 1977, *New West* magazine finally published a damning account of the People's Temple. After having failed in his attempt to block the publication of the story, Jones left San Francisco for Guyana, but not before establishing a shortwave radio communications base at the San Francisco headquarters (Conway and Siegelman, 1979:241). From Guyana, in August, 1977, Jones resigned his post as Director of the San Francisco Housing Authority and turned his attention to directing the communal activities of Jonestown.

Jones leased 27,000 acres of land from the Guyanese government in late 1973. The land was located about six miles from Port Kaituma and approximately 150 miles from Georgetown, the capital city of Guyana. This commune, called Jonestown, was related to People's Temple members as a "promised land" and described as a jungle "paradise." In May, 1977, there were approximately 70 full-time residents at Jonestown (Kilduff and Javers, 1978:96). The exodus of Jones and his followers from San Francisco later in the summer of 1977 swelled the population to several hundred and required much more work and coordination of activities. According in Conway and Siegelman (1979:241-1):

> Life in Jonestown resembled not so much a paradise as a prison. . . . The commune was run like a concentration camp. Residents were required to work eleven-hour days in 120° heat with only a ten-minute break . . . . He

[Jones] ordered disciplinary measures more harsh and punishments more brutal than those he practiced in California.

Accusations were made that Jones smuggled drugs into Guyana to control unruly members and would-be runaways and weapons to be used in case milder discipline proved ineffective. Tales of these and other atrocities came to light when Deborah Layton Blakey returned (escaped) to the United States in the Spring of 1978 and told of the prospect of mass suicide, rehearsals of which were becoming more frequent. Relatives of People's Temple members were worried that there was something amiss in Jonestown. The reports of atrocities and captivity spurred them to request investigations and eventually to form a group called the Concerned Relatives Committee. The Committee contacted Congressman Ryan, who was already interested in the People's Temple, and convinced him to lead an investigation.

Personal investigations were not new to Ryan. He had previously taken up residence with a black family in Watts in Los Angeles in 1965 and had worked there as a substitute teacher under an assumed name. He had traveled to Newfoundland to protest seal hunting and had, under an assumed identity, been placed in Folsom Prison for eight days to investigate reports of abuse (Krause, 1978:7).

Ryan had contacted Jones requesting a visit to Jonestown and had been informed by People's Temple lawyer, Mark Lane, that, while welcome, "further persecution of People's Temple . . . might very well result in the creation of a most embarassing situation for the U.S. Government" (Krause, 1978:12). Nevertheless, Ryan, two aides, nine journalists, and several members of the Concerned Relatives group arrived in Guyana on Wednesday, November 15, 1978. After several hours of telephone negotiations with People's Temple lawyers, Charles Garry and Mark Lane (who arrived in Guyana on November 17), Ryan, the press, some of the relatives, and the lawyers chartered a plane and flew into Jonestown on November 17. The rest has been given much attention in the media. Several members, after questioning, slipped notes to members of the party that they in fact wanted to leave Jonestown. When the defectors and the investigative party tried to leave they were ambushed. Representative Ryan, reporter Don Harris, cameraman Bob Brown, photographer Greg Robinson, and defector Patricia Parks were killed. At least 11 other party members were injured, and on the night of November 18, 1978, over 900 persons, including many children, were murdered or committed suicide by injecting or drinking poison. On March 15, 1979, a former press agent for People's Temple called a press conference in Modesto, California, and then went into a bathroom and committed suicide. Even at this writing there are rumors of a People's Temple "hit squad" still seeking to assassinate defectors and ex-members of the cult.

In a summary statement of the demographics on Jonestown victims, Wiencek

(1979:12) contends:

> The data show that those who died at Jonestown were overwhelmingly
> black, female and elderly. In addition, as a group they were very mobile
> and urban. . . . and more likely to be in-migrants to the state of California,
> especially from the South.

In regards to the place of birth of the Jonestown victims Wieneck (1979), using a
New York Times data set of 621 victims, found the following: 51.7 percent were
from the South, 31.4 percent were from the West, 13.3 percent were from the
North Central area of the country, and 3.6 percent were from the Northeast. In
terms of individual states, California produced 28.0 percent of the victims while
Texas produced 16.6 percent, Louisiana 8.2 percent, Mississippi 6.9 percent,
and Indiana and Arkansas 6.2 percent each. Wiencek further found, using a State
Department data set with an N of 925, that 342 (37 percent) of the victims were
male and 583 (63 percent) were female. Also, 69 percent were black and 31 percent nonblack.

Did Jonestown represent a "new expression" of religious life? We reported
earlier that mass suicide of religious practitioners has taken place before, and that
Jonestown is only "topically" a new expression. Some, however, would question
whether or not the Jonestown incident had anything to do with religion, and particularly Christian religion, in the final analysis. Krause (1978:33-34) states:

> Although his traditions were Christian fundamentalist, Jones held no con-
> ventional Christian notion of God. "Neither my colleagues nor I are any
> longer caught up in the opiate of religion. . . . " he wrote in his church's
> magazine, *Peoples Forum*, in January, 1978. In a September, 1977, inter-
> view with the *New York Times* his wife of 28 years said that Jones was a
> Marxist who held that religion's trappings were useful only for social and
> economic uplift . . . . To the religious, Jones offered religion; to the
> ideological, he offered politics; to the ignorant and gullible, he offered
> miracles.

Richardson (1979), in his critique of the journalistic and psychologized interpretation of Jonestown, has warned that it is questionable to assume that People's Temple and the new religious groups of the 1960s and 1970s share crucial
features. He also contends that even though leaving Jonestown was difficult, it
was not a prison camp, and that people who recount "How terrible it was" may
have possibly engaged in conscious or unconscious self-serving behavior. In
short, Richardson sees some accounts of Jonestown as "overdone." He draws attention to Jones' "theology of suicide" as being possibly related to his paranoia,
but he also notes that Jones possibly saw it as a positive and logical outcome of

being attacked by forces opposed to his efforts. Interestingly, Richardson notes that Jones, either by accident or design, tapped into a ritual pattern with tremendous meaning in a Christian culture. He states (Richardson, 1979:27):

> Accounts of the last few years of People's Temple all refer to group sessions in which those present were required to drink liquids that were said to be poison. If such reports are correct, this suicide-oriented ritual behavior pattern was repeated several, perhaps even many times in recent years ... they were participating in a ritual analogous to one as old as Christendom itself. Where else in Western history do we find people being administered a liquid which they then drink together with considerable symbolic meaning? Any time people take holy communion, or the Lord's supper, they are doing something with important similarities to the behavior pattern developed around People's Temple "suicide drills."

Another work (Hargrove, 1979) points to the religious nature of People's Temple by questioning whether or not one should classify it as a *new* religion. Stating that this group was not primarily made up of young people seeking alternatives to established institutions, Hargrove (1979:14-15) further contends:

> Embarrassing as it may be to the denomination, the People's Temple was a recognized congregation of the Christian Church (Disciples of Christ) throughout all the incidents of its infamy, and Jones was a properly accredited minister of that denomination. . . . Jones may not have fit many scholars' definitions of the ideal Christian minister, but it is hard to say that he led a *new* religious movement. [Emphasis in original]

Maybe Jonestown and the People's Temple cannot really be equated with other cults. It may remain problematical for some to call Jonestown a new religious expression. In addition, maybe Jonestown was more Marxist than Christian, and the theodicy, if it existed, more political than religious. We maintain, however, that due to the magnitude of the event and its novel features, we are justified in including it in this chapter on Christian-based new religious expressions. Regardless of these problems of classification, we are left with the question of "Why Jonestown?" Due to the paucity of scientific data on the actual suicide, we may never fully understand what went on during the last few months of Jonestown. There are some important ideas, however, that might lead us to a fuller appreciation of events leading up to the Jonestown suicide/murder, and we will briefly review these here.

VIEWS OF JONESTOWN

Earlier we presented the three models of cult formation developed by Bainbridge and Stark (1979); the psychopathology, entrepreneur, and subculture-evolution models. Probably only the most cynical observer would place People's Temple in the entrepreneur (cult formation as a business) classification, even though the People's Temple at the time of the Jonestown suicides reportedly had a budget running into the millions. Using the schema presented, the People's Temple probably is best categorized as having some elements of both the psychopathological and subcultural models, with different factors being more dominant at different points in the Temple's chronology. Bainbridge and Stark (1979) characterize the Temple as a group which began as an extreme but culturally traditional sect and then evolved into a cult as Jones' radical vision progressed. Indicating that the members probably encouraged Jones by requiring him to accomplish impossible goals, Bainbridge and Stark (1979:293) summarize as follows:

> Even when a single individual dominates a group, the subculture-evolution model will apply to the extent that the followers also participate in pushing the group toward cultism. In this case, the needs of the followers and their social relationships with the leader may have served as a *psychopathology amplifier*, reflecting back to Jones his own narcissism multiplied by the strength of their unreasonable hopes. [Emphasis in original]

Doyle Johnson (1979) has couched many of the happenings surrounding Jonestown in the language of the "dilemmas" of charismatic leadership. Johnson's central thesis is that charismatic leadership is tenuous and precarious and is in continual need of reinforcement. Assuming that the charismatic leader seeks to continue and strengthen his/her leadership position and power, Johnson (1979:316-319) outlines several strategies useful to the leader. The strategies are: (1) creating member dependency on the leader, (2) seeking organizational growth; (3) delegating authority to trusted close associates; (4) establishing contact with representatives of the wider society (which may be perceived as hostile); (5) seeking an isolated environment; (6) modifying and strengthening the ideology which justifies the groups existence, goals, and strategies; (7) establishing a sharp break between task activities and socioemotional activities; (8) developing special rituals which reaffirm or dramatically express member commitment; and (9) insuring that the rituals are so dramatic and overpowering emotionally that they appear sincere.

Realizing that this model applied to the Temple is an *ex post facto* interpretation, Johnson (1979:319-322) fleshes out the model with information about

Jones, his followers, Temple activities, and defectors. First, it is apparent that Jones created dependency in his followers by requiring them to contribute their resources to the Temple and later by requiring them to sign incriminating statements about themselves. Next, Jones sought organizational and political growth by moving to California, involving himself and the Temple in community activities, road trips, and recruitment drives, and in establishing contact with numerous state and national political figures. This expansion also required more coordination and led to a divison of labor involving the inner circle or Planning Commission. Possibly losing part of his control (due to size, defections, and bad press), Jones established and migrated to an extremely isolated environment (creating even more dependency) where he could control more readily daily activities and communication with the outside world. At least two accounts indicate that Jones was conscious of the relationship between an isolated environment and increased control. One source (Anonymous, 1979:46) attributes the following quote to Jones—"I'll be able to keep them in line when they're in the jungle without any place to go." The other, (Conway and Siegelman, 1979:241), quotes Grace Stoen, an ex-member of the Temple and the inner circle, as saying "I remember once in San Francisco, Jim Jones said to me, 'Boy, when we get people down in Guyana we can do anything we want to them. . . . There will be no more authorities and officials, no more police reports. We won't have to put up with any of that crap.' "

That the ideology supporting the Jonestown migration was strengthened and modified is indicated by numerous published reports. The idea of Jonestown as a "promised land," free from governmental interference and as a place of "brotherly love," signals a more intense ideology. Socialistic rhetoric also became more prevalent after the relocation, indicated by Jones' contentions that the group was being persecuted from all sides, and that the United States was a hopelessly racist and imperialistic society.

The logistics of running an isolated commune comprised of over 900 members must have been a monumental chore. The tasks of providing food, clothing, and shelter in a hot, humid, jungle forest necessitated a lot of hard work on the part of the commune members, and the leaders as well. To differentiate between the grueling work activities and the socioemotional (religious) motivation of members, Jones utilized marathon sessions of preaching and testimonials and intensified the ritualistic practices of "emergency" sessions, "education" hours, and "white night" drills. This ritualistic behavior became more and more dramatic and overpowering within a milieu that surely would have seemed bizzare to outsiders. Jones' claim to supernatural powers may have lasted right up until the end. His admonitions to his followers to commit "revolutionary suicide," and his promise that they would meet in "another place," indicates this, as well as his prophecy that the plane of Representative Ryan would "fall from the sky" (the plane, of course, never left the ground).

In analyzing charismatic leadership along these lines, Johnson (1979) down-plays the psychopathological approach and demonstrates that the processes utilized, consciously or unconsciously, by Jones are essentially normal sociological processes used in other "normal" contexts. Furthermore, the precariousness of Jones' charismatic power, and his realization that his control was limited, is possibly demonstrated by his use of armed guards at the site of the carnage—if Jones' really believed in his own, singular, omnipotence, the guards would not have been needed. As Johnson (1979:322) relates:

> The tragic choice faced by the People's Temple members may therefore not have been whether to drink the poison punch and die, or refuse and live. Rather, the only choice they may have perceived was the choice of how to die: by the cyanide in the punch, by actions of the U.S. Government in retaliation for the murder of a U.S. Congressman, or by fellow-members of the People's Temple who were standing by as armed guards to insure that Jones' final leadership decision was carried out.

This perspective is also presented by Conway and Siegelman, although in less careful language. In pointing out the "failure" of Jones' "haphazard" and "crude" attempts at mind control, they (1979:238) state that Jones "was less of a mind-bender than an arm twister. Because he had no systematic technique for controlling his members' internal thought processes, Jones was constantly forced to control them from without."

The argument over thought-reform or "brainwashing" and the more socio-logically oriented theories of "social" forces in altering persons' behavior con-tinues to exist and will not be put to rest here. It is interesting, however, to note the similarities between Johnson's (1979) treatment of charismatic leadership and Lifton's (1979) ideas concerning the "psychological principles" learned by messianic leaders over the course of their experience. Three basic principles identified by Lifton (1979:27) are: (1) control of communication, (2) stimulation and manipulation of guilt feelings, and (3) the idea of dispensing of existence. Jones did engage in communication control by isolation, censoring incoming mail and discouraging or prohibiting alternative ideological and religious expres-sions. In that he publicly humiliated persons and chastized them for not believ-ing or working hard enough, Jones stimulated and manipulated guilt feelings among his members. The dispensing of existence for Jones involved his in-sistence that the nonbelievers, ex-members, and defectors were evil and not wor-thy of engaging in the work of the movement. In his insistence that after commit-ting revolutionary suicide the members would be joined in "another place," Jones was dispensing an other-worldly existence to take the place of the tortured existence of Jonestown and this world. Ironically, Jones the Marxist utilized the typical Christian ideas of heaven and life after death to prompt his followers to commit suicide.

Some journalistic accounts, in a less abstract mode, indicate several reasons for members joining and being influenced by Jones. Kilduff and Javers (1978: 68-69), for example, state that, at least initially, Jones was a kindly preacher, a warm soul, and one who addressed the old ladies as "dear" in a soft baritone voice. He also was a caring humanitarian who was working toward social change and a new and better world. Similar to Father Divine, Jones also provided physical comfort and help with financial matters such as paying the rent, utilities, and food bills. Jones provided "miracles" in terms of "faith healing" to aid the problems of poor health for those who might not have understood the aloofness of a modern physician or the scientific nature of modern medicine. Jones offered simplicity of life-style for some and excitement for others. He was, finally, a good actor and manipulator.

These rather mundane factors have been interpreted by some to reflect patterns utilized by con artists and brainwashers in order to gain control over people for self-serving purposes. We will return to this in the next chapter in the section on programming. Another rather political view of Jonestown remains to be discussed.

Gordon K. Lewis (1979), writing as a socialist and a scholar in Caribbean studies, offers a view of Jonestown from a macro-political vantage point. Lewis sees Jones as emerging from the same tradition of American religious eccentricity as Joseph Smith, Mary Baker Eddy, Billy Sunday, and more recently, the fundamentalist movements of Billy Graham and Oral Roberts. Seeing Jones as an avowed socialist by the time he began the People's Temple, Lewis indicates that Jonestown represents a statement on the materialistic and acquisitive nature of American society and reflects the crisis of tormented souls trying to come to terms with existence and attempting to shape a coherent ideology. Believing that Jones finally became paranoid and, toward the end, possessed the tortured soul of a "charismatic psychopath," Lewis (1979:17) says that to describe and dismiss Jones' followers as "zombies" or "social deviants" shows "a complete absence of imaginative sympathy."

Lewis also describes the relationships between Jones and the Guyanese government and comments on how Jonestown came to be established in Guyana in the first place. He mentions, first, that there was an ideological similarity between the People's Temple avowed socialist doctrine and cooperative living arrangements (intermingled with the notion of self-reliance) and the Marxist ideology of the Guyana government with its emphasis on rebuilding Guyana for the "small man." Secondly, Jones preached and attempted to promote interracial harmony, a stated goal of Guyanese officials. Interestingly, Lewis (1979:24-comments that the Guyanese seemed to have overlooked the fact that Jonestown was divided into an overwhelmingly black rank-and-file and a largely white elite leadership. Thirdly, Jonestown fit well with Guyanese plans to develop the hinterland into an economically successful area. Having unsuccessfully tried to locate Guyanese workers in the Port Kaituma area, Jonestown represented a model enterprise for the successful economic development of a harsh and nonproductive environment. Fourth, Guyana deliberately used the Jonestown commune as a buffer between the Guyana and Venezuela borders. Disputes over the border began in the nineteenth century and are still unresolved. Guyana hoped to firmly establish its claim to the North West District by establishing Jones and his commune in the troubled area. Fifth, and last, Lewis (1979:35-36) indicates that Caribbean folk-peoples are deeply religious, and that the People's Temple benefited from Caribbean religious hospitality—such hospitality partially embracing, and being embraced by, other Christian fundamentalist groups, particularly the radio evangelists.

To conclude about Jonestown and the People's Temple, it must be reiterated that we do not have as much data on the phenomenon as we would like, even though, as Hargrove (1979) points out, social scientists and other academicians are readily contacted for information and comment about such happenings. Possibly fortuitously, no one was engaged in a participant observation study of Jonestown. Had there been such a study underway, and had the researcher survived, we would have been better able to understand the occurrence and to fix it more accurately into a theoretical framework, or to draw upon the raw data in an attempt to formulate new theoretical insights. As it stands now, we have to rely upon less than systematic data and to guard against overgeneralization in our *ex post facto* interpretations of the group's history and, finally, its carnage.

SUMMARY

In this chapter we have discussed a few of the aspects of some of the Christian-based new religious expressions and have presented several theoretical perspectives related to the formation, maintenance, and operation of these religious groups. We have concentrated on the Jesus People groups and on the People's Temple in an effort to document some of the ways in which new religious expressions, rituals, and beliefs can emerge from traditional religious foundations.

A basic conclusion to be drawn from our discussion is that no one particularistic explanation will suffice to explain these phenomena. Some important theoretical positions have been presented, however, in our attempt to explain and understand these complex socioreligious happenings. We reviewed and utilized three models of cult formation and found that the psychopathological, entrepreneur, and subculture-evolution models all contain elements useful to our understanding of certain religious expressions. Likewise, elements of "conversion theory" are important in any analysis of how individuals approach religious involvement. They sensitize us to the fact that one should look at the interplay of individual motivation, situational, and historical factors and the general cultural milieu within which religious expression develops.

We also presented several of the factors that have been demarcated by others as leading one to seek religious and spiritual involvement. Such variables as active seekership, secularization, quest for community, normative breakdown, and the need for a holistic conception of self are now fairly well established as important considerations for any study of socioreligious movements. We might add that human curiosity, establishing personal relations with supportive religious others, and encouragement from family members to get involved are also important features of religious exploration.

We have found that several groups may actually comprise what some consider to be the Jesus People movement, rather than it being a monolithic structure. Some of the factors appearing in association with Jesus People organizations are fundamentalism, radical evangelism, and emotionalism. The members, usually young persons, appear to be searching for transcendental experiences consisting of personalized relationships with Jesus and religious experiences they can *feel* as part of their religious identities. Some of the religious fundamentalism stressed by the Jesus People is also part of the recent "electronic church," consisting of television and radio broadcasts produced by formally organized and financially successful religious groups. Fundamental Christianity has also taken on a new form in that some utilize the "born again" label as a business calling card, refusing to do business with those not of like persuasion. Some critics have referred to this as overzealousness. The impact of the Jesus movement cannot yet be assessed. Some claim the movement is dying out as its novelty wears thin and as the political climate of the U.S. changes. Others claim it is only the tip of the iceberg of a really great spiritual awakening, merging with more traditional mainline, yet fundamentalist Christianity. Others point to the faddish and commercialized nature of some of the Jesus People activity.

The People's Temple and the Jonestown deaths have probably attracted as much attention as any religious activity of this century; thus, we have dedicated several pages to a description of the life of Jim Jones and to important events in the chronology of the group. The People's Temple was different in important respects from other new religions. It consisted mainly of blacks, females, and elderly persons who migrated to California from the southern part of the country and who utilized People's Temple as a religious and social base. They supported, in the meantime, the activities of a white man some claim to have been a crazed, drug addicted con artist and charlatan. Others describe Jones as a concerned humanitarian, burdened with the realization of the brutality and harshness of an evil capitalistic system, who attempted to lead the poor and downhearted to a promised land of self-respect and religious and social equality. Regardless of whether or not Jones was at the time of the tragedy a socialist preaching political rhetoric instead of Christianity, his movement did begin with a Christian-based philosophy.

Scholars have approached Jonestown with a variety of theoretical perspectives—some emphasizing psychological and psychiatric explanations and others employing sociological and sociopolitical frameworks. Probably all have some utility.

Many of the theoretical ideas addressed in this chapter will be reflected in the next chapter when we deal with other religious groups. We will also address some of the recent controversies over programming, deprogramming, and anticult organizations and activities.

REFERENCES

Anonymous
1979   *The Untold Story of the Jonestown Massacre.* New York: Histrionics.

Bainbridge, William Sims and Rodney Stark
1979   "Cult formation: three compatible models." *Sociological Analysis* 40 (Winter):283-295.

Balswick, Jack
1977   "The Jesus people movement: a generational interpretation." Pp. 167-176 in Chalfant, H. Paul, Evans W. Curry and C. Eddie Palmer (eds.), *Sociological Stuff.* Dubuque, Iowa: Kendall/Hunt.

Blumer, Herbert
1969   *Symbolic Interactionism.* Englewood Cliffs: Prentice Hall.

Cloward, Richard A. and Lloyd Ohlin
1961   *Delinquency and Opportunity.* Glencoe, Illinois: The Free Press.

Conway, Flo and Jim Siegelman
1979   *Snapping: America's Epidemic of Sudden Personality Change.* New York: Dell.

Davis, Rex and James T. Richardson
1976   "The organization and functioning of the Children of God." *Sociological Analysis* 37 (4):321-339.

Enroth, Ronald M., Edward E. Ericson, Jr. and
C. Breckinridge Peters
1972   *The Jesus People: Old Time Religion in the Age of Aquarius.* Grand Rapids: William B. Eerdmans Publishing Company.

Glock, Charles Y. and
Robert N. Bellah
1976   *The New Religious Consciousness.* Berkeley: University of California Press.

Hargrove, Barbara
1979   "Informing the public: social scientists and reactions to Jonestown." Paper presented at the Annual Meetings of the Society for the Scientific Study of Religion, October, San Antonio, Texas.

Johnson, Doyle Paul
1979   "Dilemmas of charismatic leadership: the case of the People's Temple." *Sociological Analysis* (Winter):315-323.

Kilduff, Marshall and
Ron Javers
1978   *Suicide Cult.* New York: Bantam.
Krause, Charles A.
1978   *Guyana Massacre.* New York: Berkley.
LaBarre, Weston
1971   "Materials for a history of studies of crisis cults: a bibliographic essay.: *Current Anthropology* 12 (February):3-27.

Lewis, Gordon K.
1979   *"Gather with the Saints at the River": The Jonestown Guyana Holocaust 1978.* Rio Piedras, Puerto Rico: Institute of Caribbean Studies.

Lifton, Robert Jay
1979   "The appeal of the death trip." *The New York Times Magazine* (January 7):26-27, 29-31.

Lofland, John
1978   " 'Becoming a world-saver' revisited." Pp. 10-23 in Richardson, James T. (ed.), *Conversion Careers: In and Out of the New Religions.* Beverly Hills: Sage.

Lofland, John and
Rodney Stark
1965   "Becoming a world-saver: a theory of conversion

to a deviant perspective." *American Sociological Review* 30:862-875.

Morrow, Lance
1978   "The lure of doomsday." *Time* (December 4):30.

Needleman, Jacob
1970   *The New Religions.* Garden City, New York: Doubleday.

Richardson, James T.
1979   "People's Temple and Jonestown: a corrective comparison and critique." Plenary address at the Annual Meetings of the Society for the Scientific Study of Religion, October, San Antonio, Texas.

Richardson, James T. (ed.)
1978   *Conversion Careers: In and Out of the New Religions.* Beverly Hills: Sage.

Richardson, James T. and Mary Stewart
1978   "Conversion process models and the Jesus movement." Pp. 24-42 in Richardson, James T. (ed.), *Conversion Careers: In and Out of the New Religions.* Beverly Hills: Sage.

Robbins, Thomas, Dick Anthony and James Richardson
1978   "Theory and research on today's 'new religions.' " *Sociological Analysis* 39 (Summer):95-122.

Rowley, Peter
1971   *New Gods in America: An Informal Investigation into the New Religions of American Youth Today.* New York: David McKay.

Straus, Roger
1976   "Changing oneself: seekers and the creative transformation of life experience." Pp. 252-272 in John Lofland, *Doing Social Life.* New York: Wiley.

Walls, Dwayne
1979   "The Jesus mania: bigotry in the name of the Lord." Pp. 177-182 in Leonard Cargan and Jeanne H. Ballantine (eds.), *Sociological Foot-*

prints: Introductory Readings in sociology. Boston: Houghton Mifflin Company.

White, Leslie
1959

The Evolution of Culture. New York: McGraw-Hill.

Wiencek, David
1979

"A demographic profile of Jonestown victims." Paper presented at the Annual Meetings of the Society for the Scientific Study of Religion, October, San Antonio, Texas.

Wilson, Bryan
1975

"The secularization debate." *Encounter* 45(4):77-83.

Zaretsky, Irving I. and
Mark P. Leone
1974

Religious Movements in Contemporary America. Princeton, New Jersey: Princeton University Press.

Chapter 10

New Expressions
from Nontraditional
Sources

Estimates of the number of new religious groups in the United States vary tremendously; some contend they number into the hundreds, others say thousands. Whatever the exact number, the last several years of this country's history has seen a very rapid growth of extremely diverse religious and quasi-religious organizations.

What kind of groups are these and where are they located? Rodney Stark et al. (1979) have provided us with important summary information on these questions by coding a set of data for 501 cults. Their analysis is based on information contained in Melton's (1978) *Encyclopedia of American Religions.* For each cult, Stark et al. (1979:349) coded the state where its headquarters is located, indicating that for most cults this state is also where the group originated and where most, if not all, of its current members reside. In terms of actual number of cults, states having fifteen or more are: California (167), New York (59), Illinois (34), Florida (20), Pennsylvania (18), and Colorado and Missouri (15 each). Alaska, Delaware, Maine, Mississippi, Montana, North Dakota, South Dakota, Vermont, and West Virginia had none.

These researchers also divided the number of cults located in a state by its population and found that the following five states have more than five cults per million residents: Nevada (10.0), New Mexico (9.1), California (7.9), Colorado (6.0), and Arizona (5.9). The District of Columbia actually has a higher rate of cult headquarters per million residents than any of the states (15.7). Looking at cult geography by region of the country and cults per million residents they (1979:350) found the Pacific region to be highest (6.9 cults per million inhabitants), followed by the Rocky Mountain region (3.5), the Southwest (2.1), the East (2.0), the Northeast (1.9), East Central (1.6), West Central (1.4), and the South the lowest (.9; with Florida omitted, .6). Using thirteen categories representing fundamental divisions among cult groups, Stark et al. (1979:352) present data on cult composition by region of the United States. These data are presented in Table 10-1.

As the volume and diversity of these data indicate, we cannot deal with each of the new groups in any detail. Rather, we will concentrate on a few of the prevalent organizations and a few of the less well-known groups in an attempt to describe some of the history of the groups, how they operate, and the foundation of some of their beliefs. We will deal below with the Hare Krishnas, the Unification Church, Scientology, the Divine Light Mission, Synanon, and briefly with a UFO cult and Transcendental Meditation.

THE HARE KRISHNA MOVEMENT

The Hare Krishna (spelled Krsna in sanskrit) movement began in this country with the arrival of Abhay Charan De, also known as His Divine Grace A. C. Bhaktivedanta Swami Prabhupada. According to Daner (1976:15-17), Charan De was born on September 1, 1896, in Calcutta, India, and attended the University of Calcutta majoring in Philosophy, English, and Economics. After terminating his education in 1920 he managed a large chemical firm. Having been raised as a Krishna-conscious child by his father, Gour Mohon De, he began studying the teachings of Sri Srimad Bhaktisiddhanta Saraswati Gosvami Maharaja. Abhay Charan De was initiated at Allahabad in 1933, and "in 1936, just days before Saraswati's death, he claims to have been specifically ordered by his guru to spread Krsna consciousness to the English-speaking people of the West" (Daner, 1976:16). Charan De remained in the Gaudiya Vaisnava Society after Saraswati's death and became editor-in-chief of *Back to Godhead* magazine in 1944. After being initiated as Bhaktivedanta in 1947, he remained a *grhastra* (householder devotee) and stayed with his family until 1954 when he became *vanaprastha* (retired order) and broke his connections with his wife and family. According to Daner (1976:16):

> He was able to do this because his children were grown annd (sic) his wife was a rich man's daughter who owned property. By 1962 Bhaktivedanta had become successful in starting his own society called the League of Devotees in Vrndavana, Delhi, and was publishing scriptural texts. In 1965, at the advanced age of seventy, Bhaktivedanta arrived in the United States to fulfill his master's sacred mission.

Another source, (Judah, 1974a:464) states that in 1954 Bhaktivedanta retired from the chemical firm and in 1959 became a *sannyasi*, or one who has accepted a renunciation of worldly life in the search for spirituality. This chronology would mean that Bhaktivedanta had moved from *grhasta*, to *vanaprastha* and finally to *sannyasi* before he left India to come to the U.S.

Daner (1976:16) states in a footnote that "Bhaktivedanta's first journey to the United States was financed by Srimatri Sumati Morarji, a woman 'industrialist' and owner of Scindia Steamship Lines. Srimati Morarji is reputed to be the richest woman in India." Regardless of the wealth of his sponsor, however,

Table 10–1. CULT COMPOSITION OF REGIONS OF THE UNITED STATES

Kinds of Cults	Pacific	South West	Mountain	West Central	East Central	East	Northeast	South	National*
1. Mormon Groups**	0%	8%	0%	24%	3%	3%	0%	0%	3%
2. Cult Communes	5	3	0	0	4	1	5	4	3
3. New Thought	6	10	11	7	3	6	21	5	7
4. Theosophy & Spiritualism	26	31	21	4	24	21	21	36	25
5. Occult Orders	4	2	5	0	4	3	0	0	3
6. Flying Saucers	6	2	5	3	3	1	0	7	4
7. Psychedelic	2	5	0	0	0	1	0	0	1
8. Psychic	12	15	10	17	0	8	16	12	11
9. Magick, Witches, & Satanists	7	8	16	21	16	11	16	24	12
10. Pagans	7	3	0	7	7	1	0	0	4
11. Asian Faiths	20	8	32	3	22	37	21	12	21
12. Jesus People	4	0	0	4	7	0	0	0	2
13. Miscellaneous	1	5	0	10	7	7	0	0	4
	100%	100%	100%	100%	100%	100%	100%	100%	100%

*Washington, D.C. Included.
**Utah Mormon Groups omitted.

Source: Stark et al, 1979:352.

Bhaktivedanta apparently arrived in the United States nearly broke. According to Rowley (1971), Judah (1974a), and Daner (1976), Bhaktivedanta started the Hare Krishna movement in New York's lower East Side.

Judah (1974a:464) in his interpretation of the first activities of Bhaktivedanta in the United States writes:

> A. C. Bhaktivedanta Swami Prabhupada, the present spiritual leader, first brought its teachings to the United States in 1965. When he arrived in New York he began chanting the names of Krishna to the rhythm of his *kartals* (small Indian cymbals), while sitting beneath a tree in Tompkins Park on the Lower East Side. Soon, however, he attracted many about him, a number of whom were hippies. The following year a temple was established in New York. Other centers soon appeared, close to the hippie community in the Haight-Ashbury of San Francisco, in Los Angeles, Berkeley, and elsewhere.

So according to accounts, the Krishna movement represents the rags to riches story of an elderly Hindu holy man who appeared on the scene as the counter-culture got under way. But what was the guru offering? What are the spiritual aspects of the Krishna philosophy?

Bhaktivedanta Prabhupada offered his followers a personality connected to Krsna through a chain of "disciplic succession" (Daner, 1976:107). Another important figure in this chain of disciples leading back to Krsna was Caitanya (1486-1533), who introduced *kirtana* (chanting the name and praises of Krsna) to Eastern India. As a result of the growth of the revitalization movement led by Caitanya some believed him to be an *avatara* (incarnation) of Krsna. Still others believed him to be "Krisna himself" (Daner, 1976:25). Krishna is believed by some to be Vishnu (or Visnu), the sustainer of the universe, who, along with Siva and Brahma are the presiders over the creation. The link between Vedic theology and the Hare Krishna movement, however, remains cloudy. Bhaktivedanta Prabhupada teaches Bhakti-yoga centering on the devotion to Krisna espoused by Caitanya and his followers. In fact, the position and importance of Krishna to Vedic worshipers remains cloudy. Judah (1974b:18-19), for example, has mentioned that:

> Krishna is popular in India; Hindus are continually reminded of him in many places and many ways. He is the cowherd diety of Vrindavan, the scene of the pasttimes, and is usually depicted as sporting in eternal loving dalliance with the *gopis* or cowherdesses, among whom Radha is his favorite . . . [However] it is fitting to note here that Chaitanya and his immediate followers were not the originators of bhaktiyoga . . . even if they emphasized the chanting of the names of Krishan publicly in their *sankir-*

tans, they had numerous important predecessors. Moreover, even if Chaitanya's particular emphasis on Krishna is perhaps most evident among Vaishnavas in India today, Krishna is not the only prominent deity. Many worship Siva or some form of his energy *(sakti)* as their favorite deity ... some worship ... Rama, as the supreme deity. The followers of Chaitanya, however, believe that Krishna is the supreme and original form. They consider Vishnu to be the same as Krishna, but he is Krishna's plenary expansion.

Regardless of the exact chronology and linkages of Krishna to Bhaktivedanta, Bhaktivedanta teaches devotion to Krishna and has translated the *Bhagavad-gita* (the sacred book of the Vedic tradition) under the title *The Bhagavad-gita as It Is* (published in 1968 by Collier-MacMillan Publishers). This book, along with the *Bhagavatum,* outlines the philosophy for devotees of Hare Krishna to follow.

The requirements of a devotee is to try to obtain Krsna Consciousness through *bhakti* or loving service to the deity Krsna. Through such devotion the devotee experiences pleasure in the search for what is beautiful and satisfying. According to Daner (1976:35), there are eight acts which are meant to bring about the proper feeling of humility and self-surrender to *bhakti:*

1. Recognizing Krsna as one's only refuge.

2. Service to a spiritual master (guru).

3. Reading and listening to the *Bhagavad-gita* and the Srinad-Bhagavatum, Krsna's pastimes, and the writings of the guru.

4. Sankirtana, singing the names and praises of Krsna...

5. Thinking constantly of the name, form and pastimes of Krsna.

6. Serving the feet of the deities, seeing, touching, and worshipping the deities.

7. Performing rites and ceremonies learned from the guru, such as putting *vaisnava* signs on one's body, taking the remains of an offering to the diety as *prasada* [usually food], drinking the water used to wash the diety and so on.

8. Prostrating before the deity forms and the spiritual master.

In addition to these aspects of *bhakti*, devotees entering an ISKCON temple are to turn over all their wordly possessions to the temple and follow four proscriptive rules. These are listed in Daner (1976:60-61) as:

1. No gambling. This rule also excludes frivolous sports and games. In addition, devotees are advised not to engage in any conversation that is not connected with the teachings of Krsna Consciousness or with the execution of duties. All other speech or reading is called mental speculation and is a luxury in which the devotees do not engage.

2. No intoxicants. This rule includes all narcotics, alcoholic beverages, tobacco, coffee, and tea. ISKCON's efficiency in getting its members to abandon the use of drugs such as marijuana, LSD, and others, has drawn commendations from the mayors of New York and San Francisco. Medicines may be taken when absolutely necessary . . . but chanting the Hare Krsna mantra is considered to be a better remedy for bodily ills. . . .

3. No illicit sex. Sexual relations are permitted only between individuals married by a qualified devotee in Krsna Consciousness. There is no dating or courtship allowed . . . A Swami stated it succinctly: "If a devotee believes he can serve Krsna better by being married, then he gets married. Marriage is primarily for the purpose of raising children in Krsna Consciousness."

4. No eating of meat, fish, or eggs. The only food that can be eaten by devotees is food prepared under strict dietary regulations and offered by prescribed ceremony to Krsna.

These rules and regulations have aided ISKCON in becoming a viable organization as well as a new expression of religious life in this country. It has grown from a storefront in New York to an international organization with temples or centers around the world.

ISKCON, International Society for Krishna Consciousness, as a sociological phenomenon, has dealt with the organizational necessities of financial stability through a variety of techniques. In addition to the collectivistic orientation requiring the surrender of worldly possessions, including money and bank accounts, upon joining the movement devotees are taught to beg for money or for donations for copies of *Back to Godhead: The Magazine of the Hare Krishna Movement.* Daner (1976:56-60), in a section entitled "Economic Activities," details numerous ways in which the organization makes money. The magazine *Back to Godhead*, for example, costs each temple nineteen cents per copy even after having been flown from New York to Los Angeles for printing and back to New York for assembly. Friends and relatives are asked for donations, and businessmen are asked to become life-time members at $1,111.00, which they may do without giving up their occupations. Another venture, which Daner (1976:59) considers the "real backbone of ISKCON's economic success" is the Spiritual Sky Incense Company. This company's profits rose from one million dollars in 1973 to double that in 1974. Incense manufacturing is done in Los Angeles by ten devotees, but sales are mainly handled by computer and persons outside of Krsna Consciousness. Other scented products made for ISKCON by Avon, such as oils, shampoo, and soap, are sold to businesses and boutiques throughout the country. This type of economic activity is positively sanctioned by Prabhupada as indicated by his following statement (quoted in Daner, 1976:59-60).

> There are many devotees who are engaged in the propagation of Krsna Consciousness and they require help. So even if one cannot directly prac- tice the regulated principles of bhakti-yoga, he can try to help such prop- aganda work. Every endeavor requires land, capital, organization, and labor. Just as in business, one requires a place to stay, some capital to use, some labor and some organization to make propaganda; so the same is re- quired in the service of Krsna. The only difference is that materialism means to work for sense gratification. The same work, however, can be performed for the satisfaction of Krsna: that is spiritual activity.

While this fiscal stability may wax and wane with ISKCON, recent publica- tions and media coverage indicate a definite solvency for the organization. Temples are being constructed in the United States (particulary a multi-million dollar structure in New Vrindaban, West Virginia) and in India (particularly the Vedic Cultural Center in Bombay, see *Back to Godhead*, Vol. 13, No. 3, 1978). The growth of the organization and its diversification in sending some devotees to rural areas and others to India has prompted one writer to suggest the "possi- ble fragmentation" (Johnson, 1977:51) of the movement. Others in the move- ment do not appear to be concerned with such fragmentation.

Another potential problem for ISKCON, however, is the succession of leaders within the movement. *Back to Godhead* (1978, Vol. 13, No. 4:1) mentions that His Divine Grace A. C. Bhaktivedanta Swami Prabhupada "passed away in In- dia's Vrndavana (the place most sacred to Lord Krsna), on November 14, 1977. His disciples are carrying forward the movement he started." The passing of Prabhupada may be producing problems for ISKCON but the succession of authority within the movement was thought out before Prabhupada's death. Ac- cording to Daner (1976:53):

> In August 1970, Bhaktivedanta decided to establish a governing body com- mission, called the G.B.C., creating a formal structure for ISKCON. The precipitating reasons for the establishment of the G.B.C. were Bhak-

tivedanta Swami's advanced age, his poor health, and the rapid growth of the movement. The G.B.C. was established in a letter sent to temple presidents. . . . Twelve men devotees, who were considered by Prabhupada to have outstanding managerial talents and to be very advanced in Krsna Consciousness, were appointed to relieve him of managerial tasks. . . . In the future, the temple presidents will elect the G.B.C. members for terms of three years each.

As to the future of ISKCON, little data is available from which to predict.

THE UNIFICATION CHURCH

Probably one of the best known "new expressions" in religious life to develop in this country is the Unification Church and its adherents—the "Moonies." The mass media has continually covered this movement probably more than any other in contemporary America. The Moonies are still embroiled in religious and legal controversy as this writing. The controversy stems from accusations of "brainwashing" of converts, to illegal solicitation of funds by members, to the tax-free status of the organization as a church, and in perhaps a more crucial domain whether the guarantes of religious freedom extends to the varied activities of the Unification Church. The church has also been investigated by the Internal Revenue Service, the Justice Department, and the Immigration Service (Lofland, 1977:334) and has been denied permission to solicit funds and/or conduct functions in many towns. Better Business Bureaus warn of the solicitation tactics of the Moonies and local newspapers and law enforcement officials "warn the citizens" of their presence.

One paper which interprets Reverend Moon's movements as "an attempt at a totalitarian response to the cultural fragmentation of mass society" states that "The Unification Church and its allied organizations represent an attempt, in the context of growing political apathy and privatism among young Americans, to redirect community and transcendence towards the civic realm and to revitalize and standardize the civil religion" (Robbins et al., 1976:113).

The brief history of the movement provided by Robbins et al. (1976:114) centers around Reverend Sun Myung Moon, a Korean evangelist who suffered imprisonment by the Communists in North Korea in 1947. He was later liberated by the Americans during the Korean war. Seeing himself as the Messiah, he also received a divine relevation, which is embodied in the *Divine Principle* (1974). The Unification Church was founded in Korea in 1954 by Reverend Moon, who first visited the United States in 1965. The movement, however, had already begun before Moon actually arrived. Sociologists, as well as others, are fortunate in that the early history of the church was chronicled in an ethnographic description by John Lofland (1966) in his book *Doomsday Cult,* which he later updated and enlarged (Lofland, 1977). While Lofland continues to use pseudonyms in his works, requiring us to make the assumption at the DP's (Divine Precepts) are actually the Moonies, Robbins et al. (1976:114) state that "It is little known among sociologists of religion that the well-known volume by Lofland (1966) and the article by Lofland and Stark (1965) represent early studies of Reverend Moon's movement." Lynch (1977:81) has also commented that "Anyone who has lingering doubts that the Doomsday Cult is the Unification Church in its embryonic form should compare Lofland's descriptions of the beliefs and practices of the Cult with journalist's accounts of the Unification Church."

The DPs, or Divine Precepts, studied by Lofland (1966, 1977) were a small group of persons who made up the American wing of a larger group of millenarians in Korea who believed in a Mr. Chang, a "Christ-Messiah," who taught that the world was going to be transformed and made perfect by 1967. In his descriptive introduction to the DP cult, which Lofland originally studied from 1959 through mid-1963, Lofland (1977:4) gives the following account of "Mr. Chang:"

> During the late 1940s and early fifties, a young Korean electrical engineer, Mr. Soon Sun Chang, received a series of what he took to be messages from God, acknowledging him as none other than the returned Christ, the Lord of the Second Advent. Chang was also convinced that through these divine encounters, a new body of knowledge, the Divine Precepts, was being revealed to him. This doctrine unveiled the laws or principles by which God governs man ... and disclosed the manner in which the perfected and eternal kingdom of God would shortly be established on earth.

From this start, the DPs grew to several hundred in and around Seoul, Korea, by the late 1950s. In 1959 Chang sent one of his earliest followers, an English-speaking former university professor, Miss Yoon Sook Lee, to the U.S. Her efforts resulted initially in only a few converts, and numerous problems in keeping those arose in the course of establishing the cult. In Lofland's (1977) Postscript he mentions that the DPs grew to only thirty-five members in the U.S. and Germany by 1963; by June 1964, there were 120 converts in some twenty-five places spread across America (and Germany). The belief in the establishment of the kingdom of God on earth (originally predicted for 1967) apparently changed in 1964. The year 1967 was still a target date, but now for the appearance of the "Spirit of Truth"which would appear in the sky and be visible to everyone in the world simultaneously. Upon this appearance, "low-level" spirits would descend to earth as "black blobs" and "hairy things." To interpret these creatures, people would have to turn to the DPs for understanding and guidance toward perfection, and would convert to the DPs. As Lofland (1977:268) states, however, this would "only be the beginning of restoring the world to perfection. The actual work of making the entire world perfect would take until about the year 2000." (See Zygmunt [1976] for similar information on prophetic failure among the Jehovah's witnesses.)

At the end of the Postscript, Lofland (1977:268) predicted that "The disciples' propensity to keep moving is likely to cause continual growth. It will not be long before they effectively blanket the country with a thin, but active layer of proselytizing true believers." While the Unification Church may be currently stabilizing at around 1,500 core members in the United States, its activities and the number of people it affects make this church's existence one of the most important in the United States today, even though Lofland (1977:280) contends that they will become a "has been" movement during the 1980s.

Particularly during the 1972-1974 "growth" period of the movement, however, the DPs utilized a rather polished recruitment method which consists of several strategies and components. Lofland (1977:305-314) outlines these as (1) picking-up, (2) hooking, (3) encapsulating (consisting of absorption of attention, collective focus, exclusive input, fatigue and logical, comprehensive cognitions), (4) loving, and (5) committing.

Picking-up involves casual contact in a public place between the recruiter and the potential convert. Examples include picking up hitchhikers or approaching persons on the streets with an invitation to a lecture and/or dinner.

After the first contact was made, *hooking* involved exuding friendship and camaraderie to possible recruits upon their arrival at the dinner. The potential convert was assigned a "buddy" who showed a personal interest in the person. The recruiter would compliment the guest on physical appearance or clothing and find out about the interests of that person. General lectures on the guiding principles of the church were given, and guests at some gatherings were invited to weekend workshops. Concerning invitations to The Farm (a several hundred acre retreat), guests were shown a slide show of the farm and its surroundings.

Encapsulating is self-explanatory in that recruits were removed from their normal sphere of activities. If the hook worked and the guest accepted the invitation to a workshop or retreat, the ideology could be presented to the recruit with a minimum of outside interference. The encapsulation process at the The Farm consisted of numerous devices which helped secure a commitment to the Church. *Absorption of attention* refers to scheduling every moment of the guest's time. Even trips to the bathroom were controlled under the accompaniment of the buddy assigned to each guest. The activities involved a *collective focus* in that group-eating, exercises, lectures, and chanting were conducted in ways conducive to focusing attention outward toward the group rather than upon individuals. *Exclusive input* was obtained by cutting the recruit off from outside contact. While prospects were not physically restrained, leaving was strongly discouraged, and "there were no newspapers, radios, TVs, or easily accessible telephones. The Farm itself was miles from any settlement. Half of the fifty or so workshop participants were always DPs and they dominated selection of topics for talk and what was said about them" (Lofland, 1977:309). *Fatigue* was obtained by speeding up work activities like gardening, and volleyball and other games were staged at a "frantic pitch." Participants were often exhausted from the days activities and sleep periods were controlled. Intermingled with such activity were brief lectures and discussions of the beliefs of the Moonies, particularly the first and most "logical" and "comprehensive" ideas of the Church.

Loving, as a recruitment method, has been mentioned numerous times in the mass media as a technique of the Unification Church. Love-bombing, as a concept, may be a singular linguistic contribution of the Church. The desire for love and positive reinforcement for ourselves and our actions may be one of the most universal of our desires. Within the confines of an intense peer group, withholding one's love while receiving gestures of love, trust, and affection from others may turn into an important conditioning element. One precept recalled the following (Lofland, 1977:311):

> Whenever I would raise a theological question, the leaders of my group would look very impressed and pleased, seem to agree with me, and then give me a large dose of love—and perhaps say something about unity and God's love being most important. I would have an odd, disjointed sort of feeling—not knowing if I'd really been heard or not, yet aware of the attentive look and the smiling approval. My intellectual objection had been undercut by means of emotional seduction. Unfortunately, I succumbed to this many times without learning what was happening.

As Lofland (1977:312) comments, "This incredibly intense encapsulating and loving did not simply happen. DPs trained specifically for it and held morale and strategy sessions among themselves. . . ." These activities were directed toward the last component of Lofland's (1977) schema of recruitment tactics, that of *committing* to the church. This stage was accomplished by not immediately demanding that a recruit commit at the end of a weekend session or workshop. Instead, he or she was invited to stay on at The Farm for a week-long workshop and then for longer periods of time. Eventually the prospect would be drawn into working, street peddling, and other church activities. One recruit was sent out after three weeks at The Farm to sell flowers and offered this comment (Lofland, 1977:313-14):

> Being out in the world again was a shock; a cultural shock in which I was unable to deal with reality. My isolation by the Church has been so successful that everyday sights such as hamburger stands and TVs and even the people, looked foreign, of another world. I had been reduced to a

> dependent being! The Church had seen to it that my three weeks with
> them made me so vulnerable and so unable to cope with the real world,
> that I was compelled to stay with them.

But what of the mechanics of this movement? What are the dimensions of
theology that make people give over their lives and earthly possessions to selfless-
ly dedicate themselves to work for the cause, involving, in some instances, the
practice of deceptive strategies. As Lofland (1977:290) contends "Parents were
sometimes milked for more money by such devices as long-distance phone pleas
for funds to pay nonexistent auto repair or medical bills."

The ideology of the movement is based upon the ideas and revelations of
Reverend Moon. Primary principles involve the following core of ideas (Lofland, 1977:15-16): (1) creation consists of three stages (formation, growth, and
perfection); (2) things exist in complementary association (i.e., male and female,
positive and negative); (3) an action of give and take exists between complementary associations; (4) God created man so that He could exist in complementary
association and experience the energy of life and the joy of love; (5) there exists a
spirit world and a material world, and man has a spirit body and a material body;
and (6) Lucifer thwarted God's plan for man's spirit to grow through the three
stages of development to perfection.

In an admittedly oversimplified summary, Robbins et al. (1976:116-17) continue the explication of the philosophy:

> God originally intended for Adam and Eve to breed perfect progeny,
> which would form the basis of a perfect God-centered family , that would
> ramify into a perfect nation, perfect society, and perfect world. Eve, how-
> ever, was seduced by Lucifer and then entered a non-God centered con-
> jugal relationship with Adam resulting in their progeny's becoming "fallen
> beings," separate from God, and incapable of truly harmonious interpre-
> sonal relationships. The goal of Reverend Moon's ministry is to enable
> man to overcome his "fallen nature" and to re-unite mankind into God's
> family, all of which is possible if enough persons internalize Unification
> principles.... Harmonious "give and take" (a key term) must prevail
> among family members, peers, social classes, and nations, and between
> God and Man. When this prevails man will fulfill his true purpose of con-
> stituting God's perfect creation.

The persons who want to commit and become "full members" of the Church
(after listening to lectures and other revealing aspects of the philosophy) usually
change their lives radically. These people, who are typically between 18 and 35
years of age and college educated, usually begin a collective existence when they
become "family members." Robbins et al. (1976:115-16) give the following

perspective:

> When one "joins the family" one gives up one's other instrumental and expressive involvements and takes up residence in a communal "Unification center," henceforth devoting most of one's energies to the movement. . . . Communal centers are coeducational, but living quarters are segregated by sex, and strict premarital celibacy is the rule. Life in a communal center is disciplined and most of the day is devoted to activities such as "witnessing" on the street, giving and listening to lectures, and attending other functions. The "center director" is appointed by the central regional office, and he supervises activities. Authority is hierarchial and flows downward from Reverend Moon. Unification centers are centrally financed; members receive free medical care plus money for clothes.

Other characteristics involve the prohibition of smoking, drinking, and drug abuse as well as, in some cases, preparing oneself for political involvement. A certain style of dress is required, and short hair is required for male members of the family. In fact, the philosophy is all-encompassing and, according to Robbins et al. (1976:117), "specifies a complex system of rules governing all dimensions of interpersonal behavior. These 'Unification principles' govern even seemingly casual social interaction which would normally be structured only by social etiquette or left to the vagaries of individual impulse." These rules may account for the mechanical or stereotypical behavior of Moon converts which make them identifiable to others.

As previously mentioned, the Unification Church has been followed, and lately attacked, by various media, governmental agencies, and families. Reverend Moon, after acquiring large real estate holdings and operating numerous "front" organizations for the church, left this country after severe criticism of his philosophy, conversion techniques, and financial status. His name has been mentioned in connection with "Korea-gate" scandals, and some have hinted at possible connections with other political agencies. Lofland (1977:329), in summarily speaking of the troubles of "Mr. Chang" and the DPs states:

> The verbal attacks contained several recurrent themes, the overarching theme of which was the accusation of deceit. The initial, and perhaps most persistent, theme concerned deceit about finances . . . from where did the millions come? Chang lived in splendor. Was that appropriate for a religious leader, especially a religious leader whose followers lived in poverty? . . . Did the money come from nefarious foreign sources (the KCIA) or nefarious domestic sources (the CIA)? . . . Funds were solicited for alleged drug programs and other civic-minded efforts, but where were such alleged programs? . . . Chang had admitted he owned a factory that made parts for

small weapons for the South Korean government. Was that appropriate to a religion? By mid-1976, a Sunday supplement magazine felt safe titling a critical article on Chang, "Prophet for Profit," a straight putdown.

As mentioned above, Lofland (1977) states that the Unification Church in the United States will eventually constitute a "has been" movement, but that core membership will decline slowly rather than having an *en masse* defection. The future of the worldwide movement, especially after emerging political pressure and post-Guyana reflections, remains for others to document. The leaders of the movement, however, are not passive at this writing. In testifying before the Dole-Ottinger congressional panel on Monday, February 5, 1979, the president of the Unification Church of America, Neil Salonen, stated that the name of Reverend Moon had been smeared (by equating the Unification Church with cults such as the People's Temple in Jonestown, Guyana) and if the Unification Church had done anything wrong, the matter should be taken over by the Justice Department. Salonen finished by stating that "to be held up to public ridicule is wrong, and we won't tolerate it" (Anonymous, *Lubbock Avalanche-Journal*, February 6, 1979:B-3).

SCIENTOLOGY

The definition of religion, as stated previously, is on the one hand limiting and on the other, expansive. Scientology would not qualify for religious status by some observers. Scientology itself, however, is billed as "an applied religious philosophy" in the small print of magazine advertisements along with statements to the fact that "The Church of Scientology of California is a non-profit organization." In numerous writings on new religious expressions, numerous figures are given as to the size of the organization. Whitehead (1974:548) places the number of Americans that are "currently active" Scientologists at approximately 30,000 and the number of people who have been "touched" by Scientology at approximately two million. Whitehead's (1974) article entitled "Reasonably Fantastic: Some Perspectives on Scientology, Science Fiction, and Occultism" provides an in-depth theoretical and historical treatment of Scientology, and serves as the major source from which the following material is adapted.

Scientology is a creation of L. Ron Hubbard, a writer of western adventure, and science fiction stories. According to one account (*Time*, December 11, 1978:36), Hubbard once said to a colleague, "Writing for a penny a word is ridiculous. If a man wanted to make a million dollars, the best way would be to start his own religion." Hubbard is also an explorer (Explorer's Club of New York, 1940), a daredevil glider pilot, and an accomplished mariner who saw naval duty in World War II. Hubbard lives part of the time on board Apollo, the flagship of the Sea Org, which is a floating community of dedicated Scien-

302

tologists. There are fourteen other orgs in the United States which are centers where advanced Scientological training occurs. Scientology was first established in Phoenix, Arizona, in 1950, and incorporated as a church in California in 1952. Recently, Scientologists have been placed under federal indictment accused of conspiracy to infiltrate, bug, and burglarize government agencies in an effort to discredit critics (see *Time*, December 11, 1978:36).

Scientology, which started out as "Dianetics," was introduced to the world in 1950 by John Campbell, Jr., the then editor of *Astounding Science Fiction*. Campbell began his own writing career while still a student at MIT in 1928 and, upon assuming the editorship of *Astounding Science Fiction*, recruited and cultivated numerous new writers, among them L. Ron Hubbard, who published the book *Dianetics: The Modern Source of Mental Health* in 1950.

Originally, Dianetics (later to become Scientology) involved a theory of the mind which divided the psyche into two parts: the *analytic mind* and the *reactive mind*. The analytic mind is operative when people are fully conscious and "rational" and contains information that is readily available to awareness. The analytic mind may mislead the person if it has obtained incorrect information; this, however, could be corrected by training and re-education. The analytic mind is similar to Freud's concept of the ego in that it sorts, assesses, and explores information and comes up with interpretations and judgments which are appropriate for the situation. The reactive mind acts, like the analytic mind, to aid the survival of the individual but does it through reflexivity or reaction which is similar to behavioristic conditioning of a Pavlovian nature. These conditioned equations are not usually accessible to awareness and are not consciously learned. This "theory" relates to a therapeutic technique through the concept of "engrams." As Whitehead (1974:574-75) explains:

> The Reactive Mind can only acquire its stored information during periods when the Analytic Mind is temporarily inoperative . . . when the Analytic Mind is out of commission, the Reactive mind continues to record information . . . the engram, which is defined as an incident containing pain and unconsciousness, is the basic building block of the Reactive Mind. All of man's apparently inappropriate or "irrational" behavior which cannot be explained on the basis of false analytic information . . . stems from the engramic contents of the Reactive Mind. These engrams are stirred into action . . . by any stimulus in the external world that resembles or is the same as something in an engram. When such a stimulus appears, the Reactive Mind "keys in" and causes the individual to react in a manner which would be appropriate were the present-time situation the same as the past-time situation of the engram . . . the contents of the Reactive Mind are responsible for neuroses, psychoses, and psychosomatic illness.

Therefore, if one was to become "cleared" of his irrationalities and neuroses, one had to consciously confront past engramic incidents, and allow them to discharge their force and influence. (Compare this to Ida Rolf's "Rolfing Techniques" and Irving Janov's "Primal Scream" therapy as well as basic psychiatric techniques, including remembering painful happenings while under hypnosis.) For Dianetics, the way for engrams to discharge was through a process of auditing or listening; auditors questioned and commanded in an effort to allow the subject, called the *pre-clear*, to recognize and recall past incidents. These incidents are also thought to be linked together or to run in *chains*, and for each chain there is a first or *basic engramic incident*. Getting the pre-clear to recognize and deal with the "basic" on the "chain" is a part of the auditing of Scientology. Hubbard audited his pre-clears through "automobile accidents, war injuries, operations, beatings by drunken fathers, falls from the crib in early infancy, the birth trauma, and back into such gruesome 'prenatals' as attempted abortions and violent parental sex acts" (Whitehead, 1974:576). Through the processing of the pre-clear through these incidents, the person would theoretically become "clear," or a totally rational person. An interesting point in early Scientology deals with the question of how far back down the chain could one be carried through auditing to get to the *Basic*. Early followers disagreed with Hubbard and split off from his organization due to his acceptance of going to "past lives." Whitehead (1974:579-80) offers a story (possibly part legend) from an early follower over this dispute.

> Before the conflict [over past lives] broke out, there were, as he recalled, two guys who always hung around the Foundation not really accomplishing much. . . . In those days Ron apparently got things going by wandering around from room to room setting up auditors with preclears, giving instructions . . . so in effect there were little sessions going on all over the building all the time. Both of the two men in question had run lots and lots of engrams, but nothing seemed to work for them. . . . Then one day, somebody opened a broom closet and found these two sitting there auditing each other on past lives. And having a marvelous time of it. . . . Hubbard's attitude was "Fine, as long as it works."

The "past lives" aspect of auditing, among other things, led Hubbard to branch off into other areas of the psyche and modify his basically psychological approach. Hubbard "began to develop a set of ideas that would account not only for past lives and the wild assortment of incidents which people found in their earlier lifetimes, but also for the whole range of uncanny pheonomena which have hitherto been relegated to the realm of the supernatural. . . ." (Whitehead, 1974:580-81). These ideas later became the cornerstone of Scientology and dealt with the notion that on some levels, man is a spiritual being, called a *Thetan*. The Thetan is the "person himself—not his body or name, the physical universe, his mind, or anything else: that which is aware of being aware; the identity that IS the individual" (Whitehead, 1974:581). From this perspective, the Thetan allowed for the development of the idea of *exteriorization*, or the sense of being outside one's body, which is one of the goals of Scientological auditing today, as is *tracking* one's past lives. Through these concepts one may be able to shed certain engrams contained in the track and achieve more and more of the analytic mind as well as spiritual abilities formerly held back by, or covered up by, engramic experiences. Therefore, at the end of the auditing road lies total freedom and total knowingness.

These ideas, admittedly oversimplified, allow for "explanations" of numerous phenomena which confront the person in day-to-day existence as well as in the "peak" of our experiences. It is easy to "understand *déja vu*, memory, fantasies, dreams, out-of-body experiences and other visual imagery when armed with the concepts of Scientology. This "understanding," however, may not be as fully developed as that of one individual's "success story" in Scientology mentioned by Whitehead (1974:584):

> I have rediscovered what telepathic communication really is. Knowing what someone is "thinking" before he says it has become part of everyday communication. I can sit at my desk and *fully* experience the reality of any place, from ocean to snow-capped Sierras. Always knowing who's calling on the phone before it rings, and being able to check the progress of my cooking hamburger without walking into the kitchen. [Emphasis in original]

Another factor usually associated with Scientology (in addition to personality tests, auditing, preclear, clear, exteriorization, and Thetan) is the "E meter." In his description of the invention, Rowley (1971:33) states:

> Disciples relate unpleasant events in their past life to an auditor, a "pastoral counselor" or confessor, while gripping two tin cans attached to an "E" meter, an invention of L. Ron Hubbard's, consisting of a small electrically operated box with a dial. Similar to a lie detector it appears to be affected by how hard or how softly one grips the cans. The Scientologists say that once a person has "seen" a painful experience, he is free of it. A five-hour session costs $175.

So, whether one evaluates L. Ron Hubbard and Scientology as hucksterism, in which basic concepts of psychology are woven into an argotic style of expression and ontology, or as the ultimate technique for arriving at the *truth*, one is confronted with the fact that for many people, Scientology is religion. As Whitehead (1974:565) proclaims, "It is part of Hubbard's genius to have invented a system which, like Alchemy, can move from the mundane to the mystical with a good long stretch of wizardry in between."

OTHER NEW EXPRESSIONS

The three examples of new expressions in religious life in America outlined above (Krishnas, Moonies, and Scientologists) represent a sample of the variety of new religions or new religious emphases which have recently surfaced in American society. There is no way, however, to address all of the new religions in one book, let alone one chapter in one book. So, we have presented below thumbnail sketches of a few other groups. The reader is encouraged to consult the original sources.

The Divine Light Mission. The Divine Light Mission is an organization whose members pledge allegiance to Guru Maharaj Ji, the "Teenage Perfect Master and Lord of the Universe." The Divine Light Mission (DLM) achieved prominence in the mid-1970s, holding a festival in November 1973 called Millennium-'73 in the Houston Astrodome (Foss and Larkin, 1978). The followers, or devotees, of the Guru are called premies and center their attention on obtaining the *Knowledge* through meditation techniques taught by the Guru, who offers a *Divine Plan* to obtain the Truth. *Satsang* is also important in that it represents the reinforcement of meditative practices through discussions with other premies. DLM members do not peddle wares on the streets for money; they rely instead on contributions to the center and tithing of members according to how much money they make at their jobs. Premies may live communally or in multiple- or single-family dwellings. If not living at a center, (*ashram*) premies are expected to attend *satsang* in communal centers. Recruitment is mainly by witnessing to friends and strangers through newspaper advertising. This recruitment has been called "soft-sell" by some (Stoner and Parke, 1979:38). Premies are encouraged to practice vegetarianism and celebacy as well as to abstain from drugs, tobacco, and alcohol. These abstentions, however, are not "demanded" but are in line with dedication to the Mission. As to beliefs concerning the Knowledge or the Divine Light, Stoner and Parke (1979:38) give the following information:

> True Premies say they are happier than before. They believe that the liquid they taste when they put their tongues to the back of their throats in one technique of the knowledge is indeed nectar, not the mucus of a post-nasal drip. They believe the light they experience when they press on their eyes is a sight through a "third eye," the pineal gland, which the guru contends is the vestige of an extra eye humans had at some point in their evolution. . . . They also believe that the vibrations they feel and hear when they cup their hands over their ears put them in touch with the source of all life.

NEW EXPRESSIONS FROM NONTRADITIONAL SOURCES

The DLM and the premie belief system has been described as "worshipping the absurd" (Foss and Larkin, 1978) in that conventional interpretations of reality are not followed by members and that the Guru is worshiped for his seemingly nonsensical and unpredictable behavior.

> The significance of the activities of the Mission lay in "service" to and execution of the "Divine Plan" of Guru Maharaj Ji. . . . But Guru Maharaj Ji was himself a *supremely incongruous divinity*; chubby, squat, enamored of expensive cars and other gadgets, and in no way saintly in his dealings with his followers. Yet it was this very implausibility which constituted a major factor in Guru Maharaj Ji's appeal. . . . " (Foss and Larkin, 1977: 159) [Emphasis in original]

The future of the DLM is uncertain. That the Guru has a taste for luxurious living, has married his secretary, and is having trouble with the distribution of power and authority (regarding conflict with other members of his family as well as in the *ashrams*) as well as financial problems, have prompted some to write of the "decline of the movement" (Pilarzyk, 1978; Messer, 1976). Others have written of the previous experiences of some members with psychotherapy and the return to treatment after rejecting the DLM (Anthony et al., 1977). Some defection may involve cognitive evaluation of certain practices of the Guru. Foss and Larkin (1978:161) report that "Guru Maharaj Ji is well known for his penchant for spraying his followers with paint, water and silly foam. All such dousings are regarded by premies as important religious experiences." Whether such practices will continue to be physically and ideationally accepted is, as mentioned above, uncertain.

Synanon. Synanon did not begin as a religion and may still fail to qualify according to rigid criteria. As will be shown, however, there are particular elements of religiosity involved for certain "true believers." This cult, like others, is precariously balanced at this writing regarding its future.

Synanon began as a self-help organization for alcoholics and drug abusers. It has received public recognition, and praise, in sociological texts on social problems, journalistic accounts, and various mass media documentaries. A recent article by Anson (1978) provides a brief history of the group as well as an analysis of its latest tribulations.

Synanon was begun by Chuck Dederich, an Ohio-born, Notre Dame dropout who drifted around the country involved in a variety of jobs and marriages. Winding up in California in the mid-1950s drunk and broke, he called Alcoholics Anonymous to help him sober up. Later he cashed an unemployment check, rented a Santa Monica storefront, and started his own treatment center. The treatment tactics he offered to alcoholics and addicts were harsh and dictatorial. Utilizing manual labor and group support as key elements in the treatment program, Dederich began "seminars" and prolonged encounter sessions in a type of "reality" training which eventually was called the Synanon "Game." (The story goes that a confused alcoholic or addict merged the two words symposium and seminar into a hardly audible "Synanon"—the term stuck.) Games were employed to strip down defense mechanisms and uncover the real person in the process. Soon, based upon contributions by wealthy sponsors and grants from businesses, Synanon grew into a multi-million dollar operation with centers across the country.

In the mid-1960s, faced with high rates of recidivism and a need to reorganize, Dederich began allowing nonaddicted outsiders to "live in." These "lifestylers" were "ordinary men, women and children who were attracted to Synanon not for its curative powers but for the communal, nonviolent, highly ordered lifestyle it afforded" (Anson, 1978:34). These persons brought to Synanon certain business and organizational skills needed to continue the growth and operation of the "community." They did not have to start out doing menial tasks in the organization, as the alcoholics and addicts did, but were given the best jobs, housing, and privileges. However, "lifestylers were expected to liquidate all that they owned—homes, personal effects, cars, bank accounts, stocks, businessess—and turn over the proceeds to 'the community' "(Anson, 1978:34).

Other changes began to take place when the sanctity of the "Game" changed from nonviolent to violent, although to some the following story may seem lacking in "real" violence. According to Anson (1978:40, 42):

> As former residents tell the story, a woman was being particularly obnoxious during a Synanon Game. Nonetheless, she was well within her rights, since within the game anything could be said, any emotion vented . . . there was only one rule . . . no violence or threat of violence. That day, however, Chuck Dederich changed the rules. As the woman became increasingly bothersome, Dederich rose from his chair, walked over to her and dumped a can of root beer over the woman's head.

From this turning point, Dederich rationalized that Synanon had often been abused by outsiders and self-defense was the order of the day. Speaking of utilizing Synanon's power to protect itself from outside assaults, Dederich, apparently, began getting "touchy" about defectors ("splitees") and "power" was used to discourage persons from leaving the organization. According to Anson (1978:35):

> Cases like the Crawford's (splitees) were rationalized within Synanon as "betrayals of Chuck." That was an unpardonable sin. For, increasingly,

the Founder was taking on the status of a secular God. He joked about it at first, dismissing suggestions that Synanon was a religion with the comment, "Yes, but with a small 'r'." But as the years passed Synanon's religious trappings grew, and with them, the adulation of Dederich. He took to wearing custom-designed priest's robes to special Synanon games, and the place where they were conducted was christened the "Stew Temples." His new wife, Betty, a former junkie and prostitute from Detroit, proclaimed herself "High Priestess of Synanon."

Apparently growing more "cultish," Synanon members were to give up the "right to bear their own children" (Anson, 1978:36) so as to care for "the children of the world"—thus, "Within a week nearly 200 men had undergone vasectomies, performed in Synanon by Synanon's own cadre of doctors, working ten hours a day, seven days a week." In addition to "changing partners," in which married couples swapped spouses, Synanon also began teaching members of it's "national guard" physical fitness and Syn-do, the Synanon version of karate.

One of the latest chapters in Synanon's life involves the alleged conspiracy of Synanon members to murder Paul Morantz, an attorney who had dogged Synanon in the courts, in the press, and in a grand jury hearing concerning violence in the organization. Morantz was bitten by a rattlesnake left in his mailbox and offered the following comment (Anson, 1978:50):

> "I feel sorry for Synanon," he says quietly. "At one time, they gave a lot to society. But they became fanatic. . . . When people believe that their group is sacred, that they have the secrets of the world, then anything to further that purpose is justified . . . and pretty soon [they're] beating people up and putting a snake in someone's mailbox. . . ." [Elipses and bracket in original].

The latest verse in Synanon's activities concerns the allegation that Dederich is back on the bottle and is being investigated to see if he should be indicted in the Morantz case. In Lake Havasu City, Nevada, it was reported that Dederich was too incapacitated in the courtroom to answer charges against him (*People*, December 18, 1978:36-37). It is reported that some members are defecting and are providing the California attorney general with information pertaining to terrorism, brutality, and other activities of the organization. (For an article that describes the organization before the changes above apparently took place, see Ofshe [1974].)

Bo and Peep. Bo and Peep, or the Two, were initiators of a UFO cult and were implicated in the disappearance of over thirty people in Oregon in the Fall of 1975 (Balch and Taylor, 1978). These people disappeared after attending a lecture about flying saucers at which Bo and Peep, a middle-aged man and woman, offered their audience eternal life in the heavens. These two claimed to be members of the kingdom of heaven but had taken human form to help mankind overcome the natural, human level of existence. Balch and Taylor (1978:62) provide the following description:

> Before their "awakening," the two apparently led rather ordinary lives. Bo, who was 44 at the time of the Oregon meeting, had been a music professor at a university in Texas, and later a choir director for an Episcopal church. Peep, 48, had been a professional nurse. After meeting in a Texas hospital in 1972, they opened a short-lived metaphysical center specializing in astrology, spiritual healing, theosophy, and comparative religions, where they first began to suspect their higher purpose on the planet.

Bo and Peep told their followers that they would be taken to heaven in UFO's if they could obtain Human Individual Metamorphosis—overcoming human emotions and worldly attachments. In order to be taken to heaven, followers were to abandon their jobs, families, and material possessions. As many as 150 persons may have eventually agreed to follow the two and traveled around the country in small families leading a spartan existence. Bo and Peep camped out with their followers as they traveled around the country making speeches about their beliefs. "Then, for reasons unclear, they went into seclusion, explaining that they would return just before the spaceships came. They never set a date, however, and most of their followers never saw them again (Balch and Taylor, 1978:46). However, Bo and Peep rejoined the remnants of their following during 1976 and have since led the group in secretive activities, "disappearing almost entirely from public view." (Balch and Taylor, 1978:63).

Transcendental Meditation. Transcendental Meditation was started in this country by the Hindu teacher Maharishi Mahesh Yogi in the late sixties. His followers have included the Beatles, The Rolling Stones, and Mia Farrow (Needleman, 1970). Transcendental Meditation is based upon the idea that one can become more in tune with cosmic consciousness and obtain a happier state of mind or inner peace by meditation and chanting one's mantra. The mantra is a word, phrase, or sound that is given to a recruit by an initiator. According to Needleman (1970:137):

> Initiation is the procedure whereby the mantra is imparted. To receive this initiation, the aspirant need only attend two introductory lectures and be interviewed. He is requested to refrain from drugs or any spiritual practice for a period of about two weeks both before and after being given the mantra. This is so he will be clear in his own mind as to the results, or lack of results, of transcendental meditation.

310

Mantras are privatized in that initiators or instructors "interview" the persons and give them the mantra that "best fits their personality." These judgments are made on information obtained about the person's health, education, profession, marital status. After receiving the mantra, one is instructed to sit quietly and comfortably for about twenty minutes in the morning and in the evening. One is to repeat the mantra quietly to oneself, and if the mind begins to wander, one slowly brings one's attention back to the repetition (Needleman, 1970:138). One is also encouraged to keep the mantra to oneself, for to tell it to someone would possibly destroy its impact in the search for transcendental bliss, the oneness with creation, or the happiness of inner solitude.

The sociological theory behind TM is that persons will become more relaxed (or "laid back," to use current vernacular), easier to get along with, and happier by meditating through chanting the mantra each day. Furthermore, "no problems of human life would remain if only enough people practiced transcendental meditation. War, poverty, injustice, and crime would vanish, permitting humanity happily to fulfill its function in the cosmos . . ." (Needleman, 1970:134).

While TM has died down in the U.S. (at least it is not as newsworthy) due to several factors (followers tiring of the practice, Maharishi returning to India for a while), the Maharishi has recently been rekindling the movement with organizational changes and, possibly, renewed political interest. According to Siegelman and Conway (1979:218):

> Now we have learned that the Maharishi has established a World Government for the Age of Enlightenment at TM headquarters in South Fallsburg, New York. According to multiple reports, the Maharishi has sent out advanced TM teams to areas of social and political turmoil in 108 countries, to "resolve outbreaks of conflict and violence" and to "create a dramatic and soothing influence in the atmosphere." His most recent announcement is of a plan "to bring invincibility to Israel," a direct appeal to American Jews to travel to Israel for a special two- month course in levitation—at $2500 per person. The program is an intense meditation regimen that purports to give "mastery of the laws of nature." It claims already to have graduated 5000 Americans, many of whom have told us and others that they have gained the ability to rise off the ground and "fly."

These sketches, of course, could go on *ad absurdum,* in that we have not mentioned Zen, Meher Baba, Subud, the Catholic Charismatic Movement, Witchcraft, Satanic cults, Nichiren Shoshu, 3HO, est, the Christian World Liberation Front, the Japanese Golf religion, yoga, and several aspects of the occult. We believe, however, that our remaining space could be better utilized in a brief analysis of a "problem" presented by several of these "new expressions" rather than to continue our descriptions of specific groups. The problem is one involving conflictual relationships between individuals, groups, corporations, and, possibly, between a government and its citizenry. The problem is best conceptualized as conflict over "programming" and "deprogramming" people into and out of religious beliefs and organizations.

THE PROGRAMMING/DEPROGRAMMING CONTROVERSY

In sociology, when we refer to taking on the ideas, mores, and behavioral styles of our family, school, nation, or religious group, the term that is used is "socialization." Socialization consists of varieties of learning, conditioning, training, and coaxing which leads, hopefully, to the individual's internalization of what has been taught or demonstrated. Internalization of values refers to the mental and cognitive aspects of socialization whereby one takes on what is taught as one's "own values." These values become instilled "inside" the person and are used to lead and guide the individual in activities and decision-making processes and to provide the person with a backdrop against which to compare "other" belief systems. Admittedly, most persons for most of their lives remain committed to their "own" way of doing things and see other nations, religions, and beliefs through ethnocentric lenses. In a pluralistic society, by definition, there exists a plurality of viewpoints, lifestyles, belief systems, and preferences. This pluralistic system often is held together by a loosely structured sense of tolerance and/or respect for the rights of others. A pluralistic system is not devoid, however, of vested interests, political power, or competition. Conflict theorists maintain that society is characterized by the exercise of power rather than consensual agreement.

Most of the "new expressions" we have been writing about, and the emerging conflict over them and their recruiting tactics, lifestyles, fund-raising techniques, and belief systems, demonstrate what many feel to be an overextension of the "freedoms" granted to persons in our society. Along this line, groups of people opposed to the new expressions have formed coalitions and have started their own anticult movement based on the premise that various marginal religions "present a clear and present danger, not only to the integrity of basic American values such as individualism, but also to the safety of individual cult members" (Shupe et al., n.d.:8). Their major claim is that cult members have been in some way duped, brainwashed, or "programmed" by some bizarre techniques and are not operating of their own free will. The tragedy at Jonestown, Guyana, involving the suicides/murder of over 900 men, women, and children in the People's Temple has highlighted the fears and concerns of the anticult movement. Weekly magazines, in their coverage of the "Jonestown massacre," often added information regarding the activities of the new religions described above (see, for example, *Newsweek*, December 4, 1978, December 11, 1978, December 18, 1978;

Time, December 4, 1978, December 11, 1978, December 18, 1978; *U.S. News and World Report,* December 4, 1978.) As we will see below, some people and groups in the anticult movement, prompted by the disappearance of sons and daughters and fears over their well-being, started the counterprocess of *deprogramming* cult members. Charges and countercharges are continuing at this writing and will for some time to come. Parents charge that their children (many of whom are over 21 years old) were kidnapped and brainwashed; cults charge that members were kidnapped or stolen and brainwashed "out" of their cultic beliefs. Programming, deprogramming, charge, and countercharge, along with the new occupation of professional deprogrammer, are recent developments possibly unanticipated by persons in the mid-1960s. In this sense, the cult as well as the anticult movements are "new expressions" for the American society.

A partial listing of words utilized in the context of the programming/deprogramming controversy demonstrate the complexity as well as the intensity of the phenomenon. Lofland (1977:331), in speaking of the period of social attack (1975-76) against the DPs (Moonies), states:

> The charge of brainwashing typically occurred in the context of certain other ideas, such as "4 cases of hysteria from [Tinkertown] in 4 months," "acute psychotic reaction," "bizarre suicide," "breakdown," "mind control," "akin to hypnosis," "mentally imprisoned," "mind manipulation," "cruel and exotic entrapments of their minds, souls and bodies," "psychological abuse," "subliminal fascism," "incredible ordeal," "zombies," "robots." A number of psychologists and others who make a living off people's troubles were enlisted to pronounce the movement unsavory because of the practices implied by labels such as those just quoted.

Other terms used in connection with the controversy are "love bombed," "blissed-out," "vacant-eyed," "glassy-eyed," "pre-taped," "duped," "entrapped," "overnight conversions," "insidious threat," "psychological enslavement," "pseudo-conversions," "mental bondage," "conservatorship," "kits of legal advice," and "the new exorcism."

The anticult movement has sprung up in this country within the last eight years. One of the first such groups was started by "angry parents" determined to find their children and "expose" the Children of God. At a meeting of like-minded families at San Diego in 1972, the FREECOG (Free the Children of God) organization was founded.

The anticult movement, as documented by Shupe et al. (n.d.) has currently consolidated efforts in an attempt to "rescue" cult members and to bring about official investigations, if not control, of the cults. While many small groups have developed independently (and aligned with larger groups or dissolved), Shupe et al. (n.d.:19) claim that the following are basically and ideologically representative

313

of the anticult organizations: Citizens Engaged in Reuniting Families, Inc. (CERF); The Individual Freedom Foundation (IFF); Return to Personal Choice, Inc.; The Citizens Freedom Foundation (CFF); The Spiritual Counterfeits Project; Love Our Children, Inc.; Citizens Organized for Public Awareness of Cults; Free Minds, Inc.; Committee of the Third Day; The International Foundation for Individual Freedom (IFIF); and the National Ad Hoc Committee Engaged in Freeing Minds (CEFM).

Shupe et al. (n.d.:6-9), in their analysis of the anticult organizations, found that the groups function in three specific roles. First, as disseminators of information, they provide persons with descriptions of beliefs, structures, and geographical movements of the cults. Pamphlets include information on the last known locations of cults as well as the names and addresses of specific persons who can provide more specific information on each group. Other memos may contain the names of "front" organizations for the different religious cults as well as a bibliography of printed materials (books, articles, newspaper stories) on the cults. Secondly, the organizations function as lobbyists, continually seeking to convince legislators and executives at local, state, and federal levels that the cults are dangerous. Thirdly, many anticult organizations function in a referral role in that they maintain files on successful deprogrammers and others who have been able to help locate and detain members until deprogramming can occur.

Certain groups also give specific advice and check lists to families who suspect their children have been kidnapped by religious groups. Shupe et al. (n.d.:19-20) provide the contents of a list subtitled "A Guide to the Parents of Children Captured by Unorthodox Religious Cults" distributed by Citizens Engaged in Reuniting Families, Inc. (CERF):

> DO record all names, addresses, phone numbers of persons known
> to be associated in any way with your child's activities.
> DO maintain a WRITTEN chronolog of events associated with your
> child's activities relating to the group.
> DO answer all communications from your child in sincere, firm,
> but unrecriminating language . . .
> DO keep your "cool;" avoid threats, be firm but remain open
> for communication at all times.
> DO file a written complaint with your County Supervisor and
> other public officials.
> DO NOT send money to your child or to the group; without economic support the group cannot survive. . . .
> DO NOT be persuaded by "professionals" to spend large amounts
> of money for "treatments" or legal actions, until you have
> verified their credentials and qualifications for handling
> YOUR problem . . .

314

DO ESTABLISH and continue an association with an organized group of parents with similar problems.

The argument represented by the anticult movement is one of "capture" and "programming" rather than "normal" socialization with a religious belief structure and religious lifestyle. The cult spokespersons asked about the difference in what they are doing and what parents and "legitimate" society does all the time. Do parents not program their children into a set of beliefs (which the cult may see as "plastic," false, or materialistic)? Why, then, they ask, cannot our system be just as true, important, and sacred as the ones parents promote for their children? The counterargument from parents is "yes, we train our children, but we do not force or coerce or trick them into believing the way we do. They do it of their own free will."

To bring home the point that a "battle for minds" is actually occurring, numerous drama-filled stories document the fact that trickery and deception, if not outright kidnapping, has been used on cult members who were taken to motel or hotel rooms, or houses with the windows nailed shut, for deprogramming. Shupe et al. (1978:148), in comparing deprogramming with exorcism, contend:

> The logic of deprogramming assumes the following: (1) that a person has experienced, through deception, hypnosis/drugs, or a lowering of normally resistant rationality by special techniques of deprivation, conversion to a new religious creed; (2) that after this conversion, the person is psychologically "enslaved" and is unable to act independently of a manipulator's directives; and (3) that a process reversal, or deprogramming of the "programmed" victim, is necessary to restore free will and rational choice.

Thus, anticultists do not necessarily perceive themselves to be violating rights of religious freedom because the cult members did not really "convert" to a new religion but were entrapped into the group. Also, if any belief change occurred, it represented at best a "pseudoconversion" brought about by brainwashing or mind control. This reasoning allows some of the anticult organizations to believe in the correctness of deprogramming (or exorcising) people who have been, in essence, "possessed." Shupe et al. (1978) compare exorcism and deprogramming along five dimensions: (1) purpose, (2) characteristics of exorcists/deprogrammers, (3) duration, (4) violence involved, and (5) alternating threats and appeals. The findings of the comparison offers a striking parallel and led Shupe et al. (1978:155) to conclude that "whatever its stated rationale, *deprogramming* bears a close resemblance to accounts of brainwashing, or radical resocialization" [Emphasis ours]. Furthermore, Shupe et al. (1978:156) maintain that "it is ironic that while modern anticultists perceive commitment to cults' doctrines as the result of brainwashing, their own attempts to restore their loved ones to 'normality' closely resemble the very phenomena they profess to despise."

One of the most famous (or infamous, depending on one's point of view) deprogrammers in this country is Ted Patrick, who, according to the March 1979 edition of *Playboy* magazine, has been arrested and convicted on numerous charges, including kidnapping and unlawful detention, since 1971. Patrick has done time in New York, Pennsylvania, California, and Colorado. Since 1971, Patrick claims to have deprogrammed nearly 1,600 people from small cults as well as from the "big five" international cults—Krishna, Moon, Scientology, the Children of God, and the Divine Light Mission. Patrick, who was interviewed shortly before and after the Guyana massacre, claims that numerous cults have the potential to turn into Guyana-type affairs. A statement made by Patrick, whose views, generalizations, and dogmatic statements were continually attacked by his interviewers, may fairly well sum up many of the views of the anticultists. When speaking of the technique used by cults to influence their members, the following comments were offered (*Playboy,* March, 1979:64, 66):

PATRICK: They *all* use the same set of techniques to turn their members into zombies.

PLAYBOY: But couldn't many of those same claims be made about the Catholic Church or any other strict religious order that makes demands on its members' time and energy? How do you distinguish between a cult, as you use the term, and a legitimate religion?

PATRICK: You look at the facts. Organized religions—Catholicism, Protestantism, Judaism—don't totally cut people off from the world. They don't teach people to hate their parents, their government and everything and everyone but them. They don't teach people to lie, cheat, steal and beg in the streets. They teach you to honor your father and mother, to love your neighbor as yourself and to do unto others as you would have them do unto you. You can't compare having a child in a cult with having a child in the priesthood. When you enter the Catholic Church to become a priest, first you've got to qualify. Then they tell you exactly what you're getting into. You know what you can do and what you can't do. If you go to become a priest or a nun, you know you aren't going to be able to get married. You know you've got to study for so many years. You know exactly what you're going to do before you go in there. But these kids don't know what they are getting into. They find out after the mind control begins, after they have been hypnotized [Emphasis in original].

In recounting several attempted deprogrammings of cult members, Stoner and Parke (1979) provide examples of how members, once they are caught by deprogrammers, may "fake" being deprogrammed so they can escape and return to their religious trappings. They also provide examples of successful deprogrammings in which cult members see the "error in their ways" and "return to society." Shupe et al. (n.d.:4) in articulating three basic types of participants in anticult organizations, state that in addition to immediate relatives/friends of cult members and professionals (e.g., behavioral scientists, physicians, educators), former cultists make up another category. As to their participation, "many of these persons have undergone 'deprogramming,' and, provided with a new perspective for reinterpreting their marginal religious experiences, remain adamant in their opposition to various cults for some time after contacts have been broken." Some cultists, then, after having returned to society become themselves deprogrammers of their previous religious peers. Stoner and Parke (1979) provide examples of deprogrammed cultists acting as "supportive others" for the deprogrammer, aiding in all night vigils and acting as guards and messengers involved in the proceedings. Singer (1979) has, in another vein, documented specific cult-related emotional problems (e.g., indecisiveness, passivity, and fear of the cult itself) with which ex-cultists are faced during "reentry" into society.

The controversy, in the final analysis, will probably be fought out in the courts. Involved is not only the tax-exempt status for the religious organizations but First Amendment guarantees of freedom of religious expression. In an article by Nat Hentoff (1979), a civil libertarian, entitled "The New Body Snatchers," the point is made that there exists a backlash reaction against the deprogrammers by the American Civil Liberties Union and by a few courts. Even ACLU members are split to some degree over the issue of the "real" meaning of the First Amendment liberties. Hentoff (1979:61) states:

> In many states, moreover, the parent kidnappers take advantage of conservator laws. The parent signs an affidavit claiming, for instance, that his adult child has shown abrupt personality changes since joining a particular religious community. That affidavit is often enough to make the parent a temporary conservator of his grown-up offspring, and he can then enlist local police to help pick up the "child" without warning. And so kidnapping becomes "legal."

On a supplemental statement as to why such "kidnapping" should continually be monitored by courts and civil liberties organizations, Hentoff (1979:61) continues:

> The First Amendment, however, does not say that the free exercise of *only* "established" religions is to be protected. Thomas Jefferson, James Madison and other founders of this country repeatedly emphasized that religion was personal and therefore was not to be defined or otherwise interfered with by the state—no matter how unpopular and seemingly bizarre its practices [Emphasis in original].

317

Supportive statements similar to the above have also been made by Dean Kelley, an official of the National Council of Churches and an opponent of the exorcism of cult members. As quoted in Hentoff (1979:61), Dean Kelley maintains:

> If a sect is a front for a foreign government, then let that be investigated and demonstrated. If it is using its tax exemption for illegal or non-religious purposes, then let that be demonstrated and the exemption revoked. But otherwise, part of religious liberty is the right of all of us to make what seems to others to be foolish choices, to be 'hoodwinked,' to be exploited for the sake of what seems to us, at the time, to be the Truth. This is not justification for acting illegally against any religious group or its members.

In an earlier chapter we spent considerable time in articulating definitions of religion and demonstrating that even within a systematic discipline such as sociology, problems continue to plague taxonomists. In our brief discussion above of the cult/anticult movements and in addressing the programming/deprogramming controversy, one perspective that comes through is that courts and possibly the U.S. Supreme Court, rather than sociologists, may eventually have to try their hand at defining religion, at least from a legalistic jurisdictional standpoint. Such a controversy over definitions is, in essence, a controversy over rights and liberties guaranteed by the Constitution of the United States (see, also, Slade, 1979). These legal disputes are simply indications that in the social evolution of a society, "new expressions" serve as a change agent and as a reflection of the times as well as a moulder of social structures and human activities.

SUMMARY

We have attempted in this chapter to present a brief overview of certain new religious expressions that have appeared on the American scene only in the very recent past. Due to the hundreds, or possibly thousands, of organizations which might qualify as new religious expressions, we have limited our attention to some of the better known organizations and have tried to provide, where possible, historical vignettes of the groups' activities. In addition, we have sought to provide some material on the theological and philosophical underpinnings of some of the religious beliefs espoused by particular groups. We have described also some of the techniques of recruitment utilized by some groups and have provided examples of the prescriptions and proscriptions of religious membership in various organizations. Through an examination of recent happenings and trends within selected groups, we have indicated that the futures of some groups are, at best, uncertain. Some organizations are apparently losing membership rapidly while others are dispersing to other parts of the country and to different nations. Finally, we have cursorily examined the latest new developments in regard to the anticult movement and have shown that some of these groups employ several of the same techniques, possibly even more harshly, as those used by the cults in the "battle for the minds." These battles will probably continue for some time into the future and may eventually result in landmark legislation regarding religious liberty for American citizens.

REFERENCES

Anonymous
1974
Divine Principle. Washington, D.C.: Holy Spirit Association for the Unification of World Christianity.

Anonymous
1979
"Playboy interview: Ted Patrick." *Playboy* 26 (March):53-54 56, 58, 60, 62, 64, 66-68, 70, 74-78, 80-81, 83-84, 86, 88, 220.

Anson, Robert Sam
1978
"The synanon horror." *New Times* 11 (November 27):28-32, 34-36, 39-40, 42-43, 47-50.

Anthony, Dick, Thomas Robbins, Madeline Douglas and Thomas E. Curtis
1977
"Patients and pilgrims: changing attitudes toward psychotherapy of converts to Eastern mysticism." Pp. 65-90 in James T. Richardson (ed.), *Conversion Careers: In and Out of the New Religions.* Beverly Hills: Sage.

Balch, Robert W. and David Taylor
1978
"Seekers and saucers: The role of the cultic milieu in joining a UFO cult." Pp. 43-64 in James T. Richardson (ed.), *Conversion Careers: In and Out of the New Religions.* Beverly Hills: Sage.

Daner, Francine Jeanne
1976   *The American Children of Krsna: A Study of the Hare Krisna Movement.* New York: Holt, Rinehart and Winston.

Foss, Daniel A. and
Ralph W. Larkin
1978   "Worshipping the absurd: the negation of social causality among the followers of Guru Maharaj Ji." *Sociological Analysis* 39 (Summer):157-164.

Hentoff, Nat
1979   "The new body snatchers." *Playboy* 26 (March):61.

Johnson, Gregory
1976   "The Hare Krishna in San Francisco." Pp. 31-51 in Charles Y. Glock and Robert N. Bellah (eds.), *The New Religious Consciousness.* Berkeley: University of California Press.

Judah, J. Stillson
1974a   "The Hare Krishna Movement." Pp. 463-478 in Zaretsky, Irving I. and Mark P. Leone (eds.), *Religious Movements in Contemporary America.* Princeton, New Jersey: Princeton University Press.

1974b   *Hare Krishna and the Counterculture.* New York: John Wiley & Sons.

Lofland, John
1977   *Doomsday Cult* (enlarged edition). New York: Irvington Publishers, Inc.

1966   *Doomsday Cult.* Englewood Cliffs: Prentice Hall.
Lofland, John and
Rodney Stark
1965   "Becoming a world-saver: a theory of conversion to a deviant perspective." *American Sociological Review* 30:862-875.

Lynch, Frederick R.
1977   "Field research and future history: Problems posed for ethnographic sociologists by the 'Doomsday Cult' making good." *The American Sociologist* 12 (April):80-88.

Melton, J. Gordon
1978   *Encyclopedia of American Religions* (2 Vols.). Wilmington, N.C.: McGrath.

Messer, Jeanne
1976   "Guru Maharaj Ji and the Divine Light Mission." Pp. 52-72 in Charles Y. Glock and Robert N. Bellah (eds.), *The New Religious Consciousness*. Berkeley: University of California Press.

Needleman, Jacob
1970   *The New Religions*. Garden City, New York: Doubleday and Company.

Ofshe, Richard
1974   "Synanon: the people business." Pp. 116-137 in Charles Y. Glock and Robert N. Bellah (eds.), *The New Religious Consciousness*. Berkeley: University of California Press.

Pilarzyk, Thomas
1978   "The origin, development, and decline of a youth culture religion: an application of sectarianization theory." *Review of Religious Research* 20 (Fall):23-24.

Robbins, Thomas, Dick Anthony, Madeline Douglas and Thomas Curtis
1976   "The last civil religion: Reverend Moon and the Unification Church." *Sociological Analysis* 37 (2):111-125.

Robbins, Thomas, Dick Anthony and James Richardson
1978   "Theory and research on today's 'new religions.' " *Sociological Analysis* 39 (Summer):95-122.

Rowley, Peter
1971   *New Gods in America: An Informal Investigation into the New Religions of American Youth Today.* New York: David McKay Company, Inc.

Shupe, Anson D., Jr., Roger Spielmann and Sam Stigall
N.D.   "Deprogramming and the emerging American anti-cult movement." Unpublished report.
1978   "Deprogramming: the new exorcism." Pp.

145-160 in James T. Richardson (ed.). *Conversion Careers: In and Out of the New Religions.* Beverly Hills: Sage.

Siegelman, Jim and Flo Conway
1979   "Snapping: welcome to the eighties." *Playboy* 26 (March):59, 217–219.

Singer, Margaret Thaler
1979   "Coming out of the cults." *Psychology Today* 12 (January):72, 75-76, 79-80, 82.

Slade, Margot
1979   "New religious groups." *Psychology Today* 12 (January):81.

Stark, Rodney, William Sims Bainbridge and Daniel P. Doyle
1979   "Cults of America: a reconnaissance in space and time." *Sociological Analysis* 40 (Winter):347-359.

Stoner, Carroll and Jo Anne Parke
1979   *All Gods (sic) Children: The Cult Experience—Salvation or Slavery.* New York: Penguin Books.

Straus, Roger
1976   "Changing oneself: seekers and the creative transformation of life experience." Pp. 252-272 in John Lofland *Doing Social Life.* New York: Wiley.

Whitehead, Harriet
1974   "Reasonably fantastic: Some perspectives on Scientology, science fiction, and occultism." Pp. 547-587 in Irving I. Zaretsky and Mark P. Leone (eds.), *Religious Movements in Contemporary America.* Princeton, New Jersey: Princeton University Press.

Wilson, Bryan
1975   "The secularization debate." *Encounter* 45(4):77-83.

Zaretsky, Irving I. and
Mark P. Leone
    1974   *Religious Movements in Contemporary America.* Princeton, New Jersey: Princeton University Press.

Zygmunt, Joseph F.
    1976   "Prophetic failure and chiliastic identity: the case of Jehovah's Witnesses." Pp. 203-215 in James M. Henslin (ed.), *Down to Earth Sociology.* New York: The Free Press.

PART FOUR

RELIGION
AND SOCIETY
IN INTERACTION

Chapter 11

Religion and Institutional Arrangements in Society

The religious realm in a society does not exist in a vacuum. Usually religion is integrated into society and culture. Sometimes, however, religion stands against other societal arrangements. American religion, historically, has been integrated into American Society and yet has remained outside other social institutions. In particular, religious sects have at times opposed the political institution and the economic system. Military service, for example, has been shunned by Quakers, by Mennonites, by Adventists, and by Jehovah's Witnesses. Communal sects, also, have advocated anticapitalistic economic systems. By and large, however, almost all of the major religious groups in society (and a majority of the minor groups as well) view their existence, their purpose, and their mission as harmonious with American society and culture.

Separation between church and state has rarely meant alienation between religion and the nation. The virtues of a capitalistic economy have been extolled from Protestant pulpits, Catholic chancels, and Jewish sanctuaries. Education, both public and private, is viewed as necessary by religious bodies who were responsible for the establishment of education in the first place. Monogamous marriage and the sanctity of family life are supported by virtually all faiths in the United States. Those groups who advocated polygamous marriage forms (notably the Mormons) quickly found their "religious right" to such practices condemned by other Christian bodies and outlawed by federal court decisions. Even sports in America contain religious symbolism, and athletic prowess is often seen as a "God given gift" by individual athletes.

All in all, religion as a social institution exists mostly in harmony with other social institutions in the United States. From a functional theoretical perspective, religion is integrated into society and contributes to the equilibrium of society. Occasionally, religion is in conflict with larger society by promoting or resisting change in other social institutions. The Social Gospel challenged the notion that capitalism had no responsibilities to the working man or to the oppressed in America. Militant black religious groups continue to challenge the economic disparities between minority and majority groups. Antiwar declarations by the National Council of Churches and by several mainline Protestant denominations condemned governmental prosecution of the war in Southeast Asia. However, interinstitutional conflict involving religion has been far less characteristic of American religion than has interinstitutional cooperation and accommodation. In this chapter we examine the relationships between religion and politics, economics, education, sports, and deviance.

RELIGION AND POLITICAL ARRANGEMENTS

The relationship between American religion and the American political structure seems harmonious—at least on the surface of society. Religious groups are free to practice particularistic beliefs with virtually no constraints by government. However, this has not always been true, nor is it completely true today.

As we illustrated in Chapter 6, diversity in religious life did not automatically occur. Colonial America did have its state churches. As Johnstone points out, the colonies with state churches were either modified theocracies or were characterized by *erastianism*, wherein the state controls religion to some extent (1975:177). In the Massachusetts Bay Colony, the state was subordinate to the Puritan Church. Colonial governmental officials were required to be members of the official church. In Virginia, Anglicanism was the official religion, but the colonial government controlled the church for the most part. This example of erastianism was characterized by the colonial government making major decisions concerning religion. It established the state Anglican church and required all citizens to attend Anglican services. Taxes were paid to support that body. For many years, non-Anglican clergy were prohibited from functioning as ministers and priests (Johnstone, 1975:180-181).

This kind of practice changed with the founding of the new nation. The census of 1790 indicated that only 5 percent of the population were church members, and the disestablishment of a state religion by the framers of the Constitution seemed to reflect the mood of the United States. However, as we mentioned in Chapter 6, evangelical churches and the rather secular Founding Fathers promoted the First Amendment of the Bill of Rights which states that "Congress shall make no law respecting an establishment of religion, or prohibiting the free exercise thereof." In spite of this, tax-supported churches in some states remained as late as 1833, when Massachusetts cut off support to both Trinitarian and Unitarian Congregational churches.

This toleration by the federal government of individual states' support of specific religious groups undergirds the description of church-state relationships in America as one of "partial separation" (Johnstone, 1975:178). Barbara Hargrove (1979:210) states that such a viewpoint can be traced back to colonial times. It was a "separationist stance" in which it is understood that the government's duty toward religion is to provide a situation in which various religious traditions may be freely practiced, with or without tax monies. As the nation expanded during the early decades of the nineteenth century, the government, under the guidance of the Constitution, remained officially neutral toward religion. It did not, on the other hand, demonstrate hostility toward the various religious groups. In fact, the United States government incorporated religious mottoes (for example, "In God We Trust") into official materials, provided for religious needs of the militia (for example, chaplains and chapels at military and naval academies), and has generally supported conventional and established Christian and Jewish religious groups.

Issues Involving Church and State

Such an orientation by the federal government toward established religions made for a strong favoring of religion, particularly Christianity (Johnstone, 1975:182). Protestantism was the ascendant religious preference in nineteenth century America. As the boundaries of the nation expanded, the Protestant establishment sent out clergy to the frontiers. The state tolerated this one-sided expansionism for several decades. When violence by church people against the Mormons flared, the government did little to provide protection for Mormon beliefs and believers. It was not until the United States' original Protestant Christian bias was challenged by the influx of millions of Roman Catholic and Jewish immigrants that the courts began to rule more even-handedly on church-state cases (Johnstone, 1975:182; Hargrove, 1979: 210). Even with this more even-handed orientation, the record of the courts has not always been consistent.

In 1870, the Supreme Court unanimously ruled in *Reynolds* v. *the United States* that Mormons were free to believe anything they desired concerning the virtues of plural marriage. However, the Court also stated that the actions of Mormons had to stay within the laws of the state (Hargrove, 1979:211). In a subsequent case, *Davis* v. *Beason,* Hargrove points out that a Mormon challenged an Idaho law which required a person to swear that he was not a member of a group that teaches, counsels, or encourages polygamy in exchange for the right to vote. In this instance the United States Supreme Court upheld the law and used the *Reynolds* case as a precedent even though no action of plural marriage was indicated (1979:211). The strongly held bias against Mormons at that time probably influenced the Court's decision since its members "did read the newspapers" each morning. In what Wilson (1978:203) calls breaches in church-state relations by the majority churches, the Mormon decision, as well as agitation for anti-Catholic and anti-Jewish governmental action can be understood in the context of the "church using the State" to its advantage.

Protestant vs. Catholic Church-State Issues. The anti-Catholic sentiment espoused by the "Know-Nothing" party in the 1840s and 1850s was as widespread as the anti-Mormon bias. There were, as we illustrated in Chapter 6, outcries for immigration limitations against Southern and Eastern European Catholics and Jews. The American Protective Association tried to persuade the federal government to restrict immigration and to prohibit parochial schools. Later in the 1920s the American Protestant Alliance lobbied for a constitutional amendment that would deny citizenship to anyone who acknowledged allegiance to the Pope (Wilson, 1978:203). A well-organized Protestant church lobby, the Anti-Saloon League, was founded in 1895. Its express purpose was to prohibit by constitutional amendment the sale of most intoxicating beverages (Pfeffer, 1953:200). Even after the Eighteenth Amendment was ratified (and subsequently ignored by a majority of Americans) this powerful religious lobby continued to enjoy support from conservative Protestants.

The most widespread attempts by Protestants to limit Catholic influence through legal and political processes have been related to the issue of *parochial schools*. Prior to 1925, Oregon required that every child be educated in public schools. However, the Supreme Court declared that parochial schools were valid alternatives (Johnstone, 1975:182). Johnstone states further that since 1925, a number of Supreme Court decisions have centered around two issues: "(1) How much (if any) state support can be given to parochial schools? (2) How much (if any) religion is allowable in public schools?" (1975:183). Since the 1940s, Protestants and Other Americans United for the Separation of Church and State (POAU) has vigorously opposed state aid to parochial schools. Although POAU is an ecumenical Protestant lobby, its chief support comes from Baptists and Methodists. It has succeeded mainly in slowing down various efforts by federal and state governments to aid parochial schools through bus transportation, subsidized textbooks, and tuition equalization. While POAU philosophically is opposed to *any aid* to or *favoritism* toward religion, it nevertheless endorses the free-exercise of religion provision of the United States Constitution, without governmental interference.

Catholic vs. Protestant Church-State Issues. American Catholicism has been less overt, historically, in its attempts to curtail Protestant influence than Protestants have been in curtailing Catholic influence. However, as Catholic immigration increased, the establishment of Catholic schools became a priority of the church heirarchy. Catholic efforts in this area were an attempt to preserve Catholicism from perceived Protestant biases in public education. After the Oregon decision Catholic attempts to gain state support for parochial schools increased. In 1930, the Supreme Court established a basis for providing free textbooks for all children regardless of whether they were enrolled in public or parochial schools (*Cochrane* v. *State of Louisiana Board of Education*). In 1947, the Court ruled that free tax-supported bus transportation for children who attended parochial schools is constitutional (*Everson* v. *State of New Jersey Board of Education*). More recently, in *Allen* v. *State of New York Board of Education*

(1968), the Supreme Court reaffirmed the constitutional right of providing free textbooks for students in parochial (and other private) schools (Johnstone, 1975:183-184).

Although other religious groups have had parochial schools for many decades (notably the Lutheran Church-Missouri Synod and the Episcopal church), the controversy surrounding public aid to religious schools has been mostly a continuing battle between Catholics and Protestants. The Catholic position historically has been to obtain as much governmental aid as possible, mainly because Catholics have placed less emphasis upon church-state separation than have either Protestants or Jews. Catholics have argued that state financial support for Catholic parochial schools is legitimate because their schools serve the public interest by admitting non-Catholic students as well as Catholic students and therefore save the state money. Some Catholics further argue that by paying property taxes for public schools and tuition fees to parochial schools they are "doubly taxed." Another argument (shared by some non-Catholics as well) states that financial aid to religiously oriented schools is not a breach of the separation of church and state as long as the monies are proportionately distributed (Wilson, 1978:208).

Yinger (1970:445) believes that this "Catholic" position of churches using the resources of state and federal governments to enhance their teachings and educational institutions is succeeding. He attributes this to the growing political and economic power of American Catholics; to the increasing number of non-Catholic parochial schools, particularly Southern Protestant denominations and Lutheran bodies; and to the overall Americanization of education, which has created a more homogenous system of both public and parochial education.

Still, suspicion among some Protestant groups remains. Southern Baptists and Seventh Day Adventists still view aid to schools, even their own, as proof of a Catholic breach of church-state separation Sorauf, 1976:52). On the other hand, some southern Baptist colleges and universities have accepted limited governmental aid for specific nonreligious programs and have also accepted, along with other Protestant bodies, vouchers for students (or parents of students) who have elected to attend a church-related college rather than a state-supported institution. Such plans provide tuition equalization for students but skirt the thorny issue of direct state subsidy to the school.

In another, more recent constitutional issue, American Catholicism has attempted to enact a constitutional amendment which would outlaw abortion except under very limited circumstances. This is in direct reaction to the 1973 Supreme Court decision to permit "abortion on demand" by upholding the constitutionality of New York state laws which were more liberal than those of most states. Not only the National Conference of Catholic Bishops, but also local and national right to life groups have lobbied for the amendment. However, not all rank-and-file Catholics are as committed to prohibiting abortion by amendment as is the hierarchy of the Roman Catholic Church. A Gallup Poll conducted in 1976 reported that 48 percent of Protestants surveyed were opposed to any constitutional amendment involving abortion and that likewise 42 percent of Catholics surveyed were opposed to such an amendment (Wilson, 1978:252). Nonetheless, for Catholics, there is less of a dilemma in church-state relations in the United States than there is for Protestants.

Other Church-State Issues. Not only have there been Protestant versus Catholic differences regarding religion and the state, but also issues involving the government versus church groups, issues between majority denominations and minority denominations, and issues involving Christian and non-Christian groups. Minority churches such as the Jehovah's Witnesses and the Old Order Amish have been accused by the government of not conforming to the laws of the state. For the Amish, the issue was compulsory school attendance for high school age children. For the present, the Amish have won their battle to keep their children out of secular high schools. Both the Amish and the Jehovah's Witnesses have been engaged in court action concerning their right *not* to salute the national flag or repeat the pledge of allegiance to the flag. Their claims to "conscientious objection" to military service have been met with both governmental skepticism and majority church disapproval. Abrams (1969:135) reports that during World War I, the thousands of religious conscientious objectors received brutal treatment.

Majority churches have attempted to use the political machinery of the state to limit minority religions and religious movements which threaten cherished religious values as well as family and political values. The actions against Mormons, previously mentioned in this chapter, is one historical example. Another was the practice of labeling clergy in minority religious groups as political and moral deviants (Wilson, 1978:204). Presently, a number of mainline Protestant denominations, the Roman Catholic Church, and Conservative and Orthodox Judaism have supported legal action against the Unification Church and the Children of God sect (David and Richardson, 1976:324).

In contrast, the three branches of Judaism have also joined conservative Protestants in attempts to prevent too much governmental involvement in religious affairs. Hargrove (1979:218) says that Jews have been prominent as a part of the "other Americans" in the "Protestants and Other Americans United" lobby. Ironically, the Supreme Court decisions, including the famous *Murray* v. *Curlett,* which established a "wall of separation" between religion and the state in the 1960s were supported by liberal Protestant denominations, Jewish groups and POAU (Johnstone, 1975:190-191). Later activity by Mrs. Madelyn Murray O'Hair has nevertheless fueled the fire for a constitutional amendment establishing the right of "prayer in public schools."

Obviously, the issue of church-state separation is not settled. While many clergy from a wide variety of denominations seem to understand the implicit limits to sectarian religion in a pluralistic society, many of the rank-and-file laity (and some clergy) oppose the actual practice of church-state separation. This is particularly true when Scripture readings and prayers are prohibited in schools or when Mrs. O'Hair attempts to remove "In God We Trust" from American currency.

Religion and Political Activity

Religion and governmental arrangements in the United States are not merely limited to church-state issues. As we earlier stated, religious groups and individuals have attempted to "Christianize" the political and governmental structure of America. The banning of alcoholic beverages by most Protestant groups through the Eighteenth Amendment is the best known example. Its failure, however, has not halted similar attempts to legislate particularistic morality. There are still laws which prohibit liquor sales on Sundays, which prescribe where taverns and liquor stores can be located in relationship to churches or synagogues, and which demand either Saturday or Sunday closings of businesses. Additionally, a candidate for political office usually must appear publicly supportive of religion, and an elected political official will be subjected to pressures from the various religious lobbies operating both on the national and state level. The success of these religious political efforts depends largely on the numerical strength of a particular religious group or several groups working in conjunction with each other.

Menendez (1977:15-16) states that since the various states fall into several categories religiously, these geographical and demographic factors influence the political behavior of various religious groups. He identifies three categories of states in terms of religious domination. First, there are twenty-two states in which one religious tradition accounts for more than 50 percent of the total church membership. Fifteen of these states are predominantly Catholic, five states are predominantly Baptist, and two states are predominantly Mormon. Second, twenty-five states are bifurcated. In other words, two religious groups comprise over 50 percent of the religious membership. In five of these states Baptists and Catholics are predominant; in five states Methodists and Catholics prevail; in eight states Catholics and Lutherans comprise a majority; in two states Catholics and Mormons make up the majority; and in five states Methodists and Baptists are predominant. Third, *only* three states are pluralistic. In these, at least three churches are required to form a majority of the religious membership in those states.

Although one, two, or three religious groups do dominate in terms of church membership in various states, this does not automatically mean that those denominations will decidedly influence political activity generally or even political activity specifically as it relates to religion. One reason for this is that the historical "fact" that only a Protestant could be elected president of the United States was eliminated with the election of John F. Kennedy, a Catholic, in 1960.

This seemed to end the issue of "Papal domination" of the Presidency. Another reason is that the Congress is pluralistic, even though representatives from the more religiously homogenous states tend to reflect that homogeneity in terms of religious affiliation. A third reason is that geographical mobility has dispersed many people of certain religious backgrounds to other parts of the country. Menendez (1977:19-20) points out that a considerable number of Jews and Catholics have moved from the East, where they were in the majority groups, to the southern states in the last ten years. Also Protestants, Catholics, and Jews have moved from the central cities into the suburban fringe areas adjacent to the nation's large cities. In such areas, there tends to be more religious diversity than in the ethnic enclaves of the central cities. Whatever "bloc voting" along religious lines that had previously existed has been considerably diluted. Thus, many state legislatures are less dominated by one religious group than in the past.

These reasons, however, are not sufficient to dismiss the religious factor as it relates to political activity. Voting behavior influenced by religion, religious lobbies and pressure groups, and the continuing efforts to legislate morality are still a significant part of American political activity. A brief description of each of these phenomena will illustrate both the accommodation of religion in politics and the occasional conflict between religion and politics.

Voting Behavior and Religion

Until 1960, all of the American presidents were either members of some Protestant Christian body or were sympathetic to religion. In fact, during the middle decades of the nineteenth century "anti-Catholicism" surfaced in several Presidential elections (Menendez, 1977:26-28). However, as more and more Catholic immigrants arrived in America, the historical link between Roman Catholics and the Democratic Party emerged. As we stated in Chapter 6, the presence of urban Catholics who were voting for Democratic machine candidates greatly disturbed the Protestant establishment and caused an overwhelming majority of Protestants to begin the historical trend of voting for candidates of the Republican Party. Only in the south did the Democratic Party command a majority of Protestant voters.

The only exception to this southern tendency was the rejection of Democratic presidential candidate Al Smith in 1928 because of his Catholicism and his opposition to the Protestant-imposed Eighteenth Amendment (prohibition). The campaign of 1928 was viciously "anti-Catholic and anti-liquor." Protestant extremists spoke out against the Roman Catholic Church and Smith's perceived subservience to it. Although newspapers and other periodicals did not overdramatize this facet of the election, the "Catholic" and the "pro-liquor" issues were in the minds of the electorate. In spite of Smith's defeat, Menendez

(1977:47-48) believes that his campaign brought into the voting fold of the Democratic Party many ethnic groups (mainly Catholic) who had never participated in politics before. However, the defeat of Smith was by no means the result of his religion alone. Evidence indicates that no Democratic candidate could have defeated Republican Herbert Hoover in 1928. As is true today, other factors were important in the voting patterns of the American electorate.

Gerhard E. Lenski, in *The Religious Factor* (1961), views religion as influencing voting subcultures, along with the strong variables of social class and race. These "socioreligious groups" that appear in his Detroit, Michigan, data demonstrate rather substantial differences between Catholics and Protestants with respect to party preference. Protestants identify with the Republican Party, and Catholics identify with the Democratic Party. These differences appear at both the middle-class level and the working-class level. Lenski's data also indicate an overwhelming preference by Jews for the Democratic Party (Johnstone, 1975:197). As recently as the 1976 Presidential election, this party-religion relationship appeared. Wilson (1978:339-340) cites poll data to indicate that Catholics and Jews are more likely to support the Democratic candidates and Protestants are more likely to support the Republican candidate. In 1976, Carter was the preferred candidate of 55 percent of the Catholics polled but of only 46 percent of the Protestants surveyed. Sixty-eight percent of Jewish persons preferred Carter over Ford. This alignment held up in spite of the fact that Carter was an evangelical Southern Baptist who, presumably, would appeal to conservative Protestants. However, his relatively high preference level among Protestants has been seen in large part as the result of the southern black Protestant voting preference for Carter. On the other hand, Wilson (1978:340) cautions that the various factors of social class and the factor of race also played a large part in voters' presidential preferences. Nevertheless, when other social factors are controlled, there is still something to the religious factor in voting. For example, *social class* can influence *religious preference*, and both can then influence *voting behavior*.

In Chapter 12, the relationships between social class and religion are discussed in greater detail, but two inferences from those relationships are relevant to the proposition stated above. Income level, occupational status, and educational attainment are, of course, important indicators of social class level. Religious denominations are characterized by having a greater or lesser proposition of numbers in various levels of the stratification system. These, in turn, correlate with degrees of liberalism or conservatism, which then influence voting behavior. The following data from National Opinion Research Center survey research illustrate the variations of liberalism and conservatism according to religious affiliation.

Table 11-1 shows first that political liberalism is *not* the ideology for a majority of members in any major religious denomination, but that Jews are far more liberal than either Catholics or Protestants. The most "liberal" group in the

335

Table 11-1. RELIGIOUS AFFILIATION AND POLITICAL IDEOLOGY

	Catholic	Jewish	Baptist	Methodist	Lutheran	Presbyterian	Episcopalian	Other	No Preference
Liberal	32%	47%	29%	23%	20%	23%	27%	25%	51%
Moderate	40%	41%	37%	44%	44%	29%	35%	40%	28%
Conservative	28%	12%	34%	33%	36%	48%	38%	36%	21%
N =	355	34	302	186	135	65	37	235	82

Total N = 1431

sample are those with no religious preference. But this data also indicates those Protestant denominations that have a higher proportion of members in the upper and upper middle social classes also have fewer people who embrace liberalism. Only 23 percent of Presbyterians and only 27 percent of Episcopalians indicate that they are liberal. The least liberal are Lutherans, Methodists, and Presbyterians, who have a majority of members in the middle-class levels. However, more Methodists and Lutherans state that they are moderate than do either Presbyterians or Episcopalians. While a moderate political ideology is characteristic of a plurality of Catholics and most of the major Protestant groups, Presbyterians and Episcopalians are less moderate and more conservative, politically, than other Protestants. In fact, 48 percent of the Presbyterians in the sample express political conservatism.

A valid conclusion seems to be that while one's religion *does* correlate with political liberalism and conservatism, so also does one's social class level. The exception, of course, is that Jews, who are relatively high in our stratification system, but continue to reject political conservatism as an ideology. Catholics, by contrast, seem to be following more closely the Protestant pattern of political ideology, one which is understood by viewing social class and religion together as these variables relate to political liberalism and conservatism.

If the Carter-Ford voting preference is further analyzed in the same fashion as is political liberalism and conservatism, similar relationships between social class level, religious preference, and reported voting behavior are seen. Table 11-2 indicates these findings. A majority of Catholics and Jews voted for the "liberal" candidate, Democrat Jimmy Carter; so also, did Baptists, many of whom are black. A majority of people from middle-class, upper middle-class, and upper-class denominations reported casting ballots for Republican Gerald Ford. Both Presbyterians and Episcopalians voted solidly for the "conservative" candidate. Methodists and Lutherans were more evenly divided: Methodists voted by a narrow majority for Ford, and Lutherans voted by a narrow majority for Carter. Again, these reports of 1976 presidential voting reflect the variables of social class and religion viewed together and their relationship to preference for a "conservative" or a "liberal" Presidential candidate.

In a very real sense, the voting behavior of religiously affiliated people demonstrates a relationship of accommodation between politics, government, and organized religious groups. No major religious denomination questioned the loyalty of either candidate to religion. Although both Carter and Ford professed to be "religious men," neither violated the unstated rule of presidential politics by advocating the virtues of one religious persuasion over another. Consequently, the religious issue, in the end, was not an important election issue, although there was less Catholic support for Carter than traditionally is given the Democratic nominee, and some journalists raised the issue of Carter's evangelical religious orientation.

Table 11-2. RELIGIOUS AFFILIATION AND PRESIDENTIAL VOTING, 1976 ELECTION

Presidential Candidate Voted for	Catholic	Jewish	Baptist	Methodist	Lutheran	Presbyterian	Episcopalian	Other	No Religious Preference
Carter	62%	65%	62%	48%	53%	38%	33%	45%	60%
Ford	37%	35%	37%	52%	45%	60%	67%	53%	36%
Other	—¹	—¹	—¹	—	2%	2%	—	2%	4%

Total N = 967

—¹ = less than 1%

Source: NORC data.

In more local political campaigns, however, there is some evidence that religion can be a more important factor. In 1978, bloc voting by certain religious groups influenced the results of several state legislative races, a few Congressional races, and at least one United States Senate race. Perceived lack of support for an anti-abortion amendment and lack of support for the defeat of the Equal Rights Amendment were seen as important reasons for the defeat of Senator Dick Clark of Iowa and several House of Representatives incumbents. Bloc voting, characteristic of many ethnic and racial groups in the past, is now being used by conservative religious groups to impose certain viewpoints on the entire pluralistic electorate. The translation of these voting efforts into legislative results remains to be evaluated. On the other hand, this kind of coercive approach by some religious groups to influence political activity and governmental decisions has been used for some time. Its main success has been realized through the formation of pressure groups and subsequently by their lobbying efforts.

Religious Lobbies and Pressure Groups

We have shown in this chapter that religious groups have always attempted to influence politics and governmental activity throughout the history of the United States. Their efforts have been both successful and unsuccessful. Protestant attempts to curtail Catholic and Jewish immigration were failures. Denying state aid to parochial schools was for many years a successful lobbying effort. Prohibition was both a success and a failure. The amendment was ratified, but its intent was never realized.

In essence, only those issues that have been perceived by a majority of politically involved citizens as good or necessary have been enacted into law or policy regardless of religious pressure tactics. That organized religion would actively lobby on religious grounds for a particular political policy demonstrates once again the less-than-absolute boundary line between church and state. Hargrove (1979:212-213) calls this kind of involvement by religious groups into the affairs of state an example of *transformationist* church-state relations. It is seen as part of the "prophetic ministry of the church." Historically, the involvement of religious groups and their leaders in projects of community betterment, the advocacy of the Social Gospel (discussed in Chapter 8) by some Protestants, and the endorsement of union organizing activities by the Roman Catholic Church have been within this tradition. More recently, efforts to further enact civil rights legislation, to end the war in Vietnam, to "restore" prayer in public schools by constitutional amendment, and to outlaw abortion by constitutional amendment demonstrate the same transformationist philosophy. Hargrove (1979:213) also points out that groups which are *Separationists,* or those who advocate a pragmatic separation between church and state, become involved in politics in order to insure the continued separation of church and state. Their activity is a conserving action in contrast to the reform-oriented action of the transformationist pressure groups.

James Adams (1970:245-248) identified nine powerful members of the "church lobby" in Washington, D.C. They are as follows: the United Methodist General Board of Christian Concerns; the National Council of Churches, representing mainstream Protestant bodies; the United Presbyterian Church in the U.S.A.; the Lutheran Council, representing the three major Lutheran groups; the Church of the Brethren, representing peace causes; the National Association of Evangelicals, representing conservative Protestants whose concerns are with moral issues; the Union of Hebrew Congregations, representing Reform Judaism; the Unitarian-Universalists, representing liberal causes and church-state separation; and the United States Catholic Conference, representing Catholic concerns. In addition, there is also a strong direct Baptist presence in the Baptist Joint Affairs Committee and an indirect Baptist presence through Protestants and Other Americans United. In recent years, the Baptist lobby has become increasingly involved in lobbying for social and moral issues along with their traditional efforts to uphold the separation of church and state by working against aid to parochial schools and against a constitutional amendment to allow prayers in public schools.

Many of the governmental programs and issues endorsed by these political arms of the churches are supported by the rank-and-file membership of the denominations as well as by "religious" Americans in general. Since the establishment of Israel as a modern nation, "Jewish" lobbying on behalf of Israel has enjoyed Protestant, Catholic, and nonreligious support. Northern Protestants, Catholics, and Jews seemed to approve of their groups' efforts on behalf of civil rights for Southern blacks. Most Baptists (and quite a few Methodists) have approved of pressure tactics to limit parochial school aid. In a more limited way, a majority of Roman Catholics have favored efforts to outlaw abortion. In a sense, this support for church involvement in political activity indicates a comfortable relationship between the political institution and the various parts of the religious institution. By enacting programs and policies endorsed by a wide variety of religiously-affiliated people, American *government* and American *religion* have appeared to be interrelated, structurally and functionally.

On the other hand, some of the efforts by religious pressure groups during the late 1960s and the 1970s have demonstrated political conflict between religious groups and government. Furthermore, particularistic lobbying by some religious organizations has alienated other religious groups as well as members within the groups. Earlier civil rights involvement was confined mostly to the South, and thus most churches comfortably supported political solutions from afar, although some clergy and laypersons were involved in marches, demonstrations, sit-ins, and voter registration drives. When the black leaders of the civil rights movement began to attract overt and covert racism and discrimination in the northern tier of states, religious leaders were put on the spot. They quickly learned that an official denominational endorsement of such issues as James Forman's demands for reparations for blacks could result in the withholding of denominational giving by the laity and condemnation of such stands by more conservative political officials. Since many of these demands called for a more radical governmental action than that which civil rights legislation and policy had provided, unified church lobbying in this arena became fragmented, as pressure mounted from conservative church members against further extension of civil rights.

A direct confrontation between religion and governmental policy also occurred in the 1960s. Most mainline Protestant denominations, Reform Judaism, and many Catholic bishops lobbied against the War in Vietnam as it dragged on and on. Hargrove (1979:215) states that "it is usually conceded that religious groups helped to increase the unpopularity of that war. . . ." In addition to challenging the prevailing foreign policy of the United States, the churches' anti-war policy also aided those in the Congress who were the "doves" against the war. Such a challenge to the nation's government by the churches also angered many members who either were for prosecution of the Vietnam War or were of the belief that governmental policy should not be questioned by religious organizations. The controversy between church leaders at the denominational level and the laity over the issue of the Vietnam War and the issue of civil rights brought about much disaffection among those members who felt that their careers, families, and lifestyles were threatened (Hargrove, 1979:215).

Catholic lobbying on behalf of a constitutional amendment to ban abortion has not generated widespread support among most mainline Protestant pressure groups or Reform Judaism. Although there is support for such political action outside of Roman Catholicism, notably among fundamentalist Protestants and the Lutheran Church–Missouri Synod, the issue is perceived by many as an attempt by one religious group to impose its beliefs upon other Americans who do not share the intensity of the Catholic anti-abortion fervor. The continuing opposition of Southern Baptists to any parochial school funding by governmental entities is not as widely espoused by other Protestants and Jews as it once was. Since so many religious schools need such aid today, it has become pragmatic for religious groups to temper their philosophical opposition to parochial school aid.

Although religious lobbying appears to be an ongoing concern, not only in Washington, D.C., but in the various state capitals as well, America's religious pressure groups do not always speak together nor do they speak for *all* of their members. In a fashion that is parallel to the relationship between religion and voting preference, religious preference and its relationship to approval or disapproval of promotion of social change through religious lobbying seems to be related to other variables—notably theological liberalism or conservatism—and to some extent variables related to social class. For example, Eckhardt (1970:199) reported that the *greater* the religiousity of the typical white church member, the *less* militant that person was likely to be in promoting civil rights reforms. The personal piety of such a church member would reflect a conservative theological orientation. The theologically liberal activists among Protestant and Catholic clergy were a highly visible minority (Hadden, 1969:84). Their *sympathy* for the cause of civil rights was shared by a majority of clergy in all major denominations, but their *direct involvement* in the struggle was not so widely endorsed by other clergy. Haden (1969:109) further reported that only one-third of his 1964 sample of clergy expressed sympathy with ministers who "manned the barricades."

This influence of theological conservativism or liberalism has been demonstrated in voting studies, the conclusions of which partially explain clergy and lay opinions concerning religious lobbying. Benton Johnson's studies of the relation between theological position and party preference are helpful in interpreting the controversy surrounding religious pressure tactics within the political arena. His findings indicate that the division between evangelical, fundamentalist, conservative, or liberal Protestantism is more meaningful than the denominational affiliations of Protestants. In two studies of Protestant laity (1962:35-46; 1964:359-366) and one study of Protestant clergy (1966:200-207), Johnson showed that these theological differences have significant effects on voting patterns. By implication, those conservative and fundamentalist church members who tend to vote for conservative candidates would also tend to be opposed to religious lobbying for liberal social causes. Conversely, theologically liberal church members would tend to be supportive of similar religious lobbying.

Although class differences are present, religious theological orientations often seem to transcend class variables. There are both working-class liberals and conservatives, and there are middle-class conservatives and liberals. Theologically, these combinations also exist, contrary to the conflict perspective that religious orientation is inherently reflective of a conservative political and economic stance. Obviously, such an orientation more often reflects a conservative rather than a liberal stance, given the opposition of many laypeople to "liberal" political pronouncements by their denominational leaders. On the other hand, liberally oriented laity do exist, many of whom are affluent. These have generally expressed approval of the reform-oriented political tactics characteristic of the mainline American religious groups.

In contrast to both the theologically conservative and liberal members of America's major religious groups, there are also individuals who continue to advocate right-wing extremism in the political arena and in the economic system. Generally these people are fundamentalist Protestants who are militantly anticommunist. Although their strength in the 1970s is not as great as in the previous two decades, religious organizations that equate a "holy war" against "Godless, atheistic communism" still exist and continue to apply some political pressure on the American governmental system. Johnstone (1975:201-202) discusses several prominent right-wing political groups whose political philosophies are intimately connected with fundamentalist Protestant theology: the "Christian-Anti-Communist Crusade" of Fred C. Schwarz, the "Twentieth Century Reformation Hour" of Carl McIntire, and the "Christian Crusade" of Billy James Hargis. Although Hargis has been somewhat discredited by a morals charge lodged against him, his group still exists.

The relationship between fundamentalists and right-wing political extremists has been analyzed by John Redekop (1969:159-178). He sees a simplistic dualism: fundamentalists recognize only two categories of thought and people, good and evil; and the right-wing radicals see American citizens as either loyal Americans or communists. Redekop also characterizes fundamentalism and right-wing extremism as sharing a conspiratorial view of the world: the Devil detours people from righteous living; and communism detours people from Christian belief and capitalistic philosophy. Finally, the individualistic concept of the idea of salvation in fundamentalism is usually connected with the fundamentalist's disapproval of social action and public welfare programs. After all, the individual can "save himself economically" if he will only try. This is parallel to the right-winger's philosophy of *laissez-faire* economics.

These symbiotic relationships are seen in the political lobbying and pressure tactics of the religiously-oriented right-wing extremists. They have consistently opposed all reform movements of the past several decades: the civil rights movement, the "War on Poverty," and the anti-Vietnam War peace movement. In contrast to the reform efforts of major religious groups, however, right-wing religious political action has been largely unsuccessful. Presidential candidates, members of Congress, state governors, and state legislators have usually avoided any entanglement with these extremists.

Religion and the Legislation of Morality

In contrast to the reform efforts of most religiously oriented pressure groups, the legislation of morality has generally been an attempt to *prohibit* certain activities by the citizenry of the United States. The ban of alcoholic beverages, the constraints on gambling, and the limitations on Sunday retail sales are historical examples of such religiously and morally oriented legislation. Currently, similar efforts to legislate morality involve the attempts to prohibit abortion-on-demand, to prevent ratification of the Equal Rights Amendment, to curtail homosexual rights, to prevent the dissemination of alleged pornographic literature and movies, and to restore the right of prayer in public schools (although the abortion and prayer issues can be viewed as "reform issues").

The legislation of a resolution to ban most abortions by constitutional amendment is more of a Roman Catholic goal than it is a Protestant or Jewish goal.

However, certain Protestant bodies also support this effort. As we stated earlier, many members of the Lutheran Church-Missouri Synod are adherents of the Right to Life movement. So also are some fundamentalist groups. Most of the lobbying for this amendment to the Constitution has been done by Catholics, including the American Conference of Catholic Bishops. Menendez (1977: 152-153) reports that although several restrictive anti-abortion amendments have been proposed, not one has yet reached a floor vote. One key vote, on the other hand, occurred in the United States Senate on April 10, 1975. Senator Dewey Bartlett, Republican of Oklahoma, introduced an amendment to a pending piece of legislation which would bar the use of Medicaid funds to pay for abortions. The motion to table Bartlett's amendment carried 54-36. Menendez further reports that senators of almost all religious traditions voted against this anti-abortion measure. Even Roman Catholic senators voted eight to seven against the Bartlett proposal. By contrast, five of eight Baptist senators and two of three Mormon senators voted for the anti-abortion position. Several other abortion votes in both the House of Representatives and the Senate indicate similar religious divisions.

In spite of these setbacks in the United States Congress, the Right to Life movement and other groups for an anti-abortion amendment still press for the necessary legislation. They also continue to demand that various federal aid programs contain prohibitions on using such money for abortions. These attempts to legislate a particularistic moral standard exist in spite of the fact that survey research indicates that a plurality of Catholics and a majority of Protestants agree that abortion is a matter between a woman and her doctor during the first three months of pregnancy (Rosten, 1975:313-317). When questioned about the merits of abortion if the mother's life is in danger, if a rape was responsible for the pregnancy, or if a deformed child would be born, an overwhelming majority of all people responding (including Roman Catholics) support the right for the woman to obtain an abortion (Rosten, 1975:313-314).

Since anti-abortion individuals and groups strongly believe that legalized abortion is akin to legalized murder of a living fetus, it is difficult to perceive that eventually this moral issue will be compromised. The tactics of those involved in the anti-abortion movement seem an example of continuing conflict over morality within the American political institution. In the eyes of many people, their tactics violate the premises that government remain neutral in matters of religion and that America's religious pluralism provides a diversity of viewpoints on moral issues. Participants in the Right to Life movement seem, at times, to constitute a "moral elite" who believe that abortion is immoral and that this is the only correct moral and religious stance.

Opposition to ratification of the Equal Rights Amendment is another issue in which the morality of women's rights is questioned. Because the enabling resolution for the amendment passed the Congress by large majorities, efforts to prevent its ratification are concentrated in the legislatures of states that have not ratified the amendment. Although support or nonsupport of the ERA is not exclusively a religious issue, there exists considerable opposition to it that is religious in nature. Because both Judaism and Christianity have traditionally taught that women are subservient to men, many Protestant fundamentalists and conservatives, Catholic conservatives, and Orthodox Jews oppose the elevation of women to equal status with men. As we said in Chapter 8, Protestant fundamentalists oppose the amendment because of their literal interpretation of parts of the Old Testament and the writings of St. Paul in the New Testament. Many Catholics see within their own church an all-male priesthood which has more prestige and power than do Catholic women's orders. They, like many Protestants, believe that each sex has a definite role and function: one as the bearer of children and the other as the provider of money and food (Wilson, 1978:265). Judaism has historically subjugated women to men. Even today, men and women sit separately in the Sabbath services of Orthodox Judaism. Only the Reform branch of Judaism ordains women as rabbis.

There is, then, within the traditions of Western religion, a bias against equality for women. For those groups who *strongly* believe in the dominance of men over women, passage of the Equal Rights Amendment is seen as unscriptural, untraditional, and even immoral. To prevent its passage is to insure a continuation of traditional moral values related to the sexes. Wilson (1978:265-266) also reports that the Roman Catholic Church has given vigorous support to organizations opposing ERA. Many Southern Baptists and Mormons, he says, are also opposed to its passage. Since many conservative Protestants are even more traditional in their perception of the roles of women and men than are Catholics, the combined strength of these Protestants, many Catholics, and some Jews makes for a formidable opposition against ratification. The endorsement of the ERA by mainline-liberally-oriented Protestant denominations and Reform Judaism is not sufficient to overcome even the religious opposition to its passage. Furthermore, recent survey research shows that a slight plurality of Americans are currently opposed to ratification, a position different from that reported earlier in the 1970s.

Defeat through state legislative action proves the "immorality" of the Equal Rights Amendment to those who oppose it. Unless the recent time extension for passage allowed by the Congress to pro-amendment lobbyists is sufficient to persuade state legislators to support the ERA, this constitutional amendment will suffer defeat.

Opposition to civil rights for homosexuals is another issue with deep religious overtones. As gay rights activists have sought to have antidiscrimination ordinances and laws enacted on behalf of homosexuals, religious opposition to such legislative acts has increased. Anita Bryant's successful campaign to repeal many of the antidiscrimination provisions enacted by Dade County, Florida, is the most well-known example of these attempts. As a result of similar successes in other cities and states, the efforts of homosexuals to obtain Congressional action against homosexual discrimination are now stymied. The conservative and fundamentalist Protestant stance against homosexuality is shared by many Catholics and Jews. In fact the issue of ordination of declared homosexuals has caused heated debate in many mainline Protestant denominations. The General Conference of the United Methodist Church voted against homosexual ordination. In 1978, the General Assembly of the United Presbyterian Church defeated a similar proposal. By contrast, the United Church of Christ has endorsed the ordination of gay individuals.

The doctrinal positions of all but the most liberal religious bodies condemn, to some degree, homosexual activity. Catholic dogma sees it as a sin; Baptist interpretation of Scriptures allows for a similar belief. Lutherans also disapprove of homosexual activity for religious reasons. United Presbyterians have officially stated that homosexuality is a barrier to Christian fulfillment, although they state that the church should minister to homosexuals. United Methodists adopted in their General Conference of 1972 the following statement: "we call upon the churches to extend to all persons, including those of homosexual orientation, the redemptive life of the church community. . . ." (Rosten, 1975:541). For many religiously oriented individuals the entire issue of homosexuality, including the ordination of homosexual clergy, is an issue of traditional morality vs. new morality; for homosexuals to gain much in terms of rights and privileges is seen as further erosion of our traditional values.

The dissemination of obscene materials is a similar issue in terms of traditional morality. Aside from the unresolved controversy concerning the effects of pornography on people, the immorality of such materials—books, magazines, and movies—is believed by many. Not only conservative Protestants and Catholics, but also many moderate Protestants, Catholics, and Jews, are disturbed by the Supreme Court's decision to protect such materials under the First Amendment. The court muddled the issue to some extent by allowing local community standards to prevail in determining whether or not a movie, a book, or a magazine is obscene. Consequently, local and regional groups, most of which have a religious base, have applied pressure to city councils and state legislatures to write more restrictive laws regulating pornography. Many states and communities have done so. Recently, some network television programming has also been attacked for being too sexually explicit or for using a controversial theme as subject matter. An example of this concerns a two-part television movie concerning incest. CBS-TV programmed "Flesh and Blood" in October 1979; and prior to its scheduled airing, religious groups around the country protested to the network. When CBS refused to withdraw the movie, local affiliates of the network were pressured by these groups, which were loosely coordinated by a Methodist minister from Tupelo, Mississippi. Some stations did substitute a local program for the network movie; other stations taped it and broadcast it during late evening hours. One Baptist church in Dallas, Texas, the Beverly Hills Baptist Church, bought a full page ad in the Sunday edition of the *Dallas Morning News* stating that church members would boycott the sponsors of the television show and would refrain from watching most CBS-TV programs. The ad was signed by hundreds of church members.

It seems that only more restrictive legislation will satisfy the more militant groups who are for what they deem a "restoration of decency" in books, in movies, in magazines, and in television programming. Other people in America view this course of action as religious censorship, which is, of course, prohibited by the Constitution. As in the case of homosexual rights, the pornography controversy has disturbed many in America's religious bodies. That such individuals and groups are seeking governmental remedy is another illustration of the intertwined relationship of religion and government in the United States.

The final example of religious attempts to regulate morality is the promotion of a constitutional amendment to restore prayer in the public schools. As we stated earlier in this chapter, two Supreme Court decisions served as a catalyst for this movement: *Abington School District* v. *Schempp* and *Murray* v. *Curlett*. These cases and their outcomes demonstrate both the interrelationship between government and religion and the tensions or conflicts between these two institutions. Furthermore, the basic issue of the relationship between religion and education is involved.

The majority opinion of the court held that America's public schools were essentially agencies of government, and should not be involved in the business of selecting prayers or Bible passages (Winter, 1977:240-241). At the same time, however, the Court did *not* endorse complete neutrality by government in matters of religion. The following pronouncement by the Court in the *Schempp* decision illustrated this: "today, as in the beginning, our national life reflects a religious people" (United States Supreme Court, 1964:853). In spite of the court's endorsement of America as a religious society, local and national movements began in order to promote a constitutional amendment that would permit Bible reading and prayer in public schools. The late Senator Everett Dirksen, then Republican Minority Leader in the United States Senate, tried twice to have passed a "prayer amendment" which would have altered the First Amendment by specifying that nothing in the Constitution could prohibit public schools from providing for or permitting students to voluntarily participate in prayers (Johnstone, 1975:190). The Senate votes failed to achieve the necessary two-thirds majority. Although the establishment churches of Protestantism for the most part adopted amendments against the amendment, their members in the Senate generally rejected these resolutions and cast decisive majorities for the amendment. Likewise, a similar attempt in the House of Representatives passed 240 to 162 in 1972 (short of a two-thirds majority), despite the mainline religious groups' opposition to it (Menendez, 1977:153).

In addition, the rank-and-file membership of many religious organizations also supports the "prayer amendment," either failing to perceive the broader Constitutional question or preferring to ignore this issue. Southern Baptists, whose political lobbies praised the original court decisions, are very much for the restoration of prayer and Bible readings in public schools. Congressional officials from the South, where Southern Baptist strength is greatest, favored the amendment by 78 percent (Menendez, 1977:154). Again, the issue is far from being settled. Many religious groups still promote the amendment in order to preserve the traditional moral and religious tenor of the United States, albeit a pluralistic morality and religiosity.

Clearly, the religious and political institutional arrangements of the United States *can be* in conflict with one another. Although the United States Constitution advocates governmental neutrality toward religion, government has often been perceived as hostile toward religion particularly by those groups who lost court decisions in matters of religion or who failed to win a specific legislative battle. More often, though, religion and politics have enjoyed a mutually beneficial relationship. Government, generally, has been friendly toward established religious groups; and religion, generally, has supported most governmental policy. There has existed, more often than not, an integrative bond between church and state and between the practice of politics and the practice of religion.

RELIGION AND EDUCATIONAL ARRANGEMENTS

Like the relationship between religion and politics the relationship between education and religion has generally been harmonious. From colonial times through the early decades of nationhood, the religious groups in America were largely responsible for education. The most prominent source for the present forms of both religious and secular education was Puritan New England. Its Calvinistic commitment to the universal education of believers and potential believers gave rise to local schools, all of which were under the control of the Puritan theocracy. Religion was in the forefront of instruction, but reading was perceived as necessary to improve the quality of Christian life. In the southern colonies, largely Anglican in religion, school curricula were less focused on religion and more oriented toward training the Anglican elite to govern the uneducated masses. From the New England tradition, the public school emerged; and from the southern tradition, the private school developed.

In a relatively short time, colleges developed. Harvard, Yale, and Brown were extensions of the two dominant religions in New England: Congregationalist and Baptist. The College of William and Mary in Virginia was officially English and Anglican. After Scottish Presbyterians settled the middle colonies, Princeton was founded. Even though the Great Awakening stressed personal piety rather than religious knowledge, formal education was not denounced by the growing number of Baptists and Methodists. For the most part, the colonies enjoyed an educational system more universal in its scope than what was then in operation in Europe. As the frontier expanded, education was expanded into the newer regions of the nation. Not only were Sunday Schools established for religious education, but schools for formal education began to appear as towns and cities developed, often housed in church buildings. In the early decades of the 1800s, a few colleges for free blacks and for women also appeared.

As a public school system emerged from the New England tradition and was extended into the western areas of the country, religion remained an integral part of the curricula. When Catholic immigrants began to arrive, they viewed this "Protestant dominated" educational system as anti-Catholic. The Catholic church began to establish parochial schools that would insure the teaching of Catholic beliefs along with reading, writing, and arithmetic. From its beginning, the parochial school has been a religious alternative to both public and private systems of education, both of which have become more secular over time.

The secular character of public schools has been taken for granted in America. In recognition of this, churches established Sunday Schools, religious retreats, and church-related colleges to supplement the secularity of public education (Hargrove, 1979:180). Jews also followed this Protestant pattern by forming Hebrew or Sabbath schools. Even though most Protestants and Jews have generally accepted the secularity of public education, many Catholics have never felt completely comfortable with it. Thus, Catholic religious training remained, until very recently, within the parochial school system. Historically, however, the easy acceptance by Protestants of public education is also a result of the dominance of Protestant culture, mentioned above, within the "secular" public schools.

As the nation became more and more education-conscious, compulsory and universal education became public policy. Smaller sects, such as the Amish, with an informal educational tradition were required to attend formal schools —public, parochial, or private. They often were able to maintain their own elementary education by having a few members of the sect become qualified teachers, but most states demanded that Amish youth attend high school as the age-requirement for compulsory attendance increased (Hargrove, 1979:182). The Amish in Wisconsin won this battle through a Supreme Court decision in 1973, *Yoder* v. *Wisconsin*. The court acknowledged that the Amish sought to return to a simple primitive Christian life by insulating themselves from the modern world. Their concept of life aloof from the world and its values was also acknowledged as central to Amish faith. As a result, the Court recognized that the Amish refusal to send their children to school beyond the eighth grade was based on that concept. Believing that compulsory high school attendance would destroy this aloofness and ultimately the Amish faith, the Court exempted

Amish youth from Wisconsin compulsory education beyond the eighth grade (Winter, 1977:249-250).

This secularity also has been extended by court decisions concerned with abolishing sectarian prayers and Scripture readings in public schools. These decisions, already discussed in conjunction with political arrangements and religion, demonstrate that whatever conflict exists between religion and public education is usually settled through the political institution. Such governmental decisions, however, do not please *all* of the religious population of the society. The "prayer amendment" is one example of such displeasure. The continuing controversy concerning how much public aid should or can be given to parochial schools, previously discussed, is another example of the dilemma of religiously oriented education versus public, secular education.

Parochial schools are an important part of the American education system. Although some Catholic schools have been closed by financial crises, the remaining Catholic schools are flourishing. Catholic parents (and non-Catholic parents whose children attend Catholic parochial schools) are demanding some relief from the rising costs of public and private education. As we earlier reported, Yinger (1970) believes that either tax relief or tuition equalization plans are here to stay. Parochial schools *will be* publicly subsidized either directly or indirectly. The unanswered question is, simply, to what extent?

Further complicating this somewhat emotional issue is the rapid growth of Protestant parochial schools. In both central city areas of the Northeast and Midwest and in recently integrated cities of the South, Protestant families are abandoning the public school systems. Although much of this flight is a response to white fears of "forced busing," some of it is attributable to a desire for a more moral education. Like their Catholic counterparts, these Protestant parents are also paying for education twice: through taxes and through tuition. Such an economic burden for middle-income families is fast becoming unmanageable. Some of the past Protestant opposition to public aid for religious schools is now evaporating.

All of the parochial schools, Protestant and Catholic, face a similar dilemma: insufficient funds with which to compete with public education. Public school teachers are better paid than are parochial school teachers, and laboratories and other facilities are generally better equipped in the public schools. In spite of these handicaps, the number of students enrolled in these schools continues to increase.

There seems to be a strong desire on the part of some parents to remove their children from modern secularized public education. Hargrove (1979:188) sees this as a protest against the notions of cultural relativity and of humankind as an evolving form of higher animal life. She writes that many of the private Christian schools teach the "creationist" understanding of the origin of human species, testing the relationship between church and state by refusing to submit to state guidelines on curricula in the name of religious freedom. Even in the public sector of education, this conservative religious reaction against secularism is also apparent. One example is the growth of religious organizations for students.

Not only in conservative, rural parts of the country, but also in the large high schools of urban areas, organized religious groups compete with other extracurricular activities for the loyalty of teenagers. These groups include Young Life, Campus Crusade, Intervarity Christian Fellowship, and the Navigators. Smaller but similar groups exist specifically for Catholics and Orthodox Jews. Hargrove (1979:189-190) ranks these organizations in terms of local autonomy and centralized authority. Intervarsity Christian Fellowship, largely a college-oriented body, is the most locally oriented and controlled; Campus Crusade for Christ is more centralized and more authoritarian in control. Young Life is the organization most concentrated on high school campuses, and usually mixes social activities with traditional moral and Biblical teachings. It also is a very standardized and centralized operation, seeking to recruit student leaders to show that Christianity in all its operations is worthy of student interest. Even though Young Life encourages student members to attend their own churches, the organization often competes with churches for both the time and the loyalty of high school students.

At the college and university levels religious organizations are also interested in supplementing the more secular aspects of education. The previously mentioned Intervarsity Christian Fellowship, Campus Crusade for Christ, and the Navigators depend upon both full-time workers and volunteers to promote an evangelical style of Protestantism. These organizations sometimes cooperate with denominational activities for college students and sometimes compete with them. The Bible Chairs and Campus Ministries of conservative and fundamentalist Protestant bodies offer programs and theological classes that are similar to both Campus Crusade and Navigator activities. The more liberal Protestant denominations, on the other hand, tend to have campus ministries that are less rigid, more socially activistic, and more oriented toward contemporary theological issues rather than simplistic Bible study. Also, these churches often form joint programs in the form of a "United Campus Ministry" consisting of Presbyterians, Methodists, Disciples of Christ, Episcopalians, Lutherans, and occasionally Roman Catholics. When Catholics are not a part of a united effort, their organizations are apart from both the evangelicals and the mainline Protestants.

That such programs exist adjacent to state colleges and universities, as well as adjacent to private universities, indicates again the blurred relationship between education, religion, and government. Furthermore, most state institutions of higher learning allow students some college credit for Bible courses taught at religious centers by sectarian clergy. In private universities, particularly those that are church-related, chaplains and religious programs integrated into the colleges and universities are the dominant patterns of relating religion to education. However, as church-related schools became more heterogenous in terms of the religious preference of students, representatives of several religious denominations began to be added to the chaplaincy programs of the established religious centers for the campuses (Hargrove, 1979:193).

The presence of campus ministries at the college and university level demonstrates organized religion's concern with higher education. Although the activities of liberal campus ministers during the 1960s in the areas of civil rights, the antiwar movement, and counterculture activities alienated many in the parent denominations, their activities during the 1970s became more pastoral and more priestly. Many are involved in clinical counseling programs as well as in more traditional religious activities (Hargrove, 1979:195-196). Since the effect of much higher education has been to erode commitment to religious institutions, organized religion's concerns are probably well-founded.

This also serves to explain the continuation of church-related colleges and universities in a secular era. At a time of increasing educational expense—both for the students as well as for the institutions—many of these colleges are experiencing large enrollments. Catholic Notre Dame University in Indiana draws a large student population from across the nation. Baylor University in Texas, the largest of Southern Baptist universities, enjoys flourishing enrollments even while being selective. Unlike many church-related colleges, it continues to emphasize its conservative religious connection. Southern Methodist University, also in Texas, has experienced enrollment increases with a high degree of selectivity among applicants. In contrast to Baylor, Southern Methodist is said by many to be "neither southern nor Methodist." Regardless of the looseness or tightness of the school's relationship to its parent denomination, that denomination is contributing *some* funds to the ongoing operation of the college or university. Thus, most religious organizations in America continue to support sectarian higher education.

Not all religious groups are supportive of higher education. Some, like the Amish, are suspicious of education beyond its rudimentary elements. Others see no value in higher education. This is true, primarily, for those sects which have a preponderance of lower-class and working-class members. Very few members of Pentecostal and holiness sects have college educations. Neither do most of their ministers. As a result, there is some suspicion on the part of both clergy and laity in regards to higher education. This type of hostility has been characteristic of other groups earlier. In earlier decades, Methodist, Baptist, and Disciples of Christ permitted the ordination of untrained clergy. Gradually a college education or at least theological training became either mandatory or expected (as in the case of Southern Baptists and Disciples of Christ). Similarly, some of the fundamentalist groups which are achieving denominational status are now stressing higher education. Examples are the Church of Christ, the Church of the Nazarene, and the Assemblies of God.

Roman Catholics, at one time predominantly working-class, have used education as a mechanism of upward mobility. As a consequence, the Catholic laity is better educated than in the past, and Catholic priests are more likely to have a college degree as well as seminary training. American Jews, more than any other group, have been upwardly mobile through education. However, Jews have depended more on the public education system than have either Protestants or Catholics. Not until after World War II was there a Jewish university. At that time Brandeis University was founded. For many decades, Jews have made up a sizable proportion of the enrollment in the City University of New York system, the city's public higher education system. In addition to attending public educational facilities, affluent Jews, like affluent Protestants and Catholics, enroll in elite private universities.

The relationship of education and religion is best understood as a multifaceted relationship. Historically, established religious groups gave rise to our educational system, private and public. Those religious organizations who most valued learning established colleges and universities. As a consequence a religious and educational elite developed early in the United States. Today, degrees of commitment to education can be seen by considering the relative social class levels within religious bodies. Those groups which have larger proportions of members in the upper and middle classes are those who, of course, have the highest level of educational attainment. These organizations support education not only in church related colleges and universities but also in the public sector of education. While the upper classes have traditionally used private schools, the upper middle and the middle classes have usually supported public education. Jews, Episcopalians, Presbyterians, the Congregationalist part of the United Church of Christ, and Methodists generally have little quarrel with secularized education. To a lesser extent, Lutherans, Disciples of Christ, Baptists, and Roman Catholics have made accommodations with secular education, also. This is particularly true of the middle and upper middle-class members of these bodies. By contrast, fundamentalist Protestants, lower-class Baptists, and Pentecostal/holiness groups demonstrate the least support toward education, particularly the more secular aspects of education. Table 11-3 illustrates degrees of support for public and parochial education and public and private higher education.

The educational institution has been intimately related to religion since colonial times. When conflict between religion and education has erupted, the resulting tensions have generally been settled in the political arena. If education continues to be the primary mechanism for upward mobility, Americans who are members of religious groups that appeal to the lower class will probably demonstrate stronger support for education in due time. Black Americans, in particular, owe a debt to the predominantly black colleges for providing educational opportunities after the Civil War. The early development of a black middle class was the result of the training available in those institutions. As black Americans con-

Table 11-3. RELIGIOUS AFFILIATION AND SUPPORT FOR EDUCATION

	Catholic	Jewish	Baptist	Methodist	Lutheran	Presbyterian	Episcopalian	Other[1]	No Preference
Support for Higher Education (Public)	Moderate	Strong	Weak	Strong	Moderate	Strong	Moderate	Weak[3]	Strong
Support for Higher Education (Private; Religious)	Moderate	Moderate	Weak	Moderate	Weak[2]	Strong	Strong	Weak	Moderate
Support for Public Education (High School)	Moderate	Strong	Moderate	Strong	Moderate	Strong	Strong	Moderate	Strong
Support for Parochial Education (High School)	Moderate	Weak	Weak	Weak	Moderate[2]	Weak	Moderate	Weak	Weak
Support for Public Education (K–8th grade)	Moderate	Strong	Strong	Strong	Moderate	Strong	Strong	Moderate	Strong
Support for Parochial Education (K–8th grade)	Strong	Weak	Weak	Weak	Moderate[2]	Weak	Moderate	Weak	Weak

[1] Includes established sects, Mormons, and fringe sects
[2] The Lutheran Church-Missouri Synod supports parochial education (K–college)
[3] Mormons support education more than sects do

tinue to enroll in increasing numbers in public colleges and universities, the proportion of college-educated members in the black denominations will certainly increase. Like the upwardly mobile ethnic group members of previous generations, blacks are realizing the importance of educational attainment, particularly in the economic arena of society.

RELIGION AND ECONOMIC ARRANGEMENTS

As we stated in the introduction to this chapter, American religious organizations have more often supported the capitalistic economic system than they have opposed it. As the nation has prospered economically so have the churches and their members. The importance of occupation and income for an American cannot be underestimated. Along with educational attainment, these are the major indicators of social class level. As we demonstrate in Chapter 12, social class and religion are highly associated with each other: affluent individuals generally participate in religious organizations that have other affluent people as members, and poor persons generally belong to religious groups whose members are also poor. On a less individualistic level, however, the relationships between the economic system and religion in a society offer insight into the interrelationships of all social institutions. These relationships also show the tension that can develop between the economic and religious realms. In terms of sociological theory, two generalizations offer basically different interpretations of the association between religion and economics. One is the thesis of Max Weber and the other is the theoretical viewpoint of Karl Marx.

Weber's Analysis of Protestantism and Capitalism

Max Weber (1958) believed that a set of religious ideas could profoundly influence secular economic behavior. His analysis was concentrated on the doctrines of John Calvin, usually referred to as Calvinism. Weber's argument was that Calvinistic doctrine determined the content of a unique system of ethics. This led to the creation of an ideal-type character important in stimulating the development of rational capitalism.

Briefly stated, Weber's elaboration of his analysis began with the Calvinistic conception of God, which emphasized his glory and holiness and his freedom and sovereignty. Since man existed for the pleasure of God, everything man does should be for the glory of God. Weber also demonstrated that these conceptions of God and man led to the doctrine of predestination, the belief that God selected certain individuals for heaven and other individuals for hell. Nothing that persons did during their lifetimes could affect God's decision; the decision had been made before they were born. This absolutism of God had an important implication for the Calvinists: a person had to go through life all alone to meet his ultimate destiny. Weber saw this as producing a tremendous psychological pressure on Calvinists to live righteously in order to convince themselves that they could be among the elect destined for eternal salvation.

These doctrines created a set of ethical standards: in addition to honoring and glorifying God through the Sacraments and on Sunday, peoples' labors during the weekdays must also glorify God. Working for the glory of God required nothing less than the believers' best efforts. The emphasis was upon *individualism* in all social relationships, including work. Those individuals who worked hardest would do the most to glorify God. Additionally, economic achievement would occur, but the use of the money must also be for the glory of God. Wealth must not be spent frivolously. Hence, it must be saved, even *invested* in order to demonstrate further a person's dedication to hard work by being able to produce more goods which would then create more *profit* and, in turn, more *investment*.

Weber did *not* attribute the development of all forms of capitalism to Calvinistic doctrine. He did, however, hypothesize that modern, rational capitalism was a product of the Calvinistic tradition of the Reformation. In what Weber calls the emergence of "ascetic Protestantism," or the devotion to a life of discipline and hard work, there was a force which produced the enterprising attitude required by modern rational capitalism. Calvinism, thus, is seen as hastening the development of capitalism in the countries where Calvinistic influence was greatest—England, Scotland, the Netherlands, and English Colonial America. It rapidly became the dominant economic activity in the Western world.

Critics of the Weberian thesis point out that the Catholic spheres of influence in Europe also allowed the development of capitalism. Others point out that later interpretations by others of Calvin's writings, and not Calvin himself, rationalized economic success and interpreted the accumulation of wealth as virtuous. The debate over the correctness of Weber's thesis has raged for many decades. Who is right? Weber or his critics? Hammond and Demerath (1969:150) write that the advent of Protestantism demonstrates the beginning of the breakdown of medieval Catholic control. This resulted in greater freedom to experiment with new political and economic forms, one of which was capitalism. The questions for a contemporary analysis of the relationship between American economics and religion are: (1) to what extent does the religious dimension influence capitalistic economics or vice versa; and (2) to what extent is the "Protestant work ethic" alive and well?

American Religion and Capitalism

If America is Protestant in orientation, in spite of its religious pluralism, does Weber's thesis find validation in the United States? The answer to this question is a qualified *yes.* The history of the relationships between organized religion and the economy shows that almost all religious bodies have supported the capitalistic economic system of the United States. The dominant Protestant denominations of the nineteenth century strongly support the emerging industrial economy, and the large Catholic and Jewish immigration supplied the workers for that system. As we said in Chapters 6 and 8 the evangelical preachers of the 1800s, notably Dwight L. Moody, preached a message which stressed the harmonious relationship between industrial capitalism and Christianity.

Today, the major churches and synagogues of America are primarily attended by individuals who are businessmen, professionals, or workers. Almost all have profited financially from the capitalistic economic system. On an institutional level, organized religion is intimately involved in the economic system. As a consuming unit, religion depends upon the voluntary financial support of its constituency. The millions of contributors to religious causes and enterprises are given a tax advantage: religious gifts are tax exempt. The religious organizations themselves are granted a tax exempt status for all operations except those which are obviously commercial. Literally billions of dollars in property and other assets are exempt from local, state, and federal taxes.

As a producing unit in the American economy, America's religious groups employ thousands of workers. Not only are professional ministers, priests, and rabbis paid, but also auxiliary personnel, such as educational directors, musicians, secretaries, and clerks are salaried employees of religious bodies. Investments in the form of time deposits, stocks, and bonds are made by the Christian churches and the Jewish bodies to increase the monies available for employees' pension funds and for capital funds of the denominations. Like private corporations and government agencies, the major religious traditions have denominational bureaucracies whose tasks include the preparation, printing, and distribution of religious literature, distribution of church funds, and coordination of denominational schools, seminaries, and programs.

American Religion and the Work Ethic

The ethics of America's religious traditions generally lend support to the dominant economic system, capitalism. In addition, many business people also attribute their success to God. Johnstone (1975) sees this as a conscious support of prevailing economic norms and institutional patterns. Although this was at one time more of a Protestant phenomenon than a Catholic or Jewish one, the other two religious traditions generally support capitalism as much as do the denominations of Protestantism. While it *is* true that Protestants occupy the highest echelons of business, government, and education in greater proportions than do both Catholics and Jews, Andrew Greeley's data on Catholics in contemporary America (1977) suggest that economic gains made by members of that tradition have created a situation of parity with Protestants. Jews have outstripped both Protestants and Catholics in general economic gains, but still are behind Protestants in access to the highest positions in the economic sphere (A lengthier discussion of this appears in Chapter 13). What was once the Protestant work ethic has become a generalized work ethic, followed by a majority of members from all three major religious traditions as well as by the religiously nonaffiliated.

American Religion and Economic Reform

In Chapter 8, we discussed in somewhat greater detail the Social Gospel movement. The attempt by religious professionals to reform the capitalistic system was a bold move at that time. Its limited success was primarily due to the fact that it was a "reform" attempt. Gladden, Rauschenbush, and others involved did *not* repudiate capitalism. Instead they fought for child and female labor laws, the rights of workers to unionize in order to achieve better working conditions, shorter working hours, and minimum wage standards (Wilson, 1978:218). The social creed of the Federal Council of Churches in 1908 spoke to the issue of capitalism's social responsibilities in a manner that seems moderate by today's standard. In fact, most of the responsibilities urged by the Council have become a part of the economic realm in the United States.

The Social Gospel, a Protestant movement, was emulated by American Catholicism. Since so many Catholics were in the labor movement, that church favored an economic system in which labor and management would exist co-equally (Karson, 1974:176-177). Although some Catholic workers advocated socialism (along with some Protestants), more Jewish Americans were involved in the agitation for socialism than were either Protestants or Catholics. As we said in reference to religious diversity, these Jews tended to be more secularly oriented than religiously oriented. All in all, the ongoing attempt to reform capitalism—not to replace it—is characteristic of American religion. In the 1960s mainstream denominations supported the war on poverty, which certainly stressed self-help and the work ethic (Hargrove, 1979).

Karl Marx's Analysis of Religion as an Alienating Institution

While it is true that religious beliefs and practices draw Americans together, politically and economically, there is some evidence that the economic cleavages present in the social class system of the United States are related to our religious traditions. In Chapter 2, it was shown that Karl Marx believed that religion was false and that adherents of religion were in a state of worshipping an *ideal* created

by mankind (1964:170-174). He regarded the dehumanization that religion promoted as the imminent feature of alienation. Marx further saw religious institutions as playing a pivotal role of sustaining the vested interests of the dominant
capitalistic class within society. According to Marxist theory, religion contributes to the exploitation of the nonpropertied class, of the lower class. Religion is
a reflection of a person's socioeconomic situation established by the society's
economic system.

Marx's theory further states that religion also sustains the dominant class
structure, and therefore aids in perpetuating the unequal distribution of wealth.
Ideologically, a Marxist analysis of the effects of religion views it as another force
which alienates individuals from their natural position. The masses of society are
not only denied the wealth and prestige available in their society, but they are
also encouraged by the dominant religious system to accept their position. In the
following chapter which deals with religion and stratification, several studies are
discussed which show a significant association between religion and social
stratification. Included are Liston Pope's study of Gastonia, South Carolina
(1942) and a later restudy of the same city—*Spindles and Spires* (1978). In both
Pope's original *Millhands and Preachers* and *Spindles and Spires,* the membership
of the Protestant churches in the community reflect the social class divisions of
society at large and Gastonia in particular.

Economic strife and conflict have been no more attributable to religious institutions than to the economy or the government. All social institutions are
culpable, according to Marxist theorists. They believe that this diffusion of
culpability is the result of denominational pluralism in the United States: no one
powerful state church dominates the economic system; and virtually all religious
groups include *some* members from the lower class, as well as from the upper
class. Consequently, almost all religious traditions support America's economic
order, capitalism. Religion, then, is viewed as an extension of the dominant and
propertied social order by those who subscribe to the Marxist tradition. Religion
is, of course, a part of the dominant economic order of America, but it is also
related to the political and educational spheres as well. Society seems to support
and maintain religious institution arrangements, and the ideal norms of society
are not only congruent with religious norms but also are given moral and ethical
validation by religion.

RELIGION AND SPORT

Although sports in America do not constitute a basic social institution, they do
form a complex and bureaucratically organized segment of social life. From the
time of organized collegiate athletics in the late 1800s until the present time,

sports have continued to capture the attention of the American public. During the twentieth century the notion of sports participation as a means of employment has also increased. Professional baseball, the oldest of the sports-for-money organizations, has been complemented by professional football, basketball, hockey, golf, and tennis. Because of television coverage, Americans have become involved in athletics as spectators as well as participants. Although the earliest baseball and football players were not necessarily the "fine, upstanding moral" young men as people were led to believe (Sacks, 1975), this image became rather permanent in the minds of spectators and in the minds of future youth who aspired to success in athletics. Early on, a religious aspect was attached to sports along with their moral and ethical qualities.

Athletic participation was seen as a "character building" exercise. "Playing the game fairly" was viewed as equal in importance to "winning." The competition necessary for athletic participation became analogous with competition in capitalistic economic endeavors. The success of Catholic Notre Dame University in football captured the attention of America beginning in the 1920s through radio and in the 1930s and 1940s through movies. When Notre Dame's legendary coach, Knute Rockne, was killed in the 1930s, his death shocked the nation. The idea of the "religious nature" of Notre Dame football became firmly planted, and other church-related colleges' and universities' athletic programs benefited from this "religious aura." Since World War II, the connection between religion and sports activities has become more solid. Now in existence are many organizations which attempt to validate the social role of "Christian athlete" as necessary to sport as an institution.

Of course "a sport is not a religion in the same way that Methodism, Presbyterianism, or Catholicism is a religion" states Michael Novak (1979:335). However, he believes that the institutions of sport generate a civil religion similar to the civil religion described by Bellah (1967). Novak describes attendance at an athletic event as half political rally and half religious service. Sports are also organized and dramatized in a religious fashion. Novak believes they serve a religious function: "they feed a deep human hunger, place humans in touch with certain dimly perceived features of human life within this cosmos, and provide an experience of at least a pagan sense of godliness" (1979:336). If Novak's perceptions about the religious symbolism and purpose in sports are correct, then the "religiosity" of some athletes in sports behavior seems logical.

Why is there an emphasis on the role of Christian athlete? Is it but one segment of a larger "sport" role? Are athletes who are socialized into this sport role taught explicitly that religious involvement is necessary for success as an athlete? The answers to these questions are not simple. The notions that athletic participation builds moral character and enhances the competitive spirit are deliberately taught by parents and by coaches. Even professional athletes, after years of experience in their sport, generally believe that sports contribute to these aspects of their life. Beckley (1975) found that a sizeable majority of active professional football players attributed their off-season and second career success to the competitiveness learned in athletics. Those former athletes who dissent from this belief seem to be in a distinctive minority (see, for example, the writings of Dave Meggysey, 1970; and Gary Shaw, 1972). In regard to the religious nature of the sport role, the answer is more complicated.

On an institutional level, organized athletics, from high school through the professional ranks, encourage the image of the American athlete as a superior moral and physical person. Part of this morality includes respect for authority and for the institutions of society. It is not uncommon for college teams to attend *en masse* religious services upon occasion, and the tradition of prayer before athletic contests is firmly established. In fact, Deford (1976) writing in *Sports Illustrated* states that:

> ... religion itself has increasingly become a handmaiden to sport. Clergymen are standing in line to cater to the spiritual needs of the deprived athletic elite, and the use of athletes as amateur evangelists is so widespread that it might be fairly described as a growth industry. . . .

A radical evangelical publication, *The Wittenburg Door,* derisively calls the movement, "Jocks for Jesus." Deford claims that it appears that a new denomination has been created, "Sportianity." Not only do all of the National Football League teams and the major league baseball clubs have Sunday chapel services at home and on road trips, but week night Bible classes have also become a part of the activities for many professional athletes. In addition, several organizations exist to promote religion and athletics together.

One of the most organized is "Athletes in Action," which has 250 full-time staff men. Eight are assigned to large cities solely to minister to professional athletes. The organization also deploys two basketball teams and two wrestling teams. These men play games against college teams or compete against individuals. These activities are then followed by witnessing and proselytizing for an evangelical-style Christianity. An older Christian athletic organization is "Fellowship of Christian Athletes." Its strategy, according to Deford, is to use older athletes to bring younger ones "to Christ." The "FCA" spreads its version of Christianity through summer camps and through staff people who organize high school "huddles." Its annual budget was $2.2 million dollars in 1976. A third organization is named "Pro Athletes Outreach," which was founded as a peace-keeping force between Athletes in Action and the Fellowship of Christian Athletes. It coordinates the activities of "Christian speakers," who are professional athletes engaged in "speaking blitzes" (Deford, 1976a:91).

The purpose of all of these sports-related religious organizations seems twofold. First, certain members of the religious community who are supportive of these groups believe that athletes need special spiritual assistance and, more importantly, that they are ideal instruments to be used in converting others to Christianity. Most of the leaders in the Christian athletic movement are fundamentalist or conservative Protestants. Although there are a few Roman Catholic athletes involved, most participants reflect the evangelical Protestant wing of Christianity. Consequently, the movement draws strength from the South and from rural areas of the nation.

These organizations have not been successful in the more urban areas of the nation, nor have they succeeded in Christianizing some of sports' most famous figures (Deford, 1976a:98-99). In fact, the use of celebrity athletes for Christian proselytizing has begun to be questioned by the venerable Fellowship of Christian Athletes. Ron Morris, a former basketball player for Southern Methodist University and an ordained Methodist minister, who is a vice president in charge of fund-raising for the FCA, is beginning to see a danger in too much evangelical fervor. As a result there is more emphasis upon the young athletes helping each other and upon counseling member coaches who are under alumni pressure or the like (Deford, 1976b:54,56). Still, emphasis is upon the virtues of fulfilling a social role which is both athletic and Christian. In parallel fashion to Young Life, the Fellowship of Christian Athletes still recruits those that it sees as the "cream of America's youth crop," the young dedicated athletes whose leadership abilities can be utilized for religious purposes.

Religion uses sport and sport uses religion. While a case can be made that the religious sport role is more individualistic than institutional, it is the organized aspects of athletics that have allowed this role behavior to develop. In addition, it can also be said that while not all religious traditions glorify sports activity, few speak out against the benefits of athletic participation. While sports do have religious overtones, these should be viewed in the larger context of an American civil religion which includes religious aspects of other institutional arrangements, namely the political and economic systems.

RELIGION AND DEVIANCE

Durkheim believed that deviant acts on the part of members of society served a cohesive function for the society. Such behavior allowed the society to pull together against a common deviant who, by violating strongly held norms, had morally offended the community (1897;1951). The responsibility of the community was to facilitate social control. Since religion was viewed by Durkheim as an integrative mechanism for society, it followed that deeply felt religious norms were a part of this control. The criminal laws of western nations reflect many of the religious norms of Judaism and Christianity that proscribe certain kinds of behavior. The injunctions against murder and theft contained in the Ten Commandments were codified into criminal law. Other religiously offensive acts, such as prostitution, homosexuality, and bestiality became criminal offenses as societies became more complex. As informal social control gave way to a more formalized social control complete with criminal statutes and specified punishments for offenses, many people continued to believe that fostering good moral character and teaching adherence to the norms and laws of society were functions of religious beliefs and behavior.

As recently as the 1960s, many juvenile courts would require that the delinquent who was granted probation attend religious services. Even today our prisons have chapels, chaplains, and regular religious services, which among other things, reflect the abiding belief that religion can "cure" the deviant. What empirical evidence is there to support this idea? Unfortunately there are few scientific studies that provide a definite answer. An examination of two acts of deviance and the impact of religion upon their commission will illustrate this lack of convincing evidence.

Religion and Juvenile Delinquency

Contradictory research conclusions are the current product of analyses of the relationship between delinquent behavior and religiosity. An examination by Richard D. and Mary S. Knudten (1971) indicates that many of these investigations suggest that high levels of religiosity are associated with lower levels of officially recorded delinquency. The Knudtens also discovered that a similar number of studies indicated little, if any, association. Other sociologists interested in this question have utilized self-reported data of delinquency. Like the evidence gathered from official records, self-reported information also reveals mixed conclusions concerning the retarding effect of high levels of religiosity upon delinquent conduct. The research of Higgins and Albrecht (1977) and an earlier study by Hirschi and Stark (1969) provide unique, but inconclusive results. Hirschi and Stark found that church attendance showed a weak positive relationship to respect for police authority, but was really related to support for moral codes. Higgins and Albrecht found that in Atlanta, Georgia, there was a negative relationship between church attendance and delinquent behavior.

Do these efforts at analyzing the effect of religion upon one specific type of behavior suggest that religion is as *ineffective* as a means of social control as it is *effective*? The answer is, not necessarily. In most delinquency studies, the adolescent peer group is seen as a contributing factor to most varieties of delinquent conduct. If the peer group of the potential delinquent demonstrates religiosity, then the youth is likely to steer away from such acts provided the religious beliefs stress avoidance of unlawful activity. If religious beliefs and religiosity decline, the youth in question could be more likely to become involved in delinquency.

Are the contradictory conclusions concerning the practice of religion and delinquency generalizable to other kinds of deviant behavior? The answer is, probably not. Contemporary explanations for adult crime and for other forms of deviance rarely include a lack of religious beliefs or religious behavior as a cause of or a connection with criminality or deviance. Current scientific theories of homosexuality and other kinds of sexual deviance also fail to attribute these conditions or acts to a lack of religiosity, in spite of the fact that many religious persons and organizations believe that these activities are morally wrong if not a sin.

Religion and Alcohol Abuse

Several recent studies indicate that involvement in religious subcultures can deter deviant behavior. Peek, Chalfant, and Milton have suggested that an exploration of deterrence theory is one valid approach to an understanding of the role of religion in deterring deviance (1979:29-39). They state that specific religious beliefs about the severity and the inevitability of particular sanctions should be examined. By using measurements of religious affiliation and religious participation jointly, these authors explored the possibility of whether or not involvement in fundamentalist and nonfundamentalist religious subcultures is associated with fear of specific sanctions for one type of deviance, drunken driving. Their preliminary findings indicate that Protestants involved in fundamentalist subcultures in a southern city are more likely to believe that they will receive specific sanctions for drunken driving than are Protestants involved in nonfundamentalist subcultures. This is probably the result of the fundamentalist religious tradition's strong proscriptive norms against *any form* of drinking. Other research would indicate that such norms can create a fear of all uses of alcohol, as well as creating a rationale for the overuse of alcohol in reaction to the proscriptive norms (Chalfant and Beckley, 1977).

Religion and the Encouragement of Deviance

Sometimes, religious groups seem to encourage abnormal behavior on the part of their members. Some of these acts of deviance cause only scorn or derision; other acts are illegal. Deeply held religious beliefs can lead to religious behavior which is "deviant" in the eyes of larger society. The quaint customs of the Amish and the ascetic qualities of the Black Muslims are examples of mild deviant behavior. By contrast, the "panhandling" of the Hare Krishnas has led to enactment of laws prohibiting such activities. These laws, in turn, have been challenged in courts by this group because of their questionable constitutionality. The lawbreaking activities aimed at changing American foreign policy by the Berrigan brothers and other members of the "Catholic Left" during the 1960s were done for religious and moral reasons. However, most of America's religious people did not approve of these activities. The mass suicides of the members of the Jonestown People's Temple cult shocked most Americans and led to outcries for laws governing the conduct of cultic groups.

There is, however, a more subtle effect that religion can have in encouraging deviant behavior. The sanctions imposed by fundamentalist Prostestant groups against drinking alcoholic beverages have been shown sometimes to encourage excessive drinking by those who are members or ex-members of these religious bodies (Bales, 1946; Calalan and Cisan, 1968). The scorn demonstrated toward homosexuals by organized religion in general has sometimes resulted in the creation of separate religious subcultures for homosexuals which attempt to justify an open homosexual lifestyle on religious grounds. Research into these relationships concerning religion's unanticipated effects on promoting deviance has been sporadic. However, these findings do indicate that proscriptive norms which imply spiritual sanctions can actually encourage deviance because of the individual's strong reaction against or rejection of these norms.

SUMMARY

Religion and other social institutions in American society share a common culture and common norms. The unique religious pluralism of this country has, by and large, been encouraged by the political institution. Occasionally, religious groups and the government have overstepped the blurred boundaries separating church and state. When such conflicts have occurred, the Federal Courts have attempted to define what is religious (and thus protected by First Amendment rights) and what is secular (and thus governed by the laws of the United States). Relationships between government and religion are largely integrative in nature.

This functional relationship is also characteristic of the relations between government and education. Religious bodies have promoted education (with some exceptions) since our colonial era. Private, parochial, and public education now coexist peacefully, although in the past governmental action has been necessary to settle conflicts between religious and secular systems of education. The conflict that has occurred between proponents of public education and parochial education also has been settled in the federal courts.

Religion in America has historically supported capitalism. Most major religious bodies have profited institutionally from our economic system; so, too, have most individual members of religious groups. Marxism, in theory, does help to explain the social class cleavages that different denominations reflect. Marxism, in practice, has failed to develop a class consciousness among a significant number of Americans that would lead to a perception of organized religion as a "tool" of the ruling class.

Sports endeavors in American society, like politics, economics, and education, have a special relationship to religion. Organized athletics stress "character building" and "traditional morality." Furthermore, religious organizations exist for athletes and encourage these skilled performers to utilize the public recognition that comes from their talents for religious purposes. Many of the traditions and practices of athletic contests form a part of our society's alleged "civil religion."

Many people believe that adherence to religious norms which are grounded in religious beliefs discourages deviant behavior, but sociological research indicates that this is sometimes true and sometimes false. Perceived "spiritual sanctions" against certain deviant acts can deter this behavior, although this is more true for those belonging to more moderate religious bodies. Deviance can actually be encouraged by religious organizations. For example, members of smaller sects and cults sometimes have engaged in deviant behavior in the name of religion. Most of this behavior results in scorn by larger society, but occasionally some deviant behavior is clearly illegal and calls for punitive sanctions. Finally, reaction against proscriptive norms that carry "spiritual sanctions" can lead to excessive deviant behavior by individuals who are reacting against such norms.

REFERENCES

Abrams, Ray
1969   *Preachers Present Arms: The Role of the American Churches and Clergy in World Wars I and II, with Some Observations on the War in Vietnam.* Scottsdale, Pennsylvania: Herald Press.

Adams, James
1970   *The Growing Church Lobby in Washington.* Grand Rapids, Michigan: Eerdmans.

Bales, R. F.
1946   "Cultural differences in rates of alcoholism." *Quarterly Journal of Studies on Alcoholism* 6:480-499.

Beckley, Robert E.
1975   *Professional Football as an Occupation: A Sociological Study.* Unpublished Ph.D. dissertation. Washington, D.C.: The American University.

Bellah, Robert N.
1967   "Civil religion in America." *Daedalus* 96:191-219.

Cahalan, D. and I. H.
Cisen
1968   "American drinking practices: Summary of find-
                             ings from a national probability sample."
                             Quarterly Journal of Studies on Alcohol 29
                             (March):130-151.

Chalfant, H. Paul and
Robert E. Beckley
1977   "Beguiling and betraying: the image of alcohol
                             use in country music." Journal of Studies on
                             Alcohol 38 (July, 1977):1428-1433.

Davis, Rex and James
Richardson
1976   "The organization and functioning of the
                             Children of God." *Sociological Analysis*
                             37:321-339.

Deford, Frank
1976   "Religion in sport." *Sports Illustrated* 44(April
                             19, April 26, May 3):88-99, 54-60, 42-44.

Durkheim, Emile
1951(1897)   *Suicide: A Study in Sociology* (trans. John A.
                             Spaulding and George Simpson). New York:
                             The Free Press of Glencoe.

Earle, John, Dean
Knudsen, and Donald
Shriver
1976   *Spindles and Spires*. Atlanta: John Knox Press.
Eckhardt, K. W.
1970   "Religiosity and civil rights militancy." *Review
                             of Religious Research* 11:197-203.

Greeley, Andrew
1977   *The American Catholic: A Social Portrait*. New
                             York: Basic Books.

Hadden, Jeffrey K.
1969   *The Gathering Storm in the Churches*. Garden
                             City, New York: Doubleday.

Hammond, Philip E. and
N. J. Demerath, III
1969   *Religion in Social Context*. New York: Random
                             House.

Hargrove, Barbara
1979   *The Sociology of Religion: Classical and Contem-*

porary Approaches. Arlington Heights, Ill.: AHM Publishing Corporation.

Higgins, Paul C. and
Gary L. Albracht
1977   "Hellfire and delinquency revisited." *Social Forces* 55 (June):952-958.

Hirschi, Travis and
Rodney Stark
1969   "Hellfire and delinquency." *Social Problems* 17:202-213.

Johnson, Benton
1962   "Ascetic Protestantism and political preference." *Public Opinion Quarterly* 26:35-46.
1964   "Ascetic Protestantism and political preference in the deep South." *American Journal of Sociology* 69:359-366.
1966   "Theology and party preference among Protestant clergymen." *American Sociological Review* 31:200-207.

Johnstone, Ronald L.
1975   *Religion and Society in Interaction.* Englewood Cliffs, N.J.: Prentice-Hall.

Karson, Marc
1974   "Catholic anti-socialism." Pp. 164-184 in John Laslett and Seymour M. Lipset (eds.), *Failure of a Dream? Essays in the History of American Socialism.* Garden City, New York: Doubleday.

Knudten, Richard and
Mary S. Knudten
1971   "Juvenile delinquency, crime, and religion." *Review of Religious Research* 12:130-152.

Lenski, Gerhard
1961   *The Religious Factor: A Sociological Study on Religion's Impact on Politics, Economics, and Family Life.* Garden City, New York: Doubleday.

Marx, Karl
1964   *The Economic and Philosophic Manuscripts of 1844.* New York: International Publishers.

Meggysey, Dave
1970   *Out of Their League.* New York: Ramparts Press.

Menendez, Albert J.
1977   *Religion at the Polls.* Philadelphia: Westminster Press.

Novak, Michael
1979   "The natural religion." Pp. 335-341 in D. Stanley Eitzen (ed.), *Sport in Contemporary Society: An Anthology.* New York: St. Martin's Press.

Peek, Charles W., H. Paul Chalfant, and Edward B. Milton
1979   "Sinners in the hands of an angry God: Fundamentalist fears about drunken driving." *Journal for the Scientific Study of Religion* 18(March, 1979):29-39.

Pfeffer, Leo
1953   *Church, State, and Freedom.* Boston: Beacon Press.

Pope, Liston
1942   *Millhands and Preachers.* New Haven: Yale University Press.

Redekop, Calvin
1969   *The Old Colony Mennonites: Dilemmas of Ethnic Minority Life.* Baltimore: Johns Hopkins Press.

Rosten, Leo
1975   *Religions of America: Ferment and Faith in an Age of Crisis.* New York: Simon and Schuster.

Sacks, Alan
1975   "The Bureaucratization of College Football." Paper read at the Annual Meeting of the American Sociological Association. San Francisco, California.

Shaw, Gary
1972   *Meat on the Hoof: The Hidden World of Texas Football.* New York: St. Martin's Press.

Sorauf, Frank J.
1976   *The Wall of Separation: The Constitutional Politics of Church and State.* Princeton, New Jersey: Princeton University Press.

United States Supreme
Court
    1964   *United States Supreme Court Reports: Lawyers Edition.* Rochester, New York: Lawyers' Cooperative Publishing Co.
    1974   *United States Supreme Court Reports: Lawyers Edition.* Rochester, New York: Lawyers' Cooperative Publishing Co.

Weber, Max
    1958   *The Protestant Ethic and the Spirit of Capitalism.* New York: Schribner's.

Wilson, John
    1978   *Religion in American Society: The Effective Presence.* Englewood Cliffs, N.J.: Prentice-Hall.

Winter, J. Alan
    1977   *Continuities in the Sociology of Religion: Creed, Congregation, and Community.* New York: Harper and Row.

Yinger, J. Milton
    1970   *The Scientific Study of Religion.* New York: Crowell-Collier and Macmillan.

Chapter 12

Religion and Social Stratification

I sing a song of the saints of God . . .
Patient and brave and true,
Who toiled and fought and lived and died
For the Lord they loved and knew.
And one was a doctor, and one was a queen
And one was a shepherdess on the green;
They were all of them saints of God—
and I mean, God helping, to be one too.

They lived not only in ages past,
There are hundreds of thousands still,
The world is bright with the joyous saints
Who love to do Jesus' will.
You can meet them in school, or in lanes, or at sea,
In church, or in trains, or in shops, or at tea,
For the saints of God are just folk like me,
And I mean to be one too.

Episcopal hymn
Lesbia Scott, 1929

Have you failed in your plan of your storm-tossed life?
Place your hand in the nail-scarred hand;
Are you weary and worn from its toil and strife?
Place your hand in the nail-scarred hand.

Are you walking alone thro' the shadows dim?
Place your hand in the nail-scarred hand;
Christ will comfort your heart, put your trust in him,
Place your hand in the nail-scarred hand.

Place your hand in the nail-scarred hand,
Place your hand in the nail-scarred hand;

He will keep to the end, he's your dearest friend,
Place your hand in the nail-scarred hand.

Baptist hymn
B. B. McKinney, 1924

It is readily apparent that these two hymns differ greatly in both tone and message. One seems to express a confidence in this life and our part in it; the other gives the impression that this life is a time of pain and suffering from which the only relief is to be found in another existence. The difference is not simply a matter of accidental choice. Each hymn is more or less unique to its denomination; and each denomination, while having members from all walks of life, is dominated by a different socioeconomic stratum or social class. The tone of the Episcopal hymn expresses the secure place in life of the upper-class members of that denomination while the message of the Baptist hymn seems attuned to the needs of the large number of lower-class persons listed as members of various Baptist groups.

Although we may seek to avoid the knowledge, it takes only limited observation of matters such as the differences in these hymns to note that our churches are as stratified as all other aspects of our society. Membership in a particular religious organization means a variety of things to those who belong to them: commitment and devotion to a specific set of beliefs and values; the continuance of a family tradition; the opportunity for business contacts; or simply a followed routine. Any of these and several other meanings will probably hold for any given church member, sometimes two or more being true for the same person.

From the sociological perspective there is yet another meaning attached to membership in a specific denomination (or sect group) and in a particular congregation. Membership is a social position and one which endows the individual with some measure of status; for to some degree, a higher or lower prestige is attached to belonging to one or another of the specific groups and congregations. Whether or not we are consciously aware of this symbolic link of church and class, subconsciously we do seem to know that those people who belong to "Old First" have higher status than those who attend "Faith Tabernacle."

In Chapter 4, in discussing the various types of religious organizations, we noted that the most certain generalization which can be made about the differences between the sect and the denomination is that, in the type case, the former is basically lower-class while the latter is overwhelmingly made up of middle- and upper-class individuals. However, the relationship between the stratification system of our society and its religious institutions is far more complex than this simple dichotomy would indicate. The effects of social stratification (the system of social class) are felt in every aspect of the operation of religious organizations, and the ways in which their members express their religiosity.

That this is true should come as no sudden revelation to the student of society. The totality of the stratification system's effects on our lives is perhaps the best established and most reliable "social fact" which we have. Although sociologists may argue the necessity of stratification, its inevitability and its value, none deny its omnipresent consequences. The partitioning of the group into groups classified by rank according to power, prestige, and/or personal psychic reward touches every corner of our lives. The eventual differential rewards that are its outcomes, the uneven distribution of society's "goodies," hits us in all areas of our selves, and our religious selves are no exception.

LIFESTYLE, RELIGION, AND SOCIOECONOMIC STATUS

The depth of this effect may well be illustrated in Hollingshead's (1949) findings concerning religion and the lives of the young people of "Elmtown." As in so many other things, the religious identity of the young people is basically that which they inherit from their parents. Catholic parents introduce the rituals, beliefs, and obligations of the faith to their children at an early age just as faithful Methodist parents do for their offspring. Even when parental faith is only tenuous, Hollingshead notes, children tend to be taught to identify with the particular group, and homes split along religious lines are frequently the scene of quarrels about sectarian identification. Hollingshead also indicates that children learn to place different valuations on the different congregations in the community (1949:243):

> He also learns in his home that to be Catholic, Methodist, or Pentecostal is desirable or undesirable socially. Thus, the young child has no more choice in the matter of religious beliefs than he does in the language he learns or the bed in which he sleeps. Finally, as is well known, religious attitudes learned in the home are carried unconsciously into the neighborhood, the school, and other areas of community life.

That the young people tend to early identify specific churches with levels of socioeconomic prestige is a good indication that social class has a powerful influence on the religious life of Elmtown. A glance at the way in which these different classes, from the "upper crust" I's and II's to the lowest stratum V's are distributed in the town's churches gives full support to the notion that class and religion are intertwined (see Table 12–1).

Hollingshead also notes that there are several important differences in the religious behavior of persons in the different social classes. For example, he notes that all families designated as being in the upper group (Class I) belong to a church and almost all of these belong to the Federated (probably Presbyterian and Congregationalist) church. However, despite the fact that they tend to con-

373

Table 12-1. CLAIMED RELIGIOUS AFFILIATION BY DENOMINATION
AND CLASS

Denomination	I and II	III	Class IV	V	Total
Federated	20	26	13	0	59
Methodist	5	31	35	2	73
Catholic	3	30	28	7	68
Lutheran	3	41	44	5	93
Baptists; and others*	3	11	40	8	62
None	1	7	23	4	35
Total	35	146	183	26	390

$X^2 = 88.2262$ p 0.01

*The denominations included, followed by the number of claimed affiliations were : Free Methodists, 5; Church of Christ Scientist, 3; Pilgrim Holiness, 5; Gospel Tabernacle,6.

Source: Hollingshead, 1949:468.

tribute financially, they do not attend church with any great regularity. Likewise, almost every family in Class II is affiliated with some church and represents the group upon which the church relies most heavily for all kinds of support. Membership in this class is heavily Protestant, with the majority (60 percent) belonging to the Federated Church.

Members of Hollingshead's "Class III" belong predominantly to the Federated and Methodist churches. For this group, regular attendance at church services appears to be some mark of respectability in the community, and both men and women from this class tend to make up the bulk of those who teach church school classes in their respective churches.

The religious situation in Class IV is confused by the ethnicity of members of this group, and there is also the problem of claimed versus real church affiliation, further confounded by the fact that "members" of Class IV avoid participation in some of the community's churches while being extremely active in other organizations. Membership in the higher-status Federated and Methodist churches seems to be perfunctory for members of Class IV who belong to it, while those who belong to lower-status churches are much more involved in the activities of these churches. Overall, members of this class are not as active in church as are their higher status community members.

For members of Class V, ties to religion are frequently nonexistent and often extremely loose. It is reported that nine out of ten families do not have an active connection with a church. Hollingshead quotes a woman who suggests that Class V persons are not really wanted by the churches (1949:117):

> One woman epitomized the situation when she said bitterly, "The Everyone Welcome signs in front of the churches should add except people like us—we're not wanted." She was right—they are not wanted by the congregations and several of the ministers of the high-prestige churches (Federated, Methodist, and Lutheran) indicate they have no objections to Class V persons coming to service and participation in church activities, but they know that members of the congregation resent the presence of these people; so they do not encourage their attendance.

In sum, Hollingshead's study of young people in the small, northern Illinois community amply demonstrated, although this was far from its central premise, that religious organizations and the social stratification system are inextricably linked. That this is true not only for a small, midwestern community at one time period, but for American society as a whole and throughout most of our history, is demonstrated by numerous studies which consistently find such a relationship, regardless of time or place.

A significant amount of research done during the 1930s and 1940s called our attention to the pervasiveness of social class in American society (despite the equalitarian ideology of the nation) and made particular reference to the extent to which this pervasive effect held for the religious organization and membership therein. W. Lloyd Warner's classic study of Newburyport, Massachusetts, (Warner and Lunt, 1941) as well as that of the mythical Jonesville (the pseudononymous Elmtown revisited), for example, demonstrated that class and religion are inextricably linked.

Other studies in the so-called community study tradition support this kind of finding. The Lynd's study of Muncie, Indiana (1929) confirmed this pattern and also reported that individuals in the upper-status groups of the society were much more likely to be members of a church, or other religious organization, than were individuals from the lower-status groups. Bultena (1949) found church membership in Madison, Wisconsin, to be linked to class, as did West (1945) in his study of a western community. In short, these and other studies consistently demonstrate the relationship between religious identification and socioeconomic status, with higher status individuals having a much higher rate of affiliation and affiliation in particular types of religious organizations.

Demerath (1965:xxi) has pointed out that this series of studies has made it a commonplace to make a distinction between the low-status sects in the community and the higher status denominations thereof. He suggests, however, that the membership pattern of American religious groups is an extremely heterogenous one, with the particular religious groups having considerable diversity within as well as between themselves. For example, he notes that although Episcopalians are generally seen to be the highest status group, there is a large number of lower-class people who have membership in that communion, and that the lower-status Baptists also include members from the middle and upper classes in their membership.

One question which is raised by these various findings is that of whether church affiliation can actually be seen as having basic *religious* significance in any sense, or whether it is merely a reflection of the general tendency of higher-status individuals to join organizations more frequently than lower-status persons and to join groups of like-minded persons. Such a suggestion follows the tendency to portray attendance at church as somewhat hypocritical and related to matters other than those which are strictly religious in nature. There is certainly evidence to suggest that, at the very least, not all participation in religious ritual is religiously motivated while, similarly, not all of those who do *not* attend church are basically Godless and without any convictions that might be called religious.

In considering this question it is important to remember that while the finding that high social status is most frequently related with more consistent involvement in the religious organization, not all studies of the matter support this result. This suggests that there is more than social class as a basis for the association of socially like individuals involved in religious affiliation; that since religious needs differ by socioeconomic strata it is logical and appropriate that different specific groups meet them at different levels. Put another way, one aspect of religiosity, other than affiliation, has to do with the kinds of beliefs which are held by different groups in the society (see Demerath, 1965). Here, as well as in reference to other measures of kind or intensity of religious involvement, many of the studies which note the higher affiliation and participation of higher-status individuals also note a difference in the beliefs of the various strata with particular reference to those of lower-status persons. The Lynds (1929:329) suggest:

> ... members of the working class show a disposition to believe their religion more ardently and to accumulate more emotionally charged values around their beliefs. Religion appears to operate more prominently as an active agency of support and encouragement among these sections of the city. A second point is the shift in the status of certain religious beliefs during the past generation—notably the decline, particularly among the business class, in the emphasis upon Heaven, and still more upon Hell.

Lenski (1961) also found, in his study of religiosity in Detroit, that lower-class individuals were more inclined to be doctrinally orthodox than were members of higher-status groups.

Indeed, it can be shown that all facets or dimensions of religiosity differ in quality, and generally quantity, according to socioeconomic status group. Referring again to Fukuyama's (1961) division of religiosity into cultic, cognitive, creedal, and devotional dimensions, we find that the involvement in each of these dimensions varied according to social class. As can be seen in Table 12-2 participation in cultic religiosity (defined as church attendance and other organizational factors) has the highest rate for those in the upper or high socioeconomic status and the lowest rate for individuals in the lowest status group. This finding confirms the general notion that lower-status persons (with lower education, occupational status, and income) are more emotionally involved in their religious behavior than are persons from higher-status groups. All of this suggests that there is no simple relationship between the social strata of the society and the way in which people do or do not express religiosity.

Table 12-2. SOCIAL CLASS AND FOUR TYPES OF RELIGIOSITY
AMONG CONGREGATIONALISTS

Four Dimensions Percent highly involved	Socioeconomic Status		
	High	Moderate	Low
Cultic	53	43	35
Cognitive	28	24	15
Creedal	27	28	31
Devotional	16	23	32

Source: Fukuyama, 1961:159.

A classic study which contributed most fully to our understanding of this complex association between religion and the social stratification system is Liston Pope's *Millhands and Preachers* (1942). Pope not only described the numerous ways in which the religious group and social class intersected, but also described in some detail the lifestyles of various churches in the milltown community of Gastonia, North Carolina. In the mid-1970s a group of researchers revisited Gastonia to replicate Pope's study, to determine what changes, if any, had occurred in the religious community since World War II (Earle et al., 1976). Although there were obvious differences in the North Carolina community and in its religious situation, the variety in lifestyles for the different religious associations which were apparent in Pope's study remain, and a brief characterization of these churches and their religious lifestyles is instructive to us in coming to an appreciation of the relationship between social class and religion. The authors note (1976:107):

> Over the past generation, perhaps the single most important sociological change in the signs that *identify* the "class" of an individual in the popular mind in Gastonia has been the decline of the mill village. In the ten years following 1945 the houses in virtually every mill village in the town of Gastonia were sold to individual owners, although this trend was slow to take hold in some of the outlying towns. The old amoeba-cluster pattern of urban organization might still have been apparent from the airplane-view of the county in 1970, but the equation "mill house =mill worker" no longer matched social reality. . . . A glance at the pattern of colored pins on the city map that hangs on the wall of many a minister's study in Gastonia speaks volumes about the change from the old days of the "mill church": residentially, the church's members have exploded outward from the local community; now they live all over town.

They go on to note that the large uptown churches have maintained their social prominence but do not dominate the religious life of the community as totally as they had at the time of the original study. Formerly rural churches have become incorporated in the cities and have taken on some of the aspects of the city churches. Some of the formerly sectarian mill churches have made the transition typical of sectarian groups which survive into a more denominational-life religious organization. All in all, they find it appropriate to delineate five sociologically significant categories of religious groups in the community at the time of their study: "uptown, transitional, middle-class, sect, and black" (1976:108). The occupational distribution of the membership of these churches (1976:109) is presented in Table 12-3.

As can be seen, there is a concentration of persons with higher-status occupations in the "uptown" and "middle-class" churches. By the same token, as the authors point out, three-fourths of the membership of the white sectarian groups are drawn from those who have lower-status occupations. As is the case in all studies of church and class, no church is without either upper or lower-status members. Nevertheless, it is clearly possible to put a status or class tag on the particular church types or categories. Because this relationship is clear, it is helpful in understanding the relationship between church and class as it is portrayed in the descriptions of the lifestyles of the various church types (Earle et al., 1976). We will now briefly examine each of these types.

The uptown church. This is a kind of church which goes back in its origin to the very founding of the city. It is the established church in the community and its membership is drawn from residential areas throughout the entire city. The

Table 12–3. OCCUPATIONAL DISTRIBUTION OF MEMBERSHIP BY TYPE OF CHURCH, IN PERCENT

Occupational category	Uptown	Type of Church Middle-Class	Transitional	Sect	Black
Professional, technical and kindred	16.6	7.5	3.6	0.7	14.8
Managers, officials and proprietors	32.7	21.0	13.5	6.4	3.5
Clerical and kindred	15.5	11.3	13.5	8.5	2.3
Sales	16.0	11.0	9.2	2.1	3.5
Craftsmen, foremen and kindred	11.2	20.4	24.4	18.4	9.6
Operatives and kindred	3.0	11.6	17.7	44.7	8.1
Laborers	2.0	10.4	11.5	12.1	23.5
Total	100.0	100.0	100.0	100.0	100.0

Source: Earle et al., 1976:109.

most prominent civic leaders are likely to be found on its membership roles. It is characterized by an extensive church plant or building and tends to have two or more full-time ministers on its staff and perceives these ministers as scholarly persons who have the responsibility of teaching the religion (as interpreted by the denomination) to the members of the church. The heads of the families involved in the church are drawn disproportionately from the ranks of upper- and upper middle-class families in the community. That is, the members of the congregation frequently have professional, managerial, and proprietary occupations, and those persons dominate the congregation. Further, a large proportion of the members of this church have a college education; a fact, the authors note, which is reflected in the kind of formal, intellectually oriented services which characterize worship in the uptown church.

On Sunday morning a visitor to an uptown church walks up concrete stairs flanked by neatly sculptured shrubbery. He or she is greeted at the door by an usher and escorted to a seat. The sanctuary has stained glass windows, carpeted floor, padded pews, and elaborately decorated pulpit furniture. About 500 people, most of whom are middle-aged or older, all well attired,

> are present for the prelude, written by a classical composer and skillfully played on a pipe organ. The printed bulletin indicates the order of service, but also lists a large number of board meetings and interest groups scheduled for the coming week. During a processional hymn, the robed choir enters, followed by the ministers. The service follows the printed program without introduction and is conducted with quiet dignity and formality. The atmosphere of the service is suffused with a sense of stability, permanence, and devotion to time-honored truth (1976:111).

It comes as no great surprise that the uptown church represents and undergirds the basic values of the dominant culture of Gastonia. In fact, a large number of the leadership of the community is in its membership and, in reality, the church has been instrumental in the shaping of that general culture throughout its long years as a part of the culture of Gastonia.

The middle-class church. What is characterized as the middle-class church is a relatively new form of religious organization in Gastonia. It emerged in the period of rapid industrial and economic expansion which followed the Second World War. All of the middle-class churches are affiliated with one of the major denominations of American society. The congregation of the middle-class church represents a cross section of the occupational groups in the neighborhood in which it is located. Unlike the uptown and transitional churches, it is rather equally divided between white-collar and blue-collar families in the community. Buildings are relatively new in construction but are not as adequate as those of the older, uptown churches. The members of the middle-class church are better educated, as well as younger, than are the members of the transitional church, but they are also less likely to be permanent or long-term residents of Gastonia. The professional staff will generally consist of a full-time pastor who will perhaps have a seminary student as a part-time assistant.

> A visitor to a middle-class church service finds it akin to the uptown church but on a much more informal level. The sanctuary is pleasantly if modestly decorated, with some carpet and modern furnishings. The bulletin indicates a formal order of worship reflecting the high educational level of the pastor and the congregation. The 200 people in attendance tend to be young—mostly in their 30s and 40s, well dressed and attentive (1976:115).

The distinctive feature of the middle-class church is that it came into being as a separate religious denomination without having the sectarian beginnings characteristic of most new religious groups in American society. It resembles the program of the uptown church in many ways, but the mixture of blue and white-collar members in the congregation distinguishes it from the uptown church and keeps it from being an institution which can always be seen as a supporter of the cultural status quo. Nevertheless, it is not likely that such a congregation would pose any serious challenge to the established order.

In transitional church. The type of church represented by this classification had its beginnings in the mill villages during the early half of the century (1920s and 30s). It has had a continuing existence since that time, and it has generally been associated with either the Baptist or Methodist denominations, although transitional churches may also be related to some other group or denomination. The dominant group in these churches, so far as class is concerned, comes from what can be called an upper-blue-collar occupational class and is varied in both income and education. Younger members of this church are generally high school graduates, in contrast to only half as many of the older members of the congregation who have achieved this level of education. The homes of the church's members are located throughout the community, however, its leadership roles are generally held by members living in the outlying areas of the community. In a sense, it can be said that the transitional church, in its shift from a mill church to its present position, has become a smaller scale version of the uptown church.

The staff of the transitional church is smaller than that of the uptown church, generally including one pastor, or at most two, with a full-time secretary. The pastor of such a church is not viewed as an "educator" but, rather, as a spiritual leader and guide. The role of the pastor, as the members of this church see it, is the cultivation and maintenance of the loyalty of the members of the church and their involvement in it.

> The visitor approaches the building from a paved parking lot, is greeted by several people at the door, and is directed to a seat by an usher. The decor of the sanctuary indicates the moderate prosperity of the congregation. In addition to an organ, there is carpeting, a divided chancel, unpretentious but attractive stained glass windows, overhead medieval-style lights, and modern, simple, pulpit furniture. Present are about 250 well-dressed persons, mostly in their 30s and 40s. The mimeographed bulletin described a rather formal structure for the service, with written and pastoral prayers, public affirmation of faith and scripture reading. In spite of the formal character of the order of service, it is frequently interrupted for announcements or other concerns. The sermon is well prepared and delivered with enthusiasm by the pastor (1976:113).

What the authors call the transitional church is no longer a mill church, but it does not yet have the status of the uptown church either. Actually, it incorporates some elements of the styles of both the uptown and the old mill churches. Its members seem to attend it because while they sense the need for some kind of religious experience, an experience which is typical of the more sectarian type of religious group, they have outgrown the totally emotional service of the sect. Thus, the transitional church does not go in for the same kind of emotional conversion typical of the sectarian group. It is thus transitional in the sense that it mixes the old traditional religious themes characteristic of the older mill sectarian church with the more formal patterns of the uptown church.

The sect. We have already discussed the general outlines of the nature of sectarian groups. Such groups have been a part of Gastonia's religious history since its founding days and are similar to such groups everywhere. Regardless of the denominational affiliation of the old mill churches, they tended to have a ·ctarian character about their organization and life. In addition to the older churches, new religious groups with a sectarian tone have continued to emerge among the poor and those outside the general social structure of Gastonia.

In a geographical sense, these religious groups are generally found in or around the older mill villages, and are located in areas of low-income housing. Services in the sect are generally attended only by people who live in the immediate vicinity of the sect building and attend this particular church because they live near it. Unskilled workers in the mills, as well as in related industries, make up the dominant portion of the sect group. The buildings in which the mill workers worship are often made of concrete blocks and tend to consist mainly of an auditorium, without extensive provisions for educational purposes. The services of the sect group are long and held frequently. Services may be led by one of a number of persons, although there is generally a "preacher" who has had only an elementary school training and possibly some correspondence courses which have been taken from a Bible Institute. There is little formal organization in such congregations.

A visitor to a sectarian service climbs three wooden or cinder-block steps to enter a small, bare room which has old, unmatched pews seating 150 people. On one Thursday night in the middle of a week-long revival, about 60 people—including 10 children—are present at the time the service is scheduled to begin. Drums, a guitar, a piano, and an electronic organ are being played, the songs having pronounced rhythms which involve the audience almost involuntarily in clapping of hands, tapping of feet, or movement of the body. The mood of those in attendance is informal. A dozen teenagers sit together and talk, while the older people move freely about the room to talk to others.

A crudely constructed pulpit and a speaker's pew are on the platform at front. . . . The preacher and his two associates move to the platform from the audience where they have been talking and shaking hands, and the service begins. After announcing the song, one of the men moves about, all the time singing into the microphone which he holds close to his face. The beat of the music is pronounced, and the people present respond with a rhythmic clapping. A prayer follows, accompanied by shouts of "Hallelujah," "Praise God," "Yes, Jesus," "Glory," and is followed by another hymn, and then another, again with rhythmic participation by the audience. . . .

The sermon begins with the preacher describing the "foolishness of most people in the world" and their careless disdain of the "fact that Jesus died for them, to deliver them from hell." Certain themes appear repeatedly in his sermon: "salvation," "punishment of the evil in these days," "the danger of giving in to the world," "God will see you through," "open your heart to Jesus." The faithful of God are pictured as being free from the bonds of religious doctrine and tradition, and willing to "let God go" by shouting, clapping, dancing, and singing (1976:116-7).

Rather obviously, the service or meeting of the sect group is in direct contrast to the kind of service which goes on in the uptown church. There is no attempt to communicate any sort of "intellectual message" in the meetings; it is an emotional religious experience for those who attend it and such an experience is their goal. To the outside observer it may well appear that their services are crudely contrived and manipulated to the end of bringing about this emotional experience. However, it is generally clear that this emotional experience is an outlet needed by the people who attend this particular church.

The black church. Inasmuch as blacks tend to represent a separate status hierarchy within the community of Gastonia, their church also represents an institution which must be seen as outside the status rankings of the white churches. Although the black church was found to be more prominent in the community in 1976 than it was at the time of Pope's study, its prominence did not develop due to the support of civil rights movements. In reality, the black church crosses most of the sociological variables of the white churches; the members of the black church having chosen it for its racial identification rather than for any class concerns.

A visitor to a black uptown service enters the building and is seated by an usher. The sanctuary is large, old, and in need of repairs. At the front is a large choir loft and a pulpit, with a piano on the side being played by a young woman. The entrance of the choir and the minister signals the start of the service, which follows a regular pattern of hymns, prayers, special music, offering, and Scripture reading. The service is similar to that in non-sectarian white churches but is conducted with greater vocal participation by the congregation. Shouts of "Amen," "Yes, Lord," and "Yes, Jesus," punctuate the minister's prayers. In the sermon, as well as in the prayers, emphasis is placed upon the ability of the people to endure in spite of the entire service gravitates around the capacity of the individual, with God's help, to resist evil and overcome personal problems (1976:119).

The authors point out that the church continues to have strong influence in the lives of the blacks of the community. They note, however, that the heavy emphasis on individualism evident in the services may lead unintentionally to support of the status quo as enforced by the white leaders of the community. The pastor of the church, who is typically the only staff except for a secretary, is generally not in opposition to the views of these white leaders.

This lengthy summary of Gastonia revisited as well as the earlier comments on community studies, hopefully serves to give us a rather holistic view of how the structure of socioeconomic status affects, as well as is affected by, the structure of the religious institution as it appears in the world. We now need to get a grasp on some of the parameters of this relationship. We will turn first to an examination of socioeconomic status and affiliation or preference for the various religious organizations.

RELIGIOUS AFFILIATION AND SOCIOECONOMIC STATUS

All indications are that one's membership or preference for a particular denomination or sect is related to one's socioeconomic status. Of course, no church is totally homogeneous as to class, but the different groups do tend to have a certain social class profile. The classic portrait of the various religious groups with regard to social status was presented by Schneider (1952). From the data presented in Table 12-4 it can be seen that there are indeed significant differences in the percentages of individuals from upper, middle, and lower classes in the different denominations or religious groups.

We note in looking at the figures in Table 12-4, that persons from each of the three social classes are found in every religious group. The Episcopal Church, for example, may have a disporportionately high number of persons in its membership who are categorized as "upper class." Yet it has more members from the "lower class" than either the somewhat lower-status Congregationalists or Presbyterians. At the same time, while about two-thirds of the members of Roman Catholic and Baptist Churches in 1952 came from the "lower class," about 8 percent of their memberships came from the "upper class" category. Still, there are clear demarcations in the class levels of the groups. In 1952, such groups as Christian Scientist, Episcopalian, Congregational, Presbyterian, and Jewish could be designated as having high status while Roman Catholics, Baptists, and Mormons would have to be seen as lower-status.

A more recent portrait of the social class composition of religious groups in American society is provided by looking at data on religious preference drawn from several of the more recent General Social Surveys conducted by the Na-

Table 12-4. SOCIAL CLASS PROFILES OF AMERICAN RELIGIOUS GROUPS

| | | Class | | |
Denomination	Upper	Middle	Lower	N
Christian Scientist	24.8%	36.5%	38.7%	137
Episcopal	24.1	33.7	42.2	590
Congregational	23.9	42.6	33.5	376
Presbyterian	21.9	40.0	38.1	961
Jewish	21.8	32.0	46.2	537
Reformed	19.1	31.3	49.6	131
Methodist	12.7	35.6	51.7	2100
Lutheran	10.9	36.1	53.0	723
Christian	10.0	35.4	54.6	370
Protestant (small bodies)	10.0	27.3	62.7	888
Roman Catholic	8.7	24.7	66.6	2390
Baptist	8.0	24.0	68.0	1381
Mormon	5.1	28.6	66.3	175
No preference	13.3	26.0	60.7	466
Protestant (undesignated)	12.4	24.1	63.5	460
Atheist, agnostic	33.3	46.7	20.0	15
No answer, don't know	11.0	29.5	59.5	319

Source: Schneider, 1952:228.

tional Opinion Research Center (NORC, 1978). The data presented in Table 12-5 are drawn from these studies in the five-year period from 1974 to 1978. The four socioeconomic status groups, referred to as upper, middle, working, and lower class, really represent the combination of income, education, and occupation divided into the four quartiles. While the class terms here are really short-hand, descriptive labels for sections of the socioeconomic status continuum, they do correspond generally to the "classes" used by Demerath (1965) in a general study of social class and American Protestantism.

As can be seen from the data in Table 12-5, based on the NORC general social

Table 12–5. RELIGIOUS PREFERENCE AND SOCIOECONOMIC STATUS

Affiliation	Upper Class	Middle Class	Socioeconomic Status Working Class	Lower Class	N
Episcopalian	40.5%	27.0%	27.0%	5.4%	37
Presbyterian	30.8	29.2	20.0	20.0	65
Jewish	30.3	30.3	24.2	15.2	33
Methodist	25.9	20.6	30.2	23.3	189
Catholic	25.8	22.4	28.3	23.5	361
Lutheran	18.7	32.1	38.1	11.2	134
Baptists	16.2	17.8	34.3	31.7	309
Sects	15.6	30.0	28.9	25.6	90
					1218

Source: NORC General Social Surveys, 1974–1978.

survey from 1974 through 1978, the relationship between social class and religious affiliation remains essentially the same a quarter of a century after Schneider's (1952) study. A difference in categorizing individuals as "upper class" has resulted in a larger percentage of respondents being classified in this way, but this does not change the relative representation of this class in the churches. The only major shift, at least for the smaller number of groups considered here, is seen in the increased percentage of upper-class persons in the Catholic church, moving it a step above the Lutheran groups; a move which probably reflects the general upward mobility of groups traditionally associated with the Catholic church. Also, although the sect groups continue to have the smallest percentage in the upper group, they have less working- and lower-class members than the Baptists; a fact which probably reflects the fact that several of the sect groups have been upwardly mobile and no longer truly deserve the designation, sect. Nevertheless, the Episcopalians, Presbyterians, and Jews maintain their position at the top of the status ladder. Again, no church is without members from the lower class. However, a clear picture of "high" and "low" status churches is shown in these data.

It can also be seen in data drawn from the N.O.R.C. sample that not only preference but strength or intensity of that preference is related to socioeconomic status (see Table 12-6). In general, it appears that lower-status individuals are

Table 12–6. SOCIOECONOMIC STATUS AND INTENSITY OF
RELIGIOUS PREFERENCE

Intensity of Affiliation	Socioeconomic Status			
	Upper Class	Middle Class	Working Class	Lower Class
Not strong	62.1	62.3	59.6	53.1
Strong	37.9	37.7	40.6	46.9

Source: NORC General Social Surveys, 1974–78.

more likely than those with upper-class status to have a strong sense of identification with the religious group to which they belong, although in none of these status groups does a majority of the respondents express such strong affiliation.

Of more interest is the fact that such differences in the strength or intensity of preference vary by denomination (see Table 12-7). Both upper-class Presbyterians and Lutherans profess greater intensity in their preference for a particular group than do their lower-class coreligionists. Conversely, a very small percentage of upper-status Methodists indicate that they feel strongly about their preference for that denomination. It can also be seen that lower-class sectarians profess a strong affiliation in more than two-thirds of the cases. In short, in some rather complex way, not only group preference, but also intensity of preference, is related to social class. It may be that many of the upper- and middle-class members of the higher status groups are recent "converts" whose preference is the result of upward social mobility rather than a traditional—even ethnic—allegiance to a religious faith that has been a family belief for several generations and is thus deeply woven in the lives of its members.

SOCIOECONOMIC STRATA AND TYPE OF RELIGIOSITY

There is little question that preference is related to social class and that other forms of religiosity are similarly related to socioeconomic position. Yet, as Demerath (1961) points out, the relationship is not clear; some investigators have found that religiosity is highest for upper-status individuals while others find just the opposite to be true. He goes on to suggest, in effect, that since religiosity is not unidimensional and thus that persons may be religious in different degrees

Table 12-7. SOCIOECONOMIC STATUS AND STRENGTH OF PREFERENCE
BY GROUP

Reference Group		Strength of Preference	
		Not Strong	Strong
Episcopalian	Upper	73.3	26.7
	Middle	50.0	50.0
	Working	70.0	30.0
	Lower	50.0	50.0
Presbyterian	Upper	65.0	35.0
	Middle	84.2	15.8
	Working	76.9	23.1
	Lower	69.2	30.8
Jewish	Upper	70.0	30.0
	Middle	60.0	40.0
	Working	50.0	50.0
	Lower	40.0	60.0
Methodist	Upper	81.6	18.4
	Middle	64.1	35.9
	Working	70.2	29.8
	Lower	52.3	47.7
Catholic	Upper	65.2	34.8
	Middle	62.5	37.5
	Working	53.9	46.1
	Lower	57.1	42.9
Lutheran	Upper	52.0	48.0
	Middle	74.4	25.6
	Working	52.9	47.1
	Lower	66.7	33.3
Baptist	Upper	52.0	48.0
	Middle	59.3	40.7
	Working	62.9	37.1
	Lower	50.5	49.5
Sects	Upper	50.0	50.0
	Middle	59.3	40.7
	Working	60.0	40.0
	Lower	31.8	68.2

Source: NORC General Social Surveys, 1974–78.

on different dimensions of religious behavior. That is, people express their religiosity not only to varying degrees but also in varying ways, or express different kinds of religiosity. It may be, then, that socioeconomic status affects not just the *extent* of one's religiosity, but also the *forms* one's religiosity takes.

An investigation by Stark (1972) into the nature of this difference finds it to be quite complex. He, too, sees class differences as ones of *kind* rather than degree. As he notes (1972:496):

> The poor are not just more or less religious than the rich, or even more or less religious in different ways, but they are more religious in some ways under some circumstances, and less religious in some ways under other circumstances.

There are several ways in which this question can be approached. We will look at four aspects of this matter of differences in kind rather than degree by socioeconomic status: (1) attendance at church services, (2) churchlike and sectlike religiosity in the same religious groups, (3) types of religious beliefs held, and (4) tolerance of those without religious faith.

Church Attendance

Among others, Stark (1972) indicates that persons from the upper class are more likely than lower-class persons to participate in such public rituals as Sunday morning worship services, saying grace before meals, and other organizational activities of the church. In particular it has been noted that attending the formal Sunday service of worship is a middle- and upper-class phenomenon.

A look at the data presented in Table 12-8, however, does not bear out this contention. Based on the combined NORC samples for 1974 to 1978, there appear to be some small differences in the attendance patterns of the four socioeconomic groups. While the difference is not great in the proportion attending church regularly, members of what we term the working class are more likely to attend church rarely than are those from other groups, while those in the middle class are least often found to attend rarely. The middle class are most likely to attend church "often" or "regularly."

A pattern does begin to emerge, however, when we examine attendance patterns for the status groups considered denomination by denomination. As can be seen in Table 12-9, there are interesting differences in attendance patterns for the different religious groups. It is true that for Catholics and Baptists the upper and middle-class members more frequently report regular attendance than do working- and lower-class communicants. However, for Methodists and Presbyterians it is the combination of middle- and working-class members that most support the worship services while the middle-class members are the most ardent supporters of the Episcopal church. On the other hand, the lower-class sectarians

Table 12–8. SOCIOECONOMIC STATUS AND ATTENDANCE AT
RELIGIOUS SERVICES

	Socioeconomic Status			
Attendance	Upper Class	Middle Class	Working Class	Lower Class
Rarely	24.1	22.8	29.0	24.6
Some	26.4	23.5	20.9	22.1
Often	16.1	18.0	16.5	17.8
Regularly	33.4	35.6	33.6	35.5
N	311	289	393	276

Source: NORC General Social Surveys, 1974–78.

give the most support to the services of those groups (the same is true for Jewish respondents but the numbers are really too small to draw any conclusions). Two things seem revealed by these data. First, there is no clear and stable relationship between social status and religious attendance; the pattern is somewhat different from the various religious groupings. Second, the middle class is, in most cases, the strongest supporter of church services. That is, it is not the upper class alone which tops the attendance lists but the middle class, either in combination with the upper or working class which provides the largest proportion of persons attending the formal Sunday morning services of the various religious groupings.

However, when a further dimension, sex, is considered in relation to church attendance further specification of the relationship can be made (see Table 12-10). It appears that there is a difference in church attendance—but only for male church members. With the possible exception of the upper-class females, who attend regularly only a bit less than females in the other status groups, there is no difference between the classes. Upper-class males, however, are most likely to attend church on a regular basis, while lower-class males are most likely to report attending church rarely. It must be noted, however, that these differences are relatively small, and no very strong conclusions can be drawn on the basis of these data. Again, the presumed differences in class for this type of religious behavior do not appear to exist to any very great degree.

Church-like vs. Sect-like Religious Behavior

As Stark and Glock (1968) have noted, there are sect-like elements in even the most formal denomination and some church-like tendencies in the most sect-like

Table 12-9.   SOCIOECONOMIC STATUS AND ATTENDANCE AT RELIGIOUS SERVICES BY RELIGIOUS GROUPS

	Rarely	Some	Attendance Often	Regularly	%	N
Catholic						
Upper	13.1 (11)	22.6 (19)	10.7 (9)	53.6 (45)	100	(84)
Middle	17.1 (13)	17.1 (13)	13.2 (10)	52.6 (40)	100	(76)
Working	20.0 (19)	21.1 (20)	10.5 (10)	48.4 (46)	100	(95)
Lower	21.3 (16)	21.3 (16)	10.7 (8)	46.7 (35)	100	(75)
Jewish						
Upper	60.0 (6)	30.0 (3)		10.0 (1)	100	(10)
Middle	28.6 (2)	71.4 (5)			100	(7)
Working	57.1 (4)	14.3 (1)	14.3 (1)	14.3 (1)	100	(7)
Lower	33.3 (1)	33.3 (1)		33.3 (1)	100	(3)
Baptist						
Upper	20.4 (10)	22.4 (11)	18.4 (9)	38.8 (19)	100	(49)
Middle	15.7 (8)	27.5 (14)	19.6 (10)	37.3 (19)	100	(51)
Working	31.1 (28)	20.0 (18)	24.4 (22)	24.4 (22)	100	(90)
Lower	17.5 (14)	26.3 (21)	27.5 (22)	28.8 (23)	100	(80)
Methodist						
Upper	33.3 (15)	31.3 (14)	13.3 (6)	22.2 (10)	100	(45)
Middle	23.7 (9)	18.4 (7)	36.8 (14)	21.1 (8)	100	(38)
Working	30.6 (15)	18.4 (9)	18.4 (9)	32.7 (16)	100	(49)
Lower	26.3 (10)	13.2 (5)	28.9 (11)	21.6 (12)	100	(38)
Lutheran						
Upper	12.5 (3)	37.5 (9)	29.2 (7)	20.8 (5)	100	(24)
Middle	28.2 (11)	41.0 (16)	15.4 (6)	15.4 (6)	100	(39)
Working	14.6 (7)	27.1 (13)	29.2 (14)	29.2 (14)	100	(48)
Lower	45.5 (5)	36.4 (4)	9.1 (1)	9.1 (1)	100	(11)
Presbyterian						
Upper	16.7 (3)	38.9 (7)	33.3 (6)	11.1 (2)	100	(18)
Middle	40.0 (6)	26.7 (4)	13.3 (2)	20.0 (3)	100	(15)
Working	50.0 (6)	16.7 (2)	8.3 (1)	25.0 (3)	100	(12)
Lower	55.6 (5)	22.2(2)	11.1 (1)	11.1 (1)	100	(9)
Episcopal						
Upper	33.5 (5)	40.0 (6)	20.0 (3)	6.7 (1)	100	(15)
Middle	11.1 (1)	22.2 (2)	11.1 (1)	55.6 (5)	100	(9)
Working	44.4 (4)	22.2 (2)	11.1 (1)	22.2 (2)	100	(9)
Lower		100.0 (1)			100	(1)

Table 12-9.   SOCIOECONOMIC STATUS AND ATTENDANCE AT RELIGIOUS
SERVICES BY RELIGIOUS GROUPS (cont'd.)

Sects

Upper	7.1 (1)	14.3 (2)	21.4 (3)	57.1 (8)	100	(14)
Middle	20.8 (5)	12.5 (3)	8.3 (2)	58.3 (14)	100	(24)
Working	22.7 (5)	13.6 (3)	4.5 (1)	59.1 (13)	100	(22)
Lower	10.5 (2)	10.5 (2)	10.5 (2)	68.4 (13)	100	(19)

Source: NORC General Social Surveys, 1974–78.

Table 12-10.   SOCIOECONOMIC STATUS AND ATTENDANCE, BY SEX

	Socioeconomic Status							
	Upper Class		Middle Class		Working Class		Lower Class	
Attendance	Male	Female	Male	Female	Male	Female	Male	Female
Rarely	23.4	17.5	29.7	16.7	31.4	22.9	27.1	18.6
Some	31.7	21.9	26.4	23.8	25.7	16.7	29.9	15.5
Often	11.0	23.7	15.4	18.5	15.0	19.8	15.0	22.5
Regularly	33.8	36.8	28.6	41.1	27.9	40.6	28.0	43.4

Source: NORC General Social Surveys, 1974–78.

groups. Further, they suggest that it is lower-class members of more middle-class churches who are responsible for what sect-like practices are found in such churches.

Demerath (1961, 1965) has worked on this assumption and studied church-like versus sect-like as it relates to differences for four socioeconomic status groups; the upper, middle, working and lower classes. For Demerath, church-like religiosity is suggested by behavior such as frequent attendance at Sunday morning services, taking part in the activities of the church, and belonging, in addition, to a number of voluntary organizations other than the church. Sect-like religiosity, on the other hand, is marked by communal involvement in the religious group at a high level; it is measured by having a number of close friends in the congregation, finding religious rewards paying off in the secular areas of life, and the tendency to disapprove of the pastor's participation in community affairs and controversy (1965:82).

Table 12-11. CHURCHLIKE RELIGIOSITY AND INDIVIDUAL STATUS
AMONG CONGREGATIONALISTS, PRESBYTERIANS,
DISCIPLES OF CHRIST, AND BAPTISTS

| Religiosity | Individual Status | | | | Denomination |
	Upper	Middle	Working	Low	
% High church-like involved	65	62	46	34	Congregationalists
N	(1346)	(1185)	(535)	(91)	
% High church-like involved	67	55	45	36	Presbyterians
N	(670)	(624)	(423)	(124)	
% High church-like involved	73	63	55	42	Disciples of Christ
N	(389)	(407)	(282)	(54)	
% High church-like involved	67	54	37	32	Baptists
N	(171)	(232)	(220)	(71)	

Source: Demerath, 1965:118.

Using these behaviors as measures of the two types of religiosity, Demerath looked at the involvement of the members in four West Coast denominations (Congregationalists, Presbyterians, Disciples of Christ, and Baptists) by social class (see Table 12-11 and 12-12). Looking at the data related to church-like religiosity (Table 12-11), for each of the denominations the upper-class members are consistently more likely to be church-like than are members classified as lower class; indeed, the upper-class members are more frequently church-like in their religiosity than are those from either middle- or working-class group.

The corollary to this is true; lower-class church members are more likely to report a sect-like religiosity than are those from the upper class, or generally, any other class of that matter. There are two points to be noted with regard to the different denominations Demerath studied. First, the Congregationalists, occupying the highest status of the four religious groups, have, in comparison, relatively few members in any class who express their religiosity in a sect-like fashion. Similarly, the lowest-status group, the Baptists, have a higher proportion of

Table 12–12. SECTLIKE RELIGIOSITY AND INDIVIDUAL STATUS
AMONG CONGREGATIONALISTS, PRESBYTERIANS,
DISCIPLES OF CHRIST, AND BAPTISTS

| Religiosity | Individual Status | | | | Denomination |
	Upper	Middle	Working	Low	
% High church-like involved	22	27	32	37	Congregationalists
N	(1386)	(1145)	(572)	(102)	
% High church-like involved	33	41	51	52	Presbyterians
N	(711)	(674)	(471)	(129)	
% High church-like involved	36	45	43	56	Disciples of Christ
N	(387)	(396)	(284)	(52)	
% High church-like involved	42	48	50	56	Baptists
N	(171)	(233)	(218)	(75)	

Source: Demerath, 1965:119.

those with sect-like religiosity than any other groups. This sect-like religiosity, like the church-like variety, is tied to social class. However, unlike church-like religiosity, the tendency to express religion in a sect-like fashion is somewhat tied to the denominations at least insofar as Congregationalists and Baptists are concerned.

Another way to look at the matter is to focus on the relationship between socioeconomic status and the tendency of church members to report having "felt religious experiences," such as sensing the divine presence (Stark, 1972). As can be seen in Table 12-13, there are social class differences in the tendency to report religious experience.

While a sizeable proportion in all four groups report religious experience (even 38 percent of the liberal protestant upper-class members report such experiences), there is a clear tendency for the lower-class members to report more religious experiences. This difference is small only in the case of the conservative churches, where there is a greater stress on such emotionality in religious behavior.

Table 12-13. SOCIOECONOMIC STATUS AND RELIGIOUS EXPERIENCE
(Church Member Sample)

| | Percentage high on religious experience | | | Percentage point difference between |
	Lower	Middle	Upper	Lower and Upper
Liberal Protestants	59 (99)	40 (313)	38 (305)	−21
Moderate Protestants	67 (123)	56 (287)	52 (229)	−15
Conservative Protestants	90 (109)	87 (149)	85 (55)	−5
Roman Catholics	62	61	41	−21

Source: Stark, 1972:499.

Summarizing the difference in kinds of religiosity by social class, Stark (1972:494) posits three types of religious commitment as typical of church-like commitment and as having a positive relationship with socioeconomic status: "public ritual involvement," "religious knowledge," and "participation in church organizations and activities." On the other hand, there is a negative relationship for: "orthodoxy (as well as particularism, ultimate meaning, and ethicalism)," "religious experience," "personal devotionalism," and "communal involvement." As he concludes, the differences found in religiosity by socioeconomic status, at least as far as church *members* are concerned, is of kind more than it is of degree (1972:495):

> The poor show greater religiousness in those aspects of faith which can serve as mechanisms for relieving their suffering: the comforts of a promised redress in the hereafter when the last shall be first and moral support through religious experiences, the catharsis of prayer, and the comforts of human relations. Thus, although the church may be relatively unable to enlist the poor, it seems able to provide traditional transvaluational and emotional comforts for those poor it does enlist.

It is to be noted, however, that this difference in kind rather than degree is generally only true for lower-class members of religious organizations. There is a difference in degree when the tendency to join a religious group, alone, is considered. Lower-class individuals do not belong to church to the same degree as persons from the upper and middle classes.

Types of Belief. In describing the differences between upper- and lower-class religiosity both Demerath and Stark have emphasized the tendency of the lower class to hold more orthodox beliefs. Stark (1972:489) notes: "Among church members, the propensity for the lower classes to exhibit greater commitment to religious belief *manifests itself on all varieties of belief measures.*" The data in Table 12-14 confirm this.

In reporting this data, Stark is seeking to answer a puzzling question: If a major function of religion is to provide comfort and support to the deprived, why don't the economically deprived (the lower class) participate more fully in religion? His conclusion is that, to the extent that the poor do participate, they participate most fully in those activities which meet the needs arising from their deprivation.

Stark notes, therefore, that the middle and upper class participate to a greater degree in those activities that confirm their worldly "success." Thus, "participation in these rituals (of the church) may . . . be seen as demonstration that one is respectable, substantial, responsible, and proper" (1972:495). On the other hand, the lower-status church members do engage more frequently in activities which will give comfort and support to their needs. Thus, firm traditional faith, as well as involvement in prayer and other emotional experiences provide answers to the needs of the lower-status individual. This relationship is summarized in Table 12-15.

Tolerance of Atheism

A final issue with regard to the differences in kind of religiosity for the different socioeconomic status groups is related to tolerance for those who do not agree with one's own religious beliefs—particularly when this disagreement takes the form of atheism. It seems likely that a variety of factors—both religious and socioeconomic—would lead to a lower level of tolerance for such an extreme position.

Looking again at the data from the General Social Survey (NORC, 1978) it can be seen that there is a definite relationship between socioeconomic status and tolerance for the expression of atheism in several forms. Combining responses to statements concerning the athiest's right to speak at a public meeting, have her or his book in a town library, and teach in a college it is found that the upper-class respondents are "tolerant" nearly one-half of the time, while lower-class respondents are at the extreme of "intolerance" at about the same proportion (see Table 12-15). The relationship between socioeconomic status and tolerance of atheists is quite direct and positive. Lower-status individuals do hold their religious beliefs in a more particularistic fashion.

396

Table 12–14. SES AND THREE SUBSIDIARY MEASURES OF
RELIGIOUS BELIEF (Church Member Sample)

	Percentage high on particularism		
	Lower	Middle	Upper
Liberal Protestants	23 (107)	15 (338)	12 (320)
Moderate Protestants	36 (131)	29 (300)	22 (239)
Conservative Protestants	76 (112)	62 (149)	69 (49)
Roman Catholics	37 (110)	37 (200)	20 (89)
	Percentage high on ultimate meaning typology		
	Lower	Middle	Upper
Liberal Protestants	30 (125)	22 (372)	21 (350)
Moderate Protestants	39 (145)	35 (345)	24 (259)
Conservative Protestants	50 (129)	42 (169)	39 (56)
Roman Catholics	52 (122)	51 (225)	50 (92)
	Percentage high on ethicalism		
	Lower	Middle	Upper
Liberal Protestants	54 (122)	49 (363)	50 (338)
Moderate Protestants	46 (149)	45 (338)	35 (256)
Conservative Protestants	56 (126)	44 (162)	35 (54)
Roman Catholics	55 (199)	58 (215)	40 (89)

Source: Stark, 1972:489.

Table 12–15. SES AND RELIGIOUS COMMITMENT
(Church Member Sample)

Mode of commitment	Direction of relationship with SES	
Public ritual involvement	Positive	
Religious knowledge	Positive	Church-like orientation
Participation in church organizations and activities	Positive	
Orthodoxy (as well as particularism, ultimate meaning, and ethicalism)	Negative	
Religious experience	Negative	Sect-like orientation
Personal devotionalism	Negative	
Communal involvement	Negative	

Source: Stark, 1972:494.

Table 12–16. SOCIOECONOMIC STATUS AND TOLERANCE OF ATHEISTS

| Tolerance | Socioeconomic Status | | | |
	Upper Class	Middle Class	Working Class	Lower Class
Intolerance	12.5	19.1	27.5	48.0
Little Tolerance	15.1	17.0	21.0	18.9
Some Tolerance	24.1	27.1	22.3	17.2
Tolerance	48.3	36.8	29.1	16.0
N	352	329	461	344

Source: NORC General Social Surveys, 1974–78.

There are some interesting differences in level of tolerance by socioeconomic status when denominations are compared (see Table 12-17). It appears that level of tolerance approximates the general social status of the various denominational groups. The highest level of tolerance is found among those denominations, regardless of class level, with the highest social status—Episcopalians, Presbyterians, and Jews. Similarly the lower-status, more conservative, Lutherans, Baptists, and Sectarians are least tolerant at all class levels. Nevertheless, the difference in tolerance holds for the socioeconomic strata regardless of denomination. With only minor exceptions, there is a direct relationship between class and the tendency to tolerate deviant religious beliefs.

RELIGION, SOCIOECONOMIC ACHIEVEMENT AND SOCIAL MOBILITY

The notion that religion might be implicated in social mobility and orientation toward achievement was implicit in Weber's major work, *The Protestant Ethic and the Spirit of Capitalism* (1858). He suggests that the values and norms of Calvinistic Protestantism lead to a rational, this-wordly asceticism that encouraged the development of a capitalist economy. From this assertion it is only a short step to the suggestion that Protestants, in Western society, have an economic advantage over other religionists, particularly Catholics.

In a review of the relationship between religious affiliation and socioeconomic achievement, Riccio (1979:200) notes with regard to Weber:

> Though primarily concerned with the religious origins of the capitalist spirit prior to the development of capitalism itself, Weber claimed that, even within the European capitalist societies of his time, religious affiliation was associated with attitudes toward economic behavior. This, he thought, explained the differential socioeconomic achievement that existed among certain religious groups. For example, he observed a greater tendency for Protestants, as compared with Catholics, to be owners of capital, business leaders, and more highly skilled laborers (1958:39). Yet, Weber also suggested that religious differences in economic behavior might decline.

What, then, is the situation with regard to socioeconomic achievement and religious affiliation today? Are Protestants still more likely to have an achievement orientation that leads to, or maintains, a more prestigious position in the economic system? Or, have the religious differentials with regard to economic behavior actually declined?

Table 12–17. SOCIOECONOMIC STATUS AND TOLERANCE OF ATHEISTS
BY AFFILIATION

| | | \multicolumn{4}{c}{Tolerance Level} | | | |
		Intolerant	Little Tolerance	Some Tolerance	Tolerant
Episcopal	Upper	6.7	6.7	40.0	46.7
	Middle	10.0	0.0	40.0	50.0
	Working	20.0	30.0	30.0	20.0
	Lower	0.0	0.0	50.0	50.0
Presbyterian	Upper	5.0	10.0	20.0	65.0
	Middle	15.8	10.5		42.1
	Working	7.7	46.2	23.1	23.1
	Lower	23.1	7.7	46.2	23.1
Jewish	Upper	10.0	0.0	30.0	60.0
	Middle	0.0	0.0	10.0	90.0
	Working	12.5	0.0	12.5	75.0
	Lower	40.0	0.0	20.0	40.0
Methodist	Upper	8.2	20.4	28.6	42.9
	Middle	28.2	15.4	17.9	38.5
	Working	38.6	19.3	21.1	21.1
	Lower	52.3	25.0	15.9	6.8
Catholic	Upper	12.9	14.0	22.6	50.5
	Middle	16.0	22.2	28.4	33.3
	Working	30.4	14.7	28.4	26.5
	Lower	45.9	15.3	22.4	16.5
Lutheran	Upper	12.0	20.0	36.0	32.0
	Middle	20.9	18.6	27.9	32.6
	Working	29.4	15.7	17.6	37.3
	Lower	46.7	13.3	13.3	26.7
Baptist	Upper	22.0	26.0	20.0	32.0
	Middle	29.1	25.5	23.6	21.8
	Working	34.0	24.5	17.9	23.6
	Lower	54.1	18.4	15.3	12.2
Sects	Upper	42.9	28.6	14.3	14.3
	Middle	18.5	18.5	29.6	33.3
	Working	11.5	46.2	23.1	19.2
	Lower	69.6	17.4	4.3	8.7

N = 1218

Source: NORC General Social Surveys, 1974–78.

These questions were addressed directly by Lenski in a study of *The Religious Question* (1961) in Detroit, Michigan. He reported that there was, at least for the males in his probability sample, a significant difference in occupational achievement according to the different religious groupings which he used. In particular, that no difference was to be found between Protestants and Catholics, especially when controls were introduced for certain intervening variables (see Gockel, 1969; Goldstein, 1969; Mueller, 1971). One study, indeed, showed that Catholics actually had a higher median family income than Protestants (Mueller and Lane, 1972).

Lenski's study seemed to demonstrate that in at least one city, Weber's thesis continued to be true. Yet a variety of criticism have been leveled at the study and its conclusions; criticisms which suggest that the religious differences in socioeconomic standing have disappeared or even been reversed.

Bouma (1973) and Gaede (1977) both reviewed a number of studies which assessed the differences in socioeconomic mobility for Protestants and Catholics and concluded that there is little evidence that any real variation remains which is based on differential religious affiliation. Bouma was concerned with three basic questions concerning religiosity and individual social mobility; first focusing his study on the differentials in the social status of Catholics and Protestants. In assessing ten different research reports, in addition to that of Lenski, he found that the results presented mixed findings. Two of the studies (Crowley and Ballweg, 1971; Porter, 1965) agreed with Lenski's findings that Protestants led Catholics in terms of social status. Another study (Morgan et al., 1962) divided Protestants into those who were liberal and those who were fundamentalist, and showed that only the liberal Protestants were ahead of Catholics in terms of status. Some other studies (Burchinal and Kenkel, 1962; Crespi, 1963) reported he indicated that white, Protestant males were more likely to attain or maintain upper middle-class status than were Catholics (or, for that matter, black Protestant males). Catholics were seen as more likely to be in the lower half of the working class than were Protestants.

Bouma also found mixed results when he looked at the question of intergenerational mobility. Three studies, in addition to that of Lenski, reported that Protestants had greater upward mobility than did Catholics (Mayer and Sharp, 1962; Crowley and Ballweg, 1971; Jackson et al., 1970). However, two other studies (Glenn and Hyland, 1967; Mueller, 1971) indicated that whatever differences might once have existed between the two religious groupings are diminishing to the point that no difference can be found. In looking at mobility within a single generation the same mixture of findings were found. Alston's (1969) study, using national poll data, indicated that a reversal had taken place in the common assumption of Protestant superiority; that is, Catholics now show greater mobility. However, both Greeley (1969) and Featherman (1971) could find no differences between Catholics and Protestants. In summary, Bouma's analysis of these eleven studies concludes that there is little evidence to show that the religious beliefs of the two traditions now lead to differences in socioeconomic mobility.

In a later review, Gaede (1977) looked at several studies not considered by Bourma. Two of these (Organic, 1963; Weller, 1963) can be added to those which show that Protestants continue to have an advantage over Catholics so far as upward social mobility is concerned. However, four studies not included in Bouma's review report that no difference exists (Greeley, 1963; Lipset and Bendix, 1959; Mack et al., 1956; Schuman, 1971). Gaede goes on to suggest that the mixed results found in these studies are likely the result of differences in the way in which the investigators controlled for intervening variables. Factors which seem to have a consistent influence on occupational mobility are "ethnicity, generation of immigration, age, region reared, and community size reared" (Gaede, 1977:60). Among these, the size of the community in which one resides, the region of the community in which it is located, and one's educational attainment seemed most important. When these factors are controlled, no differences are found in occupational mobility for Protestants and Catholics. However, a Protestant advantage was found in those studies which controlled for father's occupation, generation in this country, region of the country reared, ethnicity, and community size (Gaede, 1977).

In still another attempt to unravel the link between religious affiliation and socioeconomic status, Riccio (1979) looked at seventeen studies, eight of which had not been considered by either Bouma or Gaede. He looked at four aspects of socioeconomic mobility: occupation, income, education, and achievement orientation. Insofar as occupation is concerned six of the studies (Lenski, 1961; Mayer and Sharp, 1962; Jackson et al., 1970; Goldstein, 1969; Glenn and Hyland, 1967; and Lipset and Bendix, 1959) showed an advantage for Protestants while three (Mack et al., 1956; Warren, 1970; and Kohn, 1969) found that there was no difference between the two religious groups. When education, income, and achievement orientation were considered, the results were equally mixed. The studies were almost equally divided in finding Protestants superior to Catholics or in reporting that differences existed (in addition to studies already cited, see Rosen, 1969; Veroff et al., 1962; Greeley, 1963). The only study reporting any instance in which Catholics were ahead of other religious groups was that of Greeley (1963) in which it was reported that money was more important to Catholics than to either Protestants or Jews. Greeley and Rossi (1966) also found that Catholics who had had a parochial education had a slight advantage over Catholics who had not although Bressler and Westoff (1963) found no such difference.

Of course a specific difficulty in such research, as can be seen from many of the comments in other sections of this chapter, is that Protestantism is by no means a monolithic religious structure. The presently held social statuses of the different Protestant groups are probably the most significant factors in the mobility of members of these groups. Thus, for example, the already upper-status Episcopalians are more likely to have upward occupational mobility than are the lower-status Baptists or Pentecostals. In short, if Protestants are considered as one whole the results in Protestant-Catholic differentials in social mobility will be mixed. However, when Protestantism is considered as a number of different status groups, rather than a single whole, many of the disputes disappear (Lauer, 1975). It appears that Catholics are less upwardly mobile than *some* Protestant groups while being more mobile than others.

In summary of his own review, Riccio concludes that "religious affiliation does not explain much of the variance in socioeconomic achievement" (1979:226). Given the attention that has been paid over the years to Weber's Protestant ethnic thesis, are we now to conclude that it no longer has any significance or that it has not really been important in the history of our society? Two things may be noted. First, a number of the important institutions in our society have developed as a result of this ethic, even though they may no longer be dominated by it. Further, Protestantism has produced attitudes which have had a profound influence on the mobility of members of certain lower-class Protestant groups such as the Salvation Army and a number of Pentecostal groups. Second, it has been alleged that for some individuals a change in social status is followed by a change in religious affiliation, particularly in the case of upward mobility. We now look at this suggested tendency.

Socioeconomic Achievement and Religious Mobility

In a relatively small Presbyterian church in a suburban community in the mid-1950s a group of twenty sets of parents stands before the chancel with their 35 children, ranging in age from infants of less than six months old to ten-year-olds. They are there so that their children may receive "infant" baptism. The significance of their being there, especially those whose children are well beyond the time of their infancy, is that most of these persons had come from a church which did not practice infant baptism, generally a church which was not only more conservative than the Presbyterian church in which they now stood but also had considerably less prestige in their communities. In short, these are upwardly mobile young persons; families who have risen above the status of their parents in terms of occupation, education, and/or income. They have achieved a new social status in the general society—and their change of religion is an outward mark and sign of that change in status. As they have moved upward in society, they are also moving upward in the prestige of their religious behavior; not only as a symbol of status, but as an expression of those new needs which seem to be a part of the new status.

This vignette makes an implication common to both popular and sociological thought: that religious mobility follows social mobility. That is, as an individual moves up the social status ladder there is a tendency to shift religious affiliation to a denomination which enjoys higher prestige; Baptists become Methodists, Methodists join the Presbyterians, and Presbyterians turn into Episcopalians. Demerath (1965:71n) expresses it as "playing musical church to a status-striving tune." Warren emphasizes that this may be a two-way street (1970:149-50):

> . . . if a person rises substantially above the norm for his religious group or falls substantially below it, he may find that his religious preference no longer reflects his values nor meets his needs: and as a result, he may seek a new preference that will reinforce his new socioeconomic position.

In short, a new socioeconomic status, whether a higher or a lower social position, seems to call for a new religious status also. Such an assertion, laying aside any changes concerning hypocrisy, seems perfectly sensible. Religious affiliation not only symbolizes a new position, it tends to speak to the particular needs of the social status. However, this shift in religious allegiance may be supported more in inference than on the basis of evidence.

Lauer (1975) suggests that such is, indeed, the case. In an examination of occupational mobility in a small city of 11,000 population located in a Midwestern metropolitan area, he concludes that, in general, religious mobility is not attendant on occupational mobility. However, there is some evidence from his data to indicate that when the mobility in occupational status is extreme there is a relationship between mobility and a change in religious status; where there is considerable distance between the old and the new occupational status there will be a tendency to make a shift in religious affiliation. In addition, he found that educational attainment (a form of status movement) has an independent effect on religious mobility; attainment of a higher educational status does lead to movement to a more prestigious religious affiliation. Actually, Lauer's findings support the "up and out" idea put forth by Glock and Stark (1968). That is, for the majority of those who are religiously mobile the tendency appears to be to switch to a high-status denomination or to stop practicing the Christian faith, at least in traditional ways.

Nelsen and Snizek (1976) studied this same phenomenon, referring to it as "musical pews." Using data from a national election sample which included intergenerational measures of both religious and occupational mobility, they concluded that there was no evidence to support the thesis that religious mobility followed social mobility. Rather they contend that it is the stable worker at either the white- or blue-collar level who feel free to make a move in their religious affiliation; with stable white-collar individuals moving up and blue-collar workers making a shift downward in prestige. They did find that there was a closer relationship between religious and occupational mobility for rural residents. Nelsen and Snizek feel that this may be because religion has a greater possibility for conferring prestige in an atmosphere where ties are close and the behavior and affiliations of individuals more a matter of public knowledge. By inference, then, a change in religious affiliation would have little effect on one's status in the more anonymous relationships of the urban area.

It seems that the idea of "playing musical church to a status-striving tune" (Demerath, 1965:71n) may be based on the sort of impressionistic conclusions implied in Berger's statement (1961:74) that: "We are all familiar with the young Baptist salesman who becomes an Episcopalian sales executive." Yet the image is so familiar that it is difficult to accept the proposition that no such relationship exists.

Nelsen and Snizek's findings concerning rural-urban differences in this relationship provides an interesting clue in this regard. It may well be that playing "musical pews" is related to a particular locality. It seems reasonable to suggest that such mobility will be more likely where religion is important enough to confer meaningful status to the individual. If, as in the large metropolitan area, there is nothing to be gained by shifting religious allegiance there would seem to be little impetus to make the change; however, in the smaller community, in the South particularly, a change in denominational affiliation can give a new status in the community and thus a change may well be the result of change in occupational status.

A second suggestion concerning religious and occupational mobility is that religious mobility does follow occupational mobility—but without actually changing denominational label. The idea, as yet not investigated, is that while the occupationally mobile individual may not change denominations, there may be a change in status of the particular congregation of that denomination to which the individual belongs. It has been found, for example, that Mennonites in one small community with a number of Mennonite congregations have made such movement (Kaufman, 1972). Within the Mennonite community the congregations are status-typed and as individuals are upwardly mobile—particularly as they move from farm related occupations—there is a tendency to shift affiliation to the most liberal, and prestigious, Mennonite congregation. Informal observation of the memberships of Southern Baptist and Church of Christ congregations in the Southwest indicates a similar kind of religious mobility may go on in these denominations. Congregations in these denominations clearly show differences in status and membership does appear to be aligned, to some extent, to class differences. Thus it is reasonable to suggest that as individuals are socially mobile they will also change their membership from one congregation to another nearer their new status level. One might say that this could be related to a change in residence that accompanies the occupational or social mobility; but this is just another aspect of the total status game.

SUMMARY

In our religiously pluralistic society the variety of different religious organizations is subject to the effects of the social stratification system as are all other aspects of social and economic life. Denominations (and sects) are generally perceived to have different levels of prestige, and their memberships are drawn disproportionately from the several status levels of the community. In a particular locale the prestige of any given congregation is generally known, if only subconsciously, and membership in a given congregation may denote or seal a place in the general status hierarchy of the community.

During the first half of this century a number of community studies served to demonstrate, among other things, that the choice of a religious affiliation and style of religiosity are closely linked to one's position on the socioeconomic status ladder. Most notably Liston Pope's *Millhands and Preachers* described the membership and religious lifestyle of the religious groups in a North Carolina community. Returning to the same town in the late 1970s, another group of researchers found that while there had been changes in the specific differences between the churches, a strong socioeconomic impact could be seen in the life of each of them so that groupings of churches could be described in social class terms. Each had its style which reflected the majority socioeconomic status of the membership.

Studies based upon a number of the factors which make up one's socioeconomic status consistently characterize certain religious groups as having either high status or low. Studies separated by 25 years both indicate, for instance, that Episcopalians are disproportionately drawn from the upper levels of socioeconomic status while Baptists and sectarian members are drawn more frequently from individuals in the lower rungs of the status ladder. Further, the strength of one's affiliation with a particular church is also affected, to some degree, by social status.

In keeping with much of the thought about the church-sect dichotomy discussed in Chapter 4, it is also seen that the ways in which people are religious vary with social class. Many studies report that higher status individuals are more likely to attend church than are individuals from the lower class. It does seem true to say that participation in the public services or organizational life of the group are more characteristic of higher status individuals, as is possession of greater knowledge about the religious group. On the other hand, orthodoxy in religious belief, attributing ultimate meaning to the religious faith, and a connection between ethics and religious belief is seen as characteristic of the lower class (Pope, 1972). These connections may be summarized by saying that although sect-like and church-like characteristics are found for different members in each of the groups, there is a stronger tendency for upper-status members to display "church-like" religiosity while those from the lower status are more likely to display "sect-like" characteristics in their religiosity.

In this chapter we have really discussed just one kind of stratification—that based on socioeconomic factors. There are however other dimensions upon which the society is stratified, such as racial and ethnic group memberships. In the next chapter we will look at the relationship between such racial and ethnic status as it affects religious beliefs and participation and as religion plays a part in the lifestyle of such groups.

REFERENCES

Alston, Jon P.
1969   "Occupational placement and mobility of Prot-
                estants and Catholics, 1953-1964." Review of
                Religious Research 10 (Spring):135-40.

Berger, Peter
1961   *The Precarious Vision*. Garden City: Doubleday.
Bouma, Gary
1973   "Beyond Lenski: A critical review of recent
                Protestant Ethic research." *Journal for the Scien-
                tific Study of Religions* 12:141-155.

Bressler, Marvin and
Charles F. Westoff
1963   "Catholic education, economic values and
                achievement." *American Journal of Sociology*
                69:225-33.

Bultena, Louis
1949   "Church membership and church attendance in
                Madison, Wisconsin." *American Sociological
                Review* 14:384-89.

Burchinal, Lee G., and
William F. Kenkel
1962   "Religious identification and occupational status
                of Iowa grooms, 1953-1957." *American
                Sociological Review* 27 (August):526-532.

Crespi, Irving
1963   "Occupational status and religion." *American
                Sociological Review* 28 (February):131.

Crowley, James W., and
James A. Ballweg
1971   "Religious preference and wordly success."

Sociological Analysis 32 (Summer):71-80.

Demerath, N. J., III
1961   *Religious Orientation and Social Class.* Masters Thesis: University of California, Berkeley.
1965   *Social Class in American Protestantism.* Chicago: Rand McNally.

Earle, John, Dean Knudsen, and Donald Shriver
1976   *Spindles and Spires.* Atlanta: John Knox Press.

Featherman, David L.
1971   "The socioeconomic achievement of white religio-ethnic sub-groups: Social and psychological explanations." *American Sociological Review* 36 (April):207-22.

Fukuyama, Yoshio
1961   "The major dimensions of church membership." *Review of Religious Research* 2:154-61.

Gaede, Stan
1977   "Religious affiliation, social mobility, and the problem of causality: A methodological critique of Catholic-Protestant socioeconomic achievement studies." *Review of Religious Research* 19 (Fall):54-62.

Gallup, George
1975   *Religion in America: 1975.* Princeton, N.J.: Gallup International.

Glenn, Norval D., and Ruth Hyland
1967   "Religious preference and worldly success: Some evidence from national surveys." *American Sociological Review* 32 (February):73-85.

Gockel, Galen L.
1969   "Income and religious affiliation: A regression analysis." *American Journal of Sociology* 74 (May):632-47.

Goldstein, Sidney
1969   "Socio-economic differentials among religious groups in the United States." *American Journal of Sociology* 74 (May):612-31.

Greeley, Andrew M.
1963   *Religion and Career: A Study of College*

Graduates. New York: Sheed and Ward.

1969   "Continuities in research on the religious factor." *American Journal of Sociology* 75 (November):355-359.

Greeley, Andrew M. and
Peter H. Rossi

1966   *The Education of Catholic Americans.* Chicago: Aldine.

Hollingshead, August B.

1949   *Elmtown's Youth.* New Haven, Conn.: Yale University Press.

Jackson, Elton F.,
William S. Fox, and
Harry J. Crockett, Jr.

1970   "Religion and occupational achievement." *American Sociological Review* 35 (February):48-63.

Kaufman, Edward

1972   *Urbanization and Religious Mobility: The Mennonites.* Unpublished senior thesis. Valparaiso, Ind.: Valparaiso University.

Kohn, Melvin L.

1969   *Class and Conformity: A Study in Values.* Homewood, Ill.: Dorsey.

Lauer, Robert H.

1975   "Occupational and religious mobility in a small city." *Sociological Quarterly* 16 (Summer):380-92.

Lenski, Gerhard E.

1961   *The Religious Factor.* Garden City, New York: Doubleday.

Lipset, Seymour M., and
Reinhard Bendix

1959   *Social Mobility in Industrial Society.* Berkeley, Calif.: University of California Press.

Lynd, Robert and Helen
Lynd

1929   *Middletown.* New York: Harcourt & Brace.

Mack, Raymond W.,
Raymond J. Murphy and
Seymour Yellin

1956   "The Protestant Ethic, level of aspiration and

social mobility: An empirical test." *American Sociological Review* 21 (June):295-300.

Mayer, Albert J., and
Harry Sharp
1962   "Religious preference and wordly success." *American Sociological Review* 27 (April):218-227.

McKinney, B. B.
1924   *The Nail-Scarred Hand.* Nashville: Broadman Press.

Morgan, James N., Martin H. David, Wilbur J. Cohen, and Harvey E. Brazer
1962   *Income and Welfare in the United States.* New York: McGraw-Hill.

Mueller, Samuel A.
1971   "The new triple melting pot: Herberg revisited." *Review of Religious Research* 13 (Fall):18-33.

Mueller, Samuel A., and
Angela V. Lane
1972   "Tabulations from the 1957 Current Population Survey on Religion: A contribution to the demography of American religion." *Journal for the Scientific Study of Religion* 11 (March):76-98.

Nelsen, Hart M., and
William E. Snizek
1976   "Musical pews: Rural and urban models of occupational and religious mobility." *Sociology and Social Research* 60:279-289.

Organic, Harold Nathan
1963   *Religious Affiliation and Social Mobility in Contemporary American Society: A National Study.* Ph.D. Dissertation: University of Michigan.

Pope, Liston
1942   *Millhands and Preachers.* New Haven: Yale University Press.

Porter, John
1965   *The Vertical Mosaic: An Analysis of Social Class and Power in Canada.* Toronto: University of Toronto Press.

Riccio, James A.
1979   "Religious affiliation and socioeconomic achieve-
ment." Pp. 179-228 in Robert Wuthnow (ed.).
*The Religious Dimension: New Directions in
Quantitative Research.* New York: Academic
Press.

Rosen, Bernard C.
1969   "Race, ethnicity, and the achievement
syndrome." Pp. 131-53 in B. C. Rosen et al.
(eds.). *Achievement in American Society.* Cambridge, Mass.: Schenkman.

Schneider, Herbert W.
1952   *Religion in Twentieth Century America.* Cambridge, Mass.: Harvard University Press.

Schuman, Howard
1971   "The religious factor in Detroit: Review, replica-
tion, and reanalysis." *American sociological
Review* 36 (February):30-48.

Scott, Lesbia
1929   *I sing a song of the Saints of God.* Wilton, Conn.:
Morehouse-Barlow.

Stark, Rodney
1972   "The economics of piety: Religious commitment
and social class." Pp. 483-503 in G. Thielbar
and A. Feldman (eds.), *Issues in Social Inequality.*
Boston: Little, Brown.

Stark, Rodney and
Charles Glock
1968   *American Piety: The Nature of Religious Commitment.* Berkeley: University of Southern California Press.

Veroff, Joseph, Gerald
Gurin, and Sheila Feld
1962   "Achievement motivation and religious
background." *American Sociological Review*
27:205-18.

Warner, W. Lloyd and
Paul S. Lunt
1941   *The Social System of a Modern Community.* New
Haven, Conn.: Yale University Press.

Warren, Bruce L.
1970   "Socioeconomic achievement and religion: The

American case." Pp. 130-155 in Edward O. Laumann (ed.), *Social Stratification.* Indianapolis, Indiana: Bobbs-Merrill.

Weber, Max
1958

The Protestant Ethic and the Spirit of Capitalism (translated by Talcott Parsons). New York: Scribners.

Weller, Neil J.
1963

Religion and Social Mobility in Industrial Society. Ph.D. Dissertation: University of Michigan.

West, James
1945

Plainville, U.S.A. New York: Columbia University Press.

Zygmunt, Joseph F.
1976

"Prophetic failure and chiliastic identity: the case of Jehovah's Witnesses." Pp. 203-215 in James M. Henslin (ed.), *Down to Earth Sociology.* New York: The Free Press.

Chapter 13

Religion, Race, And Ethnicity

We demonstrated in Chapter 12 the association between religion and stratification. Just as the values of certain social class levels are reflected in religion, so also are minority group values reflected in the religious beliefs and practices of minorities in the United States. However there is a difference: the emergence of the largest minority religious organization, the black church, is more than just a reflection of the social differentiation between the majority and the minority groups imposed originally by the white, Anglo population. It developed as a result of white supremacy, segregation, and discrimination. It endures as a repository of cultural traditions and pride. It reflects society's precarious racial and ethnic relations and challenges the moral consciousness of the religious realm in society.

Evidence and data indicate that racial and ethnic prejudice are sometimes related to certain religious beliefs. Often religious beliefs benignly tolerate the prevailing prejudices and the discriminatory practices of society. Some have charged that the eleven o'clock worship hour on Sunday morning is the most segregated time period each week (Pope, 1967). Even though this may be an exaggeration, religious groups do mirror the attitudes and practices of their members, regardless of the idealistic beliefs of the organization.

In this chapter we will examine the black church as the model of a minority group's religious expression. Other minority expressions are also discussed. In addition we will present a summary of the empirical evidence related to religious belief and racial and ethnic prejudice. Finally the phenomenon of anti-Semitism, the attitudes and behavior directed against Jews will be analyzed. Since anti-Semitism is deeply entrenched in the history of Western Civilization, it has special significance in our discussion of religion and prejudice.

THE BLACK CHURCH

Historical Development

As we illustrated in Chapter 6, the all-black Protestant church began early in the nineteenth century as a result of discrimination by white Protestants against "free blacks." However, the growth of the black church as a separate religious grouping did not gain momentum until after the Civil War. The rejections of black Baptists and black Methodists by white Southern Baptists and white Southern Methodists was the major impetus for the evolution of minority expressions of these denominations. In the white backlash to the policies of political Reconstruction, black Protestants in the South were encouraged to form separate denominations. The "Christian" paternalism of the antebellum South toward slaves in matters of religion was replaced by the "caste system" in all realms of social life, including religion, resulting in segregation between whites and blacks. For the most part the freed slaves were either uneducated or undereducated. The disenfranchisement of whites during Reconstruction did allow *some* blacks to achieve political and economic advantages.

These gains, however, were cut short as white Southerners reclaimed their political rights. As a result, the euphoria of Reconstruction was either nonexistent or short-lived for a vast majority of blacks. As economic, social, and political subservience replaced parity in these aspects of societal life, the religious aspect of black life took on increasing importance. Black religion filled the vacuum for blacks in education and in both social identity and social prestige. An overwhelming majority of institutions of higher learning for blacks was church-related. Not only did they educate ministers, but they also educated teachers. During the closing decades of the nineteenth century and the early decades of this century, blacks could establish a social identity within the segregated black community as a member of Zion Methodist Church or Bethel Baptist Church. Although Presbyterians and Disciples of Christ did not encourage blacks to form separate denominations, what few blacks belonged to these denominations were, for the most part, members of segregated congregations. The few black Catholics in the Southern states were also largely relegated to segregated parishes. In general, black Protestantism and black Catholicism became a separate expression of Protestantism and Catholicism. Sometimes these religious expressions were parallel expressions, but at other times, elements of a separate black culture permeated the religious realm of social life.

E. F. Frazier (1974) views the black church, particularly the Protestant black church, as the principal source of leadership development for blacks. This happened largely because of the absence or weakness of black educational and other socializing institutions outside the home. In spite of widely held maxims among sociologists who have studied black culture and society, a good amount of evidence exists that indicates that the development of a preeminent religious institution among blacks was something more than an attempt to copy white Protestantism. The "invisible religious institution" of the plantations during slavery allowed slaves to hear slave preachers. Thus the leadership position of the black clergyman began early in the religious traditions of black Americans. Because this practice of religion provided the earliest attempts at higher education for blacks, the minister was often the most educated or the only educated person in the southern rural communities of blacks. As large numbers of blacks migrated first to southern towns and cities and later to northern and midwestern cities, they carried with them black Protestantism, much as the European immigrants had brought Catholicism and continental Protestantism with them (Drake and Cayton, 1945).

The rural and the urban congregations for blacks were in control of blacks. According to Frazier, this control in a segregated South and a discriminating North served also as an agent of social control (1974: 37-40). It could sanction, as well as reward, behavior within the community. It could withhold, as well as confer, social prestige and identity. In the rigid days of segregation the black church in the South engaged in a kind of holding action regarding political action, although, even then, it was usually the center of black political life (Washington, 1964:58-605). Mostly as an organized entity, the black church adapted itself to the customs of segregation, and the black minister was often the "go between" for the white political structure and the black community.

In spite of these limitations, Frazier (1974:49) said that in the rural South, the local congregation represented the largest social group in which blacks could find an identity in an otherwise alienating society. Participant observations studies done in the 1930s and 1940s also suggest that this function was of vital importance in the maintenance of a black religious community (Winter, 1977: 275-276). According to Mays and Nicholson (1933), the Negro church had life and vitality greater than its creeds, rituals, and doctrines because of the important social bonds established between members. John Dollard's now classic study, *Caste and Class in a Southern Town* (1937), presented the black church as a "center for social solidarity." Further studies by Davis et al. (1941), Johnson (1934), and Powdermaker (1939) all cite the networks of social relationships for blacks through the black church. Generally speaking, then, a sense of community which cut across denominational lines emerged as the historical process of black religion in America occurred (Winter, 1977:277). Joseph Washington (1964:31) described black religiosity as uniting all blacks "in a brotherhood or sense of community which takes precedence over their individual patterns for the worship of God."

Since the historical development of the black church, both among slaves and freed slaves in the South and among freed blacks in the North was overwhelmingly Protestant in origin, does a separate black religious community, a "fourth religious community" in the phrase of Alan Winter (1977), truly exist? Evidence exists which both supports and reflects this thesis. Gunnar Myrdal's *American Dilemma* (1944) described the "Negro church" as quite similar to any lower-class white Protestant church, with no innovations in theology or in the general character of the church service (1944:866). Likewise, Frazier (1974: 9, 13-14) emphasizes that because blacks were virtually stripped of their social heritage in the United States, it is impossible to establish continuity between religious practices in Africa and religious practices by blacks in the United States. Another argument marshalled against the concept of a separate black religious community is the existence of black Catholics and more recently, Black Muslims, along side of the predominant black Protestants. A separate religious community consisting of the two traditions of Christianity and a non-Christian tradition ignores the historical and contemporary conflicts between Protestantism and Catholicism and between Christianity and Islam. It is further true that recruitment by Muslims often involves members of black churches in the urban ghettos, diluting the influence of the Christian church in those black neighborhoods.

On the other hand, Winter (1977) argues that "a religious community" need not have a firm origin. He cites Will Herberg's three-generation hypothesis concerning immigrant Catholics and Jews as evidence that the concept of a religious community is a new and unique social structure which developed under uniquely American conditions (Winter, 1977:271-272). The grandchildren of the immigrants (the third generation) identified themselves as members of a religious community, whereas the immigrants had viewed themselves as members of village communities and the children of immigrants saw themselves as members of ethnic communities. Winter further argues that a religious heritage is what makes for the maintenance of a religious community. Such a "religious heritage" is, for blacks, rooted deep within an overall black heritage based upon the experiences of "blackness" in the United States (Winter, 1977:272-273). Williams (1971:267) also lends support to this idea by claiming that blacks view themselves as a community in which religion is a source of a sense of oneness which overrides the differences between denominations, creeds, and religious practices. Washington (1964:30-31) cites the presence of a black "folk religion" which unites all blacks and transcends all religious and socio-economic barriers. In this regard, it must also be remembered that, until very recently, black Catholics were members of segregated parishes served often by black priests (Joseph Fichter's *Southern Parish* [1951] gives a detailed description of this Southern Catholic practice in Louisiana.)

Black sects and cults, including the Black Muslim movement, have stressed the heritage of black oppression, and the necessity to overcome such conditions by uniting religiously. In spite of the traditional accommodation by black churches to social and economic discrimination, the more effective political assertions of blacks in the arena of civil rights had their origins in the black churches of southern cities and towns. The great prestige of the religious institution within black America has definitely contributed to the gains made by blacks by providing a base of social solidarity as well as effective moderate leadership. Obviously disagreement exists between black Muslims and black Christians over basic religious beliefs. Other areas of disagreement among blacks in general involve political militancy and the separatist movement among some blacks. The black church is both praised and condemned for its role in these issues. Nevertheless, the points of agreement among blacks in reaction to the conditions of life in America and the dual role of black religion as both comforter and innovator do support Winter's view of a "religious community" among black Americans. In the 1960s and in the 1970s religion still remains important for blacks in the South and in the urban ghettos of the Northeast and the Midwest, be it Christian or Muslim.

By tentatively accepting Winter's hypothesis, we do not imply that white Protestantism and Catholicism are permanently separated from black Protestantism and Catholicism. Instead, we recognize that the black churches have distinctive identities, purposes, apart from the common identities and purposes shared with mainline Protestantism and the Roman Catholic Church. The continuing struggle for social and economic parity with white Americans remains an issue with which black religious leaders must deal. The historical processes—slavery, the Civil War, emancipation, and segregation—that gave rise to black religion in the United States are still influencing factors in the beliefs and the practices of black churches.

Characteristics of the Black Church

If a lay person were asked to differentiate between the religion of white and black Americans, that individual would probably identify the highly expressive qualities of a "typical" religious service in a black church as compared to the orderliness of a white church. Of course, the person would be referring to a black *Protestant* service. To a large extent this stereotype is true, but there are many exceptions to this picture. Black Catholics worship in much the same manner as do white Catholics, whether they attend mass in an integrated parish or in a predominantly black parish. Black congregations within predominantly white denominations largely follow the liturgies and rituals of the United Presbyterian Church, the Presbyterian Church in the United States (Southern), the United Methodist Church, the Protestant Episcopal Church, the United Church of Christ, and so forth. It is, then, the black denominational church to which the expressive stereotype is applied. Since an overwhelming majority of blacks who espouse and practice religion in the United States are members of black denominations, our attention must be directed primarily to these congregations.

Churches affiliated with the National Baptist Convention, U.S.A., Inc., the Progressive Baptist Convention, the National Baptist Convention of America; the African Methodist Episcopal Church; the African Methodist Episcopal Church Zion; and the Christian Methodist Episcopal Church account for 11,053,493 church members in the United States. In addition, the National Primitive Baptist Convention has 1,645,000 members. Table 13-1 shows black denominational membership. Data available from *The Ebony Handbook* (1974)

Table13-1. BLACK CHURCH MEMBERSHIP IN
MAJOR BLACK DENOMINATIONS
1974[1]

Denomination	Number of Members	Number of Churches	Number of Pastors
National Baptist Convention, U.S.A., Inc.	5,500,000 (1958)	26,000	27,500
National Baptist Convention of America	2,668,000 (1956)	11,398	7,598
African Methodist Episcopal Church	1,166,000 (1951)	5,878	7,089
African Methodist Episcopal Zion Church	770,000 (1959)	4,083	2,480
National Primitive Baptist Convention, Inc.	1,645,000 (1971)	2,198	601
Progressive National Baptist Convention, Inc.	505,000 (1965)	411	450
Christian Methodist Episcopal Church	444,493 (1961)	2,523	1,914

[1]All of the membership figures are for years earlier than 1974. The date for each figure is given in parenthesis.

Source: Rosten, 1975:375.

indicates that only 793,000 blacks are members of the predominantly white mainline Protestant denominations, 722,609 blacks are communicants of the Roman Catholic Church, and a very insignificant 1 percent of Judaism are blacks. In addition, blacks account for a small percentage of the members of predominantly white Holiness and Pentecostal sects, and for approximately 30 percent of the members of the Jehovah's Witnesses (Rosten, 1975). Obviously the proportion of blacks who are affiliated with black churches is overwhelming when compared to black membership within largely white religious groups.

As is true with "white" denominations, black denominations (and their congregations) reflect the boundaries of social class, geographical region, and, of course, race. Affluent congregations and parishes reflect a more middle-class approach to religious observances than do those congregations with a preponderance of working poor members. That is, these churches are more likely to have formal services, a vested clergy, and a robed choir. In addition, the leadership positions will be filled by a more educated laity. In contrast, the poorer black congregations will be less formal in their religious services and more expressive (and sect-like). Their board and committee positions will most likely be filled with persons who are employed in semi-skilled and unskilled occupations (Pope,1967).

Both extreme types of congregations, as well as those who are somewhere between affluence and nonaffluence, are likely to offer the membership elaborate social opportunities, friendship networks, and a predominantly black validation of social prestige (Lincoln,1974:116). To a large extent, the congregations of the black Protestant denominations practice an ecumenicism which minimizes denominational differences and magnifies the common purpose of religion for blacks (Frazier, 1974). The denominations previously listed as containing a majority of black religious affiliation are all members of the National Council of Churches of Christ. By such membership, they are also involved to some extent in the larger ecumenical movement within the United States.

By construct, those sects which appeal to blacks are similar to sects which appeal to whites. That is, they are of the "avoidance" type or the "aggressive" type. The avoidance sects remain aloof from the secular work and stress rewards in the life to come, since there is little chance that life on earth will get better. In black ghettos or the black areas of smaller cities, an observer can identify the storefront churches and "temples" representative of these sects. Aggressive sects that appeal to blacks offer change either in the individual or in a drastic alteration of the world. The Jehovah's Witnesses, with their appeal to blacks, offer such an opportunity.

By and large, however, religious life for black Americans has offered solace and accommodations for its members to a mostly prejudiced society. Examples of advocacy for social reform, for an end to segregation and discrimination have always been present, but only in the last two decades has this advocacy become more public. Because of the black church's accommodation to the social and institutional arrangements in the United States, critics have charged that black Christianity has historically been an "opiate of the black masses."

Opiate of the Black Masses

Karl Marx's thesis that religion serves as an "opiate of the masses" by supporting the existing economic (and political order) is seen by some as an explanation for the lack of *radical* revolt against segregation and discrimination after the triumph of white supremacy near the end of the nineteenth century. As early as 1900, W. E. B. Dubois, one of the founders of the NAACP, wrote that the black denominations gave social and economic concerns less priority. Dubois charged that instead they were more concerned with maintaining moral standards, engaging in charity work, engaging in "social" activities, and maintaining their membership. Because of these denominations' dependence on white funds they did little to assert moral leadership against the subservient role expected of black organizations and black people (1971:77; first published in 1899).

Others have said that this accommodative function of religion began during slavery and that the black slaves were given Biblical commands that they should be obedient to their masters in order to obtain freedom in the afterlife (Stampp, 1956:158). In his analysis of race relations in the United States, Gunnar Myrdal (1944:851-853) states that, after the Civil War and well into the twentieth century, the black church in the South sublimated frustration into emotionalism and lack of opportunity into a fixation on the afterworld. John Dollard's study of the small southern town reached a similar conclusion: "religion can be seen as a mechanism for the social control of Negroes" (Dollard, 1937:248). Lincoln (1974:108) wrote that because the black denomination was the one institution under black control, black religious leaders did little to jeopardize the autonomy of the black church by challenging the segregation of the southern states.

On the other hand, as Gary T. Marx (1967:64-72) points out, the apparent acceptance by religious blacks of the prevailing social order was not without its protests historically. Marx states that "all Negro churches first came into being as protest organizations and later some served as meeting places where protest strategy was planned, or as stations on the underground railroad" (1967:66). In other words, the black church occasionally protested but usually advocated gradualism in the arena of race relations and civil rights until the desegregation decision of the United States Supreme Court in 1954 (Glenn, 1964).

Marx's empirical study sheds some illumination on the charge that the black church has served as an opiate for black people. He first considers the effect of particular denominations on militancy, and second considers the relationship between religiosity of the respondents and militancy. The data reveal that those blacks who are members of sects and cults are the least likely to advocate militancy in the struggle for civil rights. However, members of predominantly black denominations are not as militant as are the blacks who are members of largely white denominations (such as the Episcopal Church, the United Presbyterian Church, the United Church of Christ, and the Roman Catholic Church). In measuring the degree of association between expressions of religiosity and militancy, Marx reports that militancy increases significantly as the "importance of religion" for respondents decreases. He reports that there seems to be a basic incompatibility between piety and protest (Marx, 1967:64-72).

In another study, the focus is directed at the types of ministers in the black church and their advocacy of gradualism or activism in the civil rights movement. Ronald L. Johnstone (1969) indicates that there are three ideal types of black Protestant ministers: the *militant*, the *moderate*, and the *traditionalist*. In his study which consisted of interviews with a 25 percent random sample of all black clergymen in Detroit, Johnstone found that the *traditionalist* minister "is passive with regard to challenges to the prevailing social order. His attitudes and thoughts will rarely be framed in protest even to himself, nor will he join in attempts at aggressive action." The moderate clergyman is well aware of the conditions of blacks and is much more inclined to do something about the plight of his people than is the traditionalist. The moderate's methods, however, include being a peacemaker, a gradualist, and the "treader-down-the-middle-of-the-road." He or she does not see religion as completely involved only with spiritual affairs, but also with concern for the social concerns of church members. The traditionalists see their religious task as solely spiritual—preaching, converting people, and leading their people to heaven (Johnstone, 1969). The traditionalists among black clergy seem then to preach a kind of religion that is otherwordly and spirited. In Johnstone's study these ministers were older, less educated, pastors of small congregations (predominantly Baptist and Pentecostal), and from a low socioeconomic background. One can conclude, then, that religion is an opiate for escape from the conditions of poverty experienced by the congregations served by the "Traditionalist" preachers. However, the presence of moderates and militants among black ministers indicates that religion for blacks can and does serve another purpose.

Militancy

Those ministers who can be classified as moderates and militants have, since the inception of the Civil Rights movement, included the advocacy of political and economic rights as a part of black religion. In a sense, these religious leaders have sought to return their religious organizations to positions that they held when black churches began—organizations protesting the racism and discrimination of the white church (and white America in general). Barbara Hargrove (1979:148-149) reports that the local black church became an important forum for the development and expression of opinion in the black community. It also provided an arena for leadership and authority when few other arenas existed. The black church served as a welfare agency to the poor, the disabled, and the ill. Because these activities were in existence, the leaders in the struggle for civil rights, particularly in the South, utilized this structure for advocating resistance, nonviolence, and even militance.

Martin Luther King, Jr. is, of course, the best known of the black civil rights leaders who combined the moral principles of Christianity with effective political action in behalf of civil rights. Since he was trained in theology and was pastor of a Baptist church in Montgomery, Alabama, King effectively marshalled support from a large segment of the black religious community to sustain a boycott against the bus company there in 1955. It was successful, and segregation in that public transportation facility was ended.

Out of this success grew the Southern Christian Leadership Conference which utilized both the symbols and the rhetoric of black Protestantism as an underpinning to its philosophy of nonviolence in effecting social and political change. Joining King were several other black ministers in the leadership roles, most notably Ralph Abernathy, Andrew Young, and Hosea Williams. These leaders stressed the immorality of segregation and discrimination, offering as an alternative integration and brotherhood. King was particularly effective in utilizing the preaching style of black Protestantism with its cadence that allows the audience to verbally agree and show support. He added to this rich allegories from black religion: "the promised land," a "new Jerusalem," "going to the mountaintop." These phrases took on a new political and social meaning, particularly to southern blacks. Martin Luther King was most successful in appealing to southern blacks steeped in black religion. Although he offended diehard segregationists in the South, his religiously oriented movement gradually gained widespread acceptance with white moderates and liberals throughout the country. In addition Wilson (1978:376) reports that individual church people were prominent in rallies and marches and that individual congregations gave food and shelter to civil rights workers. These efforts, however, reflected the white philosophy that in the end the white majority in America would morally support the political and economic plight of black Americans.

In retrospect, however, King and the Southern Christian Leadership Conference were only mildly militant. A militancy among blacks more harsh in rhetoric, more laced with demands, and more antiwhite emerged from the earlier years of the civil rights struggle. In 1967, James Forman startled the liberal white Protestant denominations by asking for "reparations" to pay for past economic exploitation of blacks. He obviously spoke for a group of blacks unwilling to settle for moral support from white Christianity. Instead the Black Economic Development Council, a subsidiary of the National Committee of Black Churchmen, demanded that white churches make a significant contribution to show good faith in the civil rights movement. This manifesto caused considerable internal conflict within the denominations which considered the idea (Hargrove, 1979:151). However, many black churchmen opposed these reparations of James Forman, and those who did support them chose to interpret the demands as a call for better opportunities for blacks to compete in the American economy (Wilson, 1978:376).

In another aspect of militancy black churchmen and churchwomen have established "black caucuses" in predominantly white denominations. In the Roman Catholic Church there exists a black caucus that speaks out on matters relevant to the black community. It also has protested the assignment of all white staff to black parishes. There is also a Black Sisters' conference and a lay group called United Black Catholics (Hargrove, 1979:151). Similarly Protestant denominations have black caucuses that are organized and visible. Hargrove (1979:151) reports that these are "often nurtured by a denominational staff who feel keenly the charges of hypocrisy leveled against a church that shows racial separation and discrimination."

New Themes in Black Religion

The turn toward militancy in behalf of more rapid economic change for blacks also produced a militant *black theology*. This new expression of religion rejected both resignation and accommodation by blacks. Instead it stressed the more radical elements of the Christian faith. Although aspects of this "radical impulse" have been present in black religion since its separation from white religion, this liberal variant of Christianity did not receive extensive theological treatment until the 1960s. As a theological interpretation, black liberation stresses Christianity's theme of good news to the poor and oppressed which has more relevance in the black ghetto than in the affluent white suburb (Hargrove, 1979:151).

James Cone, one of the spokesmen for black theology, has stated that the church must try to recover the man Jesus by totally identifying itself with the poor and the suffering. It must, therefore, identify itself with the black power movement which advocates rights for the poor and the oppressed (1969:3). It is really a variant of a larger theology of liberation and of hope. Black theology has in common with these various theologies an emphasis upon the Kingdom of God (on Earth) and the place in it of the poor and the oppressed (Hargrove, 1979:152-153).

Another expression of black theology is expressed by Albert B. Cleage, Jr. (1974:298-301). He calls for a "revolutionary black church" totally committed to the struggle for "black liberation." Cleage argues that Christianity began in Africa as one of the religions available to blacks in Africa (the Coptic Christian Church). The whites of Europe and America have distorted Christianity and its message. Cleage sees the first task of a new "black church" as one of liberating the black person's mind away from what he calls "fairy tales" to thinking through solutions to everyday problems of living. He also advocates a Black Nationalist Movement in which the black religious institution would be liberated from its heritage of comforter.

Cleage's emphasis upon black separatism is akin to the more ascetic separatism of the Black Muslims. Although Black Muslims began as a movement in the 1930s, they did not receive much attention until the 1960s. Most of the converts to this black variant of the Islamic faith are ex-Christians in the inner city areas of the United States. C. Eric Lincoln states that blacks in America are, according to Muslim belief, the "lost Nation of Islam in North America" (1973:72). Black Muslims teach that the "white devils" have been allocated 6,000 years to rule. In a short time the chosen of Allah will be resurrected from the mental death imposed upon them by the white man (Lincoln, 1973:79-80). Elijah Muhammad, the head of the Black Muslims from the 1930s until his death in 1975, preached a militant hatred of whites. This theme was expanded by Malcolm X, and succeeded in bringing the Black Muslims many new members and national attention. An open break with Elijah Muhammad caused a bitter schism within the Muslim movement and cost Malcolm X his life (Rosten, 1975:380).

Following this assassination, the Muslims retreated into the background of the black power struggle and began to practice the purities of the Islamic faith. These include a revering of Allah as God and the Koran as sacred scripture. If Muslims are orthodox, they adhere to strict disciplines concerning food, tobacco, liquor, fasting, and cohabitation. Pork, tobacco, alcohol, and cohabitation are forbidden; fasting is encouraged. Asceticism is an ideal. The devout Black Muslims eat only an evening meal after a full day's work. The recreation of Muslims usually centers around temple work, proselytizing in the streets of the inner city, or reading the Koran at home (Rosten, 1975:381).

The manhood of blacks is stressed and, according to Islamic belief, the subservience of women is preached. According to Wilson (1978:127-128), the convert to the Muslim movement is encouraged to stop seeing old friends and to make new friendships within the movement. Black Muslims encourage new members to change their names, not only to symbolize rebirth, but to deny their "Negroness." The old name is seen as a "slave name" that must be replaced with a Muslim name. Cassius Clay became Muhammad Ali, and Lew Alcindor became Kareem Abdul Jabbar.

Despite their stress upon living life according to ascetic principles by withdrawing from as much contact as possible with the white world, there continues to be violence within the Black Muslim community. Following the assassination of Malcolm X in 1965, the several sects within the faith have fought among themselves concerning religious differences (Rosten, 1975:381). In 1978, two rival sects engaged in a shoot-out which eventually resulted in several innocent bystanders being held hostage in the Federal Court Building in Washington, D.C. Kareem Abdul Jabbar has bodyguards to protect him from possible violence inflicted by rival Black Muslim sects.

Although their numbers are small as compared with those of black Christians, the Black Muslims have increased their influence in the urban ghettos. Muslim schools have achieved recognition for their stress of basic educational techniques. According to *Newsweek* (1973:61-62), Black Muslims are believed to own real estate, businesses, shops, and farms worth around 75 million dollars. To this extent the Muslim community has chosen to work within the economic framework of the United States. This economic prosperity has legitimized the Black Muslim faith. Non-Muslim blacks recognize their success, and many are anxious to enroll their children in Muslim schools. Much of the more militant "antiwhite" hatred has become muted since the death of Elijah Muhammad in 1975. Theoretically, whites can now join this "Lost Found Nation of Islam."

It would seem, then, that both the black theology of liberation and the growth of the Black Muslim sect offer alternatives to traditional expressions of Christianity for American blacks. The new theology directly challenges the historical role of accommodation and gradual reform practiced by the black church in its relations with white America by advocating a religion that will actively solve the oppression of minorities through radical action. Black Muslims offer an alternative to Christianity, that emphasizes African heritage, black self-help, and a new black identity for the convert.

OTHER MINORITY EXPRESSIONS

America's ethnic groups, European, Oriental, and Hispanic, historically brought religious practices that were unique compared to American religious expression. The Catholic ethnic groups held on to many practices that were indigenous to their country of origin. Many of the Northern European and Scandinavian Lutheran groups maintained the practice of having services in their native language. Gradually, however, most of these groups adapted to the prevalent customs in the United States. However, even today, there are ethnic variations in religious commitment and in religious practices.

Andrew Greeley (1979) demonstrates that ethnic variations among Protestants and Catholics do exist. By using three data sources—a National Opinion Research Center General Social Survey, a Basic Beliefs File, and the NORC parochial school studies—Greeley presents some tentative conclusions concerning ethnicity in religion. Based upon the available data, Greeley demonstrates that the more devout Catholic groups—the Irish, the Germans, the Slavs, and the French—attend church regularly in greater proportion than the general American public. He reports that slightly under half of the American population goes to church at least two or three times a month; but that among the devout Catholic groups, approximately three-fifths attend that often. By contrast, Italian and Hispanic Catholics are little different from the national average (Greeley, 1979:118-119).

Greeley, in summarizing the data from the NORC General Social Surveys, says that ethnicity seems *less important* than religious affiliation as a predictor of church attendance, belief in life after death, and religiously mixed measures. German Catholics are the most likely to go to church and the most likely to believe in life after death. They are least likely to have entered into a religiously mixed marriage. Irish and Slavic Catholics demonstrate less religious loyalty than Germans; and Italian and Hispanic Catholics demonstrate the least religious loyalty. (Greeley, 1979:122).

425

In contrast to the ethnic variations in religious practices among Catholics suggested by Greeley, Charles H. Anderson (1970) states that white Protestant ethnic groups today are relatively well assimilated into "American Protestantism." Old world distinctiveness previously demonstrated among Lutherans, for example, have all but disappeared. Rarely is a Lutheran service conducted in German any longer, even in congregations of the Lutheran Church–Missouri Synod which maintained its German heritage for many decades.

However, distinctive religious expressions can be observed among Hispanic Catholics. Among Catholics of Mexican origin, their churches incorporate many folk practices into the sunday services and into the observances of Holy Days. William Martin (1979) describes one Mexican American Church in San Antonio, Texas: A mariachi band provided the music for the "folk mass"; and the liturgy of the mass, of course, was in Spanish. He also reported that the older women in the parish were more devout in observing Holy Days than were the typical Anglo Catholics. Much superstition and mysticism still permeates Catholicism as it is believed and practiced among Hispanics in the United States. In April, 1980, for example, a new church and shrine were dedicated in the Rio Grande Valley area of Texas. Many Mexican-Americans and Mexican Nationals believed that miracles and healing are available there.

On the other hand, many Hispanic Americans have abandoned Catholicism for smaller Protestant sects. There are a growing number of Spanish Assembly of God congregations, and Spanish Pentecostal groups. The former Mexican Baptist Convention of Texas became a part of the larger Baptist General Convention of Texas in 1969, but those Hispanic congregations continue to attract converts to their services conducted in Spanish. Many officials within the Roman Catholic Church are becoming alarmed at this exodus of Hispanic Catholics and are now encouraging predominantly Hispanic parishes to place greater emphasis upon the ethnicity of their memberships. Of all the ethnic groups that have been in the United States for some time, the Hispanics have maintained a distinctive minority expression of religion more than any other group, due mainly to their language difference and to their generally low level in the stratification system. In many ways, Hispanic Protestants and Catholics are similar to black Protestants in their distinctive religious practices.

Americans of Oriental origin who are members of Christian bodies frequently attend churches that are predominantly Chinese, Korean, and Japanese. Some of these congregations maintain services in native languages while others do not. With the recent influx of Indo-Chinese refugees, many Catholic parishes in cities that have sizeable refugee populations offer services in the particular languages of the refugee groups. This migration has included a number of priests and nuns, particularly from Vietnam and Thailand. Many of these individuals attend to the religious needs of the Indo-Chinese. Whether or not these newest immigrants will be assimilated into American Catholicism remains to be seen.

RELIGIOUS BELIEF AND RACIAL PREJUDICES

The very presence of a black religious community suggests that religion as a social institution reflects the prejudice present in all aspects of American society. We have demonstrated the historical bases for the development of the black church including overt hostility expressed by whites against blacks in matters of religion. In addition, we outlined the anti-Catholic (and antiethnic) prejudices of the Protestant majority as European Catholics migrated to America in the 1800s and early 1900s. Much of the antiethnic group prejudice of earlier decades has evaporated, but the prejudice against blacks (and also against Mexican-Americans, Puerto Ricans, and Indians) still remains.

Gordon Allport (1958:10) defines prejudice as "an antipathy based upon a faulty and inflexible generalization. It may be felt or expressed. It may be directed toward the group as a whole, or toward an individual because he (or she) is a member of that group. . . ." These feelings against entire groups or individuals is present among religious as well as nonreligious people. For blacks in the United States it has caused the development and maintenance of a "caste system." As Wilson (1978:321-322) states, "the precise contribution of the churches to the development of this caste system has been much debated. On the one hand, ethics of equality and brotherhood have inspired Christians to break down racial barriers and fight discrimination. On the other hand, the denominations are largely segregated, and many have long espoused and defended racist beliefs and practices. . . ." Even among the denominations with black members, these members tend to be in "segregated" local congregations or parishes. A Gallup Poll in 1977 indicated that 54 percent of whites attending church did so in churches with *no* black members (Gallup, 1977:3).

Although ethnic groups in our society—particularly those whose religious preference is overwhelmingly Roman Catholic—are no longer overtly hated and discriminated against, they still are the victims of economic, social, *and* religious stereotyping by some segments of the American population. So, too, are people whose religion is non-Christian or who are avowed atheists or agnostics. Witness, for example, the extreme uproar caused by Madylyn Murray O'Hare among church people whenever she attempts to limit some public expression of religion. It would appear that some relationship between religious beliefs and racial and ethnic prejudice do indeed exist. It is not enough to simply say that religious groups *reflect* racial and ethnic divisions in American society. Several issues are involved in the overall relationship between religious belief and prejudice: variations in levels of prejudice by different religious bodies, variation in strengths of prejudices by church attendance; and variations in prejudice between clergy and laity within the religious denominations.

Prejudice and Different Religious Groups

Just as not all social class levels or occupational groups are equally prejudiced, neither are all religious groups uniformly prejudiced. Andrew Greeley (1974:194) concludes from 1968 National Opinion Research Center data that Catholics are somewhat less racially prejudiced than Protestants. However, of the three major faiths in the United States, Jews seem the least racially prejudiced. Members of more theologically liberal Protestant denominations also tend to express less overt prejudice than do members of the more theologically conservative denominations within Protestant Christianity. On the other hand, these differences are not great and may be due to differences between social class levels and geographical regions (Wilson, 1978:328). For example Southern Baptists, who are conservative theologically and exhibit more prejudice than many Protestants are most concentrated in the south. Indeed, no white religious group of any size in America is "pure" in terms of having a completely non-prejudicial membership. Stark and Glock (1969:71) in an article concerning prejudice and the churches state that "while it is obvious that many Christians are moved by their faith to regard all men as brothers, it is equally obvious that the majority of those who throw rocks at Negro marchers, who picket schools to prevent integration, or who become agitated about keeping Jews off their local school boards . . . regard themselves as Christians. . . ."

They ask the question, "How much prejudice exists within the churches?" Their answer is to examine different levels of the organizational structure of the various church bodies at the official (or bureaucratic) level, among the clergy, or among the laity. The answer to the question also involves assessing religious prejudice (against persons of other faiths or denominations) and racial prejudice (Stark and Glock, 1969:71).

There do exist different degrees of prejudice between the various denominations' national bureaucracies. Nearly all the major denominations have spoken out forcefully against both religious and racial prejudice. However, the Lutheran Church-Missouri synod and the Southern Baptist Convention were less forceful in statements condemning anti-Semitism than the mainline Protestant denominations (Stark and Glock, 1969:72). A majority of denominations have also specifically opposed discrimination in schooling, housing, and employment.

If the examination of expressions of prejudice is extended to fundamentalist and other conservative sects, a different perspective emerges. Wilson (1978: 328-29) reports that fundamentalist churches are the most prejudiced of the religious groups. He further quotes David J. Harrell (1971:116) concerning racial prejudice and the religious sects: "The most rigid defense of racial prejudice and custom has come from the stable and well-established sects, composed of successful farmers, skilled laborers, (and) petty bourgeoisie." Wilson further states that two of the largest Pentecostal sects, the Assemblies of God and the

Pentecostal Holiness Church have always been white (1978:329). There still exists within these kinds of churches the persistent belief that the Bible prescribes the separation of races.

Thus, the official level of religious denominations largely reflects a low level of prejudice both religious and racial. However, religious groups are more than large bureaucracies. They consist also of people who claim affiliation and who demonstrate different degrees of institutional loyalty as demonstrated through church attendance and participation. If these aspects of religious life are taken into account, a further refinement of the relationship between religion and prejudice can be shown.

Prejudice and Differential Religious Participation

The overall relationship between religious participation, as measured by church attendance, and the expression of bigotry is curvilinear, according to McNamara (1974:303). He summarizes the research of Allport and later investigators as showing that those people exhibiting highest tolerance of racial and ethnic groups are on either extreme of a curve: they consist of individuals who "absolutely never attend or belong to no church; and, among attenders, those individuals who attend "more than weekly." The lowest level of racial and ethnic tolerance (and, therefore, the highest degree of prejudice) is found among people who are "regular" attenders (once a week to once a month).

After reviewing the many sociological studies concerning "religious" people and prejudice, Gorsuch and Alshire (1974:283) concluded that the studies do indicate that church members are more prejudiced than people who have never become members of churches. However, they also concluded that the occasional attender of religious services exhibits the greatest degree of prejudice.

Stark and Glock (1969:75-76) in discussing prejudice among the laity of churches report that a majority of church members are prejudiced, regardless of the frequency of their religious participation. In terms of religious prejudice, from half to two-thirds of American Christians would deny civil liberties to a person who does not believe in God. Racial prejudice also was characteristic of Christians surveyed by Stark and Glock. Among white Protestant and Catholic church members in the San Francisco Bay Area, nearly one-half said that they would move if several black families moved into their block. One third thought that blacks are less intelligent than whites. Hadden (1969) revealed that his 1967 national survey showed that 89 percent of the Christian laity felt that blacks should take advantage of the opportunities society offers and stop protesting. Although Hadden's data are a decade old, there is little reason to think that prejudice by religious individuals has vanished.

Variations of Prejudice Between the Clergy and Laity

We summarized Johnstone's study concerning black ministers and militancy, which differentiated between traditional, moderate, and activist black clergy. No doubt, a similar division exists among white Protestant clergy and white Catholic priests. However, there is little question that the white clergy are more "liberal" than their congregations and parishes concerning racial prejudice and discrimination (Wilson, 1978:329).

Stark and Glock (1969:72-74) compared the nonprejudicial pronouncements of the denominations with the state attitudes of the clergy. They found that a substantial minority of the clergy display religious and racial prejudice. Hadden (1969) reached a similar conclusion. On the other hand, Hadden found that 80 percent of the Protestant ministers surveyed expressed tolerance toward blacks and that nine out of ten supported the Civil Rights movement as it unfolded during the 1960s. Joseph Fichter also found that nine out of ten priests that he questioned supported the Civil Rights movement.

On the other hand, Hadden's study (1969) showed that while 80 percent of the clergy surveyed believed in direct action by the churches on issues related to racial prejudice and discrimination, clerical support for individual direct action is somewhat lower. Southern clergy and clergy in the more conservative denominations displayed much less support for direct involvement on their part to combat racial prejudice and discrimination (Hadden, 1969).

During the decade of the 1960s many studies indicated that the more liberal and outspoken a minister was the more likely he was to have suffered a decline in church membership or loss of some financial support (Wilson, 1978:330). Thus, lack of lay support for civil rights action was then present. Stark and Glock (1969:76-77) report that, indeed, a majority of the laity within the Christian churches opposed the collective role of the churches on behalf of civil rights for minorities. They reported that Hadden's study indicated that 70 percent of the laity denounced clerical involvement in such social issues. Stark and Glock concluded that most of the laity in the 1960s continued to bear ill-will toward other races (and religions). In a study of members and clergy of the major Lutheran bodies in the United States, Strommen (1972) found that the gap in expressed prejudice between Lutheran clergy and laity is greater than between age groupings within the laity. Clergy expressed much *less* prejudice than did the Lutheran laity.

These differences between the "spiritual leaders" of religion and those that they are leading have resulted in much hostility not only toward civil rights activism on the part of the clergy (as we already mentioned) but a reaction in the 1970s to clerical activism in general. Although denominations at the national level, congregations at the local level, and clergy and laity at all levels contributed time, money, and moral persuasion to the Civil Rights movement, there is much evidence that these actions did *not* represent the sentiments of a majority of white church members (Wilson, 1978:381). The activist ministers and laity are seen, in retrospect, as a highly visible minority who evidently lacked broad-based support from members in the various Christian churches. Hoge and Carroll (1973:81) report that while a pastor is likely to see the church as a voluntary association geared for social action programs, the laity is more likely to see it as a community for the preservation of moral values. In the 1970s activism on the part of Protestant and Catholic clergy in the arena of civil rights has markedly declined, as has much of the activism in general. There have been some Catholic priests (and a few Protestant ministers) involved in the struggle to end discrimination directed toward Mexican migrant farm workers, but these pronouncements and demonstrations have received neither the national attention nor the broad-based involvement that the earlier civil rights demonstrations engendered.

A pertinent question for the present era is whether or not prejudice among members of America's religious groups has declined since the turbulent period of the 1960s. Survey data do indicate that open hostility toward racial and ethnic minorities *has* become more muted. Yet, housing remains largely segregated as do educational institutions. Churches are still overwhelmingly divided into white and nonwhite congregations, in spite of denominational efforts to promote racial and ethnic equality. Since research on prejudice has always indicated that it is usually acted out through discriminatory practices, one can assume that many of America's "religious people" remain prejudiced against racial and ethnic groups in all the arenas of social life including the religious.

Anti-Semitism

Although the United States, on the whole, has demonstrated less religious prejudice, less economic prejudice, and less ethnic prejudice against Jews than have the nations of Europe, many American Jews believe that they are just as vulnerable as ever to anti-Semitic rampages. Furthermore, many feel that they are only a few steps removed from blacks, Puerto Ricans, Indians, Mexican-Americans, and other ethnic minorities in terms of prejudice and discrimination (Steinfield, 1970:139).

As we have stated in the chapter showing the development of religious diversity in the United States, anti-Semitism developed historically as a religious prejudice. Jews were stigmatized as the killers of Christ. Official teachings of the Catholic Church and pronouncements from the Protestant Churches following the Reformation lay this blame upon those who followed the teachings of Judaism. In later centuries, much of the expressed anti-Semitism has taken on economic and ethnic overtones. This culminated, of course, in Hitler's successful "scapegoating" of the Jews for Germany's economic and political decline in the early twentieth century. The Nazi atrocities during the Holocaust were without parallel in the history of civilizations.

In the United States, Jewish citizens have been the most successful of all ethnic groups in terms of upward mobility. The second, third, and fourth generations of the Eastern European Jewish immigrants have achieved economic and social mobility at a much more rapid pace than their Catholic immigrant counterparts. Yet, anti-Semitism, like more generalized racial and ethnic prejudice, is still present within the United States. Steinfield (1970:140) attributes this to a confusion about "who Jews are." Is a Jew a member of a religious group? Is he or she a member of a nationality or an ethnic group? Is a Jew a member of a "race," chosen or otherwise?

Although the religious Jewish person expresses belief in god, he and the secular Jew have in common the status of "non-Christian," a position shared with a majority of American Indians and American Orientals. This has led to prejudice directed against Jews in twentieth century America. The aftermath of World War I brought widespread incidences of anti-Semitism. Senator Jacob Javits of New York (1970:144-145) blames in part the anti-Semitism and the anti-Catholicism of the Ku Klux Klan revival; but he places more blame on the vicious anti-Semitic campaign waged by automaker Henry Ford through his newspaper, the *Dearborn Independent*. For seven years, beginning in 1920, the newspaper carried on a relentless campaign against Jews which publicized numerous slanders and scurrilities. One of the chief sources for such information was a forged book entitled *Protocols of the Elders of Zion*, which British, Russian, and German anti-Semites had used. American Jewish leaders exposed the fraudulent document and also sued Henry Ford for libel. He made a complete retraction and apologized for his newspaper's false accusations.

Javits also shows that during the 1930s, anti-Semitism increased under the impact of the rise of Nazism in Germany and the economic depression in the United States. New barriers against Jews were raised in employment, housing, education, and social relations. From 1933 onward, the word "Jew" appeared with increasing frequency in the press, on the radio, and on the speaker's platform. Radio sermons and publications of Catholic Father Charles E. Coughlin increased anti-Semitic emotions to a fever pitch in 1939. Also toward the end of the 1930s anti-Semitism became a factor in the American political scene complete with dramatic scenes of attack and denunciation by anti-Semitic Representatives and Senators in the United States Congress (Javits, 1970:144-145). When the United States did enter World War II, anti-Semites accused American Jews of bringing the country into conflict with Germany. Even after the Nazi atrocities became public knowledge toward the end of and after World War II, violent attacks against Jewish people, their property, and their synagogues have continued. Over six hundred such incidents were documented between the mid-1950s and the mid-1960s (Feagin, 1978: 157-158). Many of these overt acts have come from Nazi-type political organizations, but a pervasive underlying anti-Semitism is seen as responsible for the continuation of these outbursts. It is true, that much of the stereotyping of Jews is economic and political, but historically the underlying basis for the stereotyping has been religious. To what extent, then, is anti-Semitism still a religious prejudice?

The most well-known sociological study of anti-Semitism was done by Charles Glock and Rodney Stark in 1966: *Christian Beliefs and Anti-Semitism.* The contradiction between Christianity as a religion of love and brotherhood and Christianity as anti-Semitic was demonstrated in the survey data used by the authors. They do not view the Christian religion as the *sole* cause of Anti-Semitism, but they see it as an extremely important component.

Glock and Stark conclude that at least one-fourth of America's anti-Semites have a religious basis for their prejudice and another one-fourth have this religious basis in considerable part. Only 5 percent of Americans who express anti-Semitism seem to lack any religious reason for their prejudice against Jews. In extrapolating the sample finding to the larger population, these researchers estimate that about 17.5 million Americans hold fairly strong anti-Semitic views which would classify them as strong adherents to religious bigotry. Lipset and Raab (1970:441) concluded that *stronger* religious commitment on the part of Protestants and Catholic correlates with stronger anti-Semitism. In spite of the fact that the Roman Catholic Church's Vatican Council II condemnation of anti-Semitism and the centuries-old teaching of Jewish guilt for the crucifixion and similar statements issued by the major Protestant denominations, a stubborn and persistent belief in these two related factors remains.

Jeffrey K. Hadden's study of clergy and lay attitudes of prejudice (1969) indicated that a minority of clergy continue to accept the notion of collective and continuing Jewish guilt. In a summary of their earlier findings concerning anti-Semitism, Stark and Glock (1969:75-76) stated that half of America's Christians continue to blame the Jews for Christ's crucifixion. Also, the more conservative Protestant laity exhibit the strongest feeling against Jews for their rejection of Christ as Messiah. In a subsequent study, Stark et al. (1971:52) reported that the Protestant clergy are less likely than the laity to be anti-Semitic. However, the clergy were still reported to demonstrate considerable religious hostility toward Jewish people. Glock and Stark's findings (1966) did indicate that extreme religious bigotry is correlated with anti-Semitism, but Middleton (1973:35) concluded that this religious factor of religious hostility can be counterbalanced by the acceptance of norms of religious libertarianism. He further states that "those who view the modern Jew as an unforgiven crucifier being punished by God also tends to develop similar Anti-Semitic beliefs" (Middleton, 1973:35). Wilson (1978:310) concludes that the more theologically conservative the clergy are, the more likely they are to express religious hostility toward Jews; but he also states that the clergy are not as likely to demonstrate secular anti-Semitism as are the laity.

The most recent form of anti-Semitism, that perpetrated by blacks against Jewish people, seems to be more of an economic (and, therefore, secular) anti-Semitism than a religious prejudice. Out of these articulated anti-Semitic statements made by more militant black leaders there developed sometimes violent confrontations. Black rioters attacked Jewish businesses in many black ghetto areas of America's central cities in the 1960s. These business concerns were seen as exploitive of the urban poor (Feagin, 1978:158). This was particularly disturbing to Jewish intellectuals, as well as the rank-and-file Jewish community, since American Jews have always supported the struggle for equal rights. However, there is perhaps some basis for viewing black anti-Semitism as partially religious. Black Muslim antipathy toward Judaism is based upon the historic Islamic hatred of Judaism.

There also remains the fundamentalist Christian view that Jews are absolutely out of harmony with God for their rejection of Jesus as Messiah. To the fundamentalist Christian groups, this is "sin," and these religious bodies remain eager to convert the "Heathen" Jews (Feagin, 1978:175). In recent decades, a number of Christian evangelical missionary organizations, such as the American Board of Missions to the Jews, have sought to convert Jewish people to Christianity (Strober, 1974:83:98).

In a fashion similar to racial and ethnic prejudice, anti-Semitism persists in American society despite official pronouncements and educational efforts against anti-Semitism by the major Christian religious bodies. The most religiously oriented variant of this prejudice seems lodged within fundamentalist Christian denominations; but general anti-Semitism, with certain religious overtones exist among the members of *all* Christian denominations.

Religious Belief: A Causal of an Associational Variable of Prejudice

A tendency exists among some researchers concerned with religion in American society to conclude that religious beliefs do indeed *cause* racial ethnic and religious prejudice. Indeed survey data do indicate that religious people are highly prejudiced. On the other hand, sociologists who have engaged in research of prejudice and discrimination have long recognized that both these attitudes and these actions are caused by a multiplicity of social, economic, political, and religious factors.

In the realm of religion and religious beliefs, research findings are somewhat confusing. Historically, the Christian churches did indeed foster anti-Semitism through deliberate teachings. In addition, American Protestantism contributed directly and indirectly to the creation of separate black denominations. Protestants also exhibited prejudice toward ethnic Catholic immigrants, and on many occasions, committed hostile acts against these various Catholic groups. Contemporary sociological research, however, indicates that the relationship between religious belief and prejudice is associational rather than causal in most situations.

Racial and ethnic group prejudice is a *conservative* view of the world, including that part of the world which reflects religious beliefs. Stark and Glock (1969:80-85; 1973:95) note that underlying traditional Christian thought is an image of man as "a free actor, as essentially unfettered by social circumstances, free to choose and thus free to effect his own salvation. . . ." Such an image of man is an integral part of the concepts of rugged individualism and the self-made man. If someone does not display these qualities, then that person has only himself to blame. Stark and Glock interpret their empirical analysis indicating significant amounts of racial and ethnic prejudice to mean that a great many church people believe that men and women are really in control of their own destinies. Because of this, they blame the minorities themselves (particularly blacks) for their present misery. Many perhaps believe that economic and social disadvantages are the results of racial shortcomings. Stark and Glock also point to the individualistic orientation of many conservative and evangelical Protestants toward salvation as precluding their involvement in curtailing discrimination against racial groups. They call this orientation the "miracle motif," which suggests that if all men are brought to Christ, social evils will disappear through the miraculous regeneration of the individual by the Holy Spirit.

The more theologically conservative and *particularistic* a religious belief is, the more it is related to prejudice Particularism, as expressed by Stark and Glock (1973:95) in the idea that a person's own religion is true while all others are false. Any nonbeliever is, therefore, a deviant who is subject to intolerance. Practices of the religion of a different racial group lie outside of the solidarity of the "in-group." This particularism does not "cause" racial prejudice but the particularism of the religion and the expression of racial prejudice are part of the communal aspect of the "in-group" subculture (Wilson, 1978:331). Anti-Semitism, specifically, is also associated with highly particularistic and theologically conservative religious beliefs, since Jewish people and their religious beliefs are obviously *in error*, according to particularism.

Another factor which, when combined with religious beliefs, is associated with prejudice is *localism*. Roof (1974:661) noted that people with localistic orientations tend to hold intolerant and authoritarian attitudes in general. Religious beliefs come into play, but are a part of more general intolerant and authoritarian attitudes beginning with the now classic *Authoritarian Personality*.

Another study which reached similar conclusions is Strommen's *A Study of Generation* (1972). This major study of a representative sample of Lutherans from all major Lutheran denominations in the United States reported that Lutherans who felt threatened by diversity or change, and who rigidly adhered to religious law exhibited higher levels of prejudice, both racial and religious, than did the less rigid and "law oriented" Lutherans. In specifically discussing anti-Semitism, Strommen reported that this religious prejudice is not a separate entity, but just one facet of generalized prejudice.

Finally, the original Glock and Stark study of anti-Semitism (1966) concluded that *specific teachings* of Christianity have fostered anti-Semitism, and continues to do so even today. However, several studies since 1966 indicate that this is too simplistic a conclusion. As Wilson (1978:330) concludes, "there is just too much evidence of a *lack* of association between religious orthodoxy or dogmatism taken alone, and racial prejudice, for this theory to be supported." Religion is associated with prejudice against racial and ethnic minorities and with anti-Semitism, but as Hoge and Carroll (1973:75) suggest, the main determinants of prejudice are not religious beliefs as much as personal rigidity and a personal need for unchanging cognitive, as well as social, structure.

In conclusion, religious belief *alone* does not cause prejudice except for a small minority. However, religious beliefs which are *particularistic* and *conservative,* are a part of a constellation of economic, political, and social attitudes that are rigid and authoritarian. The prejudice against Mexican-Americans, Puerto Ricans, Indians, and other ethnic minorities can probably be attributed to this same configuration. Only the minority of "Archie Bunker" types in America would articulate *specific* religious prejudice against Jews, Catholics, Hindus, and nonbelievers. Even then, their list of "undesirable" Americans would probably also include blacks, Mexican-Americans, Italian-Americans, Polish-Americans, and so on. A religious white, Anglo-Saxon superiority remains, but it is manifest only when a general conservative orientation is characteristic of the individual.

SUMMARY

The emergence of an all-black, and largely separate, church structure was an historical reflection of social differentiation in the United States. Its continuing presence reflects not only a continuation of social differentiation but also minority group values in the realm of religion. The black denominations are Protestant and are divided along social class lines in parallel fashion to white religious groups. Although there are black Roman Catholics and black members of predominantly white congregations, an overwhelming majority of religiously affiliated blacks are within the black churches. In a real sense, these groups constitute a "fourth religious community."

Recent observers have charged the black churches with promoting an otherwordly orientation and with seeking a comfortable accommodation in a white society. This is true, up to a point; but the prominence of the black church, particularly in the South, during the civil rights movement cannot be underestimated. In the last decade a black theology of liberation has emerged which advocates militancy on behalf of the oppressed and the poor. In addition, an alternative to Christianity, the Black Muslim sect, competes in many urban areas for the allegiance of religious black Americans.

The existence of separate religious communities within the United States is not the only manifestation of the association between religion, race, and ethnicity. Prejudice, as well as overt acts of discrimination, against racial, ethnic, and religious minorities has continued into the second half of the twentieth century. Although much of the earlier prejudice directed against Catholic ethnic groups by Protestants has virtually disappeared, prejudice directed against blacks and Jews is still present.

Not all religious groups, however, are equally prejudiced against other racial, ethnic, and religious groups. Jews are the least racially prejudiced, and Protestants are the most racially prejudice. Catholics are more prejudiced than Jews, but less prejudiced than Protestants. The more conservative a religious group is, the more prejudice do its members demonstrate. Church attendance is a factor also in the level of prejudice expressed. Those who attend most often are least prejudiced, as are people who never attend or who do *not* belong to a religious body. The occasional attender demonstrates the most hostility toward racial, ethnic, and religious minorities. The clergy, overall, are more tolerant of minorities than are the laity, but theologically conservative clergy do express significant levels of prejudice.

Anti-Semitism, or prejudice, directed exclusively at Jews, is thought to be related to both religious intolerance as well as hostility toward Jews in secular matters. Although the United States has never "persecuted the Jews" in the manner of European countries, the society has demonstrated hostility toward Jews, based partly upon the religion of Jewish people. Fundamentalist Christians are *most likely* to seek to convert Jews to Christianity.

Religious beliefs and prejudice are associational variables, but other variables are usually present which affect prejudice and acts of discrimination. Particularism, conservatism, localism, and specific religious teachings are usually within the constellation of attitudes of religious people who express high levels of prejudice.

REFERENCES

Allport, Gordon
1958   *The Nature of Prejudice* (abridged edition). New York: Doubleday Anchor Books.

Cleage, Albert B., Jr.
1974   "The gospel of black liberation." Pp. 298-301 in Patrick H. McNamara (ed.), *Religion American*

Style. New York: Harper and Row.

Cone, James H.
1969   *Black Theology and Black Power.* New York: Seabury.

Davis, Allison, Burleigh
B. Gardner, and Mary R.
Gardner
1941   *Deep South: A Social Anthropological Study of Caste and Class.* Chicago: University of Chicago Press.

Dollard, John
1937   *Caste and Class in a Southern Town.* New Haven: Yale University Press.

Drake, St. Clair and
Horace E. Cayton
1945   *Black Metroplis.* New York: Harcourt, Brace, Jovanovich.

DuBois, W. E.
1971 (1899)   "The function of the Negro church." Pp. 77-81 in Hart Nelson, Raytha Yokeley and Anne Nelson (eds.), *The Black Church in America.* New York: Basic Books.

Ebony Handbook
1974   "Statistics: Black church membership." Chicago: Johnson Publishing Co.

Feagin, Joe R.
1978   *Racial and Ethnic Relations.* Englewood Cliffs, New Jersey: Prentice-Hall.

Fichter, Joseph
1951   *Southern Parish.* Chicago: University of Chicago Press.

Frazier, E. Franklin
1974   *The Negro Church in America.* New York: Schocken Books.

Gallup Poll
1977   "Widespread segregation found in nation's churches." *Gallup Poll Release* (April 7).

Glenn, Norval
1964   "Negro religion and Negro status in the United States." In Louis Schneider (ed.), *Religion, Culture, and Society.* New York: Wiley.

Glock, Charles Y. and
Rodney Stark
1966   *Christian Beliefs and Anti-Semitism.* New York: Harper and Row.

Gorsuch, R. L. and D. Aleshire
1974   "Christian faith and ethnic prejudice: a review and interpretation of research." *Journal for the Scientific Study of Religion* 13:281-307.

Greeley, Andrew
1974   *Ethnicity in the United States: A Preliminary Reconnaissance.* New York: Wiley.
1979   "Ethnic variations in religious commitment." Pp. 113-134 in Robert Wuthnel (ed.), *The Religious Dimension: New Directions in Quantitative Research.* New York: Academic Press.

Hadden, Jeffrey
1969   *The Gathering Storm in the Churches: The Widening Gap Between Clergy and Laymen.* Garden City, New York: Doubleday.

Hargrove, Barbara
1979   *The Sociology of Religion: Classical and Contemporary Approaches.* Arlington Heights, Ill.: AHM Publishing Co.

Harrell, David, Jr.
1971   *White Sects and Black Men in the Recent South.* Nashville, Tennessee: Vanderbilt University Press.

Hoge, Dean and J. W. Carroll
1973   "Religiosity and prejudice in northern and southern churches." *Journal for the Scientific Study of Religion* 12:181-197.

Javits, Jacob
1970   "Jews as a class." Pp. 140-145 in Melvin Steinfield (ed.), *Cracks in the Melting Pot: Racism and Discrimination in American History.* Beverly Hills, California: Glencoe Press.

Johnson, Charles S.
1934   *Shadow of the Plantation.* Chicago: University of Chicago Press.

Johnstone, Ronald L.
  1969   "Negro preachers take sides." *Review of Religious Research* 11 (Fall):81-89.

Lincoln, C. Eric
  1974   *The Black Church Since Frazier.* New York: Schocken Books.
  1973   *The Black Muslims in America* (rev. ed.), Boston: Beacon Press.

Lipset, Seymour M. and Earl Raab
  1970   *The Politics of Unreason: Right-Wing Extremism in America,* 1790-1970. New York: Harper and Row.

Martin, William
  1979   "A Joyful Noise." *Texas Monthly* 7:184–186.

Marx, Gary
  1967   "Religion: opiate or inspiration of civil rights militancy among Negroes?" *American Sociological Review* 32 (February):64-73.

Mays, Benjamin E. and Joseph Nicholson
  1933   *The Negro's Church.* New York: Institute of Social and Religious Research.

McNamara, Patrick H.
  1974   *Religion American Style.* New York: Harper and Row.

Middleton, Russell
  1973   "Do Christian beliefs cause anti-Semitism?" *American Sociological Review* 38 (February):33-61.

Myrdal, Gunnar
  1944   *The American Dilemma.* New York: Harper and Row.

Newsweek
  1973   "Black Muslims." (February 5):61-63.

Pope, Liston
  1967   "The Negro and religion in America." in Richard D. Knudten (ed.), *The Sociology of Religion: An Anthology.* New York: Appleton-Century-Crofts.

Powdermaker, Hortense
  1939   *After Freedom: A Cultural Study in the Deep South.* New York: Viking Press.

Roof, Wade
1974 "Religious orthodoxy and minority prejudice: causal relationship or reflection of localistic world view?" *American Journal of Sociology* 80:643-664.

Rosten, Leo
1975 *Religions of America: Ferment and Faith in an Age of Crisis.* New York: Simon and Schuster.

Stampp, Kenneth M.
1956 *The Peculiar Institution.* New York: Alfred Knopf.

Stark, Rodney, Bruce Foster, Charles Y. Glock, and Harold Quinley
1971 *Wayward Shepherds: Prejudice and the Protestant Clergy.* New York: Harper and Row.

Stark, Rodney and Charles Y. Glock
1969 "Prejudice and the churches." Pp. 70-95 in Charles Y. Glock and Ellen Siegelman (eds.), *Prejudice U. S. A.* New York: Praeger.

Stark, Rodney and Charles Y. Glock
1973 "Prejudice and the churches." Pp. 88-101 in Charles Y. Glock (ed.), *Religion in sociological Perspective: Essays in the Empirical Study of Religion.* New York: Wadsworth.

Steinfield, Melvin
1970 *Cracks in the Melting Pot: Racism and Discrimination in American History.* Beverly Hills, Cal.: Glencoe Press.

Strober, Gerald S.
1974 *American Jews.* Garden City, New York: Doubleday.

Strommen, Merton P.
1972 *A Study of Generation.* Minneapolis, Minnesota: Augsburg.

Washington, Joseph R., Jr.
1964 *Black Religion.* Boston: Beacon Press.

Williams, Preston N.
1971 "Toward a sociological understanding of the black religious community." *Soundings* 54

(Fall):260-270.

Wilson, John
    1978   *Religion in American Society: The Effective Presence.* Englewood Cliffs, New Jersey: Prentice-Hall.

Winter, J. Alan
    1977   *Continuities in the Sociology of Religion: Creed, Congregation, and Community.* New York: Harper and Row.

Chapter 14

Religion and American Society Today . . . And Tomorrow?

In a satirical novel concerning America at some future time, Shepherd Mead (1959) depicts a rather strange sort of church. Playing on some themes which were especially prominent in the religious life of our society in the 1950s, he paints a portrait of a religious organization which has become little concerned with such traditional matters as theology, worship, and ritual. Rather, themes of social life and personal self-improvement are stressed for the members of "People's Church"; the minister is now referred to as "The Friendly" rather than "The Reverend," and the "First Team" has taken over from the more ecclesiastically oriented groups in the management of the church. In fact, the basketball court has replaced the sanctuary as the center of religious activity, and pinball machines on which one is challenged to "light up the twelve apostles" take over for more traditional tools of Christian education.

We cannot really take Mead's "predictions" seriously, although his fabrications did seem related to a number of trends in the church life of the time he wrote. It was the end of the baby-boom, the Eisenhower years, and what appeared to be a massive religious revival (Glock and Stark, 1965) and, as religion seemed to be getting more and more popular, its expressions seemed to become less and less tied to either tradition or theology. Somehow, though, as the era ended, the forecasts of sociologists and others concerning the future course of institutional religion did not come true, leaving many new church development officials rather scarlet of face and empty of pocketbook. In short, predicting the future of religion, or even assessing its present state, is a shaky business.

Perilous as prediction may be, however, it is a task which must be addressed in any textbook dealing with the sociology of religion. Glock (1973:281) has commented on the various strands in social thought which place a consideration of the future of religion at the forefront of sociological work:

> Marx made the topic salient by raising the possibility of society without religion. In the last century when evolutionary theory was having a major impact on sociological thought, it was natural to include religion in predictions about social evolution. Structural-functional theory also made the topic pertinent through its proposition that religion is a necessary condition to the maintenance of social order. And cyclical theories of human

history . . . also included religion as an element in prognostications about where society was headed.

In making our assessment and evaluation of the future of religion, it is interesting to note, as Westley (1978) has pointed out, that many of the threads in contemporary religion seem to follow predictions made by Durkheim (1951:336) in the conclusion to one of his major works, *Suicide.* Looking across what seemed a rapidly changing social scene, accompanied by a greater division of work roles and thus a larger amount of individual differences, would lead to a state in human affairs when the only bond remaining for the members of any human group would be the simple fact that they were human beings. Human personality would be the only thing which could make a claim on the collective conscience and thus would be raised so far above all other forms of human goals that it would take on something of a religious nature.

In Durkheim's view, the central issue with regard to religion was always its ability to maintain cultural integration in an advanced, technological society. Individualism, in Durkheim's view (1969:26) was an inevitable fact of modern society; however, it did not inevitably lead to the collapse of moral restraints. Rather, Durkheim suggested:

> . . . that as a society characterized by unilateral kin group affiliations produced a totemic religion, so a highly specialized and diversified society will produce highly specialized, diversified, and individualistic religion (Westley, 1978:137).

In this "cult of man," as Westley refers to it, the sacred power binding the individual to society is to be found within the individual.

The matter is summarized by Westley (1978:139) in noting that Durkheim made seven predictions concerning "the religion of the future." First, given the greater specialization of human social roles, *humanity* will come to be the object that can be worshipped. Second, the increasing diversification of society will lead to a similar diversification for the religions of the society; religious ideals will vary with the culture of a particular religious group. Third, religion will continue to exercise the function of expressing the relationships of the individual and the society; however, the sacred will be internal rather than external to the individual. Fourth, in the religion centered around the "cult of man," science and religion will serve complementary functions; science will explain the individual's relationship to society while religion will express it. Fifth, ritual life will involve "skill testing" and will relate accomplishment to positions of authority. Sixth, these rituals will be more private than public in nature and will focus on development of the now sacred self. Finally, these rituals will be concerned mainly with the development of "purity."

In looking at the various developments within the religious life of our day, it will be interesting to keep these points in mind. Debates over the meaning of shifts in church attendance and membership, controversies over whether or not "churchly" religion is dying, as well as considerations of the presence of certain "invisible" religions and the growth of mystic, Eastern cults on supposedly secular soil may all relate to some facets of these predictions.

What, then, can we say about the situation of religion in America today, and of its future for tomorrow. Religion is assuredly a matter of concern for many. A fascinating number of events—ranging from Vatican Council II to the "death of God" movement—have set the stage for speculation and prediction. A time that has seen the reversal of the so-called religious revival, the development of a new religious consciousness among youth, as well as the renewal of evangelical Christianity, cannot be seen as dull insofar as religion and religious movements are concerned.

Yet, it is extremely difficult to assess what is really happening in religion today as well as what these events mean for the future course of religion in America. As Wilson (1978) indicates, it is not easy to determine whether religion is growing in strength or actually declining in influence. Part of the problem rests on the fact that the definition of what constitutes religion is uncertain at best. Novak (1967:249) has noted:

> . . . one reason for this uncertainty is the prior uncertainty concerning what constitutes the "specific nature of Christianity." To what propositions, to what style of life, to what symbols, to what method of resolving issues is a Christian specifically committed?

There are many who would contend that religion is definitely on the decline at least insofar as its influence in the society is concerned. As Wilson comments (1978:396):

> There can hardly be any question that there has been a decline in the influence of religious institutions in the modern West, and also a decline in the number of people for whom transcendental concerns are an everyday affair.

Yet, can there be such certainty? Is religion as a whole declining or is it that a certain kind of religious expression—that related to the traditional forms—which is in decline? To some, what many see as a decay in religion may actually be a sign of the revival of true and real religious faith. Insofar as is possible, we want to assess the situation of the religious institution and the validity of the various speculations concerning this situation.

RELIGION IN AMERICA TODAY

What, then, can we make of the situation of religion in our society today? One measure of the health of religion at this time might be found in membership statistics and records of church attendance. To be sure, these are not the most reliable of indicators. Membership records are generally inflated, unreliable, incommensurable, and frequently invalid; statistics relating to attendance are little better. However, such figures do serve to indicate, at least, whether or not the traditional, institutional religion of the society has any support.

An examination of recent response to the Gallup Poll seems to indicate ambivalence toward the religious institution. While religion seems to be supported in the sense of belief in its importance, this support is not as strong as it was in the 1950s. A larger proportion of the population now feel that religion is losing its influence (see Figure 14-1). At the same time, since the very early 1970s, there has been a renewed sense that religion is important; it might be said that the pendulum is beginning to swing back toward a more favorable situation for religion. Perhaps, as we shall see, there are cycles with regard to the influence of religion in America and these cycles are short rather than long-term in nature.

Figure 14-1. Percent Saying Religion Losing Influence

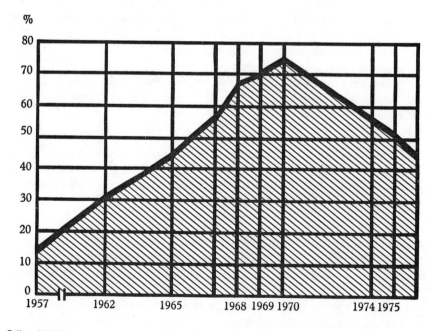

Gallup, 1978:18.

Certainly the statistics available to us seem to show "peaks and valleys" in both rates of church attendance and affiliation. Wingrove and Alston (1974) report that while church attendance is somewhat affected by age, there is no consistent pattern. Instead, looking at five ten-year age cohorts, they find that attendance is more related to the mood of the times than it is to individual points in the life cycle (1974:330). Thus, they find that all age cohorts reached peak rates of attendance during the 1950s; a time seen by many as the era of greatest interest in institutionalized religion in our century. After 1960, however, there was a decline in church attendance for all the various age groups.

In the Roper Polls covering the period from 1972 to 1978 (NORC, 1978), the number of those who reported some religious preference was extremely high. For each of the seven years, less than 1 percent of respondents indicated that they had *no* religious preference. However, the inclination to attend religious services on a regular or frequent basis declined over the same period. In 1972, nearly 30 percent (28.5) said that they attended church every week while in 1978 only about 20 percent (19.5) reported such attendance. This rate of only 20 percent who said that they attend church weekly is consistent for all years since 1972. Similarly, the proportion who report that they never attend church has risen from just under ten percent (9.2) to over fifteen percent (15.6). Of course, there is no simple dichotomy between those who never attend and those who attend weekly; however, it is these extreme points which seem to indicate a major shift in attendance patterns. There are also some contradictions in these reports; a 1976 Gallup Poll (AIPO, 1976) indicates, nevertheless, that 40.5 percent of the respondents in its national survey indicated that they had attended a religious service in "the last seven days." Further, 60.8 percent of those surveyed said that their religious beliefs were very important to them. In addition, 70 percent of the respondents reported that they belonged to a church or synagogue.

Looking at trends in church membership and attendance over the past several decades, Roozen and Carroll (1979) report that denominational membership constantly moved upward until the mid-1960s. However about the middle of that decade, a downward trend in membership began (see Figure 14-2). Since 1964 for Catholics and 1966 for Protestants, membership has declined in terms of the percent of the total population reporting that they belong to a church. Even more startling is the fact that ten of the largest, and theologically most liberal, denominations have lost membership in every year since 1966 (see Figure 14-3). Only Catholics and Southern Baptists did not actually lose membership during this period of time. This pattern for church membership is paralleled in both attendance and monetary giving (Roozen and Carroll, 1979). In short, the 1960s were a time in which there was a reversal of long-term trends with regard to religion in our society. For the first time in the entire history of the United States membership in churches did not grow.

We may add to these comments on relative membership and attendance the current interest in new kinds of religious expression, as discussed in Chapters 8

Figure 14-2: Protestant and Roman Catholic Membership
1952–1974, as a Percentage of the U.S. Population, 18 years
Old and Older

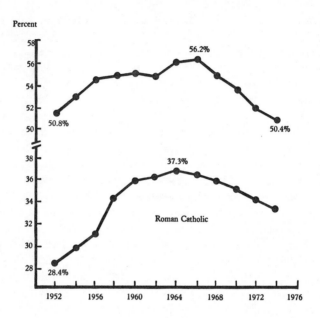

Roozen & Carroll, 1979:25.

and 9. As noted there, not only the number of such groups, but the actual number of persons involved in them has increased considerably (Robbins et al., 1978). The participants are not drawn predominantly from the economically disprivileged but from the children of that bulwark of tradition, the middle class. In addition, 30 percent of the Gallup Poll respondents (AIPO, 1976) indicated that they had had a mystical experience; indeed, between 15 and 20 percent of these respondents reported that they had taken part in one of the several forms of new religious experience.

But, what do these figures actually tell us about the state of religion today? And, what bearing do they have for the future of religion? In an attempt to see what these statistics as well as other indicators of the "health" of religion may mean, we shall keep in mind several assertions being made in contemporary sociological thought and research: (1) that religion is actually dying as adherents move from conservative to liberal denominations and finally leave traditional forms of religion altogether; (2) that religion is actually as "healthy" as ever and, in fact, may be undergoing another Great Awakening; (3) that those churches

Figure 14-3: Membership of Selected Denominations in
1950–1975
as a Percent of 1950 Membership

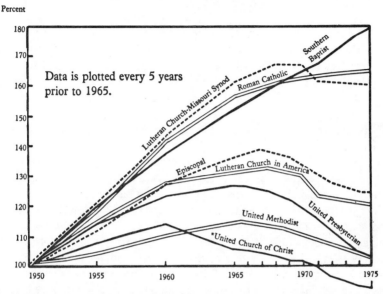

*The decline of the United Church of Christ from 1960 to 1965 is due to withdrawal of congregations after the merger.

Source: *Historical Statistics of the U.S.* (U.S. Census, 1975), *Statistical Abstract of the U.S,* (1976)
Roozen & Carroll, 1979:29.

which are still growing may be doing so largely because they appear to be more serious about religious faith and thus hold on to their members and the families of these members better; (4) that whatever the state of "church" religion may be, there exists a virulent "invisible" and/or "civil" religion which represents the true American faith; and (5) that new religious expressions are really in line with classical predictions concerning religion in an advanced society.

SLOWLY ABANDONED OR RENEWED?

As we observed in Chapter 4, the beliefs and rewards offered by traditional religious systems are to many somewhat discordant with the real value system of the larger secular society. Susan Budd (1973) notes that because of this discordance traditional religious groups in our society appear to have a much diminished influence in the contemporary world. Such an observation is in line with the early predictions of the evolutionary schools of social thought (see Chapter 2) that religion was only a vestige of humanity's primitive ignorance; a remnant that would vanish as human knowledge increased and the need to explain unexplained facts decreased.

Such thinking leads to a question like that raised by Novak (1967:237):

> The transformation that Christianity, in particular, is now experiencing is unique in its rapidity, profundity, and intensity. . . . Our task will be to sort out the ambiguities that arise from these changes: Is Christianity slowly exercising its perennial powers of assimilation over yet another culture, or is it dying the death of a thousand qualifications?

There are two opposing views concerning predictions about the future of religion. One is represented by Glock and Stark's study, *American Piety: The Nature of Religious Commitment* (1968), which sees religion as moving away from customary patterns in a direction which will end in the eventual abandonment of traditional religion. Greeley (1970, 1972), on the other hand, views the future of religion in roseate terms, picturing a renewal of faith which will include a continuance of more or less orthodox religiosity.

Stark and Glock (1968:204) present data from a sample of California church members which they say indicates that "a profound revolution in religious thought is sweeping the churches." From their findings they draw the conclusion that the major result of this transformation in attitudes toward religion will be a significant lessening of the degree to which individuals in the society find themselves committed to the more orthodox religious faiths; a diminishment which could mean a weakening of the influence of traditional faith in American society and, eventually, the demise of religion in any common sense meaning of that word. They note (1968:204-5):

> We have reached two main conclusions: that the religious beliefs that have been the bedrocks of Christian faith for nearly two millenia are on their way out; and that this *may* very well be the dawn of a post-Christian era.

As they view the responses of church members in the San Francisco Bay area, they find an interpretation of Christian faith and its symbols that is so different as to be unrecognizable as traditional Christianity. They contend that this radically altered version of religion is the dominant view today—not only for the occasional skeptic on the fringes of the religious organization but, indeed, among the religious institution's brightest theological minds and its ablest clergy. While the data do not indicate that a basic belief in a personal God had disappeared, they do show that a number of such basic beliefs which have been regarded as "fundamental" to Christian belief seem to have been discarded or at least are now viewed in only the most symbolic of fashions. In the liberal churches, which

Stark and Glock see as dominant (especially among church members under the age 50), orthodox views such as a belief in the divinity of Jesus and the reality of physical miracles are accepted as "myths" reflecting some philosophical truth but not an empirical reality. For example, the stories of creation in Genesis may be taken as "poetic" statements concerning some ultimate ground of being behind the world's existence, but not as literal accounts of an actual "construction project."

Stark and Glock also contend that the rate of attendance at Sunday morning worship services has declined significantly since its high point in the late 1950s. They see the changes wrought in the Roman Catholic Church by Vatican II and those that result from the ecumenical movement in Protestantism as indicative of the lessening grip of religious particularism on the American people. When other factors, such as the "honest to God" controversy, the "death of God" theme, and books such as Harvey Cox's *Secular City* are added to these considerations, they see a stark picture of secularization presented; traditional Christian credos such as "Christ crucified, risen, coming again" as disappearing from common belief systems.

All of this, according to Stark and Glock, has produced a "new breed" of church leaders who maintain that a literal interpretation of Christian dogma is not only not necessary but actually *incorrect*. Although this seems more like a humanistic view than traditional Christian belief and might be expected to lead to basic changes in the religious institution there has been little, if any, change in the basic structures of religious organizations in the country. Even if the liberal ministers wanted to change this basic structure, they would find it difficult to fight the interests of their most loyal members (the most theologically orthodox), as it is these more conservative members who are also most committed to the program of the organized church (see Table 14-1).

As Stark and Glock view it, this shift in theology also represents a transformation in the way in which Christian ethics are defined; a shift which entails a move from the ideal of personal holiness to a concern for social justice. Thus, the focus of this "new breed" is on humanistic values—goodness, justice, and compassion. However, while such an approach may be very satisfying to this new breed of clergy, and some of the laity, it does not have much appeal as a substitute for orthodoxy where concern for the institutional program of the church is concerned. Members concerned with social justice are far less willing to support the organized church than are those who are concerned with doctrinal orthodoxy. In fact, the concern for ethicalism does not correlate well with either church contributions or attendance at church services. As Stark and Glock show (see Table 14-2), members of the liberal denominations are more likely to be "dormant" Christians than doctrinally orthodox members.

Thus, in sum, Stark and Glock see a religious institution in great disarray. Its leaders and most of its membership no longer believe in its basic tenets, but any

Table 14-1. THE IMPACT OF ORTHODOX BELIEF ON OTHER ASPECTS
OF COMMITMENT
(Church Member Sample)

	Orthodoxy Index		
	Low	Medium	High
Percentage high on Ritual Involvement			
Protestants	19	39	71
Catholics	19	36	55
Percentage high on Devotionalism			
Protestants	20	49	79
Catholics	18	58	80
Percentage high on Religion Experience			
Protestants	25	57	86
Catholics	29	49	70
Percentage high on Religious Knowledge			
Protestants	15	19	46
Catholics	0	5	7
Percentage high on Particularism			
Protestants	9	25	60
Catholics	15	28	40
Percentage high on Ethicalism			
Protestants**	47	46	42
Catholics	48	48	56
Number of cases on which percentage are based*			
Protestants	595	729	705
Catholics	64	115	304

*With trivial variations all computations in these tables are based on this same number of cases.

**Members of Protestant sects are excluded from these computations.

Source: Stark and Glock, 1968:214.

Table14-2. DENOMINATIONAL PATTERNS OF RELIGIOUS COMMITMENT
(Church Member Sample)

	Members of Liberal Protestant Churches[a]	Members of Moderate Protestant Churches[b]	Members of Conservative Protestant Churches[c]	Members of Roman Catholic Parishes
	(982)	(894)	(450)	(545)
Percentage high on Orthodoxy	11	33	81	61
Percentage high on Ritual Involvement	30	45	75	46
Percentage high on Devotionalism	42	51	78	65
Percentage high on Religious Experience	43	57	84	68
Percentage high on Religious Knowledge	17	25	55	5
Percentage who feel their religious perspective provides them with the answers to the meaning and purpose of life	43	57	84	68
Percentage who attend weekly	25	32	68	70
Percentage who have 3 or more of their 5 best friends in their congregation	22	26	54	36
Percentage who contribute $7.50 or more per week to their church	18	30	50	6

[a]Congregationalists, Methodists, Episcopalians.
[b]Disciples of Christ, Presbyterians, American Lutherans, American Baptists.
[c]Missouri Synod Lutherans, Southern Baptists, Sects.

Stark and Glock, 1968:222.

moves for open reinterpretation of the beliefs or changes in the structure are blocked by the "holdouts" who really provide the remaining support for the "church" religion. Taking a mildly evolutionistic stance, the authors conjecture that soon, however, even this remnant will "give up," and church religion will die or become so insignificant as to be of no influence in the society.

As noted, a quite different picture of the future of religion is presented by Andrew Greeley (1970; 1972). He sees traditional religious expression remaining strong. Summing up his vision of the state of religion "in the year 2000" he feels that, except for the possibility of some severe disaster, the traditional religious organizations will not lose members and church attendance will remain at about the same level as it has for some time. Further, he feels that the majority of the population will continue to rely on religious interpretations of ultimate reality. In this way, religion will still have at least an indirect impact on the society, providing the foundation for general social consensus. In this same vein, he does not believe that secularization, in particular the effects of science and technology, will create a new kind of faith.

He does suggest that the number of full-time clergy working in the parish situation may decline in relation to more specialized types of ministry. However, such parish clergy will continue to operate as the major source of religious leadership. Further, the rituals of the church will not totally lose their aura of "mysterium tremendum," and rites having some mystical component will continue to be common. In this same vein, the traditional institutional structures will not disappear, but will get more elaborate, and will become more dependent on the work of experts; further, ecumenicism will not blur the lines of denominational distinction.

Likewise, Greeley sees no basic change in the traditional belief patterns and goals of Christian religion as projected today. Orthodox beliefs have not died, and challenges to them from liberal theological schools will not win. So, too, the drive for social and secular relevance in the place of more traditional goals of "soul-winning" will not carry the day.

It is possible, of course, to write off Greeley's predictions as the wishful thinking of an apologist for the faith (Greeley is, in fact, a priest). However, there are a number of indications that religion is far from dead. Greeley's argument is strengthened in a sense by research presented by Hadaway and Roof, Hadaway (1978) and Roof (1978) concerning denominational growth and by Kelley's (1977) research showing a growth in conservative churches. Evidence that "orthodox" evangelicism is growing, particularly through the use of the media, also demonstrates that there is a renewed emphasis on "bringing the message" to members and potential members alike.

In view of all of this, some, like Novak (1967:251-2) see a real renewal of Christianity:

My quiet conviction is that Christianity is now entering upon one of the most creative periods of its history. Dissatisfaction with the present and a longing for renewal have been generated in the almost universal anguish of two world wars. I believe that Christianity is true; it offers in the round, and in connection with other sources, the most adequate interpretation of human nature and destiny that we have.

In addition, Himmelfarb (1967:220) perceives a return to belief on the part of Jewish young people, a group traditionally not religious in the usual sense. In particular, he sees *intellectual* young Jews less antipathetic toward Judaism and sees an actual return to the traditional practices of Judaism.

While the new evangelicism (see Chapter 7) does not encompass the entire Christian population, it does show amazing growth and stamina. Viewing its advances, it is difficult to pronounce the patient, religion, "sick unto death." A Gallup Poll taken in 1976 indicated that about one-third of all adult Americans—about 50,000,000 persons—felt that they had been "born again" (*Newsweek*, Oct. 25, 1976). Further, 46 percent of Protestants and 31 percent of Catholics said that they believed that the Bible should be taken as literally true, word by word. *Newsweek* further indicates the strength of evangelicism by noting the success of the Christian Yellow Pages—a publication advertising the availability of goods and services from true, born-again Christians. In all, it is believed that such "old fashioned, true to the Bible" faith is alive and growing despite the predictions made concerning the weakening of religion in a complex society.

This is a matter which is not easily resolved, however. The complexity of the issues is seen when we look at what might seem to be a simple assertion—that conservative churches are growing while more liberal groups are declining.

ARE CONSERVATIVE CHURCHES GROWING?

A possibility not envisioned by either of our two "forecasters" (Stark and Glock, 1968; Greeley, 1970, 1972) is that churches as a whole will not decline, but that only certain churches—the more liberal ones—will do so, while others will continue to grow. Such an assertion is clearly in line with the statistics we previously cited from Roozen and Carrol (1979). Further, in an analysis of membership trends in ten denominations, Doyle and Kelley (1979) report that all groups were doing well until the mid-1960s, but in the period from 1965 to 1970 Methodists, United Presbyterians, Episcopalians, Lutherans in both the LCA and ALC, and the United Church of Christ began to suffer declines in membership. In the next five years, from 1970 to 1975, the Lutheran Church-Missouri Synod also began to decline; only the Southern Baptists and Roman Catholics, among major groups, continued to grow (see Table 14-3).

To the extent that these sorts of figures indicate the health of denominations, it

Table 14-3. MEMBERSHIP CHANGE 1950 TO 1975

Denomination*	Percentage Change					
	1950–55	1955–60	1960–65	1965–70	1970–75	1950–75
RC	18.2	19.3	10.5	4.0	2.1	65.5
SBC	19.7	14.8	10.7	8.0	9.5	79.9
UMC	4.3	5.8	3.3	-3.2	-7.1	2.6
UPC	14.3	20.5	3.2	-6.4	-13.9	14.5
EC	12.1	13.5	7.2	-2.7	-6.1	24.5
LCA	15.0	10.8	2.9	-1.1	-7.5	19.9
LCMS	20.1	18.9	12.9	3.2	-4.0	59.9
ALS	20.6	17.6	9.5	-3.0	-5.0	43.2
UCC	8.1	5.8	-7.8	-5.4	-7.2	-7.4
8 U.S. PROT	12.5	11.9	5.9	0.3	-2.2	30.7
UCN	11.2	11.4	4.6	-2.9	-7.9	15.9
U.S. POPULATION†	8.9	8.9	7.5	5.5	4.3	40.3

*All tables in this chapter arrange denominations by size of membership from the largest to the smallest. To correct membership data for mergers, the figures for groups which merged are added together for prior years. This correction was not done for the 1958 United Presbyterian merger due to its small effect on trends.
†U.S. population data in all tables in this chapter is from *Statistical Abstracts of the United States*, 1977 and earlier.

Source: Doyle and Kelley, 1979:146.

would appear that Glock and Stark's predictions about an increasingly liberal version of Christianity are totally wrong. Some studies, criticizing the methods by which Glock and Stark arrived at their conclusions, do, indeed, directly challenge the conclusion that it is liberal churches which will grow (Hadaway, 1978; Roof and Hadaway, 1977; 1979).

A major criticism of Glock and Stark's findings (Hadaway, 1978) is that the sample upon which they based their conclusions is by no means representative of the society as a whole, if only because there is such a high level of migration into California from other parts of the country. Because some of the denominations, e.g., the Southern Baptist Conference are poorly represented in California, in contrast to the areas from which people moved, there is obviously a good deal of denominational switching; switching which perforce favors the more liberal groups as these are the better established ones in California. However this does not mean a preference for the more liberal theology of, for example, the Presbyterian groups; rather, it is most likely a matter of choosing a church which is reasonably close to the residence of the "switchers."

A strong case can be made for the contention that it is really the conservative churches which are growing—and doing so at a relatively phenomenal rate. As early as 1967, McLoughlin (1967:43) suggested that this was probably the most important aspect of religious life in America at that time:

> The most significant aspect of these groups is that they have increased their membership by 500 to 700 percent over the past twenty years, while the traditional Protestant denominations and the Roman Catholics (are) ... barely keeping up with the growth in the population.

Following this argument with later data, Dean Kelley has provided evidence contrary to Stark and Glock's hypothesis in *Why Conservative Churches Are Growing* (1977). He too notes that at least ten of the major Protestant denominations have been steadily losing members since 1967; denominations which had steadily increased in membership since the Colonial era. While these bodies have frequently attempted to explain this decline in ways echoing Stark and Glock—the idea that many feel the church to be obsolescent in today's world—the argument is hard to maintain since a decline in membership does not characterize all religious bodies. Such groups as the Southern Baptist Convention, the Pentecostal and Holiness bodies, and evangelicals, in general, are exhibiting a great deal of vitality, and, indeed, growing (see Figure 14-4).

What is particularly interesting to Kelley (1977) is that these groups do not even *attempt* to be "reasonable" in terms of modern thought. They are neither "ecumenical" nor "relevant." Kelley finds it "ironic" that such groups stubbornly refuse to give in to "acceptability." It appears that the attempt to be more reasonable and relevant does not strengthen the church; rather, those groups which stick to older, more traditional formulations appear to be doing best. In

Figure 14-4: Membership Comparison: 1958–1975

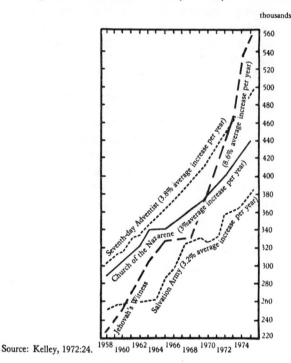

Source: Kelley, 1972:24.

U.S. population growth averaged 14% in 1960–69 and 1.1% in 1970–75.

light of this, Kelley suggests that strictness in both dogma and discipline lead to greater social strength for the churches which maintain them.

Kelley (1978), in a later article, contends that the membership trends have remained the same since his original study in 1972 except that three somewhat conservative churches (Presbyterian Church, U.S., Missouri Synod Lutheran, and the Christian Reformed Church) suffered membership losses for the first time. However, no such decline was experienced by fast-growing ultraconservative groups such as the Southern Baptists, Seventh-day Adventists, and the Church of the Nazarene. He suggests that the real "bottom line" is that the more liberal churches do not appear to be taking religion as seriously as the conservative churches are. The conservative churches have an apparent advantage over the liberal churches in that they are more serious about and do a better job of dealing with the problems of ultimate reality.

But, are there ways of explaining Kelley's data that lead to a conclusion other than that orthodox faith, and such faith alone, is growing. Bibby (1978) accepts Kelley's basic thesis but argues with his conclusions concerning the reasons for this pattern of growth (see Chapter 3). He contends that Kelley has not proven that the growth of the conservative churches is the result of their orthodox belief and the attraction of members from outside the conservative Christian community. Rather, the growth resulted from proselytizing adherents from other orthodox or conservative Christian groups, as well as to the fact that they do *hold* on to members better than do the more liberal denominations. While Kelley's two contentions might be true insofar as maintaining members already in these conservative churches, it does not apply to attracting members from outside that community.

Bibby finds that mainline and Conservative Protestants do not differ greatly insofar as bringing "outsiders" into the faith. It is not even true that the conservatives draw members away from the liberals; indeed, the opposite actually appears to be true. However, in terms of percentage, the conservatives have more children and also better success in holding these children as members of the particular group. Conservative churches, then, are really growing because of their higher birth rates and better socialization of children, rather than because of some vast turning toward orthodox belief.

This approach to the explanation of the seeming growth of conservative churches is supported in the contention that conservative groups have a growth advantage, although it may result from stability of membership and gains by switching from other groups as well as evangelism. Hadaway (1978:328-9) contends that logic should lead us to the conclusion that conservative churches would have a growth advantage regardless of the way that "advantage" might be defined. However, what looks like a clear victory for the conservative churches is diminished by the fact that sectarian groups, quite orthodox in their theology, do not display this same stability of membership.

In terms of net gains, according to Hadaway, it is not the conservative churches *per se* which show the greatest advantage, but groups at the extremes of both conservative and liberal orientation (see Table 14-4). Hadaway suggests, however, that the groups at either end of the continuum display quite different "modes of functioning," as far as membership is concerned. The sects exhibit considerable net gain through "switching," and they are growing. Their greatest gain seems to come, however, from "mobilizing" those who are not members of any church; they increase through expansion. Lutherans and Baptists, on the other hand, make only modest gains through switching, but since they hold on to the members which they have, they do not fare badly.

The moderate churches, on the other hand, make only moderate gains from switching and are not able to hold on to the members that they already have. The liberal denominations (Episcopal and United Church of Christ) have a fair or even impressive number of switchers joining them, but they are not able to hold on to existing members. In terms of commitment of those who convert, the more conservative denominations do tend to attract those members who have the

Table 14-4. THE SWITCHING OF RELIGIOUS IDENTIFICATION BY DENOMINATIONAL PREFERENCE[a]

	Episcopal (N=185)	U.C.C.[b] (N=92)	Presbyterian (N=394)	Disciples (N=100)	Methodist (N=1063)	Lutheran (N=649)	Baptist (N=1766)	Sect (N=339)
				Denominational Preference				
Stayers	60%	55%	56%	52%	61%	74%	73%	59%
Switchers to other faiths	29	39	36	43	34	22	22	36
Switchers to "none"	11	6	8	5	5	4	5	5
	100%	100%	100%	100%	100%	100%	100%	100%
Net % Gain or loss	+12%	+21%	-11%	-1%	-14%	-6%	-12%	+32%

[a]Data source is a merged file composed of the 1972–1977 NORC General Social Surveys. Switching data, however, is only available for 1973–1977. The Ns in the table refer to the number of respondents who stated that this was their religious preference when they were growing up.

[b]United Church of Christ, composed of the former Congregational Christian Church and the Evangelical and Reformed Church.

Source: Hadaway, 1978:330.

nighest rates of attending church services. This is particularly true for Baptists and sectarian groups.

Elsewhere, Roof and Hadaway (1977) have pointed out that denominational switching is very common for both liberal *and* conservative Protestants. Baptists and Lutherans tended to keep members best while sectarians as well as such staunch mainline groups as Presbyterians and Methodists lost as many as 35 per-cent of their adherents to other faiths—as well as to nonbelief. For Roman Catholics, there was a higher proportion of "defectors" to no religion at all than was true for Protestants in general. In reality, the net gains and loses vary greatly for different religious groupings.

One thing is clear to Roof and Hadaway (1977): the switching process does not follow theological lines. While the liberal Episcopalians and Congregationalists gained adherents, so too did the ultraconservative sectarians. At the same time, "liberal" Methodists and Presbyterians lost in the switching process, but so, too, did conservative Baptists and Lutherans.

Newport (1979) has also demonstrated that membership switching does not follow liberal-conservative theological lines. High- and low-status denominations gain from the switching process while Baptists, Catholics, and medium-status denominations actually lose through this process. However, the most common pattern is for individuals to switch out of participation in traditional religion altogether; a trend which applies disproportionately to young people in the society.

It is surely from this standpoint that Roof (1978) suggests that while liberal Protestant churches will not disappear, their position in society will be altered in the years ahead. He contends that they will persist, but as a "cognitive minority" institution. Further, even though there will be some continuing theological con-flict in these denominations, there will be a tendency for those who do remain committed within them to be more conservative in their views. In other words, the liberal denominations will not disappear, but it may well be that they will diminish in importance as well as lose some of their liberal theological slant. Conservative groups, on the other hand, will flourish, particularly in areas where individuals are tied together through a sense of community.

From all of this it seems clear that church growth and decline is not a simple matter, giving rise to a number of important questions which our previous discussion has not satisfactorily answered. Which groups are growing? How are they growing? What is the probable trend for the future? Are such trends long term or short term in nature? Are the factors involved in growth and decline con-textual or institutional? Are national or local factors more important in the development of such trends? Hoge and Roozen (1979a) have collected a number of essays which address these questions in *Understanding Church Growth and Decline, 1959-1978.*

In this volume, an article by Roozen and Carroll (1979) demonstrates that two questions need to be raised in analyzing trends in church membership. First, are

461

the trends due to contextual factors (those in the community, society and culture in which the church exists) or institutional ones (matters internal to the life of the church)? Second, are factors local or national in scope—the result of denominational bureaucracies or purely parish considerations?

Several things, according to Hoge (1979a:120-1) can be observed in looking at these trends from a national perspective. First, trends on a national scale tend to change quickly, often fluctuating in five- or ten-year segments. Second, the changes which have occurred nationally in the past two decades are not simply the result of such demographic trends as migration, increasing educational levels, or urbanization. Finally, changes in levels of church commitment are probably best explained in terms of patterns of value change that are broader than simply religious values, applying to the society as a whole.

Elsewhere in the same volume Hoge (1979b) reports that for the two decades in question (1955–65 and 1965–75) denominations grew or declined at rates which were consistently relative to one another. This suggests that any changes which are found in the growth of denominations from one decade to the next are the result of external factors which are common to many denominations rather than changes which have occurred in the specific groups. Hoge concludes that contextual factors explain more than half of the variation found in the growth or decline of denominations. A finding of particular importance to be drawn from the influence of contextual factors is that those factors which most affect changes in membership impinge most heavily on those denominations with the highest percentage of upper socioeconomic status members. Indeed, the higher the status of the denomination's membership, the less its growth. The encroachment of secular-humanistic views into the thinking of upper-status persons may be the most important factor in changes in membership growth, far more important than theological perspective *per se.*

Looking at institutional factors, Hoge suggests that the denominational characteristics attributed by Kelley to growing denominations are indeed important insofar as factors internal to denominations' influence, growth or decline. Emphasis on evangelism, a distinctive lifestyle and morality, and insistence on orthodox belief systems are important institutional influences. Thus trends in church membership are not to be seen as merely extensions or artifacts of socioeconomic status, family size, or religion of greatest strength for the denominations; they have an influence in their own right.

The debate, then, comes over the relative importance of contextual versus institutional factors. It would seem that the contextual ones are causally prior; a conclusion which is somewhat different than that of Kelley who puts emphasis on internal factors. "Strong" churches are strong because of the social or cultural milieu in which they exist and flourish. The suggestion of Hoge is that such churches grew in settings which were distinctive and which tended to involve some separateness from the dominant culture of the society and its centers of power. In short, when denominations attract members who feel alienated from the world, they tend to grow; those appealing mainly to those comfortable with the world and its culture tend to decline.

It would seem that in explaining trends in church growth and decline it is most useful to look at factors which have undergone short-term changes. With regard to contextual factors, denominations have maintained a rather consistent position *vis à vis* one another. This indicates that gradual, pervasive effects are at work with regard to membership trends. The main contextual factors which seem to explain growth and decline are socioeconomic status, the dominant culture of the society (churches benefited from the supportive culture of the 1950s but were hurt by the nonsupport of the 1960s and 1970s), birth rates for the nation, and changes in values about such matters as having children.

One question raised by all of this is why, if there is a liberal shift in attitudes in the surrounding culture, liberal churches do not benefit? If there is a shift in values away from traditional religious belief, why is there evidence at present of increased fervor in the more nonorthodox Christian groups? Hoge and Roosen (1979b) suggest that the broader outlines of contemporary American culture provide the answer.

Our culture has always been based on two conflicting world views: the traditional Christian one and a secular-humanistic approach. Some institutions, such as the church-related universities, have traditionally attempted to assert a unity for the two; however, the tension between these two perspectives is slowly pulling apart and polarizing in our time. It is significant that the main changes in America since the cold war years have been a rising dominance of the secular humanistic culture and its attendant emphasis on individualism and rationalism as cultural values. However, even though this is a dominant view, it is not one which provides a sustaining culture for the majority of individuals in the society. Since the late nineteenth century the secular-humanistic culture has been gaining strength in America, and mainline Protestantism has served as a bridge and synthesis for the two world views. At certain times in history, this bridge has been strong and vital, providing an accommodation between the perspectives. Since the mid-1960s, however, that bridge has been considerably weakened. In a time of increased dominance for the secular-humanistic culture among educated circles, it is not surprising that there is widespread defection from traditional and experimentation with new religious movements. The newer spiritual movements have not turned in the direction of mainline Protestantism and the bridge it had built between the two world views; increasingly there is a polarization of the two perspectives which drains the mainline groups of their more secular humanistic oriented membership who have traditionally formed their main strength.

What, then, can happen to those who seek meaning but are satisfied by neither the orthodox Christian groups or the attempts at bridging the two perspectives offered by the mainline Protestant groups and correlative movements in Catholicism and Judaism? Two suggestions can be made about the future direction of religion for such individuals.

ALTERNATIVES TO TRADITIONAL RELIGION

If traditional religion does not satisfy some, they may take two other directions. Some may simply become increasingly secularized, "dropping out" of traditional religious observances for all practical purposes. Others, however, may be finding religious answers in ways which depart from the traditional in other directions—experimentation with "cults" and "sects," or development of religious perspectives which are not tied to the institutional expression of religion we have known for so many centuries.

Increased Secularism

Many suggest that secularization is the dominant force in the life of modern, industrial society. It has been described as "perhaps the most significant development of the last several hundred years. . . ." (O'Dea, 1966). Viewed as a process through which the sacred loses more and more of its role in the legitimating of reality, this term refers to one of the central concerns of the sociologist of religion. There is, however, some confusion as to what secularization or secularism really means.

Secularization, of course, is not new to sociological thinking. In a sense, the early sociologists were dealing with secularization when they pondered the decline of religion in industrial society. Durkheim was doing so when he traced the effects of secularization in his study of suicide (1897). Weber (1947) referred to the process as the "disenchantment" of the world; that is, a seemingly irreversible trend toward the increasing rationalization of the world to the point that it becomes a self-contained nexus no longer dependent upon religion to bind it together.

Bryan Wilson (see 1966, among other works) has probably been the leading proponent of the theory of secularization. For Wilson, secularization means the process whereby religious thinking, practice, and institutions lose their social significance. He feels that the denominational diversity of modern society has in itself promoted the spread of secularization, as it provides people with such a diversity of religious choices that the effectiveness of religion to provide norms and values is greatly reduced. That is, religious values cease to be community values and religious views can diminish in the face of political realities. This has tended to reduce the association of the specifically religious agencies with other social institutions. From being the judges and determiners of moral behavior, the churches have steadily become more like reflections of the practices of the time

The suggestion that secularization is running rampant in contemporary society is not accepted by all students of religion in society, however. Such factors as ambiguity in definition and the failure of empirical evidence to support the "running rampant" contention lead many to doubt that we actually live in an age which is particularly "secular," or at least any more secular than a number of times in the past.

The fullest exploration of the various meanings of the term secularization has been made by Glasner (1977) who argues that the concept of a secularized society is, in large measure, what he calls a social myth. He notes that whether or not one feels that there is a great deal of secularization depends upon the definition of the term. By calling secularization a "social myth," he implies that it is based on the acceptance of categories of definition which have not been proven and which originate outside sociological analysis itself; for example, the preoccupation in much Western sociology with the institutionalized aspects of "religiosity." The assumption is that since a common usage definition of Christianity, for example, is concerned with church attendance, membership, and prescribed rites of passage, these constitute significant elements of a definition of religiosity, and that any move away from this institutional participation involves religious decline. Thus, secularization may not be the real trend. Rather, it may be that our society will not turn away from "religion" but simply from religion as we have known it.

New Forms of Religiosity

Our discussion of the relative strength of religion generally, and the encroachment of secularization have generally been concerned with what we might refer to as "churchly" religion or religion in the form of new expressions (see Chapters 8 and 9). Yet, unless we accept only the narrowest of substantive definitions of religion (see Chapter 1), it may well be that limiting discussion to such a narrow range of traditional religious expression cuts us off from consideration of much that can be seen as an expression of religion in contemporary society; as well as much that might be the shape of religion in the future. Indeed, Luckmann (1967), in a discussion of his concept of "invisible religion," points out the limitations of a sociology of religion which restricts itself to the "official" or traditional structures of religious life.

A number of scholars, notably Luckmann (1967), Berger (1967), and Yinger (1969), have pointed out that the functions which religion serves are such as will never be absent from the human condition; they are problems that will always need to be dealt with. In this sense, there will always be a need for that which is basic to the idea of religion. As Geertz (1966:4) has noted, it is "at the limits of his analytic capacities, at the limits of his power of endurance, and at the limits of his moral insights . . ." that the human condition cries out in need for something beyond itself. Put another way, Yinger (1969:89) phrases it as the fact that the religious is that which "refuses to let such facts be the determining ones in group interaction or in a person's fundamental outlook on life."

It is being suggested that modern humanity may be as religious as humans were in the 18th century, the 13th, or even the first. However, they may not be religious in the same fashion; the beliefs and rituals through which their religion is expressed may be quite different, in fact. It may be, as Yinger (1969) suggests, that we need ask in what particular ways is a person religious rather than asking whether the person is or is not religious.

Thus, Yinger proposes a "nondoctrinal" religion in which the strictures of dogma and creed do not bind; in which all that matters is awareness of and concern with certain essential problems of existence. As Yinger (1969:91) puts it:

> Where one finds awareness of an interest on the continuing, recurring, "permanent" problems of human existence—the human condition itself, as contrasted with specific problems; where one finds rites and shared beliefs relevant to that awareness which defines the strategy of an ultimate victory; and where one has groups organized to heighten that awareness and to teach and maintain these rites and beliefs—there you have religion.

Yinger's concept of what is included in these "basic, permanent questions" for human beings is quite broad. The questions include: social problems of the day (peace, survival in a nuclear age, poverty, population problems; relationships between persons, understanding of one another, breaking down inter-group barriers); creativity and happiness in life (happiness and a sense of creativity in life, a balancing of individual and group needs, and successful management of technology); a sense of meaningfulness and purpose in life including a sense of relationship to a sacred divine (meaning, goals, basic purposes, the concept of a soul). When any of these exist in an individual and where individuals share beliefs and ritual activity relative to the awareness of these permanent questions, it can be said that religion exists. Indeed, some would push the idea so far as to say that where the existence of these problems exists and ideas and actions are present, then there is, at least, the "invisible religion" (Machalek and Martin, 1976).

What is common to these arguments is that secularization and pluralism are not seen as having destroyed religion. Rather, these forces have pushed it to a more individual, more privatized sphere. Humans remain religious but, as Durkheim seems to have predicted, their religiosity is no longer directed at some external, objectified societal duty; it is, rather, internal and directed at what is sacred within them.

However, there may be another kind of religious substitute, or functional alternative, which is very much public; which, indeed, celebrates the most public, civic aspects of life as those which reflect that which is most sacred for society. Bellah (1967) captured the essence of this "religion" when he referred to it as "civil religion." This "religion" touches on some basic themes in American life and Christianity. McLoughlin (1967:46) notes:

> What distinguishes American from European Christendom more than anything else is the pietistic quality of American culture. To say, as Herberg does, that the traditional denominations (including Catholicism and the Jewish faith) simply embody a "culture religion" is not necessarily to say that these denominations are secularist. It depends upon the standard of measurement. If the United States is a pietistic nation, as I think it to be, even its "establishment" can be religiously radical. Many historians, foreign observers, and theologians have noted the messianic quality of the American character. In *The Kingdom of God in America*, H. Richard Niebuhr points out that Americans have always considered themselves to be God's Chosen People, a people with a divine mission in the universal destiny of man. To be an American is to belong to a pietistic sect—similar to the situation of being a Jew in the Old Testament era. Sometimes this mission expresses itself in terms of an example to the world—as in the case of the Bible Commonwealth of the Puritan city upon a hill or the new nation of 1776 dedicated to certain inalienable rights of man; sometimes it expresses itself in more aggressive forms as "manifest destiny" or "the white man's burden" to bring democracy and Christianity to the heathen or "the undeveloped"; sometimes it makes war to end colonialism (1898), to make the world safe for democracy (1917), or to prevent the immoral aggression of atheistic, totalitarian Communism (today); sometimes it dedicates its most idealistic young men to missionary endeavor and to Peace Corps evangelism; and sometimes it simply gives away its "filthy lucre" to help the poor, the weak, and the unfortunate, as in the Marshall Plan, Point Four, the Alliance for Progress, and foreign aid in general. Despite all the charges of self-interest, pragmatism, or hypocrisy that can be leveled at these actions, European observers have generally recognized that the United States is unique among nations because it professes to a conscience as well as to a mission.

As noted in Chapter 1, Bellah's conception is that there exists in this nation a "clearly differentiated" and fully elaborated set of religious beliefs and symbols which focus on "sacred" persons, events, and ceremonial rituals of the country—particularly those dealing with its history. Indeed, its history is viewed as a redemptive one in which the life and events of the American people are seen as comparable to the "redemptive history" of Israel (Herberg, 1974). Wimberly (1979) suggests that there are five basic tenets for this religion: seeing the flag of the United States as a sacred symbol; the idea that the authority of the president comes from God; the concept that God is revealed in America's history; that Americans have a divine right to liberty and happiness; and, that God grants us freedom throughout government.

This is not to suggest merely the confusion of national and Christian symbols in the minds of common folk. Rather, it proposes that the civil religion is a parallel, rival religious system. Its essence is found in such sacred documents as Lincoln's Gettysburg Address and Kennedy's inaugural address (Bellah, 1967). Again, as in the invisible religion, while the concern is with some transcendent answer to the permanent questions, the focus comes down upon the very humanity which lives out this national history and purpose. It is the sacred within each of us which is celebrated in the national story.

There is yet another trend visible in the religious life of America in the last quarter of the twentieth century. That is the proliferation of religious movements—often quite mystical and spiritual—which are clearly religious by any definition, but which depart in significant ways from the Judaeo-Christian tradition that has been dominant in American life since its inception. Some of these movements have been discussed and analyzed in Chapters 8 and 9. The question here, however, is not one of description, but that of how these movements fit into our supposedly secularizing culture and what they say for the future of religion in such a society. Surprisingly, it has been suggested by some that they fit very well into such a society and indeed fulfill the predictions of earlier students of religion and society. Westley (1978) finds them most compatible with the predictions of Durkheim concerning individualism of religion while Campbell (1978) sees them as fulfillment of Troeltsch's neglected third type of religion—spiritual and mystical religion.

The central question raised, of course, is how new religious movements can arise and flourish in a supposedly secular age. The implication derived from the work of both Westley and Campbell is that secularization is generally taken too broadly. That is, the process of secularization may well apply to the decline of church religion, but not to religiosity unconnected to the traditional structures, particularly structures of belief and organization.

Westley (1978) finds that some of these new religious movements, though not all, are reflective of Durkheim's "cult of man." There has been a tendency to view these movements as protests in opposition to the social order. It is possible, however, to see them as more positive reactions to that order in the sense that they express the mood and feelings of the time. In short, they involve approaches more compatible with the modern mind to the "permanent, persistent questions" which face humanity. The approaches of the traditional churches may be too stylized in this regard and may be unable to emphasize the unique individual who is bound to others through a noninstrumental, accepting environment.

Campbell (1978), in an essay on "the secret religion of the educated classes," continues this same kind of argument. For him secularization and the new expressions of religiosity are not contradictory developments but aspects of the same general trend. He reminds us of Troeltsch's (1931) third, much neglected category of "spiritual and mystic" religion. He notes (1978:147):

> The position adopted here, therefore, is first that the contemporary transformation of religion is best viewed as a transition from "church religion" to "spiritual and mystic religion" and secondly, following Troeltsch's own analysis, that such a change is intimately related to the processes of "secularization" that are occurring in the modern world. . . .

This "spiritual and mystic" religion is not simply a renewed emphasis on the spiritual and mystical within traditional religious systems. It is, rather, a totally new system, one whose cardinal doctrine centers around the presence of the "seed" or "spark" of God in the individual person. Obviously, if Durkheim is correct, here is an approach more compatible with the temper of an advanced, differential society than is the "Wholly Other" God of the orthodox Judaeo-Christian tradition.

The general thesis, then, is that secularization may be a process applicable to only one sort of religiosity—that related to the church. Religiosity as a general term applied to the solution of permanent, persistent questions (even when the range of solutions is limited to the transcendental) may well persist as long as there are these problems; but the forms in which it persists may take new and unfamiliar shapes. Secularization can well be sweeping away the collected religious wisdom of two or more millenia, but may not leave the void and emptiness that some have predicted.

SUMMARY

This final chapter has addressed questions concerning the state of religion at present, with a very timid look to the future. It becomes readily apparent that this is not an easy task. Not only is it difficult to define religion, it is even more treacherous to state what factors represent a decline and what represent growth in the religious institution. Yet the very rapidity with which new and sometimes startling events in the "religious world" are occurring make the question not only interesting but also vital. How have the predictions of the evolutionary schools, Durkheim, and Troeltsch, for example, fared as society has become increasingly complex and differentiated?

Poll data, from a variety of sources, is of little help in addressing this question. Basically the American people appear to give assent to the general beliefs of our three religious communities—Protestant, Catholic, and Jewish. Actual affiliation with some specific group is relatively high. Yet, support in terms of attendance and other measures of commitment is not high. We seem to go from peak periods of high support to valleys of low interest. Still, new, and often mystical, expressions of basic religious need seem to be thriving, particularly among the middle-class youth of the nation.

Some, in particular Stark and Glock (1968), see religion as being slowly abandoned. Specifically they conclude from their study in northern California that membership patterns show increasing gains for a very humanized or secularized version of the Christian faith; liberal churches are gaining at the expense of those whose beliefs are not harmonious with the contemporary world. Indeed, they indicate that many pastors and most parishioners no longer hold anything like traditional theistic beliefs. On the other hand, Greeley contends (1970; 1972) that religion "in the year 2000" will be as strong as it is today. Further, the strong showing of the "new evangelicals" in the late 1970s seems to indicate that we are ascending another peak rather than sliding inevitably into the valley of abandonment. At least one Jewish scholar (Himmelfarb, 1967) even sees some resurgence in Judaic religious life in America.

As many point out, the matter of the strength of religion in contemporary society is far from simple. Hadaway (1978), for example, has suggested that the limited regional base for the Stark and Glock study makes their findings very questionable. In reality, there is a great deal of denominational switching for both liberals and conservatives; liberal Episcopalians and Congregationalists gain but so also do the ultraconservative sects. Kelley (1977) contends that while the mainline denominations have been losing members the conservative churches have been growing rapidly. This, he suggests, is not so much a matter of theology as it is one of "seriousness." The conservative groups which are growing are more serious about their religion and thus are taken more seriously by people.

An extended consideration of the issue of church growth and decline by Hoge and Roozen (1979a) during the third-quarter of the century indicates that such decline has hit the denominations which draw their main membership from upper socioeconomic levels. These are also the groups which are most liberal. While this is true, the decline has really hit all of the denominations at a fairly constant rate as they grow and decline at about equivalent paces. This, and a number of other factors seem to indicate that patterns in church membership and attendance are really only short-term trends, influenced more by contextual factors than internal ones, and by national trends rather than local issues. Such factors as migration, the change in the birth rate, and changes in values have had an important effect on trends in church membership and attendance. However, commitment of members does have an important effect on membership and attendance. What factors are most important in affecting trends seem to impact most heavily on the upper socioeconomic status denominations. One suggestion is that there has been a cultural polarization in which the bridge between traditional Christianity and secular humanism forged by the higher socioeconomic status groups has broken down in the last ten or fifteen years.

There is one further factor in the present state of religion in our society. That is the possibility that secularized alternatives to traditional faith or religious systems which differ considerably from our heritage in the Judaeo-Christian faith will gain significant holds in our thought systems. Luckmann (1967) proposes an "invisible" religion even as Yinger (1969) speaks of a nondoctrinal one. In both cases the point seems to be that there are permanent, persistent questions which face human society and that whatever addresses these questions can be taken as religion. Yet another suggestion is that of Bellah (1967) that there is a national civil religion which forms the basic, real faith of the American people.

On the other hand a number of new expressions of religiosity have burst on to the American scene. These often have divided from ideologic systems quite alien to the Judaeo-Christian tradition which has served this society since its inception. Westley (1978) has suggested that these forms are really harmonious with our complex society and represent the individualistic religion predicted by Durkheim for such a society, a religion in which humanity itself is worshipped. Campbell (1978) recalls Troeltsch's category of spiritual and mystic religion and finds much in these new expressions which fit such a religious approach or orientation.

In sum, then, no simple statement can be made—on the basis of empirical data—about religious "health" now or in the future. The issues are exceedingly complex. While it does seem fair to say that religion will not be "slowly abandoned" in the near future, it is not certain that "new evangelicism" or the predictions of Greeley will come true. Perhaps Wingrove and Alston (1974) express the future best—a series of peaks and valleys in religious interest. As McLoughlin (1967:47) has indicated, religious life in America has always been a matter of cycles—in theology as well as interest. Most probably we shall continue to have periods of revivalism or Great Awakenings followed by times of decline.

REFERENCES

American Institute of
Public Opinion
1976   *AIPO 958.* Storris, Ct.: The Roper Center.
Bellah, Robert N.
1967   "Civil religion in America." *Daedalus*
        96:191-219.
Berger, Peter L.
1967   *The Sacred Canopy.* Garden City, N.Y.: Double-

day.

Bibby, Reginald W.
1978   "Why conservative churches really are growing:
                        Kelley revisited." *Journal for the Scientific Study
                        of Religion* 17:129-138.

Budd, Susan
1973   *Sociologists and Religion*. London: Collier-
                        Macmillan Publishers.

Campbell, Collin
1978   "The secret religion of the educated classes."
                        Sociological Analysis 39 (Summer):146-156.

Doyle, and Dean M.
Kelley
1979   "Comparison of trends in ten denominations
                        1950-75." Pp. 144-159 in D. R. Hoge and D. A.
                        Roozen (eds.), *Understanding Church Growth and
                        Decline: 1950-1978*. New York: The Pilgrim
                        Press.

Durkheim, Emile
1951 (1897)   *Suicide*. New York: The Press.
1969 (1898)   "Individualism and the intellectuals." (Trans. by
                        S. Lukes with note.) *Political Studies* 17:14-30.

Geertz, Clifford
1966   "Religion as a cultural system." In M. Banton
                        (ed.), *Anthropological Approaches to the Study of
                        Religion*. New York: Praeger.

Gallup, George
1978   "Religion in America." The Gallup Opinion
                        Index, Report No. 145.

Glasner, Peter
1977   *The Sociology of Secularization: Critique of a Con-
                        cept*. London: Routledge and Kegan.

Glock, Charles Y. (ed.)
1973   *Religion in Sociological Perspective*. Belmont, Ca.:
                        Wadsworth Publishing Co., Inc.

Glock, Charles Y. and
Rodney Stark
1965   *Religion and Society in Tension*. Chicago: Rand
                        McNally.

1968   *American Piety: The Nature of Religious Commit-
                        ment*. Berkeley, Ca.: University of California
                        Press.

Greeley, Andrew M.
1970   *Religion in the Year 2000.* New York: Sheed and
               Ward.
1972   *The Denominational Society.* Glenview, Ill.: Scott
               Forseman and Company.

Hadaway, Kirk
1978   "Denominational switching and membership
               growth." *Sociological Analysis* 39:34-37.

Herberg, Will
1974   "America's civil religion: What it is and whence
               it comes." Pp. 76-88 in R. E. Richey and D. G.
               Jones (eds.), *American Civil Religion.* New York:
               Harper and Row.

Himmelfarb, Milton
1967   "Secular society? A Jewish perspective."
               Daedalus 96:220-236.

Hoge, Dean
1979a   "National contextual factors influencing church
               trends." Pp. 94-122 in D. R. Hoge and D. A.
               Roozen (eds.), *Understanding Church Growth and
               Decline: 1950-1978.* New York: The Pilgrim
               Press.

Hoge, Dean
1979b   "A test of theories of denominational growth and
               decline." Pp. 179-197 in D. R. Hoge and D. A.
               Roozen (eds.), *Understanding Church Growth and
               Decline: 1950-1978.* New York: The Pilgrim
               Press.

Hoge, Dean and D. A.
Roozen
1979a   "Research on factors influencing church commit-
               ment." Pp. 42-68 in D. R. Hoge and D. A.
               Roozen (eds.), *Understanding Church Growth and
               Decline: 1950-1978.* New York: The Pilgrim
               Press.

1979b   "Some sociological conclusions about church
               trends." Pp. 315-333 in D. R. Hoge and D. A.
               Roozen (eds.), *Understanding Church Growth and
               Decline: 1950-1978.* New York: The Pilgrim
               Press.

Kelley, Dean M.
1977   *Why Conservative Churches are Growing.* New

York: Harper and Row.

1978   "Why conservative churches are still growing."
        Journal for the Scientific Study of Religion
        17:165-72.

Luckmann, Thomas
1967   *The Invisible Religion.* New York: Macmillan.
McLoughlin, William C.
1967   "Is there a third force in Christendom?"
        Daedalus 96:43-68.

Machalek, Richard and
Michael Martin
1976   " 'Invisible' religions: Some preliminary
        evidence." *Journal for the Scientific Study of
        Religion* 15:311-21.

Mead, Shepherd
1959   *The Big Ball of Wax.* New York: Simon and
        Schuster.

Newport, Anthony
1979   "The religious switcher in the United States."
        American Sociological Review 44:528-52.

Newsweek
1976   "Born Again!" 25 Oct., Pp. 68-70, 75-76.
National Opinion
Research Center
1978   *General Social Survey, 1974-78.* New Haven:
        Roper Poll.

Novak, Michael
1967   "Christianity: Renewed or slowly abandoned?"
        Daedalus 96:237-66.

O'Dea, Thomas F.
1966   *The Sociology of Religion.* Englewood Cliffs, N.J.:
        Prentice-Hall.

Robbins, Thomas, Dick
Anthony and James
Richardson
1978   "Theory and research on today's 'new
        religions.' " *Sociological Analysis* 39
        (Summer):95-122.

Roof, Wade C.
1978   *Community and Commitment: Religious
        Plausibility in a Liberal Protestant Church.* New
        York: Elsevier.

Roof, Wade C. and Kirk
Hadaway
1977   "Shifts in religious preference—the mid-
                            seventies." *Journal for the Scientific Study of
                            Religion* 16:409-12.
1979   "Beyond Stark and Glock: Denominational
                            switching among American Protestants in the
                            seventies." *Journal for the Scientific Study of
                            Religion.* Forthcoming.

D. A. Roozen and
Jackson W. Carroll
1979   "Recent trends in church membership and par-
                            ticipation: An introduction." Pp. 21-41 in D. R.
                            Hoge and D. A. Roozen (eds.), *Understanding
                            Church Growth and Decline: 1950-1978.* New
                            York: The Pilgrim Press.

Troeltsch, Ernst
1931   *The Social Teaching of the Christian Churches.*
                            London: George Allen and Unwin.

Weber, Max
1947   *The Theory of Social and Economic Organization.*
                            A. M. Henderson and Talcott Parsons (trans.).
                            New York: Oxford University Press.

Westley, Frances
1978   " 'The cult of man': Durkheim's predictions and
                            new religious movements." *Sociological Analysis*
                            39 (Summer):135-145.

Wilson, Bryan R.
1966   *Religion in a Secular Society.* London: Watts.
Wilson, John
1978   *Religion in American Society: The Effective
                            Presence.* Englewood Cliffs, N.J.: Prentice-Hall.

Wimberly, Ronald C.
1979   "Continuity in the measurement of civil
                            religion." *Sociological Analysis* 40 (Spring):59-62.

Wingrove, C. Ray and
John P. Alston
1974   "Cohort analysis of church attendance,
                            1939-69." *Social Forces* 53-324-31.

Yinger, J. Milton
1969   "A structural examination of religion." *Journal
                            for the Scientific Study of Religion* 8:88-99.

Index

INDEX

INDEX

INDEX

INDEX

Sacred
  beliefs and practices, 24
  cosmos, 20
  days, 222
  profane and, 21, 33, 34
  self, 444
  things, 17, 21
Sacred Canopy, 20, 41
Salvation Army, 46, 234
  Slum Brigades, 234
Sanction fear, 98
Sapp, Stephen G., 161
Schnabel, John F., 48
Schneider, Benjamin, 152
Schneider, Herbert, 384–385, 386
Schoenherr, R.A., 159
Schuler, Robert, 153, 208
Science, 25
Science and Health, with Key to the Scriptures,
    194
Scientific study of religion, 12, 31–43
Scientology, 302–305
  "clearing," 304
  Dianetics, 303
  engram, 303
  orgs, 303
  Thetan, 305
Scimecca, Joseph A., 42
Scopes, John T., 236
Scopes Trial, 232
Second Coming of Christ, 242
Second Vatican Council, 205, 214
Sectarianism
  patterns of attendance, 80
  "swamp of," 176
Sects, 11, 47–48, 123–133, 382–383
  acceptance, 127, 129
  aggressive, 129, 419
  avoidance, 129–130, 419
  contrast with denominations, 123–125
  creating new order, 131
  development, 132
  established, 132–133
  managing present order, 131
  reforming, 130
  rise of, 125–127
  withdrawing from present, 130-131
Secular City, 451
Secular ideologies, 22, 23
  increased, 464–465
  Jews, 217
  meanings, 464–465

Secular ideologies (cont'd.)
  religions, 23
Seder meal, 71
Self-concept, 37–39
Separation of church and state, 5, 15,
    177–179
  POAU, 330
  Separationists, 339
Serpent-handling ritual, 52
Session, 142–143
Shakers, 53, 54, 194
Shaw, Gary, 361
Sheen, Fulton, 243
Shupe, Anson D., Jr., 313, 314, 315, 317
Siegelman, Jim, 74, 273, 274, 280, 311
Significance of life, 18, 19. *See also* Ultimate
    meaning
Six Months in a Convent, 183
"Slave name," 424
Slavery, 186
Slaves
  freed, 414
  religious life, 414
Smith, Al, 334
Smith, Joseph, 194
Snapping, 74
Snizek, William E., 405
Social
  class, 11, 335–337, 371–407
  Gospel, 191, 233–234, 327
  institutions, 3, 25, 327
  movement of fundamentalism, 227–256
  organization, clan, 34
  participator, 247
  patterns, 13, 58
  processes, 12
  psychologists, 50
  scientists, 8
  self, 38
  status, 11
  structures, 12
  systems, cultic, 262, 263
Social Darwinism, 31
socialization, 312
  agents, 70–74
  effects, 78–93
  into the ministry, 156–158
  religious, 69, 78–93
Social Sources of Denominationalism, 119
Society
  force of, 34
  human product, 67

488

INDEX

DATE DUE